# CLARENDON LAW

*Edited by*

PETER CANE, TONY HONORÉ, AND JANE STAPLETON

# CLARENDON LAW SERIES

*Some Recent Titles in this Series*

# AN INTRODUCTION TO THE LAW OF CONTRACT

### P. S. ATIYAH

*Formerly Professor of English Law in the
University of Oxford*

**FIFTH EDITION**

CLARENDON PRESS · OXFORD

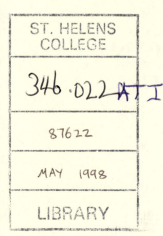
*Oxford University Press, Walton Street, Oxford* OX2 6DP
*Oxford New York*
*Athens Auckland Bangkok Bombay*
*Calcutta Cape Town Dar es Salaam Delhi*
*Florence Hong Kong Istanbul Karachi*
*Kuala Lumpur Madras Madrid Melbourne*
*Mexico City Nairobi Paris Singapore*
*Taipei Tokyo Toronto*
*and associated companies in*
*Berlin Ibadan*

*Oxford is a trade mark of Oxford University Press*

*Published in the United States*
*by Oxford University Press Inc., New York*

© *Patrick Selim Atiyah 1995*

*First published 1995*
*Paperback reprinted 1996*

*British Library Cataloguing in Publication Data*
*Data available*

*Library of Congress Cataloging in Publication Data*
*Atiyah, P. S.*
*An introduction to the Law of Contract/by P. S. Atiyah.—5th ed.*
*p. cm.—(Clarendon law series)*
*Includes bibliographical references.*
*1. Contracts—Great Britain. I. Series.*
*KD1554.A975 1995*
*346.41'02—dc20*
*[344.1062] 94–49574*
*ISBN 0–19–825952–2*
*ISBN 0–19–825953–0 (Pbk.)*

*Printed in Great Britain on acid-free paper by*
*Bookcraft Ltd., Midsomer Norton, Avon*

# Preface

The last edition of this book saw a major restructuring of the whole work, and an attempt to introduce a number of new themes, in particular, to stress the resurgence of freedom of contract ideology, and to introduce some basic economic issues in contract law. In this edition the general shape and structure of the book have been left untouched, and I have concentrated on updating and modernizing the work. It is astonishing how much even a basic text on contract law requires updating after five or six years. Looking at my annotated copy of the last edition, I see that there are few pages which have not been amended or supplemented. I have also continued the process of modernizing the text by replacing old and outdated examples with more modern questions with which the student may be assumed to be more familiar. Credit cards, to take one example, pose many unanswered questions in contract law, and I have introduced a few of these into the text.

The aims of the book remain unchanged. It tries to supply a basic introduction not merely to the law of contract but also to theories and policies and ideas underlying the subject. In addition I have widely resorted to a modern historical approach, giving the student (for instance in the chapter on restraint of trade) some sense of how the law has developed over the past hundred years or so. I have had to recognize that the book is now probably widely used as a textbook rather than a simple introduction, which partly explains why I have allowed the book to get substantially larger over the years. But I have still resisted the pressure to cover the whole subject, or even to provide references to every statement of law contained in it.

This edition was substantially completed in August 1994, but it has been possible to incorporate references up to the end of November, and I have also assumed that regulations made to implement the EC Directive on Unfair Contract Terms will be in force by (or shortly after) publication. I have also taken account of the Sale and Supply of Goods Act 1994.

P.S.A.

# Contents

# TABLE OF CASES

# The Development of the Modern Law of Contract

## I. CONTRACTS AND THE LAW OF OBLIGATIONS

THE law of contract is part of the law of obligations, that is to say, it is concerned with obligations which people incur to others as a result of the relations and transactions in which they become involved. Broadly, this is a part of private law, in the sense that obligations of a public character, such as constitutional or political obligations, are not treated by the law, or thought of by lawyers, as part of the law of obligations. Public bodies can, it is true, enter into ordinary contracts, and thus submit themselves to the ordinary law, but the broader duties of such bodies do not fall within the scope of the law of obligations as commonly understood. So also, the criminal law is not conceived by lawyers to be part of the law of obligations. The criminal law does, of course, impose duties on citizens, and these duties are in a sense legal obligations. But the duties are not owed to anyone in particular, and their enforcement normally rests with the police and other public bodies. By contrast the law of obligations deals primarily with duties owed by individual members of the public to other individuals, and these obligations are exclusively enforceable by the persons to whom they are owed. A person who has been the victim of a crime can complain to the police, who will investigate, and if they feel it appropriate, prosecute the offender. But a person who wishes to complain of a breach of an obligation owed privately to him, such as a breach of contract, must enforce his rights in the courts without the assistance of any public authority.

Obligations arise from a variety of sources, and they can be classified in various ways. They can, for example, be classified according to the social relationships from which they arise. Thus one can distinguish between obligations owed by a person to members of his family, obligations between neighbours, obligations arising from the employment relationship, and so on. But in the law it has been traditional to treat the basic distinction as that between obligations which are self-imposed, and obligations which are imposed on the citizen from outside. Broadly speaking, the law of contract is that part of the law which deals with obligations which are self-imposed. Other important parts of the law of obligations are the law of torts (which is broadly concerned with civil injuries and wrongs) and the law of restitution (which is broadly concerned with the obligation to restore money or to pay for benefits received where there has been no contract to pay for them). As will be seen later, these distinctions are by no means clear-cut, and one of the most striking phenomena of modern times has been the gradual blurring of the lines between the law of contract and other parts of the law of obligations. In particular, as will be discussed in more detail later, it will be suggested that many of the obligations recognized by the law of contract cannot be realistically thought of as self-imposed; equally, matters of consent or agreement are by no means irrelevant in the law of torts or the law of restitution.

But, for the moment, these qualifications can be left aside, and we can focus on the undoubted fact that the law of contract does enable people to impose obligations on themselves. Such a body of law naturally pre-supposes a society and a legal system in which people have the right to choose what obligations they wish to assume. In very primitive societies, the role of contract has generally been found to be small, because obligations are normally thought to arise from custom and status, rather than from free choice. Equally, in modern collectivist societies, where the State is all-powerful, and individual rights of free choice are less respected, the role of contract law may be less significant, at least in practice. But in Western democratic societies,where more extensive rights of free choice are traditionally respected, the law of contract has played a larger role. In the development of the English common law, contractual ideas came into greater prominence from the sixteenth century onwards, as the greater freedom and individualism of post-Reformation England was becoming established. No doubt the law has been influenced by a considerable number of factors, but it is probably no exaggeration to say that two of these factors have been of far greater importance than any others. These are the moral factor and the economic or business factor.

Although English lawyers and theorists are traditionally wont to insist that law and morality are distinct, it is none the less true that the law reflects to a considerable extent the moral standards and ideals of the community in which it operates. It is therefore not surprising to find that, behind a great deal of the law of contract, there lies the simple moral principle that a person should fulfil his promises and abide by his agreements. This is not to say that early English law translated this moral principle into a legal rule, for it was not, in fact, until the late sixteenth century that we acquired anything resembling a general law of contract, and when this came it was mainly under the impetus of the business or economic factor. Moreover, as will be seen later, there are still doubts and controversies over whether the law really regards a breach of contract as something wrongful, and some parts of the law do appear to countenance the view that there is really nothing wrong with breaking a contract so long as damages are paid for any losses thereby caused. And again, all sorts of qualifications would need to be made to the idea that the moral obligation to keep a promise is quite such a simple idea as it may seem. Still, for the moment it is enough to note that at least one strong undercurrent in contract law does derive from the idea that a person ought to keep his word, and that promises impose moral obligations.

With the economic and social development of modern societies, the need for a law of contract becomes far more pressing for at least two reasons. In the first place the division of labour, which is such a fundamental feature of modern societies, creates an increasing demand for the transfer of property from some members of the community to others and for the performance of services by some members of the community for others. The legal machinery by which these transfers of property and performance of services are carried out is broadly speaking the law of contract. Contract law is thus, in large part, the law of exchange, the law which regulates the methods by which individuals exchange goods and services usually in return for money.

## 2. CONTRACTS AND ECONOMIC EXCHANGE

There are, of course, many forms of exchange. Contract law is largely concerned with economic exchange, which takes place in the market, with buying and selling, leasing and hiring, employment and services, money-lending and borrowing, and so on. There are also other forms of exchange, such as take place in a family context ('You do the washing-up, and I'll do the shopping', or 'I'll pay the mortgage, and you can pay the hire-purchase on the car'). Contract law has little involvement in such non-market exchanges, although occasionally it may be invoked, for example, where unmarried partners buy a house together and then split up. Where married couples are concerned, litigation is, for obvious reasons, unlikely unless they split up or get divorced, or one of them dies and there are then disputes about the entitlement to his or her property. And such disputes are not usually solved by invoking contract law, but by different legal rules, indeed, often under a regime which rests largely on judicial discretion rather than rules at all. But even in cases of this kind many of the norms and ideas which permeate contract law will often be utilized—for instance, judges exercising their discretion to apportion the matrimonial property on divorce may be influenced by ideas of 'fair exchange' (who contributed what?), though of course family needs and other considerations may also be relevant.

In Western economic systems, economic exchange, with which contract law is particularly involved, is generally regarded as an important instrument of economic efficiency in two principal ways. In the first place, free and voluntary exchange is generally a simple but critically important method of increasing consumer satisfaction, and even of increasing a community's wealth, if wealth is defined (as it often is) in terms of consumer satisfaction. Where two parties freely agree on a contract involving, say, a simple exchange of money for goods, the seller does so because he thinks he will be better off with the money than with the goods, and the buyer does so because he prefers to have the goods than the money. Both parties thus emerge from the exchange 'better off' (in one sense) than they were before, and since society's wealth is made up of the total wealth of its members, even a simple exchange of this kind can improve social 'wealth'. In fact, the simplest of exchanges are an absolute necessity except to someone leading a Robinson Crusoe existence. Few people in a modern society could survive at all without exchanging their labour for money, and their money for goods and services. And the simplest thing which we buy in the market is itself often the product of endless earlier exchanges. Buy a pencil in a shop, and consider who grew the timber, how it was cut down, transported to a port, shipped on a vessel (itself made under innumerable exchanges), sent to a timber yard, cut again, manufactured into a pencil, distributed to retailers, and ultimately offered for sale to the consumer.

Of course, many exchanges are far more complex than simple sales: an employment contract, for instance, which continues in existence over a period of time, is much more complicated than a simple sale of goods. And, obviously, big transactions involving (for example) the construction of large engineering projects, or the sale of cargoes, or the charter of ships to carry such cargoes, will often be very intricate arrangements. In the modern world, the number of daily exchanges is immense, and their total value astronomical. By the same token, the total gain in the wealth of all the world's people, which derives from free economic exchange, is almost unimaginable. This is indeed why it is possible for international trade to exist. Such trade is obviously very costly. Ships have to be built and fuelled and crewed, all at great cost. But the gains from carrying goods across the seas, and allowing them to be sold under a system of free exchange, are so immense that there is enough to pay for all these costs, and some to spare. A moment's reflection is therefore enough to show how important free and voluntary exchange is to any society. To interfere with it is sometimes necessary; but we do need to be sure that it *is* necessary, and we need to count the cost of doing so.

There is a second reason why free and voluntary exchange is a major instrument of economic efficiency. It is free exchange which largely determines how society's resources should be allocated among different possible uses. In a free enterprise society it is not the State or the government which decides how many cars should be produced (and how many of which particular models), how much money should be devoted to the entertainment industry, whether supermarkets or corner-shops should be opened on a new site, and so on. These are matters which are to be determined by the market, operating through the medium of free exchange, and therefore contract. Consumers are the ultimate choosers. It is consumers who determine, by choosing to buy one thing rather than another, in one place rather than another, by one means rather than another, what resources should be devoted to the production and distribution of what goods and services. If consumers are free to make what choices they wish—within the limits of their own resources, of course—and suppliers are free to respond to consumer demand, then the result, in theory at least, is that the market will in the long run supply what the consumers in aggregate show that they want in the proportions that they want, and at the prices they are willing to pay. This is one fundamental reason why freedom of choice in exchange—freedom of contract—is closely associated with the rise (and sometimes decline) of belief in the free market.

But exchange alone is not enough. Only the simplest of transactions can be consummated by a simultaneous exchange, such as takes place at a supermarket checkout, where the customer unloads his trolley and hands over his money. Most exchanges of any complexity cannot be performed simultaneously. One or both parties will have to perform in the future, which means that the other party has to *trust* him so to perform, has to have confidence that he will perform. Most contracts therefore require some degree of co-operation and trust and a modern society cannot exist without an immense degree of co-operative activity. Much of this co-operation is regulated by public laws, rather than the law of contract—for instance, the maintenance of law and order is secured by the establishment of police forces, criminal courts, gaols, and so on. But a huge amount of co-operative activity is also secured by voluntary exchange, without which it would be simply impossible to collect the capital and workforce necessary for large-scale industrial projects—unless, of course, it was done by the compulsion of State power. But voluntary exchange on this scale also leads to a need for trust. In the process of transferring property and performing services, people have perforce to rely heavily on promises and agreements. Most arrangements for the transfer of goods, land, or services cannot be performed instantly and simultaneously. Often such arrangements have to be planned for in advance. Nearly always, one party has to perform before the other, and often the arrangements need to be carefully agreed in advance before any performance at all can take place. In a reasonably stable and orderly society, making such advance arrangements generates expectations about the future behaviour of other parties. In modern societies we all have reasonable expectations about how others will behave, and we all depend on, or trust, others to behave in the future as they have said they will behave.

In this sense contract law is an instrument for securing co-operation in human behaviour, and particularly in exchange. A agrees to scratch B's back if B agrees to do the same to A when called upon. But unless A is reasonably confident that B will indeed reciprocate when the time comes, A will be reluctant to help B here and now. One way of making A more confident that B will indeed reciprocate is for B to promise that he will do so. But even that is not enough by itself, because promises can be broken. Of course there are many sanctions against promise-breakers, and law is not needed for all of them. The simplest sanction is not to deal with that person again. So, even in areas where there is no real or effective law which can enforce promises or contracts, there are powerful reasons why promises and contracts tend to be observed. Consider, for instance, how rarely governments, who borrow enormous sums of money in the world's financial markets, default on their obligations, even though there is no real way of forcing them to observe their contracts. They pay because they know that if they do not they may never be able to borrow again. But sometimes sanctions of this kind are not satisfactory, and although they are better than nothing, there are occasions when co-operation will not be forthcoming because the parties know that there are no sanctions for default. Sometimes this is actually a good thing; for instance, when we are dealing with undesirable contracts, such as blackmailing or corrupt agreements. Because agreements of this kind are not usually legally enforceable, parties who want to make such agreements will have little confidence that the other parties will perform as agreed. This lack of confidence makes it more difficult for such agreements to be made, and it is often necessary for the blackmailer or the briber to arrange for some kind of simultaneous exchange, because he is unwilling to perform first, leaving the other free to default later. But simultaneous exchange is not always practicable, so these undesirable exchanges are often difficult to carry out—and this is, of course, a good thing.

But most free and voluntary exchanges are socially desirable: we want to facilitate them, not to discourage them. And in the absence of legal sanctions to enforce them, parties would be reduced to less satisfactory procedures, as in the case of undesirable exchanges. Hence we get the traditional cloak-and-dagger exchange of captured spies where the two spies walk across a bridge or frontier while guards stand at either end. This is an exchange of a desirable character, yet it is one of those exchanges which cannot easily be backed by any legal sanctions, so the parties are forced to make the exchange simultaneous. This would hardly be desirable or practicable for the great bulk of ordinary economic exchanges, and it is precisely for this reason that we need genuine legal sanctions. So most systems of law have established rules which will impose sanctions on those who break their contracts. Co-operation then becomes much easier, and exchanges are facilitated.

In sophisticated modern societies this co-operation has led to a massive and elaborate system of credit—and 'credit', of course, is simply another word for 'trust' or 'reliance'. Credit is, in effect, reliance or trust on the unperformed part of some arrangement or exchange. In the simplest sort of case, where a person provides goods or services on credit to a consumer, he trusts or relies on the consumer to pay, and in the meantime he allows the consumer to have the goods. Generally, the consumer will ultimately pay, but if he fails to do so some sanction is needed, and that sanction is provided by the law of contract. So contract law ultimately provides the backing needed to support the whole institution of credit. A moment's reflection is enough to show to what extent this is true, not only in commercial matters, but in all walks of life. A consumer's bank account, his right to occupy his house if rented or mortgaged, his employment, his insurance, his shareholdings, and many other matters of vital importance to him, all depend for their value on the fact that, in the last analysis, the law of contract will enable him to realize his rights. In the striking phrase of Roscoe Pound, 'Wealth, in a commercial age, is made up largely of promises'.[1] This is the reason the development of the law of contract, both in England and elsewhere, has been so largely associated with the development of commerce.

## 3. CLASSICAL CONTRACT LAW

Although much of the English law of contract has roots going back to the Middle Ages, most of the general principles of the modern law were developed and elaborated in the eighteenth and nineteenth centuries. These principles and, perhaps even more, the general approach of the courts to contractual questions may not improperly be referred to as the traditional, or classical theory of the law of contract. The law of contract has undergone some fundamental changes in the twentieth century, but it is quite impossible to understand the modern law without some knowledge and appreciation of the background and origins of the classical law.[2]

The eighteenth and nineteenth centuries were the heyday of theories of natural law and the philosophy of *laissez-faire*, and many of the judges, who were largely responsible for the creation of the law of contract during this period, were, like most educated men of the time, very considerably influenced by current thought. To the judges of the eighteenth century

[1] *Introduction to the Philosophy of Law* (reprinted New Haven, 1961), 236.
[2] The subject is dealt with at great length in my *The Rise and Fall of Freedom of Contract* (Oxford, 1979).

theories of natural law meant that men had an inalienable right to own property, and therefore to make their own arrangements to buy or sell or otherwise deal with that property, and hence to make their own contracts for themselves. At the same time the law was still influenced by the paternalism which was one of the characteristics of eighteenth-century ideology. So, during this period some of the potential harshness of a strict regime of freedom of contract was mitigated by paternalist doctrines and rules, which enabled the judges to protect those less capable of standing up for themselves in the free market.

During the nineteenth century, paternalist ideas waned, as the philosophy of *laissez-faire* took root. Most educated people, including the judges, took *laissez-faire* to mean that the law should interfere with people as little as possible. To the judges, the function of the civil law came to be seen as largely a negative one. Its main object was to enable people to 'realize their wills', or, in more prosaic language, to leave them to get on with their business, to conduct their commercial affairs as they thought best, to lead their own lives unhampered by governmental interference, and so forth.

By and large this meant that the law of contract was designed to provide for the enforcement of the private arrangements which the contracting parties had agreed upon. In general the law was not concerned with the fairness or justice of the outcome, and paternalistic ideas came to be thought of as old-fashioned. The judges were not even greatly concerned with the possibility that a contract might not be in the public interest. So the function of contract law was merely to assist one of the contracting parties when the other broke the rules of the game and defaulted in the performance of his contractual obligations. The judge was just a sort of umpire whose job it was to respond to the appeal 'How's that?' when something went wrong. These ideas meant encouraging almost unlimited freedom of contracting, and so the shibboleths 'freedom of contract' and 'sanctity of contract' became the foundations on which the whole law of contract was built. It would, however, be wrong to conclude that the judges of this period were uninterested in justice: they thought that it *was* just to enforce contractual duties strictly according to the letter. They came to think that paternalism was patronizing to the people who were robust enough to stand on their own feet in the market place. It would be equally mistaken to think that the judges were indifferent to the public interest. They simply thought that, in nearly all cases, it *was* in the public interest to enforce private contracts. Indeed, it was widely thought that this was proved by fundamental economic principles.[3]

---

[3] For a famous dictum to this effect, see *Printing and Numerical Registering Co* v. *Sampson* (1875) LR 19 Eq. at 465.

It is desirable to avoid over-simplification. Not all judges in nineteenth-century England were enthusiastic adherents of freedom of contract. But, at any rate after 1830 or thereabouts, *laissez-faire* ideology did have a significant influence on the development of contract law. In particular, many equitable doctrines enforceable in the Court of Chancery, and designed to protect those who entered into foolish and improvident bargains, began to be whittled away by the judges. The paternalism of eighteenth-century judges was largely repudiated by their nineteenth-century successors. This rejection of paternalism was actually part of a reform movement which was closely allied to the political movement towards democracy. It was the reformers of the 1830s who proclaimed their faith in individualism, their belief that the mass of the people could be trusted to look after their own interests, whether in the market place or at the hustings.

Like most shibboleths, that of 'freedom of contract' rarely, if ever, received the close examination which its importance deserved, and even today it is by no means easy to say what exactly the nineteenth-century judges meant when they used this phrase. At least it may be said that the idea of freedom of contract embraced two closely connected, but none the less distinct, concepts. In the first place it emphasized that contracts were based on mutual agreement, while in the second place it stressed that the creation of a contract was the result of a free choice unhampered by external control such as government or legislative interference.

To say that contracts are based on agreement or mutual assent is a statement which commands general support and, indeed, is taken as axiomatic by most lawyers. Most contracts *are* created as a result of the agreement of the parties, at all events as to the essentials. Nevertheless, some qualification of the bare statement that contracts are based on agreement is necessary. In the first place, it is one of the most fundamental features of the law of contract that the test of agreement is objective and not subjective. It matters not whether the parties have really agreed in their innermost minds. The question is not whether the parties have really agreed, or what they really intended, but whether their conduct and language are such as would lead reasonable people to assume that they have agreed. Thus the decision of the jury in the classic case of *Bardell* v. *Pickwick* was arguably correct because Mr Pickwick's language was, to put it at the lowest, capable of being understood by a reasonable person as a proposal of marriage, although nothing could, in fact, have been further from his mind.

More important than cases of such gross misunderstanding are the myriads of contracts made everyday, by consumers and even businessmen, which consist of printed and signed forms. It is well established in modern law that the printed terms of such contracts are binding on the parties, even though they may not have been read or understood by one or both parties.[4] Only in rare and exeptional circumstances of fraud or other gross mistake as to the fundamental nature or effect of the printed form can a party deny the force of his own signature.[5] Now it is obvious that the practical advantages of treating such signatures as conclusively binding are very great. At the same time it really is important *constantly* to bear in mind that these rules often mean that a person is contractually bound to provisions that he simply did not know about or understand at the time he entered into the contract.

In these respects the classical law of contract differs little from the modern law, although the objective approach has been intensified with the passage of time. But the classical law did not stop short at this point. So great was the emphasis on agreement and the intention of the parties that the judges of the nineteenth century tended to elevate the law of contract into the central position in the law of obligations as a whole. This led to two related developments. First, there was a reluctance to impose obligations on those who had not voluntarily assumed them. The law of torts and the law of restitution thus remained relatively undeveloped during this period. And secondly, where obligations *were* imposed there was a tendency to assume that they must be contractual. So, for example, the judges denied that they had any power 'to make a contract for the parties'. Similarly, they attempted to express the great bulk of the actual rules of contract law as depending on the intention of the parties. By adopting this line the courts felt that they were not imposing legal rules on the parties, but were merely working out the implications of what the parties had themselves chosen to do. Just as John Locke had argued that political obligations derived their legitimacy from the social contract to which the people gave an 'implied assent', so the judges argued that private obligations mostly depended on private contracts to which they could find a real or 'implied assent'.

Of course, there were certain overriding legal rules which could never, in any sense, be said to depend on the intentions of the parties, such as the rules relating to the contractual capacity of persons below full age, and those relating to illegal contracts, but there were, and are, a great many other rules which the courts preferred to regard as based on the intentions of the parties. The following matters, for instance, were (and often still are) traditionally regarded as dependent on the intention of the parties: the question whether the parties have entered into a contract at all; the question whether an agreement should have validity as a legal contract; the

---

[4] *Saunders* v. *Anglia Building Society* [1971] AC 1004.

[5] Moreover, as will be seen later (see *post*, 187), it is not only *signed* documents which can become binding in this way. All sorts of contractual conditions can be, and often are, incorporated in contracts 'by reference' without even being seen by one (or even both) of the parties.

interpretation of the language used by the parties, and the question whether statements made by them should be treated as contractual; the legal results of the contract, even where the parties did not expressly state what those results were to be; and—perhaps most extraordinary of all—the law of what country was to govern the contract. Furthermore, the general idea that contractual obligations derive from agreement or mutual assent is still usually insisted upon, even though the actual rules relating to the remedies available for breach are rarely treated as resting upon contractual intent. So whenever a contract is broken, the precise legal remedy available to the other party—usually an action for damages—and the kind of damages which are recoverable are nearly always determined by legal rules, and not the intention of the parties.

Now in one sense it was (and, to a lesser extent, still is) true to say that the bulk of the actual rules of the law of contract was based on the intention of the parties, because in most cases it was (and remains) open to the parties to vary or exclude the operation of these rules by express agreement. To take a simple example, the duties of the seller of goods in respect of the quality of the goods sold could be varied, or excluded altogether, if the parties expressly agreed to do so, though this is no longer always so today. To this extent, therefore, it was perfectly true to say that these rules were dependent on the intention of the parties. But it was clearly a mistake to deduce that, because the parties are free to vary the legal incidents of a contract, therefore those incidents, *when not so varied*, are the product of their agreement. Of course, this *may* be the case. The parties may have examined the legal rules operative in the absence of express agreement, and decided that those rules are precisely the ones they wish to govern their agreement, and they may therefore have decided not to vary them by any express provisions. No doubt this sometimes happens, especially in commercial contracts, in relation to particular legal rules. But it certainly does not always happen whenever the parties have not expressly varied the effect of those rules. It seems plain that classical law was wrong in treating these rules as based on the (presumed) intention of the parties merely because there was no express agreement dealing with the questions covered by them. Unfortunately we still live with the results of this mistake.

So also, the emphasis on intention and 'implied' agreements often misled courts and writers who failed to see that a good deal of the law of contract was concerned with obligations arising from what parties did, and not merely from what they agreed or promised. And in imposing obligations because of what the parties had done rather than because of what they had intended, the judges were necessarily drawing on their ideas of fairness and justice.

It has been said above that the second idea embraced by the concept of freedom of contract was that contracts were the outcome of a free choice, and this now requires some elaboration. Once again one sees the influence of political and economic theories at work, for the freedom of choice which the courts were thinking of was freedom in a rather restricted sense. It was freedom in the sense that nobody was bound to enter into any contracts at all if he did not choose to do so, freedom in the sense that in a competitive society everyone had a choice of persons with whom he could contract, and freedom in the sense that people could make virtually any kind of contract on any terms they chose. The first of these propositions was certainly very largely true, as a matter of strict law and perhaps also in a wider sense, in the nineteenth century. It was only in a very few cases indeed that a person was under a legal obligation to enter into a contract; virtually the only example in fact was the duty of a person exercising a 'common calling', such as the innkeeper and the common carrier who were (subject to certain safeguards) legally bound to contract with any member of the public who required their services. So also in the nineteenth century, industrial and commercial competition did generally provide a real freedom of choice, and it was only the coming of the railways and the public utilities which foreshadowed the later tendency to ever larger monopolies which greatly reduced competition in so many fields. But freedom in the third sense, that is freedom to make any kind of contract on any terms, was, even in the nineteenth century, somewhat restricted. For one thing there was always the overriding public interest—'public policy' as it is called in the law of contract—to be considered, and in certain types of case the courts retained the power to declare contracts to be ineffective because they were contrary to public policy. Then again, from a comparatively early date legislative interference with freedom of contract began to play a more important role. For instance, as early as 1831 the first of the modern Truck Acts was passed to protect employees from the practice of being paid in kind instead of in cash, and in 1845 the Gaming Act enacted that wagers should no longer be capable of enforcement as contracts. None the less, when one considers the enormous amount of legislation passed during the present century which restricts freedom of contract in this sense, one is inclined to agree with the judges of the nineteenth century that real freedom of contract existed at that time.

One other consequence of the stress on freedom of contract in classical law needs emphasis. Given the dogma that obligations could be created by the intention of the parties, it came to be a fundamental principle of the law that contracts were binding and enforceable as soon as they were 'made', that is, as soon as they were agreed upon. It is thus absolutely fundamental to classical contract theory that the *making* of a contract is something different from the *performance* of a contract. No act of performance or reliance needed to be shown to justify a claim based on a contract, nor need the plaintiff prove that he had suffered any actual loss through the breach of contract. It was enough that he had expected to make a profit if the contract was performed. He was entitled to recover damages for these 'lost expectations'.

Even from the beginning the classical concept of freedom of contract suffered from certain weaknesses, and in the twentieth century these weaknesses became greatly magnified. As we have seen, the classical concept of freedom of contract embraced the two ideas of contracts being based on agreement, and of contracts being the outcome of a free choice. It is doubtful if either of these ideas was ever completely valid, and certainly in the latter half of the nineteenth century changes in social and economic conditions and in the practice of the courts already foreshadowed that freedom of contract was becoming a very different thing from what it was claimed to be.

The very development of the law itself during the latter half of the nineteenth century profoundly affected the importance attached to the agreement and intention of the parties. It remained true, of course, that contracts were usually created as the result of agreement although, as we have seen, the objective approach to questions of agreement and intention gradually became stronger. But more important than this was the fact that, as the rules relating to contracts were elaborated, the sheer complexity of the law grew such that the theory that most of the rules were based on the parties' intentions became more and more a transparent fiction.

Similarly, as the detailed rules regulating most specific contracts, such as sale, agency, insurance, and so forth, were worked out, the law tended to become more standardized. The result was again that the real intention of the parties often became less important. The law of sale of goods may be taken as an illustration of this process. During the course of the nineteenth century the duties of the buyer and seller in contracts of sale were worked out in fairly considerable detail, usually on the footing that they were based on the presumed intention of the parties. As the law developed, the duties became more and more standardized until in 1893 it became possible to codify the law relating to the sale of goods in the Sale of Goods Act 1893, now replaced by the Act of 1979. The result is that nowadays the duties of the parties to such a contract are often to be found in the Sale of Goods Act and it is unnecessary to attribute these duties to any intention, presumed or otherwise. It is still true that the parties' intentions remain important in the sense that they may be able to vary or exclude the duties laid down in the Act by expressly agreeing to do so. But even this freedom of choice is greatly restricted today in the interests of consumers and others dealing on 'standard written terms of business'.

When we turn to consider freedom of contract in its other sense of freedom of choice, we again find weaknesses in the classical law. For a long time it has been customary to point to two particular weaknesses—as they were thought to be—in classical law. In the first place the classical law of contract paid little attention to inequalities between contracting parties. Freedom of contract meant that you could choose whom you wanted to contract with, and you could arrive at the terms you wanted by mutual agreement. Even in the nineteenth century this was was only true in a narrow sense, that is, if one assumed that the bargaining power of all contracting parties was equal, and this was an assumption which the classical law very largely accepted. There were, of course, the obvious cases, such as persons below the age of capacity, lunatics, and so on, for whom special provision had to be made, but by and large the law assumed that each person could fend for himself, and if he entered into a harsh or burdensome contract he had only himself to blame because there was freedom of contract and he could have gone elsewhere. Manifestly, this assumption was false, even in the nineteenth century. The bargaining strength of the employer, for instance, was usually far greater than that of his employees at a time when trade unions were prohibited altogether or were still in their infancy. The small businessman, again, was no match for the large railway company, and so on and so forth.

One reason the law traditionally paid little attention to inequality of bargaining power was that these inequalities were thought to be matters involving *distributive* justice rather than *corrective* justice. The law of obligations was traditionally concerned merely with corrective justice, with putting right, that is, things which had gone wrong as the result of a breach of contract, or a wrong done by one person to another. Inequalities in society which resulted from the way wealth and resources were distributed were thought to be essentially political matters, to be dealt with (if at all) by Parliament, and even Parliament was not overly concerned with the redistribution of wealth in nineteenth-century England.

This lack of concern with distributive questions was not unrelated to another characteristic of classical law, namely its rather abstract and general nature. It was, indeed, only during the classical period that the very concept of a *general* law of contract largely came to be developed. Previously, there had been separate bodies of law relating to different types of contract, for instance, leases, sales of goods, insurance, and so on. Now the tendency was to generalize from these types of contract, and this tendency may well have helped the law to develop its neutral approach to distributive questions. If the law has to be the same for all kinds of contract, for sales, leases, promises of marriage, and so on, then it is more difficult to develop special rules to protect particular classes of persons such as tenants or employees.

The second problem with this aspect of freedom of contract was that classical law took little account of social and economic pressures which in many circumstances might virtually force a person to enter into a contract. Even in the nineteenth century this was true in many ways. Most people had to find a way of earning a living, and this meant entering into a contract of employment. Those who could not afford to buy a house had perforce to rent accommodation of some sort. Supplies of water and gas were rapidly becoming essential for the better-off classes, and were unlikely to be obtainable from more than one source in a particular area. The railways were already becoming the modern form of travel and, certainly by the end of the nineteenth century, virtually the only form of long-distance land travel. Here, of course, there was no choice and no competition.

These apparent weaknesses in classical theory came to seem more important later, when monopolies and restrictive practices became more widespread; but in the first three-quarters of the nineteenth century, at the heyday of classical contract law, the British economy was highly competitive, and this meant that there was a considerable degree of freedom of choice in the market in reality as well as in theory.

## 4. THE DECLINE OF FREEDOM OF CONTRACT 1870–1980

For about a century, starting perhaps around 1870, changes in political thought, in social and economic conditions, and in the law, began to take place at an ever-increasing pace. After the age of freedom of contract (perhaps best placed in the century between 1770 and 1870) it is not hard to identify the period from 1870 to 1980 as a period of gradual decline in belief in freedom of contract. Developments during this period represented to some degree a reversion to older traditions which pre-dated the age of individualism and freedom of contract. For example, the paternalist ideology which began to influence much of the law between (say) 1950 and 1980 was in many respects closer to that of the eighteenth century than that of the nineteenth century. Much of this change was influenced by a widespread belief that the classical law of contract no longer accorded with the facts of the modern world in many situations. No doubt, in the purely business area in which merchants contracted with each other for the purchase and sale of commodities, or for the construction or manufacture of plant and buildings, much freedom of contract remained even in the classical sense. But even here the law had changed a good deal, and by 1980 classical contract law appeared to be crumbling fast. Three particular factors may be mentioned as having had the greatest influence in helping to destroy the coherence of classical contract law. The first was the emergence and widespread use of the standard-form contract, the second was the declining importance attached to free choice and intention as grounds of legal obligation, and the third was the emergence of the consumer as a contracting party (and perhaps still more as a litigant). These three factors are, of course, interrelated.

### Standard-form contracts

The idea that contracts are based on agreement came, in an enormous number of cases, to be true only in a very restricted sense. While it remained true that, in most cases, the actual creation of a contract (and hence the essential terms) required the agreement of the parties, it was in many circumstances no longer true (if indeed it ever was) that the detailed terms of a contract depended on the agreement of the parties. One reason for this was the development of the standard-form contract. One result of industrialization and the emergence of mass commercial market activity was that most contracts ceased to consist of individually negotiated or custom-made terms. They came to be made on standard printed terms offered by large organizations often on a take it or leave it basis. The consumer remained 'free' in theory but his choice was often restricted to 'taking it' or 'leaving it'. Thus, although nobody could compel a passenger to travel by train, if he wanted to do so he had to do so on the terms and conditions imposed by the railway companies. He could not negotiate his own terms. Similarly, if a householder wanted to obtain supplies of gas or electricity for his house, he had to enter into a contract on terms laid down by the suppliers. Even when the goods or services in question were not a monopoly of a single organization, it was frequently found that the terms and conditions which were offered to the public were largely, if not exactly, identical.

By mid-twentieth century these standard-form contracts had become one of the major problems of the law of contract. They were to be found in every walk of life. In most cases it was only true to say that the contract was the outcome of agreement in a very narrow sense. There was often no opportunity, and hence no real freedom, to negotiate one's own terms. The terms were imposed by one party, and the other had no choice but to accept them or go without. From the very nature of the case, these terms were liable to be far more favourable to the organization supplying the goods or services in question than to the individual receiving them. The organization had every advantage over the individual. It usually had the advantage of large resources, of the best legal advice and draftsmanship, of being able to litigate, if it came to that, without having to worry unduly about the cost, and, of course, of knowing that the individual, squirm as he might, could not really do without its services. One extremely common and troublesome feature of standard-form contracts was the presence of an 'exemption clause', which often provided that the organization was not to be liable in virtually any circumstances whatsoever.

Standard-form contracts also came to be widely used in transactions between businessmen. Commercial agreements for the sale of goods would normally be recorded in 'order forms' or 'acknowledgements' with printed clauses; contracts for the carriage of goods by sea would usually be recorded in a printed 'bill of lading'; insurance contracts were nearly always recorded in printed policies, and so on. In cases of this nature there might be some room for negotiation and bargaining, but it remained the case that most clauses in such contracts were not negotiated but imposed.

The whole of the theoretical edifice of freedom of contract began to seem questionable as the magnitude of this problem was perceived. It became increasingly clear that the great majority of the most important contracts made by the average citizen were made on terms more or less imposed on him. For example, the house he lived in was very likely mortgaged to a building society on terms and interest rates fixed by the society, often in agreement with all other building societies. No doubt he might have been able to get a mortgage elsewhere, but he would have found little difference in the terms, and almost certainly none in the rate of interest. Alternatively, the house might be let to him by the local authority, in which case the terms of the lease were entirely governed by the authority, and were there only to be accepted, not bargained over.[6] The supplies of gas and electricity were, as already mentioned, on terms fixed by the suppliers. The furniture or car being bought by the consumer on hire-purchase was always the subject of a contract carefully drafted by a finance corporation to safeguard its interests, and most astonished the average citizen would be if he understood these contracts, let alone agreed to them in any real sense. The insurance policy he took out on his life or car would, too, be in a standard form, although, of course, the premiums might have to be adjusted according to the status of the individual concerned. When he proceeded to his office or factory the average citizen was still pursued by standard-form contracts. For example, on the bus or train his ticket was (and indeed, still is) issued subject to innumerable terms which the citizen could peruse, if he cared to read things incomprehensible to himself, at the office of the appropriate organization. In many cases, too, his employment would be regulated by a standard contract. This is a list which could be continued more or less indefinitely, but sufficient examples have been given to indicate the extent of the problem.

All this is not to say that there was anything wrong with standard-form

---

[6] In *Liverpool CC* v. *Irwin* [1977] AC 239 the House of Lords was faced with a local authority tenancy which was recorded in a document simply listing what the tenant was required to do and what he was prohibited from doing. There was nothing whatever about the duties of the landlord. Since the Housing Act 1980 there are statutory 'implied' terms governing some of these matters.

contracts in themselves. They had the advantages of saving time, trouble, and expense in bargaining over terms. They also had the advantage that a legal decision in one case would very likely provide a guide to disputed problems in other cases. In an age of mass production it is hardly necessary to emphasize the advantages of the mass-produced article, and this applies as much to the mass-produced contract as to anything else. But what was quite clear was that many terms of the typical standard-form contract were not *agreed to* in any real sense. The reality was that the typical contract was made on a set of fixed or standard terms with a few blanks allowing for the insertion of the names of the parties, the particular subject-matter of the contract, the price, and perhaps one or two other details. These, of course, would vary with the case, and there might be some room for bargaining over some of these blanks, but the rest of the terms were just fixed, often in printed forms. Sometimes they were drafted by one party, so they might represent his intentions alone; sometimes they were drafted by neither party, for instance, standard building and engineering contract forms were (and are) drafted by the Royal Institute of British Architects and the Institute of Civil Engineers, in which case both parties may have only the vaguest 'intentions' as to what the terms of their contract actually provide. Quite often, these standard forms were standard throughout an entire industry, being, in substance, largely agreed forms of contract which were adhered to by all firms, thus depriving the consumer of the real benefits of competition and free choice.

### The declining role of free choice

As we have seen, even during the latter part of the nineteenth century the importance attached to the intention of the parties was already waning, and there were in the law technical reasons for this. One of those reasons was the simple fact that the law was growing in complexity. This process, too, continued into this century, and to some degree continues even today. For instance, in recent years the law relating to remedies for breach of contract has become very much more developed, as the courts have distinguished between different types of damages which may be awarded, and have refined and modified the rules governing breaches of contract. It became increasingly difficult to say, as classical contract theory suggested, that the only function of the courts in contract law was to 'enforce' contracts. It became more obvious that the courts rarely 'enforced' any contracts—what they did was to impose some sort of sanction for breach of contract, in particular, by an award of damages, and it also became more obvious that the selection of the appropriate sanction was a creative act of power exercised by the courts.

A second reason for the waning belief in the value of freedom of choice was growing scepticism about the reality of free choice in the market. As we have seen, inequalities of bargaining power, social and economic pressures (often the pressures of poverty), and the use of standard forms were now thought to mean that there was no real freedom of choice in many situations, whatever the theory of the market. In thus focussing on inequalities of bargaining power, and on social and economic pressures as weaknesses in the classical concept of freedom of contract (and to some degree, perhaps also, on standard-form contracts), it may well be that the critics were attacking the wrong targets. It is true that freedom of choice was less real and less extensive than classical theory assumed, especially in the period which began around 1870 or thereabouts. But the real problem here was not inequality of bargaining power in itself, nor the social and economic pressures of poverty; it was the growth of monopolies and restrictive practices of all kinds. As we shall see more fully in Chapter 17, between about 1870 and 1950 the British economy became absolutely covered with a vast network of restrictive practices and monopolies. It was these developments which restricted freedom of choice and led many critics and reformers to have doubts about the efficacy and justice of freedom of contract. But the critics misunderstood the causes of the trouble. Although economists had been warning of the increasing threat from monopolies and restrictive practices from the 1890s onwards, the politicians, the business world, and the public were not generally hostile to these developments. Indeed, they were often seen as necessary protective measures designed to enable British industry to cope with the threat of competition from the rest of the industrial world. It is only in the last decade or two that it has begun to be more clearly understood that, if the market is truly competitive, and if monopolies and restrictive practices are under firm legal control, matters of inequality of bargaining power, pressures in the market-place, and the use of standard-forms are not necessarily serious threats to freedom of choice.

But probably the main reason for the decline in belief in free choice was simply a change in political values. The period 1870 to 1980 was one when collectivist, and even socialist, values became widespread in England. The idea that free and voluntary exchange was the secret to economic prosperity, and indeed perhaps to a generally freer and more contented society, went into steep decline during that period. For one thing, there was an increased sophistication in economic understanding of the limitations of the system of free contract. In particular, the recognition of the problem of 'externalities' was a major gain in understanding. An externality is, roughly, some side effect of a free exchange which affects third parties, and it came to be seen that, even if an exchange is beneficial to the two parties who make it, it will not be in the public interest if there are externalities which outweigh the private gain. Nineteenth-century England saw massive externality problems arising from the industrial revolution—dirty towns, insanitary accommodation, disease, and pollution, and the like, could all be seen as external costs imposed by industry on third parties, that is, the public. Often these externalities were the result of private contracts, for example, for the rent of undrained lodgings which the parties freely entered into, and which they no doubt wanted to make. It was now increasingly seen that society was perfectly entitled to prohibit such contracts, if necessary by building drains and forcing the residents to pay for them.

But, even apart from the economic limitations of the system of free contract, it also came to be widely felt that such a system led to unacceptable and unjust results. The weak and the poor, the vulnerable and the exploited, were felt to be in need of protection by the law. If left to make their own contracts, it came to be increasingly thought, they would inevitably be worsted by rich and powerful contracting parties on the other side. So the law was called in aid in a multitude of ways to interfere in contracts, prohibiting some kinds of contracts, some kinds of contractual terms, or insisting that other contracts should confer rights on one or other party which were not actually contained in the contract.

For these and similar reasons it began to seem that large areas of activity could not be left to the free choice of contracting parties, and that contract law was anyhow less a matter of free choice than had previously been thought. Huge tracts of law came to be regulated by legislation, much of which interfered with or totally overrode freedom of contract. So also, some judges began to admit that contractual solutions were sometimes 'imposed' on the parties. And there were also many circumstances in which issues which were formerly said to depend on the intention of the parties came to be now dealt with as though they simply depended on rules of law. For instance, the freedom of the parties to choose what law was to govern their contract was not looked upon so favourably as formerly; the operation of the doctrine of frustration was extended and freed from its fictitious dependence on the parties' intentions; the parties' freedom to declare in advance what were to be the results of a breach of contract was limited by the doctrine of 'fundamental breach', although that was eventually abandoned after the legislature had dealt with the problem more comprehensively than the courts could ever do.

There were, moreover, many other issues, such as questions of interpretation or construction which, while they were still *said* to depend on the intention of the parties, were often decided without any real attempt being made to ascertain this intention. A key area of the law was the doctrine of frustration, which enables a court to declare that a contract is at an end when it becomes impossible to perform it without fault on the part of either party. In classical theory, it was traditional to explain the doctrine as resting on an implied term in the original contract, and hence on the intention of the parties, but this theory was later abandoned. The seminal case was the decision of the House of Lords in *Davis Contractors* v. *Fareham UDC*[7] and the following passage from the speech of Lord Radcliffe in this case explains how it was possible to move from the one theory to the other:

Lord Loreburn ascribes the dissolution to an implied term of the contract that was actually made. This approach is in line with the tendency of English Courts to refer all the consequences of a contract to the will of those who made it. But there is something of a logical difficulty in seeing how the parties could even impliedly have provided for something which, *ex hypothesi*, they neither expected nor foresaw; and the ascription of frustration to an implied term of the contract has been criticised as obscuring the true action of the court which consists in applying an objective rule of the law of contract to the contractual obligations that the parties have imposed on themselves. . . . But it may still be of some importance to recall that, if the matter is to be approached by way of implied term, the solution of any particular case is not to be found by enquiring what the parties themselves would have agreed on had they been, as they were not, forewarned. It is not merely that no one can answer that hypothetical question; it is also that the decision must be given 'irrespective of the individuals concerned, their temperaments and failings, their interests and circumstances'.[8] The legal effect of frustration 'does not depend on their intention or their opinion, or even knowledge as to the event'.[9] On the contrary, it seems that, when the event occurs, 'the meaning of the contract must be taken to be, not what the parties did intend (for they had neither thought nor intention regarding it), but that which the parties, as fair and reasonable men, would presumably have agreed upon if, having such possibilities in view, they had made express provision as to their several rights and liabilities in the event of its occurrence'.[10]

By this time it might seem that the parties have become so far disembodied spirits that their actual persons should be allowed to rest in peace. In their place there rises the figure of the fair and reasonable man. And the spokesman of the fair and reasonable man, who represents after all no more than the anthropomorphic conception of justice, is, and must be, the court itself.[11]

Lord Radcliffe's words can be paraphrased as follows. It is not the actual agreement or intention of the parties which matters, but what they are deemed, as reasonable parties, to have agreed or intended. What we require to know, therefore, is what the reasonable man would have agreed to, or intended, in these circumstances. But in fact it is the court which represents the reasonable man, and it is thus for the court to say what it thinks the parties ought reasonably to have agreed or intended. It now becomes clear that the solution which the court finally imposes is in no real sense dependent on the intention of the parties, but is simply based on a rule of law, like any other rule of law.

---

[7] [1956] AC 696.    [8] *Hirji Mulji* v. *Cheong SS Co* [1926] AC 497 at 510.
[9] *Ibid.* 509.    [10] *Dahl* v. *Nelson, Donkin & Co* (1881) 6 App. Cas. 38 at 59.
[11] N. 7 above, at 728.

Turning to developments affecting the concept of freedom of contract in the sense of freedom of choice, we again find that by mid-twentieth century the classical law of contract was increasingly felt to be out of date. It was, doubtless, still true that there were relatively few cases where a person was under a legal obligation to enter into a contract. But pressures of one kind or another, of which the common law took little notice, might be just as important as any legal obligation, and these pressures might virtually force a person to enter into a contract which he had no great desire to make. This was already true to some extent in the nineteenth century, and it became even more true later. For example, a person might be compelled to join a trade union (thus entering into a contract) in order to exercise his trade and earn a livelihood. Or again, a retailer might be virtually compelled to contract with a wholesaler to obtain the goods necessary for his business. Similarly, every householder was virtually compelled to contract with the suppliers of gas and electricity.

Other changes also began to take place which the law of contract had to grapple with. For example, a person might be given a statutory right to be supplied with goods or services in certain circumstances (for instance, under the Health Service) and questions might then arise as to the nature and incidence of the relationship between the parties. A similar development began in other areas which may yet grow in importance, at any rate if the resurgence of classical principles permits. For instance, in the 1950s a tenant of business premises was first given, subject to certain conditions, a statutory right to a new lease on the expiry of his old one. The landlord was (and indeed remains today) *legally obliged* to grant the new lease. To the traditional contract lawyer an obligation to enter into a contract seems very like a contradiction in terms, for a contract has traditionally been seen as the outcome of a free choice, yet this example is only one of many in modern law. An even more striking example, perhaps, has been the 'right to buy' legislation (contained in the Housing Act 1985) imposing a legal obligation on local councils to sell their houses to council tenants who comply with certain simple conditions. It is well known that many councils strongly objected to this legislation, but it was nevertheless passed into law, and was often enforced against them. What is more, this trend is by no means dead. In 1993, for instance, Parliament passed the Leasehold Reform, Housing and Urban Development Act which gives private tenants the right to buy out their landlords in certain situations, even against the landlord's wishes. He is forced by law to enter into a contract to sell, whether he likes it or not.

Then there are modern statutes aimed at the prevention of discrimination which are clearly based on the assumption that a party should *not* be free to refuse to enter into a contract on certain grounds. For instance, the Race Relations Act 1976 restricts the freedom of various persons, such as employers and shopkeepers, to refuse to deal with another on account of his racial origins. Similarly, the Sex Discrimination Act 1975 makes it unlawful for the providers of various services to discriminate against women (or men). These Acts now provide, in certain circumstances, for a civil remedy for compensation in favour of the person who has been discriminated against: in effect the complainant may recover compensation from a person for unlawfully refusing to enter into a contract. The curious thing is that lawyers do not generally perceive such laws as affecting the principles of contract law itself: there, free choice remains, in theory, the ultimate basis of the law.

Then there are many kinds of economic exchanges which came to be removed from the area of contract law altogether and handled by public law. Thus governmental and local authorities provide the consumer with a wide range of services, such as free education for his children, free medical services under the National Health Service, free refuse collection from his house, and so forth. These 'free' services are, of course, not free—but they are paid for by taxation in one form or another and not by contract. Here there is no free choice at all—the consumer has to pay a charge or tax fixed by legislation or by local authorities, and he often has to pay whether he needs the service or not, and whether the service is provided or not. What is more, he has no redress if the service is poor or inefficient. The householder whose dustbins are not emptied cannot refuse to pay any part of his local Council Tax, nor can he sue for breach of contract. Lawyers do not think of these exchanges as matters of contract law at all, because they are governed by quite different legal principles. It has, for instance, been said that when a person obtains a prescription from a chemist under the National Health Service he is not entering into a contract, but is exercising a statutory right. Similarly, the relationship between a doctor working in the health service and the local health authority is largely regulated by complex statutory conditions, and it is uncertain whether there is any room left for the application of ordinary principles of contract law.[12] But although these exchanges may not be contracts, they perform a similar economic function, and the more extensive such exchanges are, the less extensive will be the field of contract and hence of contract law. The law of contract may remain unchanged but it simply applies to fewer and fewer transactions, and this was one of the trends observable in our law, especially perhaps in the period between 1945 and 1980 or thereabouts.

The declining importance attached to free choice and intention as sources of obligation also appeared to lead to a number of fundamental shifts in the law and legal thinking, even though these shifts were not always obvious to the eye. There were, for example, increased signs of a

---

[12] See *Roy* v. *Kensington and Chelsea Family Practitioner Committee* [1992] 1 AC 624.

willingness on the part of the courts 'to make a contract for the parties'. Where two parties entered into certain relations (for example, a man and woman set up house together) it might happen that disputes subsequently occurred, and that one party would come to the courts for help. In such cases the courts began to show a considerable capacity for 'making contracts'. Another major shift in the law appeared to lie in an increased reluctance to enforce wholly executory contracts by an award of pure 'lost expectation' damages, except perhaps in straightforward commercial cases. As we have previously seen, damages for 'lost expectations' are only justifiable if it is accepted that a person can impose an obligation on himself, at least in principle, merely by intending to do so. During the period up to 1980 there were some signs that the courts felt unhappy with some obligations of this character. On the other hand, where actual loss was caused to a person because he had reasonably relied on what another person had said or done, and changed his position for the worse, the tendency to protect him by an award of 'reliance damages' was stronger. We return to this theme in Chapter 22. So also, there was a pronounced tendency for courts to draw distinctions between wholly executory contracts—unperformed and unrelied-upon contracts—on the one hand, and part-executed contracts on the other hand.

The decline in the importance of contract law was, to some extent, matched by a growth in importance in other parts of the law of obligations. In particular, there was a great growth in the significance of the law of tort, on the one hand, and the law of restitution, on the other. These two other parts of the law of obligations in a sense flank, and overlap with, large areas of the law of contract. The law of tort often protects a party—by giving a right to damages—who has reasonably relied upon another, even though no contract has been made by the parties. Indeed, it hardly goes too far today to state that there is a general principle of the law that reasonable reliance on another may create liability even outside the area of contract.[13] To some degree this is to recognize that the law may impose an obligation on a person who has declined to assume an obligation voluntarily. Similarly, the law of restitution may impose an obligation on a person to pay for benefits received even where he has not actually agreed or promised to pay for those benefits. Expansion of liability here is therefore also tantamount to imposing obligations on parties who have not voluntarily assumed them. So far there is no *general* principle of English law enabling a person to claim restitution for benefits rendered without

---

[13] See Lord Diplock in *The Hannah Blumenthal* [1983] 1 AC 834 at 916. As we shall see later (see *post*, 138) many cases of this kind are decided under a doctrine called 'estoppel', but whatever label is attached to the case the result is to protect someone who has relied upon another even though there is no full contract in the legal sense.

contract—for instance the House of Lords has recently decided that a person who rescues another's derelict boat, which is dangerously adrift, cannot claim a salvage reward if the rescue occurs on a river, though there has long been such a right where a seagoing vessel is similarly salvaged.[14] But more recently still the House of Lords has done much to place the law of restitution on a broader basis,[15] and development of this form of liability may indicate a reduced role for contract law.

## The growth of consumer protection

As we saw earlier, classical contract law was largely unconcerned with problems of inequality of bargaining power. But in the twentieth century, as Parliament came increasingly to use the taxation system to redistribute wealth, it also often interfered with freedom of contract in attempts to protect the weak against the strong or rich. For instance, employment legislation was passed to confer rights on employees which they could not secure for themselves by contract; hire-purchase legislation was passed to protect hirers against unfair treatment by finance companies; and similarly landlord and tenant legislation was enacted to give better rights to tenants.

Legislation for the protection of the consumer also often took the form of creating criminal offences for conduct which at common law might be only a breach of contract or even a perfectly legal action. So, for instance, the Trade Descriptions Act 1968 made it an offence to offer goods for sale in false or misleading language. A breach of the provisions of such a statute may have its effect on the contractual position, although the statute is only directly concerned with the criminal law. For example, it is now possible to obtain a compensation order from a criminal court which convicts a person of an offence which has caused loss or injury to another person.

The most important consumer protection Act dealing with contractual rights is the Unfair Contract Terms Act 1977. Further consideration is given to this Act in Chapter 16, and here it is sufficient to say that the Act greatly restricts the use of 'exemption clauses', whereby contracting parties protect themselves from legal liability. The Act extends beyond consumer protection, since it also operates, within limits, where businessmen contract on 'standard written terms'.

Legislative interference with freedom of contract is not, of course, always directed at redressing the balance between the weak and the strong. For instance, much legislative interference with freedom of contract is designed to further broad public policy objectives. For many years, for example, it was the policy of successive British governments to encourage

---

[14] *The Goring* [1988] AC 831.
[15] See *Lipkin Gorman* v. *Karpnale* [1991] 2 AC 548; *Woolwich Building Society* v. *IRC* [1993] 1 AC 70.

the development of agriculture in order that the nation should not be so dependent upon the importation of food—something which made the country particularly vulnerable in wartime. In *Johnson* v. *Moreton*[16] the House of Lords relied upon this public policy in holding that an agricultural tenant could not contract out of the protections conferred upon him by the Agricultural Holdings Act 1948. Indeed, such was the general atmosphere at that time that the House of Lords insisted that it could no longer generally be assumed that legislative rights could be freely bargained away. It was a matter of construction of the particular statute without any presumption that freedom of contract would prevail over statutory rights.

So also, it became increasingly common in this period to find legislation with public economic objectives, such as the curbing of inflation. Such legislation often resulted in limiting freedom of contract, for instance, by stipulating that a minimum deposit was required in certain hire-purchase transactions, or even (as was done more than once) by attempting to control wage increases by law. Again, in a different class of cases, international co-operation was often the origin of legislation which to a large extent codified the terms of a particular contract, for example, contracts for the carriage of goods by sea.

The courts who were responsible for handling the common law of contract rarely attempted to go down the same road, that is, they were very hesitant to develop principles requiring them to interfere with freedom of contract, to override contracts freely entered into, even where one of the parties was manifestly much weaker than the other and incapable of looking after his own interests. But by the middle of the twentieth century they were clearly often influenced by the same sort of considerations which inspired much of this kind of legislation—that is to say, they felt a sympathy for the small consumer, the weak contracting party who found himself bound by an unfair or harsh contract of employment or hire-purchase or the like. And although the courts rarely claimed the power to override the actual terms of a contract, they could and often did try to help the weaker party to a contract by less open means, for instance by 'implying' suitable terms, or by a benevolent process of 'construction' of the terms which were actually found in the contract. By the third quarter of the present century, academic writers, and then judges and lawyers generally, began to worry that the presence of inequality of bargaining power undermined the legitimacy of contracts, and so knocked away one of the props which formerly was used to justify the imposition of State coercion.

---

[16] [1980] AC 37.

## 5. DEVELOPMENTS SINCE 1980: RETURN TO CLASSICAL PRINCIPLES?

During the past fifteen years the political and economic climates have changed dramatically in England, and the virtues of free market principles have once again been proclaimed. In many different ways the policies of the government and of Parliament have gone into reverse gear since the election of Mrs Thatcher's first administration in 1979. If, as has been suggested above, the declining role of free choice in the period between 1870 and 1980 was one of the causes of the decline in importance of freedom of contract, then it must be recognized that for the past fifteen years strenuous attempts have been made to re-invigorate the area of free choice. At the same time there has been a considerable resurgence of belief in the economic virtues of the free market system, and there has also been a growing interest (especially in America) in the relationship between legal and economic principles. Some of this work has led to a re-examination of legal rules and ideas which have held sway for a hundred years or more, and this has challenged some of the assumptions underlying the decline in importance of freedom of contract. All this suggests that the decline of freedom of contract has been halted, and the pendulum is swinging in its favour yet again.

Moreover, this renewed swing of the pendulum looks set to last for some while yet, whatever the outcome of the next few elections. All political parties now accept the virtues (within varying limits) of the free market, or free contract, and even those opposed to current trends appear now to have accepted many of the recent changes as fundamentally irreversible.

These changes in the political and economic climates have, of course, produced changes in the law, especially in legislation. But the general law of contract is largely common law, and it might seem at first sight that the common law continues on its course unruffled and uninfluenced by political and economic change in the world outside the courts. It is unlikely that many books on the law of contract would even mention the change in political direction which came with the election of 1979. In England the tradition of political 'neutrality' in the courts is so strong that lawyers and judges do not generally canvass political or economic ideologies in discussing issues of contract law. But many legal questions are profoundly affected by underlying preconceptions. There is, for example, likely to be much disagreement even over the basic question, whether the law should leave parties to make their own mistakes, or whether it is one of the functions of the law of contract to protect the weak from their own folly. It is therefore necessary, even in an introductory text like this, to consider how this new swing of the freedom-of-contract pendulum is being justified, and what its implications have been, and what they may hold for the future.

Part of the justification is, of course, purely political, that is to say, there simply has been a renewed faith in some of the underlying principles behind freedom of contract—greater belief in the right of the individual to make his own free choices and increasing disillusion over the wisdom of collective and bureaucratic decision-making. So also, there has been a move away from the use of the taxation system for purposes of redistribution of wealth. State benevolence and paternalism are today less popular than they were a decade or two ago. There is less confidence that 'Whitehall knows best', a greater belief that individuals should be left to make their own arrangements. All these changes reflect a renewed faith in freedom of contract. At the same time there has been a return towards greater use of the competitive system—greater rewards for those who succeed, and less help for those who fail. Free contract tends to produce precisely these results, since non-interference with contracts means that those who are best placed to profit from the use of their skills or resources will be left to enjoy their profits. What is more, these political changes have led to an increased area of activity for contract principles at the expense of public regulation. As we noted earlier, the declining import-ance attached to free choice in the period from 1870 to 1980 led to many activities being handled by public bodies who levied taxes for the purpose. The recent privatization of many industries means that many economic exchanges which were hitherto matters of public law and regulation have now come under the general area of contract once again.

Another justification for the recent change of direction—and one which confirms that many of these changes are likely to be permanent—is that paternalism is probably less necessary today than it was a hundred or even fifty years ago. The British people are today better educated and more sophisticated than they were. They are in less need of paternalist protection. Of course there will always be the socially inadequate, the feckless and irresponsible few, who are unable to care properly for their economic interests; there will always be the unlucky, the disabled, and the unemployed, for example; and many in these groups may continue to stand in need of some paternalist protection, though it should not be assumed that those in need of financial support are also necessarily unable to handle their affairs once that support is provided. But the great majority of people are today much better equipped to make their own contracts, and to judge their own interests, without paternalist protection. The huge growth in home- and share-ownership is a significant factor in this greater economic sophistication. Furthermore the economy is much more competitive and the consumer has far more choice than was available two or three decades ago. It was, for instance, suggested above that not long ago a person who wanted to buy a house would have little freedom of choice with regard to building society mortgage terms and interest rates. But today a bewildering variety of choices is open to the consumer—he can borrow (for instance) on a fixed interest rate mortgage, or a rate which is fixed for a varying number of years (at his option) and the rates themelves vary a good deal from one lender to another.

Apart from the changes in political values there has been much new interest, as noted above, in the relationship between legal rules and their economic effect; and this has also been a major contributory factor in the current resurgence in freedom of contract. Put shortly, it is once again being said that freedom of contract is a major instrument for economic efficiency. Allowing consumers free choice means that suppliers have to produce what consumers want; and an essential aspect of economic efficiency is that society should produce what consumers want. Subsidizing inefficient industries (for example) means that excessive resources are devoted to the production of things which consumers just do not want to buy at the real social cost at which they are produced. So also, laws such as used to exist for restricting the availability of consumer credit (minimum deposits, for instance) and exchange control laws are no longer acceptable to the government because they distort the free market. They have been repealed, therefore, and the area of freedom of contract has been correspondingly enlarged.

For our purposes, it is perhaps more relevant to note how it is today recognized by economists that direct legislative interference with free contract often has disastrously inefficient results. For instance, it is now widely understood that many years of rent-control and tenant-protection laws have largely destroyed the market for rented properties in England. Because tenants are so well protected, rents provide a very low return of profit on the landlord's investment, and consequently few people are prepared to invest in providing houses for rent. This thus creates a shortage in the home-rent market which may be quite artificial, and which would not exist if landlords were entitled to charge an economic rent. A similar case is that of minimum-wage legislation. Although the matter remains politically controversial, most economists believe that this kind of legislation simply leads to inefficiency: it drives up the cost of goods or services produced by the low-paid above their proper economic value.

Furthermore, not only does such legislative interference with freedom of contract lead to economic inefficiency, it is also now widely thought that, in the long run, it tends to harm the very people that it is designed to protect. Minimum-wage legislation, for instance, increases the cost of the employee's services to the employer. But even the most elementary grasp of economics shows that to increase costs is to reduce demand. Increasing the cost of labour (that is, wages) is no different from increasing the cost of anything else. If it costs more to employ workers because wages increase (whether as a result of a minimum-wage law or for any other reason) demand for what the workers produce will fall, and so will demand for the workers themselves. So a legally-imposed minimum wage may, in the short run, give the employee more money, but may, in the long run, lead to his losing his job and, in aggregate terms, therefore, to more unemployment. Some years ago wide publicity was given to a case of a small café proprietor who was employing a waitress and paying her less than the legally prescribed minimum wage. When the facts came to light, he was required to bring her wages up to the minimum. He protested that the café could not be operated profitably at that rate and so it was closed down. The waitress lost her job, even though she was willing to work at the lower rate. Here it seems clear that both parties would have been better off if they had been left to make their own contract without legal interference. So would the public, because they would have had a café to which at least enough people resorted to pay a wage sufficient to persuade the waitress to work there. This was, of course, a very simple case, and the economic effect of such laws is often more complex and difficult to gauge. But these economic implications of legislative interference with freedom of contract are undoubtedly helping to fuel the new swing of the pendulum back to the principles of freedom of contract.

Then again, economists are now trying to remind lawyers (though here with, so far, little success) that interfering with some of the terms of a contract probably only affects the price of the bargain, and so may prove to be idle or positively harmful to those who it is sought to help—unless prices are also controlled, which is rarely desirable. For instance, if legislation 'gives' consumers who buy goods statutory rights which manufacturers cannot contract out of, the almost certain result will be to increase the price of the goods. Many consumers may not object to this price increase, because they are glad to buy the new rights at the price—but the economic argument is that *these* consumers will be unaffected by the legislation because they should be able to buy those rights in the ordinary way anyhow, if they are willing to pay for them. The consumers who *will* be affected by the legal change are those who do not think the rights are worth the extra price, whether because they cannot afford them or for any other reason. These consumers will actually be harmed by the legislation because they are deprived of the chance to buy the goods without the attached rights. It is (on this view) as though a law were passed forcing all cars to have electric windows, instead of allowing them to be sold as an optional extra. Now this particular argument has not, so far, had a noticeable impact on the law, or even on the way lawyers (and consumers) think. And it may well be that the argument is flawed, or is for some reason not applicable in certain contexts. But it is an argument which is likely to be heard more in the future, and it is certainly one which must be faced.

Similarly, it is once again being said, as it was in the heyday of freedom of contract, that inequality of bargaining power, and any resultant unfairness in contract terms, is not a matter which the law of contract should get involved in. Inequality of bargaining power is a dangerous justification for meddling with contracts. If there is a genuine competitive market, functioning well, then there should never be any problem about inequality of bargaining power, because consumers can always go elsewhere. Doubtless the ordinary shopper cannot actually try to bargain with J. Sainsbury plc, but if he does not like the goods or prices there, he can find plenty of other shops selling what he wants. In that sense even the smallest shopper has as much bargaining power as the largest business so long as there is a truly competitive market. The biggest bargaining threat of all is to take your business elsewhere. Of course, if there is a serious monopoly problem, and if that is the source of the inequality of bargaining power, then different steps may be needed to introduce greater competition into the market, or perhaps in some cases (as with public utilities) some degree of public control is needed. And that is, indeed, conceded by all, so (for example) the newly privatized public utilities, like the gas and electricity suppliers, are subjected to some measure of public control, and are not totally free to impose their contracts on the public. In either case, therefore, the argument runs, inequality of bargaining power is insufficient ground for interference with freely negotiated contracts. Indeed, the efficient operation of the market actually *requires* that those with greater bargaining power should be permitted to use it—everybody with rare skills, whether they are footballers or pop-singers, should be entitled to charge what the market is willing to pay. Anyone who happens to have what someone else wants badly has unequal bargaining power if that thing is in scarce supply, and he should be entitled to sell it for what he can get.

This means, among other things, that for the past fifteen years or so government and legislative policy has aimed, at least in the long run, to restore freedom of contract in certain areas from which it has long been absent, such as (for instance) rent-control and minimum-wage legislation. It is, of course, understood that poor tenants or very low-paid workers may need financial support from the State; but the modern trend is to provide such support direct to those who need it, rather than by trying to use contract law as a means of redistributing wealth. There is plainly much good sense in this change of policy. If tenants are too poor to pay a proper rent, they need financial help, but it is not clear why this help should be provided by landlords rather than by the taxpayer; and anyhow (as we have seen), trying to force landlords to do the work of the social security services simply means there will be too few landlords and too little investment in building property for renting. Similarly, if some work is of so litle economic value that it cannot pay a wage which is thought socially adequate, there may be a case for financial aid, but again, it is not clear why this aid should be provided by the employer rather than the State.

Modern writers on these economic issues are by no means oblivious to some of the arguments, outlined earlier, which led to the declining belief in freedom of contract. The widespread use of standard-form contracts, for instance, and the fact that contracting parties so often do not understand, or even read, the terms by which they are bound, is a problem which remains to be grappled with if freedom-of-contract principles are once again to govern. One possible approach to these difficulties is to try to distinguish between two separate questions. The first question is whether a contracting party has genuinely agreed to, or accepted, the terms in question. And the second question is whether those terms are themselves fair or reasonable. The first question is said to be concerned with 'procedural fairness'—it addresses the procedure by which contracts are made, that is, the rules operating within the market-place. It is accepted by all that this is a proper concern of the law of contract. But the second question is one of 'substantive fairness', and that relates to the *outcome* of contracts. Many modern economic writers insist that the second question is not an appropriate question for the law to ask at all: the fairness of the terms themselves will always be reflected in the price, they insist, and it is anyhow something which contracting parties must answer for themselves. In one sense the acceptability of this distinction between procedural and substantive fairness is the most fundamental issue in modern contract law and theory, but, as in the case of many similar ideological issues, rigid adherence to the distinction is difficult in practice. We return to this important question in Chapter 16.

Now the current state of the principles and policies underlying much of contract law is very difficult to summarize because we have in effect two massive trends running in opposing directions. On the one hand we have the new trend towards a revival of freedom-of-contract principles, even though this means a return to early nineteenth-century ideas. And on the other hand we have the older trend, deriving from the late nineteenth century, the trend away from freedom of contract. This older trend has been running out of steam, but it has by no means come to a complete halt. The European Directive on Consumer Protection, for instance, which is dealt with in Chapter 16 shows how, in some areas, ideas and values adverse to freedom of contract remain powerful. In any event, the older trends have left in their wake much law which will remain in force unless and until it is disposed of. Thus we still have huge bodies of law largely derived from the period 1870–1980, when freedom of contract was in decline. We have much protective and paternalist legislation on the statute book. Most of this legislation would probably be defended by lawyers brought up in the pre-1980 atmosphere, though some of it certainly seems contrary to the modern trend. Much modern consumer-credit legislation, for instance, is very protective and paternalist. It interferes with freedom of contract on a massive scale. Inevitably it drives up the cost of consumer credit, because finance companies must pass on the additional costs imposed by consumers who fail to meet their contractual obligations in reliance on the legislation. Furthermore there is the additional danger that such legislation actually protects the feckless and the irresponsible at the cost of the honest and thrifty. This kind of 'cross-subsidization' is a common characteristic of much legislation of this period. It is a natural product of a collectivist philosophy, rather than of an individualist philosophy. It seems contrary to the modern swing back to freedom of contract. But it is very doubtful if many lawyers or politicians would yet be prepared to accept that such legislation is outdated. Legislation to confer rights on contracting parties is still constantly sought by many organizations who would dispute the economists' argument that such legislation is often against the interests of those who appear to be benefited by it.

Then again the decline in importance of contract law during the period 1870–1980 was accompanied, as we noted above, by a rise in the importance of other areas of the law of obligations, particularly the law of torts and the law of restitution, both of which frequently impose liabilities on those who have not agreed to bear them. It seems unlikely that the new swing of the freedom-of-contract pendulum will make lawyers turn their backs on these legal developments of the past thirty or forty years, which have seemed innovative and meliorative to most lawyers. However, there are signs (as we shall see later) of some slight retreat of tort law in the past decade from areas where tort overlaps particularly with contract law. To that extent, it does indeed appear that the current trend is once again reviving the primacy of contract law over other areas of the law of obligations.

Of course the swing back to freedom of contract does not mean that *all* laws and all legislative interference with private contracts are now suspect, even to those who fully support the new trends. Some of this legislation, as we saw earlier, is based on broad grounds of public policy and is not motivated by paternalist and protective ideologies. So laws like the Agricultural Holdings Act which are broadly designed to promote British agriculture may still be found interfering with freedom of contract, as we saw earlier. Again, there is no turning away from the modern understanding of the problem of 'externalities'—there is no going back to the simplistic pre-1870 belief that all private contracts must be in the public interest simply because they are in the parties' interests. On the other hand, it is certainly true that the modern swing has led to the abandonment of many former interventions with free contract which rested on broad policy grounds, such as the old regulations restricting the length of hire-purchase contracts, price-control legislation, and currency exchange controls.

But other interventions with freedom of contract remain, and are not generally thought to be inconsistent with the new trends. Partly, this is due to the paradoxical fact that freedom of contract can be used in many ways which actually limit freedom of contract. So laws which appear to restrict freedom of contract may actually be designed to enhance other areas of freedom of contract. So, for instance, common law and statutory rules designed to strike down or even to prohibit restrictive practices (as we shall see in more detail in Chapter 17) are in one sense interferences with freedom of contract, but they are actually intended to enhance freedom of contract by preserving the operation of the market.

So far as the common law is concerned, the changes in the political and economic climates of the past fifteen years also appear to be having some influence, as will be seen in more detail later. There are signs, for instance, that in contracts between businessmen the age-old equity jurisdiction to relieve a contracting party from the effects of harsh penalty or forfeiture provisions is being whittled down. Whether these changes in direction are truly justifiable on a sophisticated view of what freedom of contract requires is a question that will be addressed later. So also, there are signs that the courts are today (as their early nineteenth-century predecessors were) increasingly unwilling to use the law to protect weak contracting parties from the consequences of their own folly or ignorance. And there are signs too, perhaps, of increasing doubts about the use of contract law as a redistributive device. Certainly there is a remarkable parallel between the treatment of market principles at the political level and the treatment of freedom of contract in the legal sphere. In both cases the strong tendency now is to examine the market situation first, and then consider whether there is adequate justification for interference with its results. The fudging of these two issues, formerly so common, now appears to be frowned upon, and with some justification, because it was not an aid to clarity of thought.

### 6. THE PURPOSES OF CONTRACT LAW

After this lengthy introduction, it will suffice to discuss very briefly a topic which could also be treated at length, namely the purposes of contract law. It will be evident from the above introduction that contract law serves many purposes, and it would be misleading to insist (as some jurists and theorists have done) that the law of contract is simply designed to facilitate private planning, or to bolster the operation of the market, or to enforce promises, or to protect reasonable expectations. Undoubtedly it does these things, and they are a very central element in contract law. The law of contract facilitates and encourages free and voluntary exchange, by recognizing such exchanges as having legal effect and enforcing agreements to make such exchanges. In this way the law of contract gives legal effect to the operation of the market so as to enable business and commercial activities to be carried on efficiently.

The law of contract also facilitiates and encourages private planning by individuals by giving effect to the intentions with which they make their transactions and arrangements. This enables individuals to operate effectively as consumers in the market, but also in many private aspects of their lives which may have economic implications, even though they are not within the market as normally understood. In carrying out its fundamental purposes contract law has three main aims.

First, it is inspired by the desire to enforce promises and to protect the reasonable expectations which are generated both by promises and by other forms of conduct.

Secondly, contract law is strongly influenced by the underlying institutions of property law, so that, while it recognizes and enforces transactions for the transfer of property, it does not generally support or recognize transfers of property and money which one person has obtained without any exchange; transfers without exchange are widely thought to involve an unjust enrichment of one party at the expense of the other, and this is often a ground for legal intervention. Usually this is done by invoking the separate body of rules known as the law of restitution, but contract law is itself also powerfully influenced and affected by the idea that unjust enrichment should not be permitted. There is, indeed, a sense in which the whole concept of unjust enrichment is the mirror image of the concept of exchange.

Thirdly, contract law is also designed to prevent certain kinds of harm, particularly harm of an economic nature, or at least to compensate those who suffer such harm. Above all it tries to protect those who have reasonably relied on the promises or behaviour of others from the harm or losses which they would incur through their reliance. In this respect contract law overlaps with large parts of the law of torts which also try to protect those who are harmed by others. But whereas only a small part of the law of torts is concerned with harm arising through reasonable reliance, this is the main focus of contract law's role in the prevention of harm.

Because the first of these three purposes is usually seen as the fundamental or even the exclusive function of contract law, there is a tendency (as we have seen) to treat contractual obligations as self-imposed, and therefore to think that the role of contract law is the relatively minor one of deciding which promises to enforce and how to enforce them. Community ideas of fairness and justice are then seen as having little role in contract law. There is a basis of truth in this with regard to the first of contract law's three main purposes, but even with regard to this purpose the point is often greatly exaggerated. While many contractual obligations are self-imposed, others are not; it is, for instance, the law and not the parties which must decide what kinds of expectations are reasonable and should be protected. And in any event the whole of the law's remedial system—deciding what kind of remedy to award a party for a breach of contract—is largely imposed by the law, and not decided by the parties themselves.

And as regards the second and third purposes of contract law it is anyhow evident that they require a substantial infusion of community values. Deciding what kind of enrichment is unjust, and what kind of reliance is reasonable, which are essential elements in the second and third of contract law's three main purposes, are matters which must be done by reference to the community's ideas of justice and reasonableness.

# 2

# Definition and Classification of Contracts

THE definition and classification of legal concepts for the mere sake of defining and classifying is a somewhat barren task. But it may serve a useful purpose to define a concept in order that in the ensuing explanation a glimpse of the whole subject, in the nature of a bird's-eye view, may be obtained. The classification of concepts, too, may be helpful as an introduction to the terminology rather than the substance of the subject.

## I. DEFINITION

Definitions of contract are usually cast in terms either of agreements or of promises. So English lawyers generally define a contract as 'an agreement which is legally enforceable or legally recognized as creating a duty', and there are many similar definitions cast in terms of promises. One widely used definition is that in the American Restatement of Contracts:

A contract is a promise or a set of promises for the breach of which the law gives a remedy, or the performance of which the law in some way recognises as a duty.

Some other definitions are in similar terms, but sacrifice some accuracy as the price for succinctness. Pollock, for instance, defined a contract as 'a promise or a set of promises which the law will enforce'.

But there are problems with definitions of this kind. First, they assume that the law 'enforces' contracts. There is nothing seriously objectionable about this, and in fact lawyers constantly talk about contracts being 'enforced' but, strictly speaking, this is incorrect, and in some ways it is also misleading. Courts hardly ever 'enforce' contracts themselves, and they rarely even order the parties to perform their promises. Generally speaking, the law does not actually compel the performance of a contract; it merely gives a remedy, normally damages, for the breach. In practice this means that what a breaching party is ordered to do by a court is rarely what he actually promised or agreed to do, and that may be a point of some importance for understanding the theoretical foundations of the law.

Until very recently it was always necessary, in attempting to define a contract, to take account of some anomalous cases which were at one time of considerable importance. Under the Statute of Frauds of 1677 and later replacements, including section 40 of the Law of Property Act 1925, it was necessary for certain contracts to be evidenced in writing if they were to be fully 'enforceable', even in the sense which that term usually bears in contract law. The final clause of the definition from the Restatement was inserted to take account of this problem. Where the statutory requirement of writing was not complied with the contract could not be enforced by direct legal action, but it was none the less recognized to exist and to create a duty of performance which could be indirectly relevant in other ways. In England, recent reforms have almost completely eliminated this rare type of case, and it can now be said that, if a contract exists in the legal sense, it will be legally enforceable in the same way as all contracts are legally enforceable. At the same time, it needs to be recognized that agreements and promises can be made and given some legal recognition in different contexts without always being thought of as legal contracts. An agreement by two persons to engage in sexual conduct, for instance, would not be treated by lawyers as a contract, but it undoubtedly has important legal implications—it means, for instance, that the male cannot be guilty of rape. So also, an agreement between the solicitors of two parties engaged in litigation (for example, that no objection would be made by one party to an application for an adjournment by the other) would not be regarded as a contract, but would certainly be recognized as having legal significance.[1]

Another, and perhaps more fundamental, problem is that definitions in terms of agreements or promises assume that agreements and promises are 'things' which exist outside the law and can easily be recognized as such. But agreements and promises are not physical objects which can be perceived by the senses. They are themselves abstract concepts, just as much as the concept of contract itself. Of course 'agreement' and 'promise' are ordinary English words, and do have well-understood meanings in ordinary speech, so it may be possible to recognize them when one sees them, as it were, without any legal training. No doubt this is true of some agreements and promises, but it is not true of all. There are many difficult questions involved in actually identifying an agreement or a promise. We have, for instance, already touched on the problem of the person who signs a document without reading it. Does his signature show that he 'agrees' to the contents of the document, whatever they may be; that he 'promises' to do whatever the document says, even though he has not read it? In many cases of this nature it is not possible to say whether there is an agreement or a promise until we have first of all analysed the issue in legal terms. In other words it is the law itself which provides the only precise definitions we have of the concepts of agreement and promise, so definitions of contract which use these concepts are either incomplete or circular.

Another possible weakness of the definition of the American Restatement is that it ignores the bargain element in contracts. No indication is

---

[1] For one recent example of a case giving legal effect to a promise in a non-contractual context, see *R* v. *Croydon Justices, ex parte Dean* [1993] 3 All ER 129.

given in the definition that the typical contract is a two-sided affair, something being promised or done on one side in return for something being promised or done on the other side. Thus, to say, as this definition does, that a contract can simply be 'a promise' is to overlook the fact that there is generally some act or promise given in return for the other promise before that promise becomes a contract. Even to say that a contract may consist of 'a set of promises' gives no indication that some of these promises are usually given in return for some others.

On the other hand, it would be wrong to think that all contracts are genuine bargains in which something is offered on one side for something else of equivalent value on the other. In fact, as we shall see, there are cases in which promises are treated as contractual though there is no real bargain. A promise which is simply relied upon by the promisee even though he gives nothing in return is not a bargain, though it often creates legal obligations. For instance, as will be seen in more detail later, there are well established English cases holding that an advertisement offering a reward for specified conduct can lead to a contract if the conduct is performed. Yet such cases do not seem to involve anything that could be called a bargain or an 'agreement' in ordinary speech. The person who performs the conduct does not agree to do anything, and the person offering the reward promises, rather than agrees, to pay the reward. Then there are also many cases involving other doctrines which are very close to contract (such as 'estoppel') in which a promise is enforceable because it has been relied upon by the promisee, yet there is nothing which can really be called an agreement. American lawyers, relying on the definition and approach of the Restatement would often treat such cases as contractual, which is probably why American lawyers tend to define contracts in terms of promises rather than of agreements.

A more fundamental weakness of all definitions in terms of promises or agreements is that they presuppose that people only enter into contractual relations *after* they have made some agreement or promise. The assumption of the law is thus that contract is always a planned affair—agreement first, performance later. But this is not always the case. People sometimes simply enter into transactions or relations which are not really based on prior agreements or promises. One obvious example is that of the simultaneous exchange or sale. A person who buys goods in a supermarket and pays cash for them is exchanging his money for the goods that he buys. There is no doubt at all that this is a legal contract, but it is artificial to regard it as a contract created by agreement or promises. To insist that there must be a prior agreement or a set of promises in such a case is to imply that there is a moment of time—before the handing over of the goods and the money—in which the parties are legally bound to perform their agreement or promises. But it seems very doubtful whether that is the case. In practice, it is surely inconceivable that either party would object if the other changed his mind at the last minute, in a case of this nature. For all practical purposes this is a case where the parties make an exchange or a sale without any prior agreement to do so. And there are many other similar cases recognized by the law as, for instance, where a person simply boards a bus, paying as he enters, or drives into a car park, putting his money into a slot machine, or taking a ticket which obliges him to pay on exit. In many cases of this nature the transaction does not in practice become legally binding until one party has actually *done* something, so it is artificial to regard the obligations as arising purely from agreement or promises. Still, it must be recognized that the strength of the classical tradition in contract law is great: a traditional-minded lawyer might very well argue that 'in contemplation of law' there is an implied agreement before the actual exchange of goods for money.

There is a still broader source of difficulty about all attempts to define a contract. A definition of a contract presupposes that the law recognizes a single concept of contract. In fact it is doubtful if this is really the case. Certainly there is one very central and powerful concept in the middle of contract law—and that is the concept, roughly speaking, of classical contract law. But contractual obligations arise in such a very wide variety of circumstances, and are based on such a wide variety of grounds, that there is little relationship between cases on the outer extremities of contract law. It is true that central and straightforward cases, like a simple sale of goods, are usually treated as paradigms of contract, but there are many other types of contract which can claim to be equally paradigmatic, and yet which differ greatly from a simple exchange like a sale of goods. A contract of employment, for instance, is a relationship which may subsist over a long period of time, and cannot be easily seen as a mere agreement or set of promises. Again, contract law is often used for different purposes such as regulating institutions. Bodies like the Jockey Club, for example, which are not technically speaking companies or corporate bodies, are treated in law as a group of members bound together by contract.[2] But institutions like this have a real existence and can hardly be said merely to consist of agreements or promises.

Then also, contract law often serves purposes other than merely giving effect to agreements and promises. Promises and agreements undoubtedly lie close to the centre of the concept of contract; but there are at least two other ideas which also lie very close to that centre. One is the idea that a person who induces another to rely upon him and change his position, ought not to let that person down; and the other is the idea that a person who receives a benefit from another ought generally to pay for that benefit,

---

[2] See e.g. *R* v. *Jockey Club, ex parte the Aga Khan* [1993] 2 All ER 853.

whether he has promised or not. Contractual obligations are often imposed for one or other of these reasons on persons who have not really promised or agreed to bear them.

In cases of this nature it would often be absurd to try to identify 'a contract' as though there were a *thing* corresponding, say, to a formal written contract in cases closer to the typical or paradigm contract of classical theory. There simply is no such 'thing' to be found. What is to be found is some behaviour by the parties as a result of which the law treats them as coming under certain obligations which may be called contractual. In order to reconcile this result with traditional definitions of contract, two devices are often employed. One is to rely on the concept of an 'implied agreement' or an 'implied promise'; the other is to argue that the liability being imposed is not 'truly' contractual but is in fact a legal liability of a different kind—for instance a liability in tort, or a liability arising from 'estoppel'. In the last analysis many of these issues are verbal ones. Since the law does not contain an authoritative and conclusive definition of contract, there is no way of saying what is 'truly' a contractual liability. And the fact that different legal systems may treat liabilities as contractual which English lawyers would treat as non-contractual suggests that the search for a liability which is 'truly' contractual is pretty artificial.

But the fact that there is often no *thing* which can sensibly be identified as *the contract* which the parties have made means that we need to be careful about some of the questions posed by classical law, and about some of the ways in which lawyers talk. For instance, classical law often asks such questions as, how is a contract made, or when (or where) was a contract made? This kind of question is clearly inappropriate in those cases where the law creates a liability out of the behaviour of the parties, but this is not always recognized by lawyers. And more generally, the fact that lawyers (and law books) talk of *the law of contracts* tends to reify contracts, so strictly speaking it would perhaps be more accurate to talk of the law of contractual obligations than of the law of contracts. But that would be a counsel of perfection, and it will not be attempted in this book.

## 2. CLASSIFICATION

There are a number of different ways of classifying contracts. First, there is the distinction between deeds and simple or ordinary (or parol) contracts.

### Deeds and simple contracts

Deeds, which used to be referred to as contracts under seal because they literally required to be sealed, sometimes bear little resemblance to ordinary contracts, although the liability is based on a promise. A deed (sometimes also referred to as a covenant) is a written promise or set of promises which derives its validity from the form, and the form alone, of the executing instrument. These days the 'form' of the deed is surprisingly elastic. Since the Law of Property (Miscellaneous Provisions) Act 1989 the only necessities are that the deed should be intended as such, and should be signed and witnessed, and 'delivered'. And even 'delivery' is not literally necessary provided that there is a clear intention that the deed should be operative.

Since deeds long antedate the recognition by the law of ordinary contracts they have escaped a number of the requirements attaching to other contracts. For example, a deed is valid and takes effect from the time of 'delivery', although its contents may be unknown to the beneficiary, subject always to the right of the promisee to disclaim any benefits conferred. In an ordinary contract, as we shall see in the next Chapter, the promisor's offer must be accepted in order to create the contract.

The second requirement of ordinary contracts which is absent in the case of deeds is the very important one of consideration. It is impossible to explain this in detail at this stage,[3] but at least it can be said that a purely gratuitous promise, for example, a promise to make a plain gift, is not usually enforceable as an ordinary contract, at any rate if there is no action in reliance by the promisee. Such promises may, however, be validly made by deed, and deeds are not infrequently used for this very reason, for instance, by charitable organizations when appealing for funds.

To avoid the danger of misconception it should be added that deeds are frequently used where they are not strictly necessary, for the purpose of lending added solemnity and formality to an important contract. In such a case the use of the deed is legally irrelevant, and the liability of the parties depends on the ordinary law of contract. The law sometimes also requires the use of a deed for various legal transactions, not all of which are purely or strictly contractual in nature, for example, a conveyance of a legal estate in land.

Simple, or parol, contracts are in fact ordinary contracts, that is the subject of this book, and therefore require no further mention in this classification.

### Bilateral and unilateral contracts

Another classification of an entirely different nature divides contracts into bilateral and unilateral contracts. In a bilateral contract a promise or set of promises on one side is exchanged for a promise or a set of promises on the other side. In a unilateral contract, on the other hand, a promise on one side is exchanged for an act (or a forbearance) on the other side. Typical examples of bilateral contracts are contracts of sale, the buyer promising to

---

[3] See Ch. 6.

pay the price and the seller promising to deliver the goods. A typical example of a unilateral contract is a promise to pay commission to an estate agent if he finds a buyer for the seller's house, followed by the actual finding of the buyer. At first sight the distinction between the two types of contract may appear difficult to grasp, because even when a contract is made by the exchange of promises it is not the mere making of the promises which is the object of the contract. Each party naturally looks forward to the performance of the contract; thus even a bilateral contract may appear to consist in the mutual rendering of services by the parties. However, the essential distinction is that in a bilateral contract both parties are equally bound to the performance of their promises, whereas in a unilateral contract one party only, that is the promisor, is bound to do anything. In the estate agency case, for instance, the agent is not actually bound to find a buyer; indeed, he may not be *bound* to do anything at all. But if he does find a buyer, then the promisor is bound to pay the commission.

It must be appreciated that a transaction does not usually come ready-labelled 'unilateral' or 'bilateral' contract. It is the law which imposes the label and, hence, the results associated with that label. According to the traditional theory, the law imposes the label according to the intention of the parties—did they both make promises, or only one of them? But in practice it is often unclear what the parties intended. As we have seen, a contract with an estate agent is usually interpreted as a unilateral contract, but why should this be the case? A person goes to an estate agent and invites him to find a purchaser for his house; he agrees to pay commission at a specified rate if the agent finds a purchaser. But what other promises have the parties made? There will often be nothing expressly said or written down, so it may just be a matter of inference and implication. Does the contract bind the agent to do anything? He can hardly be bound *to find* a buyer, for he clearly does not guarantee success in his search. But it could be argued that the agent 'impliedly' promises to do *something* to find a buyer, to prepare particulars, to advertise, and so on. In fact the courts have refused in general to make that implication.[4]

Traditionally, the tendency of the courts has been to construe transactions as bilateral rather than unilateral. This was the natural course while classical contract theory held sway, because it treats the contract as binding on both parties in its inception. A bilateral contract is more easily seen as an agreement or a case of mutual promises. A unilateral contract is less readily reconcilable with classical principles. It is an awkward sort of half-way house, in which one party is not bound at all, and the other is only

---

[4] See *Luxor (Eastbourne) Ltd* v. *Cooper* [1941] AC 108. The position may be different with a sole agent.

bound subject to some condition. In the estate agency case, the agent is not bound at all, and the seller is only bound to pay commission once the purchaser is found. So the liability of the seller is only partly based on his promise; it might equally be said to be based on the fact that he has received a benefit through the efforts of the agent. So also, the seller remains free to change his mind and withdraw his house from the agent's hands. That, too, seems difficult to reconcile with classical contract principles. For, after all, the chief effect of a contract is to *bind* the parties to some future performance; but in a unilateral contract like this it seems that neither party is strictly bound at all, at any rate at the time when the arrangement is first made. So it is not surprising that the role allotted to the unilateral contract has in the past been a small one. It has generally been confined to dealing with a number of odd sorts of cases, such as offers of rewards for information or for the finding of lost property, which could not easily be fitted into the mould of classical contract law at all. Fifty years ago, as the estate agency cases show, there was perhaps a tendency for the unilateral contract to come to have a larger place. It remains to be seen whether the very modern signs of a return to classical principles will lead to change here.

A number of particular problems in connection with the distinction between unilateral and bilateral contracts will be dealt with later when the problems of offer and acceptance are discussed. But it is desirable here to stress that many unilateral contracts are not really agreements, nor are they bargains in which a promise is offered *in return* for, or *in exchange* for, an act. Some unilateral contracts may be so construed (for example, the estate agency case) but others could not. For instance, a promise to donate a prize to the winner of a race could be enforced as a valid unilateral contract once the race has been won, but there is no agreement or bargain involved here. The promise to donate the prize is in no sense *exchanged* for the act of winning the race.

### Express, implied, and quasi-contracts

A third classification which will be met from time to time divides contracts into express, implied, and quasi-contracts. According to classical contract theory this is an unsatisfactory classification because express and implied contracts belong to one class while quasi-contracts really belong to an entirely different genus—in fact, they are *sui generis*. The only difference between express and implied contracts lies in the fact that, in the former case, the intention of the parties has been expressed in so many words, while in the latter case it has to be inferred from their conduct and the general circumstances of the case. For example, when a person inserts a coin in a slot machine and receives some product in return this may be said to be an implied contract, since its existence can only be inferred or implied from the conduct of the parties. Juristically speaking, there is no significant difference between an express and an implied contract, the only real distinction lying in the method by which the contract must be proved in court in the event of disputes arising.[5]

A quasi-contract, according to the classical view, belongs to an entirely different legal category which has little or nothing in common with genuine contracts beyond the accident of history which enabled the same procedure to be used for actions in contract and actions in quasi-contract. The belief that quasi-contract and contract are entirely different legal categories has to some degree been reinforced in recent years by the replacement of the very term 'quasi-contract'. Recently lawyers have begun to amalgamate the old common-law rules of quasi-contract with a number of equitable principles covering similar ground to produce a wholly new body of law called the law of restitution. Modern writers insist on the separate identity of this part of the law of obligations, based on its own principles and serving its own purposes,[6] and their efforts have now to some degree been recognized by the House of Lords.[7]

The law of restitution deals, on the face of it, with a heterogeneous collection of cases which themselves seem to have little more in common than the fact that one person is held obliged to restore or pay for some benefit received from another (or at the expense of another) in order that he should not be unjustly enriched in the circumstances of the case. If he has promised or agreed to pay for the benefit, his liability is contractual, but if he has not done so, his liability is restitutionary. A typical case of restitution arises, for example, on payment of money under a mistake of fact, or for a purpose which has failed. The common-law side of the law of restitution—what was originally called the law of quasi-contracts—was at one time connected with contract law because the same procedure was used for both types of action in the old common-law system of litigation. The result was that (in the eighteenth century and earlier periods) quasi-contracts were often thought to be a species of contract, and were sometimes said to be contracts 'implied in law'. Genuine (but not express) contracts were then said, by way of contrast, to be contracts 'implied in fact'. The contrast, according to classical contract theory, is entirely spurious, because a contract implied in fact is a genuine contract, based on a real implied promise or agreement, drawn from the facts of the case. In

[5] The same distinction will be found between express and implied *terms of the contract*. See further on this Ch. 11.

[6] For a modern academic approach to the subject, see P. B. H. Birks, *Introduction to the Law of Restitution* (Oxford, 1985).

[7] See especially *Lipkin Gorman* v. *Karpnale Ltd* [1991] 2 AC 548; *Woolwich Building Society* v. *IRC* [1993] 1 AC 70.

the case of quasi-contracts, however, the implication is a fiction.[8] It was this kind of development which led to the abandonment of the term 'quasi-contract', and the recognition that here was a new branch of the law, independent of contract law, with its own principles and creating legal obligations not arising out of agreements or promises.

Here, as elsewhere, some of the assumptions underlying classical theory are debatable. It is only partly true that contractual obligations rest on promises and agreements, as we have already noted. Moreover, it is wrong to suggest that contract and restitution are totally unconnected, even if we accept the notion that contract law differs from restitution in being promise-based. For a large part of contract law deals with promises given in return for other benefits, so contract law resembles restitution in that both of them are at least partly concerned with obligations to pay for, or restore, benefits received. Again, whatever modern theory may say, contracts implied in fact in practice often arise in circumstances where restitutionary obligations are also recognized by law, and it is not always easy to distinguish the one from the other. Further, as a practical matter it cannot be suggested that the law of restitution is of no interest to a person studying the law of contract. Even if it is true that contracts are distinct from restitutionary obligations because the former and not the latter are founded on the agreement of the parties, the points of contact between them are many and close. In particular, the distinction between contract and restitution is of less importance when remedies are being discussed. The consequences of a failure to perform a contract are usually dictated by the law and only rarely depend on agreement. In dealing with the effects of non-performance, therefore, the law of contract and the law of restitution perform similar functions and must be studied together. There would in fact be a huge hole in a student's grasp of contract law if he failed to study restitutionary remedies arising from partial performance, non-performance, or the doctrine of frustration. So these points will be touched upon in due course in the appropriate places, but it is not proposed to embark on a full-scale discussion of the law of restitution.

## Valid, void, voidable, and illegal contracts

A fourth classification of contracts is sometimes made, based on their legal effect. Thus we can distinguish between valid, void, voidable, and illegal contracts. A valid contract is, of course, simply a contract of full force and effect, not vitiated in any way. A so-called void contract, on the other hand, is really a contradiction in terms inasmuch as a contract has already been defined in terms applicable only to a valid contract. However, the

---

[8] See especially the speeches of Lord Atkin and Lord Wright in *United Australia Ltd* v. *Barclays Bank Ltd* [1941] AC 1.

term is convenient and is universally used. For purposes of exposition, it is convenient to treat void contracts as falling, broadly speaking, into two main categories. On the one hand are cases where one of the normal requirements for the creation of a contract is absent, while on the other hand are cases where all the normal requirements are satisfied, but the contract is void because the law disapproves of its purpose or the terms by which it seeks to achieve that purpose. Typical examples of contracts which are void because one of the normal requirements is absent are contracts in which the acceptance of an offer has not been communicated or in which a promise is given gratuitously. Typical examples of contracts which are void because of their terms or objects are wagering contracts and contracts in restraint of trade.

Theoretically, it should be possible to state that a void contract is simply no contract, and is therefore totally devoid of effect. But the position is not quite so simple as that, because a contract may be void on a number of different grounds, and the results are by no means always the same. For one thing, if parties enter into a void contract but proceed to deal with each other as though they had made a valid contract, it may not be possible for the law simply to wash its hands of the transaction and declare it to be entirely destitute of legal effect. The result could simply be too unjust to be acceptable. In the second place, it is impossible to treat all void contracts alike, because some are void on both sides while others may be void on one side only. In the former case no rights are created on either side, while in the latter case rights may arise on one side but not on the other. Unfortunately English lawyers have not recognized, as a special category deserving special treatment, contracts void on one side only, although it seems undeniable that there are many such cases. Sometimes a contract may be void as against one party only, as a matter of substantive law, such as certain contracts made by persons under 18 or contracts made by lunatics or drunkards. In these cases the person under 18, or the lunatic or drunkard, may acquire rights under the contract while the other party acquires none. In other cases (such as some of the so-called 'mistake' cases, dealt with later)[9] the same position is reached by refusing to allow one party to plead that the contract is void against him. Unfortunately, owing to the failure to recognize such cases as falling into a special category, there are no general rules governing them, and when they arise they are apt to be treated as anomalous and dealt with haphazardly. Juristically, however, this class appears to be necessary for an adequate law of contract, and in fact many contracts commonly stated to be voidable are more accurately regarded as void on one side only.

A voidable contract is a contract which, in its inception, is valid and

---

[9] See *post*, 85.

capable of producing the results of a valid contract, but which may be 'avoided' by one of the parties (or, perhaps, though rarely, either of the parties). This word does not have its ordinary modern meaning in this context; to 'avoid' a contract in law is to make it or render it void, that is (in effect) to cancel it or withdraw from it. For example, if a person is induced to enter into a contract as a result of fraud, the contract is voidable at his option, but if he does not exercise his option the contract will be valid and will have all the results of a valid contract, such, for example, as the transfer of the ownership of goods sold. Moreover, even if the innocent party does choose to avoid the contract, the avoidance is not necesarily retrospective and actions done on the faith of the contract, particularly where third parties are involved, may be allowed to stand.

An illegal contract is exceptionally difficult to define. It does not merely mean a contract contrary to the criminal law, although such a contract would usually be illegal. But a contract can well be illegal without contravening the criminal law. This is because there are certain activities which the law does not actually prohibit, but at the same time regards as contrary to the public interest and therefore to be discouraged, such as prostitution. While a void contract is not necessarily illegal, an illegal contract is often void. However, the consequences of an illegal contract differ somewhat from those usually produced by a contract which is simply void, so illegal contracts are usually accorded separate treatment.

### Executed and executory contracts

Another classification which has previously been touched upon is that which divides contracts into executory and executed contracts. The terms are somewhat imprecise, but broadly they distinguish between a contract which is wholly unperformed on the one hand, and a contract which is performed, or even partly performed, on the other. Lawyers often call contracts executed, even though they are only partially executed; they also tend to call contracts executory, even though they have been relied upon, so long as the acts of reliance are not themselves in direct performance of the contract. Thus, if a contractor signs a contract to build a house and proceeds at once to order various materials, he has acted in reliance on the contract in an important respect, and his position could be serious if the contract to build the house were cancelled. But since he has not actually started to build, lawyers would tend to call the contract still executory.

Since classical contract law insisted that contractual obligations arose out of agreements and promises, it usually made no difference whether a contract was partly executed or still wholly executory. No matter when the dispute arose, it was necessary for lawyers to place themselves in the position of the parties at the moment of agreement and ask what liabilities the parties intended to assume. Here too, there are many signs of change, though the changes have not always been recognized. It seems clear that today many legal rules will be applied differently according to what stage the parties have arrived at. A contract which is partly executed or even partly relied upon may well be treated differently from a contract which is wholly executory and unrelied upon. Certainly, the damages which can be awarded for breach will he different—even classical law recognized that. But in addition, many other rules may be differently applied. For instance, an executory contract is more likely to be held void for uncertainty than a contract which is part-performed. There are also other doctrines of the law, like the various forms of 'estoppel', which can apply where agreements have been partly performed but which do not apply to wholly executory agreements. For instance, an oral contract for the sale of land or a house, which is void for lack of writing while it is still executory, may become enforceable after it has been partly performed.[10]

Rules of this nature recognize that it is often more drastic to hold a purported contract to be void after it has been partly performed or even after it has been acted upon. This seems sensible and recognizes that obligations may arise as much from what people do as from what they agree. But this undermines classical contract theory. For it means that it is often not possible to say, looking back on some arrangement, whether it amounted to a binding contract when it was entered into or only became binding as a result of what subsequently happened. In many cases this does not really matter, because the question only has to be answered now that the dispute has occurred. But a traditional lawyer might reply that, even though it may not matter in this case, it matters for future cases. People who have entered into a transaction may need to know, in some similar future case, whether the transaction amounts to a binding contract there and then. Classical theory purported to answer such questions, because it insisted that the validity of the contract could be, and indeed had to be, determined at the time it was made, ignoring all subsequent events. Although this argument is not without force, some modern lawyers are sceptical of the claims of classical theory, and anyway insist that it is often impractical, and even unjust, to ignore what the parties have done in reliance on, or in part performance of, the contract after it has been made.

This contrast in attitudes between the classical and the non-classical approach illustrates an important distinction which goes to the root of the very purpose of the law of contract. Those who stress that the executory contract is the typical contract, and should be treated as the focal point of contract law tend to see contract law as an instrument of planning. Careful

---

[10] Formerly this result was achieved by means of an equitable doctrine, known as the doctrine of part-performance. Since the 1989 Act, it is assumed that similar results will be achieved through the modern doctrine of estoppel.

and prudent human beings plan for the future, and enter into agreements to deal with future risks and problems. Classical contract law was designed to reward such people, and to facilitate their planning. By contrast some modern contract lawyers tend to see one major role of contract law as that of resolving disputes after they have arisen; here the focus is on executed or part executed contracts, not on the original agreement (if any) which initiated the relationship. Somebody has received a benefit, or someone has suffered a loss through reliance on the other; planning has gone awry because unexpected events have occurred. What is to be done? It is no use pretending that the answer can always be found in the original agreement because that simply did not contemplate what has occurred. So the court must work out the fair and reasonable solution. When this is the emphasis, planning tends to be at a discount, paternalism is likely to displace individualism, and the focus shifts from executory to part-executed contracts.

Of course, all this suggests that this is precisely one of those areas of the law in which the modern resurgence of belief in classical principles, the return to free enterprise and market principles, may produce some reaction against the trends which were observable in the law until the last decade or so. And the very fact that these trends were not always recognized as such—so that the law rarely actually acknowledged a difference between executed and executory contracts—would make it much easier to revert to classical principles without giving any appearance that the law has once again turned around somewhat. It would, in any event, be misleading to suggest that the distinction between the classical and less classical approaches to contract law is always as clear cut as this; it would also be wrong to suppose that the classical approach was always adopted by courts in the last century or that it was never adopted by judges in recent times.

### Transactions and relations

In recent years some academic theorists have been suggesting that there is another classification which has not yet been properly recognized by the law, namely the distinction between contracts which are *transactions* and contracts which are actually *relations*. Although the two may shade into each other, there are certainly striking differences between transactions and relations in many typical situations. A typical transaction is a discrete event, for instance a one-off sale between a buyer and seller who are never likely to meet again—say a motorist buying petrol at a filling station remote from his home. It is a once-and-for-all transaction, over and done with on the spot, as soon as the petrol tank has been filled and the price paid. On the other hand, many contracts are not like this at all; they are long-term relationships, such as contracts of employment or business relationships between long-standing suppliers and customers. Some of these relationships consist of one single continuous contract, while others may involve a succession of distinct contracts, but these legal differences may be less important than the underlying commercial practices of the parties.

Much classical contract law appears to have been designed on the assumption that all contracts are transactions, and it is less suited to these long-term relations. Indeed, many long-term contractual relations are today heavily regulated by statute, for instance, contracts of employment, landlord and tenant relations, and the relationships involved in company law. So the long-term relationships still dealt with by ordinary contract principles often exclude the most important types of these relationships. In relations of this kind, the obligations of the parties often cannot be traced back to some agreement or set of promises which preceded the relationship. On the contrary, the obligations and rights of the parties are constantly modified and adapted as time goes on and, what is more, many of these modifications are less the result of clear agreement or promises and more often the result of actual day-to-day adjustments which are in some vague way acquiesced in by the parties. In dealing with these relations, the concept of 'promise' as a source of obligations is just too narrow.[11]

In such relations norms often seem to emerge about the way obligations are created which do not conform to the classical paradigm of promise and agreement. For example, in relations, agreement is often reached gradually over a period of time, rather than by a more or less instantaneous process. The original contract may need to be amended in ways which do not conform to the classical procedures for making and changing contracts. The parties may imperceptibly slide into a situation from which they would feel it impossible to withdraw. A concept of 'good faith', or of fidelity to the relationship, becomes important. Dispute-settlement procedures may come to be needed which are not so adversarial as those involved in litigation, because the parties may want to settle an argument amicably, while continuing their relations.

Some lawyers may acknowledge that, commercially, there are major differences between transactions and relations, but they may insist that the law is the same for both. Adjustments and gradual change may be needed in relations, but these are (it may be urged) either done as the law provides, or they are extra-legal concessions which people make for good commercial reasons. On this view there is no need for lawyers to draw a

---

[11] This idea owes its origins and development to Ian MacNeil; see e.g. 'Relational Contract: What We Do and Do Not Know' [1985] *Wisconsin Law Rev.* 483. See also Bell, 'The Effect of Changes in Circumstances on Long-Term Contracts' in Harris and Tallon (eds.), *Contract Law Today* (Oxford, 1989).

distinction between transactions and relations. This would, however, be too narrow a view. Commercial and even ethical norms arising out of long-term relations have an impact on lawyers and judges who may be called upon to apply classical principles to situations which they do not seem to fit. So even the law may have to recognize these differences in practice.

A good example of the way this can happen is provided by employment contracts. Now most employment contracts are clearly designed to last through some length of time, often indefinitely, so some machinery is almost certainly going to be needed for minor modifications of the contract, as time goes on. In classical contract law, which (as we have seen) seems to have been designed with transactions rather than relations in mind, any change in the contract has to be negotiated and agreed in the same way as the original contract. But in employment contracts this would be unreasonable: the employer surely must have the right to change minor aspects of the employee's duties without his agreement, for instance, requiring the employee to learn new techniques or to work new machines. So this problem is overcome by implying in an employment contract a term which entitles the employer to make such changes without the employee's agreement.[12] An implication of this kind would be much harder to justify in a discrete (or even short-term) contractual transaction, so it is the long-term nature of the employment relationship here which justifies the implication. This shows, therefore, how a social/commercial norm can be relied upon by lawyers as a ground for altering the normal legal effect of a contract.[13] For similar reasons, unexpected inflation may require the law to recognize as enforceable an employer's agreement to raise salaries or wages even though technically this might raise difficulties with the doctrine of consideration.[14] Again, the ordinary rules of offer and acceptance may well require some modification for renewals of contracts, although there has so far been little open recognition of this fact.[15]

Even in contracts which are not expected to last into the indefinite future, the classical paradigm of a single exchange transaction may well differ greatly from the reality. For instance, any complex building or engineering work will these days be carried out under a detailed contract which allows for all sorts of changes to be made to the work as things progress. As was said in a recent case:[16]

---

[12] See e.g. *Cresswell* v. *Board of Inland Revenue* [1984] 2 All ER 713 (holding that staff could be required to learn how to operate computer terminals, which were replacing paper files).

[13] Of course there are limits to this; see e.g. *Redbridge London BC* v. *Fishman* [1978] ICR 569.    [14] See *post*, 142–3.    [15] See *post*, 75.

[16] See *Ashville Investments Ltd* v. *Elmer Contractors Ltd* [1988] 2 All ER 577 at 591, *per* Bingham LJ.

These [contracts] contain terms which enable the contractor's work to be increased, decreased or varied, perhaps substantially, the period of performance to be extended, again substantially, and the contract price to be recalculated, upwards or downwards, in the light of events occurring during the currency of the contract.

The need for contractual relations of this kind to be flexible and to permit of change means that it often becomes necessary for such contracts to contain detailed arrangements as to *how* the changes are to be made. And when things reach a certain degree of complexity, the contract needs to have some kind of institutional arrangements built into it. For instance, a large building or engineering contract will vest many powers of decision-making in the architect or engineer in charge—he becomes a sort of arbitrator with power to adjust the rights and duties of the parties within the terms of the contract. And as we move into still more complex types of commercial arrangements, such as company law, we find that a company has to have something resembling a *constitution* which defines the powers of the various organs of the company to make changes and adjustments. In cases like this it is somewhat artificial to see the arrangements as dependent on contract, and company law has become a specialized subject of its own. But it still has roots in contract law, in that the relations between the shareholders and the directors and other insiders are treated as growing out of an original contract between them.

# 3

# Contracts Made by the Parties: Offer and Acceptance

IN discussing the definition of contract given in the American Restatement it was pointed out that one weakness of that definition, which is in terms of promises, is that it ignores the bargain element in ordinary contracts. This weakness is fully exposed when we come to examine the formation of a contract. A contract cannot ordinarily be created by a bare promise, or even a set of promises—the typical contract is essentially a two-sided bargain which can only be concluded by the actions of both parties. The purpose of this chapter will be to examine the actual mechanics of the creation of a contract. But it is necessary to stress that this chapter is primarily concerned with contracts made by the parties in the traditional sense—that is to say, with executory contracts deliberately entered into for future performance. Not all contracts (still less all contractual obligations) are of this type. We have already seen that simultaneous exchanges cannot easily be reconciled with traditional definitions of contract in terms of agreement or promise. Equally, it would be hard to analyse such a transaction in terms of offer and acceptance. Again, there are cases in which the contract is made by the parties' behaving in a certain fashion, rather than by agreement. There are also cases in which obligations are imposed (which would not always be called contractual obligations) on someone who has made a promise which has been relied upon by the promisee even without agreement. In section 5 of Chapter 6 we shall look at some examples of contracts without agreement. In addition to these cases, there are still other sorts of cases in which the contract is in effect created by the courts *ex post facto*; these also cannot be analysed in terms of offer and acceptance, for they do not really arise from agreements. Some of these cases are discussed in Chapter 4. In the present chapter we are concerned with contracts created by the parties.

We begin, then, with contracts made by agreement. In these cases it is necessary that two or more parties should have reached an agreement, as that term is understood by the law. Generally speaking, this is done (or at any rate lawyers think it is done) by the procedure of offer and acceptance. One party states his terms to the other party, and the second party accepts those terms. In the words of Pollock:

One party proposes his terms; the other accepts, rejects or meets them with a counter-proposal: and thus they go on till there is a final refusal and breaking-off or till one of them names terms which the other can accept as they stand.[1]

This sort of haggling conjures up an image of an Eastern bazaar rather than of the modern consumer transaction. But it remains a more realistic picture of business transactions; and even where this sort of bargaining does not actually take place in practice, it is often convenient to analyse the process of negotiation in order to determine precisely when the contract is concluded. For this purpose it has become traditional to look for a proposal, or an offer as it is more usually called, on the one hand, and an acceptance on the other hand. In fact these elements are usually present in a contract, even if they are implied rather than expressed, and even if it may be difficult to disentangle the offer and the acceptance from the negotiations preceding them, and even if, as we have seen, the acceptance may sometimes be virtually compelled.

There are, however, cases which depart from the simple paradigm of two parties negotiating face to face and concluding a simple transaction. And these cases may differ from the standard paradigm in a variety of ways. For example, there are contracts with many parties, rather than just two. For instance, the relationship between the members of a club or society (and to some extent, even the relationship between shareholders of a company) is regulated by a contract, namely the rules of the society, and in such cases it may be very difficult, if not impossible, to find a real offer and acceptance or to decide who is the offeror and who the offeree. Another type of problem arises in relations (as opposed to transactions) where the parties may slide imperceptibly into a contract as a result of a sequence of steps, even though they may not have gone through anything resembling the making of an offer and acceptance. As we shall see, businessmen not uncommonly commence the performance of contracts even while negotiations are still actually going on as to the precise terms of the contract. Such cases show that to insist on the presence of a genuine offer and acceptance in every case is likely to land one in sheer fiction, although it may be convenient to postulate the existence of an offer and acceptance for some purposes; for example, it helps to pin-point the exact time and place of making the contract. None the less, many cases are susceptible of explanation in terms of offer and acceptance without any undue straining of these concepts. This applies in particular (it has been stressed by the House of Lords[2]) where a contract is alleged to have been entered into by correspondence. For it is here possible to examine a sequence of letters to

---

[1] *Principles of Contract*, 13th edn. (London, 1950), 4–5.
[2] *Gibson* v. *Manchester City Council* [1979] 1 WLR 294, *post*, 56.

see whether any of them can be said to contain a definite offer which has been clearly accepted by a subsequent letter.

## 2. THE OFFER

The first requirement, then, is an offer. Now an offer is, in effect, a promise by the offeror to do or abstain from doing something, provided that the offeree will accept the offer and pay or promise to pay the 'price' of the offer. The price, of course, need not be a monetary one. In fact, in bilateral contracts, as we explained earlier, the mere promise of payment of the price suffices to conclude the contract, while in a unilateral contract it is the actual payment of the price (or performance of a service) which is required. The offer thus contains two ideas: (1) an intimation of willingness to be bound, and (2) a statement of the price required.

An offer need not be made in so many words, nor, indeed, need it be made in words at all. It may, of course, be made expressly, by using the word 'offer', but it may equally be implied from the offeror's language or it may even be inferred from his conduct. For example, a company which displays automatic machines with goods for sale is offering these goods for sale to anyone who inserts the necessary coins (or the necessary plastic card) just as much as if it had said so in so many words. But it is not every expression of willingness to make a contract which amounts to a legal offer, because an expression of willingness is frequently nothing more than a preliminary step in the formation of the contract. So it becomes important to distinguish between an offer, on the one hand, and a mere invitation to do business, or an 'invitation to treat' as lawyers usually call it, on the other hand.

The legal requirements as to offer and acceptance are well illustrated by two cases which related to the sale of council houses by the Manchester City Council. In both cases, sales were in the process of being made when a local election resulted in a Labour majority being returned, and the sale of council houses was immediately stopped. The question in these cases was whether the process had gone so far that a legally binding contract had been made. In *Gibson* v. *Manchester City Council*[3] the defendants had sent the plaintiff a brochure explaining the then scheme for the sale of council houses, together with a form in which he could apply to the council for information as to the price at which a house could be bought. The plaintiff filled in the form and sent it to the council, which replied by letter stating the price at which they 'may be prepared to sell', and also giving details of their mortgage proposals. The letter went on to say that it was not to be regarded as a firm offer of a mortgage; a further form was sent to the

---

[3] See n. 2, *supra*.

plaintiff which he was instructed to complete if he wanted 'to make formal application' to buy the house. The plaintiff duly filled in this form and returned it. The council never replied to this application, though it took the house off the list of council houses under the control of its maintenance department. It was held by the House of Lords that there was no concluded contract, but at most an offer by the plaintiff which had never been accepted. This was, it will be seen, a case in which the parties were, in effect, in a relationship before the events in question, and it was also one of those cases in which the parties were moving slowly towards the making of a contract, and could perhaps have slid into a contract without the classic steps of offer and acceptance. But the House of Lords preferred here to stick to the well-tried principles of offer and acceptance.

In the earlier case of *Storer* v. *Manchester City Council*[4] the procedure had reached a more advanced stage. Here the plaintiff had received a reply to his formal application to purchase. The reply was a letter from the town clerk forwarding a formal 'Agreement for Sale' for the tenant to sign, and stating that on receipt of that Agreement the town clerk would send a copy of it, signed on behalf of the Council, in exchange. The Agreement contained all the essential terms for the sale of the house. It was signed by the tenant and sent to the Council, but they failed to sign and return their copy in exchange. It was held by the Court of Appeal that there was here a binding contract. The town clerk's letter forwarding the formal 'Agreement for Sale' was a clear offer, containing all the essential terms, and the tenant had accepted this offer by signing and returning the 'Agreement'. The Council's failure to return a copy in exchange was immaterial.

Attempts are usually made in the books to explain the distinction between cases which are classified as offers and those which are classified as mere invitations to treat, but it is difficult to lay down any general principle except to say that an offer must be reasonably definite, and require nothing to complete it except acceptance. What the courts tend to do, it seems, is to ask themselves whether it is reasonable that the statement by the alleged offeror should be capable of being converted into a contract by a straight acceptance, or whether it is more reasonable to expect that further discussions or negotiations will take place. A few illustrations will show how this works in practice.

The issue of a catalogue, or circular, of goods for sale, even with a price-list attached, does not usually amount to an offer. The catalogue is held to mean no more than this: 'I have these goods for sale at the listed price, and if you care to make me an offer to buy some of them I shall do my best to supply them, i.e. I may accept your offer, but I am not bound to do so'.

---

[4] [1974] 1 WLR 1403. The precise result may well be different today as a result of changes made by the Law of Property (Miscellaneous Provisions) Act 1989 with regard to the requirements of writing for contracts for the sale of land.

Similarly, it has been held by the Court of Appeal that the display of goods in a shop, even in a self-service shop, with price tickets attached, does not constitute an offer in the legal sense. It is the customer who makes the offer by picking up the article and intimating his willingness to buy it at the price named.[5] The position is different from that of goods offered for sale in an automatic machine, because in that case it is obvious that the seller has waived any right to object to the particular customer or to say that he has already sold the goods, rights which the ordinary shopkeeper may in former times have wished to exercise. Unfortunately, the way in which these questions are dealt with by the courts has meant that there has never been adequate discussion of whether these are rights which the ordinary shopkeeper *should* be entitled to exercise today.

### Conceptual reasoning in the law of offer and acceptance

In order to explain how this has happened, a short digression into the nature of 'conceptual' reasoning is necessary. This is not an easy process to explain or to understand, but a correct understanding of the nature of conceptual reasoning is an important part of a lawyer's equipment, and it is desirable to devote some attention to this point.

Put very briefly, conceptual reasoning usually takes the form of reasoning *forwards* from legal concepts to the solution of a particular dispute. For instance, if a plaintiff claims that the defendant has broken a contract and the defendant denies that there was any contract, the court may approach the case by asking whether the defendant's words or conduct amounted to an offer or an acceptance. If this question is answered in the negative, the court then *deduces* that no contract was made.

But this is not the only way in which such questions can be approached; for an alternative—and less conceptual—method of approach is to reason *backwards*. For instance, if the court thinks that the plaintiff ought to have a legal remedy against the defendant for what happened, the court may reason thus: if the plaintiff is to be given a legal remedy, we must hold that there was a contract; but in order to hold that there was a contract we must first hold that the defendant's conduct amounted to an offer (or an acceptance). *Therefore* we hold that the defendant's conduct did amount to an offer (or an acceptance). This kind of reasoning is sometimes said to be 'result-oriented', meaning that the reasoning process is determined by the desired result, rather than that the result genuinely follows from the reasoning.

In practice courts in this country have traditionally adopted the first approach in preference to the second, but there is no doubt that this has

---

[5] *Pharmaceutical Society* v. *Boots* [1953] 1 QB 401. But categorically worded advertisements such as 'Special Bargain Offer' or the like may be held to be offers in the technical legal sense.

some disadvantages. It tends to lend an air of inevitability to the decisions of the courts which is most misleading. The decision only appears to be inevitable because most of the real issues are not discussed at all; though they may weigh with the courts in arriving at their decisions, their reasoning is not openly and consciously displayed. Instead, a number of other reasons which may be more or less convincing are offered for the decision.

Many of the offer and acceptance cases are good illustrations of this process. For example, the question whether a display of goods in a self-service store amounts to an offer is itself a 'conceptual' question. The answer can have no meaning except in some legal context. The most usual context would be that in which a shopkeeper refused to serve a customer (or perhaps refused to sell the goods at the price indicated) and the real question would be whether he was *entitled* to do this. The conceptual method of answering this is to rephrase the issue in terms of concepts. Instead of asking if the shopkeeper is entitled to refuse to serve a customer, or to refuse to sell at a marked price, the courts ask whether the shopkeeper has made or accepted an offer. And this question is answered with little reference to the consequences. One result is that an important social or moral question is never openly discussed by the courts, namely should a shopkeeper be allowed to refuse to serve a member of the public, or should he be allowed to refuse to sell goods at a marked price?

Another result is that the decisions of the courts often rest on demonstratively faulty reasoning. In this particular area many of the courts' reasons are shown to be unconvincing by other legal decisions dealing with a situation in which the right to refuse to serve a member of the public is *denied*, that is, in the case of 'common inns' or hotels. For example, much has been made of the difficulties which a shopkeeper may encounter if he receives more acceptances than he has goods to sell. If he is deemed to 'offer' his goods for sale, is he then to be liable to all those customers who 'accept' his offer even though he cannot supply them? But this is an unreal difficulty, as is shown by the law relating to hotel-keepers. If a hotel proprietor is asked for a room when he has no room vacant the courts have had no difficulty in adopting the common sense view that he is not liable.

It will be seen that, if it had been desired to impose liability on a shopkeeper who refused to serve a customer, the relevant legal concepts would not have stood in the way of achieving this result. The courts could have said that a shopkeeper 'impliedly' offers to do business with any member of the public, and therefore that a contract is concluded when a customer 'accepts' the offer by intimating that he wishes to buy something in the shop.

Thus in strict logic the way in which a fact or a particular piece of conduct should be conceptualized by having a legal label attached to it should depend on the result which it is desired to achieve. But it must be recognized that lawyers and courts often reason in a way which suggests that they do not accept the strictly logical position. They frequently attach the label first, and give every appearance of thinking that the selection of the correct label is something which must be done without reference to the result.

In the particular case of self-service shops, legal methods of reasoning probably mean that the law is today out of touch with modern social conditions, and also with public attitudes. Most people would probably be surprised to discover that a shopkeeper is not obliged to sell an article at the price indicated if a customer offers to pay for it, and this public attitude is confirmed by the fact that such behaviour by a shopkeeper would today probably constitute an offence under the Consumer Protection Act 1987 or other consumer protection legislation.[6]

*Other illustrations of the distinction between offers and invitations to treat*

Auction sales present nice problems in this field. Does an announcement of an intended sale bind the seller? And during the course of the sale does the auctioneer really 'offer' the goods for sale? Subject to one difficulty, most of these questions relating to auction sales were settled long ago. Certainly the mere announcement that an auction will be held does not constitute an offer capable of being accepted, because no reasonable person would regard the seller as binding himself absolutely to hold the sale. He may, for instance, accept an offer privately before the date of the sale. The announcement of an auction often says this explicitly, which is doubtless a courtesy to the public but it is not legally necessary.

With regard to the actual sale it is old law that the auctioneer is not in the legal sense offering the goods for sale, but is only inviting the public to make offers. Each bid constitutes an offer conditional on there being no higher bid. The auctioneer is not bound to accept any bid, and conversely a bidder is entitled to withdraw his bid at any time before acceptance. The contract is only completed by the fall of the hammer or the acceptance of the bid in some other way. Here again it may well be that the law is out of touch with public attitudes. Most people would today probably be astonished to be told that the highest bidder has no actual right that the goods be knocked down to him, at any rate in the absence of a clear advance announcement to this effect. In practice most auctions are these days conducted under special conditions of sale which are posted up in the auction room, and these conditions may confirm or modify the usual rules, for example they often give the auctioneer the right to reopen the bidding

---

[6] See *R* v. *Warwicks. CC, ex parte Johnson* [1993] 2 WLR 1.

after the fall of the hammer in certain circumstances, such as when there has been some dispute over who made the final bid.

An announcement that an auction will be held without reserve gives rise to more difficulty. Once again there is nothing to prevent the seller from cancelling the sale before it has commenced, but after bidding has begun it appears that the seller may be liable if he refuses to sell to the highest bidder. At least this was held to be the law by the Court of Exchequer Chamber in the nineteenth century,[7] and although the decision has been criticized on somewhat doctrinal and technical grounds it seems so eminently just that it is hard to imagine a court today not following that decision.

Another case which gives rise to some problems in this connection is that of railway and bus companies. When a person boards a bus or buys a train ticket who is to be regarded as making the offer and who the acceptance? At one time it was thought that a railway company might be making an offer merely by issuing a timetable, but the modern view is that this is just an intimation of the railway authority's intention to run its trains in accordance with the timetables. The offer is now generally regarded as being made either by the passenger when he asks for his ticket or, more probably, by the booking clerk when he actually issues it. In the case of buses it seems that the offer is made by the bus company merely by running the buses and that the offer is accepted by a passenger boarding a bus. The difference between the two cases is explained by the fact that in the former case the railway authorities retain the power to refuse to allow a person on to a train, inasmuch as he must first obtain a ticket (as the shopkeeper has a discretion not to sell), whereas in the latter case there appears to be nothing to prevent a person boarding a bus, considerations of space, of course, excepted.

A recent case shows how these old rules of offer and acceptance may still sometimes need to be applied to completely new conditions. In *Moran* v. *University College Salford*[8] the defendants, as a result of a clerical error, sent the plaintiff an 'offer' of a place on one of their courses through the Polytechnic Central Admission system (now replaced by the UCAS) and the plaintiff accepted this. The question arose whether this created a binding contract, and though this was never actually decided, the Court of Appeal clearly thought that it probably did.

### Offers to the public at large

As will have been apparent from the above examples, although an offer is usually addressed to a specific individual or to a group of individuals, there

---

[7] *Warlow* v. *Harrison* (1857) 8 E & B 647.
[8] *Independent*, 26 November 1993.

is no reason why an offer should not be addressed to an indeterminate group or even to the public at large. In such a case the offeror indicates his willingness to contract with any member of the public who accepts his offer. Frequently such a promise is made in return for an act, thus leading to the formation of a unilateral contract. So where a reward is publicly offered by advertisement to any person who gives information leading to the conviction of a criminal, or to the recovery of lost or stolen property, the offer is regarded as a definite indication of willingness to be bound to any person who performs the stipulated act. For instance, in the unique and entertaining case of *Carlill* v. *Carbolic Smoke Ball Co*[9] the defendants were the manufacturers of a contraption known as a Carbolic Smoke Ball, which was claimed to be capable of preventing influenza, as well as a variety of other ailments. By way of an advertising stunt the defendants offered to pay £100 to any person who used the smoke ball according to the instructions and nevertheless caught influenza. In order to 'show their sincerity' the defendants also stated that they had deposited £1,000 with their bankers to meet any possible claims. The plaintiff used one of the smoke balls according to the directions, but caught influenza. She then claimed payment of the £100. However, the sincerity of the defendants proved no more genuine than their smoke balls, and they refused to pay the money. The Court of Appeal upheld the plaintiff's claim, and rejected the defendants' argument that this was a contract with all the world, and that the law did not recognize such a contract. In the words of Bowen LJ:

It was also said that the contract is made with all the world—that is, with everybody—and that you cannot contract with everybody. It is not a contract made with all the world. There is the fallacy of the argument. It is an offer made to all the world; and why should not an offer be made to all the world which is to ripen into a contract with anybody who comes forward and performs the condition?[10]

A modern example of an offer made to an indeterminate group can be found in a bank guarantee card which is an offer addressed by the bank to anyone who performs the stipulated action, such as selling goods to the holder of the card and receiving a cheque in payment. The bank's liability to pay the seller is an obligation distinct from the underlying sale contract.[11]

---

[9] [1893] 1 QB 256. For a modern American case, equally unique and entertaining, see *Jennings* v. *Radio Station KSCS*, 708 SW 2d (1986).

[10] N. 9, *supra*, at 268. The problems of imposing liability for statements addressed to the public have their parallel in tort where, indeed, they have generally been found insuperable; see *post*, 262–3.

[11] See *First Sport Ltd* v. *Barclays Bank* [1993] 3 All ER 789; *Metropolitan Police Commissioner* v. *Charles* [1977] AC 177.

## Tenders

An offer is usually directed towards the formation of a single contract, but it may happen that a proposal is made which is regarded in law as a whole series of offers, each of which is capable of being converted into a contract by a distinct acceptance. This is what is known as a standing offer. So where a person invites tenders for the supply of goods over a period of months or years, and one of the tenders is 'accepted', this does not necessarily constitute acceptance in the normal legal sense because the invitation to tender may not be regarded as an offer. There are in fact three possible interpretations of the acceptance of a tender from the legal point of view. These three possibilities were lucidly explained by Atkin J as follows:

These tenders have been the subject of litigation before now, and they vary in form, but one knows that it is quite common for large bodies that require supplies over a year to ask for tenders and to obtain them, and it sometimes happens that the effect of the form of the tender with an acceptance is to make a firm contract by which the purchasing body undertakes to buy all the specified material from the contractor. On the other hand one knows that these tenders are very often in a form under which the purchasing body is not bound to give the tenderer any orders at all: in other words, the contractor offers to supply goods at a price and if the purchasing body chooses to give him an order for goods during the stipulated time, then he is under an obligation to supply the goods in accordance with the order; but apart from that nobody is bound. There is also an intermediate contract that can be made in which, although the parties are not bound to any specified quantity, yet they bind themselves to buy and pay for all goods that are in fact needed by them. Of course, if there is a contract such as that, then there is a binding contract which will be broken if the purchasing body in fact do need some of the articles the subject of the tender, and do not take them from the tenderers.[12]

Where the arrangement is of the second kind mentioned by Atkin J the legal analysis of the situation is that the tenderer makes a standing offer to supply the goods as and when they are ordered. Each order, as it is placed, is to that extent an acceptance of the standing offer, and creates a contract for the supply of the goods so ordered. On the other hand, a standing offer may be withdrawn at any time as regards goods not yet ordered.

Tenders are also sometimes invited for an outright purchase or sale of some goods, or land or shares, and here, too, it is not always easy to say whether the invitation to tender is a legal offer or whether it is merely an invitation to make offers. Invitations to tender of this character resemble auctions, except that each party only has one bid, and they are often invited by public bodies or trustees who may have a legal obligation to see

---

[12] *Percival v. LCC Asylums Committee* (1918) 87 LJKB 677 at 678–9.

that they get the best possible price. An invitation to tender for the purchase of land (or a building) would rarely be a genuine offer because such contracts must today be made by formal written agreements. But an example of an invitation to tender for the purchase of shares which clearly was an offer in the legal sense is provided by *Harvela Investment Trust Ltd* v. *Royal Trust of Canada*.[13] In this case the owner of some shares invited two parties to tender for their purchase by sealed bids, and expressly undertook to sell the shares to the highest bidder. In the House of Lords (where the case turned on a different point) it was assumed that the invitation for the bids was a legal offer, though a slightly complex analysis of the situation was made. What was said here was that there was a preliminary contract constituted by the invitation for bids and the making of the highest bid by one of the offerees. That preliminary contract was completed as soon as the highest bid was sent in. This contract then bound the owner of the shares to sell them to the highest bidder under a second, sale, contract.

There is today a complex body of new law growing up as a result of which tenders may in some circumstances give rise to legal rights and duties independently of the main contract. This subject is explained below.[14]

### Communication of offer

It is clear that an offer must be communicated to the offeree before it can be accepted. In most cases this is self-evident, but in the reward cases it gives rise to the question whether a person who has performed the necessary action can claim the reward even if he was unaware that it had been offered. One old English case holds that he can, but the decision has been universally condemned by academic lawyers, and has not been followed in Australia or the United States. The rejection of this case must be correct if the creation of a unilateral contract always requires that the act performed must have been performed as the price of, and in return for, the promise. Manifestly, this is not possible where there is no knowledge of the offer. However, this does illustrate that these reward cases do not fit easily into the general principles of contract law. From the point of view of the offeror it seems immaterial whether the acceptor knew of the offer or not. The offeror has got what he asked for and there seems no reason in justice why he should not pay for it. If an insurance company offers a reward for information leading to the recovery of stolen property, and the information is given by someone who has never heard of the reward, the company has still received the benefit that it sought, and it should surely be liable to pay for it. It would seem preferable to recognize that a promise may sometimes be enforceable as a contract even though the act requested

---

[13] [1986] AC 207.          [14] See *post*, 106–7.

by the promisor was performed without reference to the offer. As Corbin puts it:

It is probable, indeed, that the chief reason for enforcing a promise is that it has induced the promisee to act in reliance on it. One who has rendered a service without knowledge of an offered promise has not so acted. But the chief reason is not necessarily the only reason for enforcing a promise; and if it seems good to the courts to enforce a promise when the promisor has received the desired equivalent, even though the one rendering it knew nothing of the promise and rendered the service from other motives, there is no sufficient reason for refusing to call that enforceable promise a contract.[15]

At all events it seems accepted that if the offeree knew of the offer of the reward it is immaterial for what reason the action was performed. So, where a woman gave information leading to the conviction of a criminal 'to ease her conscience', it was held that she was entitled to the reward offered on proof that she knew of the offer. Yet on principle there seems little to distinguish this situation from the case where there is no knowledge of the offer, especially when one recalls the usual objective approach of the law to questions of intention.

### 3. THE ACCEPTANCE

The acceptance of an offer is the act which completes the formation of the contract—which is, of course, a totally different thing from the *performance* of the contract. The formation of a contract is the process which creates legal obligations. Until acceptance there is nothing but a revocable offer which binds nobody. After acceptance there is a completed contract which binds both parties.

The acceptance, like the offer, contains within it two ideas, namely, (1) the acceptance of the offeror's proposal, and (2) either the promise requested by the offeror or the performance of the act required. It probably follows from this that two offers, even if identical, cannot of themselves form a contract. For instance, if A and B have been negotiating for the purchase and sale of a car, and by chance they sit down and write identical offers to each other, it seems that these offers cannot create a contract. The two offers are isolated, independent acts, and are not given one in return for the other.

Acceptance must be absolute and unconditional, and must indicate a willingness to contract on the exact terms put by the offeror. A purported acceptance which seeks to add to, or vary, some term of the offer is in law no acceptance at all, although such a purported acceptance can and will be treated as a counter-offer, itself capable of acceptance. Moreover, as we

---

[15] Corbin on *Contracts* (revised edn., St. Paul, Minnesota, 1963) I, § 59.

shall see later, a counter-offer amounts to a rejection of the original offer, which then ceases to be capable of acceptance. These rules are somewhat rigid, and may well be too rigid. It often happens that a person intends to accept an offer, and writes a letter stating that he does accept it, but then adds some further remarks, or some question (e.g. 'I presume payment by cheque will be acceptable') which may be relatively unimportant or trivial. But these further remarks or questions may be held to qualify the purported acceptance to such a degree that they prevent it having the legal character of an acceptance. The offeror may then be free to withdraw at the last minute. If, however, he simply fails to reply to the additional remarks raised by the offeree, but proceeds with the performance of the contract, it may be possible to hold that the counter-offer has in turn been accepted by conduct.

It follows from what has been said above that a conditional acceptance may also fail to count as a real acceptance at all.[16] Where the acceptance is conditional on the offeror agreeing to some further term, this is clear enough. However, there is a particular class of case which tends to arise wherever parties wish to have an agreement recorded in proper legal form. Thus when A makes a definite offer to B, and B accepts, subject to a formal contract being drawn up by a solicitor, the question may arise whether this acceptance is binding before such a contract is drawn up. On the one hand, the mere fact that the parties intend to have their contract drawn up in solemn form does not prevent their earlier agreement being binding; on the other hand, if the parties have intended to reserve their freedom of action until such a contract is drawn up, then the earlier agreement is not binding. The principle is clear enough, but its application is frequently troublesome and difficult. The practice of treating sales of land and houses as 'subject to contract' may be seen as an illustration of this principle, but it will be convenient to deal with this at a later point.[17]

### The 'battle of the forms'

The rules of offer and acceptance are difficult to apply in certain circumstances known as the 'battle of the forms', where parties want to enter into a contract but jockey for position in an attempt to use the rules of law so as to ensure that the contract is on terms of their choosing. The problem, which must be extremely common in practice, has rarely been litigated in England, and there is still only one full appeal court decision on

---

[16] A conditional acceptance must not be confused with a conditional contract. If a conditional offer is made and accepted, condition and all, then the result may be a binding contract which will, however, only become operative if the condition is fulfilled. See further on conditional contracts *post*, 171–2.

[17] See *post*, 159.

this question. In *Butler Machine Tool Co* v. *Ex-Cell-O Corpn*[18] the plaintiffs were manufacturers of machinery and, in response to a query from the defendants, they sent them an offer to supply a certain machine on terms printed on the reverse of their form. The terms included, in particular, a price-variation clause, under which the price to be charged would be subject to increase as a result of increased costs prior to the expected delivery date. The buyers sent in a purported 'acceptance' of this offer, but this document also contained various terms and conditions printed on the reverse which were stated to govern the contract, and these terms naturally did not include any price-variation clause. The document also contained a tear-off slip which the sellers were required to complete, acknowledging that the sellers accepted the buyers' terms. The sellers duly sent in the tear-off slip, but they accompanied it with a letter saying that delivery would be made in accordance with their previous quotation. The matter then rested there, the sellers made the machine, and it was eventually delivered and accepted by the buyers. The question then arose whether the buyers were bound to pay an extra sum for increased costs arising after the making of the contract, as required by the sellers' original quotation. The Court of Appeal decided that the buyers were not bound to pay the extra. They held that the buyers' purported acceptance was in law a counter-offer, and that the sellers had accepted that counter-offer by sending in the tear-off slip. The reasoning is, however, open to criticism, since the letter accompanying the tear-off slip was probably intended to make it clear that the seller's original terms were to govern the transaction.

The truth is that the parties were never really agreed on the terms which were to govern the sale of the machine, but the case illustrates a fact of business behaviour which is difficult to reconcile with the legal rules of offer and acceptance. The theory of the law is that parties first make their agreement and then perform it; but the reality is that sometimes, at least, parties agree in principle on their contract, and then start performing it, while continuing to try to agree on the details. And occasionally no agreement on those details is ever finalized. When this happens, as it seems to have happened in this case, the law appears to offer the judges only two choices. The first choice was the one adopted in this case; it is to pretend that the parties *have* agreed on one or other set of terms. Clearly this is a somewhat fictional exercise. As was said by Staughton J[19] in a recent case where a very similar question arose:

---

[18] [1979] 1 WLR 401. A similar case is *Santer Automata* v. *Goodman* (1986) Build. LR 81 (sellers sent quotation on certain terms, buyers sent 'order' on different terms, and sellers then delivered goods—held buyers' order was a rejection of sellers' offer and a counter-offer, deemed accepted by delivery of the goods, so buyers' terms prevailed).

[19] *Chemco Leasing SpA* v. *Rediffusion PLC* (1985), unreported but cited by Hirst J in *Kleinwort Benson Ltd* v. *Malaysia Mining Corp* [1988] 1 All ER 714 at 720.

When two businessmen wish to conclude a bargain but find that on some particular aspect of it they cannot agree, I believe that it is not uncommon for them to adopt language of deliberate equivocation, so that the contract may be signed and their main objective achieved. No doubt they console themselves with the thought that all will go well, and that the term in question will never come into operation or encounter scrutiny; but if all does not go well, it will be for the courts or arbitrators to decide what those terms mean. In such a case it is more than somewhat artificial for a judge to go through the process, prescribed by law, of ascertaining the common intention of the parties from the terms of the document and the surrounding circumstances; the common intention was in reality that the terms should mean what a judge or arbitrator should decide that they mean.

Nevertheless the judge held that he was bound to go through this traditional exercise, though perhaps it would be more true to say he accepted that he must profess to do so, and reason openly as though he were doing so, because it is hard to see how in fact he can perform such a manifestly unreal task.

There is one kind of case where it is standard practice to regard the parties as having contracted on one party's terms in this sort of situation, and that concerns insurance. Insurance cover is sometimes urgently required—for example, when a new car is bought and cannot be legally driven until insured—and yet there is no time to issue a complete policy. In such a case temporary cover is often agreed, sometimes even by telephone, pending the making of a proper contract in the usual way. If no contract is ever made, because for instance the parties cannot agree on the terms, the temporary cover will come to an end but is not retrospectively invalidated. If the insured event occurs during the period of temporary cover, the company will be liable. So there is clearly a temporary contract of some kind, but the terms of this contract can only be found in the insurance company's standard terms. There are no general implied terms which a court can read into a contract of this kind; each insurance company has its own set of terms, so there is simply no alternative here but to treat the temporary contract as being on the insurance company's own terms, and the insured party is taken to have agreed to these terms. This is a good example of the kind of case where a lawyer finds it very easy to say that the insured 'must be taken to have agreed' a set of terms about which the insured knows nothing, and which he might protest later that he certainly never would have agreed to if he had known what they contained.

The second option open to the judge in dealing with a case of this kind is to hold that no agreement was ever reached and that there was in consequence no legal contract at all. Sometimes this may provide a neat solution to the difficulty. In *Dewar* v. *Dewar*,[20] for instance, something

---

[20] [1975] 2 All ER 728.

resembling a battle of the forms took place in a family context. A mother provided £500 to help her son buy a house in which she was going to live with him. She wanted the money treated as a gift, while the son insisted on treating it as a loan. After her death it was necessary to decide what the legal result was. The judge held that, as the parties were not agreed on the terms, there could be no contract of loan. But a gift did not require the parties to be agreed: it was enough that the mother intended to make the gift and that the son accepted the money from her. But this solution is hardly available where, as in the *Ex-Cell-O* case, a machine has been made, and delivered and accepted. Obviously there can be no question of treating this as a gift because there is no intention to make a gift. But to hold that there was no contract is not to hold that the machine must be returned and everything undone. There may be alternative ways of solving the problem. For instance, the seller may be held entitled to a restitutionary claim for the reasonable value of the goods—which may not be the same as the contract price. This was the solution adopted by Goff J in *British Steel Corp* v. *Cleveland Bridge & Engineering Co Ltd*,[21] which resembled the *Ex-Cell-O* case, although it did not actually involve a battle of the forms in quite the same way. This case is considered further later,[22] but it does need to be said here that the restitutionary claim is not always a very satisfactory solution to the problem either.

Both these alternative approaches appear to be unsatisfactory. They stem from the insistence of the law that, if any of the terms of a bargain are not agreed, there can be no contract. This is an unsatisfactory approach, because it seems wholly unreal to say that where (for instance) goods are manufactured and delivered and accepted, there *is no contract*. Indeed (though others may think differently), it is absurd. The attempt to deal with any resultant problems by invoking the law of restitution may well leave many unresolved difficulties; for instance, it is hard to see what redress the buyer can have for defective goods,[23] or for delay in performance. Restitution deals with the payment of a reasonable price but it does not deal with many other problems that can arise under a contract, and it is dangerous to decide too readily that a contract does not exist in the belief that any gaps can be dealt with by the law of restitution.

It seems obvious that there is a sufficient agreement to make a contract in this sort of case: the parties have agreed that the goods should be made

---

[21] [1984] 1 All ER 504.  [22] See *post*, 154.

[23] The buyer's interests could to some degree be safeguarded by scaling down the seller's recovery in restitution (so that the seller only recovers the actual worth of the goods to the buyer) but this would not help matters where the buyer's claim for damages actually exceeds the value of the goods, nor is it clear what remedy the buyer would have if he had already paid the price in advance.

and delivered and accepted, and they have also agreed (as Staughton J said in the above-cited passage) that if there are any arguments they should be solved by the courts. So it would seem better in such circumstances to hold that delivery and acceptance of the machine make a new contract which is on neither set of written terms, but on the ordinary (implied) terms which operate in the absence of agreed express terms, together with any further terms which the judge feels should be implied in the particular circumstances. In the *Ex-Cell-O* case that would have led to the same conclusion as the court in fact reached, because there is no general implied term in a contract of sale (or any other contract) that prices are to increase if costs increase.

There is one very common kind of case where the approach advocated here is followed as a matter of course. Where parties are negotiating for a lease over a particular property it is common practice for the landlord to allow the tenant to enter into possession, and for the tenant to start paying rent before the terms of the lease have all been finalized. If the parties then find it impossible to agree on the terms the law does not declare the contract void. On the contrary, 'the law, where appropriate, has to step in and fill the gaps in a way which is sensible and reasonable'.[24]

Of course if, in cases like these, the parties continue to argue about the terms and, failing agreement, no performance occurs at all, it would seem clear that there would be no contract because there would be no agreement. So these cases may illustrate again the importance of the distinction between executed and executory arrangements. While the arrangements are executory, it might be sensible to hold that there is no contract; but once a machine is made and delivered, or a tenant enters into possession and pays rent, that result would be absurd.

### Communication of acceptance

As a general rule it is essential that an acceptance should be communicated to the offeror and, until it is so communicated and actually received by the offeror, the contract is incomplete.[25] A bare mental intention to accept is certainly unavailing; 'it is axiomatic that acceptance of an offer cannot be inferred from silence save in the most exceptional circumstances'.[26] The reason for this is that silence or inaction is rarely unequivocal in its significance. There are many reasons a person may fail to respond to an offer, without necessarily intending to accept it.

---

[24] See *Javad* v. *Aqil* [1991] 1 All ER 243 at 247–8, *per* Nicholls LJ.

[25] See *Brinkibon Ltd* v. *Stahag Stahl und Stahlwarenhandelsgesellschaft mb H* [1983] 2 AC 34.

[26] *The Leonidas D* [1985] 1 WLR 925, *per* Goff LJ at 937. Despite the emphatic nature of this dictum there are cases where it is confidently suggested the courts would treat a contract as accepted by silence; see *post*, 75.

Furthermore, although the offeror may prescribe a particular mode of acceptance, it appears that he may not waive the requirement of communication to himself altogether. It would obviously be unreasonable to hold that a person is deemed to have accepted an offer merely because he has not explicitly rejected it, even where the original offer has stated that acceptance will be presumed unless the offeror hears to the contrary. Any other rule would enable a stranger to thrust an unsolicited offer on an offeree and impose on him the onus of replying with a refusal. But it does not follow that an offeror should not himself be held bound by his waiver of the need for a reply. If the offeree intends to accept the offer and acts accordingly, it is hard to see why the offeror should be able to plead that there has been no communication of the acceptance, if he has expressly stated it to be unnecessary. In America it appears that such a contract would be treated as complete, but the only English case, although not quite conclusive, is usually interpreted as laying down the contrary. In this case[27] the plaintiff wrote to his nephew offering to buy his horse at a certain price, and added that if he heard no more about him he would consider the horse his. The nephew did not reply, but told the defendant, an auctioneer who was selling his stock, that the horse was not to be sold. The defendant inadvertently sold the horse, and was sued by the plaintiff who claimed that the horse was his. It was held that the horse did not belong to the uncle as the nephew had never communicated his acceptance of the offer. It is by no means certain, however, that the decision would have been the same if the action had been brought by the nephew against the uncle, had the latter refused to pay the price he had offered. Perhaps in a case like this promissory estoppel could be invoked to make good any deficiencies in contract law so that the uncle would be held bound by his own waiver of the need for a reply.

There is one important exception to the requirement that the acceptance must actually reach the offeror, and that is when the acceptance is dispatched by post. In this case the rule is that the acceptance is deemed to be complete from the moment that it is posted, properly stamped and addressed, even if the letter is delivered and remains unread, or is delivered late, or even if it never reaches its destination. This rule was first propounded in 1818, and, after much fluctuation of opinion, was finally confirmed by the Court of Appeal in 1879. It was based on a number of different grounds, none of which is entirely convincing, and the rule must now be accepted for what it is, no better and no worse than any other solution of a practical problem. The rule extends to acceptances by telegram, but not to acceptances by telephone, nor to those by telex,[28]

---

[27] *Felthouse* v. *Bindley* (1862) 11 CBNS 869.
[28] *Entores* v. *Miles Far Eastern Corp* [1955] 2 QB 327.

both of which are generally governed by the normal rule that acceptance is only effective from the time of receipt.[29]

It has also been decided[30] that the rule about posted acceptance may be inapplicable wherever it would lead to manifest inconvenience or absurdity. But this case concerned an 'option'[31] and special rules may be justifiable for options. In particular an acceptance of an option may come quite out of the blue, while an ordinary acceptance is usually the last of a series of communications. This means that the failure of an ordinary acceptance to arrive when expected may lead to inquiry while this would not necessarily be so where an option is accepted.

As mentioned above, an offer may require the acceptance to be made in a certain form or dispatched by a certain method, and in this event the acceptance must normally comply with the prescribed requirements. So, for instance, an offer sent by fax may require a similar reply, in which case a letter of acceptance would be too late and unavailing. However, it would be absurd to push this rule too far, and where the offer merely suggests, rather than insists on, a certain method of communication, a reply sent by an equally speedy method has been held to be good. In the ordinary course of events the post is used as the normal means of communication, and for that reason acceptance by post (perhaps first-class post) will usually be adequate unless there is some indication to the contrary in the offer, or unless it is clear from the circumstances that a quicker reply is required than can confidently be expected from today's mail services. It is possible that in the business world fax is rapidly establishing itself as the normal method of communication in most contractual situations, and the time may come when a posted acceptance would not be regarded as adequate. There appears to be no clear decision as to when an acceptance by fax is regarded as completing a contract, but it is probably governed by the same rules as a telexed acceptance.

## Acceptance by conduct

As we have seen, in unilateral contracts, the contract is made—that is, binding obligations arise—when the act or conduct requested by the offer is performed. So this appears to be a case of acceptance by conduct, and it is usually said that unilateral contracts are therefore another exception to the requirement that acceptance must be communicated to the offeror. But because acceptance can be by conduct, it does not necessarily follow that

---

[29] Special considerations apply, however, to non-instantaneous telex communications, e.g. telex messages received outside working hours when the office is vacant. See the *Brinkibon* case, *supra*, n. 25. These considerations must also apply to fax messages.

[30] *Holwell Securities* v. *Hughes* [1974] I WLR 155.

[31] See *post*, 76, as to the nature of an option.

communication of the acceptance is not needed. It is no doubt true that it is unnecessary for the offeree to inform the offeror of his intention to perform the act requested—Mrs Carlill did not have to tell the Carbolic Smoke Ball Company that she intended to use the smoke ball she had bought. But this in any case would not amount to a communication of acceptance, because it is the performance of the act which amounts to an acceptance in a unilateral contract. From the nature of the case, it is inevitable that the offeree will inform the offeror of his actual performance of the act requested, if only to claim the reward offered. The question whether this information is actually necessary to complete the contract would only arise in a practical form if the offeror purported to withdraw his offer after the act had been performed, but before the offeree had informed the offeror of this fact. The problem has not yet arisen, but it seems unlikely that this would be held a valid revocation of the offer. So it may be correct to say that, in cases of acceptance by conduct, communication of the acceptance is not generally required.

The possibility of an offer being accepted by conduct, rather than by a communicated acceptance, in more ordinary situations is in principle recognized by the courts, and indeed it is possible for a complete contract to be inferred from conduct. But, except in some complex commercial situations, there has been little discussion in the cases of what is sufficient to constitute an acceptance by conduct. The conduct must at least point unequivocally to acceptance,[32] though it must be said that some courts have been willing to infer contracts in cases where this could hardly be said.[33] Clearly the circumstances must be appropriate for acceptance to be made by conduct: for example, the offer must invite, or at least contemplate, acceptance by these means. A simple example is provided by a bank's customer who issues a cheque which will overdraw his account, without having previously made arrangements for an overdraft. This action by the customer is an implied invitation to the bank (an offer) to lend him the amount of the cheque, by paying the cheque. If the bank does pay the cheque, it is accepting the customer's offer by conduct,[34] and no further communication of acceptance is needed, though of course the customer will eventually learn the facts when he receives his bank statement, if not earlier.

In this connection it is perhaps worth observing that the distinction between conduct and speech is becoming increasingly blurred by the proliferation of computer and similar methods of communication. When a bank customer responds to the questions on a cash dispenser machine by

[32] See Bingham LJ in *The Aramis* [1989] 1 Lloyd's Rep. 213, 234.
[33] See e.g. *The Eurymedon* [1975] AC 154, *post*, 99.
[34] *R* v. *Bevan* (1987) 84 Cr.App.R 143 (a criminal prosecution).

pressing the appropriate buttons it is by no means clear whether he is accepting an offer by conduct or by communication. This may suggest that unnecessary distinctions between communication by speech and by conduct are best avoided.

So also, there seems no reason to doubt that an order for goods may be accepted in appropriate circumstances by dispatching the goods, even without any prior communication of acceptance. This differs from the *Carlill* type of case in that this could not be treated as a pure unilateral contract. Although the contract may be constituted by an offer in return for an act, the seller in such a case would be under contractual duties regarding the quality and fitness of the goods, so this would be a bilateral contract.

Another type of case of some practical importance concerning acceptance by conduct arises when a payment is made to settle a bill or close an account. If the payor sends a cheque 'in full satisfaction' of a disputed debt and the payee simply pays it into his account, it may be argued that this is an acceptance by conduct of the payor's offer to settle the debt with the cheque. But in practice this would throw a heavy onus onto companies where the paying of cheques into the company's bank account may be a routine matter performed by clerical staff without reference to the accompanying letter. In practice it seems that the question whether such an action can constitute acceptance by conduct is treated as a question of fact in each case.

Matters become more difficult when it is asked whether there can be an acceptance by *inaction* as opposed to an acceptance by conduct. For many purposes in the law acts and omissions are equated, but if an offer can be accepted by inaction, this would seem to contradict the principle that a bare mental intent to accept an offer is inadequate. In one recent case the Court of Appeal held that it may be possible to infer an agreement to abandon an arbitration as a result of total inaction by both parties,[35] but doubts were later cast on this possibility for the very reason that it seemed to conflict with basic principles of contract law.[36] But there are certainly some circumstances in which reasonable people would expect an explicit response to a proposal if it is being rejected, and where this is the case an offeror may very well be misled by a failure of the offeree to give a definite answer. So in one old case it was held that an offer by a landlord to renew a lease at a higher rent after the old one had expired had been accepted by the tenant simply remaining in possession without comment. In a more modern decision, however, it has been insisted that this result would not

---

[35] *The Splendid Sun* [1981] 1 QB 694.
[36] *The Leonidas D*, n. 26, *supra*; *The Hannah Blumenthal* [1983] 1 AC 854; see now the Courts and Legal Services Act 1990, s. 102.

follow unless the landlord had indicated that no answer was necessary;[37] and it has also been held that a workman cannot be deemed to accept an offer to carry on working at a reduced wage, merely because he does carry on working—while protesting at the wage cut.[38]

It may be that special considerations apply to an offer to renew a contract, especially a contract where annual renewal is customary, such as an insurance contract. Suppose, for instance, an insurance company writes to its insured towards the end of the current year, inviting him to renew his insurance for another year, and telling him that if he does wish to renew he need do nothing—the company will simply continue to collect premiums by direct debit.[39] It seems inconceivable, if the insured responds to such a letter by doing nothing but intends to renew his policy, that a court could declare the new policy not to have been validly made because the acceptance was not communicated.

### 4. TERMINATION OF THE OFFER

If an offer is not turned into a contract by acceptance, it may be 'terminated', that is it may lose its ability to be converted into a contract, in a number of ways.

First, an offer may be rejected. This destroys its efficacy in so far as the particular offeree is concerned. The result is that it is no longer open to the offeree to change his mind and accept the offer after all, unless indeed the offeror renews the offer. If it is asked why the offeree should not be able to change his mind and have a second bite at the cherry, there are two possible answers. One is that it simply seems fair and right that, if an acceptance is immediately binding when communicated, likewise a rejection should be immediately binding. But another possible reason is that, if the offeree rejects the offer, the offeror may immediately act on this, for instance, by offering to make the same bargain with a third party. It would then obviously be unfair to allow the offeree to retract his rejection. If the second of these was the chief reason for the rule, then it should perhaps not apply where the offer is rejected by mistake, and the offeree immediately withdraws the rejection before the offeror has acted on it, and seeks instead to accept it. But it has been held that an offeree may not do this,[40] so perhaps the first of these reasons is the stronger.

---

[37] See *Roberts* v. *Hayward* (1828) 3 C & P 432 and compare *Palmer* v. *Sandwell MBC* (1987) 284 EG 1487. See further the discussion of these cases in a note in (1988) 51 *MLR* 517.

[38] *Rigby* v. *Ferodo Ltd* [1988] ICR 29.

[39] The present writer not long ago received a letter in these terms from one of his insurers, and he 'accepted' by doing nothing, confident that this was a valid acceptance.

[40] *Marseille Fret SA* v. *D Oltman Schiffarts* (1981) Com LR 277.

A corollary of the first principle stated above is that a counter-offer is tantamount to rejection. The classic illustration of these rules is the case of *Hyde* v. *Wrench*,[41] where an offer to sell an estate for £1,000 was met by a counter-offer to buy for £950. The counter-offer was rejected, and the buyer then wrote to say that he was prepared to pay £1,000 after all. But the seller now refused to sell to the offeree even at this price, and the offeree sued. Although the offer to sell at this price had not been withdrawn it was held that there was no contract, as the counter-offer had amounted to a rejection of the original offer. Any other rule would give an offeree an unfair advantage in the bargaining procedure, since he could pitch his first counter-offer at a low level, and then gradually edge upwards, all the while keeping in reserve the original figure. Of course, in practice this does often happen, and the offeror is perfectly happy to accept the bargain once his original figure is reached—but the legal analysis is that at that stage the offeree is counter-offering and the offeror has the right to accept or to decline the new counter-offer even though it is on the same terms as the first offer.

Sometimes an offeree may reply ambiguously to an offer or, perhaps, seeking further information, without necessarily himself producing a counter-offer or rejecting the original offer. Then the original offer may remain open for an unconditional acceptance. On principle, too, there seems no reason why a counter-offer should not be accompanied by an express intimation that it is not to be considered as a rejection. In complex cases involving many communications it is in practice sometimes difficult to say whether a reply to an offer amounts to a rejection or not.

The second way in which an offer may be terminated is by revocation. An offer may be revoked, i.e. withdrawn, at any time before it is accepted, even if the offeror has promised to keep the offer open for a specified time. Such a promise is gratuitous, and gratuitous promises are not binding owing to the absence of consideration, though if acted upon they may sometimes be enforceable under the doctrine of promissory estoppel. If a promise to keep an offer open is made by deed, or is given for a consideration (as may happen where the offer forms part of a larger transaction, for example, an offer to sell the freehold of land leased to the offeree), it would be valid as an independent contract. Such a contract is often called an 'option' or an 'option contract'. An option is for some purposes treated as a conditional contract, but for other purposes as a sort of irrevocable offer.

Notice of revocation must reach the offeree, otherwise he is entitled to treat the offer as continuing and capable of acceptance. Moreover, a revocation sent by post, unlike an acceptance, is not effective until it

---

[41] (1840) 3 Beav 334.

reaches the offeree. This means that an acceptance posted after a revocation has been posted, but not yet received, will be valid and will create a binding contract. For instance, in *Byrne* v. *Van Tienhoven*[42] an offer to sell some goods was posted on 1 October. This letter was received and a telegram of acceptance was dispatched on 11 October. Meanwhile, on 8 October, the offeror posted a withdrawal of his offer, but this did not reach the offeree until 20 October. It was held that the dispatch of the telegram of acceptance completed the contract despite the fact that at that time a revocation was already on its way. The case is a striking illustration of the objective approach of the law of contract, for there was no moment of time at which both parties were agreed on the making of the contract in question. The offeror no longer intended to make the contract after 8 October, while the offeree did not intend to accept the offer until 11 October. Hence, this is an example of a contract where the test of agreement was plainly objective or, more realistically, where there was a contract without any real agreement. In such circumstances the justification for imposing a contractual obligation on the seller is not that he has agreed, but that he may have misled the buyer who may have acted in reliance on the seller's original, unrevoked offer, and his own subsequent acceptance.

But although the revocation must reach the offeree it is not essential that the information should be provided by the offeror himself or even by anyone acting for him. Provided that the offeree is aware of facts which should have made it clear to a reasonable man that the offer was no longer open, for example, if he hears that a house offered to him for sale has in fact been sold to a third party, the revocation will be effective.

It has already been said that unilateral contracts do not always fit happily into a legal framework devised largely for bilateral contracts, and this is especially true with regard to questions of revocation. There is no reason to doubt that an offer advertised to the world can be withdrawn like any other offer, and it is probably enough that the offeror has done what is reasonable to bring the revocation to the notice of persons who may have read the original offer, even though the withdrawal may not come to the notice of every person who saw the offer. However, a classic problem is whether an offer, which requests the performance of an act, can be revoked after the performance has been embarked on, but before it is complete. For example, if A offers prizes of £1,000 to anyone who can swim the channel on a certain day, is he entitled to withdraw his offer when the swimmers are half-way across? At first sight it seems difficult to dispute

---

[42] (1880) 5 CPD 344. It is just possible that today it would be held that the offeree must actually have acted in reliance on the offer before he could hold the offeror to the contract, but the point is a very difficult one. See *The Hannah Blumenthal*, *supra*, n. 36, and my note in (1986) 102 *Law Q Rev* 363.

the offeror's right to revoke at any time before the act is completed (provided he communicates his revocation, of course) because there appears to be no contract until that moment.[43] However, the injustice to which this may give rise is so obvious that ways of escape have been sought by academic lawyers, and there is now some judicial support for them.[44] The suggestion is that, anyhow in some circumstances, an offer of this character carries with it a subsidiary implied promise not to revoke the first offer once performance has been begun. Thus, if a prospective seller of (say) shares says to the buyer: 'Turn up tomorrow with a signed contract and I will transfer the shares to you', this may be held irrevocable once the buyer appears. The seller could not revoke his offer before the buyer has a chance to produce his signed contract.

But to say that this is a possible legal conclusion is not to say that all unilateral offers become irrevocable once they are acted upon. Sometimes the offeree just takes the risk of such revocation, as in the estate agency relationship previously discussed. An estate agent has no legal ground of complaint even if he has spent time and money trying to sell a house, just because the seller decides after all that he does not want to sell. Nor, indeed, does a potential house-buyer have any right of complaint in law if he spends money on survey and mortgage fees before the making of a binding contract, just because the seller changes his mind and refuses to sell. He, too, just takes the risk, even though he may have reasonably relied on the seller's words and behaviour.[45] There is no easy test for deciding whether in this sort of case an offer becomes irrevocable when it has been acted upon, or whether it is a case where the offeree acts at his risk. The intention of the parties, if there really is an intention on this question, may be material or even decisive; but usually there will be no clear intention, and then the result will depend partly on social and commercial custom (the estate agent acts at his risk) and partly on an assessment of the unfairness of expecting the offeree to act at his risk.

---

[43] Indeed, Lord Diplock once suggested that the very concept of an offer connotes the absence of any obligation until the offer is accepted: *Varty (Inspector of Taxes)* v. *British South Africa Co* [1965] Ch. 508 at 523. But cf. Hoffman J in *Spiro* v. *Glencrown Properties* [1991] Ch. 537 for a more sophisticated and satisfactory approach. It will be seen that this is another instance of dubious legal reasoning. It is first assumed that completion of the act required 'concludes' the contract; and secondly, that it is a universal rule that an offer can be revoked before the contract is concluded. If these assumptions are correct, the conclusion follows inexorably. But of course the whole question is whether the assumptions *are* correct.

[44] *Daulia Ltd* v. *Four Millbank Nominees Ltd* [1978] Ch. 231. The *Harvela* case, *supra*, n. 13, also seems to support this analysis though it is not exactly in point.

[45] Although this is just like the estate agency situation in that one party is at risk even though he acts in reliance on the other, the legal analysis is different. In the house-purchase situation there is normally not even a legal offer on which the buyer relies, but a mere invitation to do business, or a non-binding agreement. See further on the house-purchase transaction, *post*, 159.

At this point the reader may wonder whether, even in a potentially bilateral contract, an offer may not become irrevocable as a result of some action in reliance by the offeree even though there is not yet an express acceptance of the offer. Suppose B offers to buy some goods from S, and before S actually accepts the offer he makes arrangements to acquire the necessary goods from another source, intending then to accept. Could this be treated as a sort of action in reliance which renders B's offer irrevocable? Is there any reason why there should not be a subsidiary implied promise not to revoke the offer in this sort of case, just as in the unilateral contract case? If this is not possible the somewhat paradoxical result would be that the invention of the 'subsidiary implied promise not to revoke', which was designed to help the unilateral-contract offeree, will actually place him in a better position than the bilateral-contract offeree. Consequently, in America it is now widely held that action in reliance by the offeree may make an offer irrevocable (depending on the circumstances) even in bilateral-contract situations. English law has not yet taken this step, and it is arguable that this move is unnecessary. The 'subsidiary implied promise not to revoke' is needed in unilateral-contract situations because the offeree then *cannot* accept save by performance, so he may need protection while he is in the process of performing. But the bilateral-contract offeree does not suffer this possible injustice, since he is free to accept at any time, by tendering his counter-promise in return. So the paradox tends to melt away on analysis.

The third method by which an offer may be terminated is simply by expiry. An offer may expire in accordance with its own terms, for example, if it is made subject to some condition and the condition fails. Alternatively, it may expire by lapse of time. If an offer is not accepted, rejected, or revoked, it will eventually lapse through effluxion of time. If the offerer names a time during which the offer may be accepted, this, as we have seen, will not prevent its revocation, but it will fix its maximum duration. If it is not in fact revoked, the offer will expire at the conclusion of the time fixed by the offerer. If no time-limit is set, the offer may lapse after the expiry of a reasonable time. However, it has been decided that an offer is only to be treated as lapsed when the offeror is led to assume that it has been rejected.[46] What is a reasonable time must, therefore, be decided having regard to events occurring after the date of making of the offer, because these events may show whether the offeror did believe his offer to have been rejected.

Finally, an offer will lapse on the death of the offeror or the offeree, although it may be that in the former case notice of the offeror's death

---

[46] *Manchester Diocesan Council* v. *Commercial & General Investments Ltd* [1970] 1 WLR 141. Contrast the case of rejection (*supra*, 75). Is there any justification for the difference?

must reach the offeree before he communicates his acceptance, if the offer is to be held to have terminated.

## 5. THE EFFECT OF MISTAKE IN THE MAKING OF OFFER OR ACCEPTANCE

Under the influence of the classical tradition, itself perhaps influenced by continental jurists, English law has for many years included a doctrine of 'mistake' in its law of contract, and chapters on mistake will be found in all the books on the subject. To some lawyers, it was perhaps natural to think of a mistake in the formation of the contract as impairing the 'meeting of minds' which was sometimes thought essential, but as classical law shook off this mystical approach it became more doubtful whether there was a place for any 'doctrine' of mistake. Still, people do sometimes enter into contracts, or perform actions of a potentially contractual character, while suffering from some misapprehension, and some kind of legal response to this situation is necessary. The law may classify such cases as raising issues of 'mistake' or, alternatively, it may deal with them under other headings, such as by invoking 'implied terms' or 'duties of disclosure' or even 'misrepresentation'. The student approaching the subject for the first time, however, should be warned that, although the decisions of the courts display a fairly uniform and consistent pattern, there is a good deal of controversy over the correct classification and arrangement of the subject.

In general the classical view was that there was really very little room for a defence of mistake in the law of contract. Basically, classical law took the view that people should not make mistakes. It was up to contracting parties to decide whether to contract or not, and it was therefore up to them to decide how much investigation into facts and probabilities was worthwhile. A contracting party who had made a mistake simply had himself to blame—unless of course the mistake was actually induced by something said or done by the other party, in which case there might be remedies for fraud or misrepresentation or perhaps breach of a contractual term. Moreover, as we have already seen, classical law was loath to allow contracting parties to disavow the effect of their *apparent* intentions. The law judged intentions by appearances, objectively, as it is put. Mistakes are matters which may affect subjective intentions but they do not normally affect apparent intention, so there was a strong presumption or starting point in classical law that mistakes simply were irrelevant. And this general approach was reflected in the techniques which English courts adopted in analysing cases which might involve mistakes. Broadly speaking, in classical law the only questions which English courts normally asked were (1) is there an agreement (or a promise) sufficiently certain to be enforced as a contract and, if so, (2) what are the obligations assumed by the parties or imposed on them by law? The fact that there had been a mistake by one party or the other, or even by both, might be relevant in showing that there was in fact no agreement at all, because, for instance, the rules of offer and acceptance had not been complied with, or it might be relevant in showing that there was in fact no return for a promise, i.e. that one of the promises was gratuitous, or, again, it might be relevant in showing what precisely the obligations of the parties were. But, in itself, it was generally the case that in classical law mistake had no effect on the formation of a contract. What is more, in this particular field of the law, the classical approach remained the dominant tradition throughout, and there was little sign of any trend away from its severity. Only in a handful of relatively modern cases was there any sign of a desire to adopt a more lenient or paternalist approach which could relieve parties of the effects of their mistakes. And these cases remain today of uncertain authority.[47]

There are, of course, innumerable ways in which a party entering into a contract may be mistaken. For instance, a person may be mistaken as to circumstances which affect his own purpose in contracting, but have no other connection with the contract or with the other party, as where a person agrees to buy something under a mistaken impression as to the size of his bank balance. Again, a person may be mistaken as to the quality or nature of goods he is buying. In yet other cases a mistake may occur as to the person with whom a party is contracting, as, for instance, where a contract is made by post and one party mistakenly thinks that the other party is a different person with the same name. Then again, there are cases where both parties are mistaken, sometimes mistaken as to each other's intentions and, at other times, both sharing the same mistake. At first sight these various possibilities may appear to raise similar questions, but the law draws a basic distinction between cases where the parties have the same intention, but one or both parties is labouring under some mistake, on the one hand, and cases where the parties have different intentions on the other hand. There is a world of difference between a plea of 'we never agreed because our intentions were different' and a plea of 'our intentions were the same and we agreed, but because one or both of us were mistaken, the agreement should not be treated as a binding contract'. The first plea denies the very existence of the agreement, while the second admits it. Naturally enough, therefore, the first class of cases falls to be considered in this chapter, which deals with the formation of contracts, while the latter class of cases will be dealt with in Chapter 12 when we examine the problems which arise after a contract has been found to exist.

At the moment, then, we are concerned with the effect of a mistake on

---

[47] These cases do not involve the type of mistake under discussion in this Ch. See *post*, 228 for these cases.

the rules of offer and acceptance, and this question deserves detailed examination. Three situations must be examined, namely, (1) where one party is mistaken and the other party is not aware of the first party's real intentions; (2) where one party is mistaken and the other party is aware of the first party's real intentions; and (3) where each party is aware of the real intentions of the other and these intentions do not coincide.

### Where one party is mistaken and the other is not aware of the first party's real intentions

In these cases, as we have already seen, the law interprets the intentions of the parties objectively, with the result that the mistake generally has no effect at all. The only question is whether the offeree has accepted the offer in the sense in which a reasonable person would have understood it, although it may be that he also has to show that he has changed his position by relying upon what the mistaken party has said or done.[48] Hence a mistake which only affects one party's *purpose* in contracting is totally irrelevant, because it does not prevent an agreement being reached. Indeed, a mistake of this kind may well be compatible with real subjective agreement, for a party may well intend to make a certain contract with a certain person despite a mistake of this kind. Suppose a person books a holiday starting on 1 April, thinking, mistakenly, that this is the beginning of the Easter weekend. His mistake does not alter the fact that he intended to book a holiday with that holiday company for that particular date. But even if there is no real subjective agreement, there will almost invariably be agreement, objectively judged, and that, as we have seen, is enough to make a contract. Thus, although it often used to be said that only a person to whom an offer is addressed can accept it, it is established law that any person can accept an offer if he reasonably, though mistakenly, thinks it was intended for him.

Similarly, where an offeror is mistaken about the terms of a contract of sale, the only question is, what did the offeree reasonably understand the offeror to be offering? So where A sold a yacht to B and B reasonably understood that A was guaranteeing the condition of the yacht, it was immaterial that A had not intended to give a guarantee at all. His mistake as to B's intention was thus irrelevant, and he was liable just as much as if he had intended to give a guarantee.[49] Similarly, in one well-known case[50] where the defendant was the highest bidder at an auction sale of a public house, it was held that the contract was valid and binding on him, despite his objection that he had mistakenly thought that a

---

[48] See *The Hannah Blumenthal, supra,* n. 36.
[49] *Sullivan* v. *Constable* (1932) 49 TLR 369.
[50] *Tamplin* v. *James* (1880) 15 Ch.D 215.

certain field was included in the the land being sold. Had the defendant examined the particulars of sale, as a reasonable person would have assumed he had done, he would have seen that the field was not included in the sale. The sellers were therefore entitled to assume that the defendant knew what he was bidding for. His bid, that is to say, his offer to buy the premises, was, therefore, capable of being converted into a contract by acceptance. Again, it has recently been held that an offer by a landlord's agent to fix the rent of commercial premises at an absurdly low level was binding on the landlord because it was immediately accepted by the tenant even though the agent had made a mistake which was at once pointed out on receipt of the acceptance.[51] More generally, it seems now an established principle that, when the court is construing a written document, the actual intentions of the parties as to the meaning of that document are irrelevant and perhaps even inadmissible in evidence.[52]

Thus the result in these cases of mistake is almost always the creation of a contract on the terms understood by one party or the other, according to which party's interpretation is the more reasonable. Very exceptionally it may happen that no contract is created in such circumstances because of some inherent ambiguity in the offer or the acceptance, but the absence of a contract is then due to the uncertainty, rather than to the mistake, or to the lack of any proper offer and acceptance. The question will therefore be dealt with when we consider certainty in Chapter 5.

There is an argument for suggesting that the law goes too far in altogether ignoring mistakes of this character, except in those rare cases where resulting uncertainty prevents a contract being created. The point is one of some slight difficulty because it involves a consideration of the law of remedies as well as the law governing liability. When a contract is held to exist, this means that a particular *kind* of legal liability is created—normally, a liability to pay damages for the loss of the plaintiff's bargain, damages for his lost expectations. Such a liability is normally thought to be justified either on economic grounds, or perhaps on moral grounds (or both), where there is a real bargain, a real contract in which both parties made an agreed exchange which could be expected to be profitable to them both. In such a case, if one party welshes on the deal, the other is thought entitled to have his full expectations protected by an appropriate award of damages or sometimes even by a decree of specific performance. But where one of the parties is suffering from a serious mistake, it will often be difficult to justify enforcing the resulting exchange by an award of

---

[51] *Centrovincial Estates PLC* v. *Merchant Investors Assurance Co Ltd* (1983) Com LR 158, an unfortunately inadequate report of this important case. For criticisms of the decision, see *post*, 461.

[52] *Prenn* v. *Simonds* [1971] 1 WLR 1381. But if both parties agree that a particular meaning attaches to the words of the contract, that meaning will govern.

expectation damages (or a decree of specific performance) on either economic or moral grounds. There may be neither a real subjective intention to accept such a liability nor any probability of a profitable economic exchange. The mistaken party may well have been to blame for making his mistake, and he may have misled the other party by his conduct, so it may be just that he should pay any costs which result from that mistake. But it is certainly arguable that the damages should be restricted to losses which result from the mistake (if indeed there are any) and should not extend to expectation damages. In the case about the mistake in fixing the rent mentioned above, for instance, it is not obvious why the tenants should receive an immense windfall as a result of the mistake, which was immediately pointed out before anything had been done or any costs incurred in reliance on it. If it were held that misleading another party in this way should be treated as a tort, rather than as leading to the creation of contract, this would indeed be the result. But the law of tort and the law of damages were relatively undeveloped when the current contractual rules were first adopted, which explains why the law has developed along these lines. Today there is room for reclassifying such cases as tortious ones, and so restricting the remedies available.[53]

*Where one party is mistaken and the other is aware of the first party's real intentions*

Where one party is aware that the offer or the acceptance of the other party does not represent his true intentions, but nevertheless deals with the other party without disclosing the mistake, he will normally be bound by the real intentions of the other party. In this case the law abandons the objective interpretation of the first party's intentions. There is no justification for permitting X to assume that Y meant one thing, merely because he appeared to mean it, when in fact X knows very well that Y meant something quite different. So where a person offered to sell hare skins to the plaintiff at so much per pound, but in fact it was clear that the plaintiff knew this to be a mistake for so much per piece, it was held that the plaintiff's purported acceptance did not create a contract at the price actually stated by the seller.[54] It might, in fact, have created a contract at the price really intended by the seller, but this question did not arise for decision. Had the plaintiff not known of the mistake he would, of course, have been entitled to assume that the defendant meant what he said (unless

---

[53] As already noted, it is possible that dicta in *The Hannah Blumenthal, supra*, n. 36, could be used to justify a different result in this situation. Possibly, the decision in *Moran* v. *University College Salford, The Independent*, 26 November 1993, could be interpreted as some support for this in so far as the Court of Appeal denied specific relief, although they also expressed the opinion that damages might be recoverable.

[54] *Hartog* v. *Colin & Shields* [1939] 3 All ER 566.

perhaps he ought reasonably to have known of it) but, since he was in fact aware that the defendant meant no such thing, it would have been as unjust as it was unnecessary to apply an objective test. Similarly, in the case about the mistake in fixing the rent,[55] if the tenants had known, on receipt of the proposed rent, that the landlord's agent had obviously blundered, then it is clear that they could not have held the landlord to the rent stated.

The principle is the same in the case of mistake as to the person. Obviously, a person cannot accept an offer *which he knows* is not intended for him, although in the absence of such knowledge he might reasonably have thought that the offer was intended for him. Once again, if he is perfectly well aware of the other party's true intentions, he cannot say that he is entitled to accept that party's statements at their face value. Similarly, a person cannot rely on an apparent acceptance of an offer made by him when he knows full well that the acceptance was made with the intention of accepting an offer, not made by him, but by some third party. In the famous case of *Cundy* v. *Lindsay*[56] a swindler, by name Blenkarn, wrote to the plaintiffs ordering goods from them, and signed his name to make it look as though the letter came from Blenkiron & Co, a company known to the plaintiffs. The plaintiffs sent the goods to Blenkarn, who sold them on to the defendants who were innocent of the fraud. When the fraud was discovered the plaintiffs sued the defendants claiming that the goods still belonged to them when the defendants had bought them, and therefore that the defendants had 'converted' them and were liable in tort. The legal issue which arises in such a case is whether the original contract between the plaintiffs and Blenkarn was quite void (in which case the plaintiffs would succeed) or only voidable for fraud (in which case the defendants would have got title, since at the time they bought the goods the original contract was still in force, the plaintiffs not having yet tried to cancel or 'avoid' it). It was held that there was no contract between them, because Blenkarn knew perfectly well that the plaintiffs were intending to accept an offer which they believed to have been made by Blenkiron & Co, and not by him. In saying that there was no contract in this case it must be appreciated that the court was only holding that there was no contract which could be enforced *against the plaintiffs*. If the plaintiffs had chosen to sue Blenkiron for the price of the goods it is difficult to see what defence he could have had to the action. This problem does not usually arise in a practical form because it is usually the mistaken party who is seeking to evade liability under the contract, and not to enforce it. Hence, if there is no contract which can be enforced against the mistaken party, it is usually sufficient for practical purposes to say that *there is no contract*. But if the

---

[55] *Centrovincial, supra*, n. 51.        [56] (1878) 3 App. Cas. 459.

mistaken party tried to enforce the contract this would be seen to be not wholly correct.

Cases of mistake as to the person continue to give rise to difficulties, because it is unfortunately no uncommon event for a rogue to buy goods with a worthless cheque and then resell them before the fraud is discovered. The original owner and the bona fide purchaser will then be left to fight out the consequences. Stripped of their legal dressing, these cases raise a relatively straightforward question: should the fraudulently induced sale be treated like a genuine sale (in which case the third party will be protected) or like plain theft (in which case the owner will be protected)? But the courts have often encountered difficulty with these cases because they tend to ask themselves the question: did the owner 'intend' to contract with the rogue or with the person the rogue was pretending to be? There is, in truth, no real answer to this question because the owner in these cases believes that the rogue *is* the person he is pretending to be. The most recent decisions[57] suggest that, anyhow where the fraudulently induced sale is made face-to-face, it will usually be treated as a (voidable) contract so that the third party will be protected at the expense of the owner. This seems quite reasonable, for a person who hands goods over to a stranger in return for a cheque is obviously taking a major risk, and it does not seem fair that he should be able to shift the burden of this risk on to the innocent third party.

Similarly, where bank drafts (that is, bank cheques) were issued by Bank A for delivery to Bank B, but their issue was made on the instructions of a fraudster whose messenger obtained the drafts and delivered them to Bank B, it was held that Bank B obtained a good title to them. Although the facts bore a superficial similarity to *Cundy* v. *Lindsay*, in this case Bank A knew the identity of Bank B and intended the drafts to be delivered to Bank B. So whatever the position may have been between Bank A and the fraudster, this was irrelevant to the relationship between the two banks.[58]

Less difficulty is usually encountered with mistakes as to the quality of goods. Cases of this kind are today rarely treated as raising issues of mistake, and are almost always treated as cases involving the implied terms as to quality or fitness under the Sale of Goods Act. If the seller is held impliedly to warrant the quality or fitness of the goods in the relevant respect, then he is of course liable. But in some cases there may be no implied warranty (for instance there is no implied warranty of quality where a private seller disposes of a second-hand car) and in this situation a buyer might try to raise an argument that he was mistaken as to the quality

---

[57] *Lewis* v. *Averay* [1972] 1 QB 198; compare *Ingram* v. *Little* [1961] 1 QB 31.
[58] *Citibank NA* v. *Brown Shipley & Co*, [1991] 2 All ER 690.

of the goods. Such an argument would fail because a mistake of this character does not prevent the parties being in agreement on the essential terms of the sale, *viz.*, for the sale of this car at that price between these parties.

But the position may be subtly different where the mistake is not as to the quality of the goods but as to the terms of the sale itself. So where a person sold oats to the defendant it was held that the seller could not hold the buyer to the contract if the seller was aware that the buyer was intending to accept an offer to sell oats warranted to be old, and the seller was not intending to give any such warranty.[59] Here again there may well have been a contract on the terms actually intended by the buyer.

*Where each party is aware of the real intention of the other, and these intentions do not coincide*

It is, of course, common enough for parties negotiating a contract to be aware that they have different intentions and therefore that no final agreement has been reached. But it would be less common for the parties so to conduct themselves as to give the appearance of being in agreement, while each party is yet aware that the other's real intentions are different from his apparent intentions. But this does sometimes happen, for instance, where parties are agreed about the essential terms of a written contract, and are very keen to consummate the transaction even though they know that there is some disagreement over what may appear to be minor details. As we have previously seen in dealing with the 'battle of the forms', parties do sometimes go ahead and embark on performance of a contract despite disagreements on the terms. And in such circumstances, it is impractical to argue that there is no contract at all, at any rate once the arrangements are substantially executed. In this event the parties are in effect delegating to the court the power to settle the effect of the terms which will bind them.[60]

*Other issues distinguished from mistake*

In order to avoid possible confusion it must be stressed that we have here been concerned only with the question whether a contract has been created by a valid offer and a valid acceptance. Once the contract has been held to exist, questions may arise regarding fraud and misrepresentation, or as to the obligations, express or implied, of the parties. These matters will all be dealt with in due course, but they do not arise at all unless it is first of all established that there is a contract. In many cases of mistake as to the person there is actual fraud, and as between the parties to the transaction it

---

[59] *Smith* v. *Hughes* (1871) LR 6 QB 597.
[60] See *LCC* v. *Henry Boot & Sons* [1959] 1 WLR 1069.

is usually immaterial whether the contract is merely voidable for fraud or is entirely inoperative owing to lack of a proper offer or acceptance. The only importance of the distinction lies in its effect on third parties.

One final comment needs to be made on this subject, and that is that the isolation of questions of mistake from all other problems which is common in books on contract is extremely artificial in practice. It is this very isolation which often gives defences of mistake a spurious plausibility, but in practice it is rare to find cases of mistake which are not obviously and easily disposed of on some other ground. As we have noted above, for instance, a case of sale of goods in which the buyer makes some mistake as to the quality of what he is getting would today rarely be dealt with as a case of mistake. In such a case, the instinctive reaction of a practising lawyer is to turn to the duties of a seller relating to the quality of goods sold, and not to chapters on mistake in books on contract. If there is an implied condition covering the goods in question, for example, because the buyer has indicated that he is relying on the seller's skill or judgement, and informs him of the purpose for which he wants the goods, then the seller may be liable for supplying the wrong kind of goods. It is irrelevant that the seller is mistaken about the quality of the goods, or that he has made no false statement about the goods, because if he is aware of the purpose for which the buyer needs the goods there will usually be an implied condition that the goods are fit for that purpose. On the other hand, if the law does not, in the circumstances of a particular case, place the responsibility for the state of the goods on the seller, then prima facie the buyer will have to take the goods as they are. Even if the buyer has made some mistake about the goods, and even if the mistake is known to the seller, the contract is not void and the buyer will be bound to pay the price. But in practice it is again extremely unlikely to find situations of this kind which do not involve other factors. If the buyer is labouring under some mistake it will frequently be found to have been induced by some statement by the seller; in this event there is no need to talk of mistake, for the seller is responsible for his statements. On the other hand, if the buyer has abstained from asking about the quality or fitness of the goods, the natural inference is that he took the risk of the goods not being suitable or satisfactory, in the absence of a promise, express or implied, to the contrary.

We have been speaking in terms of contracts of sale, but the principles are the same in all contracts, although the implied terms in other contracts may not be so well settled as in contracts of sale. The point to be emphasized is that it is dangerous and unrealistic to approach problems in the law of contract as though questions of mistake could be completely isolated from questions of offer and acceptance, fraud, misrepresentation and express and implied terms.

# 4

# Contracts Made by the Courts

THE heading of this chapter is, according to traditional contract theory, a solecism. That courts do not make contracts for the parties is an oft-repeated dogma. But, as the illustrations given below will show, this is misleading. In practice many contracts are held to exist by the courts in circumstances in which the parties did not intend to create one, or did not realize that they were creating one. Furthermore, many obligations are also held to exist by the courts which are not actually said to be contractual, but which nevertheless arise out of putative or failed contractual situations. Of course there are major differences between contracts 'made' by the parties, and contracts 'made' by the courts. When parties make a contract, they do so in advance: the purpose of the contract is to regulate some future arrangement, although it is also possible (as we have seen) to have a purely simultaneous exchange which lacks this element of futurity. But at least parties who make a contract are dealing with the present or the future. When the court 'makes' a contract, the operation is usually a different one, for the court always deals with the past. The court declares that, as a result of what the parties have already done, certain obligations lie upon them. And in order to justify the imposition of these obligations the court declares that there was a contract between the parties. Because cases of this kind arise after and as a result of the relevant arrangements entered into by the parties, questions of offer and acceptance are scarcely ever relevant.

On the other hand there is a sense in which it is the very failure of our traditional rules of offer and acceptance to accord with substantial justice in many circumstances which leads to these additional contracts, or contractual obligations, which can be said to be created by the courts. A great many of these contracts created by the courts will be seen to be preliminary contracts of one kind or another. They are imposed on parties who are or have been negotiating with each other (in some broad sense) but they do not arise out of any actual agreement or contract the parties may have made. Indeed, it often happens that these preliminary contracts are required precisely because the parties have not concluded any contract themselves. To lawyers with some acquaintance with foreign legal systems it will be apparent that these preliminary contracts often perform the same function as a duty to negotiate in good faith. But although there are (tort and equitable) duties not to deceive or to misrepresent the facts, no general duty of good faith is recognized by English law.[1] Parties who negotiate with each other do so, as the legal phrase goes, 'at arm's length', that is to say, each is supposed to stand on his own feet and look after his own interests. The classic rules of offer and acceptance plainly reflect this sort of tradition. But in practice these rules are often found incompatible with justice, and some kind of preliminary obligation must be recognized. Because of the absence of any general concept of good faith, the technical means by which the courts impose these duties are sometimes strained or even tortuous. The following pages will illustrate some of these problems.

Many of the cases dealt with below would not be regarded by most contract lawyers as 'leading' cases in the law of contract. And others, though well known to contract lawyers, are often thought to be anomalous or difficult to reconcile with ordinary principles, precisely because they do not fit the ordinary pattern of transactions deliberately entered into by the parties for future performance. But it is important for students to understand that the law of contract has nearly always had room for cases of this character. Judges have rarely hesitated to use whatever instruments they can lay hands on in order to achieve a just result in a particular case; and the law of contract is one of those instruments. The cases discussed below thus illustrate a second (perhaps a secondary[2]) function of contract law. If the primary function of contract law is to enable or facilitate the making of future arrangements by private people, this second function is basically a remedial one. It enables courts to do justice by imposing obligations on people as a result of what they have done, rather than what they have agreed. In practice courts often use other legal doctrines and labels to justify action of this kind, doubtless for the very reason that it seems to infringe contractual principles to 'make' contracts for the parties. But the infringement—if it is unjustified—is still there, for all that a different label may be used; while if it is justified, there seems no reason for the pretence that contract law is not being invoked.

The distinction between these two functions is, however, rarely as clear-cut as this may make it seem. So there are many cases which could be regarded as examples of contracts 'made by the parties' and equally could

---

[1] Many legal systems differentiate between a requirement of good faith in the formation of contracts and a requirement of good faith in performance. English law recognizes neither as general legal doctrines, though in particular cases good faith may be required under some other legal heading. See also *post*, 315 for the EC Directive on unfair contract terms.

[2] Whether this really is a secondary function (as most lawyers would undoubtedly say) is, however, open to challenge. My own view, which is probably seen as eccentric by others, is that this function is at least of equal importance to the so-called primary function, simply because so many doctrines of contract law impose liability which is not based on real assent or intention. Most contracts are a mix of voluntarily assumed duties and legally imposed duties.

be regarded as examples of contracts 'made by the courts'. Indeed, whenever parties are in dispute over an unforeseen result of some relationship, it is debatable whether the ultimate legal solution is 'made' by the parties or by the court, and hence whether the contract is, on that particular point, to be regarded as made by the one or the other. There is, also, the fundamental question of remedies—when a court awards damages for breach of contract, it is not easy to see this as merely carrying out a duty 'made' by the parties. The truth is that when a breach of contract occurs, the duties created by the parties (the 'primary' duties) are then replaced with new (secondary) duties, fashioned by the court.

But even primary duties cannot always be regarded as made by the parties. All manner of contracts are 'implied' in a wide range of circumstances, and it is often unclear whether the 'implication' is genuine or fictitious. Sometimes the courts insist that the implication must be genuine, and they apply traditional offer-and-acceptance analysis to the process. So in *The Hannah Blumenthal*[3] the House of Lords refused to 'imply' a contract between two commercial concerns to abandon an arbitration which had been commenced and then allowed to go to sleep for many years. There was no real intention to abandon the arbitration, they insisted, and none could be implied, because neither party actually believed that the other intended to abandon it. On the other hand, there are other cases where the courts can find a different legal pigeonhole in which to slot the facts, and then an obligation can be implied without any need to demonstrate that the implication is a genuine inference. So, for instance, in *China Pacific SA* v. *Food Corp of India*[4] the owners of a cargo on a stranded ship were held liable to pay the expenses of salvors who unloaded and stored the cargo to preserve it, although the parties had not entered into any contract for this purpose. The House of Lords held that there was a 'bailment' which is a separate legal category for some purposes, and this enabled them to impose a sort of 'implied' obligation even in the absence of express contract, but clearly the obligation here was 'made' or imposed by the court, and not by the parties themselves.

As we have seen, then, the courts are often called upon to imply obligations affecting parties who have entered into some contractual or similar relation, although it is usually possible for courts to deny that they are then imposing anything on the parties. But it can also happen that the entire relation is, in one sense, the creation of the court. The parties have simply *acted*, rather than *agreed*. Even here it is often possible for the court to 'imply' a contract, and it is then a good deal more difficult to adhere to the pretence that the court is not imposing its solution on the parties. In this Chapter we shall be mainly concerned with cases in which the whole

[3] [1983] 1 AC 834.     [4] [1981] AC 939.

contract (rather than the effect of one or more terms) is a legal construct of this kind.

## 2. IMPLIED WARRANTY OF AUTHORITY

It is a well-established principle of contract law that a person who professes to act as agent of a principal is 'taken' impliedly to warrant that he has the principal's authority to act on his behalf. If it turns out that he has no such authority, and the other party suffers some loss in consequence, the agent is liable on this implied warranty. The principle was established in the famous decision of *Collen* v. *Wright*[5] where the defendant acted as the agent of a third party in negotiating a lease of the third party's property to the plaintiff. The terms were agreed, and the plaintiff went into occupation of the property. The third party then claimed that the agent had exceeded his authority and that the lease was not binding on him. The result was that the plaintiff was (after a law suit) turned off the land. He then sued the agent, claiming reimbursement for his losses including the costs of the law suit. It was held that he was entitled to recover these losses against the agent who must be taken to have warranted, that is, guaranteed, that he had the principal's authority to grant the lease. Now it is important to observe that there was *no other* contractual relation between the plaintiff and the defendant. The lease itself (apart from the fact that it was void) was not a contract to which the agent was himself a party. So the whole content of the contract between the plaintiff and the defendant was the implied warranty. In theory such a warranty rests on the intention of the party giving it, but in practice it seems quite evident that the warranty, and the whole contract, was created by the court to recompense the plaintiff for the losses he had suffered through relying on the defendant.

If the law had developed along different conceptual lines, this sort of liability might have been called a liability in tort, arising from the fact that the plaintiff had reasonably relied on the defendant's conduct and suffered loss as a result. Or, alternatively, it might have been called a liability arising out of the requirements of good faith. As it is, it is treated as a contractual liability by English lawyers, and this has certain practical (and perhaps unfortunate) results. For instance, it means that the agent is liable whether or not he has been careless, though if it was a liability in tort, negligence might have to be proved. It also means that the agent is liable, not only for the plaintiff's wasted costs, but also for damages representing the loss of his bargain or expectations. It is not clear that this is a fair result.

The principle of *Collen* v. *Wright* has been extended to cases where it seems clear that the parties never really intended to make a contract of any

[5] (1857) 8 E & B 647.

kind. For example, in a case in 1869,[6] the directors of a company appointed C as manager and wrote to tell their bankers that C had authority to sign cheques on the company's account. C overdrew the account, which he had no authority to do without the approval of the shareholders according to the company's regulations. The bank were thus unable to claim the repayment of the overdraft from the company, so they claimed it from the directors personally. The directors were held liable, on the ground that they had warranted that C had authority to draw cheques on the company's account even where the account was overdrawn. The defendants' counsel argued with some justice that the defendants were being made liable on a contract when they had never intended to make any sort of a contract with the bank; while the company itself plainly had a contract with the bank, the defendant directors had none. Yet they were held liable on just such a contract. One can only insist, in the light of decisions of this character, that the courts do retain power to declare that, as a result of what parties have done, they must be treated as though they had entered into certain contractual liabilities.

## 3. THE REQUEST PRINCIPLE

There is a somewhat neglected principle which holds that a person may be liable to another where he has requested that other to do some act for him and the result of it being done has been to cause loss to the person doing it. Cases of this kind are also explained by the courts as resting on the idea of an implied contract. For instance, in *Sheffield Corpn* v. *Barclay*[7] the defendants had accepted from a client a certificate of Sheffield Corporation stock which was, unknown to them, stolen. They sent the certificate to the corporation to register their title, and in due course received a new certificate; this they later sold and transferred to a third party. It is well-established law that in these circumstances the third party obtains a good title to the stock, but the original owner of the stolen certificate is not deprived of his entitlement. The upshot was that the corporation found itself liable to two owners for one lot of stock. It then sued the defendants, claiming that they were responsible for this loss since they had started it all by sending in the stolen certificate. It was held that this claim was sound, and rested upon an implied contract. The defendants must be taken to have impliedly agreed to indemnify the corporation against any loss when they sent in the certificate, or alternatively they must be taken to have impliedly warranted the certificate to be genuine and not stolen. Here again, it seems artificial in the extreme to call this an implied contract, if

[6] *Cherry and McDougal* v. *Colonial Bank of Australasia* (1869) LR 3 PC 24.
[7] [1905] AC 392.

that means that the parties impliedly intended to make a contract of the kind found by the court. The reality is that the court thought that the defendants ought to be under an obligation to the plaintiffs as a result of what had happened, and to justify the imposition of that obligation they said that there was an implied contract. The contract was made by the court as a result of what the parties did.

There are many cases following this principle, although it is much neglected by writers and theorists. It appears ultimately to be a species of benefit-based liability. Because it is a reasonable assumption that something which a person requests will benefit him, it appears to be generally fair that that person should be liable for any costs or losses incurred by the other party in carrying out the request. And no doubt, it would often be legitimate to 'imply' a promise to this effect, but the principle even applies where it is quite clear that no such promise can be implied. It is therefore difficult to regard it as a genuinely contractual principle, so long as contract law is confined within classical boundaries. But although the liability seems to be benefit-based, it cannot be called a restitutionary liability because it is a claim for reimbursement of a loss, and not a claim for restoration of a gain, which the law of restitution normally deals with. This difficulty in slotting the principle into one of the traditional pigeon-holes of the law of obligations probably explains why it is so much neglected.

### 4. INFORMAL PROPERTY TRANSACTIONS

In recent years there has been a considerable number of cases concerning the rights of parties to a home in which they have been living. The cases take a variety of forms, but a typical case arises from a purchase on mortgage of a house for the occupation of an unmarried couple;[8] if the couple should split up after some years, the question may arise as to the parties' rights in the house. The problems are particularly acute if the house is bought in the name of one of the parties only, although even if it is bought in joint names, this does not necessarily dispose of all difficulty—because, for instance, there may be a dispute about whether they are entitled to equal shares.[9] In most cases the parties themselves have never

---

[8] Originally the question arose most frequently following the divorce of married couples, but these cases are now largely taken care of by statutory powers which enable the courts to make property adjustment and other appropriate orders, in their discretion. These powers make it unnecessary for the courts to invoke contract or trust or any other legitimating device in dealing with married couples.

[9] But it now seems settled that, if the property is in joint names, the parties will share in it equally in the absence of some very clear agreement to the contrary: *Goodman* v. *Gallant* [1986] Fam. 106; *Turton* v. *Turton* [1987] 2 All ER 641.

agreed, formally or informally, as to what is to happen in the event of a split—that is one contingency which is not usually discussed. So the burden of deciding what is to happen inevitably falls to the courts unless the parties are able to come to some amicable agreement when the split occurs. In making these decisions, the courts sometimes invoke the notion of an 'implied contract', though they now incline rather to use the concept of the 'implied trust' or the 'constructive trust', or even other legal concepts like estoppel. But all these are purely remedial devices used to justify the decision; they are merely tools or instruments to legitimate the decision, labels to impose on the facts. It will suffice to give two illustrations of these cases.

In *Eves* v. *Eves*[10] a young man and woman, both already married to other spouses from whom they were separated, began living together. In 1969 the woman had a child, and the man bought a house on mortgage, in his own name, to provide a home for the three of them. In fact he had told the woman that the house was to be put in their joint names but this was not done. The house was in poor condition, and both of them worked hard to improve it. After a few years the man left, and he later evicted the woman and child from the house. It was held by the Court of Appeal that she was entitled to a quarter share in the proceeds of sale—her share was less than that of the man because he had provided most of the original money and mortgage instalments. In this case the court relied upon the concept of an 'implied trust' but (as we have suggested) the label is almost immaterial.

In *Tanner* v. *Tanner*[11] a woman had twins by the plaintiff, to whom she was not married. He bought a house on mortgage, and she gave up her rent-controlled flat to move into the house with her children, and with their father. After a while the man left and tried to evict the woman. It was held that she had an implied contractual right to remain in the house until her children had grown up and left school. In this case Lord Denning MR, in his characteristically unorthodox fashion, openly admitted that the function of the court was to imply, 'or, if need be, impose', a contract, or the equivalent of a contract, on the parties.

Since these relatively early cases, the basic problem has continued to give rise to much litigation and many cases have gone to appeal.[12] The modern view[13] is that the first thing the court has to do in such a case is to see if there is anything amounting to an actual agreement or common understanding between the parties as to how the property is to be divided

---

[10] [1975] 1 WLR 1338.    [11] [1975] 1 WLR 1346.

[12] See e.g. *Pettit* v. *Pettit* [1970] AC 777; *Burns* v. *Burns* [1984] Ch. 317; *Maharaj* v. *Chand* [1986] 3 All ER 107; *Grant* v. *Edwards* [1986] 2 All ER 426.

[13] See e.g. *Hammond* v. *Mitchell* [1992] 2 All ER 109; *Lloyds Bank* v. *Rosset* [1991] 1 AC 107.

in the events which have occurred. If so, then the plaintiff must show that he (or she) has detrimentally relied on the agreement or understanding. This then enables the court to intervene on the ground of proprietary estoppel or constructive trust. If it is asked why these cases cannot be treated as themselves based on contract, given that they require an agreement or common understanding, the answer is that the court will intervene in them even though the usual formalities required for dealings in land have been omitted. This is an illustration of a curious (but very common) tendency in the law: if it turns out that the rules relating to the kind of agreements which the courts can enforce are too strict and lead to injustice, the courts tend to invent new doctrines to fill the gap rather than to modify the old doctrines. Instead of saying here that justice requires contracts of this kind to be enforced even though they do not comply with the usual legal formalities, the courts say that the agreements cannot be enforced as contracts but can be enforced provided the plaintiff chooses to base his claim on a different legal category.

If there is no actual agreement or common understanding the court must then look at the possibility of 'inferring' a common understanding from the general circumstances: here again the fact that the plaintiff may have acted in detrimental reliance on the understanding, or that he (or, more usually, she) may have rendered benefits to the other party under the arrangements, may be a ground for the requisite inference. In this case the benefits or reliance must (it seems) be rather more substantial than would otherwise be the case.

In one of the most recent cases on the subject[14] comment was made on the considerable cost of these cases: a great deal of detailed evidence is required to enable the necessary 'inferences' to be drawn. This is a good example of one of the great advantages of making a contract instead of leaving things to inference. It is also an argument in favour of marriage and against the less formal arrangements which have become so common.

Where the common intention inferred by the court is genuine, then the court is not really imposing anything on the parties, and the only reason the court has to interfere at all is that the usual formalities relating to the creation of interests in land have been neglected. The rules requring the plaintiff to show that he or she has made contributions to the house or acted in reliance are then substitutes for the usual formalities. But in so far as the 'common intention' may be fictitious, the court is actually imposing a solution on the parties to resolve the problem they have created by their conduct.

There are other types of informal property transactions in which courts invoke concepts like 'constructive trust' or 'estoppel', and which can also

---

[14] *Hammond* v. *Mitchell, supra*, n. 13.

be seen as cases in which (in effect) the courts are making contracts for the parties. One kind of case, which also arises with some regularity, concerns a person who has made it clear during his life that he intends that some property is to be transferred to a particular person who has, perhaps, lived with him and worked for him, sometimes for many years, in the expectation of receiving this property. When the owner dies, it may then turn out that he has failed to make a will or take any other steps to transfer the property to the intended beneficiary, and his legal heirs may claim the property on intestacy. The intended beneficiary may then try to find a legal way to claim the property. Legally there are formidable difficulties about such claims, especially if there is no writing to support them. But sometimes the claimant has very strong moral grounds for the claim—for instance, he or she may have worked without payment for years in anticipation of receiving the property. In such circumstances courts may strive to find an implied contract or implied trust, or they may rely upon the doctrine of estoppel.[15] Modern courts are often hesitant to use an openly contractual analysis in this kind of case because they do not find a bargain spelt out with sufficient clarity to make an enforceable contract. For this reason they often prefer some alternative analysis, justifying their decisions by invoking trust or estoppel. Once again, the result can be seen as a case of the court making a contract for the parties—supplying (or evading) the requirements of contract law.

In all these cases, it will often be found that these implied or constructive contracts created by the courts rest ultimately on some element of benefit which the courts feel ought to be paid for, or some element of loss through detrimental reliance which the courts feel ought to be made good. It is this which makes it more plausible to say that, even though the courts invoke other legal doctrines, the cases are indeed part of the law of contract. As we shall see in Chapter 6, the elements of benefit and detrimental reliance are central notions in the doctrine of consideration; and that doctrine is a central part of the law of contract.

## 5. COLLATERAL CONTRACTS

The term 'collateral contract' has no very precise meaning in the law. It is generally used as a label for a contract which is collateral to, or by the side of, another contract. A great many examples of implied or constructive contracts created by the courts are collateral in a broad sense. *Collen* v.

---

[15] For a recent example, see *Re Basham* [1987] 1 WLR 1498. Claims made under the Inheritance (Provision for Family and Dependents) Act 1975 can also help fill this gap in contract law. Under this Act the court has a wide discretion to award sums out of a deceased's estate to persons who have been dependent on him.

*Wright*, which was discussed above, is one example. There are many others.

One well-known group of cases concerns goods which are sold (or let on hire-purchase) by A to B, and in which some third party, C (the manufacturer, perhaps, or the hire-purchase dealer), gives B some assurance about the quality of the goods. Here B intends to make a contract with A, and that is indeed the main contract entered into. But if B wants legal redress he may find that he cannot get it against A (for example, because A did not give such clear assurances about the quality of the goods) and he may want to sue C. The courts have in a number of cases been willing to allow B to sue C in such circumstances on a 'collateral contract'. C's assurances are treated as warranties which B 'accepts' by entering into the main contract. Curiously, the courts have sometimes insisted that this device is only permissible where there is a clear intention to make the collateral contract,[16] but there are many cases which appear to be irreconcilable with the need to prove a real intent; and, in any event, it is standard doctrine in the law of contract that it is the appearance, not the reality, of intent that matters. So the court, even on this limited view, must ask itself not whether the third party, C, really intended to make a collateral contract with the second party, B, but whether C has so behaved that B might reasonably have thought C was intending to enter into such a contract; and it is only a small gap between that and asking whether C has behaved in such a way that it is reasonable to impose liability on him.

The device is not confined to cases for the supply of goods, but has also been imposed in contracts for services. In *Charnock* v. *Liverpool Corpn*[17] the plaintiff's insured car was damaged in an accident and the insurance company arranged for it to be repaired by the defendants; that is to say, they contracted for it to be so repaired. When the defendants were inordinately slow over doing the repairs it was held that the plaintiff, the owner of the car, could sue the defendants on an implied contract to do the work in a reasonable time. It is difficult to believe that the garage really intended to make two contracts in this case, one with the insurance company for payment, and one with the plaintiff under which they guaranteed to do the work within a reasonable time; and it is equally difficult to believe that the plaintiff thought he was entering into a contract with the garage when he knew that the insurance company was going to pay the bill. The reality is surely simpler. The plaintiff was thought by the court to have a (moral) right to have his work done within a reasonable time; in order to make that right legally enforceable, the court implied or made a contract between the plaintiff and the defendant.

---

[16] e.g. *Heilbut Symons & Co* v. *Buckleton* [1913] AC 30; *Lambert* v. *Lewis* [1980] 2 WLR 289, reversed on different grounds, [1982] AC 225.    [17] [1968] 1 WLR 1498.

A more difficult and controversial decision is *The Eurymedon*.[18] That case concerned some goods sold by an English exporter to a New Zealand buyer, and shipped by the exporter to Wellington in New Zealand. The goods were damaged while being unloaded through the negligence of the stevedores. The plaintiff was the New Zealand buyer, and the defendants were the stevedores; the action was brought in tort for negligent damage to the goods. The defendants argued that they were not liable because they were entitled to rely on a clause in the bill of lading which exempted them from liability. The bill of lading was the document containing the shipping contract which was, in the first instance, entered into between the exporter and the shipping company (the carriers). Neither the plaintiff nor the defendant was, in any obvious sense, a party to that contract. Nevertheless, it was held by the Privy Council that the exemption clause in the bill of lading did govern the relationship between the plaintiff and the defendant, because it formed the subject matter of a separate contract between them. To arrive at this result, conventional legal theory required a somewhat tortuous process of reasoning to be adopted. First, it had to be held that the plaintiffs were bound by the relevant clause in the bill of lading; that result was arrived at by saying that, when the plaintiffs claimed the goods from the carriers, for which purpose they had to present the bill of lading (duly sent to them by the exporter), they were deemed to indicate their assent to the terms contained in it. The next stage was to show how the stevedores could claim the benefit of the clause. That was done by saying that the clause was to be treated as an 'offer' of exemption by the plaintiffs, which was 'accepted' by the stevedores when they began to unload the goods. In the result, therefore, a contract was held to exist between the plaintiffs and the defendants which barred the ordinary remedy in tort for negligence.

To many lawyers the process of reasoning which the Privy Council adopted in this case was extremely artificial; indeed, there were two vigorous dissents, and the case has been criticized by some academic commentators. But the majority decision was evidently based on the view that legal concepts like 'offer' and 'acceptance' are tools designed to enable courts to reach appropriate and fair decisions, and that it does not matter if artificial reasoning is needed to arrive at sensible decisions.[19] This is made

---

[18]    Also known as *New Zealand Shipping Co Ltd* v. *A. M. Satterthwaite & Co Ltd* [1975] AC 154. The decision was reaffirmed by the Privy Council in *Port Jackson Stevedoring Pty Ltd* v. *Salmond & Spraggon (Australia) Pty Ltd (The New York Star)* [1980] 3 All ER 257. The Canadian Supreme Court has refused to follow the reasoning of the Privy Council but has reached substantially the same result by more direct means: *London Drugs Ltd* v. *Kuehne & Nagel International Ltd* [1992] 3 SCR 299, 97 DLR (4th) 261. See Waddams, 109 *LQR* 349 (1993).

[19]    Of course this assumes that the decision in this case *was* sensible and fair in the result, which may be controversial; the student should, however, appreciate that the goods were in

clear by the following paragraph of the judgment of Lord Wilberforce:

It is only the precise analysis of this complex of relations into the classical offer and acceptance, with identifiable consideration, that seems to present difficulty but this same difficulty exists in many situations of daily life e.g. sales at auction; supermarket purchases; boarding an omnibus; purchasing a train ticket; tenders for the supply of goods; manufacturers' guarantees; gratuitous bailments; bankers' commercial credits. These are all examples which show that English law having committed itself to a rather technical and schematic doctrine of contract, in application takes a practical approach often at the cost of forcing the facts to fit uneasily into the marked slots of offer, acceptance and consideration.[20]

This was not a case in which there was no real element of consent to the result. The bill of lading, which contained standard clauses, well-known to importers and exporters, did genuinely contemplate the protection of the stevedores from liability for negligence, but it is still a case in which it is hard to apply the ordinary law of offer and acceptance if those rules are taken too seriously. The decision represents something of a clash between those who believe that courts should be willing to 'make' contracts as a result of what the parties have done, to produce a sensible and fair result, and those who think the law of contract really serves the one function of enabling parties to do something themselves if they only make their own contracts. The various illustrations already given in this chapter (and many more could be given) should show that the majority were right to recognize that the law of contract is frequently invoked by courts in cases in which it cannot be seriously suggested that the parties have intentionally and deliberately created a contract between themselves by the process of offer and acceptance.

Sometimes, however, courts adopt a more technical (some might say 'legalistic') approach and refuse to 'imply' contracts from the behaviour of the parties. Two recent decisions of this character are *The Hannah Blumenthal*[21] and *The Aramis*,[22] both of which have now been reversed by statute.[23] Where such statutory reform can be counted upon it may be better to proceed in this way rather than by straining common law reasoning; but unfortunately this is not always possible.

---

all probability insured against damage, and the real plaintiff was in fact the insurer who had paid off the buyer of the goods. But equally, the real defendants were probably the stevedores' insurers.

[20] *Supra*, n. 18 at 167.    [21] *Supra*, Ch 3, n. 36.
[22] [1989] 1 Lloyd's Rep. 213; *supra*, 73.
[23] See Courts and Legal Services Act 1990, s. 102; Carriage of Goods by Sea Act 1992.

## 6. THE RELATIONSHIP OF NEGOTIATING PARTIES

The traditional view of classical contract law is, of course, that the parties make their own contracts and that the courts do not make contracts, and it was a natural corollary of this idea that the process of contract formation had hard edges. At any given time in the process of negotiation it ought to be clear that the parties either have, or have not yet, entered into a definite relationship. Before the making of the contract, neither party owes any duties to the other party (except traditional duties such as exclude fraud and misrepresentation); hence there is no duty to behave in good faith, for instance, or to proffer advice; on the other hand, once the contract is concluded, each party is fully bound, and the full panoply of remedies for breach of contract can be invoked, including the right to claim damages for lost expectations. But there have always been some limits to this view, because even though the parties may not have made a contract, some kind of legal redress for what has actually happened may be available.

Recent trends suggest that there are other respects in which the hard edges of the process of contract formation may be crumbling. For example, there are many modern decisions holding that negotiating parties may owe duties to each other (extending far beyond the traditional duties excluding duress, fraud, and misrepresentation). Because legal analysis insists that there *is no contract* until an offer and an acceptance can be identified, these duties are not thought by lawyers to be contractual duties. They are, instead, classified as duties arising under 'estoppel', or duties in tort, or perhaps duties of an equitable character, and they may not even be mentioned in books on contract law.

But, in any event, whether such claims are regarded as lying in contract or in tort or in equity it is reasonably clear that they are all examples of duties created by the law, or at least recognized by the courts to arise from the circumstances. They are not true examples of duties which are self-imposed in the classical contract sense. If they are enforced by way of the law of contract, then they are examples of contracts made by the courts rather than the parties; if they are enforced by way of tort law, or perhaps with the aid of equity or estoppel or statute law, then they are examples of non-contractual duties, but they are duties imposed on parties who are negotiating for the making of a contract. Either way, they are relevant to, and in a broad sense ought to be treated as part of, the law of contract. A practising lawyer would be failing in his professional duties (and could well be liable for negligence) if he did not appreciate that non-contractual duties might arise in such circumstances, and the time may come (though it probably has not yet come) when a student might likewise be in danger of failing in his examinations if he omitted to mention such possibilities.

## Other legal remedies: restitution

It has long been the law that, if one party actually renders services or supplies goods to the other while the negotiations are in process, then the recipient may have to pay for those goods or services even if no contract ensues—at any rate if (in the case of goods) he cannot return them, and sometimes even if he can. This has always been understood to be a restitutionary rather than a contractual remedy. The recipient is obliged to pay a reasonable price (not necessarily the 'contract' price—in the absence of a contract there is no strict contract price) and his obligation arises not because he has agreed but because he has accepted a benefit at the hands of the other party. Sometimes, too, one party may be entitled to recover from the other for wasted expenditure, incurred at the request of the latter, when negotiations break down.[24]

## Express preliminary agreement

This section is chiefly concerned with duties which may be imposed on negotiating parties by the law, independently of their own agreement. But there is, of course, nothing to prevent parties from making an express preliminary contract which should govern their relationship while negotiating or in the event of a failure of negotiations. But although there is nothing to prevent parties doing this, it is not easy to make a binding preliminary contract because of the requirements of certainty.[25] These requirements prevent the parties from making a binding preliminary contract to agree in the future, or even to negotiate in good faith. But they do not necessarily prevent all possible preliminary contracts; for instance, it has recently been confirmed that it is legally possible (and not difficult) to make a 'lock-out' agreement under which the parties are legally bound for a specified time not to enter into negotiations with rivals or competitors in respect of the very property or services under current negotiation between them.[26]

## Promissory estoppel

A negotiating party who makes representations as to his future conduct may be held liable under the doctrine of promissory estoppel if the representations are detrimentally relied upon by the other party. These are not thought of as being liabilities under the contract itself. Promissory estoppel is discussed more fully later.[27]

---

[24] *Brewer Street Investments* v. *Barclays Woollen Co Ltd* [1954] QB 428. The precise basis of this decision remains controversial.

[25] On certainty, see Ch. 5.    [26] See *post*, 114.    [27] See *post*, 145.

## Duties in tort

Legal duties may arise between negotiating parties in tort. One possibility is that the parties may owe duties of care to each other. So far, most of the reported decisions which illustrate this possibility concern cases where a contract has actually followed from the negotiations.[28] But there are now several dramatic decisions in which a negotiating party has been held liable to the other for failure to take care even where no proper contract ensued. In one case a bank was held liable to a customer who was carelessly encouraged to believe that his application for a loan would be approved, with the result that he committed himself in various ways and suffered loss.[29] And in an even more striking decision, a solicitor has been held liable in tort for negligently failing to advise a possible client that his insurance company would probably pay his legal costs, in the absence of which information the client decided not to instruct the solicitor at all.[30] Thus no contract, on traditional analysis, was ever entered into between the client and the solicitor, and yet the solicitor was held under a duty to give (presumably free) advice to the client on this point. Similarly, in America there is a famous decision holding that a negotiating party who strings another party along with prolonged negotiations, constantly changing his terms, may be held liable to the other party for actual loss suffered if no contract is eventually agreed.[31] In cases of this kind, it is clear that the disappointed party cannot sue for expectation damages—he cannot claim that he had a right that there should be a contract agreed; but he may be able to claim 'reliance damages' that is, losses he has actually suffered—for example, out-of-pocket expenses—through relying on the other party.[32]

The above decisions reflect a degree of paternalism which was characteristic of the era of decline in belief in freedom of contract. In all of them a party who relied upon another to behave in a certain fashion was protected by the courts even though, on a more freedom-of-contract analysis, the relying party had no real *right* that the other should behave in that fashion. This paternalism sometimes protects those who rely on others (especially upon others who are better informed) even though they have not bought and paid for a right to rely. On a less paternalist ideology, these decisions might seem unjustifiable. Why should a bank manager be obliged

---

[28] *Esso Petroleum* v. *Mardon* [1976] QB 801. See also *English* v. *Dedham Vale* [1978] 1 WLR 93 which comes close to imposing a duty of good faith on parties negotiating a contract in certain circumstances.

[29] *Box* v. *Midland Bank* [1979] 2 Lloyd's Rep. 391.

[30] *Crossan* v. *Ward Bracewell* (1986) 136 New LJ 849.

[31] *Hoffman* v. *Red Owl Stores*, 133 NW 2d 267 (1965).

[32] For the difference between expectation and reliance damages, see *post*, 448–9.

to warn a customer that, until his loan application has been approved, he acts at his own risk? Why should a solicitor be expected to give free advice to a potential client as to how the client's costs will be paid? Why should a negotiating party be obliged to warn the other that, until the negotiations are finalized and contracts signed, each party acts at his own risk? In all these cases, to impose a liability in tort where there is none in contract, reflects a sort of collectivist or welfarist ideology. On this view, people should behave decently to each other, should help each other, warn each other of possible risks, and so on, even though they are, in a sense, strangers dealing at arm's length in the market-place. It is possible that decisions of this character may be vulnerable to the renewed swing to freedom-of-contract principles. On such principles it might be suggested that parties should stand on their own feet and rely on themselves, unless they have clear contractual rights to rely on others. One hardly expects a man to be his brother's keeper in the market-place.

One straw in the wind is perhaps the decision of the Court of Appeal in *Banque Financière de la Cité SA* v. *Westgate Insurance Co Ltd*[33] which emphatically restates the principle that in ordinary commercial relations neither party is normally obliged to disclose facts to the other, and insists that there can be no liability in tort between negotiating parties in ordinary circumstances. This case is dealt with again later, when we look at duties of pre-contractual disclosure in Chapter 13.

On the other hand, outside the straightforward commercial sphere, there is still plenty of sympathy with the idea that consumers are in many circumstances entitled to be given careful and helpful advice before contracting. For example, the modern statutory framework governing the supply of financial services closely regulates those who deal with consumers, and much of the current agitation concerning pension contracts sold to consumers by insurance companies turns on the belief that the consumers are entitled to careful advice from the pension companies.

### Equity

Another example of duties which may arise between negotiating parties comes from equity, and the modern doctrine of 'breach of confidence'. If information is divulged in confidence between negotiating parties, and negotiations break down so that no contract is made, the party obtaining the information may be prevented by injunction from using it or, alternatively, if he does use it, he may be made to pay for it. For instance, in *Seager* v. *Copydex Ltd*,[34] the plaintiff had patented a new type of carpet grip which he had invented, and he tried to interest the defendants in

---

[33] [1990] QB 665, affirmed on narrower grounds, [1991] 2 AC 249.
[34] [1967] 1 WLR 923, and see also the sequel in [1969] 1 WLR 809.

manufacturing it. There were prolonged negotiations, but nothing came of them. Later, the defendants started manufacturing a carpet grip which the court held was an unconscious copy of the plaintiff's invention, though not within the patent. Although the defendants had not realized they were making use of the confidential information they had obtained from the plaintiff, it was held that the defendants had acted in breach of confidence, a sort of equitable tort, if such a term is permissible. The plaintiff obtained damages for this breach. This is not regarded by lawyers as having anything to do with contract law because the defendants never actually contracted to pay for the information. Yet it is clear from this and subsequent cases[35] that an essential element of such an action for breach of confidence is that there must be an 'implied obligation' of confidence, which seems to be virtually the same thing as an implied promise to respect the plaintiff's confidence. The reason such cases are not regarded as contractual is not, therefore, that there is no promise (or agreement) but that there is no consideration—that is, that the plaintiff has not paid anything for the defendant's promise.[36] Yet the paradox remains that, although there is (said to be) no contract, there is a legally enforceable duty which is derived from an implied promise or agreement. So it could equally be said that these decisions effectively extend the definition of a legally enforceable contract. It could also be said that they illustrate a limited acceptance of a duty of good faith between negotiating parties.

## Unilateral contracts

Another example of the crumbling of the hard edges surrounding the making of contracts is to be found in the decision previously cited[37] holding that a unilateral offer may become irrevocable after it has been relied upon or acted upon. Thus the traditional rule that a unilateral offer remains freely revocable until a contract is made by performance of the act requested by the offer is now seen to have more fuzzy edges. In *some* circumstances, *some* sort of acts of reliance may impose *some* sort of liability. As noted above, in America this principle has been extended to bilateral-contract situations, and it is there a regular practice to hold that a limited form of liability (for reliance damages) may be imposed where one party has reasonably relied upon an offer even before it has been accepted. A stock example concerns the sub-contractor who offers to do some job for a contractor at a specified price, which is then included by the contractor in his tender for the main contract. If the main contractor secures the contract

---

[35] See e.g. *Coco* v. *A. N. Clarke (Engineering) Ltd* [1969] RPC 41.

[36] See further, *post*, 137–41.

[37] *Daulia Ltd.* v. *Four Millbank Nominees Ltd* [1978] Ch. 231; *supra*, 78. For another 'preliminary' contract, see *Warlow* v. *Harrison* (1857) 8 E & B 647; *supra*, 61.

the sub-contractor may be held liable for the main contractor's reliance losses should he revoke his offer prior to acceptance. English law has not yet recognized such possibilities, and it is more likely that, if they come, they will do so through an expansion of tort law or possibly some type of 'estoppel'. But the practical effect is much the same. The result is to impose certain obligations on negotiating parties which do not exist in classical contract theory.

### Anti-discrimination laws

It is not customary to discuss in detail the anti-discrimination legislation in books on contract law, but it must be appreciated that these statutory (and in the case of sex discrimination, European, rights) may be highly relevant to the position of negotiating parties in particular circumstances. An employer, for example, who refuses to treat an applicant for a job as required by this legislation cannot be sued for breach of contract if no contract is made; but he may be made liable (by an Industrial Tribunal) to pay damages for breach of the legislation.[38] The same is true of commercial organizations who discriminate illegally in the provision of services and therefore do not enter into a contract.

### Public contract tenders

Those who solicit offers for goods or services by public tender are, according to traditional rules of offer and acceptance, under no liability unless and until they accept one of the tenders offered to them; and, needless to add, they are also under no liability to those whose tenders are not accepted. But all those who tender for such contracts may well have a claim that their tenders should be fairly considered according to the terms of the invitations. And there may also be a substantial public interest in seeing that invitations to tender are properly carried out so that the public service obtains fair value for the taxpayer. These two factors have prompted new law in this area, too.

The possibility of a common law claim based on an implied preliminary contract (which was adumbrated in the last edition of this book) has now been given recognition by the Court of Appeal. In *Blackpool and Fylde Aero Club* v. *Blackpool Borough Council*[39] the plaintffs had held for eight years a concession from the Borough Council to operate pleasure flights from Blackpool airport. The Council invited a small identified group of interested parties, including the plaintiffs, to tender for a new concession.

---

[38] What is more, damages for hurt feelings and even exemplary damages may sometimes be awarded in such proceedings which cannot be obtained for breach of contract at common law: *Bradford Metropolitan City Council* v. *Arora* [1991] 3 All ER 545.

[39] [1990] 1 WLR 1195.

They insisted that tenders must be delivered before noon on 17 March. The plaintiffs delivered their tender in time but the defendants mistakenly thought it was out of time and refused to consider it, and the concession was awarded to another concern. It was held that there was a preliminary contract between the parties here: the Council's invitation included an implied promise to consider all tenders submitted in due time, and this was an offer which was accepted by the plaintiffs. Of course the plaintiffs had no *right* to have the concession awarded to them, and indeed the Council could have cancelled the whole exercise. But the plaintiffs did have at least the right to have their tender considered along with all the other tenders before the concession was awarded.

The public interest in having public tenders properly awarded has now also led to a formidable new body of law designed to give effect to recent European Directives.[40] The European dimension arises from the desire to see that the massive public procurement contracts of the European Union do not discriminate as between suppliers of different member states, but in giving effect to this purpose the Directives confer new enforceable legal rights on tenderers in various circumstances. Their precise legal nature remains to be worked out by national courts but it seems possible that they will be similar to those recognized in the *Blackpool and Fylde Aero Club* case, that is, a tenderer whose tender has been wrongly refused will have a right to compensation, though probably not to the full value of the contract, nor will he have the right to upset the awarding of the contract to the successful party.

### 7. TORT DAMAGES AND OTHER REMEDIES AS A CONTRACT PRICE

There is an altogether different kind of case in which courts sometimes 'make' contracts. Suppose that A wants to make a contract with B, but B refuses all offers. This may be because he is unwilling to deal at all, or because he regards A's offer as unacceptable, for instance because the price is too low. Suppose now that A just proceeds to 'help himself' to what he has tried to buy. Obviously this is, in many circumstances, quite unacceptable behaviour, and may need to be stopped or deterred by severe sanctions. It may be plain theft. But there are some circumstances where things are not quite as simple as that.

For example, suppose that A has just been trying to 'buy' a temporary right of entry into B's land to enable necessary repairs to be carried out to A's building which abuts B's land and is not otherwise accessible. Or suppose A is a builder who wants to site his crane so that it swings over B's land and so intrudes on his air space, even though it does not actually

---

[40] See SI 1991 Nos. 2679 and 2680; SI 1992 No. 3279.

threaten any harm to B. In cases of this kind it is legally possible for the courts to prevent A intruding on B's land or air space by granting B an injunction; but it is also possible to refuse to grant an injunction and instead to award B damages. If damages are awarded in such a case then, effectively, the court is making a contract for the parties (over the protest of one of them) and is fixing the price to be paid. For example, in one recent case,[41] the defendant's garage wall encroached on the plaintiff's land by some four and a half inches, and following a neighbour's squabble the plaintiff sought an injunction ordering the defendant to remove his wall. The injunction was refused and damages in lieu were offered. Effectively the plaintiff was forced to sell her piece of land at a price to be fixed by the court. But this was an extreme case and the courts are in general reluctant to do this, for the very reason that it *does* seem to be imposing a contract on the parties.[42] It is potentially an oppressive power since it enables the court to override the unwillingness of one of the parties to make a contract on his own terms or to refuse to deal altogether. Moreover, it is to some degree an interference with a person's property rights if he is forced to 'sell' them at a price fixed by the court rather than at a price fixed by himself.

At the same time, there are some circumstances in which it would seem entirely acceptable for the court to act in this way. The totally unreasonable neighbour who simply refuses access to his land to enable necessary repairs to be carried out is abusing his property rights, and it seems to value individual property rights too highly to allow such behaviour. Yet here, too, the courts refused to 'make a contract for the parties', although they undoubtedly had the legal power to do so.[43] In this instance, however, statute has now intervened. Under the Access to Neighbouring Land Act 1992 the court is given explicit new power to authorize a person to enter upon another's land where this is necessary to do works of maintenance or repair to a building; the court may order payment for these rights of access (except where the work is to be done to a residential building). The Act contains detailed provisions for what is to happen if there is a breach of the access order which it grants, and the result is highly analogous to a breach of contract. The very fact that this Act was thought necessary even though the court already had the legal power to order compensation in lieu of an injunction shows the strength of the ideal that consent should only be dispensed with in exceptional cases.

---

[41] See *Burton* v. *Winters* [1993] 3 All ER 847, a report of the subsequent proceedings between the parties. The original case concerning the encroaching wall does not seem to have been reported.

[42] See *Shelfer* v. *City of London Electric Lighting Co Ltd* [1895] 1 Ch. 287; *John Ternberth* v. *National Westminster Bank* (1979) 39 P & CR 104.

[43] See *John Ternberth, supra,* n. 42.

On the other hand there are other cases where the courts have been more willing to interfere with property rights in this way. For instance, where a new building interferes with the rights of light of an adjoining owner, courts are often willing to award damages rather than to grant injunctions. By doing this they make the contract and fix the price for the interference, rather than leaving the claimant to fix his own, possibly exorbitant, price. There are also some other cases, such as patent infringement cases, where the courts are often (in effect) called upon to award damages as a form of fixing a price. A patent owner who is willing to allow manufacturers to exploit his patent rights on payment of an appropriate charge (called a royalty) may be awarded damages, rather than an injunction, against someone who has infringed his patent rights, and such damages represent a sort of 'price' or royalty fixed by the court. Then there are still other cases (known as 'way-leave' cases) where a defendant has, often unwittingly, infringed the plaintiff's land-ownership rights by using a right of way to which he had no right. In such a case the courts may be called upon to award damages, and they are then fixing an appropriate price for the grant of a right of way, though in this case the price is only fixed after the event.[44]

This is another area of the law in which the resurgence of classical principles may have some impact. When the court fixes prices in this way, through an award of damages, it represents, in a sense, an interference with the free market. In the market, property-owners are entitled to sell (or to refuse to sell) at their own uncontrolled discretion. And if they do sell, they are entitled to demand what price they like. Even if the property owner demands what appears to be an exorbitant price, this is not wrong according to classical principles, because it may simply show that the owner sets a particularly high value on what the other seeks to buy. Unless he gets that price, any exchange which is forced on him will not benefit both parties and is therefore prima facie unjustifiable. If the market value of my house is £100,000 but I am unwilling to sell it even for £150,000 this may simply be because I set a particular value on the house (for good or bad reasons), and I shall therefore be worse off if I am forced to sell it at a price fixed even by some impartial person like a judge.[45] So one might expect the renewed belief in market principles to strengthen the unwillingness of the courts to 'make' contracts in this way.

[44] See the note by Waddams and Sharpe in (1982) 2 *Ox. J. Leg. St.* 290, though the main point made in this note is rejected by the Court of Appeal in *Surrey CC* v. *Bredero Homes Ltd* [1993] 3 All ER 705; see *post*, 453–4.

[45] Of course this does not preclude the making of compulsory purchase orders under statutory powers, with a corresponding obligation to pay compensation at statutory rates (roughly the going market price plus a 10% sweetener). The reason for this is that it would be very difficult in such cases to establish the *real* value to the owner, who would have every incentive to claim a value far above the market rate.

## Failed contracts

Analogous problems sometimes occur when parties intend to contract, and think they have made a contract, and considerable performance occurs. If it then turns out that the contract is void for some technical reason a major adjustment of rights may be needed. Each party may claim the value of goods and services supplied and damages for some degree of non-performance. These claims must, of course, be cast in some non-contractual form, so they will usually be rested on restitutionary, tortious, or equitable principles, or some highly complex mixture of the three. This sometimes resembles a very painful and difficult attempt to construct a sort of contract after the event, but it cannot be said that the result is always very satisfactory.[46]

[46] See e.g. *Rover International* v. *Cannon Film Sales* [1989] 1 WLR 912.

# 5

# Certainty

EVEN where all the other requirements of a contract are satisfied, it is still possible for an agreement to fail to qualify as a contract because of inherent uncertainty as to the intention of the parties or as to the language used by them. This, at any rate, is the traditional way of stating the law, which is strongly influenced by the idea that a contract is a 'thing' whose identity and contours must be capable of precise statement. But it would probably be better, and certainly more accurate, if the law were formulated in a slightly different way, as follows. A party who seeks a remedy from a court for breach of a contractual obligation must be able to identify that obligation with sufficient precision to justify that remedy. The chief difference between these two ways of formulating the law is that the latter is more flexible and recognizes that different levels of certainty may be needed for different remedies.

Uncertainty may take the form of ambiguity or of vagueness or of incompleteness. It is not, however, every uncertainty which will render a contract void. For instance, many ambiguities are capable of resolution by evidence as to the intention of the parties or by interpreting the contract in an objective way. One famous instance of uncertainty due to ambiguity is provided by the unique case of *Raffles* v. *Wichelhaus*.[1] In this case the plaintiff agreed to sell some goods which were being shipped from Bombay on a ship called the *Peerless*, but he complained that the buyer refused to accept the goods when they were tendered to him. The defendant claimed that there were two ships, both called *Peerless*, one leaving Bombay in October and the other in December. While the goods offered for delivery came from the later ship, the buyer thought that the contract referred to the earlier one, and he refused to accept the goods. It was held that, on these facts, there would be no contract. The case is usually treated as an illustration of operative mistake, and no doubt the parties were mistaken as to each other's intentions, but this sort of mistake, as we have seen, does not normally render a contract void. The case is certainly unusual because (as a result of the way the case was fought) the ambiguity was incapable of resolution by the court on the basis of what a reasonable man might have thought. For even if an offer is prima facie ambiguous, it can usually be accepted in the sense in which the offeree reasonably thinks it was

---

[1] (1864) 2 H & C 906.

intended. If the case had been fought out in the usual way, the court might have found sufficient ground for construing the contract as one for the sale of the goods from one or other vessel, in which case it would not have been void at all. Given the objective way in which courts construe contracts, it is very rare for this kind of uncertainty to lead to the conclusion that there is no valid contract.

Instances of uncertainty due to vagueness and to incompleteness are far more common. These two types of uncertainty tend to shade off into each other, for if the words of the contract are so vague as to lack a definite and ascertainable meaning the contract becomes, in effect, incomplete. But a contract may be incomplete without any question of vagueness arising. For instance, the absence of agreement on some vital term may be good evidence that no contract has yet been concluded, and that the parties are still negotiating.

A simple illustration of vagueness is provided by a House of Lords' decision in 1941.[2] In this case it was held that an agreement for the sale of a van, subject to hire-purchase terms being available, was not sufficiently certain to create a valid contract. There were (and are) a large number of possible variations in hire-purchase contracts, and it was not possible to say on which terms the parties were agreed. What the parties had really done, therefore, was to agree in principle on the sale of the van, but on terms which were to be settled later when they came to agree on the particular form of the hire-purchase contract. And such an agreement in principle is insufficient to create a contract (anyhow, a wholly executory contract), because the court cannot enforce a contract unless it knows what the terms are which it is sought to enforce.

It is very old law that for these reasons 'an agreement to agree' cannot be a valid contract. So an agreement under which a builder was to construct a building for a developer was held not to be binding because no price was fixed, it being simply agreed that fair and reasonable sums would be negotiated.[3] An 'agreement to agree' would be unobjectionable if the parties had definitely agreed to enter into a contract on terms which were themselves sufficiently definite. An agreement to enter into a lease is, in fact, a very common example of an agreement to agree which is legally binding; here there is no uncertainty because the terms of the intended lease will be set out in the first agreement. What the parties cannot do is to bind themselves to negotiate *and reach agreement*, because the negotiations may quite genuinely fail to lead to an agreement.

The House of Lords has very recently confirmed this old law and insisted that 'an agreement to negotiate' is the same thing as an agreement to agree

[2] *Scammell & Nephew Ltd* v. *Ouston* [1941] AC 251.
[3] *Courtney & Fairbairn* v. *Toulaini Bros (Hotels) Ltd* [1975] 1 WLR 297.

and is likewise void.[4] Even the possibility of 'an agreement to negotiate in good faith' was rejected on the ground that the concept of a duty to negotiate in good faith is inherently repugnant to the adversarial position of the parties when involved in negotiations. In the business world, for instance, parties often make statements in the course of negotiations which are not strictly true (e.g. 'that is my last offer') and yet which are not regarded as commercially improper. For this reason the House of Lords thought it impossible to enforce a duty to negotiate in good faith as a matter of law.

It must be said that the result often seems unjust. It is true that if parties leave the details of a contract for future agreement, and they seriously and genuinely bargain over these details but fail to reach agreement, then there is little the court can do where everything still remains wholly executory. Indeed the parties themselves would probably readily acknowledge that in this situation the negotiations have simply broken down and no liabilities arise. But the problem is that the law declares such agreements void even where one of the parties makes no genuine attempt to bargain over the details at all. And although there might no doubt be difficult borderline cases over whether certain kinds of negotiating stances constitute good faith or not, there are other cases in which there seems not the slightest difficulty in identifying conduct as in bad faith. A party who agrees to negotiate, for instance, and then simply refuses to do so, or a party who agrees to negotiate exclusively with the other party and then promptly turns round and deals with a third party, is indubitably acting in bad faith, and it is a reproach to the law that such conduct cannot be dealt with by the courts.[5]

One area in which constant and especial difficulties arise concerns the sale of houses and other buildings. Because the sale procedure is so protracted in English practice[6] even a clear 'agreement' is not usually a binding legal contract, and sales often fall through because buyer or seller simply changes his mind, or perhaps because he secures a better offer elsewhere. To avoid the risk of this happening one party sometimes attempt to tie the other party down by a binding legal contract at an earlier stage than is normal in the conveyancing procedure. If it is the buyer who wishes to tie the seller in this way he may be worried that he may be unable to obtain a mortgage on the property, in which case he may find himself bound to buy without having the means to pay; attempts are therefore sometimes made to make a binding contract but express it to be conditional

---

[4] *Walford* v. *Miles* [1992] 2 AC 128, a decision much criticized by commentators.

[5] But it must be recognized that any damages that could be awarded in such cases would be very limited—the plaintiff could not in any sense get damages for breach of the contract, but at most for loss of *the opportunity* to persuade the other party to contract.

[6] See *post*, 159–62.

on the buyer obtaining a satisfactory mortgage. The effect of such a clause is uncertain in the present state of the law. On the one hand it has been held that an agreement for the sale of a house may be too uncertain to be a contract if it is made 'subject to [the buyer] obtaining a satisfactory mortgage'[7] because there are no standards by which a court can say what is a satisfactory mortgage. On the other hand there are dicta of high authority suggesting that a condition of this kind can be waived by the buyer, so the seller cannot simply welsh on the whole deal and claim that the contract is void.[8]

Another possible way of trying to make a binding legal contract at what is usually nothing more than the preliminary stage of negotiations is to enter into a 'lock-out' agreement. If a party is negotiating, for instance, for the purchase of a house, but is fearful that no matter what agreement is made the seller will simply continue to deal with other buyers behind his back, relying on the absence at that stage of a binding legal contract, the buyer may seek to persuade the seller to agree (1) that for a specified, usually very short, period the seller binds himself not to negotiate with anyone else, in return for (2) the buyer agreeing that he will enter a binding contract within that period. This is known as a 'lock-out' agreement and is legally binding because there is nothing uncertain about it.[9] The time-span is clear and the duties of the parties are clear. Breach can be readily identified without examination of the question of good faith.

These difficulties about 'agreements to agree' and similar arrangements do not mean that an incomplete agreement can never be a legal contract. The absence of agreement, even on relatively important matters such as the price, date of delivery of goods, date of payment, and so forth, is not always fatal to the establishment of a contract. This is especially true in commercial contracts, negotiated between businessmen, because the courts are able and willing to supply any necessary terms on the basis of what is just and reasonable, provided that there was a definite intention to be bound.[10] These cases differ from those discussed above because there are standards of commercial custom and usage to appeal to in deciding what terms are just and reasonable.

The courts are especially able to help in the case of contracts to be performed at some fairly distant date in the future. In such cases the parties may frequently leave unspecified important matters of the kind mentioned above. Normally these matters will be settled by agreement between the

---

[7] *Lee-Parker* v. *Izzet* [1972] 1 WLR 775.

[8] *Graham* v. *Pitkin* [1992] 1 WLR 403 (PC), *per* Lord Templeman at 405. It is not clear what Lord Templeman thinks would happen if it is the buyer who wishes to escape liability.

[9] *Pitt* v. *PHH Asset Management Ltd* [1993] 4 All ER 961.

[10] An intention 'to be bound' is not the same as an intention to create legal relations. As to this latter question, see Ch. 7.

parties when the time comes, but that does not mean that the earlier agreement is nothing more than an unenforceable agreement to agree. The earlier agreement may well be a good contract in itself when one recollects the legal implications which may be read into the agreement. These principles were discussed and applied by the House of Lords in the important case of *Hillas & Co* v. *Arcos Ltd*,[11] where the House emphasized that the problem 'must always be so to balance matters that, without violation of essential principle, the dealings of men may as far as possible be treated as effective, and that the law may not incur the reproach of being the destroyer of bargains'.[12] The following passage from the speech of Lord Wright in this case is worthy of quotation in full:

It is clear that the parties both intended to make a contract and thought they had done so. Business men often record the most important agreements in crude and summary fashion; modes of expression sufficient and clear to them in the course of their business may appear to those unfamiliar with the business far from complete or precise. It is accordingly, the duty of the court to construe such documents fairly and broadly, without being too astute or subtle in finding defects; but, on the contrary, the court should seek to apply the old maxim of English law *verba ita sunt intelligenda ut res magis valeat quam pereat*. That maxim, however, does not mean that the court is to make a contract for the parties, or to go outside the words they have used, except in so far as there are appropriate implications of law, as, for instance, the implication of what is just and reasonable to be ascertained by the court as matter of machinery where the contractual intention is clear but the contract is silent in some detail. Thus in contracts for future performance over a period the parties may not be able nor may they desire to specify many matters of detail, but leave them to be adjusted in the working out of the contract. Save for the legal implications I have mentioned, such contracts might well be incomplete or uncertain; with that implication in reserve they are neither incomplete nor uncertain. As obvious illustrations I may refer to such matters as prices or times of delivery in contracts for the sale of goods or times of loading or discharging in a contract of sea carriage.[13]

There are not wanting signs that this area is another part of the law in which there is a tendency in practice for distinctions to be drawn between executory and executed contracts. Where nothing has yet been done under the contract, and a genuine dispute arises as to the terms of the agreement, the courts seem more willing to hold that no binding contract has yet been made, and that seems perfectly sensible. But where a contract has been partly performed, or where significant acts of detrimental reliance have taken place, it is a more serious matter to say that the contract is void; the eggs cannot be unscrambled, and an attempt to do so may be unjust as well

[11] [1932] All ER 494 REP.  [12] *Ibid.*, *per* Lord Tomlin at 499.
[13] *Ibid.* 503–4.

as impractical. In such circumstances the courts may be more willing to find that there was a binding contract.[14]

This may well explain the result in such a case as *Foley* v. *Classique Coaches*[15] where the plaintiffs sold a piece of land to the defendants for use in their business as coach proprietors. A supplemental agreement provided that the defendants would buy all the petrol they needed from the plaintiffs at a price 'to be agreed by the parties in writing and from time to time'. There was also a provision for arbitration in the event of a dispute. The agreement was accepted as binding and implemented for three years, at the end of which time the defendants repudiated it on the ground that there was no valid contract. It was held that the parties had clearly evinced an intention to be bound, and that the absence of agreement about the price was not fatal to the implementation of that intention. It was one of the matters which could be settled by arbitration. So here, although there was, in a sense, an agreement to agree on future prices, the arbitration provision showed that the parties were willing for those prices to be fixed by some objective method in the absence of an agreement by themselves. But it is surely sensible to recognize that a critical factor here was also that the defendants had actually bought the land in question from the plaintiffs under the very agreement in question and had operated the agreement for three years.

In *Sudbrook Trading Estates Ltd* v. *Eggleton*[16] the House of Lords reviewed a number of problems of a similar character, though not strictly concerning an 'agreement to agree', and their decision may well be a significant move towards imposing some limited requirement of good faith in cases of this kind.[17] The case involved a grant of a lease with an option to the lessee to buy the freehold in the future, at a price to be fixed by valuers appointed by the two parties, or in default of agreement by the valuers, at a price to be fixed by an umpire appointed by the valuers. The lessee gave notice that he wished to exercise his option to buy, and appointed a valuer, asking the lessor to do the same. But the lessor simply refused to do so, and argued that the lease provided only one way in which the price could be fixed, and if no price was fixed in that way the option to buy could not be validly exercised, that is to say, any purported contract to sell the freehold would be void for incompleteness or uncertainty. This totally unmeritorious

[14] This is expressly stated by Lord Denning in *F. & G. Sykes (Wessex) Ltd* v. *Fine Fare* [1967] 2 Lloyd's Rep. 52 at 57–8.

[15] [1934] 2 KB 1. The case of *May & Butcher* v. *The King* [1934] 2 KB 17n., which has been fodder for generations of students may now be left to die in the obscurity to which the editor of the Appeal Cases thought he had condemned it.

[16] [1983] 1 AC 444.

[17] See also now *Queensland Electricity Generating Board* v. *New Hope Collieries Pty Ltd* [1989] 1 Lloyd's Rep. 205 where the PC applied the *Sudbrook Estates* case to a long-term agreement containing elaborate machinery for fixing prices after 5 years.

plea was rejected by the House of Lords. They held that the essential intention in such a lease is that the buyer should be entitled to buy the freehold at a fair or market price. The job of valuers is simply to fix that price, and the provisions of the lease for the appointment of valuers is just a matter of machinery to help ascertain the fair or market price. If that machinery fails to work, alternative machinery can be found—for instance the court can direct an inquiry as to the fair price. Of course the result might be different if the parties had agreed that the price was to be fixed by (for instance) a single named person in whom they had particular confidence, but even then alternative machinery could probably be supplied by the court unless it was expected that the price was to be fixed on some idiosyncratic, subjective basis.

It also needs to be borne in mind that even where the requirements of certainty are not met and an agreement or arrangement fails to be effective as a valid contract, the court can sometimes find some other remedy, such as by invoking the doctrine of estoppel.[18] This alternative approach is unfortunately apt to make the law more complex than it need be; there is no real need for two separate doctrines here, and it is distinctly odd to say that an agreement is too uncertain to be enforced (as a contract) but, at the same time, not too uncertain to be enforced (by way of estoppel).[19] What does need to be recognized is that the degree of certainty required for the creation of obligations varies according to whether the arrangements are still wholly executory or have been partly performed or acted upon.

So also, in relational contracts (as opposed to discrete transactions) where parties are linked together for some indefinite period, there will often be a high degree of uncertainty as to the details of the parties' obligations, but this does not render the contract void. There is often considerable vagueness about the precise details of the duties of an employee under a contract of employment—for instance, teachers' unions and their employers disagreed for many years on the extent of the teachers' duties on such matters as 'covering' for absent colleagues, but nobody suggested that their contracts were void. In such circumstances, courts may ultimately have to 'imply' or fill in the terms of the contract as best they can.[20]

---

[18] See e.g. *Crabb v. Arun DC* [1976] Ch. 179, where this seems to have been one ground why the court (and the plaintiff's counsel) preferred to proceed by way of promissory estoppel, but there may also have been others. See my note in (1976) 92 *Law Q Rev.* 174 and compare counsel's reply, *ibid.* 342. Note also the cases on informal property transfers discussed above at 94 where promissory estoppel is often invoked in cases where uncertainty is at least one reason why there cannot technically be a contract (there are often others).

[19] Which is more or less what the court said in *Crabb v. Arun DC, supra*, n. 18.

[20] See *Sim v. Rotherham Met. BC* [1987] Ch. 216; and see further, *post*, 210, as to the process of implication in this sort of situation.

# 6

# Consideration

THE 'doctrine' of consideration is generally seen by lawyers as a set of rules which limits the freedom of individuals to make binding legal promises. Only those promises which are supported by a legal consideration are legally binding; other promises are not binding, even if the promisor *intends* to bind himself by his promise. Thus to many lawyers the central function of the doctrine of consideration is to prevent people from making gratuitous promises, because the typical gratuitous promise is made without any consideration as lawyers understand that term.[1] On this view, the purpose of the law of consideration is to distinguish between gratuitous and non-gratuitous promises. This may, indeed, be one of the chief purposes of the doctrine of consideration, but it is doubtful if it is the only purpose, and certainly this has not traditionally been the only purpose of this doctrine in its very long history. Moreover, to over-emphasize this particular function of the doctrine of consideration is to risk ignoring the relationship between that doctrine and other parts of the law of obligations. Indeed, this has very largely happened in the history of this subject, and for that reason it may be worth stressing at the outset the way in which the doctrine of consideration has roots linking contract law with other parts of the law of obligations.

As will be seen in greater detail later, the doctrine of consideration has traditionally rested on two main legs. The first of these is the idea that a promise is legally binding if it is given in return for some benefit which is rendered, or to be rendered, to the promisor. The second is the notion that a promise becomes binding if the promisee incurs a detriment by reliance upon it, that is, if he changes his position in reliance on the promise in such a way that he would be worse off if the promise were broken than he would have been if the promise had never been made at all. Few would quarrel with the affirmative aspect of these two basic ideas, namely that promises given for such consideration should, as a general rule, be legally binding. But we can go much further than that (though this is the point which has been so surprisingly neglected in the traditional teaching of contract law):

---

[1] It is, however, possible to make a binding gratuitous promise by deed and (as we have seen) deeds are not infrequently used for this very purpose; the formalities required have been simplified since 1989. Deeds are in general ignored in this Ch.

we can note that the idea of recompense for benefit, and the idea of protecting those who reasonably and justifiably rely upon others, are two basic ideas underlying substantial segments of the entire law of obligations.

There are many circumstances in which those who receive benefits at the hands of others may be compelled to pay for them even if no promise has been given at all. Sometimes we explain such cases by arguing that they are cases of implied promises. But there is also a large body of law—known today as the law of restitution—which is concerned with cases where a person is liable to pay for benefits obtained even if there is nothing that could remotely be called an implied promise. A person pays money to another by mistake: he is entitled to recover it even though the recipient gave no express or implied promise to repay it. The reason given by lawyers for this right of recovery is basically that the recipient would be unjustly enriched if he were not compelled to repay. He would, in other words, receive a benefit from the payer which he has no right to retain— there would be no reason or 'consideration' why he should retain the money. Or again, a person pays money to another for some purpose (perhaps itself a contract) which later has to be abandoned; the money can be recovered because there is a 'total failure of consideration' in the technical legal phrase. In other words there is no longer any reason, any justification, any consideration, why the money should be retained. A benefit has been rendered for which there is no longer any consideration. It seems clear, although this has not been widely recognized in the recent past, that the doctrine of consideration has close associations with the law of restitution.

Similarly, the other leg of the doctrine of consideration has close connections with other branches of the law, such as the law of torts, and also various equitable doctrines, as well as the doctrine of 'estoppel' in its various forms. It is frequently an actionable tort to induce another person to rely to his loss upon one's conduct or speech, whether or not any promise has been given. For example, fraudulent or even careless speech may lead to detrimental reliance, and thus to legal liability in tort; whereas, if promissory speech leads to detrimental reliance, lawyers are apt to say that the result is a contract. Sometimes (and increasingly often today) a third legal classification is invoked, and such promises are said to be enforceable by way of 'estoppel', a concept which needs to be explored more fully later.

Since the act of rendering a benefit to another often gives rise to a right to be recompensed and, since acts of detrimental reliance often give a right to be indemnified for any resultant loss, it is not surprising that where promises co-exist with these other grounds of potential legal liability, the case for imposing liability is much stronger. If a person has rendered benefits to the other, *and in addition* the recipient has promised to pay for those benefits, the case for making him legally responsible is obviously much stronger than if either of these two grounds of liability stood alone. Similarly, where a person promises another to meet the possible results of reliance on him, the case for compensation is doubled: there are *two* grounds for imposing legal liability on the promisor. The strongest case for imposing liability is, therefore, that in which all three factors combine, as they very often do in an ordinary action for breach of contract. Take the example of a simple loan of money. A lends B £100 in return for a promise of repayment. A relies upon the promise and hands over £100. He is £100 worse off than he was before. Equally B is £100 better off than he was before. So here the three factors all operate jointly: there is a benefit to B, an act of detrimental reliance by A, and a promise by B to repay the money. Naturally, the case for imposing liability is (unless there are any other factors involved in the case) almost irresistible. Nobody would doubt that there is very good consideration for the promise in such a case.

There are, however, more difficult problems where the three factors do not coincide in this way. As we shall see later, there have been problems over the relative importance of benefits and detrimental reliance. Here it will suffice to point out that *mutual promises* are binding as a contract even though in one sense there is no real element of benefit or detrimental reliance. Once there is some element of performance of a contract based on mutual promises the doctrine of consideration will normally be easily satisfied. One party relies, or the other receives a benefit. But it has been the law for a very long time that the making of mutual promises itself creates a binding contract there and then, as we saw in the section on offer and acceptance. It is difficult (though perhaps not wholly impossible) to explain why this should be so if the doctrine of consideration is taken literally. How can mere promises be beneficial or detrimental unless it is first assumed that they are binding? But to assume that they are binding is to assume the very question at issue. This does not, of course, mean that there is any doubt about the law, for it is as well settled as anything could be that, prima facie, mutual promises do create binding legal contracts even before there is any performance or reliance.

Finally, two general points need to be made about the doctrine of consideration. As we have seen, the doctrine is in a sense a *limitation* on the free power of individuals to bind themselves as they wish. It is, therefore, a paternalistic device. If a promise or a contract is declared not binding even where there has been a clear promise, on the ground of absence of consideration, the law is in effect saying that it is better that individuals should not bind themselves unless they receive some benefit in return, or unless the other party has suffered some detrimental reliance. If, on the other hand, the law is willing to enforce a promise, or mutual promises, no matter how foolish, no matter how inadequate (or non-existent) the return may have been, no matter also that the promisee has not acted so as to change his position in any way, then the law is adopting a highly individualistic stance. It is, in effect, saying that people ought to know what is in their own interests, and that they must be held responsible for carrying out their promises once they have been made. It is right also to recall here that if there has been no element of benefit and no detrimental reliance, the promisee's only claim must be a claim to his 'lost expectations'. To hold a person to his promise, irrespective of benefits and detriments, is thus to insist that the expectations created by bare promises are entitled to full protection.

Now, after the historical introduction in Chapter 1 the reader should not be surprised to learn that in the nineteenth century the doctrine of consideration came to be widely regarded as technical and anomalous, precisely because of its inherent paternalistic tendency. What is much more curious is that in the twentieth century lawyers have continued to regard the doctrine in this critical fashion despite the very paternalistic tendencies of so much modern law. The oddity is even stronger when it is noted that two of the chief trends of modern law have been on the one side, the whittling down of the binding nature of bare promises and on the other side, the great expansion in benefit-based and reliance-based liabilities. These developments were not accompanied by recognition that their obvious corollary ought to have been a renewed faith in the value of the doctrine of consideration. But today, when there is such a resurgence in classical principles, the outlook on many of these matters looks blurred. It seems unlikely that there will be much turning back from the great increase in benefit-based and reliance-based liabilities; but perhaps criticism of the doctrine of consideration will become stronger again, as lawyers once again take their stand on the ability of individuals to make their own judgements.

## 2. EXECUTED, EXECUTORY, AND PAST CONSIDERATION

Consideration has traditionally been said to fall into one of three classes. It may be *executed* or *executory* or *past*, though only a consideration of the first two classes is legally a good consideration.

### Executed consideration

In the case of unilateral contracts the act requested by the promisor is, usually at any rate, both the acceptance of the offer and also the consideration for the promise. The performance of the act by the promisee will in most cases be both a benefit to the promisor and a detriment to the promisee. This is said to be an *executed* consideration, because the promise only becomes binding when the consideration has been actually executed, that is, performed.

### Executory consideration

In the case of bilateral contracts the consideration consists in the rendering of mutual promises. As we have seen, there is some theoretical difficulty in explaining what benefit or detriment is present in a contract consisting of mutual promises. However, it is essential that the promises themselves should be regarded as consideration for each other, otherwise there could be no such thing as a contract consisting of mutual promises at all—a bare agreement can only be a binding contract if the promises are treated as consideration for each other as soon as an offer is accepted. A consideration which thus consists of a promise is said to be *executory*, and a contract consisting of mutual promises is called an 'executory' contract.

In a contract consisting of mutual promises each promise fulfils a dual role; it is at once a promise and a consideration for the other promise. As a general rule, the validity of a promise, as a promise, cannot be divorced from its sufficiency as a consideration. If it is void as a promise there is no consideration for the other promise. Hence, as a general rule, mutual promises must stand or fall together. There are, however, certain exceptions to this principle which may be collected together within a single formula as follows. Where a promise is void under some rule of law designed for the protection of a class of persons of whom the promisor is one, the contract may none the less be enforced against the other party, at any rate if the promisor does perform his part. For instance, in *Rajbenback* v. *Mamon*[2] the plaintiff, who was tenant of rent-restricted premises owned by the defendant, promised the latter to vacate the premises by a certain date in return for a promise by the landlord of £300. The plaintiff's promise was void as a promise, i.e. it could not be enforced against him, because it is not legally permissible for a tenant to contract to give up the protection of the Rent Acts, but if he chose to carry out his promise there was no reason why the contract should not be enforceable by him, and the judge so held. Similarly, if a person performs a contract in such a way as to violate some statutory provision designed for the protection of a class of persons of whom the other contracting party is one, the contract can be enforced by the latter, even though his own promise cannot be enforced against him.

---

[2] [1955] 1 QB 283. But compare *Sutton* v. *Sutton* [1984] Ch. 184 where a wife was not allowed to enforce a contract to transfer the matrimonial home to her on divorce because her own promise (not to aply for maintenance) was void. This seems to have been because the law making the wife's promise void was regarded as being for the protection of both parties and not only the wife. Agreements of this kind are often upheld if made subject to the approval of the court, and the court may anyhow make orders of this kind even in the absence of any contract if it thinks just.

Conditional promises can sometimes present the apparent paradox of a valid promise which never binds. An insurance company promises to pay the value of a house if it is destroyed by fire during a certain year. The house is not destroyed so the insurance company never has to pay. But clearly this is a valid contract and if the insured has not paid the premium he can certainly be sued for it. The reason is that the insurance company's promise has value when made, and it is 'on risk' during the year. A more difficult modern case is the credit card company which promises to supply a credit card for life without charging an annual fee. This may seem a gratuitous offer but it is not: the customer who accepts this offer is promising that he will pay his credit card bills if he incurs any. His promise is, it is true, conditional, but is nonetheless binding. In fact (as is well known) if he always pays punctually and in full he will never incur interest charges and so in a sense receives a 'free' service. Yet this is plainly a valid contract.

## Past consideration

The third type of consideration—but a legally insufficient one—is a *past* consideration. It is a well-established rule of English law that consideration cannot normally consist of something wholly performed before the promise was made. If X renders Y some service, and thereafter Y, in consideration of this service, promises to pay X £100, this promise is not enforceable as a contract. This rule is sometimes supported by arguing that it follows logically from the rules underlying the doctrine of consideration. For instance, it may be said that the law's treatment of past consideration is no mere technicality, but depends on the whole idea of contract as a bargain, i.e. as consisting of a promise for a price. If Y has already received some service from X before he makes his promise, it is clear that the service was not performed as the price of the promise. The notion of bargain involves that the promises (or the promise and the act in a unilateral contract) should be given, each in return for the other. Where a promise is given out of gratitude for a past service it is obvious that, though the promise is given in return for the act, the act was not performed in anticipation of any promise. In effect, the case of past consideration is one where there is the element of benefit, without that of detrimental reliance. Such cases can hardly be bargains.

It may well be that some such idea underlies the traditional legal hostility to past consideration, but the law is full of inconsistencies, and it must be recognized that, though most contracts may be bargains, not all contracts are bargains: there surely was no bargain in *Carlill* v. *Carbolic Smoke Co.*[3]

---

[3] [1893] 1 QB 256; *supra* 62. The role of the concept of 'bargain' in contract law is considered again below at 137.

In any event the rule about past consideration cannot easily be justified by invoking the concept of a bargain, because this simply is inconsistent with the way the doctrine works. For instance, a promise which is in reality motivated by the desire to recompense someone for a past service will be treated as given for good consideration so long as some additional benefit or detriment can be identified, even though not bargained for. So a promise to pay a pension to an employee who has no right to it is enforceable as a contract if it is conditioned on the employee not engaging in any competing business after retirement and the employee complies with the condition.[4] Yet it is plain that in such a case the pension is not offered in exchange for the employee remaining inactive.

There are two exceptions to the principle that past consideration is not good consideration. The first is of a general nature. Where services are rendered, or goods supplied by X to Y, in such circumstances that there would be an implied promise to pay a reasonable price for the services or goods, a subsequent express promise by Y to pay a specific sum for the services or goods will be enforceable by X. It is often said that strictly speaking this is not an instance of past consideration, for in this type of case the contract is made, not when the express promise is given but when the services or goods are supplied or given in the first place. As we pointed out in the last Chapter, the absence of an agreement as to the price to be paid for goods or services does not preclude the formation of a contract, the law always being prepared to imply an obligation to pay a reasonable price. Thus the contract is formed when the services are agreed upon or the goods are accepted, and the subsequent promise does no more than fix the amount of the reasonable sum which the promisor must pay.

But it may be that this attempt to argue that the exception is not a true one is merely an instance of the common propensity of lawyers to try to reconcile legal change with traditional orthodoxy. There are cases in which past consideration has been held sufficient which cannot seriously be reconciled with orthodox doctrine along the lines explained in the last paragraph. For example, in the Privy Council decision in *Pao On* v. *Lau Yiu*[5] a benefit rendered by A to B as part of a complex commercial transaction involving the sale of shares to A and his agreement not to place them on the market before a specified date was held sufficient to support a subsequent promise by B to indemnify A against any loss arising from A's undertaking. The Privy Council reiterated the generally accepted rules governing past consideration. Such a consideration would be sufficient,

---

[4] See e.g. *Wyatt* v. *Kreglinger* [1933] 1 KB 793, though here there were other problems. Of course the position is different where the pension arrangements are part of the original contract because then the employee's work will always have been part consideration for the pension rights.                                                                 [5] [1980] AC 614.

they said, if (1) the act was requested by the promisor, (2) it was understood that the act would be remunerated, and (3) that understanding would have been legally enforceable even without the later promise. But in applying these rules to the instant case the Privy Council ignored the fact that A's act, which was now held a sufficient past consideration, was rendered as part of another transaction for which consideration was already obtained by A. Thus if it had not been for the second promise here, it is perfectly clear that A could never have obtained from B the indemnity which B in fact gave. The case cannot really be understood unless it is appreciated that the first agreement contained what was, in a commercial sense, a mistake, since A ought reasonably to have received the indemnity which B later gave him in that first agreement. Clearly the Privy Council thought that A was, in the end, only getting what he was really, morally and commercially, entitled to anyhow. So it was natural to hold that the promise was given for good consideration. This case shows also that promises are often made, not to create wholly new obligations (as legal theory tends to assume), but to recognize or confirm some existing obligation, and where a person promises to do something which judges think he ought to do anyhow there is a strong tendency for them to hold that the promise was given for good consideration and so is enforceable.

Another interesting case comes from America.[6] A saved the life of B (A's employer) in an incident which caused A severe personal injury, and disabled him from work for life. B promised A a pension which was paid for many years until B's death. The question then arose whether the promise was enforceable as a binding contract, and it was held that it was. Yet it is difficult to see how it could be argued that A's act in saving B's life was rendered in such circumstances that it was understood that the act was to be remunerated. For this reason it cannot be certain how an English court would decide such a case, but the moral appeal of the plaintiff's case would be so great that any court would surely strive to uphold his claim.[7]

The second exception to the rule that past consideration is insufficient is to be found in the law governing negotiable instruments, of which a cheque is the most familiar example. By commercial custom, now embodied in the Bills of Exchange Act 1882, 'an antecedent debt or liability' is sufficient consideration for the drawing or endorsing of a bill of exchange. It is unnecessary to examine the implications of this exception in a general work of this kind.

It seems possible that the rule which condemns past consideration as not

[6] *Webb* v. *McGowin*, 168 So 196 (1935).

[7] I overlook, as the American court did, that the moral strength of A's claim against B's executors was arguably less than that of his claim against B himself. That introduces additional complications which are best left aside at this point, but see *post*, 152.

legally a good consideration, like many other aspects of consideration, is less rigid than is commonly supposed. One case[8] opens up a way of escape from the rule which may be applicable in many (though by no means all) situations. As will be seen below, a compromise of a disputed right is accepted on all hands as a binding legal contract, the forbearance of a party from enforcing or trying to enforce his rights being a sufficient consideration for the other's promise. It is unnecessary that the forbearance related to a claim good in law; it is a good consideration to forbear *in good faith* to bring a doubtful claim or probably even one which is clearly bad in law. This means that past consideration will be sufficient wherever there is any doubt about the rights of the parties arising from the services originally rendered. It is possible that the American case previously referred to (*Webb* v. *McGowin*) could be followed on this sort of ground in England. If it could be claimed that A might have thought he had an arguable right to legal compensation from B, then B's promise could be enforced as a compromise.

In modern times, with the great developments in the law of restitution, it must be said that some further weakening of the rule against past consideration would be well justified. It is, after all, often the case today that a person who renders benefits to another is entitled to some restitutionary remedy even without a promise. But the law of restitution is, in various ways, still subject to limitations, some of which may appear unjust. For example, it has recently been affirmed by the House of Lords[9] that there is in general no restitutionary obligation on the part of an owner of goods to pay a reward to someone who has saved those goods from threatened damage or loss. Yet if, after the event, the owner actually promised to pay such a reward, the promise would strictly be given for a past consideration and would seem unenforceable as a contractual promise. Such a result compounds the injustice, and should surely be avoided.

### 3. THE VALUE OF CONSIDERATION

*Acts and forbearances*

As a general rule *any* act promised or performed by the promisee—if asked for by the promisor—will be a sufficient consideration if it was of some 'value' to the promisor or involved some real detriment to the promisee. The problem is to decide what is of 'value' for this purpose. At once we are presented with a dilemma, and an apparent (and fundamental) inconsistency in the law. On the one hand, it is widely insisted that the 'value' of all

[8] *Horton* v. *Horton* [1961] 1 QB 215.    [9] *The Goring* [1988] AC 831.

things is to be examined 'subjectively', and that contracting parties must decide for themselves whether something is worth buying and how much it is worth paying for it. It was a fundamental part of classical contract law that the *real* value of the consideration was immaterial, or (as it is put by lawyers) that the adequacy of the consideration is immaterial. If a person chose to pay an extravagant price for a promise, or if he chose to accept a nominal price for his promise, then that was his business and the courts had no right to intervene. To strike at this rule would have been to violate every principle which freedom of contract was believed to stand for, because to the nineteenth-century judges, if freedom of contract meant anything at all, it meant that the parties were free to fix their own price for their own promises. In the classic words of Lord Blackburn: 'The adequacy of the consideration is for the parties to consider at the time of making the agreement, not for the Court when it is sought to be enforced'.[10] So far was this rule carried that the most nominal consideration could (and still can) be accepted for the most valuable of promises. At one time it was traditional to stipulate for a peppercorn as nominal consideration in certain transactions, and this has always been sufficient to satisfy the law's requirements.

The principle that the adequacy of consideration is immaterial may lead to a contract being held valid when the exchange involved in it is very unequal. One party may have made an exceptionally good deal, and the other may have made a loss as events have turned out. So the adequacy principle presents a possibility of contracts being unfair. And it will be necessary to look again at this question when we examine the subject of unfair contracts in Chapter 16. But here we shall simply concentrate on the doctrine of consideration.

In 1839 it was held that the surrender of a document which turned out to be legally invalid and of no inherent value was good consideration for a promise to pay £9,600,[11] the equivalent of several hundreds of thousands of pounds in modern money. If the defendant chose to promise this enormous sum for a valueless piece of paper that (according to the court) was his business. In 1908 it was held that a newspaper which published readers' queries together with its own replies derived sufficient benefit to support an implied promise to take reasonable care in its replies. In a more recent case chocolate manufacturers offered a gramophone record to anyone who sent in some 50-odd pence and three chocolate wrappers; it was held that the wrappers (though worthless and thrown away on receipt) involved some benefit to the manufacturers and were part of the

---

[10] *Bolton* v. *Madden* (1873) LR 9 QB 55 at 57.
[11] *Haigh* v. *Brooks* (1839) 10 Ad & E 309.

consideration. So it seems that anything should be a good consideration if it is judged so by the promisor who wants it.

But this leads to a contradiction or inconsistency in the law. Obviously, in one sense, any person who makes a promise does so, if he is a rational being, because he thinks that making the promise will be preferable to not making it, or (as an economist might say) because making the promise makes him better off. Even a gratuitous promise is made for some *reason* which seems a good enough reason to the promisor. But if *any* reason for making a promise were recognized as a good consideration on these grounds this would be tantamount to abolition of the entire doctrine. And, indeed, there are some modern theorists who, in their renewed faith in classical principles, wish to go this far, and insist that the present law is fundamentally inconsistent. But the law itself continues to recognize that the doctrine of consideration exists, so this will not do. The mere fact that the promisor thought it worth his while, thought it desirable, to make a promise is not enough to show that it is given for good consideration. It must be shown that a consideration has some real 'value'.

One possible way of reconciling this contradiction in the law was extensively canvassed in America in earlier years—this was to say that *anything* could be a sufficient consideration so long as it was *bargained for*, and that nothing would be good consideration unless it was bargained for. This was known as 'the bargain theory of consideration' and although it was never expressly adopted by the courts in England there was some support for it, expressed perhaps in Pollock's definition of consideration as 'the price of a promise'. Now many contracts are without doubt bargains, and the benefit element in the doctrine of consideration may be thought to reflect the notion that a promise ought only to be binding if it is part of a bargain. But it is much harder to associate the element of detrimental reliance with the notion of bargain, unless the reliance is part of an ordinary contract in which benefit is also rendered to the promisor. Detrimental reliance without benefit is not readily reconcilable with the idea of a bargain. For instance, if a person promises to guarantee his son's bank overdraft, there is no doubt that he will be liable if the bank acts on the promise by advancing overdraft facilities to the son, but it is not evident that this can be said to be a bargain. First, the bank makes no promise (it is an unilateral contract) and, secondly, the promisor gets no direct benefit out of the arrangement. Still further removed from bargains are cases where the promisee acts on the promise in a way in which the promisor had no interest, and which he did not even ask for. Yet here, too, as we shall see, the modern trend is towards greater protection of the promisee's interests in such cases, sometimes through the doctrine of consideration, sometimes through other legal devices such as 'estoppel'. But more fundamentally, there is a great mass of case law which is really inconsistent with the bargain theory, in which incidental benefits are treated as consideration (for example in contractual variations) without any real bargain.

Another way of attempting to reconcile the fundamental inconsistency in the law is to say that consideration must be of 'economic' value, and so the mere sense of satisfaction that a gratuitous promisor obtains from his generosity is for that reason not enough. And there are some legal rules to support this. For instance, if a person makes a promise from 'natural love and affection', this is not an enforceable contract; there is no consideration. Similarly, in a nineteenth-century case it was said that a promise by a son not to bore his father with complaints was not a good consideration.

But there are also many cases which are quite inconsistent with the idea that consideration must always have economic value. For instance, mutual promises to marry were held to be good consideration for each other even at a time when a man would have been regarded as incurring an economic burden (rather than obtaining a benefit) in marrying. And such promises were still treated as good consideration until recently without any inquiry into the economic position of the parties. (Since 1970, however, actions for breach of promise of marriage have been abolished.) Again, in *Ward* v. *Byham*[12] the Court of Appeal seems to have thought that there could be good consideration in a promise to look after and keep a child happy, even apart from the economic cost involved.

Then also (as will be seen) a forbearance is often a good consideration without any inquiry as to its economic effect. If a person promises his son £100 on condition that the son does not smoke for a year, the son's forbearance would not cost him anything in economic terms (indeed it would save him money) and yet it is generally thought that this would be a valid contract. Similarly, in many unilateral contracts (for example, a promise of a prize to the winner of a race) there is not necessarily any economic gain to the promisor or loss to the promisee, although such promises may sometimes be made by way of advertising or sponsorship.

So it does not seem possible to insist that consideration must always be of economic value, nor is it possible to say that anything of economic value can be a good consideration. And it is very doubtful if any other general rule can be found which can reconcile the apparent inconsistencies in the law. It must simply be recognized that certain gratuitous promises (such as promises to charities, or promises to make gifts to members of the promisor's family) are likely to be treated as without consideration (at any rate unless they are relied upon to the detriment of the promisee) while other promises of little or no economic value may be treated as valid, because the promisor is deemed to be capable of deciding for himself what

[12] [1956] I WLR 496.

something is worth. So, too, there are a number of technical rules concerning the sufficiency of consideration in special circumstances, which will be considered below, which preclude any easy attempt at reconciliation with some universal rule as to the value of consideration.

*Forbearance*

A forbearance, like an act, can be a good consideration and, in general, the same principles apply to the two cases. But certain difficulties arise in this case which are not met in the case of an action, and these need examination. A forbearance or promise to forbear must involve giving up something which the promisor had a right to do, in order that it should constitute a good consideration. The giving up of a legal right, however slight, is thus good consideration for a promise. So also the temporary suspension of a legal right is a forbearance which may support a promise. Thus where a debtor wrote to his bank, where his account was overdrawn, and promised to deposit certain deeds with the bank as a security for his overdraft, it was held that the fact that the bank forbore to press the debtor for payment for a certain time was good consideration for the promise. The court inferred from the surrounding circumstances that the promise was made with the object of securing further time to pay. It is not necessary in these cases to show that a writ has actually been issued, nor that legal proceedings are threatened or even contemplated; it is enough that in fact the creditor has, at the request of the debtor, shown an indulgence which he was not bound to show. Nor again is it necessary to show that, if the promisee had actually sued the promisor, he would have succeeded in his action. For if the promisee has given up a bona fide claim, honestly believed in, a claim not being manifestly frivolous or vexatious, he has given up something of value, even though litigation might have ultimately shown the claim to be baseless.[13] In such a case the thing or claim given up may well have had some value at the time it was given up, even though it had none later, when the facts came to light. The value of something can change with the knowledge of the parties.

Similarly, a bona fide compromise of disputed rights cannot be attacked on the ground of lack of consideration. So if X bona fide alleges that Y owes him £200, and Y disputes the debt, but eventually promises to pay X £100 in full satisfaction, this compromise is valid and binding on both parties even though it may turn out that in fact Y owed X nothing, or that he did owe the full £200. If this were not so, no compromise would be worth the paper it was written on, for it would always be open to a party to allege that there was no consideration for it. This is plainly a strong rational

---

[13] See now *Pitt* v. *PHH Asset Management Ltd* [1993] 4 All ER 961 which shows an even more generous attitude to what is a sufficient consideration for a compromise.

argument for the present rule and one which is surely sufficient to support it. But it is not necessarily unreal to find a benefit to a party who has entered into a compromise even though it turns out to involve him in a loss. For here, too, the compromise has to be judged at the time when it was made, in the light of the knowledge of the parties at that time.

But it must be admitted that sometimes the subsequent discovery of new facts may suggest that there was no 'real' benefit to the promisor, and this may raise doubts about the fairness of a compromise. Suppose, in the example given above, that shortly after the compromise agreement is made, Y finds a lost receipt which conclusively proves that Y had already paid X the whole £200 claimed. With the benefit of hindsight it will then seem clear that Y did not in fact derive any benefit whatever under the compromise, and equally that X suffered no detrimental reliance. Where it would seem seriously offensive to the sense of justice to uphold the compromise, a way of escape may be found by holding the contract to be 'void for mistake'.[14]

## Consideration and existing duties

We must now consider the difficulties which arise when a party has done or promised to do something which he was already legally bound to do. Can such an act or a promise to perform such an act amount to a good consideration for the other party's promise? The problem is somewhat complex, for much depends on the nature of the legal duty which previously existed. The duty might have been in the nature of a public duty, imposed by the general law, and not enforceable by any individual, or it might have been a private duty, imposed by some existing relation with a third party, or it might have been a private duty enforceable by the promisor himself. These three possibilities will be dealt with in turn.

Where a person does something, or promises to do something, which the general law requires him to do anyhow, such as giving evidence in answer to a subpoena, it is usually said that this cannot constitute good consideration for the enforcement of a promise. For instance, in an old case, a promise to pay the plaintiff six guineas for answering a subpoena and giving evidence was held to be void, because the plaintiff only did what he was legally obliged to do anyhow. Everybody is obliged to answer subpoenas and give evidence when called upon to do so, subject only to payment of his expenses. Similarly, it is settled law that a policeman cannot enforce a promise given in consideration of his merely performing his duties as a policeman, though, if he goes beyond the strict call of duty, he may be entitled to any agreed remuneration; and the police authorities can contract quite validly to render policing services to those who seek them

---

[14] See *post*, 219.

(such as for large public meetings) if the authorities do not believe that their services are actually *required* for law enforcement purposes.

In modern times it is often suggested that the real basis for such decisions as these is that it is contrary to public policy for a person to demand or sue for remuneration for the performance of certain public duties.[15] A contract of this kind is too close to a bribe to be comfortable, and this is in most situations a very good reason for refusing to enforce it. It can, of course, also be said, though this is somewhat artificial, that a person who only gets what he is legally entitled to receive is not obtaining any 'real benefit' from it, and that a person who does what he is legally bound to do is not acting in reliance (or cannot claim to be acting in reliance) on a promise to reward him for doing so.

Some public duties are of a different character, and there may be no reason why parties should not be free to pay or promise payment for their performance. For instance, the mother of an illegitimate child is under a statutory obligation to maintain it; but that is only meant to regulate the relations between her and the State, not between her and the father, who also may be under a duty to maintain the child. So if she promises to look after the child in return for a promise of maintenance by the father there seems no reason of public policy why the father should not be liable on that promise.[16] The mother's promise is thus a good consideration here.

Similar problems can arise where the alleged consideration consists of an action or a promise of an action which has already been contracted for with a third party. For instance, if A promises something to B, and then makes a promise to C to do the same thing, in return for some counter-promise from C, can A sue C on the latter's counter-promise? The argument, of course, is that, since A is already legally bound by his contract with B to do the very thing he now promises to C, the promise or performance of this action is no detriment to him, and therefore no consideration. This was for long a source of academic controversy, but in recent years the arguments have died down, and the courts have twice in modern times upheld the view that, in general, performance or promise of performance of a duty owed to a third party can be a good consideration.[17] Of course, even in such contexts, there may be issues of public policy or, sometimes, of duress, but in the absence of such complications, the problem is now largely obsolete.

On the other hand, there is more difficulty about a promise in consideration of an act or promise of an act, which the promisee was already under a legal duty to perform, where that duty *was enforceable by*

---

[15] On public policy see Chs. 17 and 18.

[16] See e.g. the views of Denning LJ in *Ward* v. *Byham* [1956] 1 WLR 496.

[17] *The Eurymedon* [1975] AC 154, *supra*, 99; *Pao On* v. *Lau Yiu* [1980] AC 614, *supra*, 124.

*the promisor.* Prima facie, the promisee is here simply reiterating a duty already owed by him, and the law does not generally regard this as having any value whatever. If a debtor (here the promisee) simply promises to pay his debt, as and when it is already due, in return for some concession from the creditor (here the promisor), the creditor is prima facie entitled to insist that the promised concession is invalid because given without consideration.

For many years this rule has come under attack. The ostensible justification for it is that performance (or the promise of performance) of a duty in such a case cannot be a benefit to the promisor who is only getting that to which he is already entitled, nor can the promisee claim to be acting in detrimental reliance on a new promise, when he is merely doing his legal duty anyhow. But as a statement of fact this is clearly wrong. As Corbin said,[18] a bird in the hand is worth more than a bird in the bush and that may be why the promisor pays more to get it.

Writers have therefore argued that some more rational policy must underlie the rule than justification in terms of benefit and detriment. And this policy has been thought to be that a promise in consideration of the performance of an existing duty may be extorted by undesirable or illegitimate forms of pressure. A contractor may, for example, obtain a contract by putting in a low tender; when the work is partly done he may demand a higher price. Theoretically the employer could refuse and, if the contractor failed to complete, he could sue for damages. But the employer may in practice be reluctant to do this because he needs the work completed as soon as possible; delays may cost him dearly, and he may therefore agree to pay what the contractor demands. In such a case as this the present rule may be just.

In modern times two important developments have occurred affecting the law on this point. First, there has been increasing recognition of the concept of 'economic duress' which may invalidate a contract; and secondly, there has been an increased willingness to give effect to reasonable contractual variations which have been agreed by the parties. In effect the courts have largely adopted the view contended for by writers such as Corbin and have now accepted that the question (so far as the doctrine of consideration goes) in relation to contractual variations is whether there are practical benefits or burdens imposed by a variation. If so, there will be good consideration for a promise by the party receiving the benefit or avoiding the burden. In the important case of *Williams* v. *Roffey Bros & Nicholls (Contractors) Ltd*[19] the plaintiff was a carpenter who had agreed to do some work in some houses which the defendants had

---

[18] Corbin on *Contracts* (revised ed., St. Paul, Minnesota, 1963), § 172.
[19] [1991] 1 QB 1. An earlier decision to much the same effect (though on administrative law rather than contract law) is *Re Hurle-Hobbs* [1944] 2 All ER 261.

contracted to refurbish. The plaintiff was to get £20,000 from the defendants but, after the plaintiff had done a part of the work he found himself in financial difficulty, partly because he had offered to do the work for too low a price. The defendants were anxious to avoid incurring penalties for lateness under the main contract for which they were responsible and their surveyor persuaded them to promise the plaintiff an additional £10,300 which they therefore did. Later they denied liability for this sum but it was held by the Court of Appeal that they were liable, and that there was a sufficient consideration for their promise. They received practical benefits from it in that it helped avoid delay and saved them the trouble of finding another carpenter. The decision has been said to stand for the principle that 'where there is a practical conferment of benefit or a practical avoidance of disbenefit, there is a good consideration, and it is no answer [that is, to a claim on a variation of the contract] that the promisor was already bound'.[20]

One great advantage of treating questions of duress openly as part of the new doctrine of economic duress and not treating them as a part of the doctrine of consideration is that consideration was never a sufficiently flexible tool for this purpose. Sometimes promises of extra payment may be made where there simply is no extortion or undue pressure. Indeed, the initiative for the promise of extra payment may even come from the promisor, as actually happened in *Williams* v. *Roffey Bros.* But a minor change in the facts of cases like that may reveal that there has been some real attempt to take advantage of the situation by the party seeking the contractual variation, and that may be better dealt with as a part of the doctrine of duress.[21] Further, treating the problem as one of duress means that the courts need not find themselves (as they sometimes were formerly) driven to evade the doctrine of consideration by artificial or faulty reasoning. For instance, a promised salary increase (for a fixed term employment[22]) was sometimes enforced if the court could infer that the parties had agreed to 'rescind' the old contract of employment and make a new one at a higher salary. Yet the result was precisely the same as to recognize the validity of the promise in the first place.

Trying to deal with the dangers of extortion and unfair pressure by use of the doctrine of consideration was also unsatisfactory in another respect. For a renegotiation of a contract in fact secured by unfair pressure may

---

[20] *Anangel* v. *Hill* [1990] 2 Lloyd's Rep. 526. But there are limits to this: see *Re Selectmove, The Times*, 13 January 1994 (practical benefit to a creditor of agreeing to take payment by instalments not sufficient consideration). [21] See *post*, 273.

[22] In fixed-term employment, the employee gives nothing in return for such an increase, but in indefinite employment contracts the employee gives consideration simply by not quitting.

embody some slight variation in the original contract to the benefit of the other party. Because inadequacy of consideration is ignored, the result might then be to uphold a renegotiation obtained by such means. By treating the problem as one of duress the court may be able to avoid this result.

## 4. BENEFIT AS A CONSIDERATION

There is no doubt that in most contracts each party obtains a benefit from the other in receiving his performance and incurs a detriment in rendering his own performance. But it is not the whole contract which must be looked at to decide whether a person is obtaining a benefit or suffering a detriment. A promise or an act may be a detriment although *on balance* the promisor is making a very good bargain. A promise to pay £50,000 for a Rolls Royce worth £60,000 is a detriment, and a good consideration for a promise to deliver the car, even though the promisor has an exceptionally good deal.

As we have seen, the strongest case for imposing legal liability arises where there are both benefit and detrimental reliance. But it is not necessary that both detriment and benefit should be present in order that the consideration should be good. There is no doubt that a detriment suffered by the promisee in reliance on the promise is often a good consideration even though the promisor receives no benefit from it. The simplest example of this is the ordinary contract of suretyship whereby one person guarantees repayment of a debt to be made by the promisee to a third party. The surety may receive no benefit from this transaction (at any rate that sort of benefit which is normally regarded as relevant) but the promisee incurs a detriment by acting in reliance on the promise. There is no doubt that in principle this suffices to create a binding contract. Nevertheless, there are some peculiar rules about contracts of guarantee which may be partly explained by the fact that a guarantor derives no benefit from the transaction. For example, a contract of guarantee is one of the few contracts which cannot be sued upon in the absence of writing; there are also many special rules, often felt to be highly artificial and technical, as a result of which a guarantor may escape liability. Peculiarities of this nature may suggest that judges sometimes feel uneasy at enforcing a promise against a person who has derived no benefit from it.

It is less clear whether benefit without detriment will suffice. This may be because benefit to the promisor is rarely present without detriment to the promisee. But there are several types of case where this can occur. The case of past consideration, dealt with above, furnishes one example. A second example concerns a promise of a reward for information which is supplied without knowledge of the reward. This too we have dealt with above[23] where we saw there was difficulty in saying that an 'acceptance' could be found in such a case. A third case has also been dealt with above,[24] namely where the supposed consideration consists of something which the promisee was already bound to do. The fact that all these cases have caused difficulty in the law illustrates uneasiness about treating benefit as sufficient without detriment. But the solution to many of these cases also illustrates that the uneasiness is usually overcome in practice.

Another difficulty arises from the apparent rule that 'consideration must move from the promisee', i.e. that the promisee and not some third party must supply the consideration. If this were a universally valid rule it would certainly seem that in most situations a detriment is necessary, though there are rare cases in which the promisee can supply a consideration which benefits the promisor though he incurs no detriment in supplying it. But there are no good modern illustrations of the supposed rule that consideration must move from the promisee, and many cases which seem inconsistent with it. One instance is *Charnock* v. *Liverpool Corporation*,[25] previously discussed. Similarly, where A was indebted to B and C paid B part of the debt on the understanding that B would not sue A for the balance, it was held that B was bound by his promise and that A could rely on it though he furnished no consideration for it.[26]

In modern life there are all sorts of circumstances in which the consideration for an apparent contractual arrangement between A and B is paid for by C. For instance C may be A's employer who books hotel accommodation or obtains travel tickets for him while he travels on C's business. It is very difficult to believe that such arrangements between A and B do not amount to ordinary legal contracts, although the consideration clearly does not move from the promisee.

Because, then, detriment seems enough to make a good consideration, while it is uncertain whether benefit without detriment will do, English writers have sometimes concluded that detriment is the key concept. This may, however, obscure the fact that so much of the law of contract is to do with exchange and hence with bargains of one sort or another. Indeed, as we noted in the first chapter, the *economic* function of contract is often perceived in terms of exchange. And judges and academics often speak as though all contracts were bargains. Certainly, one result of classical law was that emphasis shifted away from factual benefits and detriments to the making of mutual promises which are treated as legally binding without (in general) any further inquiry into whether they are beneficial or detrimental. One result of this shift in emphasis was an attempt to redefine consideration in terms of bargains.

---

[23] See *supra*, 65.                    [24] See *supra*, 131.
[25] [1968] 1 WLR 1498, *supra*, 98.
[26] *Hirachand Punamchand* v. *Temple* [1911] 2 KB 330.

Of course there is a great deal of validity in this approach. Many contracts—indeed nearly all commercial contracts which are often seen as typical or paradigmatic contracts—*are* bargains. The mutual promises are, and are intended to be, the consideration for each other. They are exchanged by the parties, one promise in return for the other. Moreover, whether a promise should be treated as given for good consideration, or merely as a gratuitous promise, can often be decided by asking whether some alleged consideration was *intended* by the parties to be the consideration, or the price of the promise. What is more, it is clear that, even when courts do enforce promises which were not bargained for, they often prefer to do so by invoking equitable or other doctrines like 'estoppel', rather than by treating them as ordinary contracts. But there are also very many examples of contracts in the books which do not look like bargains, and which are inconsistent with the supposed rule that nothing can be consideration which is not intended as such. It is now necessary to say something of these.

### 5. THE PROTECTION OF DETRIMENTAL RELIANCE

Unilateral contracts provide many simple examples of contracts which are not bargains, such as the famous *Carlill* case.[27] Using the smoke ball and catching influenza were the conditions which Mrs Carlill had to satisfy to claim the promised reward, but it would be an odd use of language to suggest that these were *intended* as the price of the promise, or that there was a bargain between the manufacturers and Mrs Carlill.[28] Other examples of non-bargain contracts are many collateral contracts and other sorts of contracts 'made by the courts' which were discussed in Chapter 4. A particularly relevant example is the decision in *The Eurymedon*.[29] It will be recalled that it was held here that a contract was 'made' by an exemption clause in a bill of lading operating between the buyer of goods and the stevedores who unloaded them. The act of unloading the goods was held to be a sufficient consideration for the 'offer' contained in the exemption clause, but it is not easy to argue that this was the price of the promise. It was in truth the condition on which the stevedores were prepared to unload the goods.

The idea that all contracts are bargains and that consideration must always be the price of the promise is closely associated with the notion that the consideration must be (expressly or impliedly) requested by the

---

[27] *Supra*, n. 3.
[28] Of course there was a bargain between Mrs Carlill and the retailer from whom she actually bought the smoke ball, but the promise was made by the manufacturer, and the action was brought against him and not against the retailer.  [29] *Supra*, n. 17.

promisor in return for his promise. That such a request is necessary is also a part of the orthodox doctrine, though it, too, is not always reconcilable with the cases. But it must not anyhow be thought that a 'requested' consideration is proof that the transaction is a bargain. A person says to his nephew, 'Take a holiday and I will pay your expenses'. The nephew has in a sense been requested to take the holiday, but there is clearly no bargain. Yet few lawyers would doubt that such a promise would be enforceable once it had been acted upon, even though it was clearly gratuitous.

In fact, although lawyers often say that gratuitous promises are not legally enforceable, there are many examples of such promises being enforced once they have been relied upon to the promisee's detriment. At one time courts seemed untroubled by the absence of any real bargain. For instance, there are several cases in the books in which a person has desired to make a gift of a house to another, and has persuaded the donee to enter into a contract to buy the property from a third party on the strength of a definite promise that he will himself pay the price.[30] Such promises have been enforced. So also, during the First World War, a local authority was held liable on an undertaking to make good the wage loss of any of its employees who volunteered for the armed forces.[31] Clearly, the plaintiff acted to his detriment in reliance on the promise, but it would be very odd to call the result a bargain. In cases like this, and there are many others, the promisor has at least requested or specified the act to be performed by the promisee. The performance of such an act is regularly held to constitute a unilateral contract.

More difficulty arises when the promisee acts to his detriment in reliance on a promise, but the action taken by him was not specified or requested by the promisor. But even here the courts are often prepared to enforce the promise on the ground of estoppel, or by invoking some elastic equitable doctrine like the 'constructive trust'. For instance, in *Crabb* v. *Arun District Council*[32] the defendants told the plaintiff he could have a right of entry to his land from some land belonging to them, and in reliance on that promise the plaintiff sold the only part of his land which already had direct access to a road. When the defendants then went back on their promise, the plaintiff was left without any access to what remained of his land, but the defendants had not requested the plaintiff to sell the relevant part of his land, nor was their promise made with reference to any such action in reliance at all. Still, the court enforced the defendants' promise even though they insisted that this was being done by way of estoppel rather

---

[30] See e.g. *Crosbie* v. *M'Doual* (1806) 13 Ves. Jr. 148; *Skidmore* v. *Bradford* (1869) LR 8 Eq. 134; *Coles* v. *Pilkington* (1874) LR 19 Eq. 174; *Hohler* v. *Aston* [1920] 2 Ch. 420.
[31] *Davies* v. *Rhondda UC* (1918) 87 LJKB 166.
[32] [1976] Ch. 179.

than contract.[33] Another line of authority is exemplified by *Pascoe* v. *Turner*[34] where the defendant had lived with the plaintiff as man and wife in a house which he had bought in his name, but which he had told her would be hers. After they parted she spent money on the house and contents, and to that extent had acted in reliance on his promises or statements. It was held that she was entitled to have the house transferred to her because she had an 'equitable' right arising from his statements and her reliance on them. Here, of course, she had not been requested to act as she did, but the defendant had known what she was doing and had acquiesced.

Furthermore, tort and equity and estoppel are often invoked in circumstances in which it would seem perfectly plausible to suggest that there actually is a contract so that there is a great deal of overlap between the various categories. For example, many of the collateral contract cases discussed in Chapter 4 show how contractual liability can be imposed for misstatements of fact, even though today tort would seem the more natural category for such cases. But equity and estoppel are also often invoked today where it is not clear that a contract cannot be set up. Sometimes this seems to be done without any ulterior motive. Equity and estoppel simply become fashionable legal doctrines, and are invoked when contract might do perfectly well.

But sometimes this seems to be done because there are inconvenient technicalities attaching to contract law in particular respects—for instance if a contract is sued upon, it may need to be in writing. In these cases, equity or estoppel may be invoked as a way of evading contractual rules. Equally, equity or estoppel sometimes seem to be used because an attempt to establish a contract may fail on grounds of uncertainty. This seems odd. If there is sufficient certainty to justify the creation of legal rights it should surely not matter whether the case is classified as contract or as estoppel. If there is insufficient certainty, then rights should not be created at all. What needs to be more clearly recognized by the courts is that once a contract has been acted upon, or relied upon, it may become justifiable to recognize rights even if it would not have been justifiable before such reliance. For example, an executory arrangement may be too uncertain to be enforced as a contract, but may be sufficient to justify some degree of enforcement

---

[33] Promissory estoppel is not regarded as sufficient to found a cause of action but proprietary estoppel is. The difficulty in this case was that the facts did not seem to fall within the area traditionally thought to be covered by proprietary estoppel (the defendants did not assert that the plaintiff *had* a right but merely that they would give him one). Lord Scarman says that the difference between the different types of estoppel is anyhow not very helpful.

[34] [1979] 1 WLR 431. There are numerous modern cases of this general nature, many of which are discussed in more detailed works on contract or equity or the land law. Some of them are referred to in Ch. 4, above.

when partially performed.[35] So too, it may well be that a statement or representation, which is not intended to give rise to legal relations, may be sufficient to justify the recognition of legal rights once it has been relied upon.[36] So long as it is understood that action in reliance changes the situation even as a matter of contract law, there will be the less need to invoke equity or estoppel. But some judges and writers are reluctant to admit this because, according to classical principles, contractual liability stems from the agreement, and action in reliance cannot change the rights of the parties. Accordingly, they prefer to use concepts like equity and estoppel to protect action in reliance. It is, however, arguable that this complicates the law unnecessarily, and anyhow involves mere lip service to classical principles. It is in truth an evasion of classical principles, rather than a recognition of them.

There are thus a large number of modern cases in which detrimental reliance of one kind or another has been held to justify the creation or recognition of some rights, by way of contract or tort or equity or estoppel; and (as we saw earlier) there is now high authority for saying that English law recognizes a general principle under which injurious reliance may be a source of rights.[37] But there is, as yet, little agreement on the nature of such rights, and on the relationship between these rights and contractual rights. On one view, perhaps the orthodox view, contracts are confined to cases where there is a recognizable promise, and some requested consideration. All other cases of detrimental reliance must fall to be dealt with as cases in tort or equity or by way of estoppel. Certainly, this approach accords with some cases, especially perhaps where the plaintiff relies not on a clear promise, but on some other sort of statement. Reliance on a statement of fact, for instance, is more likely to be treated as giving rise to liability in tort than in contract. If this were a firmly drawn line, it would be necessary to decide what are the precise limits of these tortious or equitable or estoppel rights. For example, it is often said that equitable and estoppel rights must relate to specific pieces of property, indeed, perhaps, to land and buildings. But the boundaries of these equitable and estoppel rights are constantly being pushed forward,[38] so that there often appears to be little distinction in principle between them and contractual rights.

However, one major distinction is still usually drawn, namely, that rights arising from promissory estoppel (though not those arising from proprietary estoppel, nor equitable rights) are still generally said to operate only by

---

[35] See *supra* 115. For criticism of the accepted approach to this problem, see *supra*, 117.

[36] See *Kleinwort Benson Ltd* v. *Malaysian Mining Corp* [1988] 1 All ER 714; although this decision was reversed [1989] 1 All ER 785, the CA's decision is not necessarily inconsistent with the text.

[37] See Lord Diplock in *The Hannah Blumenthal* [1983] 1 AC 834 at 916.

[38] See e.g. *Re Basham* [1986] 1 WLR 1498.

way of defence, and do not give rise to a cause of action. In other words promissory estoppel is generally thought to be a way of discharging contractual obligations but not of creating them. For that reason this subject is more fully treated in section 6 of this Chapter where variation and discharge are discussed. But it must also be said that there are signs of change on this point, and it may soon become necessary to insist that detrimental reliance is simply an alternative to consideration as a source of contractual rights.[39]

## 6. CONSIDERATION FOR THE VARIATION AND DISCHARGE OF CONTRACTS

The doctrine of consideration has long been applied, not merely to the formation of contracts but also to their variation and discharge. Varying a contract, or discharging contractual duties can themselves be achieved by further contracts agreed between the parties, but these further contracts must comply with the requirements of the doctrine of consideration, and there is no doubt that this has often caused trouble.

There is one kind of situation where unilateral variation of the terms appears to be permitted without regard to the requirement of consideration, but this is not strictly a case of variation at all. In some common situations contracts are normally entered into for a fixed term, but are also very commonly renewed—for instance, annual motor insurance contracts. In these cases there is no question, strictly speaking, of variation. The renewal is a new contract, and so the insurer is free to propose that the renewal should be on different terms; for example, that the coverage should be altered, or the premium increased. (Life insurance is different— this is a long term contract and the terms are fixed at the outset and cannot be changed without agreement of both parties.)

### Variation of contracts

It is important at the outset to distinguish between a variation which is made in pursuance of the original contract, and one which is made subsequently without having been originally provided for. If a contract is made which expressly provides that the duties of the parties can be varied in a specified manner (whether by agreement or unilaterally or in any other way), then no further consideration needs to be provided for the variation. In such a case the original contract is not itself being varied at all. All that

---

[39] This is more or less the general position in American law. As American experience shows, this does not mean that such rights must be treated in all respects like other (or most) contractual rights—these rights only arise from detrimental reliance, not from agreement, and they may be protected by awards of 'reliance' rather than 'expectation' damages. See further on the damages question, *post*, 448.

happens is that the duties of the parties (or of one party) may be varied under the contract. For example, suppose that an ordinary building society mortgage provides that the borrower is to pay (say) interest at 10 per cent 'or such other rate as may be specified from time to time by the lender'. In this situation the lender may change the rate from time to time (subject to whatever restrictions the contract imposes) but this change is not a variation of the contract itself.[40] No new consideration needs to be provided by the building society simply because the rate is increased.

But where the contract itself is varied, the result may be different. It all depends upon whether the variation benefits (or may benefit) both parties or only one party. A variation such as a salary increase in a contract of employment, which obviously cannot benefit the employer but will only benefit the employee, raises a number of peculiar difficulties. Suppose that an employee is employed for a fixed period (say under a five-year contract) at a fixed salary, say £20,000 per annum. Now suppose that, after a year, the employer agrees to increase the salary to £22,000 per annum. Here, in strict legal theory, the original contract has been varied, and though the variation may have been agreed by both parties, there is, on the face of it, no new consideration. The employee has simply agreed to go on doing what he is already legally bound to do, while the employer has agreed to pay extra money for this, and there is no apparent practical benefit to him from this change. So it seems that this salary increase could not be legally enforced. But that result would not generally be found acceptable today, especially where the increase is merely inflation-proofing, so that the new salary is not more than the old one in real terms. Ways of escape may therefore be sought. It may, for example, be suggested that the original contract should really be construed as providing for 'a salary of £20,000 or such other amount as might be agreed'. Then the case would be like the hypothetical one put in the last paragraph. Or again, if the employee is not himself bound to work for a fixed period but, as is more usually the case, is free to give notice, it may be argued that, by forbearing from giving notice and continuing in his work, he has in law provided consideration for the increased salary. Alternatively, it may be argued that the parties have impliedly 'rescinded' the old employment contract and made a new one; and that would be legally valid because (as explained below) a rescission of such a continuing contract is always possible by agreement of the parties. Finally, if all arguments fail to show that there was some new consideration, the variation may be enforced if it has once been acted upon, under

---

[40] The EC Directive on Unfair Terms in Consumer Contracts (Annex, Art. 1(j), (k), and (l)) requires that a 'valid reason' should exist for such unilateral variations, and that the borrower should be informed of the variation otherwise the contract may be unfair; see further, *post*, 151 and 317.

the doctrine of estoppel. Because this doctrine has been especially used in cases of contractual discharge, it is treated more fully below.

The difficulties discussed in the last paragraph are of a highly technical character, and often allow, or appear to allow, one party to go back on a variation which he has freely and voluntarily agreed. The reason for this failure of the law to accord with the modern sense of justice may well stem from the fact that the law fails to make due allowance for the peculiar nature of continuing relations in contract law. Long-continued relations, like contracts of employment, cannot in practice be maintained without frequent adjustments to the terms of the relationship; and the reality is that even concessions made by one party which appear to be quite gratuitous are usually made for good commercial reasons. For example, the party agreeing to the concessions may wish to preserve the goodwill of the other, or may hope that future contracts may be made between them. So in making concessions he may well be motivated by belief that he is likely to receive some benefit in due course or, perhaps, has received a past benefit for which some goodwill adjustment is now due in return; yet the requirements of the doctrine of consideration could prevent the courts from recognizing that such concessions are in substance the equivalent of bargained for, and not gratuitous, concessions. It seems likely, therefore, that the modern decisions holding that a practical benefit is a sufficient consideration for a contractual variation[41] would be broadly interpreted to avoid the absurdities which would otherwise arise.

As noted above, these difficulties do not anyhow arise with a variation which benefits or may benefit both parties. Suppose there is a contract of sale of goods, in which the buyer is to pay a certain price and the seller to deliver specified goods. A change in the price, up or down, can only benefit one or other of the parties, and so some new consideration must prima facie be provided by the party benefited by that change. But a change (say) in the way in which the price is to be provided, for instance a change requiring the buyer to provide a letter of credit or a letter of credit on slightly different terms, may benefit both parties, so such a change need not be supported by any new consideration. Moreover, once there is some consideration provided, as there is by a change which may benefit both parties, that new consideration will suffice to support all sorts of other changes which may only benefit one party. So a change in the letter of credit which the buyer has to provide would suffice to provide the consideration for an increase in the price too.[42]

---

[41] See *Williams* v. *Roffey Bros & Nicholls (Contractors) Ltd* [1991] 1 QB 1, *supra*, 133.

[42] See *North Ocean Shipping Co Ltd* v. *Hyundai Construction Co Ltd* [1979] QB 705, on which these examples are based. But compare also *Re Selectmove*, *The Times*, 13 January 1994.

## Discharge of contracts

The difficulties concerning variations are paralleled by difficulties with discharges of contractual obligations. If some duties remain outstanding on both sides at the time the contract is abandoned or terminated, then there will be consideration on both sides, because there will be (or may be) benefits on both sides; and the courts will not examine the circumstances to see if in reality this is improbable. The bare possibility that both sides will benefit is enough. In contracts of a continuing nature, therefore, like employment contracts, it is nearly always possible to agree upon a termination which discharges both parties, without the need for any new consideration. Of course nothing said here detracts from the need for an *agreement* (or anyhow a new contract or its equivalent); what is being discussed here is simply the requirement of consideration. A contract can only be validly discharged without such a new contract if its original terms contain provision to that effect, and in that event (as in the case of variation) there will be no need to show any new consideration.

If, on the other hand, only one party is being discharged (either because the agreement only relates to his duties, or because the other has already fully performed) then there is, once again, a problem arising from the lack of consideration. If a creditor, for instance, accepts (or agrees to accept) part payment of a debt in full satisfaction of the whole debt, he is in law simply promising or agreeing to give up a legal right for which the debtor appears to provide no consideration. Hence his promise is not binding, and the debt remains payable. This principle, usually known as the rule in *Pinnel's case*, is a very old one, and was affirmed by the House of Lords in 1884, but it gives rise to much trouble, and many attempts at evasion are made. Most lawyers find the present law unsatisfactory, because it is generally believed—despite the fluctuations in the strength of classical principles—that a person should be free to give up part of a debt by his own free and voluntary agreement, without insisting that he should get something in return. On the other hand, if this were the law, some protection might be needed for creditors who are pressured into accepting part payment in full satisfaction.

Many limits have been placed on the rule in *Pinnel's case*. Indeed, the case itself holds that if there is any variation in the mode, time, or place of payment, the variation may be a good consideration for the waiver of the rest of the debt. So, although a debt cannot be legally discharged by acceptance of 99p. in the pound, it can be discharged by the creditor agreeing to take in full satisfaction something other than money. A book, a canary, or a peppercorn may be accepted in full satisfaction, for the courts will not inquire into their real value. But there is (as often) some inconsistency in the cases; actual benefit or detriment was insisted on in one case involving variation in place, but in other cases has been treated as immaterial.

At one time there was a suggestion that payment by cheque might be a sufficient variation to support the discharge of part of a debt. But in *D & C Builders* v. *Rees*[43] the Court of Appeal refused to apply this supposed rule in a case where the debtor had offered a cheque for £300 in payment of a bill for over £700. In this case it was the debtor who was exerting pressure on the creditor, for the debtor extorted an agreement by the creditor to accept the cheque in full satisfaction for the debt by making it clear that the creditor would otherwise get nothing. In such a situation it is unfair that the creditor should not be able to take what is offered and still come back for the rest later. It was therefore held that the creditor's promise to accept the cheque in full satisfaction was not binding. This is the kind of case where the present rule seems sound, and if *Pinnel's case* were ever reversed by statute, provision would need to be made for such cases.

Another exception to the rule in *Pinnel's case* has long been recognized. A debtor's 'composition agreement' with his creditors is binding even in the absence of consideration provided by the debtor. A composition with creditors is an agreement by which the creditors all agree to accept a proportion of their debts in full satisfaction. As between the creditors, they each give up something, so consideration is in a sense present; but the debtor provides none. Nevertheless, the agreement is binding on all parties and can be pleaded by the debtor in an action by a creditor. The rule is justified by the close similarity to judicial proceedings in bankruptcy of a composition agreement, and by the fact that an action by one creditor, after making such an agreement, would be a fraud on the others. The whole essence of such an agreement is equal treatment of all the creditors.

By analogy with this principle, it has also been held that payment of part of a debt *by a third party* (not acting as the debtor's agent) will discharge the debt if it is accepted in full satisfaction, even though the debtor is no party to this agreement and provides no consideration for it.

## Estoppel

A third method of evading the rule in *Pinnel's case* has become of great importance in recent years. The principle of 'promissory estoppel' lays it down that a simple promise to waive performance of a contractual (or other legal) obligation is binding if it is intended to be acted upon, and is in fact acted upon. 'The gist of the equity lies in the fact that one party has by his conduct led the other to alter his position'.[44] It is customary to treat such promises, though now recognized to be enforceable to some degree,

---

[43] [1966] 2 QB 617.
[44] *Per* Lord Simonds in *Tool Metal Manufacturing Co* v. *Tungsten Electric Co* [1955] 2 All ER 657 at 660.

as given without consideration. This is in line with the usual treatment of consideration, but it obscures the very close similarity between promissory estoppel and ordinary cases of consideration. For detrimental reliance seems to be the key to promissory estoppel,[45] and it is also, of course, one of the twin legs of the doctrine of consideration itself. But at least the conventional treatment has the advantage of bringing home the point that promises can be 'enforced' in different ways and to different degrees. Although a promise may be held binding by virtue of this principle, it may still fall short of the effect of a full contractual promise, supported by a counter-promise.

First, the promise will only be binding if it has been acted upon by the promisee, whereas a promise supported by a counter-promise is binding in its inception. But in this respect promissory estoppel is no different from the case of executed consideration. In unilateral contracts (as we have seen) a promise is usually rendered enforceable by the performance of some act, not by a counter-promise. But there is one difference, which has hitherto been treated as of crucial importance, between an ordinary unilateral contract and a case of promissory estoppel. In a unilateral contract, the act to be performed by the promisee is normally requested and is always at least stated (expressly or impliedly) by the promisor as the condition on which performance of the promise becomes due. But in a case of promissory estoppel, it is unnecessary to show that the act performed by the promisee was requested or even stated by the promisor. It is enough that the promisee has acted to his detriment. For example, if a person promises to waive a debt due to him from his nephew on the nephew's marriage, then the marriage would be a good consideration for a unilateral contract, and the promise would become enforceable as a contract. But if the promise were simply to waive the debt with no reference (express or implied) to the possibility of marriage, and the nephew were to marry in reliance on the promise, then the act of marriage would not be a good consideration, but would be sufficient as the basis of a promissory estoppel.

But there are a number of other possible differences between a case of promissory estoppel and a unilateral contract. First, it has for some years been insisted that promissory estoppel is 'a shield and not a sword'; that is to say, the promisee can set up such a promise as a defence to an action, but cannot himself sue upon it. So the principle applies to a promise to waive a debt, but not to a promise to make a gift. There is no doubt that

---

[45] Lord Denning frequently denied this (e.g. in *W. J. Alan* v. *El Nasr Export Co* [1972] 2 QB 189) but it is difficult to see why the promisee should improve his rights by acting on the promise in a way which does not prejudice him. There is now clear authority that the analogous defence of 'change of position' in the law of restitution does require the change to be to the actor's detriment: *Rover International* v. *Cannon Film Sales* [1989] 1 WLR 912.

this is the law in some cases, and it was so laid down as a general rule in *Combe* v. *Combe*[46] though there may have been special reasons for the decision in that case. On the other hand, there are signs of impatience with this limitation on the use of promissory estoppel in some cases,[47] and recently the courts have hived off one group of estoppel cases, now called cases of 'proprietary estoppel', in which it is accepted that estoppel does create a cause of action which can be sued upon.[48] These are said to be confined to circumstances in which a promise is made with reference to a particular piece of property; but recently this dyke, too, has been breached and it has been said that a promise which has reference to the promisor's property generally can be enforced by way of promissory estoppel.[49] In other cases yet other kinds of estoppel have been recognized. This multiplication of legal categories is, to say the least, confusing even to specialist lawyers, and it must be a nightmare to students. It is plainly time that some broad underlying principles were recognized by the courts[50] and, if distinctions are needed, that they should be clearly articulated and justified.

We have also seen that there are signs of movement towards a broader recognition of detrimental reliance as a possible source of rights, through tort law, equitable and other legal doctrines; and in the United States it has for many years been recognized that promissory estoppel can create rights as well as discharge them.[51] For the moment, this development has not yet occurred in England (which explains why this subject is still treated here under the heading of variation and discharge); but there is a strong current of movement in that direction.[52]

A second possible difference between promissory estoppel and unilateral contracts is that (it now seems) a bare act of detrimental reliance may not always suffice to establish a case of promissory estoppel. It has, for

---

[46] [1951] 2 KB 215; followed in *Syros Shipping Co* v. *Elaghill Trading Co* [1981] 3 All ER 189.

[47] See *Re Wyvern* [1974] 1 WLR 1097; *Crabb* v. *Arun DC* [1976] Ch. 179; *Taylor Fashions* v. *Liverpool Victoria Friendly Society* [1981] QB 13 (where yet another kind of estoppel was invoked).

[48] See e.g. *Western Fish Products Ltd* v. *Penwith DC* [1981] 2 All ER 204; *Salvation Army* v. *West Yorks. Met. CC* (1981) 41 P & CR 179. Perhaps *Brewer Street Investments* v. *Barclays Woollen Co Ltd* [1954] QB 428 is another example.

[49] See *Re Basham* [1986] 1 WLR 1498.

[50] See the judgement of Mason CJ in the Australian High Ct. in *Commonwealth of Australia* v. *Verwayen* (1990) 170 CLR 394.

[51] See now also the Australian High Ct. decisions (which recognize that promissory estoppel can create a cause of action) in *Legione* v. *Hately* (1983) 152 CLR 426; *Foran* v. *Wright* (1989) 168 CLR 385; *Walton's Stores (Interstate)* v. *Maher* (1988) 164 CLR 387, and the *Verwayen* case, cited in n. 50.

[52] Writing extra-judicially, Lord Oliver has suggested that these Australian decisions are likely to be mirrored in England: (1993) 67 *Australian LJ* 675 at 685.

instance, been said that it must also be 'inequitable' for the promisor to go back on his word. In particular, conduct in reliance may not suffice to establish a case of promissory estoppel if the conduct is easily reversible.[53] In a unilateral contract this particular problem does not really arise, because the nature of the act to be performed by the promisee must be requested or stated.

It has also recently been held that a case of promissory estoppel cannot be made out if the promisor did not encourage the belief that he would not change his mind.[54] It may seem odd to suggest that a promise does not necessarily encourage such a belief, but it must always be remembered that a person may be called a 'promisor' who made no express promise at all. This is especially common in cases of promissory estoppel which often arise, not out of clear promises, but from the conduct or behaviour, or even inaction, of one contracting party, which leads the other to draw inferences about the first party's intentions. These inferences may be 'reasonable' but they may, all the same, be far from what the other party really intended. Thus claims by way of promissory estoppel are quite often based on conduct which has reasonably led the claimant to believe that the other intends to behave in a certain fashion, followed by detrimental reliance by the claimant. What has recently been held is that the conduct on which such a claim of promissory estoppel is based must indicate an irrevocable intention of behaving in the way suggested. Perhaps this is only another way of saying that the conduct must really justify the inference of a *promise*.

A fourth practical difference between promissory estoppel and unilateral contracts is that—at least in some cases—promissory estoppel operates only to suspend and not to extinguish rights. A landlord, for instance, promises to reduce the rent payable by the tenant; if there is no consideration for this, the promise may indeed be binding (assuming the tenant acts upon it) but the landlord may, on reasonable notice, demand payment of the full rent again in the future. Precisely when, and subject to what limitations, promissory estoppel operates in this way is, however, still a doubtful and controversial matter. The truth perhaps is that this ought to be a matter of the construction of the promise, whether the case is one of promissory estoppel or ordinary contract. It is very hard to justify distinguishing between them in this way.

In any event, as we have already seen, all these distinctions between unilateral contracts and cases of promissory estoppel are less clear-cut than may seem here. For one thing, it is often very difficult to distinguish between them at all, because one only needs to 'imply' a request to turn an

---

[53] *Société Italo-Belge* v. *Palm & Vegetable Oils (The Post Chaser)* [1982] 1 All ER 19.
[54] *A-G for Hong Kong* v. *Humphrey's Estate (Queen's Gardens)* [1987] AC 114.

apparent promissory estoppel case into a unilateral contract. And for another thing, promissory estoppel often seems to be invoked simply as a way of evading inconvenient and technical rules of contract law. Minor modifications to those rules would often enable the case to be seen as contractual. And thirdly, in practice, promissory estoppel often seems to be invoked in cases where it would be perfectly possible, on the existing authorities, to show that a contract had been made. Indeed, it is not uncommon to find judges in the same case agreeing on the result, but disagreeing as to whether the decision should be based on contract or promissory estoppel or yet other analogous principles.[55]

## 7. THE FUTURE OF THE DOCTRINE OF CONSIDERATION

General dissatisfaction with the doctrine of consideration led to a reference to the Law Revision Committee in 1934, but the Report of the Committee, published in 1937, satisfied neither the supporters nor the critics of the doctrine, and its proposals have never been implemented. Some lawyers would still prefer to see the doctrine abolished altogether, although the issue is not at present high on the agenda of law reform.

When 'abolition' is being discussed it is normally assumed that the only function of the doctrine of consideration is to prevent gratuitous promises being enforceable. This is certainly one normal result of the rules, but we have seen that gratuitous promises are sometimes enforced (usually only if they have been relied upon) and that there may therefore be good consideration for a gratuitous promise. The function of the doctrine of consideration is therefore wider than merely to deal with gratuitous promises; in truth its function is to decide what promises should be enforced, or more broadly still (bearing in mind how wide can be the concept of an implied promise) what legal obligations should be imposed. If this is correct, talk of 'abolition' is nonsensical. There will always be a need for rules determining what promises will be legally enforceable unless (which is unthinkable) *all* promises are to become enforceable; and *a fortiori*, there will always be a need for rules deciding what obligations are to be imposed.

Plainly then, abolition of the doctrine would leave the functions it now performs to be performed by other legal rules. To some extent this might be no bad thing. For example, there is something to be said for recognizing that the reasons for *not* enforcing certain promises derive from public policy notions about illegal promises, or from objections to extortion and undue pressure. We could then rationalize the law by treating these cases alongside others involving similar problems which are not today treated as

---

[55] See e.g. *Brikom Investments Ltd* v. *Carr* [1979] QB 467.

raising questions of consideration. Furthermore, reclassifying problems in this way would force lawyers to be more open about discussing (for example) what kinds of pressure *are* to be regarded as unfair and unacceptable. To some extent the law is already moving in this direction anyhow.

But although this would be an acceptable way of reformulating the law, it must be recognized that 'abolition' of the doctrine would invite its resurgence in other major respects under a new guise. In particular, there are many promises in connection with family or social matters which the courts would probably be reluctant to enforce. Traditionally they have refused enforcement because there is no good consideration for them. But a rival theory has recently come to be advanced, namely, that in cases of this kind there is no intention to create legal relations.[56] In a few rare cases parties expressly choose to provide that their promises are not be binding in law; but in most cases where the 'intent to create legal relations' is denied, it seems quite plain that the courts are indulging in fictitious reasoning. They are simply saying that they think the promises in question are the sort of promises which *ought not* to create legal relations, and that reasonable people who make such promises should not be saddled with legal liabilities. At one time, such promises could well have been denied legal enforceability by saying that there was no consideration for them. But since the rules of the doctrine have apparently been frozen into a rigid pattern, modern lawyers have felt difficulty with this analysis. They find, for instance, a family arrangement in which there appear to be mutual promises, and so they deduce that there must be consideration. Hence to deny legal validity to such promises they must invoke a separate legal doctrine, and so they say that there is 'no intent to create legal relations'.

It should therefore be apparent that to 'abolish' consideration would merely invite the courts to consider anew what promises ought to be enforceable, using the 'intent to create legal relations' formula, instead of the 'consideration' formula. In many instances this will certainly make no substantive change to the legal result. Purely social promises (for instance to accept a dinner invitation) are not binding now, and will still not be binding if consideration is abolished. Some family arrangements which are not binding now, especially while still executory, will remain free of legal sanction, while others, especially after significant detrimental reliance, will probably still be enforced. The sort of factors which now are held to amount to good consideration (or perhaps to create liability by way of promissory or proprietary estoppel) will probably be found good reasons for holding that the parties did intend to create legal relations. But in other respects a real change might be expected. For instance, a written gratuitous

---

[56] On the intent to create legal relations see the next Ch.

promise in the language of binding commitment would in most cases doubtless become enforceable, whereas today it would often be unenforceable. So also, such a change would probably greatly simplify the law relating to serious commercial promises dealing with contractual variations and discharges, where today there is often great difficulty arising from the doctrine of consideration.

In some respects this might represent a real improvement in the law. Especially where variation and discharge of contracts are concerned, it may well be that it would improve the law to get rid of the doctrine altogether. But the doctrine is embedded deep in moral values and to get rid of it altogether might prove surprisingly difficult, even in this limited area. Although no doubt there is a wide belief that to perform a promise is a moral obligation, there are conflicting moral attitudes about the unfairnesss of expecting to get something for nothing. There is also the problem of separating out truly free and voluntary promises from those made under some degree of pressure. It seems clear, for instance, that some legal mechanism or doctrine will always be needed to prevent one party extorting a variation or discharge of the contract by unfair pressure. Traditionally that function has been performed by the doctrine of consideration, although not to everyone's satisfaction. But if the doctrine is abolished from these areas, it will need to be replaced presumably by an expanded concept of duress or unfair bargaining power, and possibly other doctrines also.[57]

At the end of the day, therefore, we must recognize the point made much earlier, that the doctrine of consideration often operates as a paternalistic device, limiting the freedom of parties in private relationships. The limits are not very serious, because in most cases a person who quite calculatedly and deliberately seeks to incur a gratuitous obligation can easily give effect to his legal intentions. There is, of course, nothing in the doctrine which prevents a person from making a gift; all that the doctrine does is to make it difficult—though not impossible—to bind oneself by a *promise* to make a gift. So to a large degree the doctrine of consideration only prevents a person from being, as it were, caught out unexpectedly by some ill-thought-out generosity or concession. Of course even this is a paternalistic measure, though many will think it a not unjustified piece of paternalism, in effect to require a person to think twice before committing himself to an act of generosity. In this respect the

---

[57] As noted above (142) the EC Dir. on Unfair Contract Terms requires that a unilateral contractual variation should only be made for a 'valid reason'. In a sense this is an alternative to the requirement of consideration (which originally probably meant no more than that a promise, to be legally binding, must likewise be made for some good reason). So the Dir. can be seen as requiring the courts to start all over again the search for principles by which to decide what are good reasons for contractual variations in this type of case.

doctrine seems precisely in line with modern consumer-protection legislation creating a 'cooling-off' period before a contract becomes binding.
Even this might seem unduly paternalistic to some, and it would not be
surprising if lawyers once again start seriously to discuss the possible
abolition of the doctrine.

It is not, however, pure paternalism that raises doubts about the
possibility of making gratuitous promises enforceable. Such a proposal
involves other problems which have rarely been discussed in our legal
literature. Making gratuitous promises enforceable does raise problems
about the relationship of such promises to other types of contracts. On the
whole English contract law seems to be framed on the supposition that
most contracts are bargains, and its rules are not wholly appropriate for
gratuitous promises. For instance, excuses for non-performance (as we
shall see later) are very narrowly confined in the present law, and it is not
clear that it would generally be found fair to treat gratuitous promises quite
so strictly. This is particularly true of *unrelied-upon* gratuitous promises,
and it must be appreciated that to make gratuitous promises enforceable
would have more impact in such cases, because promises that have been
seriously relied upon are today quite likely to be enforceable anyhow.
Then again, it is a serious question whether a gratuitous promise should
rank equally with commercial promises in the event of the death or
bankruptcy of the promisor. Indeed, it is not clear that a gratuitous
promise should generally bind the promisor's heirs at all. A gratuitous
promise is an act of personal generosity, but should a promisor be entitled
to be generous at someone else's expense? So it seems that the problem of
the enforceability of gratuitous promises is not a simple one. It is facile to
suggest that, because a person may have a moral obligation to keep his
promises, the law should be willing to enforce that moral obligation. Very
careful study of a wide variety of different factual situations would be
needed before sensible proposals could be formulated for legislative
reform as to the enforceability of gratuitous promises.

# 7

# The Intention to Create Legal Relations

IT is sometimes said that an intention to enter into legal relations must exist before a valid contract can be found, or in other words that an agreement is not a binding contract unless it is intended to have legal effect. In fact, however, this proposition can only be supported by attributing a fictitious intention to the parties. It is, therefore, more realistic to say that no positive intention to enter into legal relations needs to be shown, and that 'a deliberate promise seriously made is enforced irrespective of the promisor's views regarding his legal liability'.[1]

## I. EXPRESS AGREEMENTS NOT TO BE BOUND

If parties enter into an agreement but specifically declare that their agreement is not to have any legal effect then their intention will be respected by the courts and there will usually be no legal contract. Such cases are rare, but in the well-known case of *Rose & Frank* v. *Crompton & Bros Ltd*,[2] where two business firms made an agreement for the supply of goods by one to the other, but it was expressly declared not to be a legal contract but binding in honour alone, the House of Lords held that the agreement was not a legal contract. There is no serious policy objection to such a clause when it is entered into by business people, dealing on equal terms with one another and fully aware of what they are doing. But the emergence of such clauses in standard-form contracts could constitute a serious problem. This is especially so since in certain types of contract the advantage of excluding legal efficacy to an agreement could be all on one side. But an argument against such a clause, based on public policy, was rejected by the Court of Appeal in a case where a football-pool coupon contained a formidable clause completely ousting the jurisdiction of the courts over the matter, and it was held that no action could be brought on it. Yet it is a general principle of the law of contract that an agreement to oust the jurisdiction of the courts is void on the ground that it offends against public policy.[3] However, this principle was distinguished on the basis that it only applies where the parties intended to create a legal relationship in the first instance. This distinction seems to be highly

---

[1] Williston on *Contracts* (3rd ed., Mount Kisco, New York, 1957), I, 39.
[2] [1925] AC 445.                                        [3] See *post*, 320.

artificial, for in fact the object of an 'honour clause' is identical with that of a simple clause purporting to oust the jurisdiction of the court.

But although an express agreement that an agreement is not to have legal validity as a contract will thus be respected, there is a strong presumption that business or commercial dealings are intended to have legal affect. So, for instance, where there was an agreement to pay compensation on an '*ex gratia* basis' it was held that these words did not prevent the agreement having legal effect.[4] So also, it is these days not uncommon to find companies issuing 'letters of intent' recording their intention to enter into a formal agreement, and inviting the addressee to take necessary preliminary steps towards the performance of that agreement. Such a letter of intent (when accepted, or perhaps when relied upon) can itself be sufficient to create contractual liability, provided that there are no obvious and fundamental disagreements on the terms still to be negotiated.[5]

Furthermore, although the parties may exclude legal results flowing from their bare agreement, it is a more serious matter to prevent actual transactions from having their normal legal significance. So in the *Rose & Frank* case, where it was held that an agreement for the supply of goods was not a binding contract, it was also said that, if any goods had actually been supplied under the agreement, the normal legal remedies would have operated, including the right of the seller to sue for the price and the right of the buyer to complain if the goods had not been of the agreed quality. It is possible that the parties could have excluded even such consequences as these by appropriate wording, but evidently very clear words would have been needed to produce this result. Again, in *British Steel Corp* v. *Cleveland Bridge & Engineering Co Ltd*,[6] where a letter of intent was held not to create a contract because the parties were still negotiating over the terms and no agreement on those terms was ever reached, and yet the goods were manufactured and delivered, it was not seriously disputed that the sellers had at least a restitutionary remedy for the reasonable value of the goods. This conclusion has already been criticized earlier[7] on the ground that it is strange to deny that a contract exists when the parties are sufficiently agreed to manufacture and deliver and accept specified goods, even though they have not agreed on all the terms; but this is to some degree a disagreement over mere matters of legal technique. Whichever technique is chosen, the fact remains that, in such circumstances, rights

---

[4] *Edwards* v. *Skyways Ltd* [1964] 1 WLR 349.

[5] *British Steel Corp* v. *Cleveland Bridge & Engineering Co Ltd* [1984] All ER 504. See also *Kleinwort Benson Ltd* v. *Malaysia Mining Corp* [1988] 1 All ER 714 where a 'letter of comfort' was held a binding contract, after it was relied on by making a loan of £10 million. This decision was reversed on the facts, [1989] 1 All ER 785.

[6] See above, n. 5.     [7] See above, 69.

may arise after actions of detrimental reliance which would not arise if the whole arrangement was still executory. Here, therefore, is another instance of the law being more inclined to enforce rights arising from what people have done (executed transactions) than from what they have agreed (executory transactions).

In the absence of an express clause of the kind we have been considering, a contract will rarely be held ineffective on the ground of a lack of intention to create legal relations. For instance, until 1845 an ordinary wager or bet could be sued on as a valid contract (created by mutual conditional promises), though one might well have thought such agreements to be typical examples of agreements in honour alone. So, in *Simpkin* v. *Pays*,[8] where the plaintiff, a lodger in the defendant's house, assisted the defendant in a competition organized by a Sunday newspaper, and the defendant won a prize of £750, it was held that an agreement that the plaintiff should have a share of any winnings was a legal contract.

It must also be stressed that 'an intent to create legal relations' is not the same thing as an intent or a willingness to sue if things go wrong. Many trivial transactions are entered into (for example, the purchase of a newspaper from a street vendor, or even the insertion of a coin into a slot at a public lavatory) in which neither party is likely to contemplate litigation. But that does not prevent such transactions from being valid legal contracts.[9] So also, an arrangement by which one person regularly gives a lift to work to another, in return for some 'petrol money', has been held a valid legal contract, although it is unlikely that such an agreement would be legally enforceable while still executory.

### 2. SOCIAL AND FAMILY ARRANGEMENTS

There are some circumstances, however, in which agreements are commonly made without any thought of creating legal rights and duties, and in which agreements are treated as not amounting to legal contracts. The simplest illustration is the case of a social engagement, where all the other ingredients of a contract may be present and yet it is hardly possible for the agreement to be enforced at law, at any rate in the absence of some serious acts of detrimental reliance.

Only one step further removed are cases involving family arrangements, which the courts often refuse to enforce on the ground that the parties did not have the intention to create legal relations. In the nineteenth century

---

[8] [1955] 1 WLR 975.
[9] *Esso Petroleum Ltd* v. *Commissioners Of Customs & Excise* [1976] 1 All ER 117 (note that the headnote to this report is wrong in saying that the majority of the HL held that there was no intent to create legal relations.)

such cases would have been dealt with by asking if there was 'good consideration' for the promise. But in recent years the tendency has been to inquire whether the parties intended to create legal relations. The classic case is *Balfour* v. *Balfour*,[10] where the Court of Appeal refused to enforce a promise by a husband to allow his wife £30 a month maintenance on his departure for Ceylon. It is essential to note, however, that in this case the parties were not legally separated, for there is no doubt that on the break-up of a marriage, whether by divorce or legal separation, husband and wife will frequently enter into binding contractual relations, sometimes subject to the approval of the court. While they are living together, however, or are merely temporarily separated, their agreements 'are outside the realm of contracts altogether. . . In respect of these promises each house is a domain into which the King's writ does not seek to run, and to which his officers do not seek to be admitted'.[11] But the result in such a case probably depends not so much on the lack of intention to create legal relations, as on the courts' view that it would be unseemly and distressing to allow husbands and wives, while still living together, to use the court as an arbiter for their matrimonial differences.

In *Jones* v. *Padavatton*,[12] the Court of Appeal was divided on the enforceability of a promise by a mother to pay an allowance to her daughter while she studied for the Bar. Careful study of the judgments in this case suggests that the court was less concerned with the real intention of the parties than with the objective facts. For instance, the fact that the daughter gave up a well-paid position and comfortable home overseas in order to move to England and study for the Bar in reliance on her mother's promise plainly weighed heavily with Salmon LJ, dissenting, who thought that there was a binding contract. Another factor which clearly weighs with the courts in cases of this kind is that family arrangements are rarely spelled out in the same detail as commercial arrangements. Should unforeseen contingencies occur, members of a family on amicable terms expect to be able to change the arrangements as may be necessary to meet the new situation. Difficulties then arise if the parties fall out and cannot agree on what changes are desirable. In *Jones* v. *Padavatton* the majority of the court seems to have thought that this need for flexibility in family arrangements was so great that it was undesirable to regard them as binding contracts at all. No doubt this is an appropriate course where the arrangement is wholly executory, but it is not so easy for the courts to refuse to deal with cases where parties have actually acted on the arrangement.

In fact there are many other types of family or domestic arrangements which will certainly be recognized as creating legal rights after they have

---

[10] [1919] 2 KB 571.      [11] *Ibid.* at 578.      [12] [1969] 1 WLR 328.

been acted upon. A common type of case arises when an elderly widow (or other relative) sells her home and moves in to live with an adult child (or nephew or whatever), sometimes contributing substantial sums of money for the purchase or extension of the child's house. Such arrangements are very unlikely to be regarded as enforceable legal contracts while they are still executory; but once they have been acted upon, it would be monstrous to deny all legal rights to the widow and allow her to be driven from her child's home as a result of a family quarrel. So some kind of legal remedy may then be called for, either by invoking contract law,[13] or sometimes by drawing upon equity or promissory or proprietary estoppel.[14] Then, too, there is another line of cases in which a parent invites a child to build a house on land belonging to the parent,[15] or perhaps to move into a cottage already in existence, which may involve giving up an existing home.[16] Here also it is impossible for the courts to refuse all legal remedy on the ground that the parties did not 'intend' to create legal relations. The result would simply be too unjust to be tolerable. So some sort of remedy must be found, though its precise nature is often a matter of great difficulty; in some cases monetary compensation is awarded, sometimes an equitable decree is made which gives rights akin to ownership, and sometimes a sort of possessory right (for instance to live in a home for life) is recognized.

Then again there are a large number of cases, which have been dealt with briefly above,[17] in which cohabitants separate and disputes arise concerning the ownership of the house in which they have been living. The fact that cohabitants have deliberately chosen to live together without getting married might suggest that they are agreed on not wanting their relationship to have any legal effect; but to deny all rights on such a ground would simply be unacceptable. Some redress is usually devised by the courts for a partner in such a relationship even where the house in question is registered in the sole name of the other, at any rate subject to proof of detrimental reliance or other justificatory factors (such as that money was contributed for the purchase of the house).

As always, then, serious acts of detrimental reliance may themselves be enough to persuade the courts to recognize that legal rights have been created. Even a purely social engagement could, surely, suffice in this event, as, for instance, if one person invited another to dinner at the Ritz and pressed him to partake lavishly in the belief that his meal was to be paid for, only to refuse to pay the bill at the end of the meal. It is hardly likely that after such behaviour a court would listen to a plea from the host

---

[13] See e.g. *Parker* v. *Clark* [1960] 1 All ER 93 (agreement between friends to share a house held a valid contract after one couple had sold their own house and moved in with the other couple). [14] See e.g. *Hussey* v. *Palmer* [1972] 1 WLR 1286.
[15] As in *Inwards* v. *Baker* [1965] 2 QB 29.
[16] As in *Williams* v. *Staite* [1979] Ch. 291. [17] *Supra*, 95.

that his invitation was not intended to create legal relations. Conversely, cases in which it has been held that there was an intention to create legal relations, after the agreement was acted upon (such as the 'petrol money' case), are not good guides to the likely effect of a wholly executory arrangement.

### 3. COLLECTIVE BARGAINING AGREEMENTS

The technique of denying legal validity to an agreement on the ground of lack of intent to create legal relations has also been applied in a more controversial situation. In *Ford Motor Co.* v. *AEU*[18] it was held that a collective bargaining agreement between an employer and a trade union was not enforceable as a legally binding contract. Again, it seems doubtful if this was really the 'intention' of the parties; indeed, there seems some circularity in the reasoning in this case. The lack of the necessary intent was at least partly deduced from the fact that the Ford Motor Company's officials may have *thought* that the agreement was not a legal contract; but very probably they thought this was the case because that is what their lawyers had told them. The truth is that there are some good reasons for *not* treating collective bargaining agreements as binding contracts, though there are also arguments to the contrary. There are two principal arguments for not treating such agreements as binding contracts. First, many clauses in such agreements are couched in language more suited to vague aspiration than binding commitment (e.g. that the parties will co-operate amicably in the settlement of disputes, etc.). Secondly, it is generally recognized that litigation is not the best way of promoting good industrial relations; indeed it has been very rare for any party to a collective bargaining agreement to attempt to enforce it in the courts (at any rate in England), and this is one of the main factors which have led commentators to suppose that they are not intended to be legally enforceable contracts. But, on the other hand, arguments could also be put forward for saying that such agreements should be enforceable; for example, that some parts of these agreements, such as clauses agreeing to submit disputes to arbitration, are sufficiently clear and precise to be legally enforced, and that the unwillingness of employers to attempt legal enforcement has been due to the threat of industrial action rather than to belief that they ought not to have binding legal force. There are many countries (such as the United States and Canada) in which some parts of collective bargaining agreements are regularly enforced by courts without apparent difficulty. The Conservative Government's Industrial Relations Act 1971 provided that such agreements should be legally binding in the

---

[18] [1969] 2 QB 303.

absence of agreement to the contrary, but this Act was repealed by the Labour Government's Trade Union and Labour Relations Act 1974 which now provides that collective bargaining agreements are *not* to be treated as binding contracts unless they so provide. This provision of the 1974 Act has survived the legislation of subsequent Conservative governments, so it may be assumed that it is likely now to remain the law.

## 4. AGREEMENTS 'SUBJECT TO CONTRACT'

One of the most important practical applications of the principle that parties can exclude the intent to create legal relations by express wording is to be found in the very common custom of making agreements for the sale of houses and land 'subject to contract'. This formula means, or is taken to mean, that the parties intend their agreement to be recorded eventually in a formal legal contract and do not intend it to be binding in the meantime. The words 'subject to contract' are treated by the courts in almost all cases as excluding legal effectiveness. Once the words are used in negotiation, a subsequent agreement will be held non-binding even if the agreement itself is not expressed to be 'subject to contract'. There must be an express agreement to show that the parties have dropped their intention to make purely non-binding arrangements.[19] Because of the very widespread nature of this practice, and because it has come in for much controversy recently, it is worth devoting a few moments to it.

The present practice is the result of the procedures normally used by estate agents in England, who always advise buyers and sellers (though strictly they represent sellers only) to make their initial agreements 'subject to contract' in order to avoid legal liability. The practice has evolved as a paternalistic device to protect buyers from committing themselves legally before they have had a chance to consult solicitors who will normally explain the dangers of too early a commitment. A careful and prudent buyer may wish to safeguard his position in a number of respects before contracting to buy a house; for instance, he may wish to be assured that he will have finance available. He will, therefore, normally be advised by his solicitor to apply for a mortgage and wait for the reply before he enters into a binding contract. Similarly, if the buyer also has a house to sell, which is commonly the case, he will be advised to find a purchaser for his own house before committing himself to the house he wants to buy. The parties' solicitors will then try to ensure that the contracts are synchronized so that each party becomes bound by the contracts of sale and purchase at the same moment. Very often, a whole 'chain' develops in which A is selling to

---

[19] *Cohen* v. *Neasdale Ltd* [1982] 2 All ER 97. But compare *Alpenstow* v. *Regalian Properties* [1985] 1 WLR 721.

B, who is selling to C, who is selling to D, and so on. Usually solicitors for all these parties try to synchronize the whole chain of contracts, but this means that no contract can become binding until everybody in the chain is ready, and all the contracts can then become binding at the same time.

This procedure means that there is often a considerable lapse of time, usually several months, between the date when the parties first agree on the purchase and sale of a house, and the date when they become legally bound. The result is, of course, that either party is legally free to change his mind in this interim period, with great disappointment and possible inconvenience to the other party. Moreover, if it is the seller who changes his mind, the buyer may have incurred substantial costs (by applying for a mortgage and possibly also a survey, as well as by having instructed his own solicitor to start the purchase procedures) and these costs will be irrecoverable from the seller. Conversely, if it is the buyer who withdraws, the seller may have lost several months in his attempt to dispose of his property and he may also have incurred costs which may be wasted, such as in initial legal work, not to mention the possibility that he may have started to spend money in proceeding on a new purchase. When a long chain has developed, the withdrawal of one party may involve the collapse of the whole chain, with immense inconvenience and wasted cost to half a dozen parties. None of these costs are legally recoverable from the party responsible for the collapse of the chain, even if that party has withdrawn for some wholly frivolous reason.

Although the present procedures may have worked well at one time, they do not appear to work well today; indeed, the system appears on the verge of total breakdown. Yet it is perfectly easy to have a completely different system. In most countries buyers and sellers enter into binding contracts at an earlier stage than they do in England. Some element of risk may be involved when this happens. A buyer who commits himself to buy before he has sold may have to take the risk that he may need bridging finance from his bank if he cannot sell in time. A seller who commits himself before he has bought takes the risk that he may be homeless for a temporary period and may have to contemplate temporary accommodation arrangements. But some people may be able and willing to take these risks and, if they understand what they are doing, there seems no reason to prevent their doing so. Indeed, the present system also involves risks—that everything will fall through—so it is not clear that the risks would be worse if the present procedures were changed. The present paternalistic practice protects those who may be incapable of protecting themselves, but only at the price of also protecting those who are perfectly capable of protecting their own interests. A person who is confident of his ability to raise finance, and has (for instance) no doubt of his ability to sell his own house, may find the present practice an intolerable nuisance to him as a buyer.

The problem of the buyer who needs to be assured of a mortgage, prior to committing himself to a purchase, can be, and in some countries is, dealt with in a different way. It is, for instance, possible for a binding contract to be entered into at the outset, but expressly made conditional. For instance, the buyer could be given the right not to complete the purchase after the contract has been made if he fails to obtain a mortgage. An agreement of this kind is, of course, not a fail-safe way of binding the parties. If no mortgage is obtained, the deal will fall through, and the buyer will still be free of legal liability. But from the buyer's point of view an agreement of this kind could be advantageous. At least the seller could not 'gazump', and if the condition is satisfied (which in most cases it would be) the buyer could hold the seller legally liable on such a conditional contract. Unfortunately, difficulties have occurred in dealing with conditional clauses concerning such matters as the obtaining of a mortgage. As we have seen, an agreement 'subject to the buyer obtaining a mortgage' may be held too uncertain to be enforceable as a contract, though there should be no difficulty in drafting a clause which is less uncertain (for example, specifying the amount to be raised and the name of the proposed lender). The latest authority on the topic looks more favourably on such a conditional clause,[20] but there are still many difficulties involved. And in any event, there is always the likelihood that the seller will be advised not to sign such a contract because it binds him, while effectively leaving the buyer free.

Public complaints about present practices have led to the subject being examined by the Law Commission on more than one occasion, but the Commission has not yet recommended any fundamental changes in the law. It has pointed out that it is legally possible for the parties to bind themselves at once if they wish to do so; all that is needed is a short written agreement which any competent solicitor could draft in half an hour.[21] But in practice it is often difficult to persuade the other party to commit himself in this way, partly at least because he is likely to be strongly advised by his own solicitor not to do so unless there are some exceptional circumstances that make it advisable. Some change in the practice of the legal profession is urgently needed to break the current log-jam.

The upshot of all this is that in the great majority of cases agreements for the purchase and sale of houses are not legally binding when first made. They normally become legally binding when the parties' solicitors have drafted the formal written contract (in duplicate), when the two parts have

---

[20] *Graham* v. *Pitkin* [1992] 1 WLR 403; *supra*, 114.

[21] As noted *supra*, 114, a 'lock-out' agreement has recently been specifically recognized as possible in this situation, and such has been the public interest in this question that a daily newspaper has offered a draft of such an agreement, drawn by counsel, as a service to its readers.

been signed by the respective parties, and when the parts are 'exchanged'. The normal practice is for the purchaser's solicitor to send his copy to the vendor's solicitor (this being treated legally as the offer) together with a cheque for the deposit (usually 10 per cent of the purchase price), and for the vendor's solicitor then to return the vendor's copy duly signed to the purchaser. That is regarded as the acceptance, the mere posting of which, according to the normal rule, will complete the contract.

In modern times, because of the difficulties of synchronizing long strings of sales and purchases, it has become quite common to vary the procedure in one of a number of ways. Typically, the purchaser's copy of the contract, with the deposit, is sent to the vendor's solicitor, but the vendor's copy is not immediately returned to the purchaser's solicitor. Instead, he retains it for the time being, until the vendor is in a position to commit himself; this can then be done by the vendor's solicitor telephoning the purchaser's solicitor and giving him a professional undertaking, as a solicitor, to hold the vendor's copy of the contract on behalf of the purchaser, and to send that copy immediately to the purchaser's solicitor. This professional undertaking means that the vendor's solicitor thenceforth holds the actual copy of the contract as a trustee on behalf of the purchaser and is legally bound to hand it over forthwith. Alternatively, the copies of the contract, signed but undated, may be physically exchanged by the solicitors but only on the understanding that they are not to be treated as creating a binding contract until the solicitors so agree, usually by telephone. This enables each party's solicitor to ensure that he becomes bound both by his sale and his purchase contracts (if there are two) virtually at the same moment, since he can telephone the other solicitors in quick succession; and if need be, the first transaction can be conditioned on the later ones proceeding in the normal course. This practice has been recently approved by the Court of Appeal, which confirmed that where it is followed no binding contract comes into existence until the telephone agreement between the solicitors.[22]

---

[22] *Domb* v. *Isoz* [1980] Ch. 548.

# 8

# Formalities

As a general rule no formalities are required for the creation of a contract in English law. A contract may be created by writing, by word of mouth, by conduct, or by a combination of two or three of these methods. As we have previously noted, modern information technology is beginning to blur the lines between these old distinctions. The exceptional cases where some formality is prescribed by statute are now few and (with one exception) relatively unimportant, and can be dealt with briefly in a book of this nature. But it was not always so; for nearly three centuries the famous Statute of Frauds 1677 required various types of contracts to be evidenced in writing, and it was only in 1954 that most of these requirements were finally repealed.

Non-lawyers are often surprised at the fact that so many legal actions do not have to be in any specified form in modern times, but insistence on form is widely thought by lawyers to be characteristic of primitive and less well-developed legal systems. It reflects lack of confidence in the ability of the courts to discover the truth about a case without the trappings of formalities, and perhaps other rituals. In most modern systems of law there is little emphasis on form and a much greater emphasis on substance. In England at least this is largely due to the fact that there is confidence in the ability of the courts to discover the whole truth, even about the most complicated facts. Once this confidence exists, the requirement of formalities for legal actions becomes less insistent and is often thought to be a hindrance rather than a help to doing justice.

In the particular case of contracts, absence of any formal requirements may also reflect the emphasis of classical contract theory on the central role of intention. If a person is liable on a contract because of what he promised or agreed to do, then insistence on writing may be a hindrance to giving effect to that person's intentions. To require writing is thus a paternalistic device which may protect people from the consequences of hasty or ill-thought promises or agreements.

The Statute of Frauds, in so far as it required writing for certain classes of contracts, may have been inspired partly by these paternalistic ideals, but was more likely the outcome of weakness in legal procedure, and the prevalence of frauds. Sections 4 and 17 of the Act provided that certain contracts (and a somewhat curious list it was) were to be unenforceable in a court (but not void) in the absence of writing.[1] Today, all that is left of

---

[1] The distinction between an unenforceable contract and a void contract has already been discussed: *supra*. 47–8.

these provisions is that part of section 4 which requires contracts of guarantee to be evidenced in writing. Until 1989 another part of section 4 survived in a more modern form in section 40 of the Law of Property Act 1925 which dealt with contracts for the sale of interests in land. This section has now been replaced by section 2 of the Law of Property (Miscellaneous Provisions) Act 1989, which requires a contract for the sale or other disposition of an interest in land to be made in writing, incorporating all the terms of the contract and signed by both parties. But the Act recognizes the modern practice of exchanging contracts for the sale of land, whereby one copy is signed by one party and the other copy by the other. This Act does away with the effect of the older legislation which only rendered contracts without writing *unenforceable*, and not void. Under the new Act a contract not in writing is void. But the distinction in this context is of little practical importance because even void contracts may still give rise to rights and obligations in certain circumstances. In a book of this kind it is unnecessary to attempt a detailed exposition of the highly technical law governing guarantee contracts or contracts falling under the new Act.

The Statute of Frauds was passed at a time when English law had just recognized that mutual promises could create contractual liability, and the procedure of the courts and the rules of evidence were still not sufficiently developed to handle a fully fledged law of contract. This helps to explain why several of the most important provisions of the statute only applied to executory contracts. Where there was, for instance, 'part performance' of a contract for the sale of land, the need for writing was dispensed with. In such circumstances liability was not solely based on the agreement but arose partly from the very fact of part-performance. The 1989 Act has done away with the doctrine of part-performance, but it is assumed that the doctrine of estoppel will still enable courts to achieve just results in cases of this kind, that is where there has been part-performance or detrimental reliance.

During the nineteenth century, when classical theory was at its height, the Statute of Frauds came to seem more anomalous, and demands for repeal were frequently made. It is slightly curious that the demands were only successful in 1954 when classical theory was already giving way to a different approach, which laid less stress on promissory liability and more on paternalistic devices. At any rate, most of sections 4 and 17 of the Statute of Frauds were repealed in 1954, except the two particular cases just mentioned. The contract of guarantee was excluded from the repeal primarily because a contract of this kind is liable to be made between persons of unequal bargaining strength, and the requirement of writing was thought to give some, if meagre, protection to the guarantor. In fact this may have been a mistake, because written contracts of guarantee almost invariably strip the guarantor of his common law protective rights, so he would actually be better off with an oral contract.

It is, perhaps, desirable to add that the anti-formality approach of much modern legal thinking may not always be soundly based. As noted above, much of this derives from confidence in the ability of the courts always to discover the truth. Where an action is brought on an oral contract, the courts ought to be able to discover whether there ever was such a contract as is claimed, or whether the claim is fabricated. If there is a genuine contract, even an oral contract, it should be enforced, while if there is only a fabricated claim, that ought to be discovered and the claim thrown out. The requirement of writing, on this view, will make no difference to claims which are fabricated, and its only effect therefore must be to prevent a genuine claim being enforced where it was not put into writing. It was Jeremy Bentham who first demonstrated that requiring contracts to be in writing is liable to produce this result, and can only be justified on the assumption that the courts cannot discover the truth. And once modern procedural reforms had been introduced in the nineteenth century (also under Benthamite influence) it was confidently assumed that courts would always be able to discover the truth, so the demand for the removal of formalities in the law grew stronger.

But Bentham's argument can be over-stated for a number of reasons. The first is that even courts cannot always discover the truth, or anyhow cannot always discover the true facts except at disproportionate cost. One purpose of requiring written formalities is therefore to reduce cost. Not only does it reduce the cost of the particular legal proceedings in hand, but it also encourages people to record their agreements in writing, and may therefore have a useful long-run effect in reducing costs. A second purpose is to minimize the risk of error. For obviously, courts will sometimes make mistakes—no institution is infallible—but they are much more likely to make mistakes about the existence of oral contracts than about the existence of written contracts. So a requirement of writing does reduce the risk of error. But Bentham was right in pointing out that it means that the risk of wrongly finding that an oral contract was made is only excluded at the price of also shutting out the possibility of correctly finding that an oral contract was made. It has to be decided whether the risk is worth the price.

Another reason for thinking that the Benthamite argument may have been over-stated is that the courts are not the only institutions whose business it is to enforce and give effect to contracts. Contracts are often entered into by large organizations or bureaucracies, and in practice it will be for the members of these organizations (in the first instance and subject to appeal to the courts) to give effect to the contracts. These bodies may have far fewer facilities than the courts for discovering the truth about oral dealings—which is why all bureaucracies insist on recording everything in writing. This is why, whatever the law may say, there are many kinds of contract which it is in practice virtually impossible to make with big organizations without writing. Indeed, in practice, not only writing, but *signatures* are very commonly demanded as a kind of formal requirement for all sorts of contracts. A signature is, and is widely recognized even by the general public as, a formal device which indicates that some important legal consequences may follow from a document. As we shall see in Chapter 10 the law does today give some recognition to this modern practice because it is very difficult for a person to deny validity to a written contract which he has signed. But the law of contract, as opposed to business custom, rarely *requires* a signature.

In modern times, indeed, there are not many contracts which have any prescribed legal form at all. In a few cases only is it laid down by some statute that certain contracts must themselves actually be in writing. Apart from the case of dealings in land, already discussed, other examples of this are to be found in the Marine Insurance Act 1906, which requires contracts of marine insurance to be in writing, and the Bills of Exchange Act 1882, which lays down that bills of exchange and promissory notes must be in writing. A more recent example is the Consumer Credit Act 1974, section 61 of which provides that certain consumer credit agreements (such as hire-purchase agreements) must comply with prescribed forms and be signed by the consumer.

The policies underlying such modern formal requirements are variable. In some cases (as with the Marine Insurance Act) the policy is probably that of minimizing the risks of error in important transactions. In other cases, especially consumer contracts (such as those falling under the Consumer Credit Act), the policy may be based on the attempt to ensure that consumers really do consent to the terms of the transaction. Of course this does not always work. Consumers may not read or understand the documents placed in front of them for signature, except in the most general sense. But at least such requirements improve a little on the situation, which may otherwise arise, of contracts being made orally with reference to (or incorporating) written terms and conditions which the consumer does not even see. Another object may be to prevent one party imposing on another by unduly harsh or oppressive terms. The insistence on writing does not, of course, promote this object directly, but it does at least mean that the person entering into the contract is given the opportunity to see exactly what he is letting himself in for.

Another group of modern statutes requires certain contracts to be accompanied by the provision of written information by one party to the other. The policy behind these statutes is probably partly the minimizing of the risks of error, and partly, once again, that of trying to ensure that there is genuine consent to the contractual terms. So, for instance, an employer is required under the Employment Protection (Consolidation) Act 1978 (as amended by the Trade Union Reform and Employment Rights Act 1993) to provide a written document to his employees setting out a number of details concerning the terms of the employment; landlords under 'secure tenancies' (that is to say, local councils) have to supply tenants with a written statement as to the terms of the tenancy under section 104 of the Housing Act 1985; other landlords have to supply a rent book containing the information specified in section 5 of the Landlord and Tenant Act 1985. There are also statutes requiring the sellers of certain commodities to provide the buyers with written information so that the latter know precisely what it is they are buying. So, for instance, under the Plant Varieties and Seeds Act 1964, the seller of seeds must supply a written note to the buyer containing particulars about the goods being sold. Similarly, under the Agriculture Act 1970, a seller of artificial fertilizers must deliver to the buyer a note containing details of what chemicals it contains. Again, under the Weights and Measures Act 1985 documents are in many cases required to be handed to a buyer of goods which are being delivered at his home (such as, for example, solid fuel, sand, or ballast), stating clearly the quantity of the goods being delivered. In all these statutes the principal legal sanction is provided by the machinery of the criminal law rather than by the law of contract. Thus failure to comply with these statutory provisions is an offence and renders the seller liable to penalties. Although this may be a more efficient way of ensuring compliance with the law, it is apt to create difficulties in the law of contract, because failure to comply with the statutory provisions, being a crime, may render performance of the contract illegal, and this, as we shall see later, may involve drastic consequences.[2]

[2] See Ch. 18. In some of these modern Acts it is expressly provided that the illegality is not to affect contractual rights.

# 9

# The Different Kinds of Contractual Duties

THE law recognizes two entirely different kinds of duties on parties who enter into a contract. In the first place, the most obvious and important effect of a contract is to cast upon the parties the duty of doing what they have undertaken to do. This duty is enforceable in the sense that a failure to perform gives the other party a right to claim damages for breach of contract from the wrongdoer and, exceptionally, a decree that the other party should specifically perform the contract. These duties may be called contractual duties in the strict sense. A second kind of contractual duty of this strict type concerns *warranties*, or affirmations of fact which are strictly promised. In general discussion of the law of contract these duties are often overlooked because they do not involve anything that can be called *performance*; if a person warrants the truth of some statement, which is untrue, then he is guilty of a breach of contract in the strict sense, but it is hardly possible to perform a warranty of this kind.

But in addition to the duties imposed by the contract itself, there are other duties imposed by the law independently of the contract, duties relating not to the performance but to the making of the contract. The distinction is sometimes said to reflect the difference between the *substantive* aims of the contract, and the *procedure* by which contracts are concluded. The substantive outcome of a contract is seen by some as purely a matter for the parties, while procedural matters are more the concern of the law. The law thus polices the way bargains are made in the market-place, leaving the parties to insert whatever content they choose into those bargains. This way of putting the distinction raises problems, some of which we have already referred to, and other are discussed further in Chapter 16. But for the present it is enough to recognize that many legal duties of importance to contract law concern the way in which contracts are made.

For instance, the conduct of the parties during the course of the negotiations may raise questions as to duress, or misrepresentation, or a failure to disclose material facts, and so forth. Naturally the actual contract will be silent as to most of these matters, but that does not mean that the innocent party is without remedy. The duties imposed by the law in relation to these matters are discussed in Chapters 13 to 15.

In the present chapter we are concerned with duties arising under the contract. These duties vary considerably in their nature and importance and in this chapter we shall examine the relative importance of these varying duties. Although it is traditional to include such a discussion at this point in books on the law of contract, there is a sense in which the various distinctions to be drawn here are only of practical importance as part of the law of remedies for breach of contract, and if the law had taken a different form, it would make sense to postpone discussion of these questions. In most cases the only differences between the various kinds of contractual duties concern the remedies available to the innocent party, and the question, what are the consequences of a breach, rarely has to be determined in advance. It only has to be so determined if the parties are negotiating their contract and are applying their minds to the question of what is to happen in the event of a particular sort of breach. So far as courts are concerned, the question is always a retrospective one: a breach has occurred and the question now is, what is to be done? But the theory of the law is that the court must in general ignore the precise nature of the breach which has occurred, and must instead try to analyse the nature of the duty which was broken.

The reason behind the rather curious exercise which the court is required to perform is that, in classical contract law, the consequences of a breach of contract were supposed to be the result of the parties' own intentions. And the intentions that mattered were those which were present when the contract was made. So, in order to determine the result of a breach of contract, the court had to throw its mind back to the time when the contract was made, ignore the breach and its consequences, and ask itself, what did the parties intend should happen in the event of a breach of this sort of term? And to assist in answering that question the courts have for long divided contractual terms into different classes.

## 1. CONDITIONS AND WARRANTIES

Difficulties of terminology abound in the law of contract, and the questions dealt with in the next few pages are bedevilled by the ambiguity of the words 'terms' and 'conditions'. Now a clause of the contract—to use a neutral expression—may be either (1) a statement about a state of facts, or (2) a promise that something (not necessarily in the control of the promisor) will or will not happen in the future, or (3) a conditional clause.

Clauses of the first two kinds are often called promises, since the contracting party takes responsibility for both of them in precisely the same way. But the word 'promise' may be misleading because it suggests a degree of personal commitment which is not always required, having regard to the objective methods of interpretation used by the law. The word 'undertaking' perhaps better conveys the legal significance of a contractual duty of this kind; but in any event, the point being made here is that such undertakings cover both ordinary undertakings as to the future and also statements of existing fact. For instance, in an ordinary contract of sale of goods, the buyer undertakes that he *will* pay the price, and *will* take delivery of the goods, while the seller undertakes that he *will* deliver the goods, and also that the goods *are* in accordance with their description and, in some cases, that they *are* of satisfactory quality, and also that they *are* fit for the purpose for which they were sold. There is no legal difference between undertakings of these two kinds. Lawyers (unlike philosophers) have never had any difficulty in holding that a person can promise (or undertake) a state of facts, as distinguished from promising *to do* something in the future. To avoid confusion it should be added that a statement of fact or representation is often made *before* the contract is entered into, and such pre-contractual representations are not necessarily promises or undertakings. They may have some legal effect, however, but they are not our present concern, which is solely with terms of the contract itself.

When it has once been decided that a statement made by one party to the contract is an undertaking or a promise in the sense in which the law uses this term, the next question is to decide whether the term is a condition or a warranty or an intermediate term. The distinction between conditions and warranties is only about a hundred years old and dates from the passing of the Sale of Goods Act of 1893. In older cases the word 'warranty' is frequently used to mean any promissory term of the contract.[1] The difference between a condition and a warranty is that a breach of the former gives the innocent party the option of treating the whole contract as terminated, or cancelled, so that he is discharged from further performing himself, while a breach of the latter merely entitles the innocent party to claim damages, but does not discharge him from performing his own duties under the contract. In other words, the right to the other party's performance is conditional upon conditions (but not warranties) being performed. But this use of the word 'condition' is misleading because a condition of this sort remains an undertaking or promise, and must on no account be confused with a conditional clause. The failure of one party to perform a condition precludes him from demanding performance from the other party, but it does not render him immune from liability himself if the condition is in law an undertaking or promise. For example, if B agrees to buy goods from S and undertakes to pay the price in advance, payment is both an *undertaking or promise* by B, and also a *condition* of S's duty to deliver the goods. So if B fails to pay, S may sue B for breach of his undertaking or promise, and is also not bound to deliver the goods.

---

[1] Even today lawyers use the verb 'to warrant' meaning to promise, without necessarily implying that the promise is a warranty in the technical sense.

Although, therefore, a promise may be a condition, not every condition is a promise. Strictly, a condition is a fact or event on the occurrence of which some legal right or duty comes into existence; a party may undertake or promise that this fact is so, or that the event will take place, but it is equally possible that no party to the contract promises this. An insurance company promises to pay £100,000 to an insured person if his house is destroyed by fire; the destruction of the house by fire is a condition of the insurer's promise to pay, but obviously neither party promises to burn the house.

Conditional clauses are themselves of various kinds. The most important kind of conditional clause perhaps is a clause *on which the entire operation of the contract depends*, and such a clause is usually called a condition precedent. The vital thing about such a condition is that it is *not* an undertaking or promise, and if a contract is subject to a condition precedent it may properly be called a conditional contract. A much-quoted example of such a contract is found in *Pym* v. *Campbell*,[2] where the defendants agreed to buy from the plaintiffs a share of an invention, provided that the invention was approved by a third party. This proviso was held to be a condition precedent to the operation of the entire contract and, in the absence of the approval specified, the contract never came into operation. (We have seen earlier that in modern law there has been some doubt whether a contract for the sale of a house 'subject to the buyer obtaining a mortgage' is a condition precedent of this kind.[3])

If a condition precedent fails, the contract may loosely be described as void, but it may not be entirely accurate to say that the actual validity of a contract depends upon a condition precedent, for once the parties have complied with the rules of offer and acceptance, the contract is certainly concluded, even though it is conditional. Neither party is free to withdraw pending the occurrence or non-occurrence of the event. Hence, it may be preferable to say that the failure of a condition precedent makes the contract inoperative rather than void. The distinction between a condition which is also a promise, and a condition which is not the subject of a promise, is often one of great difficulty and importance, especially where the term is implied and not expressed,[4] and it is unfortunate that legal usage has sanctioned the word 'condition' for two such different concepts.

---

[2] (1856) 6 E & B 370.    [3] See *supra*, 114.

[4] The difficulty is particularly acute because it is often possible to 'imply' an undertaking or promise not to obstruct the workings of the contract, which in effect converts a non-promissory condition into a promissory condition, and can to a limited extent import a duty of good faith into the contract. But there is no general implication in all cases that a party will not allow a contract to fail through a condition precedent. Compare on this point *Mackay* v. *Dick* (1881) 6 App. Cas. 251 with *Luxor (Eastbourne)* v. *Cooper* [1941] AC 108, which was referred to *supra*, 43.

It would at least be desirable if lawyers could be persuaded to refer to conditions which are the subject of a promise as 'promissory conditions', a usage which it is proposed to adopt here.

Another kind of conditional clause is sometimes referred to by lawyers as a condition subsequent, that is to say, a condition on the happening of which an obligation (or sometimes the whole contract) is terminated or dissolved. A condition subsequent is simply a statement of the circumstances in which the contract (or part of it) may be brought to an end, and is usually more readily recognized than a condition precedent. Like a condition precedent, however, a condition subsequent differs from terms which are undertakings or promises, because the occurrence of such a condition does not necessarily involve the parties in any liability. There is no magic in the term 'condition subsequent', and some contractual provisions may not fall easily into any particular slot, but they are perfectly valid for all that. For example, one party may be given an express right of cancellation on the happening of a certain event without the contract being automatically terminated.

It must be added that any particular promise in a contract may also be conditional, but the presence of such a conditional promise does not make the contract a conditional contract, for other clauses will operate whether or not the condition occurs.

To revert now to the distinction between promissory conditions and warranties, the question arises, how does the law distinguish between the two? Terms do not usually bear on their face the answer to this question and, even if they do, the terminology used by the parties is not necessarily decisive, for they may have been using the words incorrectly, without full appreciation of their proper legal significance. For instance, a company appointed another as a distributor for its goods, and made it a 'condition' that the distributor should visit six customers every week.[5] It was held that this was not strictly a condition in the legal sense because the result of so holding would be that even a single omitted visit would justify termination of the whole contract. It was (said the House of Lords) improbable that the parties intended such an extreme result. But the result should really be justified by its inherent fairness because it is very common for commercial contracts to be deliberately drafted so as to produce such extreme and one-sided results. Usually this is not because the stronger party necessarily wants to terminate the contract if the other should commit a minor breach of condition, but because he wants to have *the power* to terminate so that he can, wherever it suits him, bring pressure on the other party.

If a party expressly agrees that, in the event of a breach of a particular term, the other party is at liberty to repudiate the contract, there is no

---

[5] *Wickman v. Schuler AG* [1974] AC 235.

difficulty in deciding that this must be a promissory condition, because the right of repudiation is the hallmark of a promissory condition. Similarly, where the contract makes it plain that one party is obliged to perform some act only if and when the other performs his own promise, that promise will be a promissory condition. This is also the case where one party has made it clear that he regards the matter in question as of such vital importance that he will not contract except on such terms, and the other party agrees to those terms. But where there is no clear agreement as to the importance attached to the term in question, the court has to fall back on general criteria.

Promissory conditions have been described as obligations which 'go directly to the substance of the contract, or in other words, are so essential to its very nature that their non-performance may fairly be considered by the other party as a substantial failure to perform the contract at all'.[6] The use of the word 'fairly' in this quotation is an indication of the important fact that an element of subjective judgement is involved in this decision. Whether it is correct to treat a promise as a warranty or as a promissory condition depends in many cases on whether justice and convenience are best served by the one course or the other. Unfortunately, the two considerations may point in different directions, because it often seems harsh if breach of a relatively trivial term should be treated as discharging a contract entirely; while on the other hand, considerations of convenience, especially in commercial contexts, sometimes dictate that even trivial breaches should have this consequence, in order that businessmen should be able to make instant decisions when breaches occur. The problem is well illustrated by stipulations as to time which occur in many contracts.

## Stipulations as to time

If a party fails to comply with some stipulation as to the time when a particular action is to be performed, lawyers say that the question is whether time was 'of the essence', or (that is) whether the performance of the act within the stipulated time was truly a condition. In the first instance, the answer to this is a question of interpretation or construction of the contract. If the contract expressly states that failure to perform the requisite act within the stipulated time gives the other the right to terminate the contract, then time is 'of the essence'. But more often the contract is silent as to the effect of such a failure. In that event, the court must interpret the contract, or search for its true construction, in the light of the language used, and general commercial and other considerations. In

---

[6] *Per* Fletcher Moulton LJ in *Wallis* v. *Pratt* [1910] 2 KB 1003 at 1012, a judgement approved in the HL, [1911] AC 394.

commercial contexts the House of Lords has recently reiterated the traditional English rule which is that stipulations as to time are prima facie to be treated as of the essence.[7] So in contracts of sale of goods, for example, it is a well-established rule that failure to deliver the goods (or documents of title) by the stipulated date is prima facie a breach of a condition which justifies the other in throwing up the whole contract. And in a charterparty (a contract for the hire of a ship) a breach of a term as to the time when the ship will arrive to start the voyage is a condition.[8] The charterer is entitled to treat the contract as over as soon as he learns of the breach, so that he can make alternative arrangements. It is no use the shipowner claiming that perhaps the delay will only amount to a day or two, and that the court should examine the actual nature and consequences of the breach.

This is often hard law, and it is made all the harder because English law has no general doctrine requiring contracting parties to behave in good faith. So a technical breach of condition will permit the other party to throw up the contract even though his real reason for wanting to do this may be that the market has moved against him since the contract was made. He may, in fact, be quite unconcerned at the delay in itself which may cause him no loss or inconvenience. But English law does not inquire into the reasons for which one party may wish to cancel a contract following a breach by the other—his right to cancel or repudiate is regarded as absolute, so long only as the right arises in the specified circumstances.[9]

There are, however, other contracts in which this strict rule is not followed—indeed, the general rule of equity which now prevails over the former strict rules of the common law is that time is not 'of the essence' of contracts in the absence of a contrary intention. So, for instance, in a contract for the sale of land (or a house) the failure of the vendor to convey on the stipulated date does not (unless the contract specifically states to the contrary) justify the purchaser in abandoning the contract without more ado. He must first serve a notice on the vendor, giving him a (reasonable) time in which to complete, and only then will the purchaser be able to cancel the contract if the seller still fails to complete.[10] Even in commercial contexts, the general presumption that stipulations as to time are conditions is

---

[7] *Bunge* v. *Tradax Ltd* [1981] 1 WLR 711.

[8] *The Mihalis Angelos* [1971] 1 QB 164. As to what exactly is a stipulation as to time or a 'time clause' for this purpose, see *Compagnie Commerciale Sucres* v. *Czarnikow (The Naxos)* [1990] 1 WLR 1337.

[9] See *post*, 406–7, where this question is further discussed.

[10] But damages are still recoverable for the late performance, which remains a breach of contract, even if it is not a breach of condition: *Raineri* v. *Miles* [1981] AC 1050. Many contracts for the sale of houses nowadays incorporate specific clauses stating that time is of the essence.

sometimes rebutted as, for instance, in a rent review clause which lays down a detailed timetable for the service of notices and counternotices by tenants and landlords.[11]

Where the intention of the parties is not made perfectly clear in the contract itself the question, as we have said, is one of construction of the contract. And in construing the contract the courts will certainly be influenced by the fact that it is often very harsh to treat stipulations as to time as of the essence. Sometimes this would entitle one party to terminate a substantial contract in mid-stream, as it were, with massive loss to the other party, even though the breach is of a relatively trivial character. Courts would normally be very reluctant to construe a contract so as to permit such a result where the meaning of the contract is at all doubtful. But suppose the intention is perfectly clear, what then? The possibility of very harsh results remains, but prima facie the courts will simply enforce the contract according to its literal terms, whatever the consequences. For instance, a charterer of a vessel who is one day late in paying the monthly charter-rent may find that the owner has, and exercises, the right to cancel the charter.[12] Or an insured person whose house is burnt down may find that he loses his right to an indemnity if he is one day late in submitting notice of his claim to the insurance company, if that is specified in the contract, even though the delay occurs without his fault (indeed, even though his policy is burnt together with his house!). There is no escape from results of this kind through any process of construction and they can only be avoided (in the absence of some statutory protection) if the courts are prepared to overrule the express terms of the contract in the interests of justice. Two possible legal doctrines which could be invoked by the courts to justify such a result, if they felt so inclined, are the doctrine of 'unconscionability' and the equitable rules precluding forfeiture. These are discussed later,[13] but it must be said here that the current of authority at the present time is against the extended use of these doctrines, even to avoid such extremely harsh results. The resurgence of freedom-of-contract theory (as well as the retirement of Lord Denning) seems to have quashed any tendency to assert a judicial power to override contractual terms in the interests of justice. However, in contracts with consumers, and even in some contracts between businessmen, the position is today often substantially affected by legislation.[14]

---

[11] *United Scientific Holdings Ltd* v. *Burnley BC* [1978] AC 904.

[12] *The Laconia* [1977] AC 850; *Scandinavian Trading Tanker Co* v. *Flota Petrolera Ecuatoriana (The Scaptrade)* [1983] 2 AC 694; *Sport International Bussum* v. *Inter-Footwear* [1984] 1 WLR 776.

[13] For unconscionability, see Ch. 16, at 300, and for forfeiture, see Ch. 22 at 437.

[14] See Ch. 16, sects. 4 and 5, at 305 and 313.

## 2. INTERMEDIATE TERMS

Not all contractual terms are today treated as conditions and warranties. In the past few decades it has been recognized by the courts that the classification of terms into conditions and warranties is somewhat unsatisfactory, because this classification requires the consequences of a breach of contract to be determined before the breach has occurred. If the term is a condition, then no matter how minor the breach and how trivial the consequences, the result is the same: the innocent party may treat the whole contract as discharged by the breach. On the other hand, if the term is a warranty, this result never occurs, no matter how serious the breach and how grave the consequences. At the end of the nineteenth century, it was generally assumed by lawyers that the result of this was that there were only the two sorts of terms, conditions and warranties, and the Sale of Goods Act 1893 was drafted in such a way as to make it appear that this was certainly the case in relation to contracts governed by that Act. Although the Act did not actually *say* that there were only the two sorts of terms, it only mentioned these two.

The result of limiting the classification of terms in this way was that there was something of a bias in favour of the category of conditions. For even if a particular term was broken only in some trivial way, the court had to bear in mind that some other breach of that same term might have been far more serious, and that if that had happened the innocent party would surely have expected to have the right to bring the contract to an end. Only if the court felt confident that the term was so minor that any breach of it would be certain to have had only trivial consequences would the term be treated as a warranty. The result of this was that many terms were held to be conditions even where the particular breach was relatively minor, and in contracts of sale of goods in particular, it often happened that buyers were given the right to reject goods for trivial breaches.

In the 1960s the courts began to depart from this traditional law. In a series of important cases it was held that there is an intermediate sort of term which is neither a condition nor a warranty.[15] Breach of a term of this character does not have predetermined results, fixed once for all when the contract is made. The court has to examine the nature and consequences of the breach to see how serious they are before it decides whether the innocent party is released from his liability, or whether his only remedy is to claim damages. So, for instance, where a shipbuilder contracted to construct a ship at a particular shipyard, and the ship was built at another yard, but the identity of the yard was of no practical importance, it was

---

[15] The first important case along these lines was *Hong Kong Fir Shipping Co* v. *Kawasaki Kisen Kaisha* [1962] 2 QB 26, the judgement of Diplock LJ becoming a classic.

held by the House of Lords that the charterer was obliged to take the ship.[16]

This does not mean that many terms are not still conditions, breach of which justifies the innocent party in ending the contract at once, because English courts take the view that in many commercial contexts certainty is all-important, and the parties cannot reasonably be required to wait and see how serious the breach turns out to be.[17] As we have seen above, these arguments are often decisive in dealing with stipulations as to time in commercial contracts. Businessmen are entitled to know where they stand when they are faced with breaches of contract, and should not be required to wait and see what the consequences are. Nevertheless, this is what they will have to do where these new intermediate terms are concerned, and it has now been suggested that most terms in fact are of this character. It has also been decided that, even in contracts of sale of goods within the Sale of Goods Act, some terms may be intermediate terms, for instance express terms as to the quality of the goods.[18] The peculiar result is that an express term that goods sold are in good condition is likely to be an intermediate term, whereas an implied term that the goods are satisfactory under the Act (which means much the same) is a condition, because the Act says it is.

### 3. FUNDAMENTAL TERMS

During the 1950s and 1960s there flourished another species of term called the fundamental term. A fundamental term was said to be one which was so important and central to a contract that, if it was broken, the innocent party always had some remedy, *even if the contract contained an exemption clause* protecting the guilty party from liability. This doctrine served a useful purpose in helping to protect consumers from unreasonably wide exemption clauses. It was first used most extensively in contracts of hire-purchase where vehicles were often let to consumers under contracts containing the widest possible exemptions from liability. But this particular problem was largely taken care of by the Hire Purchase Act 1964 (which was eventually replaced by the Consumer Credit Act 1974) and by the late 1960s many lawyers thought the doctrine of fundamental breach had outlived its usefulness. In particular, there were serious doubts about

---

[16] *Reardon Smith Lines* v. *Hansen Tangen* [1976] 1 WLR 989.

[17] This is one of the major differences between the commercial law of common law countries and that of modern civil law countries, where a notice demanding that the breach of contract be rectified is more extensively required. In England, such notices are sometimes required by statute (for instance, before a landlord can forfeit a tenancy for non-performance of some covenant, and before a finance company can reclaim goods let under a hire-purchase contract); but there is no general common law requirement of this kind.

[18] *Cehave NV* v. *Bremer Handelsgesellschaft (The Hansa Nord)* [1976] QB 44.

applying the doctrine to commercial contracts because it involved an obvious infringement of the parties' freedom of contract. In the famous *Suisse Atlantique*[19] decision the House of Lords insisted that the doctrine of the fundamental term was a mere rule of construction, not a rule of law. It was a rule of construction in that prima facie it was sensible to assume that exemption clauses were not designed to deal with a party who totally violated his contract; but it was not a rule of law which was to be applied even where it was quite clear that the exemption clause was designed to cover the events which had occurred.

This decision did not settle the issue. Cases still arose where consumers appeared in need of protection against unreasonably wide exemption clauses and the Court of Appeal found itself able to continue to apply the doctrine despite the *Suisse Atlantique* decision. But the Unfair Contract Terms Act 1977 changed the situation radically. For this Act gave the courts wide powers of control and regulation over unfair contract exclusion clauses, in consumer and even in some commercial contracts. Consequently, the notion of a particular term being so fundamental as to be non-excludable by contractual clauses became (or seemed to become[20]) once again an unnecessary one, and for the second time the House of Lords struck down the doctrine.[21] This time, the House appears to have made no mistake. The common law rule has been reasserted: the parties are free to put what they like into their contracts. There is no such thing as a fundamental term which is not excludable by an exemption clause. There is a rule of construction which says that prima facie an exclusion clause is not to be construed as applicable to a fundamental breach of the contract,[22] but this is a mere rule of construction which must give way to a contrary intention. If parties agree that a breach is to be non-actionable, then the agreement is binding. But if the 1977 Act or the new EC Directive on Unfair Terms applies, then of course, the courts can use them to strike down unreasonable clauses.[23]

---

[19] *Suisse Atlantique Société D'Armement Maritime SA* v. *NV Rotterdamsche Kolen Centrale* [1967] 1 AC 361.

[20] The cautionary words appear justified if one considers (to take one example) the insurance example posited above—and insurance contracts are excluded from the Unfair Contract Terms Act, and (largely) also from the EC Dir. on Unfair Terms.

[21] *Photo Productions* v. *Securicor Transport* [1980] AC 827.

[22] But this rule of construction has been held (in *Ailsa Craig Fishing Co* v. *Malvern Fishing Co* [1983] 1 All ER 101) to be inapplicable to limitation clauses as opposed to exclusion clauses, an illogical and unsatisfactory distinction which is criticized in my *The Sale of Goods* (8th edn., 1990), 209.

[23] For further discussion of the 1977 Act and the EC Dir. on Unfair Terms, see *post*, 303 ff.

# 10

# Contractual Duties Fixed by the Parties

## I. TERMS AND REPRESENTATIONS

CONTRACTS are sometimes made in writing, and sometimes orally; and they may also be made partly in writing and partly orally, and sometimes (as we have seen) they may even be made partly by conduct. Written contracts may be made in formal documents, signed by both parties, or in informal writings such as letters, fax messages, order forms, and so on. The first question to be discussed in this section concerns the identification of the terms of the contract. How are we to know what are the terms of the contract?

It might have been thought that at least with written contracts there would be no problem in identifying the terms. But this is not necessarily the case, because even written contracts will usually be preceded or accompanied by oral negotiations. And there is then often great difficulty in ascertaining what are the terms of the contract, because not every express statement, written or oral, constitutes a contractual term. It is often necessary to distinguish between a term of the contract, which is regarded as an undertaking or a promise, and statements which are not *incorporated* as terms of the contract, even though they may have some legal effect. Now a statement of *intention* which is not incorporated in the contract has practically no legal effect, although, as we have seen, it may sometimes give rise to the defence of promissory estoppel. On the other hand a statement of *fact* which is not incorporated in the contract is generally called a 'mere representation', and although it does not amount to a contractual term it may have important consequences; in particular, it normally gives the innocent party the right to rescind the contract if it turns out to be untrue.

So it becomes necessary to distinguish between 'mere' or pre-contractual representations and promissory representations which are incorporated as terms of the contract. According to the traditional method of approach, the distinction between a term of the contract and a mere representation depends on the intention of the parties. Once this intention has been ascertained the courts then apply the rules relating to contractual terms or to representations as the case may prove. If the statement is a contractual term, the breach of it always gives a right to claim damages, and may, if the term is sufficiently important, give a right to terminate the contract. On the other hand, if the statement is a mere representation then, generally speaking, it only gives a right to rescind or withdraw from the contract and (unless negligence or fraud is present) not a right to claim damages. Thus, on the traditional view, the inquiry simply becomes, did the parties intend that a particular statement should be contractual or not?

Where a formal written contract is signed by the parties this approach has some validity. The starting point then must be that oral statements, or even written statements which are not incorporated in the written document, are probably not intended to have contractual effect—although even then this starting point can be rebutted. But in many cases it is much more difficult to separate out the terms of the contract from mere representations, and in these cases the traditional approach has serious weaknesses. Indeed, this approach often obscures the real functions of the courts in these cases. For once again—as so often in the law of contract—it is reasonably clear that the phrase 'the intention of the parties' does not really mean what it says. In the first place, it is highly unlikely that the parties had any intention at all on the matter, for such an intention would virtually require an appreciation of the legal distinction between a term of the contract and a mere representation. In the second place it is almost certain that the parties will claim that they had different intentions, for if they did not, the case would probably not be in court at all. Thus we rarely find a court making any real attempt to examine the actual intention of the particular parties in order to solve this particular type of question. What we find the courts saying is something like this: 'The question is whether this statement is a term of the contract or a mere representation. This depends on the intention of the parties. Now in this case we think that the parties must have intended this statement to be a term of the contract because it is only reasonable to conclude that the party making the statement intended to accept responsibility for it'. We are then likely to find the court explaining the purely objective reasons for which it thinks that the party making the statement accepted responsibility for it, e.g. that he was a dealer in the goods in question, or that he, as owner of the land being sold, had better opportunities for discovering the truth of his statement. Alternatively, we may find the court saying that the statement in question was not 'intended' to be a term of the contract because it was made (perhaps) casually, because the parties had adopted a formal written document as their contract, by signing it, and therefore had shown that they 'intended' their legal relations to be governed exclusively by that written document, and so on.

Thus the traditional theory appears to put the cart before the horse, in that it discusses the distinction between a term of the contract and a mere representation without reference to the result. In fact, it is the nature of the result which appears in many cases to determine the answer to the question. The point is that where a representation is a contractual term the law imposes strict liability on the party responsible, which means that a party is taken to warrant the truth of a contractual statement. In the case of mere representations, however, the representor is not treated as warranting or promising that the facts stated are true. It would, on the other hand, be very hard on the other party to provide him with no remedy at all in these circumstances, and it would often be difficult to conduct negotiations for a contract if one party could not rely on statements of fact made by the other. So the law usually permits the innocent party to rescind the contract in this situation, though subject to certain restrictions. Even if the court does not consciously reason on these lines, it is difficult to believe that the judges are not aware of the consequences of their decision, and that they are not influenced by these consequences in reaching their decision.

These arguments—though primarily directed to common law principles—are to some extent borne out by a recent legislative change. Under the Package Travel, Package Holidays and Package Tours Regulations 1992 the distinction between terms of the contract and mere representations is largely abolished so far as concerns documents containing details of travel holidays, package tours, etc. Any information in a travel brochure, for instance, constitutes an implied warranty in any resulting contract; and a retailer or organizer who gives any misleading information is liable to compensate a consumer for any loss he thereby suffers. These Regulations were made to give effect to an EC Directive and it is perfectly plain that the object of the exercise was to ensure that consumers should be entitled to damages for false and misleading statements in travel brochures. Whatever the common law status of such statements, therefore, the law has simply converted them into warranties. Here it is not the intention of the parties which leads the law to classify the statements as warranties, but the desired result necessitates calling them warranties.

Of course this kind of legal development blurs the distinction between mere representations or statements and contractual terms. As we shall see later the distinction has also been blurred by two further modern developments which now enable damages to be awarded for pre-contractual misrepresentation in some cases. These developments may have improved the law in some respects but they have made it far more complex to understand and expound. There is a desperate need for a simplification of the conceptual structure of the law in this area.

## 2. WRITTEN CONTRACTS

In the case of a written document purporting to contain part or all of the contract, two questions arise. First, is the document a part of the contract at all and, secondly, if it is, does it constitute the whole contract or can anything be added to it?

*Is the document part of the contract?—signed documents*

Where a contractual document is signed by one or both parties the rule is that this signature absolutely binds the party signing and precludes him from pleading that he had no knowledge of the terms of the contract, in the absence of fraud, misrepresentation, duress, or undue influence, or a mistake of such a fundamental kind as to show that there has been no valid offer or acceptance.

Fraud and misrepresentation are dealt with in more detail in Chapter 14. Here it is enough to state the essentials. If the signature is obtained by fraud, then, in accordance with normal principles, the innocent party may take steps to repudiate the contract, but unless and until he does so, the document will be binding, and if it comes into the hands of an innocent third party before then, the signer of the document may find himself liable on it. If the signature is obtained by pre-contractual misrepresentation, then once again, in accordance with normal principles, the innocent party is entitled to rescission, that is, to withdraw from the contract provided that no innocent third parties have become involved. However, the remedy of rescission is somewhat inadequate at times, and it may well be too late to rescind the contract by the time that the innocent party has become aware of the misrepresentation. If the misrepresentation relates to a term of the contract, the innocent party may be entitled to insist that the term should be treated as it was represented to him, therefore, and not as it was actually written down. So a misrepresentation as to the scope of an exemption clause will disentitle a party from relying on that clause if he is sued for breach of contract.

Duress and undue influence are dealt with in Chapter 15, and they are only mentioned here because cases in which a person signs a document while suffering from a basic misapprehension as to its contents do often involve suggestions of duress or undue influence. If legal duress or undue influence is proved, then (as in the case of fraud or misrepresentation) the contract can be set aside by the innocent party, though subject to the usual restrictions applicable to those doctrines.

The third defence which may be pleaded to a document signed by the defendant is that he was fundamentally mistaken as to the transaction into which he appears to have entered by his signature. It is at this point (as we saw in the opening chapter) that the theory of the law of contract comes up against some fundamental questions of practical convenience. In theory contractual obligations depend on consent or on the intention of the parties. Contractual obligations are supposed to arise from promises or undertakings, and these are the products of the will or intention of the parties. But in practical terms it would often be very troublesome, if not impossible, to prove that parties intended to make every promise or undertaking which may be appropriate in a complex relationship. So for a long time it has been customary to record contracts in written documents and to obtain the signatures of the parties to these documents. Although it is not *necessary* for a contract to be made in this way—and thousands of contracts are made daily in which the terms are not written down in this way—there is a very strong legal presumption that signed contracts embody the intention of the parties. It is unnecessary to show that the party signing a contract understood it or even read it; indeed, the presumption that he is bound is not rebutted even by proof that he is blind or illiterate, or does not speak the language in which the document was written. Nor is it even rebutted by showing that the other party to the transaction *knew* that the first party had not read the document. It is, after all, an everyday affair for a consumer to be presented with a contractual document to sign, containing pages of small print (for instance, a hire-purchase contract or a bank loan contract) which he does not read, and *is not even expected to read*. Frequently the other party to the transaction is, or must be, aware that the consumer has not read the document—it would often take a considerable time to read it. And this raises a problem for the theory of the law, because it is generally held (as we saw earlier) that a party is only entitled to rely on the *appearance* of consent where he thinks that the appearance is also the reality. Although the courts have never actually attempted to reconcile the rules with the theory of the law on this point, they might do so by suggesting that a signature shows that the party signing intends to accept whatever is in the document signed, even though he has not read it. But this might only apply on the assumption that the document contains usual or standard terms for a transaction of that kind.

Of course, where responsible business organizations are concerned, one would expect that the gist of the document would be explained to the consumer and his attention directed to important or unusual terms. Occasionally, he might even be advised to consult a lawyer before committing himself to some unusual transaction, but that would hardly be likely to happen with standard everyday transactions such as hire-purchase contracts or bank loans. But all this does not alter the fact that the written contract may contain detailed terms on a variety of matters which the party signing is not actually aware of—and may be known not to be aware of—and yet if a legal dispute arises the written terms will almost always be treated as binding and conclusive.

The reality—not yet acknowledged by the theory of the law—is perhaps that signatures are treated as formal grounds of legal liability, rather than as proof of contractual intention. For if they were treated merely as proof of intention, one would expect that a person would be permitted to deny his intention despite his signature in a much wider variety of circumstances than are in fact recognized by the law. The truth is that treating signatures as a formal ground for imposing legal liability is a very convenient rule of everyday practical application. It is, moreover, a rule which is widely understood—everybody knows that when he is asked to sign a document important legal consequences may follow. So the present rule may well be highly desirable. But it is always necessary to bear in mind something that is very often forgotten, namely, that liability arising from signed documents is often *not* actually the result of an intentional assumption of responsibility with respect to the particular matter which may be the subject of a contractual dispute. It is highly dangerous to argue in favour of imposing legal liability in contract on the ground that such liability always depends on a prior showing that the defendant had promised or undertaken to accept that liability. Yet this is a very common form of argument.

Of course there are limits on the present rule. Cases occasionally occur in which a person signs a document under a complete misapprehension as to what it is that he is signing. For example, a person may be induced to sign a promissory note, thinking that he is merely signing a document as a witness; or he may be induced to sign a cheque in the belief that it is a guarantee. In theory such a signature might be valid and binding on the ground that the defendant's intentions must be judged objectively. But, of course, as we have seen, this only holds good where the other party to the transaction is unaware of the mistake which has been made by the person signing the document. In practice such gross misunderstandings are not likely to occur. Where the signature is obtained in these circumstances, it will almost invariably be found that there has been fraud, and the transaction will certainly be voidable on that ground. Actual fraud always gives the other party the right to rescind the contract as against the fraudulent party, or in other words, the right to treat the contract as 'voidable'. However, a voidable transaction remains valid until it has been rescinded, and if a third party acts upon it before it is rescinded he may acquire rights under it. But sometimes the question may arise whether the transaction is not merely voidable, but totally void, in which case third parties cannot sue on the document any more than the fraudulent party himself.

The answer at first given by the courts was that, only if the signer was mistaken as to the actual nature of the transaction and the other party was aware of the mistake, would the contract be held totally void. But the importance previously attached to a mistake as to the nature of the transaction itself has now been discarded, as a result of the decision of the House of Lords in *Saunders* v. *Anglia Building Society*[1] in which the law on this subject was reviewed and restated. The principles laid down in this

---

[1] Also known as *Gallie* v. *Lee* [1971] AC 1004.

case may be summarized as follows. First, the plea of mistake in this kind of case (known as *non est factum*) can only rarely be relied upon by a person of full age and capacity who will normally be strictly bound by any document to which he has put his signature. Secondly, in exceptional cases a person who has signed a document under a fundamental mistake as to the *nature* or *effect* of the document can plead the defence of *non est factum*; the plea is more readily admissible if the party signing was blind or illiterate, but it is not absolutely confined to these cases, nor is it automatically applicable in every case of a blind or illiterate person. Thirdly, the plea will be rebutted if the party signing fails to take ordinary care; in particular if he signs the document without taking reasonable precautions to inform himself of the contents the defence will probably fail.

The above law is now subject to an important new provision in the EC Directive on Unfair Terms which states in the Annex to Art. 3(3) that a term may be unfair, among other things, if it irrevocably binds the consumer 'to terms with which he had no real opportunity of becoming acquainted before the conclusion of the contract'. Generally speaking, it seems clear that offering a document for signature to the consumer may be sufficient to satisfy this clause, since this is the best way of giving him an opportunity of becoming acquainted with the terms in it. So the main application of this provision may lie in its effect on cases where there is no signature. But some cases of signed documents may well be covered by it as well, especially, for instance, cases where it is apparent to the other party that the consumer does not know the language in which the document is written. The general effect of the Directive is dealt with again later; here it is enough to say that unfair terms under the Directive are not binding on consumers in their dealings with suppliers and sellers.

### Is the document part of the contract?—unsigned documents

Where a written document is relied upon by one party as representing the contract, but this document has not been signed by the defendant, it is more difficult to determine whether its contents should be treated as embodying contractual terms. In principle it must be shown that such a document has been accepted by both parties as the basis of the contract. The problem arises in a variety of contexts. One common type of case—the 'battle of the forms'—has already been considered in Chapter 3.[2] Another group of cases are the so-called 'ticket cases', where one party offers to contract upon certain written terms, often contained, or referred to, in a ticket of some kind, and there is no doubt that a contract has in fact been concluded, but there is doubt whether the terms contained in the ticket have been accepted by the other party. The matter has been the subject of

[2] *Supra*, 66.

a good deal of litigation in the past hundred years, but the main principles were settled as early as 1877 in the Court of Appeal's decision in *Parker* v. *South Eastern Railway*,[3] although there has been a certain amount of embellishment and gloss added to them since then.

Before we discuss these rules one point of fundamental principle should be stressed. It is, of course, elementary that one party cannot alter the terms of the contract unilaterally after it has been finally concluded by the offer and acceptance of the two parties, unless, indeed, the original terms themselves envisage and permit such unilateral alteration. Where the contract has been completed in this way, therefore, the subsequent delivery by one party to the other of a document purporting to contain contractual terms is entirely ineffective. Similarly with a notice displayed to the other party which is only brought to his attention after the contract is concluded.[4] On the other hand a different result may be reached where it is known at the time the agreement is made that a document containing other terms may be brought into existence later. So, for instance, an agreement for the carriage of goods by sea is almost invariably recorded in a bill of lading which contains standardized, internationally agreed terms. But in practice an oral agreement for the carriage of particular goods on a particular ship will usually be made in advance, often by telephone; indeed the bill of lading is not usually issued till after the goods have been loaded. But because it is known that the bill of lading will be issued the oral contract is governed by the carrier's normal bill of lading terms even before the bill is issued, or even if it is never issued.[5]

To return to the ticket cases, the principle of *Parker* v. *South East Railway* is very simple. According to this case, a person relying on a ticket as a contractual document must show that he gave sufficient notice to the other party that the document or ticket in fact incorporated contractual terms and was intended to be part of the offer. If the party receiving the ticket reasonably assumes that it is a ticket and nothing more, or is just a receipt, and simply puts it into his pocket without reading it, then it cannot be held to be a contractual document. For instance, in *Chapelton* v. *Barry UDC*[6] the plaintiff hired a deck-chair from the defendants for use at a beach. He bought a ticket from the attendant which contained on it a clause excluding all liability for injury or damage. It was held that this formed no part of the contract as the plaintiff had simply pocketed the ticket without reading it, and no reasonable person would have assumed the ticket to be anything but a receipt.

---

[3] (1877) 2 CPD 416.    [4] *Olley* v. *Marlborough Court* [1949] 1 KB 532.
[5] *Pyrene* v. *Scindia Navigation* [1954] 2 QB 402; but compare *Burke (Raymond) Motors* v. *Mersey Docks* [1986] 1 Lloyd's Rep. 155 (here even oral contract not yet concluded, so bill of lading exclusion clause could not be applied).    [6] [1940] 1 KB 532.

On the other hand, it is well established that, where a person buys a ticket for a railway or air journey, he should, as a reasonable man, know that the ticket is bound to contain certain conditions. The question then arises whether he has been given sufficient notice of these conditions. This is a question of fact to be answered according to all the circumstances of the case, but one important point of law has been answered without, perhaps, full consideration. Does notice of the conditions mean notice of their existence or notice of their contents? Unfortunately it has been held that notice of their existence suffices. Thus it has been held that a reference on the front of a ticket to the back, and an indication on the back that the ticket is issued subject to terms set out in other documents which might be obtained at the railway station, is sufficient notice of the terms.[7] This sort of 'incorporation by reference' is quite common in business transactions of various kinds—some organizations simply print at the foot of their order forms or quotations, something like, 'All goods supplied [or All work done] according to our usual terms'.

In theory, and according to the principle of the *Parker* case, even cases like this are governed by the requirement of reasonable notice. But in practice a great deal is likely to depend upon whether the court thinks the terms are themselves fair or reasonable—or (which courts often appear to think is the same thing) whether they are standard or customary in the trade. So long as the terms which it is sought to rely upon are standard or normal in the trade, they will usually be regarded as properly incorporated in the contract even in extreme cases where a bare notice of incorporation by reference is given. Indeed, such standard terms will sometimes be held incorporated even without notice at all, as where an oral contract is concluded but it is assumed by both parties that some written agreement or document will subsequently be brought into existence.[8]

On the other hand, the courts are much less accommodating with terms they regard as unfair or unreasonable. In *Interfoto Picture Library Ltd* v. *Stiletto Visual Programmes Ltd*[9] the plaintiffs ran a library of photographic transparencies and they supplied to the defendants, as the result of a telephoned order, forty-seven transparencies in an envelope together with a document containing printed 'conditions'. These conditions required the hirer to return them within fourteen days or to pay a 'holding fee' of £5 per day per transparency for longer periods. The defendants omitted to return the transparencies for fifteen days after the expiry of the fourteen-day period and the plaintiffs sought to charge them in accordance with their conditions—a sum totalling some £3,783. According to the evidence these

[7] *Thompson* v. *L. M. & S. Rly Co* [1930] 1 KB 41.
[8] *British Crane Hire* v. *Ipswich Plant Hire* [1975] QB 303.
[9] [1988] 1 All ER 348.

charges were far higher than those generally applicable in the business—a normal charge was about £3.50 per transparency *per week* rather than the £5 *per day* which the plaintiffs sought to charge. The Court of Appeal held that such unreasonable conditions had to be more clearly brought home to the other party before they could be relied upon as being incorporated in the contract. The more unreasonable the terms, the greater the notice that must be given. Here the terms were found to be exorbitant and hence not binding on the defendants.

Similarly, in *Thornton* v. *Shoelane Parking Ltd*[10] it was held that insufficient notice had been given of an unusually wide exemption clause in a car-parking ticket issued by an automatic machine. The ticket contained a reference to conditions posted up in the car park, but by the time the customer had obtained the car-parking ticket it was in practice too late for him to withdraw.

It must be admitted that some of these cases bear an artificial look, and that the principles devised in *Parker* v. *South East Railway* do not adequately serve a law dealing with standard-form contracts. The object of giving notice of the terms on the ticket must, after all, be to warn the other party what he is letting himself in for, and to give him an opportunity to withdraw if he wishes. In practice, however, there is often no question of withdrawal because the person requires the facilities offered and must take them on the terms offered—there is often no choice.

Moreover, the decisions in some of the cases mean that the 'notice' of the terms given may be almost completely fictitious, and that the party in question may in fact have no inkling of the terms of the contract he has bound himself to observe, even though in law sufficient notice may have been given. The fundamental problem is to balance the practical convenience of enabling contracts to be made on standard terms against the risk that the terms may not be fair and reasonable from the point of view of both parties. If it is suggested by modern adherents of freedom-of-contract principles that fairness and reasonableness are subjective criteria which should have no place in contract law, the answer is that the courts tend to equate these requirements with standard or customary practice. This can be justified both on economic grounds—standard terms in a competitive market *are* fair terms; and also on the ground that it is reasonable to suppose that parties expect general contractual terms to be normal or standard in their nature.

As we have already seen, the law on this topic must now be read subject to the EC Directive on Unfair Terms. Under Article 1(*i*) of the Annex to Article 3(3) of the Directive a consumer must not be irrevocably bound by terms 'with which he had no real opportunity of becoming acquainted before

---

[10] [1971] 2 QB 163.

the conclusion of the contract'. This piece of law must be superimposed on to the general common law principles outlined above, which will certainly complicate the law and legal arguments in court. There does not appear to be a great deal of difference between the common law principles and the Directive on this point, but the Directive will of course mean that arguments can now be presented to the courts (in cases involving consumers) to the effect that the common law rules in any given situation are in breach of the Directive, and for that reason result in an unfair term. It may, for instance, be argued that lengthy terms which are incorporated by reference or printed in small print at the end of a brochure will be held invalid because the consumer does not have a 'real opportunity' of becoming acquainted with the terms before he signs. It is entirely unclear at present how these vague general principles will be interpreted, nor even whether the courts will be inclined to assume that the Directive simply restates the common law principles.

The Directive's provisions on this point are somewhat complicated by the fact that Article 1($i$) of the Annex deals entirely with procedural fairness, that is with the rules governing the way terms become part of a contract. Once a term is held to be part of the contract, there are many other provisions in the Directive which enable the courts to strike the terms down as a matter of substantive unfairness. There is nothing in the Directive which prevents a court from holding that Article 1($i$) is satisfied but then going on to hold that a term in the contract is unfair under some other part of the Annex.

This means that a court may be inclined to lean in favour of treating Article 1($i$) as satisfied where the matter is doubtful. There are signs that this—or the corresponding—approach is being followed in relation to the Unfair Contract Terms Act, that is that the courts are more likely to treat clauses as incorporated into the contract under the common law principles where the Act applies so that they can then, if necessary, deal with the clause under the Act. The *Interfoto* case referred to above was, however, not one to which the Act applied, because it did not concern an exclusion clause, and the Act (despite its title) does not deal with all unfair contract terms.

All this does not mean that the question of notice may not still have an important part to play in dealing with standard-form contracts. For it is clear that, if no notice at all is given, there can be no question of incorporating a document (except where it was clearly intended by both parties to be so incorporated).

## Is the document exclusive evidence of the contract?

Assuming that the document in question is held to be part of the contract, the next question which arises is whether it is exclusive evidence of the transaction. The answer to this is once again said to depend on the intention of the parties, but it is at least settled that in two classes of cases the writing will not be held exclusive. In the first place, where the parties have entered into a definite and clear contract and the contract has been reduced into writing, but owing to some mistake the written contract does not exactly conform with what the parties had agreed, the court has power to order the contract to be rectified. Naturally, a person who impugns a written contract on this ground undertakes a heavy burden of proof, for normally the writing will be accepted as the best evidence of the contract, but if the plaintiff can satisfy the court of the mistake, there is every reason why it should be put right. Refusal to rectify the written agreement in these circumstances would enable one party to take advantage of a mere clerical slip. So, for instance, where A agreed to let certain premises to B at a rent of £230 per annum, but the lease by mistake stated the rent to be £130, and both parties signed the lease without noticing the mistake, it was held that the tenant could not take advantage of the slip and insist on having the premises at the lower figure.

Rectification will only be ordered where it is clear that the document departs from the intention of *both* parties. In *Riverlate Properties Ltd* v. *Paul*,[11] a lease was granted to a tenant which failed to impose on the tenant any obligation to contribute to the cost of external repairs. The landlord had intended to require such a contribution, so from his point of view there was a mistake. But the tenant knew nothing of the landlord's intention or mistake, and it was therefore held that she could enforce the written lease as it stood.

When it is said that a contract may be rectified if the writing does not represent the parties' real intentions, it must be understood that we are again referring to the apparent and outward intention of the parties. To put the rule in an objective way, a written contract can be rectified if, but only if, it is not a correct record of a prior oral agreement.[12] Thus, where A made a contract to buy horse-beans from B, both parties being under the erroneous impression that horse-beans were just another name for feveroles, it was held that the contract could not be rectified by substituting feveroles for horse-beans. The parties had in fact made a contract for the sale and purchase of horse-beans and, although they were mistaken as to the nature of this article the written contract was a correct record of their oral agreement.[13]

Although it is often convenient and advisable to have a written contract rectified by a formal order of the court, especially if it has anything to do

---

[11] [1975] Ch. 133.
[12] It has been held that it is not necessary that this oral agreement should itself have been a binding oral contract: see *Joscelyne* v. *Nissen* [1970] 2 QB 86.
[13] *F. E. Rose* v. *W. H. Pim* [1953] 2 QB 450.

with rights in land, modern developments suggest that this is not usually strictly necessary. Indeed, it seems that rectification can probably only be ordered when the legal effect of the document is already what it would be if rectified. In law, the contract itself (it must always be remembered) is not a piece of paper, but a set of rights and duties. The court does not alter these rights and duties with a decree of rectification, it only rectifies written documents so that they are a correct record of the parties' rights and duties.

The second type of case in which written documents are often supplemented with other evidence of intention relates to 'collateral contracts'. Although the normal presumption is that the parties intend a written contract to be exclusive evidence of their intentions, it is always open to a party to show that in fact the writing did not exclusively represent their intentions, because of a 'collateral' contract made during the negotiations but not incorporated in the written instrument. A collateral contract is a second contract, by the side of the main contract, but it is often implied or even invented by the court, rather than expressly made by the parties. The basic principle is often called the 'parol evidence rule', and according to this rule evidence is not admissible to contradict or qualify a complete written contract. The rule is usually stated in the form of a rule of evidence, but it is probably best regarded as a rule of substantive law. The question is not really whether evidence can be admitted which might vary the written document, but whether, if the evidence is admitted, it will have the legal effect of varying the document. If so, the evidence is always admissible, but if not, it is inadmissible because there is no point in admitting it—it is simply irrelevant. The question then arises, how do we decide whether the evidence would have the effect of varying the document if admitted? Unfortunately, the question whether the writing is exclusive or not is said to depend, like so many other questions, on the intentions of the parties, and it is hard to think of a more elusive criterion in this connection.[14] It is, of course, standard doctrine that this does not mean the actual intention of the particular parties involved, but the intention which reasonable men would have had in their shoes. It would not be inaccurate, in other words, to say that the writing is exclusive unless the court thinks that a reasonable man would not regard it as such. But since the court represents the reasonable man, what this means is that the court is only to hold that the writing is exclusive if the court reasonably thinks it should be held to be exclusive. When the matter is viewed in this way, it becomes clear that this is in fact merely a statement of the rule, and provides no guidance for deciding whether the writing is exclusive or not.

---

[14] No doubt there are some cases where this intention is clear enough but these are not the cases which come into court.

All that can be said by way of general guide is that 'the person who claims that the written agreement was not intended to be exhaustive must in practice, if not in law, be able to point to something said or done by the other party at the time the agreement was concluded'.[15] Where, at the time the agreement is being negotiated, one party gives oral assurances to the other which a reasonable person would rely upon, it is nowadays accepted almost without question that the assurances override the written contract. This is particularly so perhaps in consumer transactions, but it is often also applied to commercial contracts. So where forwarding agents orally undertook to ship the plaintiff's goods under deck, it was held that this overrode a printed bill of lading clause which permitted shipment on deck.[16]

Similarly, where leases were entered into which required the tenants to contribute to the cost of external repairs, it was held that the tenants were entitled to rely on the oral assurances of the landlord's agent that the landlords would repair the roof at their own expense.[17] This was a particularly striking example of oral assurances overriding a formal, signed contract, because such leases are not usually entered into lightly or without legal advice. In the nineteenth century it may be that such a case would have been differently decided under the parol evidence rule, but this rule seems today almost obsolete in practice, though the courts have not yet admitted this openly. The change may be due to the fact it is today often regarded as perfectly reasonable to rely on clear and categorical oral assurances, rather than to insist on everything being written and the last 'i' dotted, the last 't' crossed. Of course, in practice, this may be 'reasonable' in one sense; but it is not *advisable*, because it will often involve a lawsuit before the oral assurances are recognized as overriding the written terms.

It is also possible, of course, to show that a written agreement has been varied by a subsequent agreement, or even by some unilateral action, where the original contract permits such unilateral variation. In recent times this principle has caused some problems in connection with employment contracts, because it is not always clear what changes can be introduced by the unilateral actions of the employer,[18] but these cases have little to do with the subject of this Chapter. More relevant perhaps is the fact that many contracts of a kind which formerly allowed unilateral change of terms on notice nowadays often dispense even with the requirement of notice. So, for instance, building society mortgages are today often made

[15] Cross on *Evidence* (3rd ed.), 508–9. This passage does not appear in later editions but the general gist remains unchanged.

[16] *J. Evans & Sons (Portsmouth)* v. *Andrea Merzario* [1976] 1 WLR 1098.

[17] *Brikom Investments* v. *Carr* [1979] QB 467, where varying reasons for the decision were given by the three judges of the CA; *Rigby* v. *Ferodo* [1987] ICR 457.

[18] See e.g. *Miller* v. *Hamworth Engineering Co* [1986] ICR 846 (employer cannot unilaterally reduce pay); *Kerr & Williams* v. *Hereford & Worcester CC* [1985] IRLR 505 (employer cannot unilaterally withdraw 'perks').

on the terms that the building society can vary the interest rate charged without giving individual notices to the borrowers—it is often unnecessary to give individual notice (which can instead be published in the press) because payments made by direct debit can be increased without new instructions from the borrower, or adjusted once a year. (For the possible effect of the EC Dir. on Unfair Terms, see *post* p. 317.) Of course, all this is only permissible if authorized by the original contract, but it does illustrate how far removed we sometimes are from the notion that all contractual duties are based on assent or promises.

### 3. ORAL CONTRACTS

If the problem of isolating the terms of the contract from other statements is difficult enough in the case of written contracts, it is even more so where the contract is purely oral. In the former case the writing is at least a useful starting point, whereas in the latter case there is no real starting point at all. There is first the purely practical problem that it may be difficult to establish what exactly (or even approximately) was said anyhow, but because this is treated as a question of fact it does not figure prominently in the books. The difficult questions of law only arise after this first hurdle has been surmounted, and it has been found as a fact what was actually said. It must then be decided which words used by the parties are to be treated as contractual terms or promises. The negotiations may contain a large number of statements which eventually result in agreement, and it is very difficult to draw a line between the terms of the contract and mere statements or representations not 'intended' to have contractual effect. Once again the distinction is said to depend on the intention of the parties, but, as we have already pointed out, this is of very little assistance in this connection. Moreover, as we have said above, the question whether a statement is a promise or a mere representation is usually discussed without reference to the result, but there is good ground for thinking that the courts, consciously or unconsciously, tend to prefer the former alternative when they think it is just to hold the defendant liable in damages, and the latter alternative when they do not. The problem has been before the courts again and again, but in a book of this nature it will suffice to refer to two or three of these cases, few of which appear to lay down any general principle beyond the importance attached to the intention of the parties. Moreover (as we shall see later), the distinction may prove of less importance in the future than in the past; the reason for this is that even a misrepresentation will now give rise to a liability in damages if it was made negligently. And it will therefore often be immaterial whether a statement was intended to have contractual force or not.

In *Schawel* v. *Reade*[19] the plaintiff required a stallion for stud purposes, and he was examining a horse in the defendant's stables. While he was doing this, the defendant entered and said: 'You need not look for anything; the horse is perfectly sound'. The plaintiff thereupon ceased his examination, and eventually (though not in fact for several weeks) he bought the horse. The House of Lords affirmed the jury's decision that the seller's statement was a term of the contract of sale. Lord Moulton said:

It would be impossible, in my mind, to have a clearer example of an express warranty where the word 'warranty' was not used. The essence of such a warranty is that it becomes plain by the words and the action of the parties that it is intended that in the purchase the responsibility of the soundness shall rest upon the vendor; and how in the world could a vendor more clearly indicate that he is prepared to and intends to take upon himself the responsibility of the soundness than by saying: 'You need not look at the horse because he is perfectly sound', and sees that the purchaser thereupon desists from his immediate independent examination?[20]

As put by Lord Moulton, therefore, the question is whether the person making the statement has assumed the responsibility for the truth of what he has said. As a very general rule it may be said that a statement is a term of the contract when the person making it is in a better position to know the truth than the other party, but even this is by no means always the case.

Conversely, in *Oscar Chess* v. *Williams*[21] a majority of the Court of Appeal laid it down as a very rough guide that a person is not usually to be assumed to be accepting responsibility for the truth of a statement as to which he had no personal knowledge. In this case the plaintiffs, who were car-dealers, bought a car from the defendant which was believed by both parties to be, and was stated by the defendant to be, a 1946 model. In fact the seller did not know and had no means of knowing the true age of the car, and was merely passing on the information contained in the log book, which, as it turned out, was wrong. It was held that this statement was a mere representation. But where the role of the parties is reversed the position will normally be different, because a dealer who states that a certain car is a model dating from a particular year should know whether this is true or not, and if he does not know he can discover the truth by application to the manufacturers. Certainly a statement made by a dealer as to the quality of goods being sold will rarely be held a mere representation. This is borne out by the decision in *Dick Bentley Ltd* v. *Harold Smith (Motors) Ltd*,[22] where a dealer supplied a car to the plaintiff

---

[19] [1913] 2 I R 81.

[20] It is strange that this case was for long less well known than the English case of *Hopkins* v. *Tanqueray* (1854) 15 CB 130, which appears contrary but is of lower authority. But in this last case the sale was at Tattersalls, where it was well known that all sales were without warranty.        [21] [1957] 1 WLR 370.        [22] [1965] 1 WLR 623.

as a '20,000 mile Bentley'. In fact the car had done considerably more than 20,000 miles and the plaintiff obtained damages for breach of warranty. This case is thus a good illustration of the point that the courts tend to place the responsibility on the person who they think reasonably ought to bear the responsibility, rather than on the person who has agreed to bear it, for the simple reason that it is often not apparent whether anybody has agreed to bear it.

Our final illustration is a more recent case which shows the interplay of common law doctrine and the Misrepresentation Act 1967. In this case[23] a company hired two ocean-going barges to carry out some excavated waste matter and dump it at sea. The plaintiff's manager had mistakenly told the defendant's manager that the barges had a capacity of 850 cubic metres each. In fact they did not, and they proved inadequate for the job. The Court of Appeal held (by a majority) that no warranty had been given but that the defendants were entitled to damages under the Misrepresentation Act. Lord Denning MR dissented and thought there should be no liability at all. The result of this case may well be to limit the practical importance of the distinction between a warranty and a misrepresentation to two situations. First, where the representor can show that he was not negligent, he will not be liable under the 1967 Act; and secondly, where the representee wants to claim damages at the contractual rate, that is, expectation damages for loss of his bargain, the Misrepresentation Act will not suffice.[24]

## 4. THE INTERPRETATION OF EXPRESS TERMS

So far we have been attempting to explain how a court decides what is a term of the contract and what is not. When this task has been performed the court's function is to interpret these terms and give effect to them. The court has, in theory at all events, no power at common law (with rare exceptions) to add to or alter or override the terms which the parties have made. (In Chapter 16 we shall discuss these exceptions and an important statutory power of this nature.) Even the formulation of implied terms is theoretically, as we shall see, merely a reading in of terms already implicit in the contract, and does not add anything to it. However, the court will, if possible, interpret the terms of the contract in a manner consistent with the rules normally applicable to contracts of the class in question, but the interpretation of the contract is no formal or mechanical task. On the contrary, it is one of the most intractable tasks which a court has to face, and it is not made easier by the inadequacy of the rules which the courts have forged to assist them.

[23] *Howard Marine & Dredging Co* v. *A. Ogden & Sons* [1978] QB 574.
[24] For the difference between expectation damages and other damages, see *post*, 444.

These rules are based on the assumption that words have a 'plain' or 'simple' or 'ordinary' meaning, and that the only function of a court in interpreting a document is to find out what that meaning is and give effect to it or, in other words, that the judge is just a kind of legal dictionary. Generally this means that the actual intention of the parties (as opposed to the intention which appears from their words) is irrelevant, as also is the fairness or justice or even rationality of the outcome. In fact the fallacies in this assumption have been exposed many times, first by modern philosophers and secondly by lawyers, with particular reference to the problems of legal interpretation. Yet the courts are bound by precedent, and even more by their traditional ways of thinking, to ignore ideas of this kind. The result is not necessarily that the courts reach worse results than they would if they abandoned the safe haven of the 'plain meaning of words', but the result certainly is that the interpretation of contracts is an unpredictable business for the simple reason that the courts often say one thing and do another. They say that they are looking for the intention of the parties as expressed in their written contract, and that for that purpose they are merely searching for the 'plain meaning of the words', whereas in truth, where the meaning of the contract is doubtful, they have to choose between the various possible meanings available, and the choice is dictated by a large number of considerations, of which the literal or grammatical factor is only one. However, the difficulties of interpreting written documents reach beyond the confines of the law of contract, and in a book of this nature it is impossible to develop this theme more fully. It must suffice to say that the problem of interpretation is far from being a mechanical one, but on the whole English judges remain true to their usual formal approach to law and legal doctrine and legal documents.

### Interpretation of exemption clauses

There is one particular aspect of the problem of interpretation which does require more extended examination, and that is the treatment by the courts of exemption clauses. An exemption clause may take many forms, but all such clauses have one thing in common in that they exempt a party from a liability which he would have borne had it not been for the clause. In some cases an exemption clause merely relieves a party from certain purely contractual obligations, for example, the duties of a seller in a contract of sale regarding the quality and fitness of the goods. In other cases exemption clauses go further and protect the party not merely from contractual liability but even from liability which would otherwise have arisen in tort. For example, a shipping company's bill of lading may exempt the company from liability for damage to the goods being carried, however caused. Now if the goods are damaged as a result of the negligence of the company's employees, that would, in the normal way, give rise to an action in tort for negligence, quite apart from the contract. But the exemption clause may operate to exclude the cargo-owner's right of action in both contract and tort. In yet other cases exemption clauses may be only partial in their operation, e.g. by restricting the time during which a claim may be made, or by limiting the amount of damages recoverable. Clauses of this latter kind are sometimes called 'limitation clauses' and are occasionally distinguished from exemption clauses.

During the past forty or fifty years consumer hostility to exemption clauses has grown, and has gone hand in hand with judicial and legislative law reform. The clauses in question appear in many cases highly objectionable. They are frequently drafted in the widest possible terms, and contained in standard form contracts which the individual member of the public apparently has little choice but to accept. We have already emphasized that in many such contracts it is a fiction to regard the detailed terms of the contract as based on agreement, even if the contract itself may be the outcome of a genuine agreement. Nowhere is this more apparent than in dealing with these exemption clauses. Nobody in his senses would agree to a contract which permitted the other party to commit negligence with impunity—unless, perhaps, by doing so he were to get the goods or services offered at a cheaper price, an important point to which we shall return. Especially where a body supplying the public with goods or services is able to dictate its own terms because it has an effective monopoly, the blunt truth is that the ordinary law of contractual and tortious liability can simply be set aside at the pleasure of this body.

It has been widely thought that changing business and commercial practice has often rendered these exemption clauses unnecessary as a protection to the companies using them. If the individual whose right of action is excluded has to bear the loss or injury himself, the burden may be a grievous one, and he is unlikely to be insured against the eventuality which has occurred. Where, however, a company supplying goods or services to the public is liable for loss or damage, the company will in most cases have insured itself against these liabilities. This has a twofold result. In the first place the cost of insurance becomes an overhead of the company and is passed on to the consumer in increased charges. In this way the general body of consumers become in effect insurers for each other, and it is arguable that this method of apportioning liability is to be encouraged. In the second place, the premiums payable to an insurance company may vary according to whether the insured is a good or bad risk. In this way insurance can act as an indirect method of enforcing standards of behaviour in compliance with the law.

It has not, however, always been recognized that exemption clauses are not necessarily unreasonable or undesirable from a social and commercial point of view. Apart from cases in which personal injury is involved (and perhaps special considerations affect such cases) there are many situations in which an exemption clause is in practice merely an agreement about the allocation of responsibility for insuring against certain risks. For example, a company whose business is the carriage of goods by road may incorporate clauses in its contracts under which it excludes all liability for loss of, or damage to, the goods. In this kind of case the exemption clause is merely an indication that the responsibility for insuring the goods against loss or damage is intended to rest on the owner and not on the carrier. There is nothing necessarily unreasonable or undesirable about this. No doubt the carrier could insure the goods, though he would then have to increase his charges to cover the cost of insurance; but it may well be better for the consignor of the goods to insure them himself. In particular he would know more about the nature and value of the goods, the way they have been packed, and their vulnerability to damage—all factors which would be very relevant to the question of insurance.

A recent decision of the House of Lords is a welcome recognition of the fact that that such insurance-type clauses may be perfectly reasonable in a commercial sense even though they appear at first sight to offend fundamental legal sensibilities. In *Scottish Special Housing Association* v. *Wimpey Construction UK Ltd*[25] builders contracted to modernize eighteen houses for a client. The contract provided that the contractors were to be liable for damage caused by their negligence except for loss which was declared at the risk of the client under another clause in the contract. That clause required the client to maintain insurance on the houses against damage by fire. The question arose whether the builder was liable for fire-damage to the houses caused by their negligence. In the lower courts it was thought outrageous if the builder were not liable because the result would be that the fire-damage would have to be repaired by the builder who would then get paid twice (according to the contract) for doing the same work. But in the House of Lords it was insisted that there was nothing commercially strange about such a result. It was standard practice to insure against fire—the only question was whether the builder or the client was to provide the insurance. So long as the contract made it clear that the client was to insure it was wrong to throw the liability on to the builder even where he had been negligent. As so often happens in these cases, the real contest was probably between two insurers—the builders' insurers and the client's insurers. But the client had clearly paid a premium for this insurance, whereas the builders' insurance premiums were (presumably) fixed on the assumption that he was not liable for this fire damage. So the result seems sound.

There are also some situations (of which the above may have been an

---

[25] [1988] 1 WLR 995.

example) in which property is likely to be already insured by the owner in the ordinary course of events. For example, many car owners carry comprehensive policies which cover them against the risk of loss or damage from any cause. If a car owner takes his car to a garage for repairs, therefore, it may be positively desirable for the garage to exclude its normal liability for causing damage by negligence. If the garage company is unable to do this it will have to insure against the risk and charge the customer accordingly. This would simply mean that the owner would pay twice over for his insurance protection.

The problem of exemption clauses produced a great deal of contractual litigation in the decades after the Second World War, and the courts adopted a variety of methods of dealing with them. We have already seen something of one of those methods, namely the invention of the idea that certain terms were so fundamental as to be non-excludable by exemption clauses altogether.[26] Another device was to permit the aggrieved party to sue someone other than the contracting party: for example, he might sue an employee or contractor employed by the contracting party. Such an action, of course, had to be brought in tort, but liability in tort for negligent injury to the person or damage to goods is so widespread that it is usually possible to sue some third party for negligence in this way. The third party was generally held by the courts to be unable to protect himself by invoking the exemption clause.[27] Yet another possibility was to hold that insufficient notice had been given of the incorporation of an exemption clause in an oral contract, or that such notice had been given too late. Then there were a number of statutory provisions for the protection of consumers, though until recently these were of a piecemeal character.

But much the most important procedure by which the courts tended to nullify or modify the effect of exemption clauses was the simple process of 'construction'. Words have to be interpreted, and if the words appear to produce a result which seems unreasonable, it is often possible to give a strained interpretation to the words to avoid that result. Scores of cases from the 1950s onwards illustrated how judicial ingenuity was able to cut down the effects of drastic exemption clauses by strained interpretation. But eventually it came increasingly to be felt that all these devices, and especially the methods of construction used in dealing with exemption clauses, were somewhat unsatisfactory. Although no doubt much justice was done by these means, they tended to go too far in some ways, and not far enough in others. These devices tended to go too far because they did not distinguish between reasonable and unreasonable exclusion clauses. As we have seen above, it is too simple to condemn all such clauses as unreasonable or unfair: some of them are positively desirable in the

---

[26] See *supra*, 177.    [27] See *post*, 376.

interests of the parties or in the public interest. But strict construction and other devices mentioned above were used by the courts quite indiscriminately against all sorts of exemption clauses. On the other hand, these devices did not seem to go far enough in the other direction. For if it was accepted that the courts had in the last resort to give effect to clear language, the draftsmen of exemption clauses only had to go on rewording their clauses more carefully, and in the end the courts would have had to give effect to them. What appeared to be needed was some sort of substantive power to override certain unreasonable exemption clauses, and during the past twenty to thirty years these powers have been increasingly forthcoming from Parliament. In 1964 the Hire-Purchase Act of that year first gave a substantial measure of protection to those who bought goods on hire-purchase; in 1973 similar protection was at last extended to purchasers of goods who paid cash, or who financed their purchases with loans from banks or other sources. In 1977 the Unfair Contract Terms Act enacted a fairly comprehensive code on the subject of exemption clauses generally, and in 1994 Regulations were made to give effect to the EC Directive on Unfair Contract Terms, which are also of a very general nature. The Act and the Regulations are considered further in Chapter 16.

One indirect result of this legislation has been to modify the way in which the courts approach the problem of interpreting exemption clauses. For it has now been stressed by the House of Lords[28] that courts should no longer strain to interpret exemption clauses narrowly in order to avoid injustice. Such a clause should be interpreted according to its ordinary meaning in the usual way. If it is found applicable to the case in hand, the clause can then be tested against the criteria in the Unfair Contract Terms Act (or, now, the EC Directive) and, if necessary, struck down. Unfortunately, it must also be added that more recently still the House of Lords appears to have endorsed a distinction between exemption clauses and limitation clauses[29] which seems to imply that the former are still to be construed in a stricter manner than the latter. This may prove a temporary aberration only, and it is to be hoped that the House of Lords will eventually make it clear that strained interpretation of all exemption and limitation clauses should now be avoided.

---

[28] *Photo Productions Ltd* v. *Securicor Transport Ltd* [1980] AC 827; *George Mitchell (Chesterhall) Ltd* v. *Finney Lock Seeds* [1983] 2 AC 803.
[29] *Ailsa Craig Fishing Co* v. *Malvern Fishing Co* [1983] 1 All ER 101. See *supra*, Ch. 9, n. 22, as to this decision.

# Contractual Duties not Fixed by the Parties

## 1. THE NATURE OF IMPLIED TERMS

In the previous chapter we saw that the duties of the parties to a contract may be defined and fixed by themselves with great precision if they so choose, and in this event the function of the court is—in theory—merely to give effect to the rules which the parties have chosen to impose on themselves. But in practice there are several reasons why it rarely, if ever, happens that the function of the courts is thus restricted, as we have stressed already. First, the courts must interpret the language used by the parties, a matter referred to in the last chapter. Secondly, parties tend naturally to anticipate performance rather than breach, so only in complex and legally drafted contracts do they usually deal with the question of remedies for breach. But even leaving aside the question of remedies— which is not the subject matter of this chapter—there is nearly always an important role for the law in delimiting the precise extent of the parties' duties under the contract. Parties simply cannot and do not define their duties in such detail that there is no room for applying the ordinary rules, at least in part. It would simply be too costly to be worthwhile. Moreover, the parties do not and cannot know all the relevant facts when they make their contracts, nor can they foresee what the future is likely to bring, let alone anticipate completely abnormal contingencies. In practice many contracting parties simply agree on the bare essentials and leave everything else unexpressed. In these circumstances the courts have to decide what is to happen when disputes arise in the performance of the contract. And even the most complex and intricate commercial contracts often give rise to disputes or litigation, despite the efforts of the parties and their lawyers to anticipate all contingencies.

Fortunately, most contracts fall into certain well recognized classes, such as sale of goods, hire purchase, agency, employment, partnership, insurance, and so forth. Each of these contracts has its own 'law' just as much as the general law of contract, although in both cases the parties are normally free to contract out of these rules if they wish. But if they do not expressly contract out of them, the usual thing is for the court simply to apply the rules relating to the particular contract in question. As we saw earlier, the existence of these rules may frequently prevent a contract from failing for uncertainty.

Traditionally, many of these rules relating to particular contracts are regarded as resting on 'implied terms' in the original contract, and these implied terms are themselves regarded as resting on the presumed intention of the parties. In cases of a commercial character there is some legitimacy for this approach, because many implied terms in these contracts originated in commercial custom, and it is reasonable to assume that business people who make business contracts intend to abide by the normal commercial customs if they say nothing to the contrary.

But there are other cases in which obligations arising in a contractual context are treated as legal duties, created by law, not arising from the intention of the parties, and it is not always apparent why the legal basis of different contractual duties should differ in this way. For instance, in a contract of sale of goods, the seller's duties in respect of the quality of the goods are rested on implied terms. On the other hand, the seller's duties in respect of the quantity of goods to be delivered are not based on an implied term, but are simply treated as legal obligations, deriving from the general law. Again, in the relationship of employer and employee it has been said, for instance, that there is an implied term that the employee shall not be required to do an unlawful act. On the other hand, the employer's obligation to provide a safe system of work is always stated as a legal duty, and not as based on an implied term.

Further, some of these duties which are regarded by lawyers as created by the law, rather than by the contract itself, are treated as contractual in their character, and some as belonging to the law of tort. An action for personal injuries brought by an employee against his employer is, for instance, treated by lawyers as an action in tort and not for breach of contract, even though it would have been conceptually perhaps more natural to base the employer's duties on implied terms of the contract. Probably the reason this has happened is that an action for personal injuries brought by an employee more closely resembles other personal injury actions (for instance, those arising out of road accidents or, indeed, actions brought by employees against third parties) than a typical action for breach of contract. So there has been a tendency to lump the employee's personal injury action together with other such actions even though most of the others clearly arise in tort. This itself perhaps shows that the way such claims get classified has more to do with practical convenience than with careful theoretical analysis.

Generally speaking these differences between legal duties said to arise in tort or in contract, or between duties arising in contract from implied terms and those arising from the general law of contract, have anyhow no practical importance, and are mere matters of labelling. Sometimes, indeed, identical duties (especially a duty of care) may co-exist in contract and tort. But occasionally legal rules come to be associated exclusively with the law of contract or of tort, and it may then matter precisely how a duty is classified. For example, it has recently been held that the (exceptional) duty of the parties in an insurance contract to give pre-contractual information to each other does not derive from the law of tort, nor from an implied term in the contract, and consequently cannot be enforced by an action for damages, but only by the rescission of the contract.[1]

In modern times it must also be noted that the complexity of legal relationships, and of the law itself, often means that contracts 'incorporate' all kinds of terms laid down elsewhere. For instance, employment contracts often incorporate, expressly or by implication, all sorts of terms negotiated in collective bargaining agreements between the employer (or employers' representatives) and the relevant trade unions. So also there are areas where statute law is heavily involved, such as in the employment contracts of doctors working in the National Health Service. The terms of employment of such doctors are today largely laid down in statutory regulations which do not depend on the intention of the parties, nor on the usual tests for the implication of terms in a contract.[2]

Of course even traditional 'implied terms' in a contract cannot always be attributed to the intention of the parties without indulging in fictions, and until recently there were increasing signs of a willingness on the part of the courts to recognize this fact, particularly perhaps in relation to the doctrine of frustration. For example, only a few years ago Lord Wilberforce said:

> I think that the movement of the law of contract is away from a rigid theory of autonomy towards the discovery, or I do not hesitate to say imposition, by the courts of just solutions, which can be ascribed to reasonable men in the position of the parties.[3]

But since then (as we have seen) there have been many signs of a renewed swing of the pendulum, and in 1985 Lord Scarman, giving the opinion of the Privy Council in *Tai Hing Cotton Mill Ltd* v. *Liu Chong Hing Bank Ltd*[4] rejected the use of the language of 'imposition' in connection with implied terms. Nevertheless, this renewed faith in the idea that implied terms are the work of the parties rather than the court is no more convincing than the old. Of course, the idea of the implied term has been used to serve many different purposes. Sometimes, when a court implies a term it is merely reading in what is already logically implicit in the language of the contract. Sometimes a court is adding something to the contract which the parties probably had in mind but did not actually express. Sometimes, again, the court is adding terms which the parties

---

[1] *La Banque Financière de la Cité SA* v. *Westgate Insurance (UK) Ltd* [1990] QB 665, affirmed on narrower grounds [1991] 2 AC 249, but with dicta of Lord Templeman at 280 supporting the CA.
[2] See *Scally* v. *Southern Health and Social Services Board* [1992] 1 AC 294.
[3] *National Carriers Ltd* v. *Panalpina (Northern) Ltd* [1981] AC 675 at 696.
[4] [1986] AC 80.

would probably have expressed if the matter had been brought to their attention. In yet other cases a court adds terms to a contract which it thinks the parties ought in fairness and justice to have included even though they might not have done so if the matter had been brought to their attention. In the first type of case the phrase 'implied term' is unobjectionable. In the last type of case, on the other hand, it seems clear that the court is merely applying a rule of law, albeit a rule which can be excluded by express agreement. But in the intermediate positions it is difficult to dogmatize about which approach is more accurate, particularly as the different cases tend to shade off into each other.

## 2. IMPLIED TERMS IN STANDARDIZED CONTRACTS

The theory that implied terms depend upon the intention of the parties is especially thin with respect to particular types of contracts, such as those referred to above, and in these cases the position is that the so-called implied terms have come to be standardized, and are always implied unless they are expressly excluded. In implying terms in these cases the courts must have regard to wider considerations than the presumed intention of the particular parties. These wider considerations include especially considerations deriving from the very nature of the contract in question—is it an employment contract, for instance, or a landlord and tenant contract? It also seems clear that in these cases questions of reasonableness cannot be excluded: the court can hardly imply terms unless they are reasonable, when it is examining the implication of general terms in standardized cases, although that does not mean that a term can be implied just because it would be reasonable to do so.[5]

In fact in some cases the implied terms have become so well settled that they have been incorporated in statutes, such as the Sale of Goods Act 1979 and the Partnership Act 1890. In these contracts the search for the parties' intention is a sheer fiction, for the courts will apply the terms implied by these Acts as a matter of course unless they are expressly excluded. With this one qualification, therefore, it is probably best to regard these rules as positive rules of law in no way dependent on the intention of the parties. And even this qualification does not always apply, for under the Unfair Contract Terms Act (as we shall see) the parties cannot always exclude the terms even by express agreement. In other cases modern statutes have added comparable implied terms to contracts which have never been covered by similar terms at common law, though the statute does not represent any real new policy—for instance the Supply of

---

[5] See the speeches of Lord Wilberforce and Lord Cross in *Liverpool City Council* v. *Irwin* [1977] AC 239 at 256 and 257–8. See further on the question of reasonableness, 206.

Goods and Services Act 1982 provides in section 13 that there is an implied term that all contractual services are to be supplied with reasonable care. This was never expressly laid down at common law but it is hardly a great innovation to hold that such a term should be implied.

Even in a case of a standardized term of this nature the Privy Council restated the traditional dogma that implied terms depend on proof of contractual intention in the *Tai Hing Cotton Mill* case, and it is worth pausing over this case to show how unsatisfying that dogma is in cases of this kind. The case arose out the relationship between a company and its bankers. Over a period of some years the company's accounts clerk had forged the signature of the managing director on some 300 cheques and thus fraudulently obtained very large sums of money. When the fraud was uncovered, the company sued the bank, demanding the recovery of these sums which had been debited to its account. In the normal way the bank would have had no defence to the action because a bank cannot debit a client's account except in accordance with his instructions and a forged cheque, of course, is not the client's own authority to the bank. But the bank here argued that the company was to blame for allowing the fraud to continue so long undetected, because of the negligent supervision of the accounts clerk. There was nothing peculiar about the particular case, other than the allegation of negligence, so the case turned on the ordinary duties of bankers and customers. Now previous authorities of the House of Lords had established that a customer owes two duties to his bank to protect it from being defrauded in the handling of his account. First, he must not so make out his cheques as to facilitate their alteration by some third party, for example, by leaving blank spaces where figures can be added. Secondly, if a client learns that forged cheques have been drawn on his account, he must inform the bank promptly so that it can proceed against the forger and indeed prevent further forgeries from escaping undetected. Now in the *Tai Hing* case the bank argued that these duties should be extended, and that a company owed a more general duty to its bank not to permit the negligent operation of its accounts department so as to facilitate fraud or forgery. That was the point at issue in the case.

The bank argued that the law of negligence had been extensively developed in recent years, and that it was right that the loss in this case should be borne by the company whose negligent supervision of their accountant was to blame. In rejecting this more extensive duty the Privy Council relied on the traditional tests that are often used in some cases of implied terms. But these tests were not really appropriate in cases of standardized relations such as this, and it now seems clear from later House of Lords authority[6] that (subject to one point to be discussed

----

[6] See the *Scally* case, *supra*, n. 2.

later) they only apply in more individual types of case. What is at any rate clear is that the question at issue here was a general question about the duties between a bank and its customers, and had nothing to do with the intentions of the particular parties in that case. On this general question, perhaps the strongest point against the bank is that banks themselves tend to set the terms on which they contract, so if they want special protection against frauds by clients' accountants, they should stipulate for it. The Privy Council might also have used an argument sometimes relied upon in the past, namely, that banks are better placed than most customers to cover themselves, or to insure, against losses of this kind. But this is perhaps a distributive sort of argument (which on analysis may amount to little more than saying that banks are normally richer than their customers) and that sort of argument is also going out of fashion today.

### 3. REASONABLENESS AND NECESSITY

One test which constantly recurs in the cases is that of necessity. Is the term to be implied *necessary* to make sense of the contract, or (as is said in the more individual, one-off cases) to give it business efficacy? The leading case on this point is *Liverpool City Council* v. *Irwin*[7] which concerned the contractual obligations of a local authority to tenants living in a block of flats. The flats in question were the notorious 'piggeries' in Liverpool which were eventually made uninhabitable by vandals, though at the time of the proceedings the plaintiff was still living in the flats and they were still fully used. The plaintiff's main complaint was that although the flats were ten storeys high the lifts were constantly out of order, and that even on the stairs lights were frequently broken or missing. But the defendants' reply to this complaint was that, as fast as they put right faults, lifts and lights were damaged again by vandals. The defendants had already spent far more on repairs than they had received in rent for the whole block of flats. The legal question was whether the defendants were under any, and if so, how strict an, obligation with respect to the lifts and lights on the stairs. The plaintiff argued that an implied term had to be read into the contract of lease requiring the defendants to maintain lifts and lights. The defendants for their part said that no such term was to be implied, and that their only obligation was to permit the tenants to use the lifts and stairs in such a way as not to cause unnecessary risk of danger. In the result the House of Lords decided that the landlords did owe a duty to the tenants to do what was reasonable to ensure that the lifts and lights remained in working order: there was an obligation but it was not an absolute obligation.

[7] [1977] AC 239.

On the question of the 'necessity' test the case involved an apparent conflict of opinion between Lord Denning, in the Court of Appeal, and the House of Lords. Lord Denning had said in the lower court that it was always possible to imply a term into a contract whenever it was reasonable to do so, but the House of Lords rejected this in favour of the more traditional view that such implications can only be made when it is strictly necessary. The difference in opinion between the judges on this point seems, however, to have been somewhat unreal. For it is evident that the formula that implications can only be made when necessary is not to be taken too literally. It is not *necessary* to have lifts in blocks of flats ten storeys high (indeed high-rise buildings existed long before lifts were invented), though it would no doubt be exceedingly inconvenient not to have them. So 'necessary' really seems to mean 'reasonably necessary', and that must mean, 'reasonably necessary having regard to the context and the price'. So in the end there does not seem to be much difference between what is necessary and what is reasonable.

The point is borne out even more strongly by the later House of Lords decision in *Scally* v. *Southern Health and Social Services Board*.[8] The plaintiff was a National Health Service doctor who argued that there was an implied term in his contract of employment that his employers, the local Health Board, would notify him of some of the very extensive and very complex legal rights to acquire pension entitlements which he had under the statutory regulations governing his employment. Lord Bridge insisted that even in such a case of a standardized contract a term of the kind sought could only be implied if it was *necessary* to the contract, but he held (and all the Law Lords concurred with him) that the test was satisfied on these facts. It is hard to take the finding seriously. Plainly the plaintiff *could* have found out his legal rights in other ways—he could have employed a solicitor, for instance, or at least consulted a trade union. Clearly, what Lord Bridge meant was that it was 'reasonably necessary' to imply the term in question, not that it was absolutely necessary. It is a pity that the House of Lords seems so reluctant to admit what it is doing in these cases.

This reluctance may stem from the belief that it is dangerous to argue that any 'reasonable' terms can be implied in a contract, because what is reasonable cannot be decided in abstract, or in general terms as it is in the law of tort. And this may also be why in the *Tai Hing Cotton Mill* case, Lord Scarman suggested that it was not appropriate to invoke the tort of negligence when examining contractual implied terms. Of course it should go without saying that in a contractual context the question of what is reasonable must be decided by reference to what the parties have agreed about; the nature of the contract and, above all, the price are obviously

[8] *Supra*, n. 2.

relevant in deciding what is reasonable. Moreover, it would generally be wrong to permit tort law (or the imposition of 'implied' contractual duties based on reasonableness, which is virtually the same thing), to circumvent a clear refusal to assume a liability in contract. It is one thing to *supplement* a contract with 'implied' terms or with tort duties of reasonable care; it is quite another thing to alter it or contradict it. Lord Scarman's remarks in the *Tai Hing Cotton Mill* case may well reflect the resurgence of freedom-of-contract principles in emphasizing this vital point.

The difficulty, of course, is to know when the failure of a contract to impose a particular duty amounts to a deliberate non-assumption of liability, and when the contract is simply neutral on the question of duty or no duty.[9] It is right to beware of 'supplementing' a contract in ways which really alter it or contradict it because, for instance, the 'supplementation'— if expressed at the time the contract was made—would have affected the contract price. But on the other hand judges should not fear supplementing a contract where the addition would not have affected the price. Indeed, if expressing these supplementary duties would not have altered the price, this would seem a clear indication that the duties really are, or ought to be, 'implied'.

Where implied terms or tort duties of reasonable care would actually alter or contradict a contract, so that the price plainly would have been affected if the parties had known of the implied term or tort duty when the contract was made, then warning signals should flash, although it may still sometimes be permissible to proceed with caution. There are several reasons that caution is needed in such cases. First, in such circumstances adding the implied term (and in this discussion we include in this term tort duties) would clearly be redistributive in the particular case. One party is simply given a legal right at the expense of the other party, and it behoves the court to be extremely careful in doing that. Redistribution of income or wealth is normally a political exercise, for Parliament. Judges and the law are expected to be neutral as between different classes of the community. The rich are entitled to justice no less than the poor, landlords no less than tenants, employers no less than employees, consumer-credit companies no less than buyers.

But although adding an implied term may be redistributive in the particular case, it may not be redistributive in the long run, because once the new decision establishes itself as law, prices will be adjusted to reflect that law. Sometimes this is regarded as a ground for not adding the implied

<hr />

[9] See e.g. Mann LJ in *Greater Nottingham Co-operative Society Ltd* v. *Cementation Piling* [1988] 2 All ER 971 at 991: 'I ask myself whether it is just and reasonable to impose a duty in tort where the parties are united by a contract which is notably silent on the liability which it is sought to enforce in tort'.

term—it seems hardly worthwhile, where the redistributive effects of the decision are so easily circumvented. But there are some circumstances where it may be right for the courts to press ahead and add the implied term. For instance, the market may be working so imperfectly in the relevant area that the claimant has not been given the choice of paying extra for the benefit of the implied term. A legal decision may then provide just the shaking up the market needs, so that, in future, contracts provide a genuine choice. Occasionally, even this element of choice may not become available, for some technical reason, so that the alternatives lie between giving all relevant parties the benefit of the implied term, even with some eventual price adjustment, or giving none of them that benefit, with a consequentially lower price. Here, too, there are circumstances where it may be, on balance, preferable to give the benefit. Finally, even if (as may happen in special circumstances, especially in the short run) some redistributive results of the decision remain, judges may be entitled to behave in this way if they are following some clearly defined Parliamentary policy which emerges from the legislation.

The above arguments may sound abstract and theoretical, but they are well illustrated by the problems concerning the liability of surveyors for negligent valuations conducted on behalf of building societies and other lenders. Although this is seen as (at any rate in the first instance) a problem in tort law, it precisely parallels the questions which arise when a term is implied into a contract. When a borrower was first held entitled to sue in tort for negligence in such a case,[10] the result was clearly redistributive in that particular case. The borrower had not paid an appropriate charge for the survey, including a 'premium' entitling him to rely upon it. Later, some surveyors' charges were adjusted to reflect this fact, while other surveyors attempted to disclaim their liability. The market thus came to work more effectively, giving borrowers some degree of choice; still, the choice was often limited, because the particular building society, or surveyor, might choose one or other method of responding to the duty of care, without giving the borrower the right to choose. Since then the House of Lords has decided that such disclaimers are generally invalid under the Unfair Contract Terms Act, a point discussed again in Chapter 16.[12] The result of this decision is to change the way the market works in this sort of case. Borrowers will now have the right to sue surveyors for negligence but they will also pay a little more for their surveys to cover the insurance cost of this form of liability.

Subject to these caveats it is difficult to see why the judges are so

---

[10] *Yianni* v. *Edwin Evans & Sons* [1982] QB 438.
[11] See *Smith* v. *Eric S. Bush* [1990] 1 AC 831.
[12] See *post,* 308.

reluctant to admit that reasonable terms are implied into contracts. In tort law the judges are every day imposing obligations on parties for no better reason than that they seem to be required by the demands of 'reasonable care'; it is not easy to see why similar obligations cannot be imposed on contracting parties—and indeed they are, all the time.

One recent example is provided by an important test case brought to settle the question whether teachers are under a contractual duty to 'cover' for absent colleagues, or whether they can insist that, once their own classes have been allocated to them by the timetable, they can refuse to undertake any further teaching duties.[13] In this case, as in most cases concerning the employment of professional persons, the contracts traditionally did not spell out the nature of the teacher's duties in any detail. But the judge held that teachers were under an obligation to 'cover' because of their basic professional responsibility. This required consideration of the general background governing the way schools operated, which (among other things) meant that classes could not be left unsupervised and timetables had to be adhered to. It seems clear that this was tantamount to holding that the question was one of reasonableness, but reasonableness in the particular context of the contracts in question, not reasonableness in the abstract.

## 4. WIDELY APPLICABLE IMPLIED TERMS

In addition to those duties which are the creation of the rules relating to particular contracts, there are a number of other duties or 'implied terms' which apply to practically all contracts, again almost as a matter of course. For example, in nearly all contracts there is an implied term or duty that work will be done competently and not negligently. This applies to contracts for the supply of services as well as to contracts of employment; indeed in the case of services the duty is now laid down in the Supply of Goods and Services Act 1982. So, too, in the absence of any agreed time limit, it would usually be implied that a contract must be performed within a reasonable time. Again, the courts have had no difficulty in laying down a rule, which would probably apply to all contracts, that a contracting party should not be required to do an unlawful act. Similarly, there is a rule, laid down in *Southern Foundries* v. *Shirlaw*,[14] that a party must not put an end to a state of affairs necessary for the performance of the contract. That, however, is far from being a universal rule, because sometimes one party is *entitled* to do this, that is, owes no duty not to do so,[15] so perhaps this

---

[13] *Sim* v. *Rotherham Met. BC* [1987] Ch. 216.    [14] [1940] AC 701.
[15] For a recent discussion of this difficult area of the law, see *Thompson* v. *ASDA-MFI Group* [1988] 2 All ER 722.

principle should not be seen as on a par with the other cases referred to in this paragraph.

Again, where parties have contracted against the background of a particular trade, the customs of that trade (or local usages) are normally imported into the contract. This is usually done under the guise of an implied term, but it is in truth simply a rule of law that parties must perform their contracts in conformity with relevant customs and usages unless they have expressly decided the contrary. There is, of course, no doubt about this latter qualification.

## 5. IMPLIED TERMS IN SPECIAL CASES

So far we have been dealing with contractual duties of a standard nature, either because they apply in most contracts where they are relevant at all, or because they are implied in all (or anyhow most) contracts of a particular standard type. The position is naturally more difficult where the court is considering the duties of the parties under some non-standard contract, and the duty itself does not fall into any well-recognized category. Here the court cannot fall back on precedent or statute. In these cases it may be more accurate to speak of implied terms, because the principle is that the court can only read a term into the contract if it is essential to give 'business efficacy' to the agreement, or if the matter is so obvious that it goes without saying. It seems, in other words, that the courts here really are trying to find out what the parties would have said if the matter had been brought to their attention, and they are not prepared to add terms to the contract merely because they are fair and reasonable, as they have done in some other cases. The implication of terms in cases of this kind, is often called the principle of *The Moorcock*[16] following the case of that name, and there is no doubt that this principle is sparingly and cautiously used. The test universally used in these cases was stated by Mackinnon LJ as follows:

Prima facie that which in any contract is left to be implied and need not be expressed is something so obvious that it goes without saying; so that, if while the parties were making their bargain an officious bystander were to suggest some express provision for it in their agreement, they would testily suppress him with a common, 'Oh, of course'.[17]

That this test is more easily stated than applied, however, is shown by the somewhat ironical fact that, in the case in which it was laid down, a divided Court of Appeal was only affirmed by a bare majority in the House of Lords. Perhaps a better test, for reasons given above, would be to ask

---

[16] (1889) 14 PD 64.      [17] *Southern Foundries* v. *Shirlaw* [1939] 2 KB 206.

whether the price of the contract would have been different if the term in question had been expressed.

A good modern example of an implication of this kind is provided by the decision of the House of Lords in *Harvela Investment Ltd* v. *Royal Trust Co of Canada Ltd*[18] where a trustee was negotiating for the sale of shares to two bidders. In order to ensure that the best price was obtained the trustee invited the two bidders to make sealed bids stating the highest prices they were prepared to pay, and undertook to sell to the highest bidder. One bidder offered $2,175,000, while the other bidder offered '$2,100,000 *or* $101,000 higher than the other bidder'. The question was whether this last bid was valid, or whether such a bid was by implication ruled out. It was held that there was a necessary implication in the original invitation that such bids could not be made—the whole point of asking for sealed bids was that each bidder had to state an amount. Nevertheless, even in this case the Court of Appeal had held that business efficacy did not require this implication, only to see their decision overturned by the House of Lords.

Even in cases of this nature, however, it is unreal to think that the courts have no power to modify the literal meaning of the contract by a generous process of construction. It will be sufficient here to mention *Staffs. Area Health Authority* v. *South Staffordshire Waterworks*[19] as an illustration of this possibility. Here the court construed an agreement to supply water at a fixed price 'at all times hereafter' to mean 'at all times hereafter during the subsistence of the agreement'. These words meant that the suppliers were entitled to give notice to terminate the agreement, and then offer to enter into a new one at a much higher price. The addition of these words was not treated as falling under the *Moorcock* principle, still less as a violation of that principle. Although the principle itself is often said to be applicable in very limited circumstances, the truth is that the ordinary process of construction can often be used to justify a result which the court wants to reach. But it must also be recognized that courts often appear to think that their powers in this respect are more constrained than they really are, and that their duty is to pursue literal methods of interpretation, even at the expense of justice or (sometimes, it seems) common sense.

## 6. NO GENERAL IMPLIED DUTY OF GOOD FAITH

It is worth adding a word about an implication which is *not* made as a matter of course in English law, namely that contractual duties will be performed in good faith. Good faith is of course very difficult to define or even to summarize, although it is usually easy to recognize examples of bad

---

[18] [1986] AC 207.          [19] [1979] 1 WLR 203.

faith when they are seen. We have noted earlier that there is no general duty of good faith in the making of contracts in English law, so the law relating to performance falls into place alongside that relating to formation. In many legal systems a general duty of good faith in the performance (as well as the making) of contracts is a normal requisite, and it may seem a reproach on English law that such a basic requirement as good faith is not given legal recognition. Of course there are many cases in which terms can be implied in a contract which, in the particular circumstances, are the equivalent of duties of good faith, but the absence of any general duty of good faith can probably be best explained as an illustration of English legal formality. Judges do not like to have or to wield the power to make decisions on whether parties have acted in good faith or not. The parties must comply with their contractual duties, and courts can recognize these (although not without difficulty sometimes) but the broader concept of good faith was probably thought (anyhow by nineteenth century judges) to be equivalent to a general recognition of ideas of moral right and equity in the law which was inconsistent with strict commercial dealings. Modern judges would probably not be nearly so unhappy if the law recognized a general duty of good faith.

# 12

# The Construction of the Contract

## I. STRICT DUTIES IN THE LAW OF CONTRACT

ONE of the most important and difficult questions which arises in examining the extent of the parties' duties under a contract is to decide whether the parties are absolutely bound to do that which they have contracted to do or whether they are merely bound to do their best to secure performance of the contract. Or, to put the matter in another way, the question is whether a party to a contract is to be held liable for a breach which occurs through no fault of his own.[1] This is obviously a question raising social and commercial issues of great importance, and in the law of tort the desirability of liability without fault has been extensively discussed. In the law of contract, however, the matter is not usually put in this way: the question is usually assumed to be one of construction of the contract. This is thought to be a mere matter of interpreting the extent of the parties' obligations under the contract—is the obligation absolute or is it to be read subject to implied stipulations that a party is not to be liable if he is unable to perform through no fault of his own?

Speaking very generally, the answer to this question is that contractual obligations are absolute, and that absence of fault is no defence. It is axiomatic that in relation to a claim for damages for breach of contract it is in general immaterial why the defendant failed to perform.[2] For instance, a seller of unascertained (i.e. non-specific) goods will be liable for damages if he fails to deliver goods answering the contract description, notwithstanding that he simply cannot obtain such goods. Again, the implied conditions in a contract of sale, that the goods must correspond with the contract description, or must be satisfactory, or must be fit for the purpose for which they are sold, may be broken despite the complete absence of fault on the part of the seller. Thus a shopkeeper who is simply selling goods made by a reputable manufacturer may be liable for a breach of these duties even though he had no possible means of knowing whether the conditions had been complied with or not.[3] Again, a person who has

---

[1] 'Fault' in law generally means either wilful wrongdoing or negligence, that is a failure to take reasonable care where there is a duty to take care.

[2] *Raineri* v. *Miles* [1981] AC 1050 at 1086 (Lord Edmund-Davies).

[3] In *Grant* v. *Australian Knitting Mills* [1936] AC 85, for instance, a shopkeeper who sold pants containing (unknown to him) an excess of sulphites, was held liable for damages of £2,450 to the plaintiff who contracted dermatitis from wearing the pants. The manufacturers were also held liable (in tort) and it is probable that the shopkeeper would have been entitled to an indemnity from them.

contracted to sell his house in a 'chain' under which he has also contracted to buy another house is liable for damages if he fails to convey his house on the due date even though the reason he has so broken his contract is that *his* seller has failed to convey the other house to him.[4]

The position is often different where the breach of duty complained of is not the failure to perform a contractual obligation but the falsity of a contractual statement. Certainly a party to a contract who expressly or impliedly affirms a state of facts to be true may be held to 'warrant' the truth of his statement. If it should turn out to be false it will then be no defence for him to say that he honestly believed it to be true, or even that he had reasonable grounds for believing it. But statements of fact are less generally treated as promissory representations—or binding commitments—than promises. As we shall see below, courts often prefer to limit liability even for promissory misrepresentations to cases where the representor was careless or negligent.

In some of these cases it may appear hard to condemn a contracting party for a breach of contract not due to his fault in any way. Certainly, if the contract is still wholly executory, this may be some ground for caution over the imposition of liability on either party without some requirement of fault. For where a contract is wholly executory neither party will have suffered any actual loss, other than a loss of expectations. And bare expectations do not generally warrant such extensive protection. But even expectations may be entitled to some protection, and if a contract is primarily a risk-allocation device, this may be a sufficient ground for imposing liability even without fault in certain circumstances.

The case for imposing liability without a requirement of fault is evidently much stronger where a contract has been partly performed or relied upon. To take a simple example, a person who borrows money obviously cannot argue that he is unable to repay it because of some event not due to his fault in any way. He has had the benefit of the loan, and clearly must repay it. Similarly, where actual loss has been caused by a breach of contract as a result of something done in reliance on the contract, liability may be imposed without any requirement of fault. The justification for this is that if loss or damage occurs it must fall somewhere. The question is not merely whether a defendant is to be liable for loss or damage caused without fault, but whether the loss or damage is to be borne by the plaintiff or the defendant, neither of whom may have been at fault. If the question is put in this way it will be seen that the sensible answer must be for the courts to place the loss on the person they think has, or ought to have, taken the risk

---

[4] *Rainieri* v. *Miles*, n. 2 *supra*. He would probably be entitled in his turn to recover all these damages (plus his own damages) from the seller who had defaulted in the contract with him—but the seller might not have the resources to pay.

of the contract not being properly performed, or who has, or ought to have, accepted responsibility for the proper performance of the contract. For, speaking very broadly, one of the chief functions of a contract is to shift on to the parties the risk of non-performance of their promises. So a person who promises to do something (in exchange for another's promise) assumes the risk that he may be unable to perform his promise through no fault of his own.

This means that, prima facie at least, a contractual obligation is usually absolute in its nature. But this is by no means invariably the case. Courts do not always find it just to impose liability on a contracting party who is unable to perform what he has undertaken; nor do they always find it just to impose strict liability for a misstatement of fact. There are some situations in which the courts prefer to impose liability only if the defendant has been at fault in some way and, in particular, where he has been guilty of fraud or negligence.

Unfortunately, it is often very difficult to understand why the law adopts one course rather than another. This is largely because the courts have rarely articulated clearly the reasons which motivate them in making decisions of this nature. Instead, they explain their decisions in 'conceptual' language, that is, they place the case in a certain legal category and they then apply the rules appropriate to that category. The decision then appears to be dictated by pure logic, but in fact the crucial part of the decision is the initial categorization of the case. It is therefore impossible to lay down what are the actual policy considerations which determine whether a contractual duty will be treated as strict or as requiring proof of fault. But we can at least draw certain broad distinctions which appear to be recognized in practice, and we can also show how these policy considerations may be taken account of underneath the skilful deployment of legal concepts and doctrines.

One notes, to start with, a striking distinction between promises and representations of fact. Promises are usually strictly interpreted; and the inability to perform a promise (even without fault on the part of the promisor) is rarely a good defence in law to an action for breach of contract. But the law relating to misrepresentations displays a much more confusing and complex pattern. Many misrepresentations are treated as warranties or promissory representations and thus enforced strictly in the same way as promises, more particularly if they are part and parcel of a wider transaction in which there are promises as well as representations. But sometimes even representations standing alone are treated as promissory representations. For instance, a broker sends a share transfer to a company for registration; unknown to him, this transfer is forged, and the company suffers a loss in registering the transfer. It is held that the broker is liable because he has impliedly represented the transfer to be good by sending it in for registration.[5] He has not been negligent or at fault; but he has represented a state of facts to be the case and invited the plaintiff to act on that representation.

But in other cases the courts have been unwilling to treat representations in this way, and they have insisted that the defendant should be shown to have been at fault before he is held liable. This is particularly so where professional services are concerned. It is very rare that a professional person is held liable at law where he has not been negligent. Professionals are not treated, in other words, as 'warranting' the soundness of the advice they give, or of the services they render. They do not generally 'guarantee' results.

This absence of warranty has important effects on damages as well as on the basis of liability itself. For instance, a surveyor, who has negligently failed to spot some obvious defect in a house that he has been instructed to examine, will certainly be liable for his negligence, but he is only liable for the difference between the value of the house as it actually was with the defect, and its value as it was thought to be without the defect. He is not liable for the cost of the necessary repairs, because he has not *guaranteed* that the house is defect-free.[6] Similarly a surgeon who negligently performs an operation will be liable for the damage he has done in so far as he has made the patient's condition worse; but he will not be liable for damages representing the difference between the patient's original condition and the condition he would have been in if the operation had been properly performed.

Why are professionals treated in this way? At first sight this may appear inevitable, because it looks unreasonable to expect a professional person to do more than exercise all professional care and skill. Is a solicitor to be held liable to a client who has relied on his advice when the solicitor has exercised all due care and skill but failed to foresee, for example, that a Court of Appeal decision might be overruled by the House of Lords? Is a surgeon to be liable merely because his patient has died, even though he has performed the operation with all due skill?

But in fact these results are not inevitable at all. Where goods are sold or commercial services (as opposed to professional services) are supplied, liability of this nature is regularly imposed by the law. A builder who fits defective tiles to a roof is liable although the tiles appeared to be perfectly sound and have been bought from a reputable manufacturer—and what else can a builder do than buy from a reputable manufacturer and check the tiles for apparent defects? A painter who uses defective paint is liable without inquiry into the question of fault. Sometimes, the relationship

---

[5] *Starkey* v. *Bank of England* [1903] AC 114.
[6] *Watts* v. *Morrow* [1991] 4 All ER 937 is a recent illustration.

between commercial and professional services is very close and strange results may follow from the distinctions drawn between them. An anæsthetist in a hospital injects an anæsthetic into a patient and the anæsthetic has been contaminated in a manner which could not have been reasonably foreseen: the anæsthetist is not liable because he is not at fault.[7] But a veterinary surgeon who inoculates some cattle with contaminated serum is liable despite all due care and skill on his part.[8] Similarly, an architect is liable for negligence only; so if he tells the builder to use a certain material which turns out to be unfit for use (despite all due care) he will not be liable;[9] but if the builder himself selects unsuitable material (despite all due care) he is liable. Indeed, a builder is liable even if he designs and constructs the whole work.

These distinctions are not always easy to understand, and, as we have seen already, the justification for them is rarely openly discussed. They are probably due in part to a reluctance to impose liability on professional persons in the absence of fault because of the great importance of reputation to the professions. But there is perhaps also the feeling that a professional client is more likely to appreciate that he is buying a service or advice which may be right or may be wrong. A person who buys goods or commercial services is not likely to be so philosophical about the possibility of the goods or services proving unsatisfactory. This may explain why, in the case of routine and straightforward professional services, clients may nowadays sometimes feel that they have been guaranteed a successful result, and not merely competent services. For example, a client who has a routine sterilization operation may think—if he is not warned otherwise— that permanent sterilization is guaranteed, but even in such cases the courts have followed the traditional view that results are not guaranteed.[10] The doctor is only liable for failure to exercise due care and skill.

We have said that promises are much more readily treated as binding, even in the absence of fault, than promissory representations, but we must now go on to examine some of the cases in which even a promisor may be absolved from liability where he is unable to perform his promise without any fault on his part. There are two main classes of cases in question here. Where the entire performance of the contract proves substantially impossible, either because of pre-existing facts or because of unforeseen

---

[7] *Roe* v. *Minister of Health* [1954] 2 QB 66.

[8] *Dodd* v. *Wilson* [1946] 2 All ER 691.

[9] But for a rather special case, see *Greaves & Co (Contractors)* v. *Baynham, Meikle & Partners* [1975] 1 WLR 1095, where architects were held to have warranted the soundness of a design.

[10] See *Eyre* v. *Measday* [1986] 1 All ER 488 and *Thake* v. *Maurice* [1986] QB 644, in both of which cases it was held that sterilization procedures carried out by doctors did not carry any warranty of success or irreversibility, and courts should be slow to interpret anything said by a doctor as amounting to such a warranty.

and unforeseeable developments occurring without anybody's fault, the courts have been loath to hold a contracting party liable, especially in the latter case. In other words, the law does not usually treat a person who has contracted to do something as having taken the risk that the whole performance may prove utterly impossible, either initially or owing to later events.

But impossibility is too narrow a concept to explain all the decisions which the courts have made in this area. For cases occur in which the performance of the promise is not necessarily impossible, but yet in which it would seem excessively hard on one of the parties to compel performance or hold him liable in damages. Sometimes this is the result of pre-existing facts which were unknown to the parties, sometimes it is the result of subsequent events which were not expected or foreseen by the parties. In the former case the problem is said to be whether the contract is void for 'common mistake'. In the latter case the problem is whether the contract is 'frustrated'. The discussion of the two problems is usually separated in law books, and all cases of mistake are often lumped together in one section while frustration is dealt with in a later chapter on discharge. Yet the different types of mistake often have little or nothing in common. And although frustration is certainly one of the ways of discharging a contract, the doctrine of frustration has the equally important function of defining the scope and extent of contractual obligations. Hence, these two problems are dealt with in the ensuing sections of this chapter.

## 2. COMMON MISTAKE AND PRE-EXISTING FACTS

The question to be discussed here is to what extent the validity of a contract is affected by a common[11] but mistaken belief held by the parties at the commencement of the contract. This belief may frequently, but not necessarily, be that the contract is capable of performance, when in fact it is not. The rule is usually stated to be that the contract is void if the mistake is sufficiently fundamental or basic. This is a common, though somewhat dangerous, way of stating the law: it is dangerous in particular because many fundamental mistakes are actually at the risk of one or other of the parties and, where that is the case, the mistake will not render the contract void. Putting the point the other way, the risk of the facts turning out differently may be allocated by express or implied terms of the contract, or even by other clear rules of contract law, and once it has been decided that certain risks lie on a party there is no room for him to argue that the contract should be rescinded for mistake.

In practice, it will be found that mistakes are rarely regarded as

[11] Cases of 'common mistake' are more usually, but less grammatically, referred to in older cases as 'mutual mistake'.

sufficiently fundamental or basic to invalidate a contract, perhaps partly because the courts feel that one or other of the parties could have discovered the pre-existing facts, and partly because the courts dislike holding apparent contracts to be inoperative. This is particularly the case where the contract has been partly performed because serious practical difficulties can arise in adjusting the rights of the parties if the contract is then held to be void or inoperative. So also, where third parties have become involved it may be particularly undesirable to hold a contract to be void or inoperative.

However, it does sometimes happen that both parties enter into a contract on the clear understanding that it is only to operate if certain assumptions are correct, and in particular on the assumption that the contract is, initially at least, capable of performance. For example, a sale of some specific chattel is normally based on the assumption that the chattel exists, and this assumption is, in many cases at least, fundamental to the operation of the contract. Moreover, there are certainly some cases in which the seller is not responsible for this state of facts—so if there is an implied term that the goods exist, that term will be a condition precedent and not a promise by the seller. So if it should prove that the goods do not exist at the date of the contract, it may be held to be void or inoperative.

This is what happened in the famous case of *Couturier* v. *Hastie*,[12] where the seller sold a cargo of corn which the parties believed to be on its way to England, but which had in fact become overheated and been sold by the master of the ship *en route*. The House of Lords held that the buyer was not liable to pay the price of the cargo, and it is generally assumed (although it was not decided) that the seller likewise would not have been liable for damages if the buyer had suffered some loss from non-delivery. Thus the contract in this case is usually stated to have been void. This is a doubtful conclusion, but even if correct it is not a universal rule that a sale of perished or non-existent goods is void for mistake. In traditional language, the question depends on the true construction of the contract. One possible construction involves implying a condition precedent that, if the goods do not exist, the contract should be void. But there are two other possible constructions to choose from. The court may conclude that the seller was impliedly promising that the goods existed, so that if they did not exist, he would be liable to pay damages for affirming a state of facts which was not true. On the other hand, it is also possible that the buyer might have taken the risk of the goods having perished or been disposed of (for example, because he expected to receive the insurance proceeds), in which case he would be bound to pay the price even if the goods had ceased to exist.

---

[12] (1856) 5 HLC 673.

Now, as we have seen, the courts tend to base implied conditions on the presumed intentions of the parties, but rather than search around for what is probably a non-existent intention, it would seem preferable to put the matter as follows. Where both parties enter into a contract in the belief that certain assumed facts are true, and it turns out that they are not true, the question is, which of the parties bears the risk that the facts are not as they were thought to be? This question can be sub-divided into two further questions. First, has either party expressly assumed that risk by accepting the responsibility for the truth of the assumed facts; and secondly, if not, is it reasonable to treat one of the parties (and which one?) as having taken the risk of the facts turning out otherwise than as expected? If neither party has assumed this responsibility, and if the court does not feel it reasonable to treat either party as having the risk solely imposed on him, the falsity of the assumption will render the whole contract void or inoperative. But this is an unlikely eventuality, and if it is clear (as it usually will be) that one party was accepting the responsibility for the facts assumed to be true, or that it is reasonable to treat that party as having accepted that responsibility, then the contract will not be void. And this may be so whether the initial impossibility is due to the facts or the law. So, for instance, where a person sold to another a shipwrecked tanker stated to be on a certain reef, it was held by the High Court of Australia that the existence of the tanker was not an implied condition precedent to the operation of the contract.[13] On the contrary, it was a promissory representation or an undertaking, and, as the tanker did not in fact exist, the seller was liable for having broken his promise that it did exist. Manifestly, the seller had impliedly accepted responsibility for the existence of the tanker, and the plaintiffs would certainly not have agreed to any terms which would have had the effect of rendering the whole contract inoperative, and leaving themselves without any remedy, if the ship did not exist.

Had the facts of *Couturier* v. *Hastie* occurred in modern times the result in that case might well have been that the seller would have been liable for contracting to sell goods which did not exist. In fact the contract in *Couturier* v. *Hastie* was not held void or inoperative, for the simple reason that this question did not strictly arise. The decision is perfectly consistent with the possibility that the seller promised that the goods existed, but as the buyer did not claim damages for breach of this promise it was unnecessary to decide this point. It is true that in 1856, before the days of modern methods of communication, it might have been reasonable to hold that a seller did not undertake that the goods existed, especially when, as in that case, the goods were on their way to England by sea. But today a seller

---

[13] *McRae* v. *Commonwealth Disposals Commission* (1950) 84 CLR 377.

who sells goods in such circumstances would probably be to blame for not knowing what had happened, unless perhaps there had not been sufficient time for the information to reach him. Unfortunately, section 6 of the Sale of Goods Act (now the Act of 1979) has fixed the law in the state in which it was believed to have been left by *Couturier* v. *Hastie* with the result that, even today, a seller of goods cannot prima facie be held to contract that they exist. In view of the revolution in methods of communication which has taken place since 1856, section 6 now appears to be based on an anachronism. At the present day it would accord better with principle to hold that a seller of specific goods normally undertakes, or promises, that they exist, for the simple reason that he should know whether they exist or not.

Cases concerning the sale of perished or non-existent goods are not very common in the modern world, but the underlying problem still occasionally surfaces. In *Associated Japanese Bank* v. *Crédit du Nord SA*[14] one JB entered into a sale and leaseback transaction with the plaintiffs, under which he sold four large machines to them for over one million pounds, and they leased the machines back to him. Commercially such a transaction is not unusual—it is simply a way of raising money, rather like a mortgage of goods. But what was unusual in this case was that the four machines did not exist at all, and the whole arrangement was a fraud by JB. However (as commonly happens in such cases), the fraudulent party was unable to repay the money when the fraud was discovered, and the plaintiffs sued the defendants who had guaranteed the performance of JB's obligations under the leaseback transaction. The defendants argued that their guarantee was void because they and the plaintiffs had supposed that the whole arrangement was about four specific machines which did not exist and, consequently, the guarantee imposed wholly different risks on the defendants from those they thought they were undertaking. Of course, as between JB and the plaintiffs there could hardly be any doubt that JB was actually warranting the existence of the machines, just as in the *McRae* case, the sellers were held to have contracted that the supposed shipwrecked oil tanker existed. But the guarantors were not in the same position as JB, and there was no reason to hold that they were expressly warranting the existence of the machines. Was it then reasonable to impose on them the risk that they did not exist? Steyn J held that it was not, and that the contract was void because of the mistake. The risk which the defendants thought they were undertaking was totally different from that which would be imposed on them if it was held that their guarantee was binding in the events as they were.

It has already been said that it is rare for common mistake to render a

---

[14] [1988] 3 All ER 902.

contract void, or in other words that implied conditions precedent of this kind are unusual. This is especially so as regards mistakes as to quality in contracts of sale of goods, and it may well be that the ground in such contracts is so well covered by the terms implied by the Sale of Goods Act that there is little room for any implied conditions precedent in such cases, except for the one case covered by section 6, that is, where the goods have perished. Where the question is as to the quality or fitness of the goods for any particular purpose, there are really only two alternatives. Either the terms implied by the Act apply, in which case the seller is responsible for the state of the goods, or the terms are excluded (or satisfied), in which case the natural inference is that the buyer takes upon himself that responsibility, that is, he accepts the risk of the goods proving defective or unsuitable. For a buyer to argue that a contract of sale of goods is void for mistake about the quality or fitness of the goods is, in effect, to attempt to add new conditions to those already implied in his favour by the Sale of Goods Act. Since these are now very extensive, very favourable to the buyer, and, at least in consumer sales, non-excludable, there will rarely be any room for a buyer to invoke arguments based on mistake.

The position of the seller may be rather different. A seller has no implied terms to protect him under the Sale of Goods Act, no doubt because most sellers are business sellers who are assumed to be able to look after their own interests. But not all sellers are businessmen. Individuals sometimes sell goods, and they occasionally sell them to dealers, for example, second-hand cars, antiques, or farm produce. An individual seller may sell something for very much less than its true value because the parties are mistaken as to its nature or qualities, and he will have no remedy under the Sale of Goods Act. It is in this sort of situation that a court might be expected to invoke the idea of fundamental mistake, as an American court did in the famous case of *Sherwood* v. *Walker*.[15] In this case a cow was sold for $80 because it was believed by both parties to be barren; in fact it was already with calf and its true value was about ten times the agreed price. The contract was held to be void, although there was some difficulty about the result because the buyer attempted to argue that he had not ruled out the possibility that the cow could be got to breed.

It is not surprising that the courts are reluctant to hold that a contract is void for mistake, or on the ground that it depends for its operation on some implied condition. It is one thing to imply a promise *in* a contract; it is quite another thing to imply a condition precedent which makes the whole contract void or inoperative. This is a drastic proceeding which would threaten the sanctity of contracts if it could be invoked whenever a party claimed that he (or even both parties) had made a serious mistake. This is

---

[15] (1887) 33 NW 919.

one reason common mistake operates much less frequently than the doctrine of frustration, for in the latter case there is no question of declaring the contract void or inoperative from the outset. Frustration (as we shall see) dissolves a contract but not retrospectively. Another reason common mistake applies so rarely is that the courts are less reluctant to hold a party liable where the contract proves initially impossible, because it is not unreasonable to hold that a person should not enter into a contract unless he is able to perform it, or, in other words, that, prima facie, a person who contracts to do something takes the risk that performance may prove difficult or even impossible in the circumstances existing at the date of the contract. The position is otherwise when the court is dealing with subsequent events. Here the reasonable and just solution is more likely to be to declare the contract dissolved because it is unreasonable to insist that a person impliedly undertakes, not merely that he can perform in the circumstances at the date of the contract but that he will continue to be able to perform, no matter what cataclysms the future may bring. Thus the courts will more readily place on a person responsibility for a state of facts necessary for the commencement of the contract than for its continuance in circumstances which it is impossible to foresee, although that does not mean that even the doctrine of frustration can be lightly prayed in aid.

A contract which turns out to be quite impossible to perform is so dramatically different from the contract the parties had in mind that impossibility seems to be a special legal category of its own. But it would be wrong to think that these are the only types of case which can be dealt with as matters of 'mistake' or 'construction'. Wherever the facts existing at the date of the contract turn out to be different from what the parties thought, questions may arise as to the liabilities of the parties. These questions are usually dealt with as questions of construction, and implied conditions, although occasionally they are treated as involving an independent 'doctrine' of mistake.

For instance, in the famous case of *Bell* v. *Lever Bros*[16] the defendant was manager of a large company under a contract which still had some years to run. Although he had rendered very valuable services to the company, they wanted to reorganize their business in such a way that they had no further use for him. They therefore paid him £30,000 for loss of office though this was substantially more than he would have earned even if he had worked his contract out to the end. It was then discovered that the defendant had been guilty of certain minor breaches of his contract which would have justified his dismissal without any compensation. It was held nevertheless that the plaintiffs could not recover the £30,000. The case was largely discussed in terms of 'mistake'. Was the 'mistake' sufficiently

---

[16] [1932] AC 161.

fundamental to make the compensation agreement void? The decision has been much criticized, but most of the criticism overlooks the all-important fact that the compensation was partly a reward for the value of the services rendered which were in no way affected by the defendant's technical breaches of his contract.

There has been much controversy about what this famous case is authority for. It is perhaps difficult to go beyond saying that it stands for the rather vague principle that a common mistake may render a contract void if the mistake was sufficiently fundamental. If it should then be asked which kinds of mistake are sufficiently fundamental, the answer tends to take the form of illustrations, rather than of further elaboration of the principle. But in the *Associated Japanese Bank* case[17] Steyn J suggested that a mistake is sufficiently fundamental for this purpose if it renders the subject-matter of the contract essentially and radically different from what it was believed to be. This is (as we shall see) the accepted modern test applicable to frustration cases, and though the application of the same test in the two areas may not always produce identical results for reasons which have already been given, it makes good sense to equate the two tests. But it must be realized that the application of such tests is never simple or mechanical, because all tests of this kind tend to be somewhat vacuous in practice.

A case apparently similar to *Bell* v. *Lever Bros* which was decided differently is *Magee* v. *Pennine Insurance, Ltd.*[18] In this case the plaintiff's car was destroyed in an accident and the defendant insurance company agreed to pay him £385 as representing the value of the car. But before the money was paid the insurance company discovered certain misrepresentations in the application for insurance which would have justified them in repudiating the policy altogether. The question was whether the agreement to pay £385 was vitiated by this fact. By a majority the Court of Appeal held that it was.

As in the analogous question of frustration, there has been much controversy over the juridical nature of the question involved in these mistake cases. Do they, for instance, depend on implied conditions, or on a separate doctrine of mistake? This is, in the last analysis, a question of judicial technique, and not one of substance. It thus seems odd to hold (as was done in the *Associated Japanese Bank* case) that there was an implied condition precedent (implied in accordance with the *Moorcock* principle) that the machines existed, and *also* that the contract was independently void for mistake at common law. This is to give two identical reasons for the decision, albeit with different labels. The only issue of substance in this sort of situation is whether the parties accept (or ought to have imposed

[17] *Supra*, n. 14.     [18] [1969] 2 QB 507.

upon them) the risk of the facts being as they actually were (the service contract being invalid in *Bell* v. *Lever Bros*, the insurance policy being voidable in *Magee* v. *Pennine Insurance*, the machines being non-existent in the *Associated Japanese Bank* case). Undoubtedly the possibility of pre-existing facts turning out to be different from what the parties had supposed is normally a risk which the parties assume. In *Magee's* case, for instance, the parties clearly took the risk of the destroyed car being more or less valuable than £385. The insurers took the risk that it might have been worth less; the plaintiff took the risk that it might have been worth more. But the question in these cases is whether the facts are so different from what the parties had supposed that it would be unreasonable or unjust to regard them as having accepted those risks. Sometimes this is indeed so, but it must be remembered that whenever an apparent contract is held void the fundamental objectives of contract law (e.g. the protection of reasonable expectations, or reasonable reliance) are being set aside. So the courts must weigh the injustice involved in disappointing reasonable expectations or reliance against any injustice involved in imposing on a party risks entirely different from those which he thought he was assuming. In performing this exercise, two very general considerations appear to influence the courts.

The first is that they start with a strong general disinclination to hold a contract void because of some unknown pre-existing facts, because as a rule pre-existing facts could have been discovered by the parties. In the *Magee* case, for instance, the insurance company could have satisfied itself of the validity of the policy before agreeing to pay anything; or it could have agreed to pay but made its agreement expressly subject to the validity of the policy. Insurance companies are not usually slow to make express stipulations where they feel these are necessary for their protection. Accordingly, the decision may be thought to be unsatisfactory. But the second broad consideration relevant to the weighing exercise mentioned above is that the courts may be *less* inclined to hold a contract void once performance has begun and acts of reliance have taken place. The injustice of imposing on a party risks entirely different from those he had intended to assume may thus outweigh the injustice of disregarding a mere expectation where it would not outweigh serious acts of reliance. Perhaps the decisive distinction between the *Magee* case and *Bell* v. *Lever Bros* was that in the former case the money had not yet been paid, while in the latter it had been paid. Traditional legal reasoning would reject this as a relevant distinction, and there is no reference to it in the *Magee* case itself. But it does not seem unreasonable to treat the actual payment of money in this kind of case as finally settling certain issues, such as whether the payer was under any liability at all. Certainly it seems clear that less injustice was done in disappointing Mr Magee's expectations than would have been done if Mr Bell had actually had to *repay* the £30,000 after it had been paid to him and perhaps spent.

A point which is in some ways parallel to the *Magee* case arose in *Harvela Investments Ltd* v. *Royal Trust Co of Canada*[19] which has already been discussed in another context. In this case, it will be remembered, the seller of some shares had invited sealed bids from two buyers, A and B. A's bid was later held invalid by the House of Lords, but when the bids were first opened it was thought by the seller and A that the bid was good, and it was therefore 'accepted' by the seller. It was held that this 'acceptance' did not create any valid contract in itself: if A's bid was valid, then this second 'acceptance' was unnecessary, while if A's bid was (as it turned out) invalid, then it was simply 'unthinkable' that it would create a separate contract. And the reason it was unthinkable was that all parties knew that, if A's bid was invalid, the seller would be bound to sell the shares to B. So it could be said that the seller's acceptance of A's invalid bid was either void for mistake or based on the implied condition that the bid was valid. The decision on this point is plainly incontestable.

As we have seen, the cases raising issues dealt with by the law under the heading of common mistake or, sometimes, as matters involving implied conditions, are, in the last analysis, risk-allocation questions. Which party is to be treated as having assumed which risks? It is now necessary to note that the allocation of risks is sometimes a relative business. A may be treated as having assumed a risk as against B, but as between A and C the risk may be placed on C. This possibility is well illustrated by some recent decisions concerning the sale of shares at a valuation.[20] Suppose A contracts to sell to B certain shares at a price to be fixed by an independent valuer, say an accountant. Suppose also that the valuer grossly undervalues the shares so that, if the contract between A and B is carried out, A will only receive a small fraction of their true value. As between A and B the question is whether the parties have assumed, or must be treated as having assumed, the risk of a serious mistake on the part of the valuer. In general, the answer to that is clearly, yes, though in an extreme case the mistake may show that the valuer did not really comply with his instructions, in which case the valuation would not be within the contemplation of the contract, and so not binding.[21]

But, whatever the position may be as between the parties themselves, the position as between them and the valuer may well be different. If the valuer is a professional person, being paid for his valuation as an ordinary

---

[19] [1986] AC 207; see *supra*, 212.
[20] *Campbell* v. *Edwards* [1976] 1 WLR 403; *Baber* v. *Kenwood Manufacturing* [1978] 1 Lloyd's Rep. 175.
[21] *Jones* v. *Sherwood Computer Services plc* [1992] 1 WLR 277.

professional service, he normally owes the parties a legal duty of care. So if he grossly undervalues the shares, the seller may be bound to sell them to the buyer at that price, but may also be entitled to be recouped the amount of his loss from the valuer himself. In other words, he may have a right of action against the valuer for negligence so that the risk of the valuer's negligence, as between him and the parties to the sale contract, is on him and not them.

*Mistake in Equity*

As we noted above, the decision in *Bell* v. *Lever Bros* has long been controversial, and one of the chief controversies arising from the case is whether there is any difference between common law and equitable principles in this area of the law. On one view *Bell* v. *Lever Bros* was a decision at common law alone, and did not involve any equitable principles, so that it is theoretically arguable that the case might have been differently decided in equity. This is undoubtedly a bold suggestion, because the House of Lords does not usually overlook such a simple matter as the difference between common law and equity, but there has been a slender stream of authority to support this view since it was first proposed by Lord Denning.[22] It has also gained the support of the High Court of Australia,[23] whose views on such matters are usually given great weight by English courts. But it is not entirely clear what the role of equity is supposed to be, especially if the common law is as flexible and as reasonable as has been suggested above. The supporters of an equitable jurisdiction appear to think that the common law is unjust in refusing to hold certain contracts to be void for mistake, because the applicable test as to whether a mistake was sufficiently fundamental is too narrow. But according to the view put forward above the question is always at bottom (in the absence of an express allocation of risks) how risks ought *reasonably* to be allocated. If that view is right, then it is difficult to see what role there can be for equity in this area: it could hardly be supposed that equity would require risks to be allocated in an *unreasonable* manner.

The truth seems to be that some lawyers find the common law allocation of risks hard in certain cases, because parties may be landed with risks that they did not contemplate, even though the difference between the facts as supposed and the facts as they were is not so great as to justify declaring the contract to be void. The owner of a house, for instance, contracts to sell

---

[22] For Lord Denning's views, see *Solle* v. *Butcher* [1950] 1 KB 671, and the *Magee* case, *supra*, n. 18. Other cases supporting this view include *Grist* v. *Bailey* [1967] Ch. 532 and the *Associated Japanese Bank* case, *supra*, n. 14. Differing opinions were expressed in the CA in *Sindall (William) PLC* v. *Cambridgeshire CC* [1994] 3 All ER 932, Hoffman LJ taking a view very close to that stated in the text, while Evans LJ was prepared to concede a wider role for equity.     [23] *Taylor* v. *Johnson* (1983) 45 ALR 265.

it for a low price because he thinks the occupant is a protected tenant under the Rent Acts, and it turns out that both he and the buyer were mistaken, so the house is worth much more than the price. It seems hard if the seller is unable to get out of his bargain, particularly, perhaps, if the contract is executory and the mistake is speedily discovered so that it would be easy to undo the transaction. But it is dangerous to relax the rules as to risk-allocation too readily. In this sort of case, for instance, there are standard conveyancing procedures which mean that plenty of time is available to the parties and their solicitors to examine the status of a tenant. If those procedures have for some reason failed to work properly in the instant case, the better solution may be to uphold the contract but (perhaps) to enable the seller to sue his solicitor for negligence.

Nevertheless, it must be admitted that there may be cases, especially, perhaps exclusively, where the contract is wholly executory, where the usual allocation of risks may not appear just. This does not require us to commit the absurdity of suggesting that a reasonable allocation of risks may be unjust, but it requires us to recognize that there may be special reasons, especially with executory contracts, why the usual way of allocating risks is unreasonable. If that is recognized there would not seem any reason to invoke a separate equitable jurisdiction in this area of the law.

### 3. FRUSTRATION AND SUBSEQUENT OCCURRENCES

As we saw in the last section, parties sometimes contract on the basis of certain assumptions which turn out to be unfounded because the pre-existing facts were different from those which they had assumed. The same can and does happen with respect to subsequent events which may also turn out rather differently from what the parties had anticipated. So here, too, it may be necessary to decide who has assumed, or who is to be treated as having assumed, the risk of the events turning out in this way. Here also there has been a tendency to treat questions of impossibility as falling into a special legal category. Just as a contract may turn out to be impossible to perform because of some pre-existing facts, so also may it turn out impossible because of some unexpected development in the future. In the former case, the traditional legal approach (as we saw earlier) is to put the case under the common mistake heading, and ask whether the mistake was sufficiently fundamental to invalidate the contract. We saw, however, that these cases could also be dealt with by other techniques, for instance, by treating them as raising questions of construction, but that the substantive issues raised ought to be distinguished from the legal techniques adopted to deal with them. Very much the same could be said with regard to subsequent events. Here, too, there has been a tendency to separate off questions of subsequent impossibility and to put them in a doctrine of their own, called the doctrine of 'frustration'. But other changes in the facts affecting the performance of a contract tend to be treated as raising straightforward issues of construction, and are not regarded as involving the doctrine of frustration. To take a simple example which has been referred to before, the *South Staffordshire Waterworks*[24] case raised the question whether a contract to supply water was affected by a fifteen-fold increase in costs over a fifty-year period. Strictly speaking, all that the court decided in this case was that the contract was terminable on reasonable notice, but the effect of that holding was to throw on to the buyers the risk of increases in costs as from the expiry of a period of reasonable notice.

In principle there is no essential distinction between cases of frustration and other cases involving the allocation of risks of subsequent events. The only real justification for separating off cases of impossibility is that there is an established body of case law here which enables one to say with some confidence that a promisor does not normally assume the risk of total subsequent impossibility simply by making a promise as part of a contract. In other cases, the effect of subsequent events tends to be treated very much more as a matter for the construction of the particular contract and less as something falling under any general rule.

The differences between the cases as to pre-existing facts and those as to subsequent facts is blurred, because in some situations it may not be wholly clear whether the relevant facts are indeed pre-existing or subsequent. For example, in some of the cases which arose out of the postponement of the coronation of Edward VII (the 'coronation cases') the contract was made very shortly before the official announcement was made that the coronation was being postponed. But in some of these cases the fact that the King had become seriously ill was itself a pre-existing fact, and the parties who were contracting for the services in question were ignorant of that fact. Some of these cases were dealt with as cases of pre-existing facts, raising the question of common mistake, and some as cases of subsequent facts, raising issues of frustration. Some cases could perfectly well have been treated as falling into either category. A similar situation arose more recently in *Amalgamated Investment & Property Co* v. *John Walker & Sons*[25] where a contract was made to buy a property for redevelopment at a very substantial price, and unknown to the parties the appropriate authorities were already considering 'listing' the building, which rendered redevelopment impossible. The result was that the property was very much less valuable, but it was unclear precisely when the internal decision of the authorities had effectively been made. The decision was not officially

---

[24] [1979] 1 WLR 203.    [25] [1977] 1 WLR 164.

communicated until after the contract was made, and it was eventually held that the case ought therefore to be treated as a frustration case and not as one of common mistake. In fact, however, it was held that there was no frustration because in contracts of this kind the buyer must be prepared to accept the risk of listing as from the date of the contract. In cases of this nature, it may seem strange and unreal if the legal result varies according to whether the risk is seen as arising from pre-existing or subsequent facts.

We proceed to consider in greater detail the nature of the doctrine of frustration.

### Frustration through impossibility of performance

Where the entire performance of a contract becomes substantially impossible without any fault on either side, the contract is prima facie dissolved by the doctrine of frustration. For instance, where a person contracted to let a hall to the plaintiff for use for some concerts, and the hall was accidentally destroyed by fire before the date of the first concert, it was held that the contract was dissolved.[26] So also, a contract of personal service will normally be dissolved by the death or prolonged illness[27] or (at any rate in some cases) the imprisonment of the employee.[28] Similarly, where a ship is chartered for a particular voyage but she is unable to arrive at the required port owing to some disaster at sea, the whole contract is dissolved.[29] Again, a contract for the charter of a ship for a certain time will be frustrated if the ship is requisitioned by governmental authorities acting under statutory powers, at all events where the requisitioning is likely to continue for such a length of time that the substance of the contract is removed.[30]

The position is more difficult where the contract is one of long duration and the performance is merely interrupted and not actually prevented in full. In these cases the contract is prima facie dissolved if the interruption is likely to prove so lengthy that to compel the parties to resume the contract later would, in effect, be to compel them to enter into a new contract. So, for instance, a contract for the construction of a reservoir, which was scheduled to take six years, was held frustrated when, after less than two years, all further work was temporarily prohibited owing to wartime restrictions. As it was impossible to foresee how long these restrictions

---

[26] *Taylor* v. *Caldwell* (1863) 3 B & S 826.

[27] *Notcutt* v. *Universal Equipment Co (London) Ltd* [1986] 1 WLR 641.

[28] *F. C. Shepherd & Co Ltd* v. *Jerrom* [1986] 3 All ER 589. The reason for the qualifying words in brackets is that an employee may be arrested and charged with an offence, but may be released on bail, in which case there is no urgency about deciding what is to happen to his contract of employment.

[29] *Jackson* v. *Union Marine Insurance Co* (1874) LR 10 CP 125.

[30] *Bank Line* v. *Arthur Capel Ltd* [1919] AC 435.

might last, it was unreasonable to hold the parties to the contract when it was at least certain that the conditions would be quite different after the end of the war. The real principle behind these cases of delay or interruption in performance is that 'businessmen must not be left in indefinite suspense',[31] and for this reason the courts are not inclined to be wise after the event, and say that the parties should have realized that the interruption was only a temporary measure which would not seriously interfere with the contract. On the other hand, where the interruption, even on the most pessimistic view, is unlikely to affect more than a small fraction of the contract, it is not frustrated. For instance, in *Cricklewood Property Trusts, Ltd* v. *Leighton's Investment Trust*,[32] a building lease for ninety-nine years was held not frustrated merely because building on the land (which was the object of the contract) was prevented by wartime restrictions. There was no reasonable likelihood of these restrictions continuing for more than a fraction of the duration of the lease, and the contract therefore remained binding.

A similar problem occurs when the performance of the contract becomes not impossible, but illegal, after its creation. In these cases, again, prima facie the contract will be dissolved by such a change in the law because 'there cannot be default in not doing what the law forbids to be done'.[33] So, for instance, where a person sold land and covenanted that no buildings would be erected on adjacent lands retained by him, it was held that he could not be sued for breach of the covenant when a railway company, acting under statutory powers, compulsorily acquired the land from him and built a railway station on it.

### Frustration of the common venture

The application of the doctrine of frustration becomes more difficult when what has been prevented is not the actual performance of the contract but the ultimate purpose or venture. If the contract is to be held frustrated it is obvious that 'it is the common object that has to be frustrated, not merely the individual advantage that one party or the other might have gained from the contract'.[34] For instance, if a person buys a specific chattel, and after the contract is fully executed the chattel is accidentally destroyed, there can obviously be no question of frustration. The chattel belonged to the buyer and it was at his risk: *res perit domino* (the loss of something falls

---

[31] *Per* Lord Wright in *Denny, Mott & Dickson* v. *Fraser* [1944] AC 265 at 278.
[32] [1945] AC 221.
[33] *Per* Lord Macmillan in *Denny, Mott & Dickson* v. *Fraser, supra*, n. 31. A person may, however, contract in such a way as to take the risk even of supervening illegality if the intent is clear enough.
[34] *Per* Lord Sumner in *Hirji Mulji* v. *Cheong Yue SS Co* [1926] AC 497 at 507.

on the owner). The buyer cannot show that the object *of the contract* has been frustrated, even though *his* object may have been frustrated.

Similarly, where a person buys something for a specific purpose which proves impossible of fulfilment, it is no concern of the seller for what purpose the buyer bought the goods, and the failure of this purpose will not normally affect the contract. The seller is, indeed, concerned with the purpose for which the buyer requires the goods in the sense that he may be under a legal duty to ensure that the goods are fit for that purpose under the terms implied by the Sale of Goods Act. But the seller is not concerned with the purpose for which the buyer requires the goods in so far as that purpose is unknown to the seller or depends on facts outside his control. Thus, if the buyer contracts to buy machinery for his factory there may well be an implied term that the machinery will be suitable for use in the buyer's factory. But if the factory should happen to be accidentally destroyed before the machinery is delivered, this will not affect the contract, because it is no concern of the seller what the buyer proposes to do with the machinery once it is established that it is fit for the purpose for which it was sold.

Just as normally it is no concern of a seller what the buyer proposes to do with the goods, so also it is normally no concern of the buyer where or how the seller expects to procure the goods to be sold. Hence, in a contract for the sale of unascertained goods, e.g. 100 tons of corn or the like (but not some specific chattel), the fact that the seller is unable to procure any goods does not normally excuse him from non-delivery, although it may do so in exceptional circumstances. On the other hand, an agreement to sell some specific chattel is normally frustrated if the goods are accidentally destroyed before the risk has passed to the buyer; indeed, this is expressly provided by section 7 of the Sale of Goods Act 1979.

There are a number of situations in which it is not easy to distinguish between the common object of both parties and the individual motives of each party. Most of these cases involve contracts of hire or leases, and it seems no coincidence that nearly all the difficult cases on the law of frustration involve facts of this kind. For in a contract of hire or lease, both parties may make a plausible case for their claims. The owner of the thing hired or leased may say, in effect, 'What you do with the thing (or land) is no concern of mine; all I want is the rent. If you are unable to use the thing (or land) for the purpose for which you wanted it that is your misfortune, not mine'. On the other hand, the hirer may say that, where his object in hiring the thing is well known to the owner, the use of the thing is the common object of both parties and its prevention frustrates the contract. Broadly speaking the attitude of the law to these opposing viewpoints is a compromise. The courts have taken the view that, provided the hirer can use the thing or land for *some* purpose (or perhaps for some purpose envisaged by the contract), it is immaterial that he cannot use it for the particular purpose that he had in mind. Hence, if the thing is destroyed or requisitioned, the contract is prima facie frustrated. But where the thing may still be used for some purpose, although not the purpose for which it was required, the contract stands. So, for instance, in a case in 1916 it was held that a lease of a flat was not frustrated merely because the tenant was an enemy alien and was unable to occupy the flat himself owing to war-time restrictions.[35] The tenant could still use the flat for other purposes, such as subletting; moreover, in a lease alternative uses are, in a sense, always envisaged by the contract precisely because the lessee can use the property how he pleases. Again, in one of the famous 'coronation cases' the defendant had agreed to hire a ship for the purpose of viewing the naval review by King Edward VII and for a day's cruise round the fleet, and it was held that the contract was not frustrated by the cancellation of the naval review owing to the King's illness.[36] The day's cruise round the fleet was still possible, and, indeed, the ship could have been used for many other purposes.

On the other hand, in *Krell* v. *Henry*[37] the same Court of Appeal held that a contract for the use of a flat to view the coronation procession on two successive days was frustrated by the cancellation of the coronation. This decision is a borderline one, and it has been said that 'the authority is not one to be extended'.[38] But it may, perhaps, be justified on the ground that, where the owner is aware of the purpose for which a person hires something, and where he well knows that the thing would certainly not be hired for any other purpose and would in fact be useless for any other purpose, and where the price is grossly inflated because of the special use contemplated, then it is reasonable to say that this use is the common object of both parties, and not merely the motive of the hirer. Gross inflation of the price is often akin to a form of insurance, and may be an indication that special risks are being assumed. But the mere fact that the owner is aware of the hirer's motives in hiring the thing does not necessarily mean that the contract is frustrated because the purpose becomes incapable of fulfilment.

If the owner of goods is not normally concerned with the purpose for

---

[35] *London & Northern Estates* v. *Schlesinger* [1916] 1 KB 20.
[36] *Herne Bay Steamboat Co* v. *Hutton* [1903] 2 KB 683.
[37] [1903] 2 KB 740.
[38] *Per* Lord Wright in *Maritime National Fish Co* v. *Ocean Trawlers* [1935] AC 524 at 529. Surprisingly, the argument does not seem to have occurred to counsel or the court (or to many later commentators) that it might seem unjust if the landlord were able to retain the large windfall profit paid by the defendant, and then make a similar windfall when the coronation was eventually held. (But in fact when the coronation was held the procession was much curtailed, and it is not known whether the procession did still pass within view of the landlord's windows.)

which they are hired, the position is even stronger in the case of a lease. A lease, unlike a contract of hire, confers proprietary rights on the tenant; in technical language, it confers an 'estate' in the land, and in some respects a lease, and especially a long lease, is therefore more analogous to a contract of sale than to a contract of hire. Hence, it may be reasonable to hold that a tenant, like a buyer, takes the risk of anything happening to the land or premises leased for the duration of the lease. If the house leased is burned down, the owner loses his house for all time after the expiry of the lease, so why should not the tenant be the loser for the duration of the lease? Of course this would mean that he would be bound to continue paying the rent even though the house had been burnt down, and this may seem an unfair and unacceptable result, but it must be remembered that houses are usually insured and, in the case of a long lease, there will often be a clause requiring the premises to be rebuilt.

In fact, for these and similar reasons it was for a long time doubtful whether the doctrine of frustration could ever apply to a lease at all. But the House of Lords have now decided[39] that there is no reason of principle why frustration should never apply to a lease, though they also made it clear that this will only occur in quite exceptional circumstances, for example on a short-term letting of a holiday home. Perhaps, indeed, a short-term lease, such as a weekly or monthly lease, where there is no security of tenure is in rather a special category, since it is unlikely that the parties would envisage re-establishing relations if the premises were totally destroyed in such a case.

In other cases it may be suggested that a lease will be frustrated only in circumstances in which it is perfectly clear that the object of both parties has been defeated. Normally, this will not be the case, no matter what happens to the premises, for land cannot be physically destroyed and the precise use to which the land is put is no concern of the owner so long as it can be used for something. But where the owner is vitally interested in the proposed use of the land, frustration may occur if, for instance, building is totally prohibited for the duration of the lease by some new and unexpected development. Of course, such prohibition is today common enough under *existing* planning regulations, but a tenant is expected to inquire about the planning position before he takes a lease, and nobody could claim that a lease had been frustrated merely because planning permission was refused for some use which the tenant had in mind.

Frustration must obviously be distinguished from breach of contract by one party or the other, but there are cases where the distinction is not always easy to draw. If the performance of the contract is rendered impossible by the fault of either party, then that party is guilty of breach of

---

[39] *National Carriers Ltd v. Panalpina (Northern) Ltd* [1981] AC 675.

contract and will have to pay damages to the other party. 'The essence of "frustration" is that it should not be due to the act or election of the party'.[40] This is sometimes expressed by saying that a 'self-induced frustration' cannot be relied on, but this is a somewhat misleading term. In fact a self-induced frustration is not frustration at all, but breach of contract. In practice, however, it is not always easy to draw the line between genuine frustration and breach, because it is not entirely clear what meaning is to be given to 'fault' in this connection. Certainly it includes deliberate action which prevents the performance of the contract, and equally certainly it will often include the negligent destruction of, or damage to, property without which the contract cannot be performed. It is not, however, settled whether a person who, through his own carelessness, becomes ill can plead that a contract requiring his personal services is frustrated.[41]

### Juridical basis of the doctrine of frustration

It is tempting to think that, when a contract is held to be frustrated because of impossibility of performance, the law is merely recognizing the inevitable. How, it may be wondered, can a person be legally obliged to do what is impossible? But, as in the analogous case of mistake, this is not an inevitable result. Apart from the fact that this argument anyhow does not explain cases of frustration of the common venture, it is perfectly possible for the law to impose duties which cannot be performed. Indeed, people often impose duties on themselves, through contract, which cannot be performed. The result is quite simply that damages must be paid in lieu of performance.

In principle it is plain that, when a claim is made that a contract is frustrated, there are really three legal possibilities. To take a simple example, suppose that A charters a ship from B and that, before the ship is delivered, it is requisitioned by government authorities. Prima facie the contract is frustrated with the result that both parties are discharged from their obligations. But there are two other alternative results which the law might, and sometimes does, adopt. The law might say that A has contracted to pay rent for B's ship, and that he must pay this rent, ship or no ship, or alternatively the law might say that B has contracted to supply A with a ship and that, having failed to do so, he must pay damages to A for breaking his contract. In the former event, of course, B will not be

---

[40] *Per* Lord Wright in the *Maritime National Fish* case, *supra*, n. 38 at 530.

[41] Perhaps illness would be treated as one of the hazards of ordinary life, and not therefore as self-induced frustration, see *The Super Servant 2* [1990] 1 Lloyd's Rep. 148 at 156. It has also been held that a party is not entitled to set up his *own* breach of contract, so as to convert a frustrating event into a case of self-induced breach, where on the particular facts this would have been advantageous to him: *F. C. Shepherd & Co Ltd* v. *Jerrom*, *supra*, n. 28.

liable for failing to provide a ship and in the latter event A will not be liable for the rent. In what circumstances, then, does the law reject the prima-facie rule that the contract is frustrated and apply one or other of these alternatives? As with the problem of mistake, the question ultimately is always one of risk-allocation. The question to be answered therefore is whether one or other party has expressly assumed the risk of the events which have occurred or, if not, whether the court thinks that one or other party ought reasonably to be treated as having assumed that risk.

But before attempting to answer this question it is desirable to take a brief look at a problem which has been much discussed by academic lawyers, and sometimes by judges as well. This problem is said to be an inquiry into the juridical 'basis' of the doctrine of frustration. Is the doctrine 'based' on an implied term, or more generally on the 'construction of the contract', as the traditional view has it? Or is it based on some positive rule of the law which enables courts to qualify the literal 'meaning' of a contract? Or is it 'based' on the fact that a radical change of circumstances would make the enforcement of the contract something fundamentally different from what the parties had contracted to do?

The traditional theory is to explain frustration as based on the presumed intention of the parties, or in other words as based on an implied term in the original contract. In contrast to the implied term in cases of common mistake, which is a condition precedent, the implied term in cases of frustration would be a condition subsequent. Support for this theory is to be found in numerous judgments from the mid-nineteenth century right down to the present day. But there were always serious weaknesses in the implied-term theory, weaknesses which in fact exist in any attempt to base the consequences of a contract on the intention of the parties. In particular, it was always well established that the actual intentions of the particular parties did not matter—it was the intention which could be attributed to them as *reasonable men* which was determinative. Again, a problem arose from the fact that frustration was generally held only to be a possible legal conclusion if it was caused by some *unanticipated* or perhaps *unforeseen* event. But then how was it possible to attribute an implied intention to the parties with regard to something which they just had not foreseen?

For these and similar reasons, the implied-term theory became unpopular with some judges, particularly those who favoured greater candour as to the nature of the judicial function. Some judges began to say that it was not the intention of the parties which decided whether a contract was frustrated, but the court which exercises the necessary power of declaring the contract at an end. What happens is that the court decides what is reasonable in the circumstances of the case, and says that the parties ought to be discharged or not, according to these circumstances.

This theory was originally put forward by a distinguished Lord of Appeal, Lord Wright, in three cases in the 1940s, and it later attracted the support of Lord Denning. After various vicissitudes, it was substantially adopted in the speech of Lord Radcliffe in *Davis Contractors* v. *Fareham UDC*.[42] We have already quoted a passage from this speech, and reference should again be made to this passage.[43] Lord Radcliffe's view, like that of Lord Wright, was that frustration depends on the operation of a rule of law rather than the intention of the parties, but Lord Radcliffe went on to define a little more precisely when and how this rule of law would operate. According to this view, which has now been repeatedly endorsed by the House of Lords in later cases,[44] a contract is frustrated when events have occurred which have changed the substance of the obligations assumed by the parties, so that to compel them to perform would be to make them do something radically different from what they contracted to do. Of course, even this approach does not discard the intention of the parties as an irrelevancy altogether. The whole point of the doctrine, as thus formulated, is to enable the parties to insist that they should only be legally obliged to perform what they had intended to perform, not something radically different. What the new formulation effectively does is to depart from the literalness which might once have insisted that parties had to do something they never intended to do, merely because the contract might literally appear to oblige them to do so.

The rejection of the implied-term theory eventually took place when the principle of freedom of contract was at a low ebb, but earlier attempts to discard it by judges like Lord Wright and Lord Denning were frigidly received by traditional-minded judges like Lord Simon and Lord Simonds.[45] It remains to be seen whether the modern resurgence of freedom-of-contract principles will lead to attempts to resuscitate the implied-term theory here, on the ground (for instance) that it is not the function of the law to 'impose' solutions on contracting parties.[46] But it is desirable to point out that earlier support for the implied-term theory was often based on a serious misconception. It seems to have been thought (by judges like Lord Simon and Lord Simonds) that, if the power to declare a contract frustrated was (as Lord Denning suggested) a power to qualify the literal terms of the contract, then this would replace certainty in the law with arbitrary, discretionary justice. The judge would be imposing *his* views on the parties, instead of enforcing their *own* intentions. But this was

---

[42] [1956] AC 696.               [43] *Supra*, 21.

[44] See the *Panalpina* case, *supra*, n. 39, and *Pioneer Shipping Ltd* v. *BTP Tioxide Ltd* [1982] AC 724.

[45] See *British Movietonews* v. *London & District Cinemas* [1952] AC 166.

[46] See Lord Scarman's remarks in *Tai Hing Cotton Mill Ltd* v. *Liu Chong Hing Bank Ltd.* [1986] AC 80, referred to *supra*, 203.

a serious mistake. Like all rules of law, those relating to frustration are a mixture of firm principle and judicial discretion. Judges do not have wide-ranging discretion to do whatever they think just; but they do, and must have, the power to decide border-line cases, and most lawyers think that when they do so they are exercising a discretion, though there is disagreement among theorists as to the precise nature of this discretion. But these border-line cases are relatively unusual, taking the law as a whole, though they may be common in the appeal courts. And clearly, as the doctrine of frustration is refined and applied, precedents will multiply, and the law will become clearer, even though there will always be difficulties of application in some cases. In this respect there is no difference between the doctrine of frustration and any other set of rules of contract law.

But there has not merely been controversy over the source of the court's power to declare a contract frustrated; there has often been controversy over the precise test to be adopted for this purpose, and the two controversies have sometimes become entangled with each other. This was because it was often asked, what is 'the basis' of the doctrine of frustration? Much of the difficulty here arose out of a failure to inquire precisely into the nature of the question being posed. When it is asked what is 'the basis' of a doctrine (whether it is frustration, or mistake, or any other legal doctrine), the first question is really as to the nature of the inquiry itself. If this question is analysed more precisely it will be found that an inquiry as to 'the basis' of the doctrine may involve several quite distinct questions. First, it may involve the question: Is a contract dissolved by frustration because the parties have so willed it, or independently of the will of the parties? This is the question which is usually being considered when the discussion centres around the reality of implied terms. Secondly, 'the basis' of the doctrine may be a reference to judicial techniques or methods of reasoning. This is a matter of empirical fact; if the courts do (as they still often do) discuss frustration in the language of 'implied terms' or 'construction of the contract', then it is true to say that remains 'the basis' of the doctrine *in this sense*. A third possibility is that discussion about 'the basis' of the doctrine is really an inquiry into the circumstances in which the doctrine may be invoked. This is the question which is being answered when it is said that 'the basis' of the doctrine is that to enforce the contract after a radical change of circumstances is to enforce obligations quite different from those undertaken by the parties.

It will be seen, therefore, that there is a great deal of truth in all these 'theories' as to 'the basis' of the doctrine of frustation. The common belief that only one of these theories can be the 'true basis' is unfounded, because the different theories are not necessarily mutually inconsistent.

## Frustration as a risk-allocation procedure

In the light of this discussion, it should now be possible to define with a little more precision when exactly the doctrine will operate. It must be repeated that the ultimate question is always about the allocation of the risks of certain events. Of course where these risks are clearly allocated by the contract itself, there can be no question of frustration. All insurance contracts involve an express assumption of risk, and therefore the occurrence of the event insured against cannot frustrate the contract. If I insure my house against fire it would be absurd to suggest that destruction of the house by fire could frustrate the contract.[47]

But if the contract does not expressly allocate the risks, the question is how the law (or the court, speaking for the law) should allocate them. If it is not reasonable to place the risk of the relevant events on either party the contract is frustrated whereas, if the risk is placed on either party, that party will be bound to perform or to pay damages if he cannot do so. The following factors may be considered as very general guides in deciding whether the court will place a certain risk on one or other of the parties.

First (as in the case of mistake), it can be said that a party takes the risk of any changes in circumstances which affect only his own purposes in contracting, and do not affect the common object of both parties. Similarly, a change in circumstances which only affects *the way* in which one of the parties is to carry out his obligations does not normally frustrate a contract. So where a seller sold Sudanese groundnuts under a c.i.f. contract for shipment to Hamburg, the contract was not frustrated by the closure of the Suez Canal.[48] In a c.i.f. contract the seller undertakes to ship and insure the goods and pays the freight himself, so the price of the goods covers all these items. Accordingly the seller normally takes the risk of an increase in freight charges; in this case the increase was very great, because the seller had to ship the goods round the Cape instead of through the Suez Canal, but even this was not held to frustrate the contract.

---

[47] The case in the text would of course be too clear for argument. But in 1987 there was a great deal of argument (though not in the courts) over the liability of the insurers who underwrote the BP privatization share issue, that is to say, who undertook to buy any of the shares which remained unsold after they were offered to the public. When the stock market crashed two days before the shares were to be issued (thus making the issue price far too high to attract public buyers), underwriters round the world stood to lose many hundreds of millions of pounds. The underwriters (and foreign governments) put intense pressure on Nigel Lawson, the Chancellor of the Exchequer, to withdraw the share issue, which he resisted, saying later that 'they were inviting [him] to abandon the right to claim on an insurance policy'. Margaret Thatcher, the Prime Minister, also strongly took the view that 'the sanctity of contract and the reputation of the City of London required that the underwriters should meet their obligations'. See Nigel Lawson, *The View From Number Eleven* (London, 1992), 766, 771.

[48] *Tsakirogolou* v. *Noblee and Thorl Gmbh* [1962] AC 93.

Secondly, it may happen that a party enters into a contract whereby he receives remuneration so abnormally large that it is clear that in effect he is receiving a sort of insurance premium against special risks. Then it must be reasonable to place on him those risks. This, it may be suggested, is the best explanation of the decision in *Tatem* v. *Gamboa*.[49] In this case the plaintiffs, who were shipowners, agreed to charter a ship to the Spanish Republican Government during the civil war at £250 per day, which was about three times the normal rate of freight prevailing at the time, for use in evacuating government supporters from a Spanish port. It was manifest that the dangers of the ship being sunk or damaged, if not captured, must have been appreciated by the parties, and the high rate of freight was only explicable on the assumption that the owners realized the risk and were prepared to accept it. Hence, when the ship was captured by the rebels, it was held that the contract was frustrated, and that the owners were no longer entitled to recover freight.[50]

The third rule is perhaps the most important of all: generally speaking, a person who undertakes to do something takes the risk that performance of his undertaking may prove more onerous than expected, or even impossible, as a result of changes in circumstances which are normal, or merely slight deviations from the normal, whereas he does not take the risk of performance proving impossible owing to utterly abnormal or extra-ordinary occurrences. So, in *Davis Contractors* v. *Fareham UDC*, which we have referred to above, where a builder contracted to build a number of houses for some £94,000 in a period of eight months, but owing to shortages of labour and materials the work took twenty-two months and cost some £115,000, it was held that the contract was not frustrated. 'In a contract of this kind the contractor undertakes to do the work for a definite sum and he takes the risk of the cost being greater or less than he expected'.[51] Similarly, Lord Simonds pointed out that, merely because 'there has been an unexpected turn of events, which renders the contract more onerous than the parties had contemplated'[52] that is no ground for invoking the doctrine of frustration. The question in such cases is whether the entire nature of the contractual obligations has been changed, or whether they have merely become more costly or more onerous. It is of course quite common in inflationary times for building contracts to include price-variation clauses, so that the price may be increased if costs increase

---

[49] [1939] 1 KB 132; [1938] 3 All ER 135.
[50] This case is an excellent illustration of the point that the stress on the implied intention of the parties is apt to mislead people (even lawyers) as to the real grounds for decision. The most important fact, namely the high rate of freight payable, is not even mentioned in the report in [1939] 1 KB 132, as the reporter obviously thought it irrelevant. Yet it formed one of the main planks in the defendants' arguments. The other report is fuller.
[51] *Per* Lord Reid, *supra*, n. 42 at 724.         [52] *Ibid.* at 716.

during the period of the contract. This means that a fixed-price contract is more obviously than ever a way of allocating to the builder the risk of these increased costs, and no doubt he allows for this when making his bid for the contract.

Fourthly, even though a person does not normally take the risk of non-performance where performance is rendered impossible as a result of utterly abnormal developments, he does take the risk, or at all events the courts think it reasonable to place on him the risk, of non-performance, if the result of the impossibility is to give him a remedy over against some other person.[53] Although the actual decisions appear to justify this rule, the courts are for some reason extremely reluctant to acknowledge it. But the cases show a consistent approach to the problem. For instance in a case in the First World War[54] a ship was chartered for five years, and when only two years had run it was requisitioned by the Admiralty, but the Admiralty paid compensation at a far higher rate than the rent being paid by the charterers to the owners. Both parties apparently thought that, if the contract stood, the charterers were entitled to receive this compensation and merely to pay the rent for the ship to the owners, whereas if the contract was frustrated the owners would, of course, be entitled to the compensation. The House of Lords held that the contract was not frustrated, and although little weight was placed in the speeches of the law lords on the fact that compensation was being paid, it is difficult to believe that it did not play an important part in their decision. Indeed, in a later case Lord Dunedin thought that this was the decisive fact, and that if no compensation had been paid, the contract would certainly have been frustrated.

This case also shows that, although (as it is usually put[55]) in theory frustration is automatic and does not depend on the choice of either party, yet in practice a court is reluctant to hold a contract frustrated where one party receives exactly what he bargained for, but alleges the contract to be frustrated, while the other party, who is the only one affected by the alleged frustrating event, denies that the contract is frustrated.

Finally, it may be laid down as a very rough general rule that, if parties make a contract which is only to be performed at some distant future date, one or other of them will be held to have assumed the risk of performance whatever the future may bring. The point is that the whole object of such contracts is frequently to eliminate the dangers of later events.

---

[53] See also the analogous cases as to mistaken valuations, cited *supra*, 227.

[54] *Tamplin SS Co* v. *Anglo-Mexican Petroleum Co* [1916] 2 AC 397.

[55] This may not be wholly accurate. In *F. C. Shepherd* v. *Jerrom, supra*, n. 28, Mustill LJ suggests that this only means that a promisor is entitled to regard himself as discharged without giving notice.

If a contract is really a speculative contract . . . the doctrine of frustration can rarely, if ever, apply to it, for the basis of a speculative contract is to distribute all the risks on one side or on the other and to eliminate any chance of the contract falling to the ground. . . . No one can tell how long a spell of commercial depression may last; no suspense can be more harassing than the vagaries of foreign exchanges, but contracts are made for the purpose of fixing the incidence of such risks in advance, and their occurrence only makes it the more necessary to uphold a contract and not to make them the ground for discharging it.[56]

## Force majeure clauses

The doctrine of frustration is in practice of rather limited application and it may not reflect commercial expectations very well. At any rate business parties very commonly insert clauses into their contracts which excuse them from failure to perform in a very wide range of circumstances where it can be said that the failure was not the fault of the party in question. The clauses, usually called *force majeure* clauses, must of course be interpreted but they do not affect the general law and so call for no further discussion in a work of this kind.

There is, however, one point which may be worth making. One of the limitations affecting the doctrine of frustration is that it generally only operates where it is the whole performance of the contract which is affected. Frustration is no defence to a party who wishes to plead merely that one or more duties under the contract could not be performed. For example, frustration cannot be relied on as a defence where the performance of the contract has merely been delayed rather than prevented altogether. But *force majeure* clauses are of course not restricted in this way; indeed delay is one of the main types of events covered by these clauses.

## Consequences of frustration

It is usual to deal with the consequences of frustration of a contract at this point, but in this book detailed discussion of this question is deferred to a later point, where remedies can all be conveniently considered together.[57] Here a number of points of more general interest will be made. First, the consequences which follow frustration in certain circumstances may sometimes influence a court in deciding whether frustration has indeed occurred. Cases sometimes occur in which it is claimed that a contract was frustrated even though the contract was, in one sense, fully performed, perhaps with modifications. The *Davis Contractors* case, discussed above, was a case of this kind. The builder here did not throw up the contract when prices rose faster than he had expected—he went ahead and built the houses and then proceeded to argue that the contract was frustrated. In such a case the purpose of claiming that the contract has been frustrated is

[56] *Per* Lord Sumner in *Larrinaga* v. *Société-Americaine* (1923) 92 LJKB 455 at 464–5.
[57] See Ch. 22, 433–4 and 453.

to justify a claim for payment at a higher rate than was agreed by the contract. So long as the contract remains in being, all the work done under it has to be paid for at the contract rate, but if the builder can persuade the court that the contract was frustrated, he may then be able to make a restitutionary claim for payment at a 'reasonable' rate—which of course may well be higher if prices have in fact risen. As we have seen, in the *Davis Contractors* case the claim failed; and it seems reasonable to suggest that most such claims are likely to fail. There is something decidedly odd about a claim that a contract was frustrated even though all the work contemplated by it has actually been carried out.

Nevertheless, in extreme circumstances this may be a justifiable course. In an Australian case a few years ago,[58] a contract for the construction of a section of an underground railway was rendered far more onerous and protracted because injunctions were obtained by third parties restraining the contractor from working (as the contract had envisaged) at night or on Sundays, because of noise and vibration from the work. It was held by the High Court that the contract had been rendered radically different from what the contractor had originally undertaken, and he was entitled to be paid at a different rate altogether. So the contract was held frustrated. Although this general result may be acceptable, there must remain doubts about the invocation of frustration in this sort of case. Surely the terms of the contract in this case (which was the usual voluminous detailed contract found in such cases) must have continued to govern all the other details of the case—except for the rate of payment. But if the contract really was frustrated the *whole* contract would have ceased to apply, with difficult or even absurd results. The law of restitution—while it may cope with a simple claim for payment for services rendered—is hardly able to handle the huge number of minor and ancillary issues which are usually regulated by detailed construction contracts.

This leads on to a second point of some general importance. Remedies for frustration are generally highly inflexible—the result of frustration is that the contract is terminated, and the parties' rights must then be worked out on that footing. But what the parties often want is that the contract should be adjusted, rather than that it should be terminated. And this is a perfectly legitimate commercial need which the law at present fails to meet through the doctrine of frustration. This is another reason for the widespread use of *force majeure* clauses, because these clauses often make provision for adjustment of the contract if unforeseen difficulties arise, rather than for its complete termination. For instance, if performance is held up by serious delays, the *force majeure* clause may allow more time for performance, and so on.

---

[58] *Codelfa Construction Pty Ltd* v. *State Rail Authority of NSW* (1982) 149 CLR 337.

# 13

# The Duty to Disclose Material Facts

## 1. NON-CONTRACTUAL DUTIES

BEFORE we embark on an examination of the particular duties which arise independently of the contract, it may be as well to devote a few words to the relationship between contractual and non-contractual duties. We saw in Chapter 9 that, traditionally, contractual duties have been seen as duties which the parties have voluntarily chosen to assume while non-contractual duties (in the special sense here relevant) were duties imposed by the law on the parties to the bargaining relationship. But according to classical contract theory the law's concern was in general limited to ensuring that the bargaining process was properly conducted. The law, as it were, set the rules of the contest: no fraud, no misrepresentation, and no coercion. As for the rest, it was up to the parties to conduct the bargaining process according to their respective skill and ability. If one party emerged with a good bargain, and the other with onerous obligations, that was a proper outcome of the bargaining process.

In modern times this neat dichotomy between self-imposed and externally imposed duties has broken down. As we shall see in more detail in Chapter 16, it is unreal and incorrect to assume that the law is totally unconcerned with the fairness of the bargains which result from the bargaining process. Equally the rules for the conduct of the bargaining process (no fraud, no misrepresentation, no coercion) often seem to be applied as much for the purpose of seeing that fair bargains are struck as for the purpose of enabling the parties to choose freely and voluntarily what obligations they will assume. The consequence is that some of the traditional distinctions have almost completely broken down, for instance that between pre-contractual representations and promissory representations. It must therefore be appreciated that the traditional distinctions, though partly maintained here for purposes of exposition, are often somewhat unreal. When the substance of a particular situation is examined, it will often be found that contractual and non-contractual duties are both applicable, frequently covering the same ground, and some attempt is made below to show how this can happen.

One other preliminary note of warning is in order. We have said before that it is dangerous to treat the various parts of the law of contract in complete isolation. To take a simple example, the question of illegality in contracts and the implication of terms in a contract appear at first sight to be poles apart, and are usually treated in separate parts in books on contract. But the criminal law may often play an important, if indirect, part with respect to contractual duties. As we shall explain later, an illegal contract is often unenforceable, so that, if a person makes a contract which involves the commission of some offence, this may give the other party a good defence to an action on the contract.

Statutory obligations of this kind, backed by the sanction of the criminal law, do not generally give rise to civil rights of action as opposed to defences. For instance, if a person sells noxious food or drugs, contrary to the provisions of the Food and Drugs Act, he is liable to criminal penalties, but he cannot be sued by the person to whom he has supplied the food or drugs merely because he has broken the criminal law. (However, in practice, the provisions of the Sale of Goods Act are usually wide enough to protect most buyers.) For this reason it is not usual to discuss such matters in books on contract, except in so far as they arise incidentally in chapters on illegality. Nevertheless, from the point of view of a contracting party, duties in respect of the contract are all legal obligations which must be obeyed. What is more, in many relatively minor cases, it is now not uncommon for criminal proceedings to be brought (for instance, under the Trade Descriptions Act) against sellers who have used misleading sales or advertising language, and it is also possible for compensation orders to be made in these criminal proceedings in favour of any person who has suffered loss or damage. So, for instance, a person who has been misled by the language of a holiday brochure may be able to persuade the local Trading Standards Office to initiate criminal proceedings against the company, in which he may obtain some compensation. This would save him the necessity of bringing civil proceedings to enforce his civil rights which would today plainly exist in such a case. In practice this is beginning to make nonsense of the idea that these criminal statutes do not create civil rights.

## 2. THE DISCLOSURE OF MATERIAL FACTS

English law has traditionally taken the view that it is not the duty of the parties to a proposed contract to give information to each other. Each party must make up his own mind and exercise his own judgement in deciding whether to contract or not, and it is not the duty of either party to put before the other facts in his knowledge which may influence the other in deciding whether to enter into the contract or not. There is no doubt that in the commercial sphere this approach is closely associated with the economic basis of our society. The whole essence of trade and business in a free-enterprise society is that parties compete with each other 'at arm's length', as the lawyers say, that is, on a footing of equality. Each party is entitled to make use of what information he has in order to obtain the best bargain he can get; neither party is under any obligation to assist the other party. In a sense all this is of the essence of freedom of contract and free enterprise, and it is doubtful if trade and commerce could operate in the way it does on the basis of any other rule in the ordinary way.

One obvious reason there cannot be *general* duties of disclosure in commercial dealings is that there must be some economic incentive to invest in the acquisition of skill and knowledge, and that incentive is in part provided by the ability of parties to make use of their knowledge and skill in negotiating contracts. If oil companies, for instance, engage the best experts in the world in order to assess the probability of oil being discovered on this or that piece of land (or under this or that part of the sea) it would be absurd to expect them to divulge to landowners or concessionaires what they know or have discovered with the help of these experts. This would simply be a way of depriving them of the fruits of their knowledge, or compelling them to share it with the other party, who has made no equivalent investment. In the same way someone who has devoted a lifetime to the study of antiques or Old Masters is clearly entitled to use his knowledge for his own benefit in judging what to buy, or what to bid for some item or painting at an auction. He has no obligation to disclose to the seller that the dirty old canvas he is selling has in all probability a Rembrandt hidden under the layers of dust or later painting.

However, this robust individualism can get taken so far that it offends the sense of justice. While the general principle denying duties of disclosure works well enough in the commercial area in most cases, it does not always work well in other cases, and even in commercial cases, it will be found that the law effectively permits what many would consider sharp practice. There is, it must be remembered, no general principle of good faith in English law, although of course ideas of good faith are often incorporated into the law through specific legal doctrines like mistake or implied terms. But this means that, unless one party can bring his case under some specific legal rule of this kind, he cannot complain that the other party was under some general duty to disclose some fact, even though honourable dealing would have required such disclosure. And there are many special cases in which some legal systems would regard disclosure of special facts as required by honest dealings. Nor can all cases of denial of duties of disclosure be defended by the need for economic investment in skill and knowledge. Sometimes, for instance, one party has acquired information in some illegitimate way—information which is denied the other party as in the case of insider information in stock market dealings; and in other cases one party may have acquired information by pure chance which is not generally available, but which was not the product of any particular skill. Then again, there are cases of personal relations where economic incentive arguments appear inappropriate.

A famous American case raises the general problem in an acute form. In *Laidlaw* v. *Organ*[1] a tobacco merchant learned, early on the morning of 19 February 1815, that a peace treaty had been signed between Britain and the USA (ending the war of 1812), and he contracted to buy 111 hogsheads of tobacco from the defendant, Laidlaw, before this fact became public knowledge an hour or two later. Once the news broke, the price of tobacco rose sharply. Laidlaw considered that Organ's failure to disclose his knowledge was sharp practice, and he refused to deliver. In an appeal to the Supreme Court of the United States, judgment was given for the buyer. Marshall CJ rejected the idea that a duty of disclosure could be imposed on buyers or sellers in such circumstances, largely because of the great difficulty that would be found in imposing any sensible limits on it. Obviously a buyer or seller cannot be obliged to disclose everything he knows which may influence his judgement, and a more limited duty would clearly be difficult to define.

An English case which perhaps comes closer to shady conduct than *Laidlaw* v. *Organ* is *Turner* v. *Green*.[2] Here two parties, who were already engaged in litigation, entered into a compromise to settle their dispute after a preliminary hearing in London before the Chief Clerk. The Chief Clerk had made it evident that he did not think much of the plaintiff's case, and the plaintiff's solicitor, who was present, had telegraphed to his country associate advising settlement. The other party's solicitor had, however, no knowledge of what had transpired at the London hearing. When these facts came to light the defendant protested that the plaintiff's solicitor had acted dishonestly, but the settlement was upheld, even though the judge clearly thought that there had at least been shabby behaviour by the solicitor concerned.

Perhaps even more striking is a modern case, *Wales* v. *Wadham*[3] in which a husband and wife were negotiating a financial settlement while divorce proceedings were pending. The wife did not disclose the fact that she was intending to remarry a wealthy man as soon as the divorce became absolute, and in fact she did so. In the meantime the first husband had agreed to a financial settlement which assumed that his wife would be financially dependent on what she obtained from him. Even in these extreme circumstances it was held that there was no duty to disclose. This decision has now been overruled by the House of Lords,[4] but only on the ground that under the relevant statutory provisions, full disclosure is necessary so that the court can properly exercise its statutory discretions.

---

[1] 15 US (2 Wheat) 178 (1817).        [2] [1895] 2 Ch. 205.
[3] [1977] 1 WLR 199.        [4] *Jenkins* v. *Livesey* [1985] AC 424.

As a matter of common law, the decision might have stood, yet it seems plainly unacceptable. The wife's conduct here bordered on (if it did not amount to) the dishonest, and no question of economic investment could be relevant in the circumstances. This was a case in which the law of the market was applied to a transaction not taking place in the market in the ordinary sense.

In contracts for the sale and lease of houses and buildings also, the rule still holds sway unchallenged. A person who is selling his house is under no obligation to disclose that the drains leak, that a Borstal is located round the corner, that there are plans for building a motorway across the road, that the local schools and post office are about to shut, that the house is subject to flooding, that the timbers are riddled with woodworm, that the central heating does not work. It is up to the buyer to make his own inquiries. Of course one way of making these inquiries is actually to ask the seller about them, and if the seller answers these, or other questions, he must answer truthfully; but he is perfectly entitled to say (and some sellers do say, in response to some kinds of queries) that the buyer must make his inquiries elsewhere. It may seem surprising that there is so little modern case-law to illustrate these legal rules in this area, but that must be because the law is so clear that buyers would be told they have no chance of success in suing.

It will be seen that many cases of this general nature are closely associated with the narrow operation of the principles governing common mistake. As we saw in the last chapter, it is unusual that a contract can be set aside or held void because both parties shared some fundamental mistake. In these disclosure cases, there is no shared mistake, but one party is labouring under the mistake, and the other is aware of it. In one sense, the party aware of the mistake has behaved less honourably or honestly than if he had shared the mistake, so there might be a stronger case for relief in these cases than where the mistake is common to both parties. Certainly it would be very odd to allow relief where the mistake is shared, and refuse relief for the same type of mistake, if one party is instead aware of the mistake. Yet it is often assumed that a contract may be held void for common mistake (or by virtue of an implied condition precedent) even where it is almost certain that there would have been no duty to disclose if one party had been aware of the mistake. In *Bell* v. *Lever Bros*,[5] for instance, there does not seem to be any doubt that the contract would have been valid if Bell had been aware of the other party's mistake, because an employee is under no duty to disclose his misdeeds to his employer. This oddity is perhaps due to the general belief that a mistake must be common, or shared, before any relief can be given for the mistake,

---

[5] [1932] AC 161; see *supra*, 224.

or before a condition precedent can be implied with regard to the facts in question. But this does seem to be a misconception, though it is one widely shared by English lawyers. There is no compelling reason why a condition precedent cannot be implied into a contract even though one party is aware of the facts while the other is not, just as there is no compelling reason why a promissory condition cannot be implied in the same circumstances—and, as we shall shortly see, this is in fact one common way of by-passing the narrow scope of duties of disclosure.

In cases involving consumers the other party frequently has more information than the consumer because of greater technical expertise, or knowledge, and in some such cases the economic arguments might be stronger for allowing the other party to retain the benefits of that knowledge and expertise. Yet these are often cases where this result is found particularly offensive and unacceptable. An art dealer calls on a 'little old lady' and offers to buy her old canvas for a song, well knowing that it is a Constable worth many thousands of pounds. If he is not allowed to retain the fruits of his bargain, what incentive is there for art dealers to search out hidden treasures which may otherwise be lost to the public for ever? Whatever the explanation, this is a classic sort of case where there is no duty of disclosure, but it is also just the sort of case where courts might be expected to strain to discover some sort of operative mistake or implied condition, or actual misrepresentation.

Perhaps more important, and certainly more common, than these sorts of cases are those in which consumers obtain financial services of one kind or another, insurance, for instance, or advice on pensions. There is today a widespread belief that consumers are not given all the information which they should get when they enter into such contracts. It is, for instance, clear that very large numbers of people take out life insurance policies which are surrendered after a year or two, at great loss to the consumer. If consumers were given clearer information about the surrender value of such policies it is possible that fewer people would incur these losses.[6] There is also a widespread belief that consumers are entitled to clearer information about the commission of insurance brokers which, because it is nominally paid by the insurance companies, is often not disclosed to the consumer. Statute has begun to impose limited duties of disclosure in such cases but there is constant pressure by consumer groups to extend the duties.[7]

---

[6] See the Report of the Director-General of Fair Trading on *Fair Trading and Life Insurance Savings Products* (HMSO, London, 1993) in which he recommends legislation requiring disclosure on many of these matters.

[7] See the Financial Services Act 1986, Sched. 3, paras. 5–8 of which require financial services practitioners to disclose various facts to consumers dealing with them.

As mentioned above, many legal systems—France is a notable example—today impose extensive duties of disclosure in particular circumstances, on broad grounds of good faith. Yet in England the law relating to duties of disclosure has not developed a great deal in this century. But it must also be noticed that exceptions to the rule of non-disclosure have been indirectly created, or perhaps it would be more accurate to say that the rule has been by-passed, by the imposition on a party of responsibility for a state of facts, irrespective of his knowledge. Thus, in most contracts of sale of goods, the seller is liable if the goods prove unsatisfactory, so that a duty of disclosure of defects in the goods is unnecessary. The seller is liable whether he knows of the defects or not, so it would be pointless to invoke a less extensive duty of disclosure. Hence the statement which will be found in most of the books to the effect that a seller of goods is not bound to disclose any defects in them may be strictly accurate, but is completely misleading. It could, however, be important in those cases where there are no implied conditions, for instance, where a private seller of a second-hand car knows but fails to disclose that the car is in a dangerous state.

If a problem of this kind, not covered by the precedents, were to arise today, the courts could, in principle, approach it either by way of an implied term, or by way of a duty of disclosure. The choice between these two approaches is largely a matter of judicial technique or legal method, but there appear to be at least three reasons why the courts have recently favoured the implied-term technique over the creation of duties of disclosure. First, the implication of terms is traditionally (as we have seen) rested on the intention of the parties; this means that the doctrine of precedent is less rigid in this area than in others. A court can always justify a decision to imply a term by stating that it is merely giving effect to the presumed intention of the parties in the case before it, even though in previous similar cases no such term has been implied. But duties of disclosure are more obviously dependent on positive rules of law and the category of cases in which such duties exist has been thought for some time to be now closed. New cases cannot, therefore, be dealt with by inventing a duty of disclosure unsupported by precedents.

Secondly, the duty-of-disclosure technique suffers from an inherent limitation which in some cases seriously affects its utility; the courts have said, not unnaturally, that even where a duty to disclose exists, a person cannot be required to disclose what he does not know. But there are in fact many situations in which justice would not adequately be done if a party was under no duty in regard to facts unknown to him; for instance a consumer who buys some defective product is clearly entitled to some legal remedy even though the seller was not aware of the defect. If this sort of case is dealt with by implying suitable terms, this difficulty does not arise.

And a third advantage of the implied-term technique over the duty of disclosure technique is that the former offers a more flexible range of remedies. Prima facie the only remedy for a breach of a duty to disclose is to rescind the contract;[8] this is not always a very satisfactory remedy and there may well be situations in which damages would be more appropriate. If the problem is approached by means of implying a term there is a considerable degree of flexibility in the remedies which can be made available. The court may, for instance, imply a suitable warranty which would give rise to a right to damages only; or it may imply a promissory condition which gives the aggrieved party a choice between obtaining damages or rescinding the contract; or it may imply a condition precedent to the operation of the contract which would release both parties from all liability.

There seems little doubt that for these reasons the law relating to duties of disclosure has remained relatively static for some time, while continuous developments are taking place by the implication of terms. Unfortunately, this has occasionally led to decisions which seem quite unreasonable because the circumstances raise no duty of disclosure and the facts arise outside the areas where terms are regularly implied. One such example is *Wales* v. *Wadham*, referred to above.

The absence of a duty of disclosure can also be by-passed by other means in particular cases, for example, by allowing an action in tort for negligence. We have already seen, in dealing with some cases concerning the relationship of negotiating parties in Chapter 4, how a number of recent cases have imposed (rather paternalistically) duties of care on negotiating parties. Obviously, if one party owes a duty to take reasonable care to prevent the other party from suffering loss through some contract being negotiated between them, he will be bound to disclose all sorts of things which might have been required by a specific duty of disclosure. But the most recent case on this topic pours a certain amount of cold water on this method of by-passing the absence of a duty of disclosure, by re-affirming that in ordinary commercial dealings the parties do not owe duties of care to each other.[9]

In this chapter we are concerned with positive duties of disclosure but throughout the chapter it must always be borne in mind, therefore, that the absence of such a duty does not necessarily mean that there can be no other legal technique which can provide relief, such as an implied term or a duty of care.

---

[8] See *Bank of Nova Scotia* v. *Hellenic Mutual War Risks Association* [1989] 3 All ER 628, reversed on grounds not affecting this point, [1991] 3 All ER 1.

[9] *La Banque Financière de la Cité SA* v. *Westgate Insurance Co Ltd*, [1990] QB 665, affirmed on narrower grounds, [1991] 2 AC 249. Compare the more paternalistic decision of the House of Lords in *Barclays Bank* v. *O'Brien* [1994] 1 AC 180, discussed below, 277.

Cases where there is a duty to disclose facts to the other party to a proposed contract fall, broadly speaking, into two classes. On the one hand, there are certain general principles applicable to all contracts, and, on the other hand, there are certain special contracts which have received special treatment.

## General principles

As we have seen, there is no general duty of disclosure of material facts in one's possession before entering into a contract. A person is not compelled to open his mouth and speak, but if he does so, the law is particularly careful to ensure that the other party is not misled by what he says. If he actually makes a false statement, of course, then that is a misrepresentation, and the law provides relief which will be discussed in the next chapter. But a person may make a statement which cannot be condemned as false, and yet which may mislead the other party to the contract. This is a possibility which cuts across the subject-matter of these two chapters because it might be dealt with by an extension of the duty not to make false statements, or it might be dealt with as a case of a duty to speak.

Typical instances of such duties arise where a person makes a statement which is literally true, but which none the less creates an impression contrary to the truth. For instance, in *Curtis* v. *Chemical Cleaning Co*[10] an assistant in a dry cleaner's stated that a receipt signed by the plaintiff exempted the defendants from liability for loss of, or damage to, any beads or sequins on the plaintiff's dress which was to be cleaned. This was true, but the assistant did not state that in fact the receipt exempted the defendants from any liability whatsoever for loss of, or damage to, the dress. Obviously the assistant's statement created an impression quite contrary to the truth. It was held, therefore, that the defendants were not entitled to rely on the exemption clause and the plaintiff got her damages.

A duty to speak may also arise where a person has made, during the course of negotiations, a statement which was true when made but which ceased to be true before the contract was finally concluded. For instance, where a doctor, selling his practice, stated truthfully what the practice was worth, but later omitted to inform the buyer that it had dwindled almost to nothing by the time the contract was signed, it was held that the contract could be rescinded, as the seller should have informed the buyer of the change in the value of the practice. This duty only arises where the party concerned knew of the change in the circumstances; but even where he did not know, it may be possible for the courts to give appropriate relief by implying a term that the situation has not changed.[11]

---

[10] [1951] 1 KB 805.
[11] See, e.g. *Financings Ltd* v. *Stimson* [1962] 1 WLR 118.

## Particular contracts

In a certain restricted group of contracts good faith is peculiarly necessary owing to the relationship between the parties, and in these cases—known as contracts *uberrimae fidei*—there is a full duty to disclose all material facts. By far the most important instance of such contracts is the contract of insurance. Here the duty to disclose all material facts to the insurer arises from the fact that many of the relevant circumstances are within the exclusive knowledge of one party and it would be impossible for the insurer to obtain the facts necessary for him to make a proper calculation of the risk he is asked to assume without this knowledge. This, at least, was originally the justification for giving contracts of insurance special treatment. In modern conditions, however, the law is often extremely oppressive. Insurers are generally well able to take care of their own interests by requiring a prospective insured to complete an application form giving information on a wide range of matters. The ordinary consumer might well be justified in assuming that if he gives the information specifically requested he has complied with his legal obligations. Unfortunately, this is not so. He must also disclose any other material fact known to him even though he does not realize its significance. This duty, moreover, applies not only when an insurance policy is first obtained, but on any renewal thereafter, when an application form is not usually filled in. There is no doubt that the present law is sometimes a source of grave injustice, and the Law Commission has published some proposals for change. Although there has not yet been any change in the law, there has recently been some welcome change in insurance practice, because companies now regularly draw the attention of the insured (on application forms, and when renewals are requested) to the need to disclose any additional information which may be material, of which examples are sometimes given.

Ever since the days of Lord Mansfield it has been stated that contracts of insurance impose a duty of disclosure on the insurer as well as on the insured, but there are very few cases illustrating such a possibility in the books. Recently an important such case arose in *La Banque Financière de la Cité SA* v. *Westgate Insurance Co Ltd*.[12] Here, insurers accepted a proposal to insure a bank against certain credit risks, without disclosing that the broker through whom a similar contract had previously been negotiated had been guilty of gross frauds in connection with that previous contract. Because a broker is in English law deemed to be the agent of the insured, the insured bank was unable to recover on this second policy when a claim was made, which was again vitiated by the broker's fraud. It was held that the insurer should have disclosed this fact which was most

[12] See *supra*, n. 9.

material to the recoverability of the loss insured against. However, the court went on to hold that the only remedy available to the insured for breach of this duty of disclosure by the insurer was to rescind the contract of insurance and recover the premium, a remedy which was hopelessly inadequate to do justice after the event insured against had actually occurred. The court refused to hold that this duty of disclosure could found an action for damages, thus confirming the point made above about the inflexibility of the remedy for breach of a duty of disclosure. But the chief reason for this holding seems to have been the rather conceptual view which the court took, that this duty of disclosure arose from general equitable principles, rather than from an implied term at common law, and equitable duties have never been remediable in damages. The result will seem to many an unhappy example of the law failing to be even-handed in its dealings between insurers and insureds, because the latter are penalized severely for breaches of the duty to disclose, whereas it now seems that the insurer's duty to disclose can be breached at little cost to him.

Another case where duties of disclosure are recognized by the law to exist is the contract of partnership where the duty is imposed mainly because it is obviously impossible to carry on a partnership without the fullest confidence between the parties.

Closely analogous to these cases are those involving what Courts of Equity have always called a 'fiduciary relationship', such as the relationship between a trustee and a beneficiary. In these cases the person in the fiduciary position is under a duty not to abuse that position, and this duty involves the duty to disclose all material facts. The same is also true of many cases which fall within the doctrine of 'undue influence' which (it is important to emphasize) is not solely concerned with what might be called undue influence in the ordinary sense. However, in both these and other relevant cases the duty to disclose is obviously much less extensive than the general one of not abusing the position of trust, or exploiting the relationship between the parties. These cases are, therefore, reserved for special treatment elsewhere.[13]

It should not be thought that there is any general principle requiring disclosure merely because a judge thinks that a particular contract requires good faith. Unless the case falls within one of the classes mentioned above, or is closely analogous to the cases in these classes, there will be no such duty.

In all these cases the rule is that a party is under a duty to disclose all material facts. The duty does not as a matter of general law extend to facts not within the knowledge of the person under the duty, but insurance contracts nearly always contain a severe clause, known as the 'basis of the contract clause', under which it is declared that the insured has disclosed all

[13] See Ch. 15.

material facts, whether known to him or not. The severity of the law as against insureds is aggravated because the judge of the materiality of the facts is the law and not the insured himself—indeed, in insurance contracts, it is effectively the insurer who is judge of the materiality of the facts. In these cases, the hardship which the present law can cause is particularly severe because the definition of materiality is so very wide. Any fact which would influence a prudent insurer is material for this purpose,[14] and prudent insurers may be influenced by facts which many members of the public would regard as irrelevant—for instance a householder insuring his house or belongings has been held obliged to disclose previous convictions for robbery, because many insurers would regard such a person as a 'moral hazard', raising the possibility of bogus claims. The duty is, moreover, absolute, in the sense that it can be breached without intentional wrongdoing or even negligence.

There are today numerous examples of statutory duties of disclosure in particular contractual situations. Only a few of these need mention here. Under the Companies Act 1985 a prospectus which is issued to the public inviting them to subscribe for shares must contain information on a large number of points, all of which are specified in the Act, and are obviously matters which might influence a person intending to buy shares.

A somewhat similar duty of disclosure is provided for by the Consumer Credit Act 1974 in connection with advertisements offering to supply credit or loans to consumers. Such advertisements have to comply with Regulations designed to ensure that the advertisement contains 'a fair and reasonably comprehensive indication of the nature of the credit or hire facilities offered by the advertiser and of their true cost to persons using them'.[15]

We may also refer briefly to those cases which have already been mentioned in dealing with formalities which require certain written information to be supplied to the buyers of certain commodities such as seeds, fertilizers, and coal.

Finally reference may be made again to the modern financial legislation requiring information to be given by dealers in financial services (such as insurance brokers, or advisers on financial matters like investments).[16]

---

[14] The extreme severity of the law here is, however, now partially mitigated by the fact that the insurer must show, not only that a prudent insurer would have been influenced by the non-disclosure, but that he in fact was so influenced. See *post*, 259.

[15] Consumer Credit Act 1974, s. 44(1).     [16] See *supra*, n. 7.

# 14

# Misrepresentation

ALTHOUGH, as we have seen, there is no general rule imposing a duty to disclose material facts, there is a general, indeed a universal, rule of great strictness, that a party must not make any false statements to the other party, and thereby induce him to enter into the contract. To compensate for the absence of a duty of disclosure the law scrutinizes the conduct of the parties with an eagle eye to ensure that there has been no misrepresentation. 'Simple reticence does not amount to legal fraud. . . . But a single word, or . . . a nod or a wink, or a shake of the head or a smile'[1] may amount to a misrepresentation of facts which justifies rescission of the contract or some other form of relief.

What precisely amounts to a misrepresentation, however, is not such a simple matter as it might appear. It is often said that a misrepresentation of law as opposed to one of fact has no effect on a contract entered into on the faith of it, unless it was made dishonestly. But in practice it would be rare that a party would enter into a contract with another in reliance on his statement of some abstract proposition of law; and a statement of private rights is not generally treated as a representation of law, but of fact.

In the second place, a promise to do something is not a statement of fact, and cannot therefore be a misrepresentation. There can be no question of such a promise being true or false at all. Such a promise can only be sued on if it is incorporated in a contract and is supported by some good consideration, although as we saw earlier a non-contractual promise may, to a limited extent, operate as a defence to an action under the principles of promissory estoppel. Thus, if a person makes a non-contractual promise and merely refuses to fulfil his promise, the other party has no direct remedy whatever. But, perhaps for this very reason, the courts are generally more reluctant to regard a promise as non-contractual than to regard a statement of fact as non-contractual. So it would today be relatively unusual for an actual promise made while a contract is being negotiated to be treated as non-contractual. The tendency would be for such a promise to be regarded as incorporated in the contract, or at least as constituting a collateral contract, which legally comes to much the same thing.

---

[1] *Per* Lord Campbell in *Walters* v. *Morgan* (1861) 3 De G F & J 718 at 723.

But occasionally even a promise may be held to be distinct and separable from a contract induced by it, or (more probably) a statement of intention may be made which is clearly non-promissory in character. Such a promise or statement of intent cannot itself be treated as a misrepresentation, but it does at least involve an implicit representation as to the state of mind of the speaker. Even the making of a promise involves a representation that the promisor intends to fulfil his promise, and 'the state of a man's mind is as much a fact as the state of his digestion'.[2] Hence, if a promise is made with no intention of carrying it out, this is a misrepresentation of fact, for it misrepresents the state of the promisor's mind. This is, of course, quite different from the case of a promise, honestly made with the intention of carrying it out, even though it is not eventually carried out. So to borrow money without any intention of repaying it is fraud, whereas to borrow money and simply fail to repay it is purely a breach of contract.

In the third place, an opinion is not a fact, and the law recognizes that a contracting party must be allowed a certain latitude in advertising his wares. For instance, the estate agent's cliché, 'a very desirable residence', is not a statement of fact which could be complained of as a misrepresentation. And more generally mere 'puffs', as they are sometimes called, are disregarded by the law as statements which would not influence any reasonable person. So, for instance, a seller's statement that what he offers is worth the asking price is not usually regarded as a representation at all.

Even statements which look more like real statements of fact may be disregarded by the law if they turn out, on analysis, to be matters of opinion. So where a person sold some land and gave his opinion on the sheep-carrying capacity of the land, this was held to be a mere matter of opinion. But the vital feature of this case was that the land had never been used for sheep before (as the buyer knew), so that the information was necessarily a matter of opinion. But on the whole the courts are reluctant to entertain the plea that a statement is only one of opinion, especially if it is based on facts not known to the other party. It is also well settled that even a statement of opinion involves an implied representation that the person making it knows no facts which would make the opinion untenable. A fortiori, a statement of opinion involves an implicit representation that it is honestly believed to be true. 'A representation of fact may be inherent in a statement of opinion, and, at any rate, the existence of the opinion in the person stating it is a question of fact'.[3]

In some recent cases the courts have had to consider the effect of statements which are not readily classifiable as 'fact' or 'opinion', for

---

[2] *Per* Bowen LJ in *Edgington* v. *Fitzmaurice* (1885) 29 Ch.D 459 at 483—one of the most famous of all legal dicta.
[3] *Per* Lord Merrivale in *Bisset* v. *Wilkinson* [1927] AC 177 at 182.

example forecasts or advice about the sales potential of a petrol station.[4] Cases of this kind suggest that perhaps the real issue is not whether a statement is one of fact or opinion, but whether it was reasonable to rely upon it in the circumstances. Reliance on statements of fact is usually more easily justifiable than reliance on the other party's opinion, but in particular circumstances even this may be reasonable. It must also be remembered, as we saw in Chapter 4, that the courts have in some rare cases recently held that one party may owe a duty of care to the other in pre-contractual negotiations (though not usually in an ordinary commercial contract between two business parties) and that one result of such a duty of care may be that one party comes under a duty to explain what the effect of the contract may be.[5] Similarly, a duty to explain the nature and effects of the proposed contract may be imposed on a party who is, in the special circumstances of the case, under a fiduciary duty or is aware of facts from which undue influence by a third party may be presumed.[6]

When it has once been established that a representation of fact in the legal sense has been made, the next question is whether that representation was false. Generally speaking there is little difficulty about this, and in modern times it is likely that statements which are misleading even though literally true would be held to be misrepresentations.

It is usually said[7] that a misrepresentation must also be material if it is to ground relief, but this requirement is most commonly stated in connection with the non-disclosure rule in insurance contracts. Now clearly a requirement of materiality is a necessary part of a rule requiring disclosure because one cannot be required to disclose everything one knows. But it is not a necessary requirement of the rule against misrepresentation that the facts misrepresented should be material, and there is no good modern authority to this effect.

The next requirement for a successful plea of misrepresentation is a causal one. The representee must prove that he was in fact influenced by the representation in deciding whether or not he would enter into the contract in question, and this causal requirement does apply both to cases of non-disclosure and of misrepresentation.[8] Hence even a fraudulent misrepresentation has no effect where it exercised no influence on the

---

[4] *Esso Petroleum* v. *Mardon* [1976] QB 801.

[5] See e.g. *Esso Petroleum* v. *Mardon, supra*, n. 4.

[6] See *post*, 277.

[7] *See e.g. Lohnro* v. *Fayed (No.2)* [1991] 4 All ER 961 at 966.

[8] *Pan Atlantic Insurance Co Ltd* v. *Pine Top Insurance Co Ltd* [1994] 3 All ER 581. This decision, to some extent, takes away with one hand what it gives (to insurers) with the other, because in cases where it is held that a non-disclosure was barely material, the court may well now go on to hold that it did not in fact have any causal effect.

other party's judgement. So if he knew the statement to be untrue, or if he did not know of the misrepresentation at all, or if he relied on his own judgement and not on the other party's false statement, then he has nothing to complain of. On the other hand it is not necessary to show that the misrepresentation was the sole inducement to enter into the contract, and the mere fact that the innocent party has taken independent advice does not mean that he has not relied, in part at least, on the false statement. If such a case actually comes to court, much will depend on the evidence of the person to whom the representation was made, and if he is prepared to swear that he was influenced by it, and if he is unshaken in cross-examination, it will be extremely difficult to maintain that the misrepresentation had no causal effect.

It is no defence to a plea of misrepresentation to allege that the other party might have discovered the true facts by reasonable diligence.[9] Provided that the innocent party did in part at least rely on the false statements, he is entitled to have the contract rescinded, although he might easily have discovered the falsity of the statements. It lies ill in the mouth of a person who is found to have made a false statement to say that the other person ought to have realized that it was false. However, there must be some limits to this, for an extreme want of due care by the representee would show that his reliance was unreasonable. And although the courts have not recognized a distinct principle requiring that the reliance should be reasonable, this may be implicit in the cases. Moreover it now seems possible that, where the misrepresentation is being used to found a claim for damages, it would today be possible to apportion the damages for contributory negligence, thus reducing the amount which would otherwise be payable because of the plaintiff's own share of the responsibility. Naturally the primary responsibility for a false statement must always lie with the maker of the statement[10] but there are some circumstances in which apportionment would be fully justified. Of course where the plaintiff's claim is for rescission of the contract this alternative is not possible, and in that event it seems the plaintiff could only be defeated by such extreme carelessness on his own part that it could be said that the representation had no causal effect.

---

[9] See *Redgrave* v. *Hurd* (1881) 20 Ch.D 1, an extreme case where in a claim for damages some apportionment would surely be justified today; see later in the text and *post*, n. 10.

[10] *Gran. Gelato Ltd* v. *Richcliff (Group) Ltd* [1992] Ch. 560. But continued reliance in this case on dicta in *Redgrave* v. *Hurd* (see *supra*, n. 9) and other old cases hardly seems justified since, at that time, the alternatives were full damages or none. It has also been held that there can be no apportionment of damages in an action of deceit or for fraud: *Alliance & Leicester Building Society* v. *Edgestop Ltd* [1994] 2 All ER 38, but the reasoning here is not very satisfactory either.

## 2. FRAUDULENT AND INNOCENT MISREPRESENTATION

At common law, only two classes of misrepresentation were originally recognized, fraudulent and innocent. Of these, only fraudulent misrepresentation was held actionable in damages, though innocent misrepresentation leading to the making of a contract gave a right to rescission. In more modern times, negligent misrepresentation has become a separate category, and may nowadays be actionable in damages, both at common law and under the Misrepresentation Act 1967.

It was settled once and for all by the House of Lords in the famous case of *Derry* v. *Peek*[11] that a statement is only fraudulent if it is made with knowledge of its falsity, or recklessly, without knowing or caring whether it is true or false. In one sentence, a statement is fraudulent if it is made without honest belief in its truth. The essence of the decision is that mere carelessness or negligence is not to be treated as dishonesty. No matter how negligent a person may have been in making a false statement he is not to be condemned for fraud if he honestly believed his words to be true. It is sometimes said that, although negligence cannot amount to fraud, gross negligence may be evidence of fraud. This, however, is almost as misleading as saying that gross negligence may amount to fraud, for the fact is that negligence, gross or otherwise, is the very antithesis of fraud. Strictly speaking, negligence can no more be evidence of fraud than it can amount in itself to fraud. But what is evidently meant by this somewhat elliptical expression is that the facts of the case may be consistent with fraud or with gross negligence, but not with both, and that the latter explanation is simply not credible because it is not possible to believe that anybody could have been so grossly negligent as is alleged. To take a hypothetical example, suppose that a person were to sell his own second-hand car and were to state that the brakes were in good working order. If in fact it transpired that the brakes did not work at all the seller would find it difficult to convince a judge that he had merely been negligent rather than dishonest.

## 3. NEGLIGENT MISREPRESENTATION

As mentioned above, in modern times, negligence, even without fraud, is itself a ground of liability in tort in many circumstances, and recent developments have shown that *Derry* v. *Peek* will be much less important in the future than it has been in the past. At common law it was first held in the House of Lords in *Hedley Byrne* v. *Heller*[12] that there could in special circumstances be liability for damages for negligent misrepresentation,

---

[11] (1889) 14 App. Cas. 337.          [12] [1964] AC 465.

even in the absence of fraud. This is a liability in tort, as generally understood, but there are circumstances in which the liability is very close to being contractual. Indeed, in some cases it was said that the liability only arose where the representor *voluntarily assumed the obligation*, and although this test is not always relevant, many of the cases which arise are very close to the borderline between contract and tort and could easily be classified as contractual if the law adopted a different conceptual approach. In the *Hedley Byrne* case itself, for example, liability would have been imposed (but for an explicit disclaimer of liability) where a bank negligently gave a misleading reference to a customer's clients, at the request of the customer. The plaintiffs here were the customer's clients, who had no direct contractual relationship with the bank, yet the bank clearly voluntarily assumed the duty of giving them information, and it would not be stretching things to suggest that they intended to assume the obligation (as intent is understood in contract law) to give reasonably careful information.[13]

Similarly in *Smith* v. *Eric S. Bush*[14] the House of Lords held that a surveyor commissioned by a building society to value a house for the purposes of a mortgage could be liable for negligence to an applicant for a mortgage with the building society. The normal procedure in such a case is for the building society to require the applicant for the mortgage to pay the surveyor's fee, and this is passed on to the surveyor who reports directly to the building society. At one time these reports were not made available to the applicant even though he paid the fee, and it was thought that this would protect the surveyor from liability for misrepresentation. But that proved mistaken, and in this case the surveyor's report was passed on to the applicant, but with a disclaimer of liability. But the House of Lords held that a duty of care arose because of the close proximity between the parties—the surveyors knew the applicant's name, they knew the particular transaction contemplated, and they knew that the applicant would in all probability rely on their report. It will be seen that the relationship between the surveyor and the buyer is very close to an ordinary contract. The buyer even pays the surveyor's fees, although the money is channelled through the building society, and legally speaking it is they who strictly 'pay' the surveyor.

On the other hand the House of Lords has recently held in *Caparo Industries plc* v. *Dickman*[15] that a company's auditors are not liable for negligence even to existing shareholders in the company who have bought further shares in reliance on the auditors' report. Strictly speaking, it is the

---

[13] The House of Lords has now reasserted the importance of the voluntary assumption of responsibility for liability in many tort cases of this kind: *Henderson* v. *Merrett Syndicates Ltd* [1994] 3 All ER 506.    [14] [1990] 1 AC 831.    [15] [1992] 2 AC 605.

company itself which employs, contracts with, and pays the auditors, but in commercial reality the auditors are the watchdogs of the shareholders, employed and paid for their benefit. So the situation is in a sense similar to that which arose in *Smith* v. *Eric S. Bush*. The difference between the two cases cannot easily be put into technical language—except for the fact that the plaintiff in the *Smith* v. *Bush* situation is a known individual whose reliance is the very purpose of the transaction, while this was not the case in *Caparo*. In the leading speech in the House of Lords Lord Bridge relied on this as the key distinction:

The situation is entirely different where a statement is put into more or less general circulation and may foreseeably be relied on by strangers to the maker of the statement for any one of a variety of different purposes which the maker of the statement had no reason to anticipate.[16]

Shortly after the decision in the *Hedley Byrne* case, the Misrepresentation Act 1967 substantially modified the common law rules as to misrepresentation, so that it is now often possible to claim damages for negligent misrepresentation under that Act as well as (or as an alternative to) damages at common law. The result is a confusing conceptual tangle, and it will suffice here to say that the Act gives a right to claim damages for misrepresentation to a person who has been induced to enter into a contract by a representor, if the representor had no reasonable grounds for believing in the truth of his representation. To a large degree, in effect, the Act permits a misrepresentee to treat a negligent misrepresentation as though it had been made fraudulently—in which case, of course, damages could be claimed for the falsity.

### 4. EXCLUSION OF LIABILITY FOR MISREPRESENTATION

Another important statutory development is that any attempt to exclude liability for misrepresentation now falls within the Unfair Contract Terms Act 1977, and is void in so far as the exclusion is 'unreasonable' as that term is used in the Act. So, for instance, where a buyer at an auction bid for and bought some land in reliance on various statements as to planning permission, which were held to be false, an attempt in the contract to exclude liability for such misrepresentations was held unreasonable and void.[17] And in *Smith* v. *Bush*,[18] which has been discussed above, the main issue in the case concerned the application and effect of the Act to

---

[16] *Supra*, n. 15 at 621. But note how the very similar argument of the defendants in *Carlill* v. *Carbolic Smoke Ball Co.* [1893] 1 QB 256 was disposed of a hundred years before *Caparo*. Of course *Carlill* involved a *promise*, and *Caparo* a statement of fact, which may well be a valid distinction.

[17] *South Western Property Co* v. *Marton* (1983) 2 Tr. L 14.          [18] *Supra*, n. 14.

disclaimers attached to surveyors' reports which were passed on to the
applicant. Here it was held that with an ordinary home-purchase
transaction it was generally unreasonable for building societies or
surveyors to attempt to disclaim their liabilities under the Act, and such
disclaimers are therefore invalid. This aspect of the case is discussed again
in Chapter 16.

## 5. REMEDIES FOR MISREPRESENTATION

It is customary to discuss the remedies for misrepresentation at this stage,
but it seems more convenient to postpone further discussion of this subject
to the end of the book, where all the various remedies for breaches of
contractual and non-contractual duties can be dealt with together.

## 6. MISREPRESENTATION IN THE PERFORMANCE OF CONTRACTS

When lawyers talk of 'misrepresentation' in a contractual context, they
usually confine the term to *pre-contractual* misrepresentations—that is, to
the sort of statements discussed above, which are made before any contract
exists between the parties. Because these misrepresentations are made at a
time when no contract exists, they cannot be governed by obligations
arising out of the contract itself. But entirely different principles govern
liability for false statements made *during the performance of contractual
duties*, which can be governed by ordinary contracual duties. A solicitor,
for instance, or a surveyor giving advice to a client, is performing the duties
imposed on him by the relationship (and contract) between himself and his
client, and this contract imposes a duty (via an implied term) to be careful
in the making of any statements. Hence there has never been any doubt
that negligence alone would be a sufficient ground of liability in such a
case. Moreover, many of the principles of the law relating to the effect of
pre-conceptual misrepresentation are clearly irrelevant to cases of negligent advice. For instance, the distinction between a statement of fact, on the
one hand, and a statement of law or of opinion, on the other hand, is
clearly immaterial where the liability of a solicitor for negligent advice is
concerned. And the same is true of advice given by any professional person
during the course of his employment.

# 15

# Duress and Undue Influence

ALL persons over the age of 18 and of sound mind are generally treated as of equal capacity for the purpose of contracting, and the law is reluctant to admit the direct plea that the contract is unfair, and that one party was in a position to dictate the terms to the other. But while maintaining the sanctity of contracts as a general principle, the law has, from time to time, stepped in to redress the balance between the strong and the weak. It has sometimes done this indirectly, as, for instance, in its treatment of exemption clauses. There is also a great deal of legislation (most of which shows no signs of being dismantled even in the present era) which is designed to prevent one party being overreached by the other by controlling or regulating the conduct of contracting parties through some sort of licensing system; some of this legislation is briefly referred to in Chapter 16. In the present chapter we deal with much older and more traditional law, which is concerned with redressing the balance between the parties in particularly gross cases of inequality, namely the doctrines of duress and undue influence.

Like the law relating to misrepresentation and duties of disclosure, these doctrines are concerned with pre-contractual relations, that is, with the way that a contract has been made. They are, in other words, part of the rules that police the way the market works. But at the same time (as we shall see) they are by no means irrelevant to the outcome of contracts and to issues of substantive justice.

It is obvious that every civilized legal system must have rules deterring the use of violence and threats of violence, and these rules operate in the market-place, as they do elsewhere. But in the market-place these rules have a special significance. Not only is it a crime to hit someone over the head or to point a gun at an innocent victim, it is also necessary for the law to refuse legal validity to transactions entered into under threats of violence or the like. If a person signs a contract at the point of a gun there is no doubt that the contract will be held at least voidable, and perhaps even void for duress. Further, the legal definition of duress extends to threats of a more general nature, provided that they are illegal. For instance, a promise extorted by a blackmailer is clearly void and unenforceable.

Although in extreme cases of this kind there can be no difficulty or doubt about the legal result, there is considerable doubt about the theoretical justification for the rules of duress, and perhaps even more for those of undue influence, which we shall come to shortly. Traditionally, it used to be said that these are simply cases where there is no 'true consent', or where the promisor's 'will is overborne' so that his promise is not a genuine act of free will at all. But this explanation has been much criticized, especially by American writers, and some of the grounds for the criticism go back to Aristotle. A person who does something under the most severe constraints (such as throwing his cargo overboard to save his ship during a storm), is, said Aristotle, still acting voluntarily, of his own free will. He is choosing between two very unpalatable courses, but he is still making a free choice. Similarly, a person who signs a contract at the point of a gun may be said to be simply choosing between being shot and signing the document. He signs, not because he has no will—indeed, the more strongly he believes in the gunman's threats, the more willing he is likely to be to sign—but because it is the lesser of the two evils open to him.

But this analysis leads to a new difficulty. If even the gunman's victim is acting of his free will, then we must say that all (or anyhow nearly all[1]) contracts are made voluntarily, but we must also admit that all contracts are made under pressure of some sort. Not only is there no such thing as a totally involuntary contract, there is equally no such thing as a totally unconstrained choice. Every contract we make is made under some form of pressure, every contractual offer is made backed by some sort of threat. The pressure and the threats are implicit in the whole concept of exchange, because the offeror is always demanding something in return for his offer, which is only another way of saying that he is threatening not to supply what you want, unless you can give him what he wants in return. This means that some way must be found of distinguishing between the kinds of pressure and the kinds of threats which will be permissible, which will not invalidate a contract, and those pressures and threats which will be ruled out, and which will invalidate a contract. The distinction which the law seeks to draw, therefore, must be that between legitimate and illegitimate pressure, or threats, and has nothing to do with 'overborne wills'.

This excursion into theory is not without practical import, because the questions raised by these two possible approaches are quite different. If the law were truly concerned with the degree to which a choice was an exercise of free will, the question before the court would presumably be a psychological (or even philosophical) question[2] of no little difficulty, and it

---

[1] This qualification is needed to meet the rare case where one person falls so far under the complete domination of another that he acts as though in a trance, scarcely aware of what he is doing at all.

[2] Or possibly a linguistic question. It could be argued perhaps that the question is whether in ordinary language we would say that a person had acted of his free will, but the difficulty is

would also be a question of fact in each case: has the will been overborne? On the other hand, if the true question concerns the legitimacy of the pressure or threats used, the question must be one of law which has nothing to do with the psychological state of mind of the party in question. Unfortunately, the courts have not yet shaken off the 'overborne will' theory, despite the fact that the House of Lords appears to have disposed of it in a slightly different context.[3] The result is that judges sometimes say that the question is simply one of fact, and 'find' that the party's will was (or was not) overborne, even though there appear to be no criteria by which such findings can really be made. It is time that this approach was discarded, and some attempt made to face up to the difficult problem of deciding what are legitimate forms of pressure, and what are illegitimate.

Obviously there are two extremes which cause no difficulty. On the one hand are the perfectly ordinary pressures existing in any competitive society. These include, not merely the inherent threat in all exchanges that you cannot get what is on offer unless you pay the price, but also more substantial social and commercial pressures, such as the blandishments of the salesman or the pressure to keep up with the Joneses. These are the threats and pressures of any competitive society, and clearly they must not be allowed to invalidate contracts in the ordinary way. At the other extreme there are the cases of gross personal violence discussed above, such as that of the contract signed at the point of a gun. There is no difficulty about ruling these out as impermissible, and invalidating the resultant contract, because this kind of violence is anyhow illegal. Quite apart from the law of contract, there are criminal laws which define and control the limits of permissible violence of this kind.

But between these two extremes, there are far more difficult cases. Historically, for instance, contracts of employment were often entered into under extreme pressure—when the choice was between one particular local industry and the workhouse, it was often stark indeed. Yet contracts of employment were never invalidated on grounds of duress or pressure at common law. Similarly, moneylending contracts are often entered into by very desperate borrowers, and we know that such people are often willing to sign almost anything to lay their hands on the money they need, or want.

that ordinary language is not a sufficiently precise guide to the fine distinctions which the law has to draw.

[3] This analysis was accepted by all members of the House of Lords in the (criminal) duress case of *Lynch* v. *DPP of Northern Ireland* [1975] AC 653. (The actual decision of the majority in *Lynch's* case was overruled in *R* v. *Howe* [1987] AC 417 but this does not seem to affect the theoretical analysis approved in *Lynch*.) See also *Universe Tankships of Monrovia* v. *ITTF* [1983] 1 AC 366 and *Dimskal Shipping Co SA* v. *ITWF* [1992] 2 AC 152 in which there are further HL dicta casting doubt on the 'overborne will' analysis. But lower courts have not yet begun to use this analysis, and still tend to speak in terms of the 'overborne will' theory.

These contracts, too, were never regarded as entered into under unacceptable pressure or threats in the ordinary course of events, although it is possible that this kind of pressure was one of the reasons underlying the readiness of Courts of Equity to interfere with such contracts where the results were thought to be grossly unfair.

If the law of duress and undue influence was confined to threats which were illegal in themselves, actually criminal, these distinctions would be intelligible, if harsh. But the law of duress and undue influence has never been quite so limited as this. The threat of many an ordinary blackmailer (for instance, to give some information to the police, or to an employer, or to a spouse) is quite often not criminal in itself. Indeed, it sometimes actually is the duty of the blackmailer to give the information (where it is itself information about a serious crime, for instance, there may be a duty to inform the police), so the threat is not to do anything which is itself illegal. What makes the blackmailer's conduct criminal is the attempt to extort money by use of the threat—but is that not what everyone does in the market? Clearly, it is necessary to distinguish between threats which are acceptable or legitimate, and those which are not acceptable or legitimate, even in cases where the threats are not themselves illegal. And this is a source of real difficulty, because there are no general criteria by which we can draw these distinctions.

Yet in modern times, commercial and economic pressures are of enormous importance, and they often reflect major conflicts of political power. Gross cases of duress by personal violence are rare in modern societies. It is the more subtle and insidious forms of pressure that one finds today. Until very recent times economic or commercial pressures were almost entirely ignored by the common law. No matter that a contract was entered into under sheer commercial necessity, and that the terms were dictated by one party to the other, it could not generally be attacked on this ground. For instance, few pressures could be greater than that imposed by manufacturers' threats to place a trader on a 'stop-list', with the result that he might be driven out of business. Yet a promise to pay money in return for not being placed on the stop-list was enforceable at common law, and has only been outlawed by legislation since 1956. Similarly, an agreement by an employer to pay increased wages is frequently made under great pressure; but it would be very surprising if a court were to hold that the agreement is for that reason unenforceable. So long as strikes, and threats of strikes, are treated by the law as permissible ways of exerting bargaining power (subject, it may be, to various conditions), it would be inconsistent to treat contracts made under pressures of this kind as vulnerable to attack.

On the other hand there are a number of recent cases in which the courts have begun to recognize the concept of 'economic duress'. For instance, many strikes and threats of strikes are today unlawful in some sense, such as where they are called without a statutory ballot of the workforce or where they involve secondary boycotts, threatening parties not directly involved in the dispute. Such strikes are not criminal, but tortious, so that they can be restrained by injunctions, and the threat of such a strike may well have invalidating effects on subsequent contracts. For instance, where a union demanded payments to a sort of 'slush-fund' as the price of not (unlawfully) blacking a ship and so allowing it to leave port, it was held that the money could be recovered.[4] So also, in another modern case, where a contracting party was compelled to agree to a variation of his contract (by paying more) because of a strike threat by the *other party's* work-force, it was held that the contract-variation was invalid, as made under economic duress.[5] This situation differs from that in which an employer agrees to some demands by his own work-force, because his relations with his workers is at least *his* business, and it is his responsibility to decide whether to give way, or to face the consequences. But where the strike threat comes from the other party's workers, the victim of the threat has no responsibility for the relations between the workers and their employer.

Clearly, if the law is to avoid the danger of economic duress being widely used to invalidate contracts, some limits must be placed on how this new doctrine is to be used, and these limits are gradually emerging from the modern cases. First, it is clear that the nature of the threat must be strongly coercive, so that the innocent party may truly be said to have had little real or effective alternative but to submit. This means, among other things, that if there is any real opportunity to go to law and have the issue thrashed out in court, this should be done. A party should not, in general, hoodwink the other by pretending to submit to the threats made to him, and then challenge his conduct later. The challenge should come at the outset.

Some of the most coercive threats occur in monopoly situations of one kind or another—indeed, it is arguable that (truly understood) these are really the only kinds of coercive threats to which the law pays attention, other than manifestly criminal threats of violence and the like. Obviously, in the ordinary competitive market, a threat to refuse to supply goods or services is not coercive, because the threatened party can simply go elsewhere in the market. But in a monopoly situation enormous coercive power can lie behind threats not to deal, or only to deal on certain terms, and in the ordinary commercial market-place monopolies often do use their power in ways which would seem unfair to the impartial observer. Yet English courts are still loath to strike down contracts entered into under such monopolistic pressures. Two examples of this kind of thing can be given.

---

[4] See the *Monrovia* case, *supra*, n. 3.
[5] *B. & S. Contracts & Design Ltd* v. *Victor Green Publishers Ltd* [1984] ICR 419.

When a business closes down as a result of insolvency the first thing that happens is usually that a receiver or liquidator comes in—literally comes in to the office or premises of the business. His first task is obviously to examine the books, to obtain control of the assets, and to ascertain the liabilities of the business, but he will have very great difficulty in doing any of these things if he cannot switch on the lights or use the telephone. But until recently it was the practice of the public utilities to cut off supplies and to refuse to restore them unless and until the receiver or liquidator agreed not merely to be responsible for future supplies, but also to pay all past unpaid bills. The result was that these public utilities obtained payment of their bills in preference to other creditors simply by using their monopoly powers. This practice was never challenged at common law but it is now barred by section 200 of the Insolvency Act 1985.

The second example illustrates how, even in the ordinary commercial market, a monopoly situation can still exist and still be exploited. In *Leyland Daf* v. *Automotive Products Ltd*[6] a motor manufacturer became insolvent and a receiver was called in who attempted to carry on the business pending a possible sale. The defendants were sole suppliers of spare parts to the manufacturer, and as a condition of continuing to supply the receiver they required him to pay all existing debts due to them from the manufacturer, even though the receiver was not of course liable for past debts. It was not disputed that the whole of the manufacturer's business could be halted for lack of one part which only the defendants could supply so that their coercive power was plainly enormous. Even in this situation the lawfulness of the contract was not (apparently) challenged on grounds of economic duress, though the defendant's conduct was unsuccessfully challenged as a restrictive practice rendered unlawful under Article 86 of the EC Treaty, which strikes down conduct which is an 'abuse of a dominant position'.[7]

These two examples show that the new doctrine of economic duress still requires considerable amplification if it is to be clear when it applies and when it does not. If it cannot be invoked even in extreme cases of monopoly such as these, it is not obvious why it should be available in less extreme situations. Yet there are a number of cases where the law has intervened which certainly do not involve monopoly pressure as normally understood. But here we come to a point of considerable importance. Monopoly situations are far more common than is generally recognized, because monopoly is a matter of degree. While economists are usually interested in large-scale monopolies which have an influence on the nation's whole economy, the lawyer must recognize that monopolies often exist on a very small scale and, furthermore, that they are often mere

---

[6] (1993) BCC 389.     [7] See *post*, 336.

matters of degree. A small-scale monopoly, or what I have elsewhere referred to as a micro-monopoly, may, for instance, exist in a particular place: there is only one supplier for some commodity or service. This is rarely a problem in modern societies, because ease of travel and transportation prevents such local monopolies having much coercive power. But occasionally a local (and temporary) monopolist may have immense coercive power as, for instance, when a vessel is in distress at sea, and a solitary salvage vessel offers to lend assistance on its own terms. Extortionate contracts entered into in such circumstances have long been liable to be set aside by the courts.[8]

Other micro-monopolies exist between parties who are already locked into some relationship. For instance, where two contracting parties try to negotiate a variation of their contract, the parties are in a situation which economists term 'bilateral monopoly'. They are, in a sense, *both* monopolists—the contract variation can *only* be negotiated between these parties. If either party is dissatisfied, he cannot go into the market to renegotiate that contract—he can, of course, try to extricate himself from the relationship altogether, and form a new one elsewhere in the market, but there are often enormous practical difficulties over such a course, and frequently it would anyhow be irrelevant to the problem in hand. For instance, a trade union and an employer are almost permanently locked into a bilateral monopoly—neither party can break off the relationship, realistically speaking. In these situations, it cannot be said, *a priori*, that one or other party has the more powerful bargaining position, but in particular circumstances, this kind of monopoly situation can give one party great coercive powers over the other. These bilateral monopoly relations are very common in situations which give rise to legal problems. Apart from cases mentioned above, other common examples are cases of husband and wife negotiating a financial settlement on divorce, and cases of accident victims, negotiating a settlement in a tort claim against the tortfeasor or his insurer.

Another common type of micro-monopoly arises out of the constraints of time. Someone needs something in a hurry for good reasons; inability to obtain what he needs may threaten him with great loss. Perhaps he has a regular supplier, and that supplier tries to extort extra payment because of the situation, or perhaps he can only find, for the moment, one possible supplier. Here again, the supplier may have great coercive power. Or again, someone is using a professional adviser, such as an accountant or a lawyer, to prepare documents for him. The documents are needed in a hurry—perhaps they have to be filed by a certain date, or sent out by a certain date to be legally effective. At the last moment, when it is far too

---

[8] *Akerblom* v. *Price* (1881) 7 QBD 129, and *The Port Caledonia and The Anna* [1903] P 184 are two of many such cases.

late to obtain help elsewhere, the adviser demands extra payment as a condition for getting the work done on time. Here the adviser has a micro-monopoly position because of the time situation, and his coercive power may be enormous.

Of course, care must be exercised before it is concluded that all such use of monopoly power is wrongful. It must be remembered that the whole system of private property also rests (in a sense) on recognition of the monopoly rights of the property owner—only he owns the property, and only he has the right to use it. So a property owner can sell his property (or rights over it) at whatever price he chooses, and he can therefore (tautologically) threaten *not* to sell it unless he is paid whatever price he wishes to ask. The same goes for human labour: every person can sell his labour at whatever price he can get in the market. He is a monopolist owner of his own labour.

But despite this need for caution about the nature of small-scale monopoly, it seems clear that one of the major causes of coercion, and hence of unfair contracts, arises from these monopolies; and it is here therefore that some relief is most likely to be needed for parties who have entered into contracts under threats or pressure. Many cases bear out this need and, indeed, some cases also show that the courts are particularly prepared to respond in cases of this nature. And although the courts do not use the language of 'monopoly' they often use similar language, more traditional for lawyers—for instance, they place great stress on the effectiveness, or reality, of the choices open to a party, and of course it is precisely here that monopoly tends to bite.

Some modern cases illustrate how these micro-monopolies can arise in the renegotiation of existing contracts. In an interesting modern decision upholding the plea of economic duress, it was held that the purchaser of a ship from a shipbuilder could have refused to honour a promise of extra payment extracted from him as a condition of delivery of the ship.[9] In such circumstances it may be unreal to suggest that the buyer should resist the demand and go to law to enforce his right to the ship without extra payment. For there may be simply no time for appeal to the law, and the buyer's need for the ship may be urgent. Yet even this buyer was held to have lost his right to complain of economic duress, because he had paid the extra and made no further protest until some months after taking delivery of the ship—this was held to amount to an affirmation of the contract-variation at a time when the duress had ceased to operate. In other words, the buyer complained too late. So also, a person who, faced with an unjustified demand of this kind, carefully considers his alternatives and

[9] *North Ocean Shipping Co Ltd* v. *Hyundai Construction Co Ltd* [1979] QB 705; see also *Atlas Express Ltd* v. *Kafco (Importers and Distributors) Ltd* [1989] QB 833. But compare *CTN Cash and Carry Ltd* v. *Gallaher Ltd* [1994] 4 All ER 714.

decides to submit, may be held to have lost any right to complain of economic duress even from the outset.[10]

There are also signs that in other cases the courts might be more willing to pay attention to various forms of economic pressure in modern times. For instance, a debtor who pays only part of what is due to a hard-pressed creditor, and extracts from him an agreement not to sue for the balance, may receive an unsympathetic hearing from a court today.[11] Although fiction is fond of portraying the misfortunes of the debtor who is harassed by his creditors, every lawyer knows that an unscrupulous debtor can in fact lead his creditor a long and merry dance before he gets any money; there are thus some cases in which the real pressure comes from the debtor and not the creditor. This too is a micro-monopoly situation.

We saw earlier[12] how at one time the doctrine of consideration was used as a way of controlling the validity of contractual variations which might have been obtained by undue pressure, and how modern decisions are beginning to shift the basis of the law away from consideration towards the new doctrine of economic duress. The result, in particular, of the decision in *Williams* v. *Roffey Bros & Nicholls (Contractors) Ltd*[13] may well be that in future little difficulty will be encountered with the doctrine of consideration when considering the validity of a contractual variation, and it also seems from that decision that one way of testing the variation against the doctrine of economic duress is to ask whether it was commercially reasonable. Where the variation makes good commercial sense as a result (for example) of some change in circumstances it is clearly unlikely that there will be any arguable case of economic duress.

### 2. UNDUE INFLUENCE

The rather narrow traditional limits of the doctrine of duress have long been supplemented by the equitable doctrine of undue influence. This is rather a peculiar doctrine, because (as we shall suggest) many of the most important cases falling under it have very little to do with 'undue influence' in any ordinary sense. There are two classes of cases which fall within the doctrine, first, those in which actual undue influence is proved, and secondly, those in which there is a 'presumption' of undue influence.

### 'Actual' undue influence

In the first type of case it must be shown that the defendant obtained a dominating influence over the plaintiff, and used this influence to coerce or

---

[10] *Pao On* v. *Lau Yiu* [1980] AC 614. Perhaps if the complaining party only submits under protest, or subject to a reservation of rights, this might make a difference.
[11] *D. & C. Builders Ltd* v. *Rees* [1966] 2 QB 617.      [12] See *supra*, 134.
[13] [1991] 1 QB 1.

pressure him into a contract which he would not otherwise have agreed to. In most such cases the party exercising the influence has done so to take advantage of the other by extracting from him some highly favourable transaction, but in these cases of 'actual undue influence' it is not necessary that the resultant contract should be unfair in the result. Exercising 'actual' undue influence is a legal wrong, akin to fraud, and as in the case of fraud the innocent party is entitled to have the transaction set aside irrespective of the fairness or unfairness of the result.[14] This book is concerned with contracts, so we speak in terms of contracts, but in practice such cases of undue influence are often alleged where it is a gift or a will that is in question, and the principles applicable in all these cases are broadly the same.

Occasionally such cases arise even where the defendant has not acted in any way irrationally. The courts are sometimes prepared to hold a contract voidable when it can be shown that, although it was entered into 'at arm's length' (i.e. between parties in no way dependent on one another), yet in fact one party exerted unfair pressure on the other. For example, in a leading nineteenth century case it was held that a promise by the defendant to guarantee payment of certain promissory notes was voidable because the promise had been extorted under implied threats that the defendant's son would be prosecuted for forging endorsements on the notes.[15] This sort of contract is particularly objectionable, not only because of the element of pressure or duress, but also because it is generally against the public interest that serious crime should be hushed up in this way. So contracts of this kind are often void on public policy grounds even without the complicating factor of illegitmate pressure. There is, however, nothing objectionable about a promise to make good defalcations for which the promisor is personally responsible, even under threats of prosecution, so long as it is quite clear that the promise is not given as an inducement to withhold information from the police, or to suppress a prosecution.

But most modern cases of undue influence involve defendants who (it is claimed) were not wholly normal or rational. Typical cases arise where a senile person, no longer fully able to get about and seek advice, has fallen under the influence of a companion or nurse or relative who has been taking care of him. Other typical cases arise where a person joins a religious organization or group, and falls totally under the domination of a leader of the group, so as to be apparently incapable of exercising any independent judgement of his own. Often the allegation is that the party said to have been suffering from the undue influence has made over valuable property to the other, whether by way of contract or gift, or made

---

[14] *CIBC Mortgages plc* v. *Pitt* [1994] 1 AC 200.
[15] *Williams* v. *Bayley* (1866) LR 1 HL 200.

a will in his favour, when in the ordinary course of human relationships other persons would have been expected to have a stronger claim to be named beneficiaries of the will. Of course, care must always be taken not to confuse undue influence with eccentricity. A person is entitled to make strange contracts or gifts or wills, if he really understands what he is at, but in practice many of the cases reek with suspicious circumstances—for instance, the seclusion of the person in question from other normal advisers or relatives, the fact that long-maintained plans or wills are often upset by the dispositions being challenged, and so forth.

Cases of actual undue influence do not, on the whole, raise many difficult questions of law, although they often give rise to prolonged factual disputes, which can only be resolved by lengthy judicial hearings.

## Presumed undue influence

The second class of cases—those in which there is said to be a 'presumption of undue influence'—are more difficult, as a matter of law, and also tend to be more numerous. These cases developed from an ancient equitable jurisdiction over trustees and other persons in what is called a 'fiduciary' relationship. Courts of Equity, with their emphasis on conscience and good faith, developed an extremely valuable and elastic principle to the effect that a person must not abuse a position of trust or confidence. This principle extends far beyond the confines of the law of contract, and finds its main application in the duties of trustees. For instance, it is a well-established rule that a trustee must not profit from his position unless expressly empowered to do so. Indeed, the position of a trustee is so capable of abuse that in some respects the law prefers to put temptation out of his way altogether, for example, by completely prohibiting a purchase by a trustee of trust property. This does not mean that such a purchase is void, but that it is voidable, and that its voidability does not depend on any proof that the trustee did in fact take wrongful advantage of his position. No matter how fair the contract itself, the law permits no inquiry into the transaction but simply declares it voidable.

But trustees are not the only persons who fall under this doctrine. Any relationship in which trust or confidence is reposed by one party in another to such a degree that the former becomes dependent on the latter, falls within the doctrine, and gives rise to the 'presumption of undue influence'. In some circumstances, the 'presumption' arises merely out of a standard type of relationship—for instance, it arises (in addition to the case of trustee and beneficiary) between principal and agent, solicitor and client, parent and child (at least if the child is unmarried and under age), and religious adviser and disciple, but not between husband and wife.

But the category of fiduciary relationships has never been strictly defined and is not to be confined within any narrow formula. So even where the relationship does not fall into one of the standard classes which raise the 'presumption of undue influence', it is possible to establish that the presumption arises from the particular facts. In any case where one person turns to another for advice or assistance, and the court thinks that the relationship between the parties, for example, their relative ages, or experience, or blood relationship, is such as to require confidence and good faith, the duty not to abuse that confidence may be imposed. For instance, in a nineteenth century case, where a young man, heavily indebted and estranged from his father, turned to other relations for advice, it was held that a contract for the sale of his estate for a price which the other party, a distant cousin, knew to be considerably less than its real value, should be set aside.[16]

One modern example of a case of this kind is *Goldsworthy* v. *Brickell*[17] in which the plaintiff, a man of 85, who owned a valuable farm worth about one million pounds, came to trust and depend a great deal on the defendant, a neighbouring farmer, for advice and help in running his farm. This was not a case in which any 'actual undue influence' or any personal domination was shown—the plaintiff was mentally and physically quite fit, and had a strong personality, but it was nevertheless held that the relationship between them raised the 'presumption of undue influence', and could be invoked to invalidate an agreement by the plaintiff to let his farm at a very low rent to the defendant, with a favourable option to purchase as well.

So also, even in cases which do not fall within the presumption because they are one of the standard cases, it is often relatively easy to establish the necessary degree of trust and confidence, if the case resembles the standard cases. For instance, if a young girl, just over the age of majority, is advised by her father to settle her private fortune on trusts which are by no means in her best interests, the settlement may be set aside even though there is no question of her father having put pressure on her, and even though there is no evidence that he sought any unfair profit for himself out of the arrangement. So too, as between husband and wife, a case of presumed undue influence may arise if it is shown that the wife simply did what her husband wanted, signing documents put in front of her, and so on, without questioning his advice in any way.

In *Lloyd's Bank* v. *Bundy*[18] in 1974, the Court of Appeal applied these principles to the relationship between a bank and one of its customers. The customer in this case was an elderly man whose only substantial asset was his house. He was persuaded to grant a mortgage over his house as a security for advances made by the bank to a business owned by the customer's son. The business was in financial difficulties and heavily

---

[16] *Tate* v. *Williamson* (1866) LR 2 Ch. App. 55.   [17] [1987] 1 All ER 853.
[18] [1975] QB 326.

indebted to the bank which nevertheless induced the father to increase the amount of the guarantee covered by the mortgage. Shortly afterwards, the son's business failed completely and the bank attempted to enforce the mortgage. It was held that, in the particular circumstances of this case, the bank should have advised its customer to take independent advice before granting the increased mortgage. As a customer of the bank, he was entitled to frank and honest advice, but the bank's interest in obtaining the security meant that that advice was never given.

Since then it has been made clear by the House of Lords in *National Westminster Bank* v. *Morgan*[19] that the presumption of undue influence does not arise from the mere relationship of banker and customer: it must be shown that in the particular circumstances the customer reposed such confidence and trust in the bank that the presumption arises. The actual decision in the *Bundy* case may, therefore, be correct, though of course the circumstances will vary from case to case.

## Undue influence by third parties

A question which has caused some difficulty (as anticipated in the last edition of this book) concerns the possibility of undue influence being exercised by a third party, and not the contracting party being challenged. A typical case involves a mortgage of a matrimonial home granted to secure the business debts of the husband. If the wife is joint owner of the home, and signs the mortgage as surety or guarantor under the domination or influence of her husband, is the mortgagee affected by this even though not itself guilty in any way of undue influence?

The law on this point was reviewed and restated in modern terms by the House of Lords in *Barclays Bank* v. *O'Brien*.[20] According to this decision the first task is to examine the situation as between the husband and wife. There is no automatic presumption of undue influence between husband and wife, but if in the particular circumstances of the case the 'presumption' arises, that is, if the wife has not really exercised any independent judgement of her own, but has habitually confided in her husband and signed documents without question, then, as between them, the case of undue influence is proved. Strictly it also needs to be shown that the contract is to her manifest disadvantage, but a contract of guarantee is nearly always to the disadvantage of the guarantor who derives no benefit from it.[21]

---

[19] [1985] AC 686.                    [20] [1994] 1 AC 180.

[21] The *O'Brien* case (*supra*, n. 20) seems to accept rather lightly the assumption that a wife can rarely benefit from a transaction by which she guarantees her husband's business debts. But in practice wherever a couple draw their income from the husband's business—a common event—it is likely that the wife would benefit from such a transaction. See on this point the *Morgan* case, *supra*, n. 19.

The second question is then whether the mortgagee is affected by this undue influence. There are two ways in which it can be so affected. The first is by showing that the husband acted as agent of the mortgagee, but this is unlikely and can be disregarded in most cases. The second and much more important possibility is by showing that the mortgagee is affected by 'notice' of the husband's undue influence. The mortgagee may, of course, have actual notice, but much more likely is that the circumstances are such as to put the mortgagee on inquiry. Indeed, the House of Lords appears to have thought that the mortgagee is put on inquiry merely because the wife stands surety or as guarantor for her husband, first because she can derive no real benefit from such a transaction,[22] and secondly because of the informality of everyday domestic arrangements between husband and wife which makes it very possible that the husband has concealed or misrepresented important facts.

Where the mortgagee is thus put on inquiry as to the possibility of presumed undue influence it must arrange a separate interview with the wife, warn her of the risks involved, and counsel her to seek independent advice.

These principles apply also between cohabitants (even of the same sex) so long only as the mortgagee is aware of the facts. But they do not apply where the wife (or other partner) is simply a joint debtor who joins in an ordinary mortgage of the common home to secure money borrowed to buy the home. There is no reason why such a transaction should be to the manifest disadvantage of the wife or other partner, and therefore nothing to put the mortgagee on inquiry.

### Rebutting the presumption of undue influence

The next question which needs to be answered is what precisely is the effect of establishing that the 'presumption of undue influence' arises. The answer is that, unless the presumption is rebutted, the transaction is liable to be set aside. Moreover, it is liable to be set aside *even though no personal domination or actual undue influence is shown*. It is for this reason that the references to the 'presumption of undue influence' have been placed in quotation marks in this section, because (although judicial usage is inveterate) it is clear that the term is highly misleading. Many of these cases do not involve anything that could reasonably be called 'undue influence' in the ordinary sense of the term. The so-called 'presumption of undue influence' cannot in fact be rebutted by proving that there was no undue influence. It would be closer to the truth to say that in these cases there is a presumption that the contract is invalid for unfairness, though

---

[22] It is necessary again to warn that this inference may not always be justified, see *supra*, n. 21.

that way of stating the law is, of course, liable to arouse the hostility of the traditionalists.

But it seems clear that this would be a more accurate way of stating the law because, although the 'presumption of undue influence' cannot be rebutted by showing that there was no undue influence, it can be rebutted by showing that the contract (or other transaction) was not unfair. In practice there are three ways in which this can be done, some cases emphasizing one way, and some another, according to their relevance to the context.

First, it can be shown that in fact no undue advantage was taken, so that the contract was not to 'the manifest disadvantage' of the complaining party. This possibility was emphasized by the House of Lords in *National Westminster Bank* v. *Morgan*,[23] where it was held that the 'presumption' did not arise on the facts, but even if it had arisen, the transaction was perfectly fair and reasonable. The wife in this case had joined in granting a mortgage over the matrimonial home to secure her husband's debts, but in the particular circumstances, this was a perfectly fair and reasonable course from which the wife derived a significant benefit. (There remains at present some doubt as to who has the burden of proof in relation to showing whether the contract was to the manifest disadvantage of the complaining party.[24])

In order to show that no undue advantage was taken, it may be necessary to examine the particular nature of the relationship between the parties with some care. The precise way in which the duties imposed on fiduciaries are applied varies according to the nature of the relationship. The principal–agent relationship, for instance, varies from the case of the office boy who is sent out to buy a few stamps to that of the company director managing the business of a large company in which many thousands of shareholders may be interested. Naturally, the duty not to take unfair advantage of the confidence reposed in the agent will vary in intensity with his position. In the case of company directors, for instance, the duty is exceptionally strict, and, indeed, their position nearly approaches that of trustees if they attempt to sell property to, or buy property from, the company. In such a case they may find it hard to satisfy a court that there has been nothing unfair or unconscionable about their conduct. The strictness of the duty in this case is probably justified because the directors, being in charge of the company's business, are subject to practically no real

---

[23] *Supra*, n. 19.

[24] The *Morgan* case appears to lay the burden of proof on the party seeking to set the agreement aside, but there are earlier authorities possibly inconsistent with this: see *CIBC Mortgages plc* v. *Pitt, supra*, n. 14.

[25] Compare on this point the *O'Brien* case, *supra* n. 20.

control by the really interested parties, the shareholders, at least in the case of public companies.

The second way in which the 'presumption' can be rebutted is by showing that the challenged transaction was fully understood and intended by the party claiming to have been prejudiced. If the transaction was truly a spontaneous act of free will,[26] by someone who fully understood what he was doing, this may itself be enough to rebut the 'presumption'. As we have said above, the purpose of the law is not to prevent people from disposing of their property in strange or even eccentric ways. The law is (rightly) suspicious of such dispositions of property, because they may be evidence that the owner did not wholly understand what he was doing, but if it is quite clear that he did so understand, that he wanted (for instance) to be extremely generous to a mere friend or neighbour, even at the expense of members of his family, the transaction may well be upheld.

There is, in practice, a third way in which the 'presumption' may be rebutted, and that is by showing that the party alleged to have been prejudiced was independently advised by some suitable person—for instance, by a competent solicitor, not also acting for the other party to the transaction. There are many cases in which the question of independent advice has played a prominent part, and gifts and contracts are very much more suspect where they are entered into solely on the advice of someone in a position to exercise influence. It is of the utmost importance in such cases that the party in question should receive the disinterested advice of a solicitor or similarly trustworthy person who can point out exactly what are the disadvantages of what is proposed to be done, and suggest possible alternatives. It is, of course, equally important that the advice should not come (as it often has in the cases) from the solicitor acting for the other party to the transaction. Indeed, a solicitor would probably be failing in his professional duties if he acted for both parties in a case where one of them was manifestly under a duty of a fiduciary nature.[27] On the other hand, the courts have refused to hold that a transaction of this nature can never be upheld in the absence of independent advice, although some of the cases indicate that in particular circumstances this is an unlikely eventuality.

It will be seen that the question of independent advice may be relevant to either of the first two ways of rebutting the presumption. A solicitor, for instance, may be able to weigh the fairness of the proposed transaction, and advise the party in question that it appears to be a perfectly reasonable

---

[26] These are the terms used by the CA in *Goldsworthy* v. *Brickell* (*supra*, n. 17) and it is clear enough what they mean in this context, though in one sense they are pretty vacuous.

[27] In *Clark Boyce* v. *Mouat* [1993] 4 All ER 268 it was held that a solicitor can act for both parties to a transaction provided there is full discolosure and informed consent, but this case did not concern parties one of whom owes fiduciary duties to the other.

transaction, and that there is little prospect of securing better terms elsewhere. This would be evidence that the transaction was objectively fair and reasonable. Alternatively, the independent adviser may be able to explain in careful detail precisely what is involved in the transaction, so that (even though he may personally think it strange or unwise or even unfair) he can ensure that the transaction is at least the fully considered act of the party concerned.

In practice it is often clear that, in many cases of this kind where there has been no independent advice, the most likely advice would have been that the contract should on no account be entered into on the proposed terms. For instance, if the defendant in *Lloyd's Bank* v. *Bundy* (which has been mentioned above[28]) had consulted a solicitor or accountant it is very probable that he would have been advised that it was folly to give the bank the extra security they were asking for, as he would only be throwing his money away. Similarly, where a separated wife is asked to sign away her interest in the matrimonial home, receiving in return nothing more than a release from her mortgage liabilities, it is clear that an independent adviser could give only one piece of sensible advice: Don't.

---

[28] *Supra*, n. 18.

# 16

# Unfair Contracts

## I. FAIRNESS AND CONTRACT LAW

WE have seen that many contracts are bargains, and that the bargain is the central, or paradigm, kind of contract addressed by classical contract theory. According to this theory, the role of courts in handling contract cases is very limited, and the same is true for the role allotted to ideas of fairness and justice. Classical theory distinguishes fundamentally between fairness in the process of negotiating and concluding a bargain, on the one hand, and fairness in the result or outcome of the bargain, on the other. Making a contract is thus rather like participating in a contest or game. There are rules designed to regulate the way in which the contest is conducted, to outlaw fouls, to decide upon the appropriate penalty for fouls, and so on. The rules must themselves be fair, if the contest or game is to be perceived to be fair, so (for instance) the rules must apply equally to both sides, and provision must be made for the interpretation of the rules by neutral and impartial umpires. But if the game is played according to the rules, there is really very limited scope for any concept of a 'fair outcome'. Both participants should benefit from taking part in the game, and the best contestant should 'win'. The rules are designed to produce this result—they are not designed to equalize the chances of all contestants, because some are more skilful or better equipped than others.

This kind of vision of the nature of contract law permeates classical theory, and has probably always been an extremely powerful vision affecting a very large number of contractual disputes—certainly for the last three or four hundred years. And with the apparent revival in the influence of classical theory in recent years, this vision has once again become of great importance. According to this vision, the function of the law, in so far as fairness and justice are concerned, is largely confined to ensuring *procedural fairness*. Bargains must be made according to the rules, and there are indeed rules to ensure that. For example, there are fundamental rules which outlaw the use of fraud or misrepresentation, violence or coercion in the making of contracts. There are rules designed to ensure that parties are only bound by terms to which they have actually given their assent, and there are rules protecting parties from trickery or (to a limited extent) even from the effects of gross mistakes. There are rules designed to ensure that the parties are not wholly unequal in their capacity to make contracts, so for instance, there are rules protecting minors under the age of 18 or persons suffering from mental illness. There is also the doctrine of undue influence protecting a party who is under the domination of the other to such a degree that his judgement may be seriously impaired. In all these ways, then, the law is concerned with fairness, procedural fairness.

But according to classical theory, the law has no concern with the results or outcome of a contract. This is a matter of substantive fairness or justice, and here, ideas of fairness are said to be out of place, just as much as they would be out of place in considering the outcome of a sporting event. Each party has assessed the desirability of making the contract or not making it, and has decided to make it. Each party, as a responsible adult, must therefore be assumed to have weighed the value of what he proposed to give in exchange for what he expected to get. If each party is satisfied with that exchange, how can it be said that the result is 'unfair'? Furthermore, (according to classical theory) there is no real cause for concern here, because if contract law works well, if the procedures are properly adhered to, and parties are only held to bargains they have freely and voluntarily entered into, then both parties ought anyhow to be better off as a result of the contract. The exchange which they have made will have produced what economists call 'gains from trade', a sort of happy surplus, and that surplus will be divided between them as a result of their contract. Suppose S sells his house to B for £100,000. Perhaps S would have been willing to take £98,000, so he is £2,000 better off. Perhaps B would have been willing to pay £105,000, so he is £5,000 better off. Both parties are gainers for having made the contract. True, B has done rather better than S in this example, but that may be because he was more skilful at bargaining (he successfully concealed the fact that he was willing to pay more) or it may be because B had more bargaining power (S had to sell urgently for private reasons, perhaps, while B was prepared to take his time looking for a house). Whatever the reason, both parties have gained, and each has decided that the gain is worthwhile. The same is true, though the gain less measurable, even where the price fixed is the least S would take, and the most B would pay; even here there are gains to both parties for the simple reason that S prefers to have the money and B prefers to have the house and these preferences have some value though it may be difficult to put a precise figure to them.

This theoretical analysis leads to the view that the law must simply respect the contract which the parties have made, and must enforce the contract according to its terms, without concern for the fairness of the outcome. Indeed, in one extreme version of this approach, it is not even possible in principle to say what a fair contract is—there simply is no such thing as a substantively fair contract. On this view, all values are purely subjective, and if the two parties are content with their bargain, there is no basis on which some third party (such as a judge) can pronounce the contract unfair at all. This view somewhat resembles a basic position in political theory often held by (American) liberals which denies that there is such a thing as substantive justice in the abstract. There are merely just procedures, and the outcome of just procedures must be respected, wherever they lead.

Of course, this does not mean that in practical reality the only function of the court is the purely mechanical one of enforcing what the parties have agreed to do. Because even on this extreme view of the nature of contract law, there will always be borderline cases, disputed questions of fact, for instance, about whether one party crossed the line between misrepresentation and simply keeping quiet, and there will always be a need for 'implications' to deal with points which the contract has not expressly dealt with. And there will always be a need for rules concerning remedies for breach of contract which are rarely expressly stipulated for by the parties.

There is no doubt that this distinction between procedural and substantive fairness is a fundamental idea which has influenced and continues to influence much of contract law, and the application of the law to individual cases.[1] At the same time, there are problems about this theoretical analysis, and in practice the law and the courts never seem able to withdraw wholly from concern with the substantive fairness of contractual outcomes. There are many reasons for this, but perhaps we should first attempt to address head on the question, what is an unfair contract?

Most lawyers would say that contracts—or particular contractual terms—can be unfair for all kinds of reasons. An employment contract might be unfair (it may be said) because, for instance, it allows the employer to dictate that the employee move to another place of work; a building contract may be unfair because, for instance, the builder may be entitled to demand extra payment for having to redo work previously done badly; a contract for services may be unfair because, for instance, the supplier of the services excludes his liability for negligence. This approach is mirrored in the EC Directive on Unfair Contract Terms which is discussed in more detail later in this chapter. But it is possible to take a different and much simpler approach to the problem of identifying an unfair contract or unfair term. It can be argued that an unfair contract is simply one in which significantly more (or less) than a fair market price is paid. Economists would probably suggest that this is a completely comprehensive answer (if they admit that the question can be answered at all) because, in theory, everything in the contract can be, and is, allowed for in the price. Every extra burden imposed on one party, every exclusion from liability demanded by the other, will enter into the calculation of the price in the market. Even where the extra burdens or exclusions are

---

[1] This distinction is to some extent recognized by the PC in *Hart* v. *O'Connor* [1985] AC 1000 at 1017–18.

contingent, the answer is in principle the same, because the market can and does take account of risks and contingencies, as well as of certainties. It only needs to be recognized that what is unfair at one price may be perfectly fair at another to appreciate that, in the last analysis, it is (nearly) always the price which determines fairness at the end. To test the correctness of this suggestion one only has to ask whether a price adjustment would be sufficient to persuade a party to agree to a term which is claimed to be unfair. Provided that some price adjustment—no matter how big or small—could be made which would satisfy the party affected, it should then be clear that if that adjustment were made the contract would (at least prima facie) be fair.

It must also be recognized that the common argument that all prices are subjective is fallacious. No doubt there is a subjective element in many prices, such as in the price of a house, or of a work of art, but even things of this kind have a market price—though it may sometimes be difficult to gauge it exactly. And many other things available in the market have a very precise market price. So when it is said that, if a person who has made a purchase is satisfied with the price, it is impossible to contend that the price is 'unfair', this simply fails to recognize that the buyer may have been mistaken. If he later discovers that he has agreed to pay much more than the fair market value in the belief that he was only agreeing to pay a market price it would seem absurd to contend that there is no basis on which it can be held that the contract was unfair. This does not mean that all such contracts should be held invalid; but it does mean that the common argument that a free and voluntary contract *cannot* be unfair is grossly overstated.

It therefore seems clear that in most cases fairness comes down to the amount of the price at the end, and this saves us from the need to pursue more esoteric definitions of fairness and unfairness. However, some qualifications may be needed to this answer, which it is not possible to pursue at length here. The reason is that there are certain rights which are not saleable—which we are not permitted to sell—and therefore which have no price in the market. A contract which (for instance) purported to penalize a party for issuing a writ would be void, because the right to apply to the courts is not saleable, and no matter what the consideration for this contract, it would remain an 'unfair contract'. But these complications can be left aside for our purposes, and it will suffice to assume in the following discussion that an unfair contract simply means one in which the price is grossly excessive or deficient.

We turn now to consider why it is so difficult for the law to concern itself exclusively with procedural justice—with fairness in the way contracts are made—and not to get involved with substantive justice—the fairness of contractual outcomes.

First, then, it is difficult always to put aside ideas of distributive justice in handling contract cases. The outcome of contractual negotiations will always be affected by the input: from what position did the parties start? If one of the parties is much richer and more powerful than the other, the outcome is likely to reflect this fact. Many people will not find acceptable the idea that the outcome of market bargains must always be accepted as made by the best procedures we have. This answer will not satisfy everyone, because the fairness of the outcome of bargains in the market-place is dependent on the initial distribution of wealth and resources with which the parties have entered the market. If that distribution is assumed to be acceptable, or itself fair, then bargains made in the market may also be assumed to be fair. But if the initial distribution of wealth is thought to be unfair, then any resulting bargains will simply mirror that unfairness. The analogy of contests and games is misleading in this connection because the participants in such contests are normally more equal than those in the market-place. Indeed, many sports grade contestants and teams for the specific purpose of eliminating the grosser inequalities.

Classical theory ignores these inequalities because (it is claimed) these are questions of morality or justice with which economics is not concerned. If we are concerned only with questions of efficiency, then market theory tells us that so long as there is a flourishing and genuinely competitive market inequalities do not matter. But even if we leave aside questions of morality and justice, we cannot be certain that bargains in the market-place are always, or even generally, efficient. In practice, markets notoriously suffer from many weaknesses which prevent perfect competition. There is, for instance, the problem of monopoly, and we have already seen that micro-monopoly raises many problems in contract law.

Then there are also informational difficulties: even private enterprise economics has to concede that markets provide efficient solutions only in conditions of 'perfect knowledge'. It is certain that parties who enter into free and voluntary exchanges will both gain (and so will the public) only if they actually know all the relevant facts. But this condition is never satisfied in practice. Nobody has perfect information, so parties often do enter into contracts which turn out disadvantageous simply because they did not know the full facts.[2] Suppose someone buys a house from a seller

---

[2] Some economic writers attempt to argue their way out of this difficulty by suggesting that information can always be bought in the market, and that those who lack information have decided that they are better off without it, because it would not be worth the additional cost of buying it. It is then argued that if they are indeed better off without the information, they should be bound by contracts just as if they had it. But the argument is flawed, because those who lack information often do not *know* that they lack it, and they may anyhow assume (often reasonably) that the law protects them if they do not have it (for instance, information that a new car they are buying is defective).

who knows but does not disclose that the house is suffering from a bad case of dry rot. Such a contractual exchange does not necessarily produce gains for both parties, and there is no economic justification for insisting that it should be enforced by the law. It is not at all clear that in such a case the outcome must be accepted because of the 'fair procedures' involved in the making of the contract.

In many cases, such as that discussed in the last paragraph, contracts are made in the market, but it is not clear whether the price agreed is really a market price. In fact we cannot say what the market price is, until we have first decided whether the market price means the price in a market in which the parties *know* the full facts, or the price in actual everyday markets, where the full facts are not known. Suppose a person buys a seriously defective second-hand car at a price which does not reflect those defects. Most people would probably say that he had agreed to pay more than the market price, and for that reason the contract would be regarded by them as substantively unfair. The assumption that, because something is sold in a competitive market, it will be sold at market prices is no doubt a reasonable assumption, but it does not take account of the fact that perfect information is not actually available in the market. So outcomes in the market will often seem unacceptable (and will often be economically inefficient too) where one party was much better informed than the other.

A second problem with classical theory is one we have already touched upon. The whole of this theory is based on the premiss that contracts are binding only on those who freely and voluntarily enter into them, and assent to their terms. But in practice the law has always adopted a fairly broad-brush approach to the question of determining whether there is assent. So contracting parties are often bound to terms which they have not read, or understood, or whose legal significance they have not grasped. This is not (as is often thought) a matter of marginal significance. Because in practice it is impossible for parties to read, understand, and keep in mind lengthy and complex written contracts—unless they employ expensive lawyers to do this for them—because also of the great importance of concepts like objective interpretation of intention, of induced reliance and estoppel, many contractual obligations are not supported by any real element of assent. Such liabilites are, in truth, closer to tort liabilities in their justification, and this means that most contracts rest on a mixture of voluntarily assumed obligations (which are assented to) and legally imposed obligations (where there is no real assent). Where these latter obligations turn out to be important in the particular circumstances of a case, there is no presumption whatever that the outcome will benefit both parties. One party may actually suffer heavy loss, while the other gains.

A third reason why it is impossible always to separate out procedural and substantive fairness is that they are closely inter-related in several ways.

One possibility, in particular, is that the requirement of assent (which goes to procedural justice) and that of fairness in outcome (which is a matter of substantive justice) are to some degree balanced against each other. This arises because each of these requirements can clearly be met in various degrees, and it seems quite likely that, the more unfair we find a contract to be, the more the law demands that it should be clear beyond a peradventure that a true and genuine assent has been given. Where a contract is reasonably fair (or perhaps only slightly unfair), however, a lower degree of assent will meet the requirements of the law. This possibility is suggested by the recent decision of the Court of Appeal in the *Interfoto* case,[3] which was discussed in Chapter 10 in connection with the rules governing the ticket cases. In that case, it will be remembered, the plaintiffs supplied some transparencies on hire to the defendants, together with a note setting out their terms. These terms included 'a holding charge' which was about ten times the charge made by similar agencies. The defendants were held not bound by these terms because they had not been sufficiently brought to their attention, given their extreme nature. Yet it is clear that sufficient would have been done to make the terms binding if only the charges themselves had been reasonable. In this kind of case, therefore, and there may well be many others (many of the undue influence cases also seem to raise a similar issue) it seems clear that procedural fairness and substantive fairness are inextricably inter-related.

There is a another fundamental problem about classical theory. Its basic premiss is that the law is neutral and impartial, once the rules of the market-place are observed and enforced. But this is debatable. The rules of the market-place are *not* neutral—they clearly benefit some people more than others. They benefit not merely the rich and more powerful, but the shrewd and farsighted. Now, that may be economically desirable in the long run: a society may prosper as a whole if markets are free and are allowed to operate freely—indeed, history strongly suggests that this is the case. But this does not alter the fact that the rules of the market-place are, in a sense, loaded. Here again, the analogy of games is misleading. Most games have rules which are similarly 'loaded'—the rules of tennis are loaded towards the powerful server, the rules of cricket to the batsman with a sharp eye—but these are not seen as involving any unfairness. They are simply part and parcel of the game, and a game is, after all, nothing but a game. But markets are not games, and the outcome of bargains in market-places has a social significance which games do not have. So if the rules of the market-place are 'loaded' in favour of one group, some will inevitably find contractual outcomes unfair and unacceptable.

---

[3] *Interfoto Picture Library Ltd* v. *Stiletto Visual Programmes Ltd* [1989] QB 433, *supra*, 187.

Again, this alleged neutrality of the market-place means that the law has to treat all sane adults equally; only gross abnormalities like insanity or drunkenness can be allowed for by law. But of course there are many feckless and irresponsible people in society with little experience in financial and legal matters. People like this can easily fall prey to 'loan sharks' and others who can exploit their vulnerability. They may only have themselves to blame if (for instance) they borrow money at exorbitant rates of interest with harsh accompanying terms, but a civilized society—which, after all, has the ultimate responsibility for enforcing the laws of the market-place—cannot wholly wash its hands of people at the bottom of the social heap. This may be paternalism but all modern societies indulge in some degree of paternalism, if only (but probably not only) because ultimately society has to pick up the bill for the destitute.

There are other problems with classical theory which we will encounter. But enough has been said to show that the distinction between procedural and substantive fairness is not and cannot always be adhered to. No doubt it is a good working rule for courts to concentrate on securing procedural fairness, but it is not possible, and perhaps it is not desirable, for courts always to ignore the fairness of contractual outcomes.

Finally, it is necessary to add another word of caution here about the scope of contract law. It has been repeatedly stressed that not all contracts are bargains, and we shall see many examples of contractual (and similar) obligations which are recognized by the courts in the absence of bargains and exchanges. Concepts of fairness and justice are clearly different in such circumstances, particularly where no exchanges are involved, though there are often overlaps in difficult borderline cases.

We must now turn from this theoretical approach to demonstrate how in practice the law does often concern itself with just outcomes. This can be done relatively briefly at this point, because we have throughout the book pointed to the ways in which courts do find themselves involved in trying to impose just solutions in contractual disputes—many of the doctrines and rules of the law permit the courts to use ideas of justice and fairness in particular situations.

## 2. CONTRACT LAW AND SUBSTANTIVE JUSTICE

One of the principal doctrines of the law which leads lawyers to think that contract law has little to say about substantive justice is the rule that adequacy of consideration is immaterial to the validity of a contract. This rule appears to mean that even if a person enters into a contract which is extremely one-sided, so that the consideration he pays is grossly excessive for the consideration he receives in return, the contract is binding and must be enforced as it stands. Nevertheless, it is today profoundly misleading to adopt without qualification the traditional dogma that adequacy of consideration is immaterial. No doubt it may still be true that an adult and mature person who deliberately, and with his eyes open, contracts to pay more than something is worth in the market is bound by his contract. But it is rare that consideration is grossly inadequate (or excessive) in such circumstances. After all, why *should* a sane and rational person knowingly pay more than the market price for something? Unless he wants to make a present to the other party to the transaction there must be a strong presumption that if there is a serious unfairness in the value of the two parties' performance it is because one, at least, of the parties did *not* enter into the transaction fully appreciating the circumstances. If the consideration is grossly inadequate there may be a strong suspicion of fraud or misrepresentation, of duress or undue influence, which would justify a court in setting the contract aside.

Now these doctrines—of fraud, misrepresentation, duress and undue influence—appear to deal solely with the procedural aspects of contractual fairness, that is they seem to be about the policing of the market-place, to ensure that bargains are fairly arrived at. But we have also seen that there are cases in which this theory wears very thin indeed. For instance, the rules about the 'presumption of undue influence' (as we saw in the last chapter) are not easily defensible solely on the ground that the law must ensure that parties are only bound by a true assent. In fact it seems clear, as we suggested, that this so-called presumption is concerned with fairness of outcomes, as much as with fairness of contractual procedures.

This is also confirmed by another point. We saw in the last chapter how the House of Lords decided in *National Westminster Bank* v. *Morgan*[4] that the 'presumption of undue influence' can be rebutted by showing that no unfair advantage was taken of a fiduciary position. So here it seems that the law has shifted its interest from procedural fairness—ensuring that there is no undue influence—to substantive fairness—to a greater concern with the fair outcome.[5] It is true that, if a real case of fraud or misrepresentation or duress or actual undue influence is proved, the plaintiff may have the contract set aside even if in fact it was a fair contract in itself, that is, even if the consideration was quite fair. And this may suggest that these doctrines are indeed more concerned with the fairness of the bargaining process than with the fairness of the outcome. But obviously in practice, plaintiffs are not likely to complain unless the consideration was inadequate and, in any event, there may well be good reasons why we

---

[4] [1985] AC 686, *supra*, 279.
[5] It must be admitted that another modern decision appears inconsistent with this approach: see *Hart* v. *O'Connor*, *supra*, n. 1, where an executory contract at a very unfair price with a mentally ill person was upheld because the other party did not know of the mental illness. I can only say I find the result here offensive to the sense of justice, as did the NZ CA.

wish to deter fraud and misrepresentation and similar wrongs, even though the result in some (presumably rare) case is not in itself unfair.

One or two other modern cases, historically deriving from the doctrine of undue influence, are worth mentioning here because they seem to have far more in common with cases of inadequacy of consideration than with the general run of undue influence cases. In the nineteenth century a few isolated cases in equity had kept alive some older paternalistic doctrines holding that conveyances or contracts could be set aside if made at a gross undervalue by poor, ignorant people who did not appreciate what they were doing and who acted without independent advice. These decisions did not in general have much following, probably because they were widely thought to be anomalous and contrary to fundamental principle. But in the past few decades they have been revived in two cases on similar facts.[6] Each case concerned a wife who was joint owner of a matrimonial home, subject to a mortgage. In both cases, the marriages had broken down, the wives had left the home, and had been persuaded (though with no overt signs of pressure or undue influence) to sign agreements surrendering their interests in the matrimonial home in return for an indemnity against liabilities on the mortgage. The indemnity was almost valueless since it is of no importance so long as the house is worth more than the mortgage, and in those days of rapidly rising house prices this was nearly always the case—the situation may well have changed in more recent years. Of course, it could not be said that the indemnity was no consideration since there could be very remote contingencies which would have given it some value. Nevertheless, in the first case the contract was set aside, and in the second the judge would have done the same if it had been necessary for the decision. In the first, it was held that in modern times, a person could be treated as 'poor' if he or she was a member of the 'lower income group'; and he could be treated as 'ignorant' if he was 'less highly educated'. In the second case, the same principle was treated as applicable even though the wife was not destitute for she was, if not poor, 'certainly not wealthy', and she was also not 'ignorant' but 'an intelligent woman'. It is difficult to see what ground is left for saying that these contracts ought to be set aside except the bare fact that they were grossly unfair because one person gave up a lot, and received very little in return. Of course, these are cases of bilateral monopoly, which may not be irrelevant.

Then there is another problem with the classical theory that courts have no concern with substantive justice, and that stems from the incompleteness of most contracts. Courts are constantly called upon to resolve contractual disputes because something has happened which the contract

---

[6] *Cresswell* v. *Potter* [1978] 1 WLR 225n; *Backhouse* v. *Backhouse* [1978] 1 WLR 243. But cf. *Butlin-Sanders* v. *Butlin-Sanders* (1985) *Fam Law* 126, where the wife was advised, knew exactly what she was doing, and where anyhow the transaction was not unreasonable.

does not in clear terms seem to contemplate. Classical theory says the court must then simply 'imply' suitable terms, and in doing this it must not impose its ideas of fairness on the parties, but just give effect to what it thinks the parties should have agreed. But here too, as we have seen, the theory is flawed because it turns out that in implying terms the courts must sometimes give effect to their sense of fairness and justice—courts speak for the reasonable man, and so represent the 'anthropomorphic conception of justice'.

Indeed, the whole process of construing and interpreting contracts is suffused with the notion of *fairness in exchange*, so that it is a major part of the function of the court in contract cases to strive to ensure some reasonable reciprocity in exchange. This has not been recognized by the traditional books and cases because it conflicts with traditional contract theory, and also perhaps because it tends to be done covertly rather than openly through some clear doctrine or principle. But when the cases and doctrines are put together, it is impossible to avoid the conclusion that fairness of outcome, and even adequacy of consideration, are indeed a very important part of the law of contract. Of course, that does not mean that, when the consideration is felt to be seriously inadequate, the court will declare the contract void. That is only one way of remedying a serious imbalance in the fairness of the exchange, and it is also a rather clumsy way of doing so, except perhaps where the contract remains wholly executory. In other cases, it is simpler to hold the contract to be binding but to adjust the obligations of the parties so as to ensure that—within broad limits— some sort of fairness in exchange does occur. In a book of this kind, it is not possible to deal with this subject with the detail that its importance deserves, but some examples must be given of cases in which the adequacy of consideration can be a most important factor in settling the obligations of the parties.

There are, first, many cases concerning the quality of goods where the amount of the consideration may be most material to the outcome. In particular, where the interpretation of the contract is doubtful the amount of the consideration may be an important factor in deciding precisely what obligations the parties have assumed. For example, suppose a manufacturer contracts to sell cloth to a buyer, and he supplies cloth of Grade B while the buyer contends that the contract was for the more expensive Grade A. In such a situation the amount of the consideration—the price— would be most material, because if the price paid was substantially more than the usual cost of Grade B cloth this would be a strong indication that the contract was indeed for Grade A cloth. It would not, of course, be conclusive proof of this, because another possible explanation of the high price would be that the buyer had simply made a bad bargain—that he had agreed to pay much more for Grade B cloth than it was worth.

Then there are the standard implied conditions in contracts of sale of goods which are read into all such contracts (subject to some exceptions) under the Sale of Goods Act. Under this Act, it is normally an implied condition of a contract of sale of goods that the goods must be 'satisfactory' in quality. This is a somewhat imprecise term, which remains imprecise despite the fact that the Act now professes to give a definition of it. But what is quite clear is that it is not possible to decide what is satisfactory quality without having regard to the price paid, and to some rough notion that a buyer is entitled to get value for money. Suppose that a person buys a second-hand car which turns out to be defective in some serious way. The court does not ask itself openly whether the buyer has got value for money,[7] or whether he was 'done' and paid far more than the car was worth. But as a practical matter this is very much what the court actually does in the end. If the car is not of 'satisfactory' quality, having regard among other thing to the price paid, the buyer is entitled to damages. In effect, he gets some of his money back. Of course this does not mean that the court is going to try to adjust every trivial imbalance between the value of the goods and the amount of the price paid; it would be an intolerable and inefficient process for the courts to attempt to do that. But it does mean that where there is a serious imbalance in the contract—the buyer having paid far more than the goods are worth—it is very likely that he will be able to claim damages on the ground that the goods were not of 'satisfactory' quality.

More generally, questions of construction and interpretation are liable to be approached by courts with a strong bias in favour of the idea that a contract should ensure some substantial reciprocity in exchange. Many of the mistake and frustration decisions illustrate how the courts deal with cases where, as a result of unknown or unexpected contingencies, the contract would impose unfair obligations on one or other party, beyond what they *really* had expected to bear, and therefore beyond what the price of the contract allowed for.

A striking example of an ordinary 'construction' case which does not fall within these traditional categories is *Staffs. Area Health Authority* v. *South Staffs. Waterworks*[8] (which has been referred to several times already) where the court was concerned with a contract made in 1929 whereby a water company contracted to supply water to a hospital at seven old pence per 1,000 gallons 'at all times hereafter'. By 1975 the price of water was in general fifteen times what it had been in 1929. Clearly, the contract was by then operating in a very unbalanced fashion. The water authority was

---

[7] So I wrote in earlier editions, but a judge has now blurted out the truth. See *Rogers* v. *Parish (Scarborough) Ltd* [1987] QB 933 at 944, where Mustill LJ actually says in such a case, 'the buyer was entitled to value for his money'.          [8] [1979] 1 WLR 203.

having to supply water at far less than its true value. But the contract looked on the face of it to be binding in perpetuity. The Court of Appeal held that the contract could be interpreted so that the price fixed in it was only chargeable 'at all times hereafter during the subsistence of this agreement'. They went on to hold that the water authority could give reasonable notice to bring the contract to an end; once that had happened, of course, the water authority was free to offer a new supply at a new price. Traditional contract theory would say that the court was merely giving effect to the intention of the parties. But this seems wildly improbable for it is scarcely possible that the water authority could have determined the contract within a year or two of its original formation. The truth appears to be that the court was simply offended by the idea that the hospital should, nearly fifty inflation-ridden years after the agreement was made, still be buying its water at far below cost.

Another type of case where the amount of the consideration is now likely to be regarded as highly relevant concerns contracts containing exemptions from liability. In *Photo Productions Ltd* v. *Securicor Transport*[9] the House of Lords was concerned with the liability of the defendants for a fire which was caused by one of their security guards while engaged in providing security services at the plaintiffs' factory. The factory was wholly destroyed by the fire, and the plaintiffs claimed over £600,000 in damages. The contract under which the security guards were provided by the defendants required them to visit the factory four times a night on seven days a week, with extra visits on Saturdays and Sundays, at a total charge of £8.75 per week or about 26p per visit. One of the factors which the House of Lords regarded as highly relevant to the construction of an exemption clause in the contract was the very small charge for the services in question. So here again, the amount of the consideration was regarded as most important in settling the liabilities of the defendants. This kind of case would now be governed by the Unfair Contract Terms Act 1977 which was not in force at the time of the contract in the *Securicor* case, and which is discussed further in Section 4 of this chapter. But it is unlikely that this would lead to a different result on the facts of that case, because the House of Lords made it clear that on such facts they regarded the use of an exemption clause as perfectly reasonable. And reasonable exemptions are still permitted in such cases under the 1977 Act.

It is true that there are still modern decisions which may appear to contradict this unorthodox emphasis on unfairness of outcome, and inadequacy of consideration as a ground for relief. For example, in *Mountford* v. *Scott*[10] the grant of an option for £1 entitling the grantee to buy the defendant's house (at a price of £10,000) was held binding. No

---

[9] [1980] AC 827.          [10] [1975] Ch. 258.

inquiry was permitted into the question whether this clearly nominal consideration was or could have been a reasonable price for the option. So, too, in *Multiservice Bookbinding Co* v. *Marden*[11] a loan agreement was upheld by the judge even though he thought it was an unreasonable or unfair agreement. The capital sum in this case was subject to a 'Swiss franc' clause whereby the amount to be repaid was revalued in accordance with the value of the Swiss franc; that by itself might not have been thought an unreasonable or unfair provision, for the lender was simply trying to ensure that his money retained its value when out on loan, but the loan was also subject to very high interest rates which were only justifiable on the assumption that the capital was at risk from inflation. So the agreement as a whole seemed hard. But it was upheld.

Some of these decisions, on careful examination, do not turn out to be such serious obstacles to the view being contended for here as they seem at first sight. For instance, in *Mountford* v. *Scott* (the case about the option) a careful reading of the case suggests that the seller may well have received some benefit in addition to the nominal consideration, because there were several houses concerned, all of which were needed by the buyer for redevelopment. Had he not been able to obtain options, he would probably have been unable to buy any of the houses, so the very possibility of a sale was created by the grant of the option. But it is true that the judges still pay lip service to the principle that inadequacy of consideration is not a matter for the courts, and no doubt it is also true that where parties have entered into a commercial agreement, with legal advice and with a clear understanding of what they are doing (as in the *Multiservice Bookbinding* case), there is still a powerful tendency to uphold the contract however unfair the outcome may appear to be. Clearly, it would be wrong to suggest that the traditional values of free bargaining never have any influence on judicial decisions. They clearly do, and indeed may be on the upsurge once again. What is being suggested here is that nobody can understand how the law of contract works in practice today if he does not appreciate that judges, like the man in the street, dislike very unfair contracts in which the consideration is grossly excessive or inadequate. And when judges dislike a result sufficiently strongly they normally try to avoid reaching it if they can do so by acceptable legal techniques. Such techniques do exist, and are capable of use.

There are, of course, also a considerable number of situations where statute law provides, by one means or another, for some method of adjusting the consideration for a contract. An obvious example is the system of rent regulation which enables a tenant to apply for a 'fair rent' to be fixed by a rent officer, which then overrides any contractual agreement.

---

[11] [1979] Ch. 84.

Another example is to be found in the Consumer Credit Act 1974 which invalidates grossly exorbitant interest rates on loans. Examples of this kind may be important, not merely for what they do in the precise fields where they operate, but for the contribution they make to the general sense of justice. In earlier editions of this book I wrote that there was little doubt that most people in Britain did believe in the concepts of 'fair prices' and 'fair wages', despite recent signs of an increased faith in the principles of the free market at the governmental level. The reader must form his own judgement on whether this remains true.

There are many other statutory methods of ensuring fair contracts. One very common technique is to control or regulate, by licensing procedures, the persons who are permitted to make certain kinds of contracts. It is common knowledge that many kinds of work require special qualifications—for instance, being a doctor or a lawyer—and that the authorities responsible for giving or approving these qualifications exercise control over their members. Many commercial types of business, especially those involving dealings with the general public, also come under complex bodies of law designed to protect the public from unfair dealings, or from risky financial enterprises—so, for instance, consumer credit suppliers must be licensed by the Director-General of Fair Trading and insurance companies likewise by the Department of Trade and Industry. It may be said that this kind of control is designed to regulate the procedural proprieties, to make special provision for the policing in the market-place of these special sorts of contracts, rather than to ensure fair outcomes. Of course this is to some extent true. The new procedures regulating those who deal in financial markets, like stockbrokers and investment advisers, do little to interfere directly with the terms of contracts which may be made by these parties with the general public. They are designed rather to ensure that this kind of work is done by responsible and reputable people who can be called to account for shady or fraudulent behaviour. At the same time, control over the persons who may enter into certain types of contracts is often one way of controlling the outcomes of those contracts. The Law Society's control over solicitors, for instance, extends to cases of overcharging, which is a matter of fairness in outcome rather than in the bargaining process.

### 3. THE STRIKING DOWN OF EXPRESS CONTRACT TERMS AT COMMON LAW

So far in this chapter we have discussed ways in which the law seeks to do substantial justice within the general parameters of the contract itself, by 'interpretation', supplementation, or minor adjustments. Occasionally, the methods discussed above permit the courts to strike down or set aside the actual contract terms, or even complete contracts, as with the doctrine of undue influence. But most of the cases so far discussed do not involve the actual overriding of the contract terms themselves, still less the striking down of a complete contract. But obviously if the law is to be seriously concerned with substantive justice, there will be occasions in which it will be necessary to override the actual terms of a contract. That is something that the common law has been most reluctant to do, particularly since the the nineteenth century development of classical contract theory. But even the common law—including in this term, the rules of equity—has sometimes been willing to take this extreme course.

## Agreements contrary to public policy

Of course the common law has always been willing to override a contract (or contractual terms) in certain select cases on the ground that they are contrary to the public interest—contrary to public policy in the legal terminology. That is in most cases obviously a different matter from overriding contractual terms on grounds of *unfairness*. Yet it is clear that in some cases the line between these two purposes has been blurred and, indeed, it sometimes seems almost as if public policy is invoked merely to overcome the general common law principle prohibiting the courts from interfering on grounds of fairness. Once this element of public policy is admitted, the court is able to rove freely over the question of fairness as well as over the public interest. This, in particular, seems often to be the case—and it was frankly admitted to be the case by Lord Diplock in the House of Lords in 1974[12]—where the principles of 'restraint of trade' come into question.

These principles (the modern term would be 'restrictive practices') are dealt with in Chapter 17, and here it is enough to note that certain types of agreements have long been held contrary to public policy if they involve restrictive practices contrary to the public interest. One major class of such agreements, of particular concern here, is an agreement by which a person undertakes not to compete with another, by using his own labour or skill in a certain profession or trade. Although such agreements may be valid within reasonable limits, excessively wide restraints are void as contrary to public policy. The important point to note in this chapter is that it seems quite clear that in many cases of this nature the courts are just as much concerned with fairness between the parties, as with the public interest. And in examining the question of fairness in this context, the courts are usually driven, as they must be, to look closely at the amount of the consideration for the promise in question. A person who is paid handsomely for his promise not to compete is likely to find it difficult to challenge the agreement, while if the consideration appears inadequate,

---

[12] See *A. Schroeder Music Publishing Co Ltd* v. *Macaulay* [1975] 1 WLR 1308, *post*, 331.

the agreement is likely to be held void, so this is one type of case in which adequacy is often necessary.

## Penalties and forfeitures

A second major class of case in which the common law (originally, equity) has long been willing to override express contractual terms concerns penalties and forfeitures. Contracts often provide that if one party fails to perform some stipulated obligation, he is to suffer additional contractual penalties or some forfeiture. Such penalties and forfeiture provisions are often void. The oldest example of these rules comes from the law of mortgages. Originally a mortgage commonly provided that, if the borrower failed to pay the loan and interest off on the due date, the property should be forfeited to the mortgagee, even though it might be worth much more than the amount due. Centuries ago, the Court of Chancery began to override these forfeiture provisions, and to permit borrowers to pay off mortgage debts long after the due date, and so reclaim their property. Similarly, it was for long very common for written contracts to be made in the form of 'penal bonds' in which a debtor would 'acknowledge' that he owed the creditor a stipulated sum of money, but went on to add that this debt should be void if he performed such-and-such an act before a certain date. The stipulated sum inserted in these bonds was commonly *twice* the value of the contract itself, so for instance if the debtor borrowed £100, he would grant a bond, 'acknowledging' that he owed £200 unless the £100 plus interest was paid at the due date. The penal element in these bonds was also held invalid first in equity, and then at common law, so that the remainder of such a bond had to be enforced as a simple contractual obligation in which the debt or damages had to be claimed and proved in the usual way.

The rules are discussed further in Chapter 22, and here it will be sufficient to consider the justification for this departure from freedom-of-contract principles. In modern times, with the new swing to these principles, there has been some attempt by law-and-economics writers to explain why, in this particular area, the parties should not be left free to make their own bargains, as they are elsewhere. There have been several economic arguments canvassed about these rules. One view is that penalty clauses are inefficient because they may provide an incentive to perform even where the cost of doing so exceeds the net benefits. On this view a penalty clause is just like a rule which permits the plaintiff to recover more damages than he has lost. Another view is that the rule against penalties is unjustified, and that penalties should be enforced according to their terms. It has, for instance, been argued that a penalty clause is like an insurance clause, inserted where the plaintiff fears that breach may cause him losses which will not be recognized by the ordinary rules on damages. If the plaintiff insured with a third party against the risk of such a breach, the third party would have to pay if there were a breach. So why cannot the plaintiff, in effect, insure with the defendant himself? The trouble with this argument is that it is fanciful—there is no empirical evidence to suggest that penalty clauses are intended to operate like insurance contracts. In any event, since most loss insurance like this is indemnity insurance, the plaintiff still cannot recover more than the amount of his losses so the insurance explanation explains nothing.

The best justification for interfering with these contractual stipulations is in fact the one given by the courts themselves, namely, that these stipulations are designed *in terrorem* as deterrents, and not as ordinary contractual provisions. Penal and forfeiture clauses are intended to *punish* a contract-breaker in order to discourage him from breaking the contract. But once he *has* broken the contract, the deterrent has failed to work and the only point in inflicting the punishment would be to deter future breaches, either by the same party or by other contracting parties. There is no need to *compensate* the innocent party with an award of damages in the form of the penalty. But if the penalty is not to be awarded as compensatory damages, then there is no justification for awarding it as a deterrent either, because this form of deterrence is generally regarded as the responsibility of the state, and of the courts, and not of contracting parties. This argument can be developed by suggesting that penal and forfeiture clauses are not usually genuine promises or undertakings at all— nobody wants or expects them to be carried out, because the parties contract in the belief that contracts will be performed, not broken. Indeed, it may not be going too far to suggest that such clauses are bogus promises, cast in the *form* of promises so as to attract the general moral and legal sanctions attaching to promise-breaking, but not amounting to real promises. In particular, great stress is laid in modern times on the protection of reasonable expectations as the justification for the legal enforcement of contracts, but if neither party believes that a penal or forfeiture clause will ever apply, then such clauses do not actually create expectations. So Antonio's bond in *The Merchant of Venice* should have been void because the reasonable expectations of the parties were that Shylock would receive his money and interest, but not his pound of flesh.

If the law were entirely consistent with this justification, it would probably be necessary to distinguish cases where the penal or forfeiture clause does create expectations, and thus influences the consideration being paid, from other cases where it does not do so. Only the latter should, perhaps, strictly be held void; in fact this does not seem to be the rule, but this may only be because the law is not entirely consistent, or perhaps because penal and forfeiture clauses are themselves often instruments of oppression, and it is felt desirable to offer some deterrent against their use.[13]

## Unconscionability and inequality of bargaining power

There is a third, possible, type of case where express contractual terms may be overriden at common law, though this one is more general, and also more suspect. It is possible that a court can strike down a contract (or a clause) on the rather hazy ground that it is simply 'unconscionable' in the legal terminology or, in other words, that one party has extracted an extortionate and grossly unfair bargain, by taking advantage of the other in some unfair or tricky way. It is curious that the existence of so important a potential power should remain uncertain at this late date in the history of contract law, but the uncertainty stems from the fact that courts have rarely been willing to apply such a doctrine (outside a limited class of cases), though they have also been unwilling totally to renounce it.

The jurisdiction over 'unconscionable' contracts—if it exists—comes from history. Courts of Equity, in the eighteenth century in particular, often set aside express contractual provisions on grounds of unconscionability, but nearly all these cases fell into certain special classes. There were the mortgages, and the penal bonds, discussed above. There were also all sorts of loan agreements, often similar to mortgages, in the sense that security was given in one form or another, which parties often tried to dress up so as to escape the Chancellor's eye in equity. These ruses failed, and all loan agreements were capable of being opened up, and the terms rewritten if necessary, so as to require the borrower simply to pay off what he owed, plus interest, allowing him to reclaim any surplus.

Then there was another extensive type of case, also related to these other classes—the sale or mortgage of a reversionary interest. Today that would be a very odd sort of transaction because a reversionary interest is today a rather odd sort of property, but it was a great deal more common in past centuries. When property was tied up in trusts and settlements, and when the sons of the aristocracy had no real occupation in their lives but to await the parental death, and particularly when the line of succession often passed outside the immediate family, to nephews, or cousins, or more remote kin, it was not uncommon for a person to have very little income, but large expectations. Such persons were, not surprisingly, often tempted to raise money on these expectations (usually reversionary interests in the legal sense) by borrowing against or, in extreme cases, selling, their interests. Since they often had little income, and since they were also often brought up to extravagant ways of life, the bargains they struck were often

---

[13] The EC Directive on Unfair Contract Terms also deals with penalties and forfeitures, and may have some impact on the law: see *post*, 316.

highly disadvantageous to them, although, to be fair to the lenders, there were often high risks to them too. Contracts of this kind also fell into the jurisdiction of Courts of Equity, and were liable to be set aside for unconscionability, simply leaving the lender to have his capital plus reasonable interest. Indeed, this particular jurisdiction was so widely exercised that it came to be a complete matter of course to reopen all bargains with 'expectant heirs', so that it ceased to be necessary even to show any element of unconscionability in these cases. That, however, proved over-protective (some have seen signs of class bias in these cases), and by the Sale of Reversions Act 1867 these cases were, in effect, returned to the general category of cases in which contracts could be set aside provided that they were unconscionable.

This equitable jurisdiction was, of course, also closely related to the cases on undue influence, and extended, in odd and isolated cases (as we have already seen in Section 2 of this chapter), to setting aside grossly unfair contracts entered into by 'poor and ignorant' persons.

What was never made wholly clear was whether these cases were merely to be treated as illustrations of a broad equitable jurisdiction to deal with *any* unconscionable contract or contractual term, or whether it was to be confined to these particular classes of cases. Towards the end of the nineteenth century, this whole area of law fell into disuse, partly because conditions changed, partly because the Moneylenders Act of 1900 gave statutory control over some of the activities formerly regulated by this jurisdiction, and partly for the more general reason that the jurisdiction seemed contrary to the fundamental basis of classical contract theory. So the basic question as to the *extent* of the jurisdiction remained largely unanswered.

In modern times there have occasionally been attempts to revive the old equitable jurisdiction.[14] The best known of these was the attempt of Lord Denning in dicta in *Lloyd's Bank* v. *Bundy*[15] (which we dealt with earlier) to suggest that there was a general equitable jurisdiction to set aside contracts where the parties were of unequal bargaining power, and one of them had used his superior bargaining power to extract some unfair or unconscionable advantage. He also suggested that cases falling within the 'presumption of undue influence' were in reality illustrations of this principle. These dicta were not approved by the House of Lords in *National Westminster Bank* v. *Morgan*[16] (which has also been referred to before) where it was suggested (somewhat pedantically, perhaps) that

---

[14] In Australia the High Ct. has several times reasserted the continued existence of a wide jurisdiction over unconscionable contracts in recent years, while also stressing the need to be hesitant in the exercise of this jurisdiction. See *Legione* v. *Hateley* (1983) 152 CLR 406; *Stern* v. *McArthur* (1988) 165 CLR 489.         [15] [1975] 2 QB 326, *supra*, 276.

[16] [1985] AC 686, *supra*, 277.

inequality of bargaining power could not explain the cases of gifts which were not bargains at all. But even the *Morgan* case does not wholly close the door to the possible recognition of a broader equitable jurisdiction over unconscionable contracts, though certainly Lord Scarman, who delivered the opinion of the House, 'questioned' whether there was today any need for any general principle affording relief in cases of inequality of bargaining power.

Two further comments may be made. First, it is clear that Lord Scarman's doubts about the need for any general principle of this character today, stemmed largely from the enactment of the Unfair Contract Terms Act in 1977 (which is dealt with in the next section) and which today does give some wide measure of statutory control over unfair contract terms. But neither this Act nor the EC Directive on Unfair Contract Terms which has recently come into force is all-embracing, and it is arguable that some residual (rather than general) principle remains necessary to deal with unconscionable contracts in cases not caught by the 1977 Act or the EC Directive or other statutory provisions.

But the second point that needs to be made is that stress on inequality of bargaining power may well be a mistake. As we have previously noted, bargaining power is nearly always unequal and, in free markets, it must be unequal. But mere inequality of power does not normally matter in free and competitive markets—it is chiefly when one party has some *coercive* power, usually arising from a monopoly position, or possibly from superior information, that inequality of bargaining power matters. So even if some residual equitable power remains to strike down unconscionable contracts, there is no doubt that some very serious unfairness must be shown, some real use of bargaining power to take advantage of another person. In *Alec Lobb (Garages) Ltd* v. *Total Oil GB Ltd*[17] the plaintiffs sought to invoke unconscionability to invalidate a 'petrol tie' contract, under which they sold their leasehold garage, and took a leaseback with various onerous covenants. Some members of the Court of Appeal appeared willing to apply the old equitable jurisdiction, but they held that no case for its application had been made out. All that had happened here was that the plaintiffs, in deep financial trouble, had entered into the best deal they could get (at their own promptings) from the defendants, who had driven a fairly hard bargain.[18] The plaintiffs were independently advised by their

---

[17] [1985] 1 WLR 173.

[18] The chief complaints of unfairness were that (1) the plaintiffs were unable to raise money on their garage by dealing with anyone else, because the defendants already had a 'tie' agreement under which the plaintiffs had to buy all their petrol from them (so the case was one of bilateral monopoly), and (2) the defendants refused any modifications to the terms of the contract in question, offering it on a 'take it or leave it' basis.

own solicitor (who in fact advised them not to enter into the transaction), but they had gone ahead anyhow.

So also in *Boustang* v. *Pigott*[19] the Privy Council held that if it were sought to set aside a contract as unconscionable it must be shown that the defendant was guilty of some moral culpability or impropriety, some actual or constructive fraud. It was not enough to show that the contract was a hard or unreasonable or foolish bargain. In the terms used earlier, unconscionability is thus a matter of procedural and not substantive justice.

### Fundamental breach

Before we proceed in the next section to deal with the Unfair Contract Terms Act, a reminder may be in order about one other modern attempt to develop a judicial power to override unfair contractual clauses. As we saw in Section 3 of Chapter 9, the doctrine of 'fundamental breach' was at one time thought to give the courts power to declare that such a breach overrode express contractual terms exempting the breaching party from liability under the contract. This doctrine was eventually overruled by the House of Lords, after the enactment of the Unfair Contract Terms Act, in *Photo Productions* v. *Securicor Transport*,[20] and there are dicta in this case, like those of Lord Scarman in the *Morgan* case, suggesting that there is no longer any need for courts to search for a power to override contractual terms on grounds of unfairness. This is, in general, it was said, a matter which could now be left to Parliament. Even these dicta, however, appear to be directed largely to commercial contracts between business parties, and perhaps still leave open the door in cases where consumers or other small parties are involved.

### 4. THE UNFAIR CONTRACT TERMS ACT 1977

This Act is the first general statutory attempt to deal with the problem of unfair contract terms. There are many other statutory provisions (probably hundreds, perhaps thousands) which invalidate particular contractual clauses in particular kinds of contracts. For example, there are all sorts of provisions in the Consumer Credit Act 1974 which invalidate a variety of clauses formerly found in consumer loan agreements and especially in hire-purchase agreements. Among these may be mentioned in particular the power to strike down 'extortionate credit bargains' which is reminiscent of the old equitable jurisdiction dealt with in the last section. There are many provisions in a variety of statutes invalidating what are thought to be unfair clauses in employment contracts. There are many statutory provisions

---

[19] [1993] NPC 75.   [20] *Supra*, n. 9.

invalidating contractual attempts to bargain away rights conferred on tenants by rent-protection legislation. And so on. But the 1977 Act is the first general statute dealing with unfair contracts.

This Act is a most intricate piece of legislation, and only the barest summary can be attempted here. It should perhaps first be stressed that the Act deals only with exemption clauses as that term is commonly understood. It does not, despite its title, deal with the whole subject of unfair contracts. Contracts can, in a broad sort of way, be said to be unfair as a result of one or two causes: either the contract may impose an excessive burden on one party, or it may impose too light a burden on the other party—for example by exclusion clauses. The 1977 Act only deals with one of the ways in which too light a burden may be imposed on one of the parties; it does not in general have anything at all to say on contracts which impose too heavy a burden on the other party. Some examples of that possibility are dealt with by other statutory rules, and it may also be possible occasionally to invoke common law rules to evade an apparently over-burdensome contractual clause.[21] But there is no general statute dealing with excessive contractual burdens.

The simplest reform carried out by the 1977 Act is that it imposes a total ban on exemption clauses which concern negligence actions for personal injury or death. Thus, ordinary tort liability for personal injury or fatal accidents is now unaffected by contractual exclusion clauses. The same goes for notices such as are sometimes posted up warning persons that they may be permitted to enter buildings or land at their own risk. But a notice may still have some effect as a warning, because a person who gives another due warning of some danger may be held in some circumstances to have discharged his duty to take care.

Next, the Act continues the effect of previous legislation so far as concerns defective and dangerous goods.[22] Broadly speaking, the effect of the Act is that exclusion clauses in contracts of sale and hire-purchase no longer avail as against a person buying the goods *as a consumer*. Consumers buying or acquiring goods on hire-purchase are, in general, entitled to goods of 'satisfactory' quality and reasonably fit for their purposes, and no exemption clause can exclude the seller's responsibility for defective goods. These provisions, however, only apply to goods purchased from a person selling in the course of business, because it is only on such sales that the relevant conditions are implied under the Sale of

---

[21] See *Interfoto Picture Library* v. *Stiletto Visual Programmes, supra*, n. 3.

[22] I have elsewhere argued that sense cannot be made of the detailed effect of these provisions on the statutory implied terms under the Sale of Goods Act without realizing that the concept of 'reasonable reliance' substantially underpins them: Atiyah, 'The Move from Agreement to Reliance in English Law and the Exclusion of Liability Relating to Defective Goods', in Harris and Tallon (eds.), *Contract Law Today* (Oxford, 1989), 21, esp. at 30–37.

Goods Act. So a person who buys a second-hand car from a private seller does not get the protection of the implied terms in the Sale of Goods Act, not because they may be expressly excluded from the contract, but because a private seller does not have the implied terms imposed on him by the Act. On the other hand, where goods are sold by a dealer, even the sale of second-hand goods, such as cars, falls within the requirements of the Sale of Goods Act, and is likewise protected by the Unfair Contract Terms Act. Of course nobody can reasonably expect a second-hand car to be as good as a new one, but the buyer is still entitled to a car of satisfactory quality and one which is reasonably fit for its purpose, having regard to the price and the general circumstances.

There is one exception to the rule that these cannot be excluded in consumer sales, and that applies to auctions. Auction sales of second-hand cars have for long been regarded in the motor trade as the only way to dispose of old 'bangers' which are almost at the end of their useful lives; if it were not permissible to exclude all liability on the part of the seller for the condition of the car being sold, it was thought that these auctions would have been effectively closed down.[23] The Act therefore permits exclusion of all terms relating to the quality and suitability of goods sold by auction; the same holds good for competitive tenders which are in effect another form of auction.

Where goods are bought by business firms, the total ban on exemption clauses does not apply. But even business buyers have some degree of protection. Exemption clauses which are contained in contracts of sale of goods or of hire-purchase and which protect the seller from liability for defective goods are only valid as against a business buyer if they are *reasonable*. This standard of reasonableness is widely used in the 1977 Act, as we shall see, and its implications are discussed below.

Outside the two fields of personal injury, on the one hand, and sale of goods and hire-purchase on the other, the 1977 Act relies very heavily on the standard of reasonableness. Thus, in all other contracts (as well as in purported disclaimers of tort liability), exemption clauses are generally only valid against a consumer if they are reasonable and, as against business parties, they must also be reasonable to be valid if they are contained in 'standard written terms of business', or if they arise from negligence. The result is that business parties can invoke the 1977 Act and attack the validity of a contractual exemption clause on the ground that it is unreasonable in three main cases: (1) if it is a case of defective goods in a contract of sale or hire-purchase, or (2) if the clause excludes liability for negligence, or (3) if the clause is contained in the other party's written standard terms of business.

---

[23] But (as we shall see shortly) auctions are not excluded from the EC Dir. on Unfair Contract Terms, though its effect remains to be seen.

   The Act provides some guidelines on the term 'reasonable' in relation to exclusion clauses, though these may not always be helpful. But at least certain relevant factors are clearly spelt out.[24] For instance, it is relevant to inquire into the relative bargaining position of the parties. So an exclusion clause contained in a standard contract imposed by a monopoly supplier on a consumer may well, for that reason, be regarded as unreasonable. It is also expressly provided by the Act that it is relevant to consider whether the customer received some inducement to accept the exemption clause: for example, if the customer is told that (say) his goods can be carried at owner's risk at a lower charge than at carrier's risk, and he opts to have them carried at owner's risk, he will have received an 'inducement', in the form of the lower charge, to agree to have his goods carried at his own risk. This may well be held to be perfectly reasonable, at least where it is clear that the customer fully understood the choice being offered to him. A third relevant factor concerns the possibility of insurance. Many of the risks which are commonly litigated about are also insurable risks, and many battles about exemption clauses are effectively battles between one party and an insurance company, or even between two insurance companies. But where insurance is simply unavailable, a complete exemption clause may be reasonable, or if insurance is only obtainable up to certain limits, it may well be more reasonable for a person to exclude his liability beyond those limits. There will also be cases where only one party has the relevant knowledge to enable insurance to be bought, and other cases where insurance is more readily obtainable by one of the parties.[25]

   All these matters are themselves referred to in the Act. What the courts will do with them is slowly becoming clearer. There are now several important cases giving some indication of what the courts are likely to hold to be 'reasonable' in the sense used by the Act, though it has also been stressed (perhaps unfortunately) that reasonableness is a matter to be decided by the trial court in each individual case, and should not generally be regarded as raising issues of principle. In *George Mitchell (Chesterhall) Ltd* v. *Finney Lock Seeds Ltd*[26] the plaintiffs were farmers who had ordered late cabbage seed from the defendants, who were seed merchants. The defendants supplied an inferior variety seed, which indeed was not a

---

[24] The Act inexplicably limits the application of some of these factors to some of the various cases in which reasonableness is relevant. But it is likely that the courts will tend to regard them as relevant to all cases arising under the Act, if only because they are anyhow directed to have regard to all the circumstances which were known or contemplated when the contract was made.

[25] See *Wright* v. *British Railways* [1987] CLY §424, where a suitcase was lost by the defendants, but an exclusion clause was upheld as reasonable, largely because the plaintiff was much better placed to insure than the defendants, having sole knowledge of the contents.

[26] [1983] 2 AC 807. See also *Stewart Gill Ltd* v. *Horatio Meyer & Co Ltd* [1992] 1 QB 600.

late cabbage seed at all, and the plaintiffs suffered considerable losses (over £60,000) in wasted labour in planting and clearing the fields where the crop completely failed. The contract contained a term limiting the liability of the defendants to some trivial sum, but it was held that this clause was void as unreasonable under the predecessor to the 1977 Act. The most important factor relied upon by the House of Lords in reaching their decision seems to have been that seed merchants often negotiated settlements and paid proper compensation in cases of this kind even where their contracts contained (as they all did) the relevant clause. This seemed to demonstrate that even those in the trade did not themselves think their own contractual clauses were reasonable, or possibly did not intend that these clauses should always be strictly applied anyhow.

It should perhaps be added that this case did not fall under the 1977 Act but under an earlier Act, and there is some difference between the two Acts. In the earlier Act, reasonableness was a matter to be judged at the time of the decision; but under the 1977 Act it is the *terms of the contract* which must be tested for reasonableness. This probably would have made no difference to the *George Mitchell* case, but it may affect other cases.

An earlier case of a similar kind provides an interesting contrast with the *George Mitchell* case. In this case[27] a farmer bought some seed potatoes which turned out to be defective, and the crop failed. The sale contract contained two exemption clauses, the first of which required the buyer to give notice of any complaints within three days of delivery to him of the potatoes, and the second of which excluded the liability of the seller for any consequential loss. Thus, under the second clause, the seller was responsible only for refunding the buyer's price, but was not liable for the loss caused to the buyer as a result of his having spent time and money sowing a crop which failed, nor for any resultant loss of profit. The first clause was held unreasonable because it was proved that the disease from which the potatoes suffered was not discoverable until the crop began to grow, and it would therefore have been quite impossible for the buyer to make his complaint within three days of delivery. But the second clause which excluded the seller's liability for consequential loss was upheld. There were a number of factors which told in favour of the view that the clause was quite reasonable: first, the parties were of roughly equal bargaining power, and, secondly, the seed potatoes in question were uncertified and somewhat cheaper than certified potatoes, so the buyer was in a sense buying an inferior product with some element of risk attached.

Another group of cases under the 1977 Act has dealt with plant-hire contracts. Excavators and other large mechanical plant are today often

---

[27] *R. W. Green* v. *Cade Bros Farms* [1978] 1 Lloyd's Rep. 602.

owned by companies which are let on hire to those who actually use them. They are often supplied together with the driver or operator. The standard terms of business of these companies nearly always impose liability for damage to the plant on the hirer, even though the damage may be caused by the negligence of the operator, who is actually an employee of the owner. It may be thought that such clauses are merely designed to allocate responsibility for insurance, and should therefore be upheld as reasonable. But the difficulty with that view is that the owners are experts in the business and are well acquainted with the insurance situation, whereas hirers sometimes require this sort of plant at short notice, for short periods or simple one-off operations, and may have no time to arrange insurance. For these reasons it was recently held that a clause of this kind was void as unreasonable,[28] but further litigation in such cases may well occur because much plant is hired on these terms.

Another area which has caused much difficulty concerns disclaimers of liability by surveyors undertaking valuations for the purposes of building society mortgages, as well as by building societies themselves. If a surveyor is employed and paid by a building society to value a house and negligently fails to discover serious defects so that his valuation is grossly excessive, a borrower from the building society is prima facie entitled to sue the surveyor for damages in tort. But many surveyors used to attempt to avoid this liability by suitable disclaimers, and in 1988 two cases of this kind were taken to the House of Lords.[29] It was there held that in cases of ordinary 'consumer' house-buyers these disclaimers were generally unreasonable, and therefore invalid under the 1977 Act. They were unreasonable because it was clear that the great majority of such buyers would rely on the surveyor's report and not commission an independent survey, because this fact was well known to surveyors and building societies, and because the buyer would otherwise be unprotected against a serious risk, whereas surveyors could insure against their liability. Of course the cost of the insurance would have to be added to the surveyor's charges, but it was not thought that this would greatly affect the cost of surveys. The House of Lords went on to suggest, however, that the result under the 1977 Act might not be the same where the case concerned large commercial property (such as a block of flats) and the buyer was a concern which could reasonably be expected to commission its own survey.

### Theoretical justfication for legislative protection of the consumer

It is worth concluding this section by adding a few thoughts on the theoretical justification for these interferences with freedom of contract.

---

[28] *Phillip Products Ltd* v. *Hyland* [1987] 2 All ER 620.
[29] See *Smith* v. *Bush* [1990] 1 AC 831.

As we have already seen, the resurgence of freedom-of-contract principles in the last decade or so has raised questions in the minds of some academics (especially in America) about whether—or at least when—it is justifiable for the law to strike down contractual clauses, even where they appear harsh and unreasonable. The argument, which has already been briefly adverted to in Chapter 1, is basically that striking down exemption clauses must drive up the price of the goods or services being supplied. The buyer who wants the goods or services without an exemption clause does not need statutory protection because he should be able to buy them at the higher price which the absence of the clause will entail; the buyer who prefers to have the goods at a lower price even with the exemption clause is deprived of his freedom to do so without any obvious good reason. While it remains essential to ensure that parties are not bound by clauses to which they have not really assented, where they have actually been aware of, and understood the effect of the clauses concerned, this argument thus suggests that the legislative banning of exemption clauses is simply a mistake.

Undoubtedly the argument is a powerful one in some contexts, and where it really is forceful one could expect that the courts would indirectly be influenced by it in applying the statutory test of reasonableness. Indeed, the Act's own guidelines provide some justification for doing this, by requiring the courts to ask whether some inducement has been given for the presence of an exemption clause. Where some modern economists and the Act part company is that the former might insist that the presence of an exemption clause means that there *must* always be an inducement in the form of a lower price. And in general terms, and in the long run, this surely must be right. Banning exemption clauses must have an impact on prices in the long run. And once this is recognized the whole concept of an 'unreasonable' exemption clause becomes open to challenge, for the question in every case is whether the contract with the clause is worth the price being paid, and that (according to freedom-of-contract principles) is for the parties to decide themselves.

But one partial answer to this is that the market just does not work as well in practice as theory suggests. The position regarding building society mortgages shows that in the short run, and in particular cases, the market does not always work very well. It might seem that this would be a good case where greater choice ought to be available in the market, so that the best solution would be to require surveyors to offer two alternative ways of presenting their report, with liability and without, leaving the borrower to decide whether he wishes to pay the extra charge. In fact it appears from *Smith* v. *Bush* that at least one building society did offer this choice to applicants for mortgages, but the extra charge for survey reports with liability was very large, and probably unwarranted by the cost, and taken up by very few applicants. The House of Lords appeared to think that these facts meant it was still unfair to exclude liability where the more limited survey report was requested.

Still, there may well be other areas of commercial activity where the market works a great deal more effectively, and in these areas great care may need to be taken before protection is (in effect) forced on consumers, together with the bill. The requirement in the guidelines that regard should be had to the availability of insurance may also compel the courts to face up to these economic arguments. Insurance is often available to *both* parties to a contract—it is simplistic to assume that even in consumer contracts only the other party can insure against the risks involved, although no doubt this would sometimes be the case. And where the person adversely affected by an exemption clause can insure, but chooses not to do so, there are obviously strong economic (not to say moral) arguments for saying that he should not then be able to demand that the clause be held void, and thus obtain the benefits of insurance via the other party.

The arguments against a blanket ban on exclusion clauses regardless of reasonableness are even stronger. As we have seen, in some cases the 1977 Act altogether bans clauses excluding or restricting the seller's liability for breach of the implied terms relating to quality or fitness in a contract of sale of goods. An illustration of a case in which this could cause practical problems comes from the personal computer industry. It is the almost universal practice of retail sellers of personal computers to restrict their liability for breach of the implied conditions by requiring the buyer to return the computer to the seller for repairs. As many computers are sold through mail order catalogues, and they are often quite heavy and bulky items, this could plainly be a costly and troublesome business. At the same time the seller almost always offers the buyer the option of buying, for an extra sum, what is called an 'on-site warranty' under which the seller undertakes to put right faults at the buyer's own home, or place of business. There does not seem to be anything in the least objectionable about this practice, so long as the buyer clearly understand the choice he is being offered. But the practice almost certainly falls foul of the 1977 Act because it involves a restriction on the seller's liability for breach of the implied terms under the Sale of Goods Act. (Sellers may sometimes recognise this technically by proclaiming that their conditions of sale are without prejudice to the consumer's 'statutory rights' but in practice a consumer who has not bought an on-site warranty probably faces a very uphill task to have his statutory rights fully respected.) If a test case to this effect is ever decided and receives widespread publicity the probable result will be that buyers will no longer be given the option of buying computers *without* having to pay extra for an on-site warranty. So an Act designed for the protection of consumers could have the effect of depriving consumers of a right which they currently enjoy. In this situation the free-market arguments against the 1977 Act are hard to refute.

In this connection it is right to note that consumer choice is far more real and widespread than it used to be. When hostility to the present widespread use of exemption clauses first surfaced some forty or fifty years ago it was nearly always difficult, if not impossible, for consumers to contract *without* such clauses for the purchase of a very wide range of consumer goods and services—there was no question of buyers or consumers having the choice between two different sets of terms at different prices. But things have changed a great deal in this respect in recent years, so that buyers and consumers now often do have a wide (indeed often a bewildering) range of choices in such matters. For instance, buyers of cars and consumer durables can now often buy, as optional extras, an extended period of 'guarantee' cover, so that defects appearing in the goods for periods of up to five years may be repaired free of charge. Yet even the availability of these 'guarantees' (which are actually often insurance policies sold quite independently of the manufacturer of the goods) is not without problems. It is widely claimed by consumer bodies that many of these guarantees are sold at extortionate prices, and consumers do not know (and are not told) of the differing guarantees which may be available, often at much lower cost. So the availability of insurance to the consumer may well not settle the question: courts will have to inquire into how effective the market for that kind of insurance is.[30]

Even now there may also be circumstances where a choice of terms—with or without warranty cover—is simply not available, as apparently it was not to the seed buyers in the *George Mitchell* case, for instance. And there are also many risks which are simply not insurable in today's insurance markets, or anyhow not readily insurable by buyers or consumers.

There are a number of other reasons for thinking that the theoretical economic arguments do not necessarily conclude the question of the desirability of controlling or banning unreasonable exemption clauses, apart altogether from the problem of ineffective markets. First, there is the

---

[30] Some years ago the author acquired a car with an ordinary 12 months' guarantee and also (for a substantial extra premium) an extended guarantee. The fine print on this extended guarantee revealed that, to make the extended guarantee valid, the buyer was obliged at the end of the 12 months to send by recorded delivery a specially supplied card to 'register' his extended guarantee; it further provided that if no reply was received in 21 days (as in fact happened) the buyer was to write again to obtain 'confirmation' of its receipt. As the author habitually reads fine print he followed these instructions to the letter, but could not help wondering how many other buyers would have done so.

constant difficulty that the rules of contract law (as we have repeatedly stressed) do not require that the parties assent to and understand all the terms of the contract except in the most general and vague sense.[31]

Secondly, there is some ground for thinking that, as also is illustrated by the *George Mitchell* case, many exemption clauses are inserted into contracts even though they are not really designed to be taken literally. They are often (it seems) inserted, not to protect the beneficiary from all liability, but to enable him to decide which claims to pay and which he will reject. They are, in other words, clauses designed to protect the beneficiary from the courts, rather than from liability. And that is something which there is strong ground for banning on altogether different grounds—that it contravenes the fundamental principle of justice that a person should not be a judge in his own cause.

In any event, all these arguments seem extremely theoretical today. While economic theorists may contend that the 1977 Act enshrines a degree of paternalism which seems out of tune with current trends, the EC Directive on Unfair Contract Terms, which is examined in the next section, shows that support for this kind of legislative protection of the consumer has not yet waned.

## 5. THE EC DIRECTIVE ON UNFAIR CONTRACT TERMS

The EC Directive on Unfair Contract Terms[32] was approved in 1993 and given statutory force in the UK by Regulations made under section 2(2) of the European Communities Act. It applies to contracts made on or after 1 July 1995. There appears to have been very little need or point to the Directive so far as the UK is concerned. The subject is already covered by the Unfair Contract Terms Act and, if there are arguably gaps in that Act, it can hardly be said that they are specifically addressed by the Directive. In fact the Directive overlaps substantially with the Act, and is bound to introduce considerable uncertainty into the law because it is not drafted with the precision which English lawyers are accustomed to in legislation. All this is not to say that there may not be some welcome results from the Directive in areas where the 1977 Act does not apply. The Directive shares one feature with the Act, namely that it appears complex and intricate. Only a summary of its effects can be offered here.

The main effect of the Directive is to make certain unfair terms in contracts between a consumer and a seller or supplier not binding on the

---

[31] See *supra*, 183. And see also *R. & B. Customs Brokers Co Ltd* v. *United Dominions Trust* [1988] 1 All ER 847 at 852, where, in discussing the application of an exclusion clause under the 1977 Act, Dillon LJ mentions in passing that the printed terms were brought to the plaintiff's attention though he did not trouble to read them.

[32] [1993] OJ L 95/29.

consumer. Each of these concepts is the subject of careful definition in the Directive and the Regulations.

As the Directive and the Act of 1977 will plainly overlap in many cases it will now be open to consumers to challenge contracts terms—where they are not declared void outright in the 1977 Act—on the ground, either that they are unreasonable under the 1977 Act, or that they are unfair and so contrary to the Directive. In most circumstances it is probable that the two tests will lead to the same result. But because the legal concepts are different, and the legal route to be followed in the two cases is different, it is clear that the law will now become a great deal more complicated. Both sets of laws will need to be studied, and their effect considered, wherever they are both applicable.

### Application of the Directive

The application of the Directive differs substantially from that of the 1977 Act. First, the Directive only applies to protect consumers, and a consumer means a natural person (excluding, therefore, all companies) who is acting for purposes outside his business. In addition, the consumer is only protected in so far as he contracts with a seller or supplier who is acting in the course of his business. So the Directive has no application (for instance) to a consumer who buys a second-hand car from a private seller not acting in the course of business. And though the Directive applies to contracts for the sale of land it will only do so where the seller is acting in the course of business, so (for instance) a sale by a builder or developer would be within the Directive. The Directive also contains no exclusion for auction sales, differing in this respect from the 1977 Act. So it will remain for judicial decisions to make it clear whether the auction of second-hand cars can continue to exclude all implied conditions and warranties or whether this will be regarded as unfair.

A curious omission from the Directive is that it only protects the consumer who is *buying* goods or services. As with the implied conditions in the Sale of Goods Act there is absolutely no protection for a private consumer who sells to someone goods being acquired in the course of business—for instance, antiques, farm produce, or a second-hand car. In some cases it may not be clear whether the Directive applies because it is not clear whether the other party is supplying a service. For instance, is a publisher who contracts with a private author (not writing in a professional capacity) supplying a service? If so, such an agreement is caught by the Directive, but this would be of no help to an author writing in a business capacity.

The Directive does not apply to contracts of employment, contracts relating to succession rights, contracts relating to rights under family law, or contracts relating to the incorporation and organization of companies or partnerships. Unlike the 1977 Act, however, the Directive does apply to insurance contracts, except to those terms which define and circumscribe the insured risk and the insurer's liability. This means that it will not be possible to attack terms in an insurance contract as unfair because they exclude certain risks—for instance, flood damage from a householder's policy, or accidental damage from a motorist's third party, fire, and theft policy. On the other hand, it will now be possible to attack as unfair conditions of liability which are at present extensively imposed on insured persons. If a householder's policy declares, for instance, that it is a condition of the insurer's liability that the burglar alarm should be properly maintained, it will be possible to contend that this is an unfair term, for example, if there was no apparent defect in the alarm. Many conditions in ordinary insurance policies are very harsh, or are at least capable of operating very harshly, and it may well be that this will prove one of the most significant practical changes made by the Directive. Of course the application of the Directive is one thing; whether any particular contract term is unfair is another.

## Unfair terms

We now come to the central part of the Directive. A term which has not been individually negotiated is an unfair term if contrary to the requirements of good faith, it causes a significant imbalance in the rights and obligations of the parties to the detriment of the consumer, taking into account the nature of the goods or services, and the circumstances attending the making of the contract. Each of these concepts is then supplemented by further provision.

A term cannot be attacked as unfair under the Directive if it was 'individually negotiated'. A term is not individually negotiated where it was drafted in advance so that the consumer was unable to influence its substance; but it may also be claimed that a term was not individually negotiated even where it was not drafted in advance. That would, presumably, be a question of fact.

The Directive also explicitly provides that a term should not be considered unfair by reason of the definition of the main subject matter of the contract or the adequacy of the price and remuneration, in so far as these terms are in plain, intelligible language. The intention behind this is plain enough: if a person agrees to buy a particular car for £10,000 he should not be able to complain that the term of the contract containing the price is unfair, because it must have been perfectly obvious to the consumer what price he was committing himself to pay. But this really is a bit of nonsense, though fortunately in many cases it will be harmless nonsense. It is nonsense because (as we suggested earlier[33]) unfairness

---

[33] *Supra*, 284.

always (or anyhow nearly always) comes down in the end to the question of price. Suppose, for instance, that the car in this example has defects so serious that a fair market price for the car would only be £3,000. Almost certainly a car being sold *at the price of £10,000* would be considered unsatisfactory if it has defects rendering it worth only £3,000. This contract could be considered unfair either because the price is excessive or because the car is not good enough. But under the Directive the consumer cannot complain that the price is too high, only that the car is not good enough. Of course it all comes to the same thing, whichever way it is put. And that is why we are able to say that it is a piece of harmless nonsense.

But it may not always be harmless nonsense. Indeed, in some cases, the greatest difficulty may be found in the application of this provision. Consider a case like *Multiservice Bookbinding Co* v. *Marden*[34] which was discussed earlier in this chapter. In this case a loan agreement at a high rate of interest was also subject to a Swiss franc clause, providing for a revaluation of the amount to be repaid in the event of the pound sterling falling below its then value against the Swiss franc. In a contract of this kind what is the price or remuneration which cannot be challenged under the Directive? Is it the sterling sum, or the Swiss franc sum?[35]

### Good faith

In assessing good faith, particular regard must be had to the bargaining position of the parties, whether the consumer had an inducement to agree to the terms, whether the goods or services were sold or supplied to the special order of the consumer, and the extent to which the seller or supplier has dealt fairly and equitably with the other party whose legitimate interests he has to take into account.

Clearly this concept differs substantially from the general principles of English law as hitherto known. At common law it is very rare that a seller or supplier has any duty to take into account the legitimate interests of the other party. Now this will become relevant in assessing whether he has acted in good faith. But there are, all the same, similarities between the requirements of good faith under the Directive and aspects of the test of reasonableness under the 1977 Act. In particular, the first three factors listed above as relevant in assessing good faith all appear as guidelines in Schedule 2 of the 1977 Act, and it is this in particular which suggests that the two pieces of legislation will very often lead to the same result where they both apply.

---

[34] *Supra*, n. 11.

[35] The Annex list of suspect terms excludes price-indexation clauses, but the problem in the *Multiservice* case was that the contract was (possibly) unfair because of the combination of the price-indexation clause with the very high rates of interest normally justified by the risk of inflation—which was avoided by the price-indexation clause.

## Significant imbalance

This, too, is a completely new concept, at least according to the conventional way English law is presented. The English doctrine that adequacy of consideration is immaterial means that English law appears to have no doctrines at all corresponding to the idea that there should be no significant imbalance between the parties' rights. However, we have already seen[36] that in many circumstances this is by no means a realistic portrayal of English law as it currently operates. When, for instance, an eminent judge declares that in a contract of sale of goods, 'the buyer is entitled to value for his money'[37] this shows that the concept of balance between the two sides of the transaction is surely already reflected in the law. But to say that English law and English judges already lean against contracts which are significantly imbalanced does not mean that an explicit provision of this kind may not have a substantial effect in certain kinds of cases.

## The Annex

The Annex to the Directive contains an 'indicative and non-exhaustive' list of terms which *may* be considered unfair. The Annex is plainly intended to be of limited force: a term contained in it may not be unfair in a particular contract; a term may be held unfair even though not listed in the Annex. Yet the Annex is of considerable length, and it is not difficult to foresee that there will often be considerable argument over whether a particular contract term falls within the Annex list. A brief summary only of some of the most important items on the list can be given here.

Paragraphs (*a*) and (*b*) deal with exclusion clauses, the former being of no importance in England in that it deals with clauses excluding liability for personal injury or death. Any such contract clause is already void in England under the 1977 Act.

Paragraphs (*d*) and (*e*) deal with penalties and forfeitures. The second probably only restates the English law rule against penalties. But paragraph (*d*) reads strangely to an English lawyer, because it suggests that a term may be unfair simply because it provides for the forfeiture of sums paid by the consumer if he should cancel the contract, without providing for an equivalent payment of compensation should the other party cancel the contract. This could have a significant impact on the drafting of package holiday contracts. In these contracts it is customary to provide that the consumer cannot recover his deposit if he cancels at too late a date, but it is not customary to provide for the payment of equivalent compensation

---

[36] *Supra*, 293.
[37] Mustill LJ in *Rogers* v. *Parish (Scarborough) Ltd, supra*, n. 7, at 944.

if the holiday company itself cancels the holiday. Holiday companies will now have to decide whether to include such provision, or run the risk of having to argue that the forfeiture of deposits is not unfair.

Paragraphs (*f*) and (*g*) apply to contracts of indefinite duration, restricting the freedom of the supplier to terminate without notice, or to retain moneys paid in advance of such termination. But suppliers of financial services (banks, for instance) retain the right to terminate such contracts without notice, where there is a valid reason, provided the supplier informs the other party at once. The words 'where there is a valid reason' presumably mean that a bank could not rely on a contract term to terminate an account or withdraw a credit card (if issued indefinitely) unless there really is a valid reason which it is prepared to disclose, subject to its running the risk of having the term declared unfair.

Paragraph (*i*) refers to a term which irrevocably binds the consumer to 'terms with which he has had no real opportunity of becoming acquainted before conclusion of the contract'. This paragraph has already been discussed.[38]

Paragraphs (*j*) and (*k*) deal with terms which allow the seller or supplier to alter contract terms, or the specification of goods, unilaterally without a valid reason—and in the case of alteration of the terms, the reason must be specified in the contract. There is a limited exception for suppliers of financial services who have the right to alter interest rates payable by or to a consumer 'where there is a valid reason', so long as notice is given immediately to the consumer, and provided that the consumer is then free to dissolve the contract. These paragraphs could have a significant impact on certain types of consumer contracts. For instance, an ordinary building society mortgage commonly gives the building society the right to vary rates of interest unilaterally, by giving notice in the press or the like. Such a clause might now be held unfair because it does not provide for notice to be given to the consumers themselves; or because it does not give the consumer the right to dissolve the contract. The same is also true of the converse situation where investors in building society accounts may be at risk of their rates of interest being reduced, without then having the right to withdraw their deposits. Building societies have estimated that the annual cost of compliance with the Directive could be £60 million,[39] presumably because of the notices that they will be required to give in future. These costs will, of course, have to be borne by the borrowers and investors who are the very people the Directive is intended to protect.

[38] *Supra*, 188.
[39] See DTI, *A Further Conultation Document, Implementation of the EC Directive on Unfair Terms in Consumer Contracts* (93/13/EEC) (1994), 38.

Paragraph (*l*) deals with terms in contracts of sale of goods which provide for the price to be determined at the time of delivery, or for the price to be increased, without giving the buyer the right to withdraw from the sale if the increase is 'too high' in relation to the original price.

# 17

# Void Contracts

GENERALLY speaking, when the requirements for the creation of a valid contract have been duly complied with, that is to say, when there has been an offer and an acceptance of reasonable certainty, by capable parties, and there is consideration, and any necessary formalities have been complied with, the resulting agreement will be enforced as a legal contract. If any of these requirements is not present the contract may be 'void', but strictly speaking this means no more than that the alleged contract is not in fact a real contract. But even where all these requirements are present the law sometimes refuses complete validity to the resulting transaction, because of its objects or terms, and here again the contract may be said to be 'void'. In the last chapter we examined a number of situations in which agreements (or particular terms in agreements) might be held void on the ground of unfairness; in this chapter we are more concerned with agreements that are held void because of the public interest, but we also saw in the last chapter that it is not always easy to be sure precisely why agreements are held void, and that there are certain cases in which questions of fairness and questions of public interest overlap. Furthermore, although some kinds of agreements are held void for obvious reasons of broad public policy, many (perhaps all) agreements of that kind would generally be regarded as unacceptable on grounds of fairness also. For instance, a contract which imposes a condition of slavery or servitude on one party is certainly void, but it is obvious that both the public interest and fairness as between the parties demand the same result.

The public interest, or public policy as it is usually called in contract law, can affect a contract in one of two chief ways. Sometimes, a contract or a contractual term is void on grounds of public policy, and sometimes it (or the performance of the contract) is actually *illegal*. In both cases these results derive from the fact that the contract is believed to be contrary to the public interest, but where a contract is merely declared void the parties remain at complete liberty to make and perform it if they want to do so. All that the law does is to refuse legal enforcement to the contract. But an illegal contract is often *prohibited* as well as void—it may be illegal to *make* such a contract, or illegal to *perform* it (or to perform it in a certain way). In other words illegality is a more drastic way of expressing the public interest, and is therefore usually reserved for cases in which the public interest is more seriously infringed. But the terminology of the law is often inconsistent. For example, some contracts which are merely void (such as contracts in restraint of trade) are sometimes said to be 'unlawful', and it is therefore necessary to bear in mind that this is not the same thing as 'illegal'. In this chapter we deal with void contracts, while illegal contracts are dealt with in the next chapter.

A contract may be void either at common law or by statute. The public interest can be affected by contracts in so many different ways that a complete list of contracts or contract terms rendered void by statute could probably never be compiled—it would certainly include many hundreds and perhaps even thousands of possible cases. So in this chapter we shall be concerned mainly with cases where contracts are void at common law, although even in these cases, statute now obtrudes so frequently that there are few areas left of pure common law invalidity.

## I. AGREEMENTS TO OUST THE JURISDICTION OF THE COURT

An important and ancient common law principle renders void any agreement to oust the jurisdiction of the court. The rather technical language in which this principle is always couched should not disguise its importance. It is a fundamental, indeed a constitutional principle of the highest importance, that civil disputes can only, in the last resort, be settled by the courts, and any attempt to contract out of this principle is against public policy. Decisions on the law and on legal rights are, after all, entrusted to the courts, and this principle is respected by all political parties and all governments. It is of the highest public importance that this ultimate power should remain available, even though today many other bodies also handle legal disputes at lower levels. Prima facie everybody has the right to apply to the Queen's courts for redress against legal injuries, and nobody can deprive himself of this right by contract.

After this rather high-sounding language it may seem contradictory to recognize that contracting parties are today entitled to incorporate arbitration clauses into their contracts, under which they bind themselves not to apply to the courts until the dispute in question has been submitted to an arbitrator. Such a clause often severely limits the court's powers over the dispute, because the arbitrator may be given sole power to decide all questions of fact and even law that arise out of a contract. Generally speaking, however, there can be no objection to this course because an arbitrator is very much in the position of a (private) judge himself, and must follow and apply English law,[1] unless the contract specifically incorporates the law of some other country. Moreover, leave to appeal to

---

[1] But it must be admitted that since the Arbitration Act 1979 this requirement may be somewhat unreal, because there will often be no way of enforcing it.

the courts on questions of law can be granted although in recent years the courts have begun to insist that such leave should only be granted in special cases, in order that appeals should not be used as a matter of course to delay and clog up the arbitration process. Many business contracts, especially international contracts, today incorporate very wide arbitration clauses, because business people often prefer arbitration to litigation. It is usually quicker, cheaper, and more convenient in that parties can agree hearing dates and places with the arbitrator. Furthermore, in international contracts it means that the parties can avoid the invidious problem of deciding which country is to be entrusted with any litigation arising out of the contract. London in particular has a very high reputation in the commercial world as a centre of international arbitrations, and many cases are heard there before English arbitrators which have no connection at all with England or English law. There is certainly nothing contrary to the public interest in these arbitration clauses. Indeed, they are a useful source of 'invisible earnings' and so contribute to the balance of payments.

Sometimes, however, arbitration clauses are not so innocuous, especially when they are found in standard-form contracts which are imposed by one party on the other. For instance, it is notorious that insurance companies insist on arbitration clauses in all their contracts, partly because they prefer to dispute claims in the quiet of an arbitrator's office, and not in the glare of publicity which a High Court action might involve. An action of this kind might do the insurance company much harm, especially if it is relying on technicalities rather than on the merits of the case. The Arbitration Act 1979 provides some small degree of consumer protection in this respect: the right to appeal to the courts from an arbitrator cannot be excluded in an insurance contract. It can only be excluded in an insurance case if the parties agree to do so after a claim is made. The EC Directive on Unfair Contract Terms also includes in its Annex of suspect terms a clause requiring disputes to be referred to arbitration 'not covered by legal provisions'. But the meaning of these last words is obscure and may deprive the provision of any real effect.

## 2. CONTRACTS PREJUDICIAL TO FAMILY RELATIONS

Family relations present peculiarly difficult problems to the law of contract, because by and large these relations depend on status, the incidence of which is almost entirely fixed by law, and is largely independent of the agreement of the parties. The result is that many agreements concerning family relationships are void and cannot be enforced by the courts. For instance, an agreement by a parent to renounce his rights over a child is void, although it may be possible to achieve the desired result today by the procedure of adoption. Of course this requires a court order. Traditionally these contracts are said to be void as being prejudicial to family arrangements.

Many examples of such void agreements exist. For example, an agreement *not* to marry has always been held void on this ground, although an agreement to marry entered into by two parties was for centuries a legally enforceable contract. Since 1970, however, engagements to marry have not been enforceable as contracts.

That these old principles still have modern applications is shown by the fact that (almost certainly) a surrogacy contract would be held void.[2] Such an agreement is one under which a mother agrees to bear a child for another person in return for payment. While the agreement is executory, it would surely be held void—that is, no action would lie against the mother if she decided to keep the child. It is perhaps less clear whether she would be able to keep any advance payment, or sue for such a payment after she had handed over the child.

Again, agreements for *future* separation between married couples are void, an old principle which presumably means that the law does not recognize the modern idea of preparing a contract on marriage which will determine how the parties' assets are to be divided on separation or divorce. Of course, when a marriage has actually broken down and separation has become inevitable, there is no reason in policy or law why the parties should not provide for the many problems which may arise without recourse to the courts[3]—unless they want a divorce. Needless to say, a divorce can only be obtained by petitioning the court in the usual way. And even agreements as to maintenance or the division of the matrimonial assets are not usually binding in the same way as ordinary contracts. They are, however, often made the basis of a 'consent order', that is to say they are incorporated in a court order which means that the court retains a supervisory jurisdiction over agreements of this nature. Such agreements may thus be treated as prima facie evidence of what is fair and reasonable between the spouses, but are not absolutely binding unless confirmed by the court.[4] Questions of public interest and of fairness are clearly both involved in these agreements, because divorced wives who are

---

[2] Under the Surrogacy Arrangements Act 1985 it is an offence to negotiate a surrogacy agreement or arrangement, but this only affects agents and middle persons, not the parties directly concerned.

[3] But since many separated wives find themselves forced to claim social security benefits there is a sense in which these agreements have high externality costs. The establishment of the Child Support Agency is an attempt to recoup some of these costs by the taxpayer.

[4] See e.g. *Dean* v. *Dean* [1978] 3 All ER 758; *Sutton* v. *Sutton* [1984] 1 All ER 168. There are signs that these cases are beginning to give rise to more difficulty, as one or other of the parties often change their minds, and seek to persuade the court not to confirm the agreement.

not maintained by their husbands often become a charge on the social security system.[5]

Another kind of agreement which falls within this traditional heading is a marriage-brokage contract. These also have long been held to be void, but it is hard to see what is wrong with them in modern times. Indeed, many of these contracts are made by perfectly respectable marriage bureaux whose object, albeit for gain, is to introduce suitable persons to one another with a view to matrimony. Although such a method of meeting one's life partner may not appeal to the majority of the population, it seems entirely unnecessary to condemn all such contracts as void.

### 3. CONTRACTS IN RESTRAINT OF PERSONAL LIBERTY

Restrictions on personal freedom have traditionally been kept to an absolute minimum in English law, and contractual restrictions on this freedom are generally void. Of course, contracts of employment are valid, even if made for life, but such contracts must not contain servile incidents. Hence a contract which imposes unreasonable restrictions on a person's right to live where he pleases, or to come and go as he chooses, is void.

The law also, and obviously, permits parties to consent (whether by contract or otherwise) to conduct which would otherwise constitute the tort of 'false' or wrongful imprisonment. Clearly a person may validly contract to work in a coal mine, and in that event he cannot throw up the contract and demand to be taken to the surface at a moment's notice, though he certainly can expect to be taken to the surface as soon as reasonably practicable. Any contractual clause which deprived him of this right would almost certainly be void. So also, a person may obviously contract to travel by ship or air even though, in the process, some limits on his personal freedom of movement are involved. It is not clear whether similar restraints on freedom would be legally valid where they are less strictly necessary as, for example, if a theatre company stipulated on its tickets that clients would not be entitled to leave the theatre while a play was in progress.

### 4. CONTRACTS IN RESTRAINT OF TRADE

Contracts in restraint of trade are one of the most important categories of void contracts at common law. The modern term would be 'restrictive practices' which is, indeed, somewhat wider than 'agreements in restraint of trade', but the economic and legal problems are the same whatever the label. Broadly these are agreements in which one or both parties limit their

---

[5] See n. 3 above.

freedom to work or carry on their profession or business in some way, such as (for instance) by agreeing not to compete with each other in certain places. Such agreements, as we saw in the last chapter, may be attacked because they conflict with the public interest, and because they are unfair in unduly restricting personal freedom. At one time the former of these factors predominated, while at another time it was the latter. Today it sometimes seems to be the public interest and sometimes the question of fairness between the parties which is the most important factor in agreements involving restraints of trade.

Contracts in restraint of trade are merely one aspect of a very large and complex problem with important economic and social implications. From the legal point of view it straddles the law of contract, tort, and crime, and is now subject to much public law regulation, as well as the law of the EC. Essentially, the question is to what extent the law should interfere with the freedom of businessmen to do business in such a way as to limit or restrict competition in the market, and thus to harm the public interest as a whole. The problem has arisen in a number of different legal contexts, such as the tort of conspiracy and the crime of blackmail, as well as in connection with the doctrine of privity of contract, with which we have still to deal. Broadly speaking the traditional attitude of the courts was to leave businessmen to use their own methods of conducting business, even if this was likely to lead to the creation of monopolies, or unfair competition, or the enforcement of restrictive practices of various kinds. Once again the influence of economic theories, and in particular of *laissez-faire*, can be seen in many important cases. Some of the speeches in one of the leading cases at the end of the nineteenth century read almost like part of a Liberal Party tract advocating free trade.[6] But in this field the influence of *laissez-faire* was reinforced by the difficulty of the courts' taking positive action without getting even more deeply involved in political or economic theories. In modern times, however, legislation has become increasingly important in handling the wider implications of anti-competitive practices, and the role of the common law is now of relatively minor importance.

It is against this background that the particular problem of contracts in restraint of trade may be considered. Most of the case law concerns contractual clauses which prohibit a person from working in a certain trade or profession, usually subject to limitations of time and space. Clauses of this kind are commonly found in two types of contract. First, they are frequently found in contracts for the sale of the goodwill of a business or a professional practice. Manifestly, the buyer of a shop or of a practice will not be satisfied with what he buys unless he can persuade the seller to

---

[6] See *Mogul Steamship Co Ltd* v. *McGregor, Gow & Co* (1889) 23 QBD 598, and on appeal, [1892] AC 25, especially the speech of Lord Bramwell.

contract that he will not immediately set up a competing business next door and draw back most of his old clients or customers. Hence the buyer will usually want the seller to agree not to enter into competition with him. In fact a sale of goodwill necessarily involves some degree of limitation on the seller's freedom to compete—that is what a sale of goodwill means. Secondly, clauses of this kind are often found in written contracts of employment, the employer requiring his employee to agree that he will not work for a competing employer or set up a competing business of his own after he leaves his present work. Such clauses are also often found in similar relationships, even though they are not strictly contracts of employment, for example, the relationship between a self-employed person, such as a pop singer, and his music publisher, or a professional boxer and his agent or manager, and in general they are governed by the same principles as apply to employment contracts.[7]

The general principle of the common law has long been that restrictive agreements are void unless they are 'reasonable' in the interests of the public and of the parties. Of course reasonableness in the interests of the parties is the kind of thing which classical contract law said was for the parties themselves, but in this area of the law (which long antedates the development of classical principles) both the public interest and the fairness of the contract to the parties may be raised in the courts.

## What kinds of restraints?

Until relatively recent times little attention has actually been given to specifying what kinds of restrictions fall within the common law principles. As noted above, there were two very common kinds of cases, but all sorts of other restrictive agreements exist which until recently were rarely challenged. Modern cases, however, show that the courts are now willing to develop this part of the law after a long period during which legal changes have been left to Parliament.

In particular, in *Esso Petroleum Co Ltd* v. *Harper's Garage*,[8] the House of Lords decided that the categories of restraint of trade are not closed, and that other types of contract may be held void as being in restraint of trade, e.g. (as in that case) contracts relating to 'tied' garages, that is, garages (or filling stations) where only one brand of petrol may be sold. This decision brings many problems in its wake. In particular, it now becomes necessary to decide what *is* a contract in restraint of trade. Most contracts involve *some* restriction on the freedom of the parties, for example, an employee is not free to work except for his employer during

---

[7] See e.g. *A. Schroeder Music Publishing Co* v. *Macaulay* [1974] 1 WLR 1308, *post*, 331; *Watson* v. *Prager* [1991] 3 All ER 487.　　　　　　　　　　　[8] [1968] AC 269.

ordinary working hours, and a buyer who contracts to obtain all the supplies of some commodity which he needs from a particular seller (a common enough form of business agreement) is restricting his freedom to buy from anyone else. But it would certainly be wrong to conclude that *all* contracts containing restrictions are now open to challenge as contracts in restraint of trade, and must be shown to be 'reasonable' if they are to be valid.

Many customary and accepted forms of business agreement are probably still unchallengeable (at any rate under the common law rules), even though they may strictly involve some degree of business restraint. In particular, it has been held that a person who buys land (or a building) may validly enter into some restrictions on how the land is to be used without falling foul of the restraint of trade doctrine—in other words he cannot challenge the validity of the agreement on the ground that it is an unreasonable restraint.[9] This limit on the scope of the doctrine has been justified on the ground that, if a seller could not validly demand from the buyer some restriction of this kind, he might choose not to sell at all, which would be even more restrictive of competition.[10] But this argument is implausible: it could equally be said of any agreement whereby a seller of a business takes an unreasonably wide restraint from the buyer.

### Restraints to be justified must protect a 'legitimate interest'

In deciding whether a restraint of trade is reasonable, the courts have long taken the view that regard must be had to the 'interests' which the restraint is designed to protect. The principle governing these clauses is that they are valid if, but only if, they are no wider than is reasonably necessary to protect the legitimate interests of the promisee. The nature of these interests differs according to the type of case. Thus in the case of the buyer and seller of a business the courts quite naturally think it reasonable for the buyer to protect himself against competition by the seller in order to protect the value of the business which he has bought. It is, indeed, in the interests of the seller that such contracts should be upheld because he would not otherwise be able to get such a good price for his business. In fact once the courts had recognized the concept of goodwill as being property with a money value attached to it, this conclusion was inevitable. It is still true that the restraint must not be wider than is reasonably necessary to protect the buyer's purchase. For instance, he must not request the seller to refrain from opening a new business in a town where the old business had no customers, nor must the clause operate for a length of time disproportionate to the type and size of the business.

---

[9] *Alec Lobb (Garages) Ltd* v. *Total Oil GB Ltd* [1985] 1 WLR 173.
[10] *Ibid.*

Generally speaking, as the restraint grows wider in space and longer in time, so must the interests of the buyer be correspondingly large if the restraint is to be justified. In an extreme case, extreme restraints may be justified. For instance, in one leading case on the subject, a company which bought an armaments business for the huge sum (in 1897) of £287,000 was held justified in taking a contract from the seller that he would not enter into competition with this business anywhere in the world for a period of twenty-five years.[11] In view of the fact that the business was world-wide in its operations, and that its customers were mainly governments, any attempt by the seller to re-enter the armaments business anywhere in the world might well have affected the value of the buyers' purchase. This, however, was an extreme, indeed a unique, case, and in most cases the restraint would have to be much narrower in space, or for a much shorter time, or both, if it is to be upheld.

The case of restraints in contracts between employer and employee presents rather different considerations. For one thing, in such cases the employer is frequently in the stronger bargaining position—he presents the terms to the employee, and the employee must accept them or go elsewhere for his work. Of course this is not always the true position at the present day, particularly in industries with strong trade union traditions. However, it is probably true to say that these covenants in restraint of trade are more often found in employments which are not highly unionized. They are also often found in partnership agreements, restricting the freedom of ex-partners to compete after the departure of one partner. But because of the element of mutuality involved here, each partner benefiting from the restrictions, the courts seem more favourably inclined to them than in employer–employee cases. For instance, in *Bridge* v. *Deacons*[12] the defendant was a solicitor who had formerly been a member of a firm in Hong Kong. The partnership agreement prevented him for five years from dealing with any client of the firm, or anyone who had been a client within the previous three years. The defendant argued that this covenant was unreasonably wide because the firm's business was divided into some ten branches (some of them even physically dealt with in separate premises) and he had had no effective dealings with about 90 per cent of the firm's clients. Yet it was upheld by the Privy Council. This was undoubtedly a severe decision, because it must have greatly limited the defendant's capacity to work as a solicitor in Hong Kong at all, and the decision seems to have afforded the firm a large degree of protection against bare competition. It would surely not have been the same if the case had involved a former employee rather than a partner.

[11] *Nordenfelt* v. *Maxim Nordenfelt Gun Co* [1894] AC 535.
[12] [1984] AC 705.

## Employer–employee cases

Where employer–employee cases are concerned, the courts have insisted that an employer cannot protect himself against bare competition. Even though, as is commonly the case, the employer has trained the employee, or enabled him to develop into a skilled craftsman or professional worker, he cannot demand that these skills should not be used against him. The skills or experience obtained by an employee do not belong to the employer—they are assets of the employee alone, and prima facie everyone has the right to earn his living by using his own experience, skill, and knowledge, even if it was acquired in the employment of another.[13] In the absence of some explicit contractual restriction an employee is entirely at liberty to enter the same field of business on leaving his employment, and even to target his former employer's customers.[14] The employer is not even permitted to take a contract which prevents the employee using these skills or experience in competition with the employer unless he has some legitimate interest which requires protection.

Basically, there are only two interests which an employer may protect by a contract of this kind. These are 'trade secrets' and business connections. Both are somewhat nebulous and ill-defined concepts, but both are interests which an employer may reasonably ask to be protected. It would obviously be unjust that an employee should work for a rival and impart to him special methods of manufacture, or the like, which he has learnt while working for a previous employer. So, for instance, a restraint was upheld in *Littlewoods* v. *Harris*,[15] where the defendant had worked as a senior executive for the plaintiffs, a large mail-order firm, and then left to work for their only serious rivals, after having helped prepare the new season's catalogue for the plaintiffs. So, also, where an employee comes into contact with clients or customers, it is generally felt unacceptable that he should later attempt to use his personal influence with these clients in order to draw them away for a new employer, or for himself, if he chooses to set up business on his own account. So, for instance, a hairdresser's assistant would not be permitted to work for a rival salon in breach of a reasonable restraint.[16] Restraints in cases of this nature must normally be much more limited in time and space if they are to be upheld than in the case of business sellers. Thus in a hairdresser's assistant case, a restraint covering twelve months, but only a half-mile radius of her previous employer's salon, was held reasonable; and in *Littlewoods* v. *Harris*, referred to

---

[13] *Faccenda Chicken Ltd* v. *Fowler* [1987] Ch. 117.
[14] *Universal Thermosensors Ltd* v. *Hibben* [1992] 1 WLR 840.
[15] [1977] 1 WLR 1472.
[16] *Marion White* v. *Francis* [1972] 1 WLR 1423.

above, a ban on working for the one rival employer for twelve months was also upheld.

Indeed, in this sort of case the law gives limited protection to the employer even in the absence of a special contractual prohibition, perhaps under an 'implied term' or perhaps simply as part of the general contractual or equitable duties owed by an employee to his employer. The former employee will not be permitted to infringe 'trade secrets' acquired during his employment even in the absence of an express contractual prohibition. But the employer cannot protect himself against the use even of confidential information acquired during the employment unless it amounts to a 'trade secret', in the absence of express contract. In *Faccenda Chicken Ltd* v. *Fowler*[17] a group of employees of the plaintiff company left together and set up a rival concern. The plaintiffs' business had involved the selling of frozen chickens from refrigerated vans to butchers and similar establishments, and the ex-employees made use of their knowledge of customers, prices charged, suitable routes, times of the week, and so on, in their new business. The Court of Appeal held that, in the absence of express prohibition in their contracts, there was nothing to stop the ex-employees competing in this way. Such confidential information would only be protected if it amounted to a trade secret, and confidential information had to be 'highly confidential' before it could be classed as a trade secret, e.g. it might be information as to some secret manufacturing process, or possibly a list of customers. Here only the prices charged by the plaintiffs were truly secret or private information which they had a right to keep to themselves, for their own use, but the knowledge of these prices could not in the present case be severed from the other information which the ex-employees had used, none of which was truly secret.

The court said that in deciding whether information amounts to a trade secret, regard must be had to (a) the status of the employee and the nature of his work, (b) the nature of the information itself, (c) whether the employer impressed the confidentiality of the information on his employees, and (d) whether the information could easily be isolated from other information which the employee was free to use. A good practical working rule is that information normally carried in the employee's head may be used, but if the employee takes or copies or even memorizes lists of customers or other similar information, this may well be a breach of the employee's duties even in the absence of an express covenant.[18]

Because of the difficulty of defining 'trade secrets' or confidential information employers often try to impose wide general covenants on their employees, but these may well be struck down as too wide, and in any

[17] *Supra*, n. 13.
[18] *Universal Thermosensors Ltd* v. *Hibben, supra*, n. 14.

event the employer often cannot get an injunction for breach of such a covenant because of the difficulty of proving real loss or damage.[19]

Even where the ex-employee is breaching his duties to his former employer, and can be stopped by injunction from doing so, the clients themselves cannot of course be compelled to continue to patronize the previous employer. But it has been held[20] that, even if a customer or client makes it clear that he will not deal with the former employer, an injunction can still be granted against the ex-employee (assuming of course a breach of duty) to stop him dealing with that client. This is disturbing because it seems to limit the right of the third party to do business with whom he chooses, and he, after all, owes no duty whatever to the former employer, but it is perhaps an inevitable result of the former employer's right to control the work of the ex-employee. Effectively, he can only be treated as offering to do business with those with whom he is entitled to contract.

No magic attaches to the words 'trade secrets'. In particular, it must be remembered that the doctrine of restraint of trade applies to all sorts of professional and business activities, and is not limited to trade in the usual sense. For instance, it applies even to professional sports, many of which impose highly restrictive rules on the players—preventing them from playing for certain teams, or banning them from selection for national teams. Such restrictions have to be reasonable, like all other restrictions, if they are to be legally valid.

### Marketing as a legitimate interest

Now that the courts have enlarged the categories of cases in which agreements may be held to be in restraint of trade, it obviously becomes necessary to determine new criteria for deciding these cases. For example, in dealing with the matter of 'tied garages' it is not entirely clear what are the 'legitimate interests' which a petrol company is entitled to protect. Here, it seems that the simple desire of a business for an orderly and regular marketing of its products was enough to be a 'legitimate interest' which could be protected.

### Sports authorities

In *Greig* v. *Insole*,[21] (which arose out of an unauthorized commercially sponsored tour of Australia), it was held that the cricket authorities had sufficient interest in the organization of the game at test and county level to justify the imposition of reasonable restraints on the players. But it was also held that the restraints in question—a test and county ban on any

---

[19] *Universal Thermosensors Ltd* v. *Hibben, supra*, n. 14.
[20] *Michael Design PLC* v. *Cooke* [1987] 2 All ER 332.
[21] [1978] 1 WLR 302.

player playing in the tour—was far too wide to be justified. Bans on sportsmen who associated with or played cricket in South Africa in the days of apartheid never came before the courts in England, but if challenged would also have had to be justified in the same way. Probably, sports authorities would be held to have sufficient interest in the general management of their sports to try to prevent players consorting with countries which are the subject of an international boycott (as South Africa was) though even that is arguable, because it is not wholly clear why sporting authorities should have a legitimate interest in such political matters. Of course any restrictions or bans imposed on the players (and sometimes on other players who then consort with those players—a sort of secondary boycotting system) would also have to be justified as 'reasonable'.

## Other cases

In *A. Schroeder Music Publishing Co Ltd* v. *Macaulay*[22] the House of Lords had to examine a restraint in a contract between a song-writer and a music publisher. The contract required the writer to offer all his songs to the publisher for five years, and the publisher had the option to renew the contract for a further five years; the contract imposed almost no obligations on the publisher, however, except to pay a royalty on songs actually published. It was held that the publisher was entitled to impose some reasonable restraint on the song-writer because the business was clearly a speculative one, and the publisher was entitled to a reasonable return if the speculation should succeed; but it was held that ten years was too long, particularly as the publisher was not obliged to publish any of the songs. Effectively, what the contract meant was that if the song-writer became (as this one did) highly successful, the publisher would have the benefit of his songs for ten years even if he had not really helped him to 'hit the jack-pot'. Clearly, the House of Lords thought the contract unfair, as well as contrary to the public interest. But the decision has been criticized on the ground that music-publishing is (and was) a highly competitive business, and that the mere fact of inequality of bargaining power in such a case is no evidence of oppression or unfairness. Because there are very many people who want to be song-writers, and very few of them ever reach the pinnacle of success, it is inevitable that contracts with beginners will not be very rewarding, and will contain clauses demanding that, if the writer does become highly successful, some of the profits should be diverted to the publishers. If publishers are not permitted to make contracts like this with would-be song-writers, fewer beginners will ever have a chance to have their songs published. Thus the decision may be seen as dating from

[22] *Supra*, n. 7.

the time when freedom-of-contract principles were in the decline, because it effectively prevents economic forces operating properly in the market.

## Reasonableness in the interests of the parties and of the public

In all these cases the principle applied by the courts is that the restraint must be shown to be reasonable in the interests of the parties and of the public.[23] The burden of proving the first is on the person suing on the contract, while the burden of proving that it is contrary to the public interest is on the other party. In practice, however, it has been extremely rare for the courts to hold that the contract is reasonable in the interests of the parties, but is void as contrary to the public interest, a fact which illustrates the point that the courts have often been more concerned with fairness and justice between the parties than with the public interest in these cases. For instance, in the *Alec Lobb (Garages)* case[24] a petrol tie of twenty-one years was upheld as reasonable in the particular circumstances of the case, even though twenty-one years is in general far too long from the public interest point of view. But in this case, the new contract was a rescue operation for a business in deep financial distress, and so in danger of closing down altogether, and indeed the petrol company was reluctant to enter into the transaction at all.

The truth is that the courts are much better equipped to handle questions of reasonableness between the parties—contractual fairness (though under challenge from the new freedom-of-contract extremists) is a traditional sort of judicial issue, suitable to the processes of the courts. Public interest questions are far more difficult for courts to handle, which is largely why, in modern times, the broader issues arising out of restrictive practices have been dealt with by different methods.

## Statutory developments

The common-law rules concerning agreements in restraint of trade suffered from four weaknesses which became increasingly serious after the Second World War. First, an agreement in restraint of trade was *void* but it was not *prohibited* to make or carry out such an agreement. An agreement in restraint of trade is not a breach of the criminal law; nor is it even a tort of which a third party can complain in a civil action for damages, unless unlawful means are used in carrying out the agreement. In the famous case of *Mogul Steamship Co. Ltd.* v. *McGregor, Gow & Co.* in 1892[25] a number

---

[23] Reasonableness must be tested by the terms of the contract, not how they have been applied or operated.      [24] *Supra*, n. 9.

[25] [1892] AC 25. It is interesting to note that almost contemporaneously with this decision the US Congress passed the Sherman Anti-Trust Act which converted agreements in restraint of trade into *prohibited* agreements.

of shipping companies combined to offer discounts off their freight charges for the China tea trade with a view to preventing the plaintiffs, a rival shipping company, from obtaining a foothold in the trade. These discounts, however, were only available to those who used the shipping companies concerned for *all* their trade. Clearly, this was a severe disincentive to any trader to use other ships at all, and therefore a highly anti-competitive device, as economists were by then beginning to appreciate. Although the defendants' agreement was clearly in restraint of trade, and possibly unreasonably wide, it was not an illegal agreement and the plaintiffs lost their case. The courts felt unable to lay down standards of permissible behaviour in trade competition short of actual criminal acts or other illegalities. It was simply assumed that, if in the long run all was permissible in competition, everything would come right in the end.

But this proved a great mistake. The result of this case was that agreements in restraint of trade were frequently made and frequently abided by. So long as it was in the interests of all parties to reduce or eliminate competition, the agreements, though void, were in fact complied with. Moreover, even though these agreements could not be legally enforced against the occasional recalcitrant trader, the business world soon found very effective extra-legal methods of enforcement. In particular, the 'stop-list' (a collective agreement between suppliers to refuse to supply the party who broke the 'rules' and competed more actively) soon forced him to toe the line or drove him out of business altogether.

The second principal weakness of the common-law rules was that the public was not represented in litigation concerning agreements in restraint of trade. Although we have seen that in theory such agreements can be declared void if they are contrary to the public interest (even though they are reasonable in the interests of the parties) the public is not represented at the bar of the court. Accordingly, evidence that such agreements are contrary to the public interest is not presented—indeed, it is strictly inadmissible, because what is in the 'public interest' is supposed to be a matter of law, within the knowledge of the judges, even where complex economic issues are involved. Hence (as we have seen) once the agreement is found to be reasonable in the interests of the parties it is very rare that the courts proceed to hold it void as contrary to the public interest.

The third weakness of the common law was that the practice and procedure of ordinary courts is ill-suited to an inquiry into the effect on the public interest of many types of restrictive agreements. Such an inquiry may raise wide issues of social and economic policy and may require prolonged and careful examination of the likely effect of such agreements on the national economy or important parts of it. Moreover, these are often matters of opinion, though economic or business expertise may be helpful in coming to an informed opinion. Judicial procedures, with their tradition of oral evidence and cross-examination, and their assumption that issues of fact are just matters for ordinary evidence, are not suited to the handling of issues of this kind.

The fourth weakness of the common law principles was that they were confined to dealing with agreements and contracts. Although in the seventeenth century there had been signs of a wider set of doctrines dealing with restraints on competition, very little remained by the nineteenth century except the rules dealing with agreements. This left a huge hole in anti-competition policy. In particular, it left out of account the restrictive effects of monopolies and mergers. A monopoly is obviously more effective as a form of restriction on competition than an agreement between rivals not to compete, but if the rivals merge to form one large monopoly, the common law rules against restraint of trade simply have no operation at all.

The result of these weaknesses in the common law was that restrictive practices flourished exceedingly between the last decades of the nineteenth century and the Second World War. By 1950 British industry and trade were riddled with a vast network of restrictive practices of every kind. Resale price maintenance, to take one prominent example, was a system whereby manufacturers combined together to agree to compel retailers to abide by the retail prices set by the manufacturers themselves. First the manufacturers agreed their own prices so as to reduce or eliminate competition among themselves, and then they ensured that every retailer was forced to observe these prices, so there was no price competition between retailers either. Those whose memories go back to the 1950s and even the early 1960s will recall that there was virtually no price competition at all at that time on a very wide range of consumer (and other) goods. The whole system was rigidly enforced by a system of stop-lists so that any retailer who dared to sell an item at a cut price was liable to be 'fined' by private courts or have his supplies cut off, not merely by the supplier whose goods were in question, but also by all other suppliers too. The common law proved powerless to control these activities and, indeed, many judges seemed to sympathise more with those trying to enforce the restrictions than with those who tried to break them down—though (to be fair) most other people originally did so too.

Many other restrictions were widespread during this time. For instance, someone who wanted to open a newsagents' shop had to get the permission (!) of rival traders who naturally had no wish to see competition increased, and were able to ensure that unwelcome intruders were unable to obtain newspapers from suppliers. Manufacturers often carved up areas of the country as markets, so that they did not compete among themselves. Tenderers for large contracts often agreed to parcel out the contracts among themselves, in some sort of order, rather than to compete for individual contracts. Manufacturers and trade unions (in a rare spirit of co-operation) were even held entitled to boycott the importation of material which competed with Harris Tweed in the Scottish islands, thus enabling Harris Tweed prices to be maintained without the pressure of competing goods.

These failures of the common law led eventually to much legislative activity in an attempt to restore competition to the British economy. The first significant sign of the new approach was the passing of the Restrictive Trade Practices Act 1956 (now replaced by the Act of 1976) which created a new court—the Restrictive Practices Court—whose members include non-lawyers with experience of economic matters and of trade and industry. Under this Act many restrictive agreements are required to be registered with the Director-General of Fair Trading. These agreements are then brought before the Court, which is charged with the task of deciding if they are in the public interest. The Director-General has the function of representing the public in these proceedings and he is represented by counsel before the Court like an ordinary litigant. If the Court finds the agreement to be contrary to the public interest it then becomes illegal to carry out the agreement or make any other agreement to the like effect.

After the Act was passed a number of important decisions were made by the Court which made it clear that a huge number of restrictive agreements would in all probability be found eventually to be contrary to the public interest. Consequently many such agreements were abandoned or modified and the purposes of the original Act were thus to some degree achieved. Later amendments to the original Act extended it to many restrictions relating to the supply of services as well as goods, though in general professional services still fall outside the jurisdiction of the Court.

Another important development was the passing of the Resale Prices Act 1964 (now replaced by the Act of 1976) which gave the Restrictive Practices Court jurisdiction to deal with resale price maintenance arrangements and to decide if these are in the public interest. Here again, the work of the Court has now resulted in the almost complete collapse of resale price maintenance, except for the (almost) unique case of books.[26] Nearly all agreements for resale price maintenance are now void, and it is illegal to try to enforce resale price maintenance by boycotts, stop-lists, or even by refusing to supply a dealer.

Another statutory development has been the creation of the Monopolies and Mergers Commission, which is an administrative body whose only

---

[26] Resale price maintenance for books under the so-called Net Book Agreement is still subject to challenge under the Treaty of Rome, but pending a judicial decision the Agreement remains legally valid. See *Publishers Association* v. *EC Commission* [1992] 4 All ER 70.

powers are to inquire and report into various questions. These questions include the effect of restrictive agreements in the supply of professional services (as opposed to goods and commercial services, with which the Restrictive Practices Court is concerned) and also with various monopoly situations. The appropriate Minister has statutory powers to prohibit arrangements contrary to the public interest on the strength of a report from the Monopolies and Mergers Commission.

Much of the relevant legislation was consolidated in the Fair Trading Act 1973, which established the office of Director-General of Fair Trading who is charged with a general oversight of restrictive and anti-competitive practices. The Act also created an Advisory Committee to which may be referred various sorts of trade practices which may be harmful to consumer interests. A report of the Advisory Committee may lead to the prohibition or regulation of such practices by statutory Order; further powers are granted by the Competition Act 1980.

Finally, there are important provisions in Articles 85 and 86 of the EC Treaty which (in very broad language) are designed to limit anti-competitive devices and arrangements so as to prevent the distortion of competition over the whole or any part of the EC. These Articles deal not only with restrictive practices, but also with the 'abuse of a dominant position' in the market by a monopoly or dominant firm. As the Treaty is now part of English law, these Articles (and the powers conferred under them on the European Commission, the Council, and the Court) are now also part of English law. A considerable body of law now exists on these provisions, including case law of the European Court, and rulings of the Commission, but this law is too specialized for treatment here.

There is no doubt that the British economy is today far more competitive than it was forty or fifty years ago as a result of this legislative activity. It is today obvious that consumers have far more choice available to them in a variety of ways than they used to have when restrictive agreements were so common. Not only is there now plenty of price competition, but competition on contract terms on offer to consumers has also become available in a very wide range of transactions. This is a matter of some general importance to contract law, because it greatly affects the validity of the argument, still often used with regard to consumer transactions, that consumer contracts are 'imposed' on them by those with superior bargaining power.

There can be little doubt that it is largely due to this outburst of legislative activity that the courts have taken a renewed interest in restrictive practices, as shown first by the *Esso Petroleum* case, and many subsequent ones. One problem which this may raise is how far it is desirable for the ordinary courts to pursue their reawakened interest here, rather than leave these matters to Parliament, and the various statutory bodies charged with responsibility for dealing with anti-competitive practices. On the whole there is a good deal to be said for the courts confining their attention to minor matters, or perhaps more specifically to the question of reasonableness in individual cases, and exercising great caution about invoking considerations of the public interest. The reason for this is quite simply that the statutory authorities have much more suitable procedures to obtain evidence and information on the wide issues raised by many restrictive practices. This is illustrated, indeed, by the particular problem raised in the *Esso Petroleum* case, because the question whether the tied-garage system is in the public interest was itself considered, more or less contemporaneously with that case, by the Monopolies Commission. The Commission came to the conclusion that in general the tied-garage system operated in the public interest for two principal reasons. First, tied garages bought one brand of petrol only, and therefore bought in larger quantities, so helping to reduce the cost to the public. Secondly, the system had encouraged petrol companies to lend money to garages for improving facilities for repair and services to the public. In addition, the very wide availability of petrol filling stations meant that a motorist rarely had to drive far to find one selling a competing brand of petrol. Considerations of this nature involved an inquiry into facts and figures which was far more extensive than could be presented to an ordinary court in ordinary litigation, as is shown by the *Esso Petroleum* case itself. In fact the result of that case was more or less in line with the Monopolies Commission Report (that only ties exceeding five years were undesirable in the public interest) but it obviously cannot be assumed that divergences will not occur in the future if the courts are active in areas where the statutory bodies also function.

Despite all that has been achieved, it is now apparent that much remains to be done to compel industry to be more competitive. The existing legislation, it is now felt, is no longer as effective as it once seemed, although it has certainly had significant results. The chief problem, it is now generally agreed, is that the existing law identifies anti-competitive practices by formal, legal criteria, and in particular, of course, by looking for *agreements*. Even though the existing legislation does strike at some informal arrangements as well as formal agreements, it is now being said that many anti-competitive arrangements operate in a less formal way even than this. Business concerns may act in concert without actually agreeing or arranging to do so. There are phenomena, such as 'parallel pricing', where it is found that large firms simply adopt a practice, without agreeing or arranging to do so, of pricing their goods in an uncompetitive way. There is 'price leadership' whereby whenever one large and dominant firm adjusts its market prices, all other firms follow suit—but without agreeing or arranging to do so. And so on. Because these anti-competitive practices do not involve agreements or 'arrangements' they do not fall within the jurisdiction of the Restrictive Practices Court, and indeed that court has not now been active for some years. New legislation to deal with these anti-competitive devices is anticipated, but this very shift in the shape of the law is likely to take the subject still further away from the law of contract.

## 5.  WAGERING CONTRACTS

Another kind of agreement which is void by statute is worth a few comments because it illustrates how the law's policies can vary in different cases. At common law a wager or bet was a perfectly valid contract consisting of mutual conditional promises or, sometimes, of one conditional promise in consideration of a fixed stake. For instance a bet on the outcome of the boat-race would involve a promise by A to pay B say £5 if Oxford wins, and a similar bet by B to pay A £5 if Cambridge wins. In the event, only one of the two promises will need to be performed, but since it is uncertain at the outset which that one will be, each promise is good consideration for the other. Similarly, a bet at a fixed stake involves a promise by (say) a bookmaker to pay at odds of (say) five to one if a certain horse wins a race. If the horse loses, the bookmaker keeps the stake, of course.

At common law such agreements were valid contracts, but section 18 of the Gaming Act 1845 declared all such contracts to be null and void. The policy of the law does not seem to be to prevent or perhaps even to discourage betting as such, because there is nothing in the Gaming Act to prevent parties making and paying bets. Bets, once paid, cannot be recovered and there is, of course, an enormous betting industry which survives perfectly well without the ability to enforce unpaid bets by legal action. Furthermore, this industry presumably serves a public purpose, since it provides mutually satisfactory gambling facilities to the public and the bookmakers, and Parliament has not seen fit to prohibit the activity altogether. Indeed, it taxes it and, with the introduction of the national lottery, even authorises it.

So it looks rather as though the policy of the law here lies in two other directions. One perhaps is the feeling that the courts have more important things to do than solemnly to adjudicate on matters of this kind. Courts cost money, after all, money which is provided by the taxpayer in order to subsidize peaceful methods of settling disputes. But there seems no reason why the taxpayer should subsidize the cost of settling betting disputes. In other words the law prefers to deal with wagers as though they were social engagements or family matters to be settled outside courts of law. Secondly, it may well be that what the law particularly objects to with betting agreements is the enforcement of an *executory* contract to pay a lost bet. The fact that bets can be freely made in cash, and can be paid when lost without any legal difficulty, confirms that there is nothing wrong with *executed* contracts of this character. All that the law does is to prevent a person from binding himself by an *executory* agreement to a bet. So there may be a degree of paternalism in the present law; and perhaps it is not unjustified in this particular area. Even the most devoted adherent of freedom-of-contract principles may have qualms about the possibility that a person should be able to pick up a telephone and make a binding legal contract to bet £10,000 on a horse.

## 6. CONTRACTING OUT OF STATUTES

Contracts which bind a person to do something which a statute says he is *not* bound to do are often invalid. And similarly, a contract which binds a person *not* to do something which a statute says he may do may also be invalid. Sometimes the invalidity is spelled out by the Act itself, but it is often a matter of inference from the general statutory scheme.

For example, a statutory body set up for public purposes cannot stultify the intentions of Parliament by contracting not to use those powers. So also a person who is a tenant of rent-restricted premises cannot surrender this protection by contract, although he can do so by actually giving up the possession of the premises. Similarly, the House of Lords has held that an agricultural tenant cannot by contract surrender his statutory right to demand security of tenure from his landlord.[27] It can no longer be treated as axiomatic, said their lordships (though in fact it never was), 'that in the absence of explicit language, the courts will permit contracting out of the provisions of an Act of Parliament'.

In some cases, on the other hand, the courts have reached a different solution to this kind of case by holding that a promise to surrender a power is enforceable by an action for damages, although the actual surrender is invalid in the sense that the power can still be exercised. Thus a person may retain the *power* to do something while giving up the *right* to do it. Again, it may be possible for contracting parties to bind themselves so as effectively to restrain a third party from exercising its statutory powers. For example, a registered company has power to alter its articles of association under the Companies Act. If it should make a contract which would prevent it from exercising this power in some respect, the contract may be void, but there is nothing in law to prevent the shareholders from contracting that they will not vote for a company resolution to alter the articles of association.[28] But this approach would clearly be inappropriate in cases where the statute is in effect a consumer-protection statute.

[27] *Johnson* v. *Moreton* [1980] AC 37.
[28] *Russell* v. *Northern Bank Development Corp Ltd* [1992] 1 WLR 588.

## 6. THE CONSEQUENCES OF A VOID CONTRACT

If a contract is void because of its objects or terms, the primary and obvious consequence is that it cannot be sued upon and enforced as an ordinary legal contract. However, other normal legal consequences may still follow, and remedies other than contractual ones may be available to the parties. For instance, if a person pays money or transfers property under a void contract he may be able to recover it, not because there is a contract, but on the contrary because there is no contract, with the result that there is, or may be, a total failure of consideration. That is to say, there may be a total failure of the purposes for which the money was paid or the goods transferred. There is no public interest in refusing a right of recovery in such circumstances as a general rule, although there may be objections to recovery in special circumstances. As we have seen, a person who pays his betting losses cannot recover them, although the contract is void, because he is regarded as having waived the benefit of the Gaming Act. More realistically, this is because (we have suggested) the policy of the law is against *executory* and not *executed* contracts of this kind.

Again, if part of an agreement is void, for example, on the ground that it is in restraint of trade, or that it involves an ouster of the jurisdiction of the court, this will not normally affect the validity of other parts of the agreement. Thus a restraint-of-trade clause will not prevent other terms in a contract of employment from being enforced. Moreover, a court is sometimes able even to sever the offending part of the void clause itself, and declare the rest binding. However, the principles governing this question, whose practical application lies mainly in the field of restraint-of-trade clauses, are extremely difficult to ascertain. It is, in fact, difficult to resist the conclusion that the courts have sometimes acted on an unacknowledged discretion rather than on fixed rules of law. Where they are faced with a covenant in restraint of trade drafted so widely as to be really oppressive, the courts have not felt at all inclined to assist the promisee by removing the offending part of the clause from the rest. They have often preferred to treat the whole clause as void.[29] On the other hand, especially in buyer-and-seller cases, where a covenant is only slightly too wide, for example, in that it covers areas where the seller has never done business, the courts have never hesitated to strike out the excess, while enforcing the rest of the clause.

---

[29] Otherwise there would be no incentive on employers to comply with the law: *J. A. Mont (UK) Ltd* v. *Mills* [1993] IRLR 172. But there is undoubtedly power to sever even in employer–employee cases: see *T. Lucas & Co* v. *Mitchell* [1974] Ch. 129.

# 18

# Illegal Contracts

## 1. CONTRACTS TO COMMIT A CRIME

It is obvious that a contract which is entered into by the parties for the deliberate purpose of doing some act which involves a breach of the criminal law is void and unenforceable. Thus an agreement to perpetrate murder, robbery, rape, or indeed any other crime is manifestly illegal and cannot be the subject of an action for breach of contract. In economic terms, these are classic cases of externalities outweighing the benefit to the parties. Moreover, owing to the extreme width of the crime of conspiracy in English law, it must be remembered that many agreements may themselves be conspiracies, and hence criminal, even if the actual object of the agreement is not in itself criminal. This remains the case to some degree even after the enactment of the Criminal Law Act 1977, although that Act in general now confines the crime of conspiracy to agreements involving the actual commission of an offence. For instance, if two parties make an agreement to defraud the Inland Revenue authorities (such as the common agreement to pay fictitious 'expenses'), it is probable that they commit indictable conspiracy. So also a contract involving bribery or corruption, even though it may fall short of these actual offences, may amount to criminal conspiracy.

So far we have been considering cases which involve crimes of a fairly serious nature, crimes requiring moral culpability at all events. In the modern world, however, it must be remembered that the vast bulk of the criminal law is not made up of these offences, but of petty infringements of various statutes and statutory rules and regulations. Most offences of this kind are triable summarily by a magistrate, without a jury; many of them involve little or no moral culpability; and in many of them the maximum penalty is a fairly small fine. It is criminal offences of this sort that cause the most trouble in the law of contract, because the blind application of the rules concerning illegal contracts to agreements of this kind may well be harsh and unjust. For instance, if A and B make an agreement involving large sums of money, but knowing that this contract can only be performed by committing some trivial statutory offence for which the maximum penalty may be a fine of £50 or £100, it seems unreasonable to treat the contract in the same way as an agreement to rob a bank. The result may well be that one party obtains an entirely unmerited windfall, for which he cannot be made liable to account, while the other party, instead of being fined a few pounds by a magistrate, loses perhaps thousands of pounds. It must also be remembered that, when a person is tried for a criminal offence, the judge or magistrate always has a discretion as regards the sentence, which will be tailored to the gravity of the particular offence and of the accused's culpability. A particular accused may be, and frequently is, simply given a conditional or absolute discharge or put on probation. Thus the criminal law may regard the accused as not deserving any punishment or, at any rate, as only deserving a relatively trivial punishment. But in the law of contract these factors have little weight. Either the law has been broken or it has not. In the former event the contract may be treated as illegal, and there is an end of the case. The consequences of this Draconian rule are not always satisfactory, and caution is needed in applying the rules as to illegality.

There is even more difficulty in those cases in which the law is violated, not in making the contract, but in performing it. Here there is no question of the contract itself being illegal or void, but the consequences of an illegal act in the performance of the contract may be no less drastic than where the illegality is actually contemplated by the contract. This matter is more fully discussed later.

The law on this subject is undoubtedly in a difficult and confused state and it is very difficult to deduce principles of general validity which will explain all the decisions of the courts. This may be partly due to the fact that the policy considerations involved in this branch of the law are often conflicting. It is perhaps also partly due to the fact that here, even more than elsewhere in the law of contract, the courts have generally eschewed discussion of policy. But no apology is needed for a brief excursus into the policy considerations involved, for this is only another way of saying that legal rules must in the last resort be justified on some rational basis, and it is sensible to inquire into this basis.

The policy considerations involved here appear to include at least the following factors, though not all will be involved in every case. First, there is the desirability of deterring parties from criminal or anti-social conduct, and the associated (though different) object of punishing them if they commit such conduct. Normally it is the criminal law that performs these functions, but there may be forms of anti-social conduct which are not criminal, and yet which it may be desirable to deter (e.g. prostitution), and there may also be advantages in using contract law as an additional deterrent over and above that provided by the criminal law. To take the latter point first, there are situations in which contract law may deter more effectively even than the criminal law, though this may seem surprising at first sight. For instance, for many years there used to be statutory controls over hire-purchase transactions for the purpose of reducing the volume of consumer credit, though these have all been abolished in recent years.

These controls usually took the form of requiring a minimum deposit and a maximum repayment period. It was well established that a finance company which let goods on hire-purchase in violation of these controls could not enforce the resultant hire-purchase contract on grounds of illegality. In this kind of case the unenforceability of the contract may well have provided a more serious deterrent than the criminal law, if only because discovery and threat of prosecution were never very likely. Similarly, with exchange-control regulations (now also abolished): most probably the legal unenforceability of an illegal agreement to buy foreign currency was more effective as a deterrent than the criminal law. To put it at the lowest, the unenforceability of illegal contracts in this kind of case may be a useful additional deterrent to illegal conduct. But this is by no means always the case. It is rarely the case with a cash transaction, for then neither party usually needs the law to enforce the promises of the other.

A second policy consideration which is undoubtedly involved in some cases is the undesirability of jeopardizing the dignity of the courts. Respect for law and Courts of Justice is an important aspect of public policy, and this respect could be gravely impaired if courts were required to adjudicate on certain types of illegal transaction. It will be noticed that policy here suggests that the courts should refuse even to *hear* cases of this kind, and indeed the law recognizes this policy by requiring a court to dismiss an action forthwith if it becomes apparent that it is based on some illegality. Even the normal rules of pleading are ignored here because the courts will, of their own motion, take note of the illegality of a transaction even if neither party himself raises the issue.

A third possible policy consideration may in some cases be the desirability of bringing an illegal or undesirable state of affairs to an end. If, for instance, a woman takes a lease of a flat and then uses it for prostitution, it may be desirable that the landlord should be able to evict her by legal process, in order to terminate this state of affairs.

It will be seen that some of these factors may well conflict in any given case. For example, if a landlord knowingly lets premises to a prostitute and then seeks to evict her for non-payment of rent, the first and third policy considerations would conflict. The desirability of deterring landlords from similar conduct in future suggests that the action should be dismissed: the desirability of bringing the situation to an end suggests the contrary. But apart from conflicts of this nature in the relevant policy considerations, there is often likely to be conflict between the considerations suggesting that illegal contracts should not be enforced, and the general desirability of upholding contracts. In any given case, the considerations which normally render it just to enforce a contract may be present despite the illegality— for example, the plaintiff may have paid for some goods or services which the defendant has promised; or the plaintiff may have changed his position in reliance on some promise by the defendant. In such cases there is an acute conflict between the desire to do justice between the individual parties and the more general considerations set out above concerning the undesirability of enforcing illegal contracts. In this situation the traditional result has been to ignore the injustice which may be done in the individual case in the belief that this is outweighed by the public interest in refusing redress in such cases. But in recent years there has been a perceptible trend in the reverse direction, particularly where the illegality in question is thought to be of a technical nature which does not involve moral turpitude.

## 2. CONTRACTS INVOLVING SEXUAL IMMORALITY

Illegality in the law of contract is not coterminous with illegality in the criminal law, for a contract may be illegal without involving any breach of the criminal law at all. The most obvious illustration of this possibility is a contract involving sexual immorality. For instance, although prostitution is not, as such, criminal, a prostitute cannot sue her clients in a court for remuneration for her professional services. Nor, indeed, can she be sued by a person who has supplied her with goods or premises which he knows are to be used by her for her professional purposes.[1] In fact if he takes an inflated price, for example, by way of rent, he may even be prosecuted for living on the earnings of a prostitute.

Few people would quarrel with the law thus far. But changes in social customs and moral beliefs have in recent years produced a silent and dramatic revolution in the courts' attitudes to other forms of conduct which used to be regarded as sexually immoral. So, as we have previously seen,[2] the courts have been willing to 'imply' and enforce contracts (or trusts) between cohabiting partners as to their respective rights in the home in which they have been living. Earlier authorities concerning the illegality of sexually immoral contracts were totally ignored in these modern decisions, and it may be said with some confidence that many of them would not now be followed. But it is no doubt still the law that a contract actually designed to reward someone for sexual favours would be illegal.

## 3. OTHER AGREEMENTS CONTRARY TO PUBLIC POLICY

There are a number of other types of illegal agreements which do not involve the commission of a crime or sexual immorality, though many of them would have been criminal conspiracies under the old law. Such agreements are said to be illegal as being contrary to public policy. Such cases include agreements which tend to prejudice the administration of

---

[1] *Pearce* v. *Brooks* (1866) LR 1 Ex. 213.          [2] *Supra*, 95.

justice, such as stifling a prosecution; agreements involving bribery or corruption; agreements to defraud national or local revenue authorities; and so on.

The doctrine of public policy is strictly limited by the precedents. It cannot be too strongly emphasized that it is not open to a judge to reject a contract merely because he thinks that it is contrary to the public interest. It is only when a contract falls under one of the well-established categories stigmatized as being contrary to public policy that a judge can interfere and, as we have already said, most of these categories are so obviously matters contrary to the public interest that agreements falling under them are (or were formerly) criminal conspiracies. Indeed it was at one time suggested that courts could no longer invent new heads of public policy, although existing heads could be extended by analogy to new situations. But this is probably too extreme a view; and in any event the distinction between a wholly new 'head' of public policy and a 'head' analogous to an existing category is likely to be unreal in practice. No doubt this is an area in which it behoves the courts to move with caution. But public values do change, and the change these days sometimes seems to come about very quickly; provided that the courts avoid idiosyncratic views there seems no real reason why they should not treat agreements as contrary to public policy in wholly new situations. In *Initial Services, Ltd* v. *Putterill*[3] the Court of Appeal seems to have come very close to doing just this. In this case, at a time when there was widespread public concern about increased prices and all forms of 'price-fixing', the plaintiffs' former manager threatened to disclose to the newspapers certain confidential information. This information was to the effect that laundry companies were agreeing in concert to raise their prices. The court held that an agreement by the manager not to disclose such information would probably have been contrary to public policy. It is hard to find any previous case dealing with this sort of situation.

## 4. THE CONSEQUENCES OF ILLEGALITY

### Enforcement of the contract not generally permissible

The consequences of an illegal contract are drastic. In the first place it is obvious that the contract cannot be enforced by either party. This may sound reasonable enough, but in practice it is sometimes far from satisfactory. For one thing, if the actual contract is illegal it is immaterial that the parties did not know it to be illegal. The result may sometimes be that, as a consequence of a statutory regulation prohibiting certain kinds of contract, one party is presented with an entirely unmerited and technical

---

[3] [1968] 1 QB 396.

defence to an action for breach of contract, when neither party to the contract had any intention whatever of breaking the law. For instance, in one case an Englishwoman, residing in France during the war, borrowed money (repayable in sterling) contrary to emergency regulations.[4] The parties were in fact aware of the regulations, and they specifically provided that the money should only be repaid when it was legal to do so. Nonetheless, the contract was held illegal and void, and the lender was unable to recover his money. It is difficult to see what public interest is served by cases of this kind, especially when the only person who committed an offence was the very person who benefited by the defence of illegality.

One of the least satisfactory aspects of the law relating to illegal contracts is that the law strikes blindly at all parties concerned, with the result that the only person to benefit from the illegality is usually the defendant. His position is invariably better than that of the plaintiff, because a successful plea of illegality involves the automatic dismissal of the action. Unfortunately it is often pure chance who is the plaintiff and who the defendant, and complete refusal of all assistance to a plaintiff may encourage him to take the law into his own hands, especially since it is not impossible that any subsequent action against *him* may also be defeated by the same plea. Another troublesome feature is that the courts are reluctant to enter into any examination of the *relative* guilt of the parties in these cases, and if the contract is itself illegal it is immaterial that one party knew of the illegality and expected to benefit from it, while the other did not, even if the former is the defendant and the latter is the plaintiff. There are, however, signs in some recent cases that the courts are making inroads into this principle. At any rate where the plaintiff is not directly seeking to enforce the illegal contract itself, but is seeking to enforce some collateral right (for instance, by claiming damages for fraud, rather than for breach of contract), the courts have now accepted the need for some inquiry into relative fault.[5]

It is relatively straightforward to identify cases where the plaintiff is seeking to enforce a contract whose actual purpose was itself illegal. But the law also deals with more troublesome cases where the contract was not itself designed to perpetrate some illegality but where it is 'tainted' by some collateral illegality. It is often very difficult to say whether a claim is 'tainted' with illegality, but two principles are now differentiated in the cases. First, there is the rule that a plaintiff cannot succeed if he has to *found his claim* on an illegal contract; but conversely, if he can set up an independent cause of action which does not depend on, or arise from, or

---

[4]  *Boissevain* v. *Weil* [1950] AC 372.
[5]  *Saunders* v. *Edwards* [1987] 1 WLR 1116.

require the support of the illegality, he may be able to sue. And secondly, there is another principle (it is too general and subject to too many exceptions to call it a rule) which seeks to prevent a person from benefiting from a crime.

Both these principles give rise to many difficulties and many fine distinctions, though the essential problem is usually the same—namely to decide whether the claim is close enough, or sufficiently directly connected with the illegality, to be 'tainted' with it. For instance, in *Alexander v. Rayson*[6] a landlord was held disentitled from enforcing a lease when it was shown that the landlord had prepared two separate documents for the tenant to sign in order to defraud the rating authorities by making it appear that the rent was lower than it really was intended to be. Here the landlord was trying to sue on *both* documents, so his claim was founded upon the very documents that made up the illegality. By contrast, in *Saunders v. Edwards*[7] the buyers of a flat were held entitled to sue the seller for fraudulently stating that the flat included a roof terrace (when he knew it did not belong to him) even though the buyers had apportioned £5,000 of the price to fixtures in order to defraud the stamp-duty authorities. Here it was held that the claim, being for fraud, was not directly founded on the contract; the court also took account of the relative fault of the parties in this case.

Another pair of cases illustrating a fine distinction comes from the law of insurance. In *Geismar v. Sun Alliance and London Insurance Ltd*[8] the plaintiff was held not entitled to claim from his burglary insurers for goods stolen from him, because they had been illegally imported without declaring them to the customs authorities. Here the plaintiff had been in the possession of smuggled goods, and his claim to their value included, of course, an element which represented the unpaid customs duty. On the other hand, this case was distinguished in *Euro-Diam Ltd v. Bathurst*[9] where the plaintiffs had despatched diamonds to German buyers with an invoice understating their value, to assist the buyers in defrauding the German customs authorities. The diamonds were lost or stolen after they reached the buyers but before they had agreed to buy them, and were therefore still covered by the sellers' insurance policy. Here it was held that the attempt to defraud the German authorities (which was treated as on a par with a violation of English law) was only marginally for the benefit of the sellers, and did not taint their claim to the proceeds of the insurance policy. They themselves did not smuggle the goods, they did not make use of the fraudulent invoice, and they did not have possession of the goods at the relevant time.

[6] [1936] 1 KB 169.    [7] *Supra*, n. 5.    [8] [1978] QB 383.
[9] [1988] 2 All ER 23.

The second of the above-mentioned principles—that a person should not be allowed to benefit directly from criminal conduct—is illustrated by the well-established rule of insurance law that an insured cannot claim under a policy if he actually causes the insured event to occur by deliberate criminal conduct. So in *Beresford v. Royal Insurance Co Ltd*[10] it was held that sane suicide by an insured (at a time when suicide was a crime) debarred his administrators from claiming the proceeds of a life insurance policy—even though the policy itself did not exclude such a claim. This was not a case of an illegal contract, because the insurance policy was not in itself illegal; but the claim to the proceeds was held to be tainted with the illegal act. So, too, at common law, a person who killed another, whether intentionally or recklessly, so as to be guilty of murder or manslaughter, was debarred from recovering any benefit from an insurance policy. And this was the result whether the policy was a life policy whose proceeds might have passed to the killer by succession, or an indemnity policy, which the killer had himself purchased, and which covered his liability to pay damages. The rule did not, however, apply to an accidental or even negligent killing, so that (for instance) a person whose negligent driving causes death or injury has never been prevented from getting an indemnity from his insurers— indeed the whole road traffic insurance system assumes that he will do so. Even with deliberate killing, there is now some chance of relief (through judicial discretion) in the Forfeiture Act 1982, though unfortunately this is of very limited application.[11]

By way of contrast to the *Beresford* case, in *St John Shipping Corp v. Joseph Rank Ltd*[12] it was held that a shipowner, who committed an offence in allowing his ship to be overloaded, could still sue for the freight payable by cargo-owners, despite the fact that this was, in a sense, to enable him to benefit from his crime. Here it was held that it was not possible to identify or earmark the portion of the profits made by the shipowner from committing the offence, and this prevented the application of the *Beresford* principle.

### Recovery of money or property transferred under illegal contract

The next consequence of an illegal contract (or of a contract tainted by illegality) is that it normally prevents recovery of money or goods even by a non-contractual remedy, differing in this respect from a merely void contract. But this is subject to the same qualifications as the general rule noted above, so that it does not (for instance) prevent a person from recovering his own property even though it may have been transferred to another in connection with an illegal contract, provided that he does not have to rely on the illegality to assist his cause of action. The leading case

---

[10] [1938] AC 586.                    [11] See *Re K* [1985] 1 All ER 403.
[12] [1957] 1 QB 267.

on this difficult area of the law is now the House of Lords' decision in *Tinsley v. Milligan*.[13] In this case the plaintiff and defendant bought a house together as a joint venture, each contributing to the purchase price. The house was conveyed into the sole name of the defendant to facilitate a fraud on the social security authorities, but it was held that this illegality did not prevent the plaintiff claiming a share in the house when the parties split up. While it is clear that the court will not enforce an executory contract designed to facilitate such frauds, the court will recognize a transfer of property where the contract is executed, as it was here, and the plaintiff does not need to rely on the illegality to make good her claim. Here the plaintiff was able to make good her claim by relying on the normal equitable rules that a person contributing part of the price of a property is presumed to be entitled to a share in the property.[14]

The position is different in cases involving the 'presumption of advancement'. If, for instance, a father conveys property into the name of his son to defraud the tax authorities, but intending all the while to retain the right to the property, the result of the presumption of advancement is that the intention of the owner will be presumed to have been to transfer the beneficial right in the property to the son. In the absence of any illegality the father would be entitled to adduce evidence to show that he did not have this intention, and thus to rebut the presumption of advancement; but in this situation the illegal purpose would prevent him adducing this evidence. He would not be able to make good his claim without showing the very illegal purpose underlying the arrangement.

Again, a person may be able to recover property transferred under an illegal contract if he has repented of his illegal intention, and decided to withdraw from the transaction, at all events where it has not been substantially performed. But it has been held that this course is not open to a person who has shown no real change of heart, but who merely discovers that his guilty colleague simply refuses to do what he agreed to do.[15] More recently there has been a distinct tendency to take a more sympathetic view of 'technical illegalities', especially in favour of someone who did not realize he was breaking the law. In *Shelley v. Puddock*[16] a buyer of a house overseas who paid the price in breach of exchange control regulations was permitted to recover it from a fraudulent seller who failed

---

[13] [1993] 3 All ER 65. See also *Bowmakers v. Barnet Instruments Ltd* [1945] KB 65 which was for long the leading case.

[14] Lord Goff dissented, arguing that the decision would enable terrorists to recover a house which they had put into a third party's name to facilitate their activities. The answer to this appears to be a forfeiture order under the Prevention of Terrorism (Temporary Provisions) Act 1989, s. 13. Confiscation orders under s. 71 of the Criminal Justice Act 1988 are also possible but may not extend to such a case; perhaps the 1988 Act needs amending to cover this sort of case.  [15] *Bigos* v. *Bousted* [1951] 1 All ER 92.

[16] [1980] 1 All ER 1009.

to convey the house. The buyer was found (perhaps generously) not to know anything about the exchange control regulations, and in such circumstances the technical illegality committed by one party is grossly outweighed by the fraud of the other. Of course, even in this sort of case the court could not permit an action to *enforce* the contract—what was in question here was an action to recover the money paid under the contract when it was clear that performance of the contract had been abandoned.

### Other parts of illegal contract also unenforceable

Next, illegality in a contract affects not only the part directly concerned, but may 'taint' the whole contract with invalidity. For instance, a contract of employment will be wholly illegal and unenforceable if the parties agree on the payment of fictitious 'expenses' with the object of defrauding the income-tax authorities.[17] So the employee cannot recover damages for wrongful dismissal in such circumstances, let alone the fictitious expenses.

### Effect of illegality on collateral transactions

It is commonly stated that the effect of illegality goes still further and affects other, collateral, transactions, or contracts only indirectly connected with the illegal agreement. Although there may be circumstances in which this is so, recent cases show that the tendency these days is to restrain the rules relating to illegality within reasonable bounds, and to avoid this extreme result if possible. One successful method of evading the severity of some of the older cases has been to hold that, although the actual contract may be illegal, one of the parties is liable to the other because he warranted that the contract would not be illegal. For instance, an architect who promised a builder that he would obtain a licence for some work to be executed by the latter was held liable on this promise to the builder, although the licence was not obtained and the actual contract to do the work was hence illegal.[18] Similarly (before the abolition of actions for breach of promise of marriage) where a married man promised to marry and did 'marry' another woman who did not know him to be already married, this actual promise to marry was illegal since the man could not perform it without committing bigamy. None the less, the Court of Appeal was able to give the second 'wife' much-deserved damages, when after the man's death his real wife claimed his estate as next of kin, on the ground that the defendant had *contracted* that he would be able to marry her.[19] Again, where a carrier contracted to carry goods in a van for which

---

[17] *Napier* v. *National Business Agency* [1951] 2 All ER 264.

[18] *Strongman (1945) Ltd* v. *Sincock* [1955] 2 QB 525.

[19] *Shaw* v. *Shaw* [1954] 2 QB 429. Since the 1971 Act which abolished these actions the second 'wife' may be able to claim contribution from the deceased's estate in a different sort of proceeding.

he did not have the requisite licence, it was held that the carrier impliedly warranted that he would carry the goods legally.[20] The contract was not therefore an illegal contract at all. In all these cases the implication of a warranty of legality enabled damages to be obtained despite the possible illegality; but the courts have refused to imply a warranty of legality so as to *defeat* a plaintiff's claim, where he was suing on an insurance policy. An insured does not by implication warrant that he will never commit an illegal act in connection with goods being insured,[21] for that would lead to the absurdity of defeating a legitimate claim where (for instance) the owner of the goods had stored them in a building that did not comply with fire regulations, or were carried in a vehicle whose MOT certificate was overdue.[22]

Moreover, the cases noted above (concerning the question whether a claim is founded upon an illegality) have made it clear that there must be a reasonably direct and close connection between the claim and the illegality, and this principle will *a fortiori* apply where the claim is brought upon a collateral or related contract, rather than the principal contract concerned. It has also recently been held more generally that if a purely ancillary provision of a contract is illegal, but is solely for the benefit of one party, he may be able to waive the benefit of that provision, and enforce the rest of the contract without it, if the justice of the case so requires.[23]

## Illegality in performance

So far we have been considering mainly cases of contracts which are themselves illegal. There are, however, many circumstances in which the law is broken in the performance, and not in the making, of a contract. For instance, if a person sells goods without delivering to the buyer a note containing certain particulars which may be prescribed by statute, his conduct may amount to a petty offence, punishable by a fine. Again, if a lorry-driver discovers that the lorry he is driving is uninsured he will find that he, as well as his employer, is committing an offence. In such cases the actual contract—of sale in the first case, and employment in the second—is not itself illegal (unless indeed both parties made it with the deliberate intention of breaking the law) because it might have been performed quite legally. When the contract was made there was nothing on the face of it to suggest any breach of the law. The only breach has been in the performance.

[20] *Archbolds (Freightage) Ltd* v. *Spanglett Ltd* [1961] 1 QB 374.
[21] *Euro-Diam Ltd* v. *Bathurst, supra*, n. 9.
[22] See the judgment of Kerr LJ, *ibid.*, 33.
[23] *Carney* v. *Herbert* [1985] AC 301.

In these circumstances there is no objection to the contract being enforced by the innocent party, but great difficulty arises as to the rights of the guilty party. Some of the cases discussed above, dealing with contracts illegal in themselves, may also be relevant to claims under this category, where, for instance, the guilty party may benefit from his crime, or where he founds his claim on the illegality, but the cases in this category sometimes raise independent problems of their own. The modern cases hold that a breach of a statute in the performance of a contract does not necessarily disentitle a person from enforcing it. It will only do so if the statute in question expressly or by implication prohibits that kind of contract. Thus the merchant who omits to supply a statutory note is breaking the law in the very act of performing a prohibited contract, and may accordingly be unable to enforce it. But the company which commits an offence by overloading its ship will not be debarred from recovering freight, and the car-driver who negligently injures a pedestrian will not thereby be debarred from claiming against his insurance company. In all these cases the statute in question is intended to strike at a certain action but not necessarily at contracts which may involve the commission of this action. For example, the provisions of the Merchant Shipping Acts prohibiting the overloading of ships might render illegal an actual contract for loading goods on a ship in excess of the permitted amount, but do not render illegal a contract for the carriage of goods which are transported in an overloaded ship.[24] On the other hand, if a statute actually forbids a contract of a certain kind *to be performed* then it has been insisted that damages cannot be awarded for its breach, even though the whole purpose of the statute is to protect a class of persons of whom the plaintiff may be a member. So where a statute prohibited the making or performance of a certain type of insurance contract (without the necessary authorization) it was held that the contract could not be enforced by the insured, even though the whole point of the statute was to protect insured persons from unauthorized insurers.[25] This decision seems to defy commonsense, and has now been reversed by Parliament.[26]

These results are justified by the courts by invoking the 'presumed intent' of Parliament as deduced from the statutory provisions in question. But in practice there is little doubt that in many circumstances this 'intent' is a fiction. The courts are, in effect, taking into consideration the sort of policy considerations we have adverted to above under the guise of giving effect to the 'intent' of Parliament. But because this is not done openly,

---

[24] Compare the *St John Shipping Corp* case, *supra*, n. 12, with *Ashmore, Benson, Pease & Co Ltd* v. *Dawson Ltd* [1973] 1 WLR 828.

[25] *Phoenix General Insurance Co of Greece* v. *Halvemon Insurance Co* [1988] QB 216.

[26] Financial Services Act 1982, s. 132. See also *Fuji Finance Inc* v. *Aetna Life Insurance Co Ltd* [1994] 4 All ER 1025.

arguments cannot be addressed to the real issues, nor can the decision be evaluated by reference to those issues. This explains why sometimes the results seem to be outrageous, as in the case discussed at the end of the last paragraph.

### Illegality as a personal disability to enforcement

We have distinguished above between cases where a contract is 'itself illegal' and cases where illegality is involved only in the performance of a contract because this is the distinction conventionally drawn in expositions of this subject at the present time. But it is doubtful whether this is a completely satisfactory distinction. In particular, it is usually said that, if both parties intend from the outset to break the law in the performance of the contract, then this intention places the contract in the category of 'contracts illegal in themselves'. Yet the policy arguments for limiting the effects of illegality in the law of contracts may be just as applicable in this situation as where only one party is guilty of a breach of the law in performing the contract. For instance, if both parties to a contract of carriage intend the goods to be carried in an overloaded ship, or in a van without the necessary road licence, it is very doubtful whether the intention of the parties should be treated as the critical consideration.

It may well be that the effect of illegality on contracts is too complex a matter to be solved by the division into two categories only—that is, contracts illegal 'in themselves' and contracts where the illegality lies only in the performance. There are so many degrees of illegality (including agreements contrary to public policy at common law) and so many ways in which illegality may in fact be involved in a contractual relationship, that greater flexibility may well be desirable. That the courts appreciate this in practice is shown by a number of decisions which seem to recognize the special consequences of illegality.

For instance, it was at one time common to regard illegal contracts as necessarily 'void', but it now seems clear that this is too inflexible and simple a view. Thus it is now well settled that, if goods are delivered by a seller to a buyer with the intention of transferring ownership of the property, this intention will be effective despite some element of illegality in the transaction. Again, it now seems clear that an illegality which may debar one party from enforcing a contract against the other will not necessarily prevent an innocent third party from doing so. Thus a road-traffic third-party insurance policy may be enforceable by an accident victim against the insurer even though it might be contrary to public policy for the insured himself to enforce it, for example, where he has deliberately run down the victim. Again, it has been held in Northern Ireland that a wife was debarred from claiming on her husband's life insurance policy when he was killed in the course of a robbery in which she also took part.[27] Yet if the husband had had children, or other heirs, who were not involved in the robbery, it seems that they might have been able to claim the proceeds of the policy. Even in cases of murder where it is plain that the murderer cannot enforce an insurance policy on the life of the victim, it seems that third parties (such as mortgagees or co-owners) may be able to do so.[28] This part of the law has not yet been fully developed and there can be acute difficulty in distinguishing between cases in which the plaintiff is affected by the principle that a person cannot benefit from his own illegality, and cases in which he is simply seeking to enforce his proprietary rights.[29]

These possibilities suggest that it may be unwise to generalize too much about the effects of illegality on a contract. In some cases it seems more accurate to treat illegality as merely rendering that contract unenforceable at law by a party implicated in the illegality. But in other cases its effect may be more drastic. The truth seems to be that the balance between trying to do justice between the parties and giving effect to the general policy considerations against enforcing contracts involving some illegality is a very delicate one. In the last edition of this book it was suggested that it was probably best approached by a careful consideration of all the circumstances of a case rather than by a mechanical application of general rules, and there were a number of lower court decisions which favoured this approach. But in *Tinsley v. Milligan*[30] the House of Lords rejected this approach, and insisted that at least where proprietary claims are at stake they must be judged by fixed rule and not by anything in the nature of a discretion.

---

[27] *Hewitson* v. *Prudential Assurance* [1985] 12 NIJB 65.
[28] *Davitt* v. *Titcumb* [1989] 3 All ER 417.          [29] *Ibid.*          [30] *Supra*, n. 13.

# The Enforcement of Contractual Rights
# by Third Parties

## I. THE DISTINCTION BETWEEN CONTRACT AND PROPERTY

It is an elementary principle of English law—known as the doctrine of 'privity of contract'—that contractual rights and duties can only be conferred or imposed on the parties to a contract, and this principle is the distinguishing feature between the law of contract and the law of property. True proprietary rights are 'binding on the world' in the lawyer's traditional phrase. Contractual rights, on the other hand, are only binding on, and enforceable by, the immediate parties to the contract.

It is, of course, not true that a contract can never have some indirect *effect* on the rights or obligations of third parties. There are, in fact, very many circumstances in which this is the case. For instance, the obligations of a guarantor are affected by what happens between the creditor and the debtor. If the debtor pays the debt, the guarantor derives a benefit from this in that he will not have to pay the same debt; while if the creditor and debtor vary the debt by a new contract, the guarantor may be discharged from liability. Much the same is true of a co-debtor. And sometimes also an insurer may be affected by a contract between his insured and a third party; for instance the insurer may have no rights of subrogation if the insured has contracted with a third party in such terms as to exclude that party's liability for damage. Or again, the right of a plaintiff to sue in tort under the doctrine of vicarious liability may depend on the terms of the contract between the tortfeasor and the defendant. The doctrine of privity is narrower than this: it states that, prima facie, a person cannot enforce a right arising under a contract if he was no party to it, even where it was intended that he should have such a right. Likewise, a person cannot have any obligations enforced against him if the obligations arise under a contract to which he was no party.

On the other hand, it would also be a mistake to suppose that it is the privity doctrine which always regulates the inter-relationship of many parties in complex commercial transactions. These days there are numerous highly complex commercial relationships between groups of business parties where there is never any intention that rights should be conferred across the contractual boundaries. For instance, to take a simple case, manufacturers often sell goods to wholesalers, who in turn resell the goods to retailers, who in turn resell to members of the public. So there may be four parties to the distributional chain (and often a great many more), but there is rarely any deliberate intention to afford contractual rights except as between each pair of contracting parties. The ultimate buyer (that is, the consumer) rarely has direct contractual rights against the manufacturer in this example. But this result does not flow from the doctrine of privity—it follows from the fact that no rights are intended to be conferred by the different contracts on those who are not direct parties to them. And, generally speaking, the law still respects the intentions of the parties. Of course there is nothing sacred about these intentions, and statute here, as elsewhere, can tear down a carefully constructed set of business arrangements. For instance, under the Package Travel, Package Holidays and Package Tours Regulations 1992 a holiday tour operator can in certain circumstances be liable to a consumer for the defaults of hotels or airlines, even though the tour operator claims to act solely as agent and disclaims liability for these defaults.

A slightly more complex situation, which has recently caused much trouble in this connection, concerns the major building or engineering contract. Here there is usually a main contractor who enters into the main contract with the client or owner. The main contractor then subcontracts parts of the work to many different, often specialized, firms. For instance, the plumbing, electrical, or plastering work may be subcontracted. In complex cases, the owner often nominates the sub-contractors, but generally he does not directly contract with them, though he may do so to some limited degree in special cases. Here, too, there may be no rights which cut across the contracts, but this is not because of the privity principle, but because the parties prefer, for good business reasons, to operate in this fashion. Indeed, the arrangements they make often seem deliberately designed to insulate some parties from others, so as to prevent privity of contract arising between them, again, no doubt, for good business reasons.

### Third parties and representatives of a second party

In the modern law all contracts, save those of a highly personal nature, can be enforced by or against a party's personal representatives, i.e. his executors or administrators, in the event of his death. And in the event of insolvency of the debtor contractual duties can generally be enforced by a trustee in bankruptcy (or company liquidator) and, to the extent of the assets in his hands, against him. Lawyers are so accustomed to these cases nowadays that they are inclined to regard personal representatives and trustees in bankruptcy as not being third parties at all. Their rights are derivative, and they are merely representatives of the second party.

But although cases of this nature are not often discussed in connection with the doctrine of privity, they do sometimes raise important policy questions related to the doctrine. For instance, in modern times it is very common for goods to be bought by one person from another, in such a way as to leave a proprietary right in the unpaid seller as security for the price under a 'retention of title' clause; and it is, of course, even more common for mortgages or charges over property to be given by a debtor, in such a way as to confer proprietary rights on the creditor. In the event of the debtor becoming insolvent, his creditors will then find that their rights to the debtor's assets turn upon a detailed examination of the contract between the debtor and the party claiming the proprietary right, a contract to which the other creditors are, of course, not party. In one sense this is simply a result of the law of securities—it has long been recognized that a debtor can grant a mortgage or charge over his assets so that the other party obtains priority over that property in the event of insolvency. What has not always been recognized is that freedom of contract makes it very easy to manipulate the rules relating to property rights between a debtor and a creditor so as to give the creditor such priority, even in circumstances where other parties may not have any warning or notice of what has been done. In such a case, the rules of privity are actually evaded in circumstances in which there is a case for their application: third parties are held bound by contractual clauses when they are not party to the contract by the simple device of treating the third party as not being a third party at all.

### Property law and privity

There has also been a tendency for certain contractual cases to bridge the gulf between contract and property, and so become generally enforceable against third parties, especially in connection with the land law. Thus a mere contract to buy or rent land has itself become, over the years, something in the nature of a proprietary interest in land. Originally such contracts became enforceable against third parties when they had notice of them, but nowadays this requirement has been replaced by a system of registration. If the contract is registered it becomes virtually as good as an actual transfer, that is, a conveyance of the land. Quite recently mere licences, hitherto always thought to be purely contractual in their nature, were added to the list of interests in land which could be enforced against third parties, and (at least in some cases) thus crossed the bridge between contract and property.

Leases are a striking instance of the interplay between contract and property conceptions. When two parties execute a lease they enter into certain obligations of a contractual nature, such as the obligation to pay rent on the one hand, and the obligation to allow the tenant possession on the other. However, these obligations are of a somewhat impersonal nature since they are intended to be effective, not so much between the particular parties concerned, as between the landlord and tenant for the time being, whoever they may be. Hence, from a very early date it came to be recognized that obligations of this kind 'run with the land', that is, they are enforceable by and against the landlord and tenant for the time being. If the tenant assigns his lease (but not if he merely sublets) the new tenant can be sued for the rent by the landlord and if the landlord sells the freehold, the new landlord can sue, or be sued by the tenant, whether he is the original party or an assignee. Recently these old principles were reaffirmed and applied by the House of Lords to the case of a guarantor of the rent of a tenancy, the freehold of which was sold to new buyers. It was held that the buyers—the new landlords—were entitled to the benefit of the guarantee, and could sue the guarantor even though they were not strictly parties to the same contract.[1]

But there are still relics in the law of leases of the contractual origin of many leasehold rights. A lessee of a long lease who 'sells' his lease is in law 'assigning' the contract, but a person cannot get rid of his contractual duties by assigning them, because these duties are thought to be personal matters arising out of the contract. So the result is that although the assignee (or 'buyer') of the lease becomes the person primarily responsible for performing the tenant's duties under the lease (such as paying the rent) the assignor remains liable in the background as a sort of guarantor. If the assignee becomes insolvent the assignor may be sued—and that remains the position even if (as is usually the case) the landlord retains the right to veto an assignment if he is dubious about the assignee's business reputation. In the recent recession many business tenants who had assigned long leases have been shocked to discover this liability being enforced against them on the insolvency of the assignee. Now that long leases of residential flats have become a lot more common than formerly there is a real danger of ordinary home owners being faced with the same sort of liability. The law on this point desperately needs amendment.

The position in the law of trusts is similar in some respects. A trust is far too complex an institution to be squeezed into the law of contract, although a great many trusts are the creation of contractual agreements. Until comparatively modern times, indeed, a trust was regarded as consisting essentially of personal and not proprietary rights. Nowadays, however, it is clear that rights under a trust are in many respects proprietary, although they cannot be enforced against one type of person, namely the bona fide purchaser for value without notice. This person, however, is a very rare figure in the law of trusts.

---

[1] *P. & A. Swift Investments* v. *Combined English Stores Group* [1989] AC 643; see too *Coronation Street Industrial Properties Ltd* v. *Ingall Industries plc* [1989] 1 All ER 979.

## General principle of privity

Despite these considerations, the general principle remains that a contract can be enforced neither by nor against third parties. In *Tweddle* v. *Atkinson*[2], which is generally taken as the starting point of the modern doctrine, the fathers of an engaged couple contracted with each other to pay some money to the son on the marriage taking place, and it was held that the contract could not be enforced by the son. In *Beswick* v. *Beswick*[3] this principle was reaffirmed in a case of classic simplicity. In this case a man sold his business to his nephew, who agreed in return to pay an annuity of £5 per week to the seller's widow after the seller's death. It was held that the widow could not enforce this contract in her personal capacity because she was no party to it. But, as we shall see shortly, a way was nevertheless found of doing justice in this case.

Although the doctrine of privity of contract still stands, a very considerable number of exceptions has gradually nibbled away at the principle that rights cannot be conferred on a third party to the contract even where the parties intend that they should be. Indeed, it must be said that there are probably few circumstances of practical importance today in which the principle is liable to be applicable and to work serious injustice or inconvenience. This is an illustration of an interesting juridical phenomenon, namely a 'general rule' which is no longer in practice the general rule. Apart from these exceptional cases, objections to the existing law must now rest largely on its form, and the lack of uniformity and consistency, rather than on its content. As to the lack of consistency there can be no doubt. In particular, since the recognition and development of assignments of rights the refusal to recognize the enforceability of third-party rights as a general rule has become pointless and anomalous.

There is today widespread agreement among lawyers that the doctrine of privity requires reform, and the subject is on the Law Commission's agenda.[4] So far the Law Commission has been thinking in terms of a very limited reform which will only give enforceable rights to a third party where it was the intention of the parties (*a*) to confer a benefit on the third party, and (*b*) that that benefit should be legally enforceable. But the Law Commission's final report on the subject is still awaited; and it is conceivable that judicial reform may pre-empt it. This is an area in which the judges may well feel that, if statutory reform is very long delayed, they will themselves need to depart from old doctrine. English lawyers tend to think that statutory reform is preferable because it leaves fewer loose ends and less uncertainty than the major upheavals caused by reversal of old

---

[2] (1861) 1 B & S 393.    [3] [1968] AC 58.
[4] See Beatson, [1993] *Current Legal Problems*, 1.

doctrine at common law; but it is possible that they tend to exaggerate the certainty of statutory reforms and also the uncertainty caused by judicial activism.

## 2. ENFORCEMENT BY THE PROMISEE

Although the principle of privity of contract prevents a third party from enforcing in his own name a contract intended for his benefit, there are many situations in which the promisee may enforce the contract on behalf of, and for the benefit of, the third party. In particular, the promisee may be able to obtain a decree of specific performance (i.e. a court order directing the promisor to carry out his promise). In *Beswick* v. *Beswick*, which was referred to above, it was held in the outcome that the administrator of the seller's estate was entitled to sue for specific performance of the nephew's promise. It so happened that in that case the widow herself was the administratrix of her husband's estate, and in that capacity she obtained a decree of specific performance compelling the nephew to perform his contract for her benefit in her personal capacity. What was particularly striking about this decision was that one of the chief reasons given by the House of Lords for permitting the contract to be enforced by specific performance was the very fact that this might be the only way in which the contract could be enforced at all. Generally speaking, as we shall see later,[5] specific performance is not available where damages would be an adequate remedy, but in these privity cases damages may never be an adequate remedy because the third party cannot sue at all, and the promisee may not be able to obtain damages—a point considered further below. It thus seems that specific performance may now be available to bypass the privity rule in very many situations.

Even where the third party and the promisee are not represented by one party as they were in the *Beswick* case, there may be many cases in which the promisee can obtain specific performance of such a contract. If the promisee is in some close relationship with the third party (as he often will be) he may be willing to take proceedings on his own initiative. Even if he has no interest in doing this, the third party may still be able to sue in the name of the promisee. Provided that the third party is able to furnish satisfactory security to see that no liability (e.g. for costs) falls on the promisee, there will often be no reason why he should not give permission for his name to be used in litigation. The case may then be brought and conducted by the third party in all but name.

The only type of situation in which the promisee is likely to refuse permission in practice is where he himself has some interest in conflict with

---

[5] See Ch. 22, 425.

that of the third party. For example, if the promisee in *Beswick* v. *Beswick* had died bankrupt, his personal representative would have represented the interests of the creditors who might very well have wanted to obtain payment of the annuity to themselves rather than to the widow. Even in this situation, however, the most likely outcome now seems to be that the third party and the promisee will come to some arrangement between themselves. It may be that neither promisee nor third party could enforce payment by suing alone; jointly they could obtain payment with little difficulty. Clearly, therefore, in practice they would most likely agree on some division of the receipts, and then sue jointly. Once all the relevant parties are before the court, it seems that the doctrine of privity is almost irrelevant. In *Snelling* v. *John G. Snelling Ltd*[6] three brothers, who were interested in and had lent money to a family company, agreed among themselves that any of them who resigned from the company would forfeit his money. The company was not itself a party to this contract, but it was nevertheless held that the company could rely on the agreement by making the other brothers parties to proceedings brought against it by one brother.

But if all else fails, there is still one further avenue which may be explored as a result of *Beswick* v. *Beswick*. This is the possibility of the third party obtaining an order from the court compelling the promisee to allow his name to be used by the third party in an action for specific performance, or permitting the third party simply to add the promisee to the case as a defendant. While a third-party donee might have difficulty in obtaining such an order, there may well be cases in which the court would be willing to grant one, for example, where the promisee has actually contracted to see that the third party is paid by the promisor. This sort of procedure was precisely the method by which assignments first came to be legally recognized, though that development occurred many years ago, when it was still necessary to apply to a Court of Equity for the necessary order permitting the assignor's name to be used in proceedings at law. In modern times the normal procedure is simply to add a person as a defendant to the case where he is unwilling to be joined as a plaintiff.

Whether the promisee can sue for *damages* to enforce a contractual right on behalf of a third party is (as presaged above) more difficult and controversial. It was at one time thought that the promisee could not claim damages for breach of a contract where the beneficiary was a third party, on the ground that the promisee would not then have suffered any loss himself, and damages are generally awarded only for losses suffered by the plaintiff. But it is almost inconceivable that the courts would deny all remedy to the promisee if they also insisted that the third party could not enforce the contract because of the doctrine of privity. Where the contract

---

[6] [1973] QB 87.

is executed this would mean that the promisor could retain the benefits of the contract and be free from any sanction for non-performance. As has been well said, if this were the law the promisor's liability to damages would disappear down a sort of black hole never to be seen again. It is virtually certain that, by one means or another, the courts would find some way of preventing so intolerable an injustice.

There are anyhow some well recognized situations where damages may be recovered by a plaintiff on behalf of a third party even though the plaintiff has suffered none himself. For instance, an owner of goods who has been paid for damage done to them by an insurance company can sue on behalf of the insurer (and indeed the insurer can sue in the owner's name). Another broad exception to this rule (if it exists at all) has anyhow recently been recognized by the House of Lords, which may well cover a number of different situations.[7] In contracts for the sale of property, and perhaps also of services, where it is in the contemplation of the parties that the property or services will be transferred to a third party, then if the buyer has resold the property or services before it is discovered that the seller has been guilty of a breach of contract (e.g. by supplying defective goods) the buyer is still entitled to recover damages from the seller. The promisee's right to damages crystallizes at the moment of the breach and is unaffected by the later sale of the property, even though he may in a sense be said to have suffered no damage. Another exceptional case which may also be justified by this principle is settled law as well: where a person sues for damages for breach of contract in respect of a 'family holiday', he can recover for his family's disappointment and inconvenience, as well as for his own.[8]

### 3. ASSIGNMENT

In the modern law there is nothing whatever to prevent a contracting party assigning, that is, transferring, to a third party contractual rights which are already in existence. Furthermore, the formalities necessary for such an assignment have been kept to a bare minimum. Although a written assignment and a written notification to the debtor (to inform him whom to pay) are necessary to transfer a full legal title to the right in question, even a verbal assignment will suffice to transfer an equitable title. In practice

---

[7] *Linden Garden Trust* v. *Lenesta Sludge Disposals* [1994] 1 AC 85. There are powerful dicta in Lord Griffiths' speech in this case arguing for a much wider exception on the ground that, wherever the promisor fails to perform, the promisee does suffer actual loss in that he does not receive that for which he bargained, even though the direct beneficiary of the performance would have been a third party.

[8] *Jackson* v. *Horizon Holidays Ltd* [1975] 1 WLR 1468, approved by the HL in *Woodar Investments Ltd* v. *Wimpey* [1980] 1 WLR 277.

this is almost as good as a legal title, the only important difference being that if, the assignment is equitable, the assignor may have to be joined as a party to an action by the assignee against the debtor.

It would be unfair if the debtor was prejudiced by an assignment of contractual rights, and this gives rise to two important rules. In the first place a debtor is not affected by an assignment of which he has no notice. For this reason it is highly advisable for the assignee to give notice to the debtor, even if the assignment is merely equitable. Once he has notice of the assignment the debtor must pay the assignee and not the original creditor. Indeed, a payment to the latter will not discharge the debt, and the assignee will still be able to recover it. In the second place, all assignments are 'subject to equities'. This means that the debtor will be entitled to plead against the assignee any defence which he may have against the assignor. For instance, if the debtor has a right of set-off against the original creditor he will be able to plead it against the assignee.

Debts and other straightforward commercial rights are often and easily assigned, but not all contractual rights are assignable. Rights of an essentially personal nature, for instance, cannot be assigned at all. So an employer cannot assign the right to his employee's work to another. And it is also possible for a contract to declare specifically that any rights arising out of it are not to be assignable.[9] There are, too, some rules of public policy which declare void an assignment of a 'bare right of litigation'. But (at any rate in the absence of a specific agreement) ordinary money debts are usually assignable, for it can make little difference to a debtor to whom he has to pay the money. Indeed, even where it does make a difference, as where the creditor is a friend of the debtor who is likely to be indulgent to him, this does not prevent the debt being assigned.

A question which used to give rise to some difficulty is the extent to which consideration is necessary for an assignment. But the modern view is that this is a relatively simple matter. An assignment is a transfer of rights which, in the widest sense, are a form of property. Like the transfer of any other form of property an assignment will be valid if executed with any necessary formalities, even without consideration. It will be valid by way of gift in exactly the same way as a gift of a chattel will be valid if it is completely executed. If, however, the assignment is not properly made, or if it only relates to a future right, it cannot take effect as an actual transfer, but can be effective at most as a promise or contract to transfer. In this event, of course, consideration will be necessary as it is for all other contracts.

The law relating to assignments, like the whole law of privity, probably works smoothly enough in practice in the great majority of cases. Indeed, a

---

[9] See the *Linden Garden Trust* case, *supra*, n. 7.

large industry (known as factoring) has grown up which depends on the law of assignments, under which small traders assign debts to financial institutions, so as to receive cash today (at a discount, of course) instead of payment of the debt tomorrow. But the concepts with which the courts work are exceedingly confused and technical. This is an area in which the notion of 'equitable' rights, distinct from and inferior to 'legal' rights, has survived the abolition of the separate rules of 'equity' by over a century.[10] It seems high time that a general simplification of this branch of the law was undertaken.

The fact that the law is prepared in principle to accept the simple assignability of contractual rights makes the doctrine of privity particularly anomalous, and hard to justify on rational grounds. If the law is perfectly prepared to allow a contracting party to transfer his rights, once created, to a third party, there can hardly be any valid objection to his creating the rights for the benefit of the third party in the first instance. For example, if A makes a contract with B under which B is to pay A £100 in return for certain services then and there rendered by A, there is nothing to stop A forthwith assigning to C the right to receive the money. Once B has notice of the assignment he must pay the money to C, and can be sued by him if he fails to do so. There seems, then, no possible reason why A should not be able to make the contract for the benefit of C in the first place. Of course, B could not be sued in any event, whether by A or by C, if the money has not yet been *earned*, or is not yet *due*; but once it is due, there can be no objection of principle to allowing C to sue. Nevertheless, the law has not yet accepted this simple principle.

The fact that assignments are generally so easily made means that privity can often be evaded by careful prior planning, though this will often require skilled legal advice—which must moreover be deployed before problems arise. But difficulties are now common as a result of contractual clauses declaring the benefit of the contract to be non-assignable. Suppose that a building is constructed by a builder for client A (who may be a mere developer) and who intends to sell the completed building to client B. If defects show up in the building after it has been conveyed to B what remedies does he have? B cannot sue the builder in contract because of privity and it is now also established that he cannot sue the builder in tort for negligence. How can A and B try to ensure that B obtains some legal protection against the builder when he buys the property? In the absence of a prohibition against assignment of the contract it is perfectly simple for A to sell the property together with an assignment of the contract. But

---

[10] For a recent case which to some degree turned on a minute analysis of the distinction between a legal and an equitable assignment, see *Deposit Protection Board* v. *Dalia* [1994] 1 All ER 539 (reversed with less reference to these questions, [1994] 2 All ER 577).

builders often do insert prohibitions against assignment for legitimate commercial reasons. B's only remedy in this situation is to try to persuade A to bring suit in his own name against the builder (which is now possible as a result of the *Linden Garden Trust* case[11]) or, more realistically, to permit B to bring the action in A's name. To ensure that this will be possible the contract between A and B should therefore give B the right to enforce the contract by suing in A's name, while at the same time protecting A's interests by requiring B to give adequate security for costs. In this way the doctrine of privity can ultimately be overcome in this situation but only with the aid of skilled legal advice and at some cost.

## 4. AGENCY

English law recognizes a very wide doctrine of agency, most of which would be irreconcilable with any strict application of the principle of privity of contract. Agency is a very large subject in the law, and here we can do no more than indicate briefly the part it plays in the law of contract.

A contract of agency may create two entirely different relationships. First, there is the relationship between the principal and the agent himself. This is simply a contract like any other contract, and the rights and duties of the parties between themselves are regulated by the express and implied terms of that contract. For instance, there is a term, implied by law, that the principal must reimburse the agent for any expenses incurred by him in the performance of his principal's business, and, on the other hand, there is an implied term that the agent must strictly abide by his instructions, and must not exceed his authority.

For present purposes, however, we are concerned with the possibility that the agency may be created for the purpose of establishing a further relationship between the principal and a third party; and indeed for this purpose it is unnecessary that the relationship between the principal and his agent should itself be an enforceable legal contract. A principal may, for instance, authorize an agent to do something on his behalf (including making a contract with a third party) without any consideration passing between the principal and the agent. If the agent makes a contract with a third party on behalf of his principal, that contract is regarded by law as having been made by the principal himself. Hence he can sue on it and be sued on it. So far it may be thought that there is no real breach of the principles of privity of contract, for when the agent avowedly acts on behalf of his principal it would be pedantic to insist that the principal is not really the contracting party.

However, the law does not stop at this point. In the normal way the

[11] *Supra*, n. 7.

principal will have authorized the agent to make the contract, or anyhow to make contracts of that class, but the agent's power to bind his principal frequently extends beyond his actual authority. In the absence of notice to the contrary the third party is entitled to assume that the agent has in fact the authority that an agent of that class usually has (usual authority), and the authority that he appears to have or is held out as having (apparent or ostensible authority), even if in the case in hand it is proved that the agent was specifically prohibited from making the particular contract in question. In that event the agent can no doubt be sued by his principal for acting in excess of his actual authority, but that does not prevent the third party from holding the principal to the contract made by the agent. The basis of cases of this kind is close to the principle insisting that apparent rather than real intentions are the law's usual concern. A person may mislead the other contracting party, either by saying or writing something in a misleading way, giving a false impression as to his intentions; or he may mislead him by permitting his agent to appear to have authority which he does not have. In both cases the underlying rationale for holding the principal liable probably depends on the fact that he has induced the reasonable reliance of the third party—it certainly cannot depend on the intentions or consent of the principal, which by hypothesis do not exist in this situation. However, the principal himself can enforce the contract even if made in excess of the agent's authority provided that he ratifies the agent's action.

English law goes even further in departing from ordinary contractual principles, in recognizing the 'undisclosed principal', that is to say it recognizes the right of a principal to enforce a contract in fact made on his behalf by an agent, even though the agent was not known to be acting for a principal. This is even more inconsistent with any strict application of the doctrine of privity of contract, especially when viewed in the light of the usual objective approach of the law to questions of intentions. The third party who has no knowledge of the principal's existence may thus find that he has made a contract with a person of whom he has never heard, and with whom he never intended to contract. In a sense, the resulting contract is based on the subjective intention of the agent. However, as is the way with English law when it departs from principle, the departure is rarely pushed to inconvenient extremes. Thus the doctrine of the undisclosed principal is hedged about with certain limitations to safeguard the interests of the third party.

In the first place, the third party can always enforce the contract against the agent personally if he chooses, since he is permitted to judge the agent's intentions in the usual objective way. In the second place, the principal must prove that the agent did in fact have authority to make the contract at the time when it was made. If the agent exceeds his authority the principal cannot ratify his action unless the agent was known to have been acting for a principal. And, thirdly, the principal will not be able to enforce the contract if it is of a personal nature. Obviously, for instance, a person cannot agree to paint another's portrait and then explain that he was acting for an undisclosed principal. Less obviously, a person cannot normally make a contract with a third person by using an agent when this is merely a ruse to obtain something with which he knows the third party is not prepared to supply him. However, this will only be the case where the third party was justified in regarding personal considerations as important. But ordinary commercial contracts (for instance, insurance contracts) can usually be enforced by an undisclosed principal provided only that they were made by the agent intending his principal to have the benefit of the contract.[12]

Despite the width of the English law of agency, it will be seen that a third party cannot enforce a contract simply on the vague plea that it was made 'on his behalf'. Before he can do so he will have to prove that he actually authorized the agent to make the contract on his behalf, or else that he has ratified the agent's action, and this, as we have said, he cannot do unless the agent disclosed that he was acting for a principal when he made the contract. This means that many people, who in a commercial sense are called 'agents', are not strictly agents in the legal sense unless actual, apparent, or usual authority is proved in relation to some particular transaction. For example, the ordinary car dealer may be called a 'Ford agent' or a 'Toyota agent' but generally such dealers buy and resell cars as principals, not as agents, in the strict legal sense.

## 5. INSURANCE CONTRACTS

There are many statutory exceptions to the rule that a third party cannot enforce a contract to which he was not a party. Here it will be sufficient to refer to a number of such exceptions which are all concerned with contracts of insurance. In these contracts rigid insistence on the doctrine of privity of contract is liable to cause serious inconvenience and injustice. Hence various statutes have intervened to permit actions on insurance policies by persons declared to be beneficiaries under such policies. For instance, a life insurance policy expressed to be taken out for the benefit of a wife or a husband or a child may be enforced by the beneficiary—indeed the policy in a sense *belongs* to the beneficiary. But a policy taken out for any other person is still subject to the common-law rule, although its effect can easily be met by assigning the policy to the beneficiary or by disposing of the proceeds of the policy by will. In this particular situation the doctrine of privity may serve a useful purpose, because a person who insures his own

---

[12] *Siu Yin Kwan* v. *Eastern Insurance Co Ltd* [1994] 1 All ER 213.

life will normally be better advised to dispose of his policy by will than by naming a beneficiary in the policy. For use of a will leaves him as the owner of the policy and this may be useful if he later wants to borrow on the security of the policy. Furthermore, if he leaves the policy to a named beneficiary in his will, he retains the right, which may be useful later, to revoke or vary the intended beneficiary. On the other hand, a valid nomination of a beneficiary in the policy itself might be irrevocable, if there were no doctrine of privity, as it is when the insured's spouse or child is named as the beneficiary.

Another case in which statutory intervention has proved essential in modern times is in the field of road-traffic insurance. The scheme of compulsory third-party insurance which has existed in England since 1930 makes it imperative that an ordinary motor insurance policy should be enforceable by every person whom it purports to cover, notwithstanding that the driver may himself be no party to the contract of insurance. For instance, a lorry-driver is normally covered by an insurance policy taken out, not by himself, but by his employers. Obviously, the intention is to give him a right to an indemnity if he should be held liable to pay damages for injuries caused in an accident, but even though the policy may purport to cover anyone driving the vehicle with the consent of the owners he could not enforce it at common law. This situation was met by the Road Traffic Act 1930 (now the Act of 1960), which permits the driver to enforce the contract directly against the insurance company.

Yet another insurance problem in connection with privity has proved of some practical importance, especially in connection with road-traffic insurance cases. In these cases an injured person may wish to claim directly against the insurance company instead of against the driver, who will in turn seek an indemnity from the insurers. Indeed, in practice, in all motor insurance third-party claims, arrangements for a settlement and, if necessary, litigation will be handled directly between the injured party and the insurers, the actual driver or insured simply dropping out of the picture. But the injured person is, of course, also a stranger to the contract of insurance (he is the 'third party' after whom third-party insurance is named), and he would normally be debarred from pursuing this course. In the ordinary way this would not matter very much because the injured person would claim against the driver, and the driver would claim an indemnity from the insurance company. In most cases the claim would be negotiated and settled directly between the injured person (or his solicitors) on the one hand, and the insurance company on the other hand. If, however, the driver of the vehicle should happen to be insolvent, his creditors might attempt to intervene and claim a share of the damages which would be payable by the insurance company, while leaving the injured person to take his place in the queue, as it were, with the other creditors. This seemed unjust to Parliament, which accordingly enacted that in such circumstances the injured party should have (subject to various conditions) a right to sue the insurance company directly, thus creating one more exception to the doctrine of privity of contract.

There are, however, still a variety of insurance arrangements in which policies are clearly taken out for the benefit of third parties, and yet are not enforceable by those third parties. For instance, employers often take out insurance designed to provide accident or sickness benefits to their employees, and these cannot be enforced by the employees. So also retailers sometimes insure against their liabilities under extended guarantees for consumer goods, and these too cannot be enforced by the consumer. No statutory exceptions to the privity principle exist in these cases, and though, doubtless, reputable insurers would never refuse to pay under these policies, difficulties may still occur where the insured himself is insolvent or in receivership. In such a case an insurer may simply decline to pay and the third party may have great difficulty in proceeding.[13] The Australian High Court has recently decided to abandon the principle of privity of contract in insurance cases, but the basis of the decision is unclear as a result of differences of opinion among the judges.[14]

## 6. TRUSTS

It has already been mentioned that the law of trusts, being closely associated with the law of property, is not subject to all the restrictions of the doctrine of privity of contract. So A and B can create a trust for the benefit of C without the participation of C at all. Indeed, it might happen that C is not even in existence when the trust is created, as frequently used to happen with the classic marriage settlement, where the beneficiaries would include the children of the marriage, as yet unborn. Nevertheless, such trusts were enforceable, and the doctrine of privity of contract was, and remains, irrelevant. The trust creates proprietary rights, so that the creation of the trust operates to transfer property rights (in equity of course) to C, rather than to create merely personal rights in favour of C. Even if the trust is not completely constituted, so that it has to take effect as a contract, and not as an actual transfer of property (for example where the settlor merely covenants to transfer future property to the trustees, rather than making an actual transfer then and there), C will be able to enforce the trust if he is a child of the marriage in question. Despite his being a stranger to the contract and supplying no valuable consideration, he is said to be 'within the marriage consideration'. Any other person, however, who attempted to enforce an imperfectly constituted trust would

[13] The Insurance Ombudsman is likewise powerless to take on such cases.
[14] See *Trident General Insurance Co Ltd* v. *McNiece Bros Pty Ltd* (1988) 165 CLR 107.

be met by the plea that he was no party to the contract and had supplied no consideration.

Towards the end of the nineteenth century attempts were made to use the device of the trust as a general method of escape whenever the doctrine of privity proved a serious inconvenience. Thus it came to be suggested that, whenever a contract purported to confer rights on third parties, the third party could claim that a trust in his favour had been created, and could enforce his rights by way of trust, if not by way of contract. This was more or less the process by which assignments first came to be enforceable, for here also the common law refused to permit an assignee to sue on the contract because he was no party to it. In equity, however, the assignor came to be treated as a trustee for the assignee, and once this result was reached it became possible for the assignee to enforce the assignment himself. At first this had to be done in the name of the assignor, but after the Judicature Act even this was usually unnecessary.

For a while it looked as if a third party beneficiary might be treated in a similar way to an assignee, and permitted to enforce the contract in equity as though the promisee was a trustee for him. At first this method of escape proved fairly successful and looked full of promise for the future, but during the present century the judicial attitude to its use gradually hardened until it was almost rejected altogether.[15] While it is still, of course, open to a person to enforce a genuine trust without having been a party to its creation, it is not now possible (unless the circumstances are wholly exceptional) to allege a fictitious trust merely as a device for the enforcement of contractual rights by a third party. Moreover, although it may be possible to find that a genuine trust has been created without the word 'trust' having been used, the cases show that this is a very unlikely eventuality.

There do remain, however, a number of standardized situations in which the courts are still willing to impose a constructive trust on the parties, such as (for instance) where husband and wife make 'mutual wills' under which they agree to leave all their property in an agreed way. In these cases (and subject to various limitations), it is still possible to enforce the arrangements after the death of one of the parties by means of a 'constructive trust'. Although these cases must arise out of agreements—because an enforceable legal contract is a necessary requirement of the holding that there is a trust[16]—they are not thought of as being contractual in nature, but as concerning 'equitable' rights.

The principal reasons for the failure of the trust mechanism as a device

---

[15] See especially *Re Schebsman* [1944] Ch. 83; *Vandepitte* v. *Preferred Accident Insurance Corp* [1933] AC 70; *Green* v. *Russell* [1959] 2 QB 226.
[16] *Gray* v. *Perpetual Trustee Co Ltd* [1928] AC 391; *Re Dale* [1993] 4 All ER 129.

to avoid the privity doctrine are of some interest because of the light they throw on the processes of legal reasoning. In refusing to develop the trust device for this purpose, the courts appear to have been motivated by the following considerations. A trust, once constituted, is prima facie irrevocable except with the consent of the beneficiaries; and if some of the beneficiaries are under age, or still unborn, it may be irrevocable altogether. If a contract between A and B which professes to confer rights on X is treated as creating a trust, it would follow (the courts have reasoned) that the contract was irrevocable as soon as it was made. A and B would lose the right, normally possessed by contracting parties, of agreeing to vary or rescind their contract, without obtaining the consent of X; and still further difficulties would arise if X was a child, or included children or persons as yet unidentified or unborn. Therefore, it has been held, even though A and B have never shown the least desire to vary or rescind their contract, the fact that they *might have wanted to do so* is a very strong argument against holding that a trust has been created.

So, for instance, if a man makes a contract with his employer that the employer will pay the employee's widow a pension if the employee dies in his employment after (say) twenty years' service, the courts have refused to treat the widow's claim to the pension as enforceable by way of trust.[17] The reason given for this is that the employer and the employee might have wanted to vary or rescind the pension arrangements; but the result is precisely the same if the employee has served out the full twenty years and then died and there has never been any desire to vary the contract at all. It seems that in truth the reasoning of the courts has been based on faulty logic in some cases of this kind; and they have also made the mistake of treating a fiction as a fact. It seems absurd that legitimate claims are refused legal recognition because of what might have been rather than what has actually happened. There seems no reason why the trust device should not have been more widely used to avert the worst injustices of the privity doctrine without clashing with the desire to maintain the variability and revocability of contractual rights. This could have been done in at least two ways had the courts shown any desire to do so. First, they could have held that a contract for the benefit of a third party does create a trust, but a revocable trust. The concept of a revocable trust is by no means unknown to the law; and if it is legitimate to 'imply' a trust in order to do justice, there is no greater difficulty in 'implying' a power to revoke the trust for the same purpose. Alternatively, the courts could have held that the promisee holds the right of action to enforce the contract on trust for the third party. It is unnecessary to regard the contract itself as creating a trust in its inception; the need to invoke the concept of a

<hr />

[17] *Re Schebsman, supra,* n. 15.

trust only arises when enforcement is sought. At that date the third party could be treated as the beneficiary of a trust.

Thus, it can be seen that here, as so often in the law, results which appear to be dictated by the logic of legal principle are not so dictated at all. Legal rules can often be made to yield up a wide variety of results without any violation of fundamental principles; whether they do so or not depends to a large extent on the willingness of the courts to mould the law to new conditions. Sometimes—as in this area—the courts have taken the easy (one is tempted to say 'lazy') way out and refused to modify the law at all. On other occasions, in different areas of the law, the courts have been much more willing to adapt rules to new situations.

### 7. COMMERCIAL CASES

Businessmen have never been very fond of the doctrine of privity of contract, in so far as it stands in the way of giving effect to their intended arrangements. As so often in the past, the law has had sometimes to give way to the demands of commercial practice. Thus one very important exception to the privity rule is to be found in the law relating to negotiable instruments. Bills of exchange, promissory notes, and cheques, for instance, are generally negotiable, that is to say they may be passed from hand to hand (subject sometimes to endorsement) and they may be enforced against the original drawer by any holder in due course. So if A draws a cheque in favour of B, and B endorses the cheque in favour of C, C may sue A on the cheque if it is not met when presented to A's bank. And this is so notwithstanding that C was no party to the original transaction, and that he has supplied no consideration to A. Indeed, the law goes further, and declares it irrelevant that the plaintiff has not supplied any consideration at all for a cheque, provided that some consideration has been given for it by someone. To avoid confusion, it should be added that the payee of an ordinary cheque acquires no rights against the bank on which the cheque is drawn: a cheque is regarded in law as a mandate or instruction by the drawer to his bank to pay the person named on it, or any person to whom it should be endorsed. The payee is not a third party beneficiary of the contract between the bank and the customer, nor is a cheque an assignment of funds held by the drawer in the bank.

Negotiability differs from assignment, with which it has obvious affinities, in at least two respects. In the first place no notice need be given of the transfer of a negotiable instrument, and in the second place the transfer of such an instrument is not subject to equities. Thus whereas an assignor only transfers his rights subject to any defences which could be pleaded against him, a transfer of a negotiable instrument to someone in good faith passes a good title, free from any such defences. For instance a person who receives a cheque in good faith obtains a good title, even though the cheque may have been stolen. It is not, of course, any document which has the attributes of negotiability. Only those documents recognized by law or the custom of trade to be transferable by delivery (or endorsement) are negotiable. Other documents can only be transferred by assignment.

Other examples of commercial situations where normal privity rules are by-passed are provided by the rules relating to the transfer of bills of lading. When goods are consigned by sea, the consignor usually makes a contract with the carrier which is evidenced in a bill of lading. The transfer of the bill of lading to the consignee (and, sometimes, to other transferees such as sub-buyers) is treated as transferring the whole contract of carriage. This result was originally provided for by the Bills of Lading Act 1855, but drafting problems in this Act often caused technical difficulties in the way of this result. To fill the gaps resulting from these difficulties common law 'implied contracts' were sometimes invoked, but these also gave rise to difficulty. Fortunately the need for these implications has been greatly diminished by the Carriage of Goods by Sea Act 1992 which has replaced the Bills of Lading Act with modern and better drafted provisions.

## 8. PRIVITY AND THE LAW OF TORT

During the past half century or so an enormous amount of litigation has centred around the relationship between the doctrine of privity of contract and liability in tort, especially in negligence. In a nutshell, the essential question usually is whether it is permissible, or legitimate, for the courts to impose tort liability on parties who are (or one of whom is) involved in some contractual relationships, not necessarily with each other, in such a way that the tort liability may add to the burdens or obligations created by the contract. Is this, in some sense, an illegitimate development and, if so, what is wrong with it? The problem is still giving rise to great difficulties, and it is not possible to treat the subject here with the full consideration that it really requires—particularly because, as yet, no clear solutions of principle are in sight. The question is usually treated as one for books on the law of tort, but it has become clearer from a series of recent House of Lords' decisions that the correct answer to many of these tort problems actually lies in contractual principles, so some discussion is desirable here.

The starting-point for this problem was a series of nineteenth-century cases in which actions were brought by plaintiffs injured by goods made or repaired by the defendant, or by services supplied by the defendant under a contract with a third party. One typical case was that in which defective goods were sold by A to B, and the defects caused injury to C. Another typical case was that of a railway passenger who bought a ticket from one company, allowing travel partly over a second company's lines, and was then injured in an accident caused by the negligence of the second company, while on their train. For a long time the courts grappled uneasily with these cases, sensing that two fundamental principles clashed here: on the one hand the defendant ought not to have imposed upon him a liability, growing out of his contract, to compensate a plaintiff who was no party to the contract and paid nothing to the defendant; and on the other hand, the injured plaintiff ought not to be prejudiced in claiming damages by the terms of the contract between the defendant and the third party. In one sense, either solution appeared to involve problems with privity. If the plaintiff was allowed to sue, he seemed to be building his cause of action on a contract to which he was no party; and if he was debarred from suing, it seemed that the contract, to which the plaintiff was no party, somehow operated to protect the defendant from liability.

Eventually, as all lawyers know, this problem was settled (or was at least thought to have been settled) by the great decision in *Donoghue* v. *Stevenson*.[18] The unfortunate consumer (who was not also the buyer) of the ginger beer with the (alleged) snail in the bottle was there held entitled to sue the manufacturer for injuries suffered by her from drinking (and seeing) the unpleasant contents. The existence of these contracts was, said the majority of the House of Lords, not a ground for denying liability in tort to the plaintiff. It was a fallacy (the famous 'privity of contract fallacy') to suppose that, because the plaintiff could not sue on a contract, he could not sue in tort either. Liability in tort and liability in contract were two entirely different things. Furthermore, this analysis seemed supported by the fact that the standard of liability was different in the two cases. In tort, the defendant had to take reasonable care; but in contract his obligations were to do what the contract required, which might be an entirely different matter.

With the 'privity of contract fallacy' apparently disposed of by this decision, this branch of the law seemed now to have no connection with privity of contract at all. It became a part of tort law alone; and for a long time it seemed that the expansion of tort liability, especially for negligence, could proceed in blithe disregard of contractual relations. Manufacturers of defective goods now came to be held liable for negligence to members of the public injured through that negligence, even though the plaintiff was no party to the contract under which the goods were made or sold to the public. So also, those performing services under a contract came to be generally liable for injuries negligently caused to third parties while the services were being performed. A duty to take care in tort even came to be

18 [1932] AC 562.

regularly imposed *as between the parties*, in many contractual situations. It eventually came to be said that in many contractual relationships (especially those between professional persons and their clients) parallel duties of care existed in tort and in contract. In most such cases there was no great harm in this. It usually made no difference to the result whether the liability to take care, as between the parties, was treated as a matter of contract or of tort. And where it did make a difference (as with the application of the Limitation Acts) the result was arbitrary, rather than a matter of fundamental principle. There was no illegitimacy in imposing these tort duties, because there was no real difference between doing that and implying a contractual term to take care. The results were usually the same, and the criteria should have been the same. Moreover, the courts never committed themselves to holding (what certainly would have been illegitimate) that a contractual exclusion clause could not operate to protect against liability in tort as well as in contract.

For several decades, then, the decision in *Donoghue* v. *Stevenson* seemed to have solved the problem. It was gradually extended to all sorts of analogous situations, so that repairers and professional people and others came to be covered by the rule. It was even extended to work done by builders, though that proved (and still proves) to have been much more problematic. But throughout these early decades, the liability was confined (it seemed) to cases where the plaintiff suffered physical injury or physical damage to property.

One consequence of this expansion of tort liability was that there was less pressure to expand contractual liability, and therefore the concepts of contract law itself. In the absence of this form of tort liability it might well have come to be thought that concepts of privity and consideration were too narrow in the modern world. For instance in the *Smith* v. *Eric S. Bush*[19] situation, where a building society client pays a fee for a mortgage survey to be conducted by an independent surveyor, strict application of contractual concepts leads to the conclusion that the client has not actually supplied any consideration to the surveyor (because strictly the client pays the building society) and therefore there is no contract between the client and the surveyor. In *Smith* v. *Bush* itself the House of Lords held that, *as a matter of tort law*, it was unreal to regard the situation in this light, and therefore the surveyor owed a duty of care in tort to the client and, further, this duty was non-excludable by disclaimers which were unreasonable under the Unfair Contract Terms Act 1977. Of course the actual result of this sort of development was not very different from recognizing that traditional contractual concepts are too narrow and need to be modified.

---

[19] [1990] 1 AC 831.

*Privity of contract and exemption clauses*

The first real indication that the privity of contract 'fallacy' had not been totally disposed of by *Donoghue* v. *Stevenson* did not come, perhaps, until the 1950s. What happened then was that a series of cases came before the courts in which attempts were made to by-pass exemption clauses in contracts by suing third parties in tort. This was (it will be recalled) a time when exemption clauses in standardized contracts were coming to be viewed by lawyers with distaste and hostility, and it seemed an excellent idea to many lawyers that a 'way round' the use of such clauses could be found by invoking the privity principle.

So, for instance, where a passenger travelling first class on a ship, was given a ticket exempting the company from all liability for personal injuries, even though caused by negligence, it was held that the shipping company's *employees* could still be sued for negligence in tort.[20] In this case the contract in the ticket did not actually purport to protect the employees from liability, but it soon became clear that, even if it had, the result would have been no different. The same result was arrived at when a passenger with a free pass was injured on a bus by the negligence of the driver; although the pass stated that the holder would not make any claim for negligence against the driver, the driver could not in law defend himself by relying on the terms of the pass—he was no party to the contract.[21]

Decisions of this kind may have produced acceptable results, because they were clearly motivated by the desire to ensure that an accident victim actually recovered damages. And nobody doubted that, although these actions were brought against the defendant's employee, in fact the employer (or his insurer) would pay. The only reason for suing the employee was, of course, the exemption clause protecting the employer himself. Now, although these decisions relied upon the privity principle, it seems clear that in one sense they were actually evasions of the principle. They were evasions in that the employee was made liable in tort in a contractual situation under which he assumed no such liability. The employees in the two cases mentioned above plainly did not contemplate that their work might render them legally liable for negligence to passengers, and doubtless if such a possibility had occurred to them they would have demanded protection from that liability by their employers. The paradox was that the 'privity of contract fallacy' by this time was taken to mean that the injured plaintiff could sue in tort a third party to his contract, while not being bound by the restrictions on liability which his contract imposed. There is much truth in the comment made by Lord

---

[20] *Adler* v. *Dickson* [1955] 1 QB 158.
[21] *Gore* v. *Van der Lann* [1967] 2 QB 31.

Denning in a later case[22] that this was a strange perversion of the law. Either privity of contract should have been fully applied, so as to prevent the plaintiff suing the employee (which is probably what would have happened in the nineteenth century); or it should not have been applied at all, so as to permit the employee to defend himself by pleading the terms of the contract between the passenger and the employer.

So in one sense, these decisions were an illegitimate extension of tort liability—permitting tort law to be used to impose a liability which was plainly not being assumed in contract. But of course the decisions were, as noted above, a response to the perceived unfairness of the exemption clause and the way such clauses were imposed in printed tickets without the ordinary passenger probably being aware of them at all. So the 'illegitimacy' of using tort law in such a situation was, in a sense, justified by the fact that the contractual exemption clauses were not truly assented to by the plaintiff, though legal doctrine held that he was bound by them. These decisions are now largely obsolete, since the Unfair Contract Terms Act 1977 anyhow bans altogether clauses which exclude liability for personal injury; so recourse to this device will not be needed in the ordinary way.

Unfortunately the privity rules were applied, perhaps unthinkingly (or perhaps in the belief that rules must be applied whatever their origin or purpose), in various other circumstances where the result seemed much less acceptable. In particular, they were applied in cases of damage to property consigned by sea, where the bill of lading explicitly extended protection to third parties such as stevedores who load and unload ships.[23] In these circumstances there is really very little wrong or unreasonable about the use of exemption clauses; indeed, their use is often commercially desirable, though this remains to some extent controversial. The point is that goods consigned by sea are almost invariably insured, and the relations between carrier and owner are anyhow largely regulated by international conventions. If the stevedore is not entitled to be protected against liability for negligence, stevedore firms will have to insure against that liability, and hence charge more for their services. Quite possibly, this will increase the total insurance bill.

Perhaps as a result of considerations such as these, there seems to have been some change of heart about these cases, though judicial disagreements are by no means over. As we have already seen, in *The Eurymedon*[24] the Privy Council upheld an argument that a stevedore could

---

[22] In *Scruttons* v. *Midlands Silicones Ltd* [1962] AC 446. Lord Denning himself was an enthusiastic party to *Adler* v. *Dickson, supra*, n. 20, where the privity principle was also misused in this way, but he justified himself in much the same way as we have done, see below.         [23] *Scruttons* v. *Midlands Silicones Ltd, supra* n. 22.

[24] [1975] AC 154, *supra*, 99.

rely on an exclusion clause in a bill of lading, where the carrier purported to act as agent of the stevedore. Another similar device which has also been upheld is for the bill of lading to include a clause whereby the owner of the goods undertakes that he will not sue third parties such as stevedores. This undertaking, being part of the binding contract between the owner of the goods and the carrier, can be enforced by the carrier, who can therefore prevent the owner suing the stevedore.[25] These cases appear to illustrate a new trend. Since the Unfair Contract Terms Act it will usually be possible to challenge the substance of an exemption clause of this kind on the ground that it is unreasonable. So if it is valid at all, it will be because the courts think it is reasonable; and if it is reasonable, it clearly ought not to be evaded by the simple device of suing third parties. It is unfortunate that the 1977 Act did not contain a simple provision declaring that an exemption clause which is held to be reasonable is valid and effective to protect third parties.

The cases dealing with the liability of building society surveyors have raised similar problems. In these cases the surveyor, as we saw earlier, is usually commissioned and paid by the building society, and often limits his responsibility with disclaimers, or with instructions that his report is not to be shown to the ultimate clients. And here, too, there was a danger that the privity principle would be by-passed to the extent of permitting the building society's client to sue the surveyor in tort, while refusing to permit the surveyor to limit or disclaim liability. But this danger was averted, and the true question faced, namely whether the disclaimers are reasonable under the Unfair Contract Terms Act.[26]

Even more striking is the Court of Appeal decision in *Norwich City Council* v. *Harvey*.[27] Here the plaintiff council contracted for an extension of a municipal swimming pool with a builder under a contract which threw on to the council the responsibility for fire damage and insurance against such damage. A fire was caused by the negligence of a sub-contractor who had contracted with the main contractor on the basis of the main contract. The council (or more probably, its insurers) sued the sub-contractors in tort for negligently causing the fire. Plainly there were privity difficulties about allowing the sub-contractors to rely on either of the two contracts here: the sub-contractors were not parties to the main contract, and the council was not a party to the second contract. But the Court of Appeal neatly side-stepped these difficulties by holding that there was no duty of care, and hence no liability in negligence. This is a striking reversion to nineteenth-century principles, and in effect adopts the dissent of Lord

---

[25] *The Elbe Maru* [1978] 1 Lloyd's Rep. 206.
[26] See *Smith* v. *Eric S. Bush, supra,* n. 19.
[27] [1989] 1 All ER 1180.

Denning in *Scruttons* v. *Midland Silicones*.[28] There are also dicta indicating that, if the individual workmen employed by the sub-contractor who were responsible for the fire had been sued, they too would have been held to owe no duty of care in the circumstances. Thus, an exemption clause in a contract which cannot be relied upon by the defendant can be used as a ground for negativing the duty of care in tort, so that the liability in tort is effectively evaded just as much as if the exemption clause were capable of being relied on by the third party.[29]

### Concurrent duties in contract and tort

Although this question does not necessarily involve privity problems, it is convenient to add a paragraph here about the possibility of concurrent duties in contract and tort. This is closely related to the privity problem because so many cases of concurrent duties involve an attempt to evade contractual privity difficulties by invoking tort law. We saw above how, after *Donoghue* v. *Stevenson,* the idea developed that there could often be concurrent duties in contract and tort between the parties to a contractual relationship. So the liability of a doctor or solicitor or other professional person came to be said to be a liability either in contract or in tort, and it was generally immaterial whether the plaintiff sued in contract or in tort.[30] For a while the authorities began to seem less favourable to this entangling of contract and tort. We saw earlier, for instance, how Lord Scarman in *Tai Hing Cotton Mills* v. *Chong Hing Bank*[31] suggested that implied terms in contract cases were solely a matter for contractual principles, and that it was undesirable to import ideas from tort law when applying these principles. It began to look as if the courts would decide that where a contract exists between the parties the liability must be contractual and contractual only. But an attempt to persuade the House of Lords to revert to this view has now been made head on and has failed. It has been held[32] that concurrent duties may co-exist in contract and tort and that the plaintiff is entitled to sue on either cause of action so long only as there is no contractual restriction or limitation on tort liability.

---

[28] *Supra,* n. 22. But an attempt to argue that the *Norwich* case was *technically* inconsistent with the decision in *Midland Silicones* failed in *Marc Rich & Co AG* v. *Bishop Rock Marine Co Ltd* [1994] 3 All ER 686.

[29] See also the decision of the Supreme Court of Canada which is to very much the same effect, though rejecting the privity rule more openly: *London Drugs Ltd* v. *Kuehne & Nagel International Ltd* (1992) 97 DLR (4th) 261.

[30] *Midland Bank Trust Co Ltd* v. *Hett Stebbs* [1979] Ch. 384.

[31] [1986] AC 80; and see also *Lancashire & Cheshire Assocn. of Baptist Churches Inc* v. *Howard & Seddon* [1993] 3 All ER 467.

[32] *Henderson* v. *Merrett Syndicates Ltd* [1994] 3 All ER 506.

## Privity of contract and liability for omissions

An area which has not yet been properly explored by legal writers or by the courts concerns liability for omissions. Generally speaking there is no liability in tort for merely failing to act. A person must be under a duty to act before he can be liable in negligence for not acting. But supposing the only duty to act is imposed by a contract with a third party? To take a simple hypothetical example, suppose that A contracts to keep B's driveway clear of snow and ice in the winter and, because he fails to do so, C is injured by slipping on the drive. C may, of course, be able to sue B, but perhaps B is uninsured and not worth suing; can C sue A? Clearly, privity prevents C suing A on A's contract with B. So if A is to be liable at all, he can only be liable in tort, and this will require proof of negligence. There is no doubt that, until very recently, there would have been a strong tendency to say that A could be liable in tort if he was negligent in failing to perform his contract. But, as we shall see below, the latest cases raise serious doubts about such a possibility because it is difficult to establish a proper standard of care in these circumstances apart from the contractual duty. The contract may require A to clear the driveway within twenty-four hours after a snowfall, or may merely require that he should use his best efforts to clear the driveway as soon as practicable. Either possibility—and many others—is perfectly legitimate as a matter of contract law; and the price of the contract can be expected to reflect the extent of the duty undertaken. It might thus alter the nature of the contractual burden in an unacceptable way if A were to be held liable in tort to third parties, irrespective of the standard imposed by the contract.

## Economic loss and privity of contract

Many modern tort cases have attempted to push the boundaries of tort law forward by claiming damages for economic loss for negligence. Now a claim for economic loss is often, perhaps usually, a claim based on a lost *expectation*, rather than any other kind of loss. A person who claims he has suffered economic loss usually means that he has not been able to obtain certain benefits which he expected to obtain. But the protection of expectations is generally the province of contract law; it is because a contracting party has a *right* to the performance of the contract that he generally has a right to have his expected profits protected by the law. Tort plaintiffs do not have such extensive rights; they are only entitled to be put in the same position they were in before the tort, which is a different matter altogether. This distinction is well established in the law of damages, although it has been somewhat obscured by the fact that so many tort claims are personal injury claims in which damages to put the plaintiff back in the position he was in before he was injured actually include damages for his lost expected earnings.

This means that claims to economic loss in tort are somewhat suspect; they are usually attempts to obtain through the medium of tort law compensation for the breach of a contractual duty not owed to the plaintiff, or not owed by the defendant, because of the privity principle. Thus many claims to economic loss are illegitimate attempts to circumvent the privity principle. In some circumstances, however, such a claim is wholly justified for special reasons. In *Ross* v. *Caunters*[33] the plaintiff was the intended beneficiary of a will which failed to take effect because of the negligence of the testator's solicitor, the defendant. Here the plaintiff's claim in tort was upheld, although in effect the plaintiff was permitted to sue on the contract between the testator and the solicitor, and in other countries such a claim might be classified as an action in contract. The reason this was not an illegitimate evasion of the privity principle is that nobody other than the plaintiff could have enforced the defendant's duty to take due care. The testator was dead, and his representatives had suffered no loss (because the testator's estate was not diminished by the negligence—it was merely distributed in a way which was not what he had intended). So the evasion of the privity principle here did not impose duties which were not owed by a contracting party—indeed, quite the reverse, because the result was to enable the solicitor's contractual duty to take care to be effectively enforced.

Apart from this rather exceptional type of case there has been a great deal of very difficult litigation in recent years on the possibility of liability for economic loss in tort, and on the contract/tort boundary. The upshot of these cases is that the House of Lords has now insisted that the test of liability in tort is the existence of sufficient *proximity* between plaintiff and defendant,[34] while at the same time recognizing that proximity is not really a test of liability at all but a 'convenient label' which is attached to the varying features of different sets of circumstances in which liability arises.[35] This makes it very difficult to summarize the law accurately, but fortunately this book is on the law of contract and not the law of tort. Our task does not require a detailed analysis of the circumstances in which tort liability for economic loss may arise, but only requires us to show how contractual principles may affect this kind of tort liability.

### Cases of reasonable reliance

It is quite clear that one key feature of cases where this kind of tort liability exists is the existence of *reasonable reliance* by the plaintiff on the

[33] [1980] Ch. 580, followed and extended in *White* v. *Jones* [1993] 3 All ER 481 (under appeal to the HL).    [34] *Murphy* v. *Brentwood DC* [1991] 1 AC 398.
[35] *Caparo Industries* v. *Dickman* [1992] 2 AC 605.

defendant. This at once shows that we are in the contract/tort boundary area because the most obvious circumstance in which it is reasonable for one person to rely upon another is where the latter has committed himself by making a definite promise and so entered into a contract. But in modern times complex commercial (and indeed social) relations may exist in which reasonable reliance is shown without contract, either because of privity principles or because of the lack of consideration or some other factor. The classic illustration of this kind of liability is *Hedley Byrne & Co Ltd* v. *Heller & Partners Ltd*,[36] where the defendant bank would have been liable (but for a disclaimer) when it negligently gave a misleading reference to the plaintiffs who were not customers of the bank, at the request of a third party who was a customer. Clearly this case is very close to contract, and in some systems of law it might be that the plaintiffs would have been held entitled to sue in contract.

### Owners, contractors, sub-contractors, and suppliers

We saw at the beginning of this chapter that in building and engineering contracts a long-established practice exists under which the owner or client contracts with a main contractor, who in turn enters into contracts with sub-contractors, and they, in turn, may buy goods for their sub-contracts from suppliers. Each one of a pair to this chain of parties is, of course, in a contractual relationship with the other; but the long-established under-standing has been that (unless there are special legal arrangements) privity of contract does not exist between one pair of parties and others lower down or higher up in the chain. In *Junior Books Ltd* v. *Veitchi Bros*[37] this established tradition was upset by a decision of the House of Lords which has caused much trouble ever since, and has now been largely relegated to the sidelines as a precedent. In the *Junior Books* case an owner was permitted to sue a sub-contractor directly for the negligent construction of a floor, which meant that the floor had to be relaid. The floor was not dangerous and there was no damage to property in the ordinary sense, so the claim was purely for the financial loss, or economic loss, arising from the defective floor. It was very much as though the plaintiff in *Donoghue* v. *Stevenson* had not actually drunk the ginger beer, but had sued the makers for the *value* of the (uncontaminated) ginger beer which she had expected to have.

It seems that the *Junior Books* decision was an illegitimate use of tort law to evade the privity principle. As Lord Brandon pointed out in his dissenting speech, it is impossible to see by what standard of care the defendant's conduct could be judged. In laying the floor, he was carrying out a contract, which may have imposed on him detailed requirements as

[36] [1964] AC 465.
[37] [1983] 1 AC 520.

to how the floor should be laid. How could he, at the same time, be under a contractual duty to his own co-contractor (the main contractor in the case) and under a tort duty to the owners which might have conflicted with that contractual duty? As Lord Brandon's speech has now, to all intents and purposes, been endorsed by the House of Lords in a subsequent case,[38] and the *Junior Books* decision confined to its own very special facts as a case in which some reasonable reliance was shown,[39] it seems unnecessary to elaborate further on this case here.[40]

Another attempt to evade the privity principle in this type of commercial situation was rejected in *Simaan General Contracting Co* v. *Pilkington Glass*.[41] Here the defendants supplied glass to a sub-contractor who installed it in a building which the plaintiffs were erecting, as main contractors, in Abu Dhabi. The glass was not dangerous or faulty, but it was the wrong colour, according to the contract, and had to be replaced at considerable cost to the main contractor. The main contractor attempted to sue Pilkington Glass, the suppliers, direct in tort, but their claim failed. The proper procedure, insisted the Court of Appeal, was for the main contractor to sue the sub-contractor, who could claim against the supplier. In that way, the liability of each party would be determined by the contractual burdens he had undertaken, subject to any contractual defences available to him.

## Builders and buyers

The above cases concern contracts for the construction of buildings. But of course many people buy buildings (or strictly, the land on which they stand) after they have been constructed, sometimes years afterwards. In such a case the buyer has a contract with the seller, and that seller no doubt may have a contract with the person from whom he bought, and so on. But the buyer of a completed building has no contract with earlier owners, still less with the original builder. Suppose, then, that serious defects exist in the building as a result of the negligence of the builder, can the buyer sue

---

[38] *D. & F. Estates Ltd* v. *Church Commissioners* [1989] AC 177.

[39] *Murphy* v. *Brentwood DC, supra*, n. 34.

[40] But a footnote may be permitted. The puzzling thing about the case (as it is reported) is to understand why the owners did not sue the main contractors directly, because the main contractor in a building contract prima facie assumes liability for the proper carrying out of the entire works, even those parts which are done by sub-contractors. It appears that the owners could not have sued the main contractors because, before the damage to the floor became apparent, they had compromised a whole series of other claims against the main contractor. This compromise had fully covered all the contractors' liability arising out of the main contract. So in making this compromise, the owners must have already received from the contractors damages for the risk that the floor would prove defective. So on this ground also it was an illegitimate evasion of the privity principle to permit the owner to sue the sub-contractor in tort when the risk eventuated.

[41] [1988] 1 All ER 791.

the builder in tort for negligence? It is clear that if the buyer (or anyone else) is physically injured because of the defects, an action lies against the builder under *Donoghue* v. *Stevenson*. But after a great deal of troublesome case law in the 1970s and 1980s it was finally decided by the House of Lords in *Murphy* v. *Brentwood D C*[42] that no action will lie against the builder in tort if the occupier is aware of the defect and fails to eliminate it; and certainly no action lies against the builder for the purely economic loss involved in the house being less valuable than was thought, or for the cost of repairs. Several earlier decisions (including one in the House of Lords itself[43]) were overruled in *Murphy*.

Once again, the best policy justification[44] for thus limiting tort liability is that it would otherwise encroach on contractual and privity principles. The buyer of a building is prima facie expected to satisfy himself that the building is worth what he pays; he does not usually have any contractual remedy against the seller (unless the seller is also the builder) for defects in the house, and it is now clear that he will not normally have any tort remedy against anybody else.[45] Although this result may seem hard, and somewhat contrary to the trend of much modern law, which has seen such an expansion of liability for negligence, there seems no doubt that it is ultimately based on the contractual idea that the price of anything in the market (buildings or goods) should reflect the risk of defects, except in so far as they are expressly or impliedly covered by warranties given by the seller himself.

## Manufacturers and distributional chains

As with the case of owners, contractors, and sub-contractors, we have also seen that similar chains of supply often exist with goods manufactured and distributed through the market. Here also, the usual way of proceeding if the goods are defective is for the ultimate buyer or consumer to sue the retailer with whom he has contracted; the retailer may bring third-party proceedings against his supplier; and so on up the distributional chain to the ultimate manufacturer. There are, however, problems about this method of proceeding (which even in straightforward cases must also be rather costly and cumbersome) where one of the intermediaries cannot be found, or is abroad, or is insolvent. In these circumstances attempts may

---

[42] [1991] 1 AC 398.          [43] *Anns* v. *Merton London BC* [1978] AC 728.
[44] Though not the one given in *Murphy* which was mainly based on the difficulties and uncertainty of defining the limits of the earlier decisions, and the confusion and litigation they had caused.
[45] But there is a limited statutory right against the builder of a *dwelling-house* for negligence under the Defective Premises Act 1972. There are also extra-legal compensation schemes to protect the buyers of relatively new houses (up to 10 years old) where defects subsequently develop.

again be made by one party in the chain to jump a tier, as it were, and sue in tort a defendant with whom he has no privity of contract. Of course, these difficulties only arise where the claim is for economic loss: if it is for physical injury, the action lies in a straightforward application of *Donoghue* v. *Stevenson*.

But it is now clear, as a result of dicta in several recent decisions of the House of Lords, that a claim for economic loss in such circumstances will not lie.[46] A person who buys defective goods can only sue the manufacturer for negligence if the defect causes physical damage to the person or property. If the only complaint concerns defects *in* the goods, no claim in tort lies. So we now know that the plaintiff in *Donoghue* v. *Stevenson* could not have sued the manufacturers for the value of the ginger beer.

There are, however, further complications. One is illustrated by *Muirhead* v. *Industrial Tank Specialities*[47] where physical damage is followed by consequential economic loss; here it now seems clear that the economic loss is recoverable but only if it really follows from the physical damage. Care must be taken, as it was in the *Muirhead* case, to see that the plaintiff is not in effect given damages for his lost *expectations* against the maker of the goods. There is no case for these damages, and it would be a bare evasion of the privity principle to award them in tort.

[46] *D. & F. Estates*, *supra*, n. 38 and *Murphy*, *supra*, n. 34.
[47] [1986] QB 507.

# 20

# The Enforcement of Contractual Rights
## Against Third Parties

ALTHOUGH there are no strong reasons against allowing the contracting parties to confer rights on third parties, the same obviously cannot be said of imposing liabilities on third parties. Naturally enough, it is generally speaking impossible for the parties to a contract to impose liabilities on third parties without their consent, and although criticisms are frequently levelled against the doctrine of privity of contract, it is not to be thought that anyone would wish to see this part of the principle altered. However, there are circumstances in which a person may consent to the imposition of duties under a contract to which he was no party. There are also cases in connection with property where a person may become bound by contractual obligations even without his consent. Finally, mention will have to be made of a number of other legal devices which may enable contractual obligations to be enforced against third parties in special circumstances.

We have already briefly discussed the position of agency in the law of contract, and need not advert to it further here, except to emphasize once again that a principal may be liable on a contract made by an agent on his behalf, even though the agent has exceeded his actual authority.

### I. NOVATION

In the previous chapter we discussed the assignment of rights, and pointed out that by a relatively simple legal process a contractual right may be transferred to a third party. It must now be observed that contractual duties cannot be shaken off in this way, save with the consent of the other party to the contract. It is, of course, possible for a party to a contract to perform it through his employees or agents, at all events if personal considerations are not important. Indeed, in many cases it is not for one moment expected that a contracting party will actually perform in person, and when the contracting party is a corporation this would anyhow be a physical impossibility. But the fact that a party is not expected to, and does not, perform in person does not mean that he is not still the contracting party. On the contrary he remains the only person liable on the contract (although others may sometimes be liable in tort) and the only person able to enforce it.

The only way in which it is possible actually to *transfer* contractual duties to a third party is by the process of novation, which requires the consent of the other party to the contract. Strictly, novation amounts to the extinction of the old obligation and the creation of a new one, rather than to the transfer of the obligation from one person to another. So if B owes A £100, and C owes B the same amount, B cannot transfer to C the legal duty of paying his debt to A without A's consent. But if A agrees to accept C as a debtor in place of B, and if C agrees to accept A as his creditor in place of B, the three parties may make a tripartite agreement to this effect, known as novation. The effect of this is to extinguish B's liability to A and create a new liability on the part of C.

The necessary consents may be implied or inferred, as well as expressed, but it is sometimes difficult to decide whether a new debtor has been accepted by the creditor *in place* of the old debtor (which would be a novation) or as an additional source of payment, leaving the original debtor still liable if that source of payment fails to materialize. An assignment of a lease, even though the landlord's consent may be required (as is customary), is not in general treated as a novation. As we saw in the last chapter, an assignment makes the assignee liable on the lease, but leaves the assignor also liable as a sort of guarantor. Similarly, where a buyer of goods in an international trade transaction agrees to pay the price with a banker's letter of credit, it is generally held that the bank's undertaking to pay does not displace the buyer's liability. If for some reason the bank fails to pay, the seller may still sue the buyer direct. But an interesting modern example of a genuine novation is provided by many credit-card transactions. Where a customer buys goods and pays for them with a credit card, it has recently been held that his obligation to pay the price is actually replaced by that of the credit-card company, with the implied consent of the seller.[1] So if the credit-card company fails to pay, the seller can no longer claim against the buyer.

It will be seen that the result of these rules is that it is not normally possible for a complete contract to be assigned to a third party. While the benefit may be assigned, the burden cannot be transferred except with the other party's consent. This can cause problems when a complete business changes hands (unless the change is carried through by selling the shares in a limited company) because it may then become necessary to obtain the consent of all the customers of the business to the transfer of existing contracts. In America such difficulties are largely avoided by the simple expedient of requiring the transferee of the business to promise to honour all existing contracts, and allowing the other parties to these contracts to

---

[1] *Re Charge Card Services Ltd* [1989] Ch. 497. In some cases there is no prior obligation to pay in cash at all, because the seller has made it clear that he will accept payment by credit card from the outset.

sue the transferee on this promise. The interests of these other parties are safeguarded by the fact that the transferor of the business remains liable as a sort of guarantor or surety.

In England, the obstacle of privity stands in the way of this procedure, so that when a business changes hands the consent of all existing contracting parties to a novation may have to be obtained. Sometimes it is possible to 'imply' a novation, for example, where a retiring partner in a firm is replaced by a new partner. Parties who continue to deal with the firm with knowledge of the change in partners may be held to have consented to an 'implied' novation whereby the old partner is replaced by the new one in any continuing contracts.

It has been held[2] that, even in the absence of circumstances justifying the implication of a novation, a person may be held to have assumed the burdens of a contract simply by virtue of having taken or accepted benefits under it. If this rather surprisingly wide principle becomes accepted it will furnish another illustration of the tendency (perhaps now obsolete) for benefit-based liabilities to supersede consent-based liabilities.[3]

There is now also an important statutory exception to the above rule about the transfer of complete contracts. Under the Transfer of Undertakings (Protection of Employment) Regulations 1981 (which were made to give effect to an EC Directive), contracts of employment are transferred in their entirety when the employer's business is transferred to a new owner. This is generally beneficial to the employee, which is presumably why his consent is dispensed with, but the Regulations may not be unrelated to the view, perhaps still widely current in 1981, that to require the consent of the employee in such a situation is pedantic. This may explain the original failure of the Regulations to make any provision for cases in which the employee may be seriously prejudiced by being transferred without his consent to a new employer—as, for instance, where he has no desire to work for the new employer, and yet would be bound by a severe restrictive covenant if he left.[4] The Regulations have since been amended to make it clear that an employee cannot be transferred to a new employer if he objects, but in that event he is not deemed to have been dismissed by the transferor, and so cannot claim compensation for unfair dismissal.[5]

---

[2] In *Tito* v. *Waddell* [1977] Ch. 106.

[3] See *supra*, 24–5 as to this tendency. In fact the principle laid down in *Tito* v. *Waddell* was curtailed in *Law Debenture Trust Corp* v. *Ural Caspian Oil Corp Ltd* [1993] 2 All ER 355.

[4] It seems clear that this is indeed the result of the Regulations. See *Morris, Angel & Son Ltd* v. *Hollande* [1993] 3 All ER 569 where, however, the CA interpreted the restrictive covenant so as to restrict the employee from soliciting business from the transferor's customers, and not the transferee's.

[5] So the amendment would presumably not help an employee subject to a restrictive covenant as in the example put in the text.

## 2. OBLIGATIONS RUNNING WITH PROPERTY

Just as the benefit of certain obligations (e.g. a landlord's right to receive rent) will 'run with the land' and be enforceable by the owner of the property for the time being, so also the burden of certain contracts may run with the property in the same way. In particular, where contractual duties relating to land are created, they frequently run with the land, and are binding on anybody in possession of the land. This principle was established very early in regard to leases, with the result that landlords' and tenants' duties are generally enforceable against whoever happens to be landlord or tenant for the time being.

It was not until the middle of the nineteenth century that this principle was extended to cases of the sale of freehold land. In the famous case of *Tulk* v. *Moxhay*[6] it was held that a person who bought land with knowledge that the former owner had entered into a 'restrictive covenant' in respect of it (limiting the uses to which the land could be put) would be bound by the covenant. The development and elaboration of the rule in *Tulk* v. *Moxhay* went a long way to supplying England with a system, admittedly crude and imperfect, of private planning law, but in doing so it really passed out of the realm of the law of contract into that of the law of property. Since 1925 restrictive covenants have been registrable, and registration has taken the place of the requirement of notice. Thus when a person agrees to buy land he, or his solicitor, will search the Register to discover if there are any covenants restricting the use to which the land may be put. An unregistered covenant will not be binding on him, while a registered covenant will be binding, whether he actually has notice or not. In the great majority of cases he will have notice, and so may reasonably be treated as buying the land subject to the covenant. But the principle of *Tulk* v. *Moxhay* has been confined to restrictive or negative covenants. A covenant which imposes a positive obligation (such as a covenant to repair) does not run with freehold property and cannot be enforced against a buyer.[7]

It was perhaps inevitable that attempts should sooner or later be made to extend the principle of *Tulk* v. *Moxhay* to goods, and the system of resale price maintenance provided the testing ground. This system (as we saw in Chapter 17) constituted an attempt on the part of manufacturers to lay down the minimum price at which their goods could be sold to the public. Since in most cases the goods are sold to the public by retailers who themselves buy, not from the manufacturers, but from wholesalers, it is apparent that the doctrine of privity of contract was a stumbling-block to the enforcement of resale price maintenance.

[6] (1848) 2 Ph 774.
[7] Old law, but reaffirmed by the HL in *Rhone* v. *Stephens* [1994] 2 All ER 65.

Attempts were made, therefore, to persuade the courts to permit the manufacturer to sue the retailer directly, at all events where the latter had bought with notice of the conditions. First of all it was argued that the retailer was liable on the contract made between the manufacturer and the wholesaler on the principle of *Tulk* v. *Moxhay*, and when this failed it was argued that the manufacturer could sue the retailer on the contract made between the wholesaler and the retailer himself. This also failed owing to the doctrine of privity, with the result that the manufacturers devised their own methods of enforcing resale price maintenance—namely, the 'stop-list'. 'Stop-lists' were outlawed by the Restrictive Trade Practices Act 1956, and after various other legislative changes which it is unnecessary to examine in detail, resale price maintenance has now largely disappeared, except in the case of books. Privity of contract, therefore, is now of little consequence in this connection.

The possibility of contractual duties running with goods has also arisen in another connection, that is, in cases of hire. If a person lets goods on hire to another for a fixed term, and subsequently sells the goods to a third party, can the third party disregard the contract of hire and recover the goods from the hirer before the expiry of the term? There is, of course, no doubt that a purchaser of land is bound by a lease created by the seller, but the general principle is that a hire of goods creates merely personal and not proprietary rights. The buyer is generally free to disregard the contract of hire and recover possession of the goods at his pleasure. However, in 1926 the decision of the Privy Council in *Lord Strathcona SS Co* v. *Dominion Coal Co*[8] extended the principle of *Tulk* v. *Moxhay* to the case of a ship. Here it was held that a person who buys a ship with notice that it has been let to a charterer for a fixed period is bound to respect the charter. Although the decision appears to have served the ends of justice, it met with a great deal of criticism on the ground that the doctrine of *Tulk* v. *Moxhay* could only apply, for various reasons, to cases of land. Nevertheless, the case does not seem reasonable or unjust, and it is perhaps regrettable that it has been dissented from in the High Court.[9]

There is no doubt that, even if correct, the *Strathcona* case must be confined to cases involving goods of exceptional value and importance, but changes in commercial practices may well make it necessary to extend the *Strathcona* principle rather than to limit its effects. It is today becoming very common for large concerns to hire (or 'lease') plant, equipment, and vehicles on a substantial scale, and serious practical problems could arise if

---

[8] [1926] AC 108.
[9] *Port Line Ltd* v. *Ben Line Steamers* [1958] 2 QB 146. See also *Law Debenture Trust Corp* v. *Ural Caspian Oil Corp, supra*, n. 3.

such contracts were to be treated as creating only 'personal' rather than 'proprietary' rights. If, for example, A hires a fleet of lorries on a long-term basis from B, and then B sells its business to C, it would be absurd if C could demand immediate possession of the lorries from A, and perhaps bring its business to a standstill. Not only is this result unreasonable, but it would make it very difficult for a business like B's to be sold at all. B may wish to ensure that, after the sale of its business, its old customers' rights to the continued use of their fleets of lorries are respected, and it may insert into the sale contract with C a clause insisting that C will respect those contracts; but even that clause would make no difference to the relationship between A and C. There is still the privity gap, and A cannot prevent C demanding the return of its lorries. Of course, this might very well be a breach of contract on the part of B (which remains liable to pay damages despite the sale of its business), and B may in turn be able to claim an indemnity against that liability in damages from C which has thus violated the specific clause in the contract requiring it to honour existing hire contracts. But to recognize that A has a right to damages from B in this situation might be no adequate substitute for an enforceable right to retain the lorries themselves. The only way out of this difficulty is for B to require, as a part of its arrangements for the sale of the business to C, that C should enter into direct contractual arrangements with the existing clients, like A, to honour their contracts.

### 3. OTHER WAYS OF ENFORCING OBLIGATIONS AGAINST THIRD PARTIES

We saw in the last chapter how efforts have been made in many cases to enable third parties to a contract to sue one of the parties in tort, thereby evading the privity principle that a contract cannot be enforced *by* third parties. It should come as no surprise that similar attempts have been made to overcome the privity principle that contractual burdens cannot be enforced *against* third parties. Here, too, these attempts have generally taken the form of trying to invoke tort law against third parties, though attempts have also (and rather more successfully) been made to use other branches of the law, such as equity, for this purpose.

### Inducing breach of contract

The first possible way of trying to enforce contractual obligations against third parties is to argue that these obligations must not be interfered with by other people—that there is a general duty, enforceable in tort, not to interfere with the contracts of other parties. In 1853 it was decided for the first time that a person who persuades one party to a contract to break that contract may be sued by the other contracting party for damages in tort.[10] During the last fifty years or so this tort has been developed and elaborated by the courts and its principles may now be stated with reasonable confidence. The vital element in this tort is knowledge by the defendant of the contract when he induced one party to break it. If this is established the defendant will be liable unless he can set up some reasonable justification for his act.

In one sense there is no doubt that the recognition of this tort creates something akin to a further exception to the doctrine of privity of contract. In particular there seems no reason why it should not be invoked in the cases of hire or charter discussed in the last section. If A makes a contract to charter his ship to B, there is no doubt that C will be liable to B if, knowing of the charter, he persuade A to sell the ship to X who does not intend to honour the charter. Is there any reason, then, why he should not be liable if he buys the ship himself, and proceeds to renounce the charter for his own benefit? There are, in fact, some cases which come very close to deciding just this, and it may yet be that the *Strathcona* case will be justified on such grounds as these.

### Other attempts to sue third parties in tort

A defendant who by his negligence causes physical injury or damage to the plaintiff or his property is of course liable for that loss; and any contracts which the plaintiff may have made may be relevant in showing what the amount of the loss actually is. So, for instance, in the ordinary personal injury case the plaintiff's contract of employment is relevant in showing what salary or wages have actually been lost by the plaintiff. There is no breach of the privity principle in requiring the defendant to make good these losses.

But the position is otherwise where the plaintiff has not himself suffered any personal injury or physical damage. It is now clear that a third party cannot be sued for negligence, merely because he has caused some physical damage or injury to one person, which has interfered with the contractual rights of another. A charterer of a ship cannot sue a third party for damages for negligence which has resulted in damage to the ship.[11] This is justified as a matter of tort law by saying that the loss to the charterer is merely economic loss unless he is actually owner (or strictly a lessee) of the ship, and then insisting on the general principle that economic loss cannot be recovered in tort. Another way of putting the point would be to say that a third party cannot be liable in negligence to one contracting party for

---

[10] *Lumley* v. *Gye* (1853) 2 E & B 216.
[11] *Candlewood Navigation* v. *Mitsui Lines* [1986] AC 1 is the leading modern case, but there are many others.

conduct which prevents the other contracting party from performing his obligations under the contract.

The chief reason which has usually been given for this limitation on tort liability is the sheer impossibility of coping with the extent of legal liability if any other rule were adopted. Suppose a factory is burned down by the negligence of the defendant: hundreds of parties may be indirectly affected by this, and may suffer economic losses—workers laid off, contractual suppliers or buyers of the factory's products, and others still more remotely affected, such as landlords of the workers, or publicans with whom the workers used to spend their earnings. If all these parties were entitled to claim damages from the negligent tortfeasor the liability would be immense and the legal difficulties enormous. And this seems quite enough to justify the limit on liability. But there may also be genuine privity of contract reasons underlying the rule too. Contracting parties (other than the immediate owners of property damaged) should, perhaps, look to their contracts, and their contracting partners, to settle issues of this kind, rather than to impose them on third parties.

It is thus possible to avoid what may otherwise appear to be some odd results flowing from the rule: if a charterer is obliged to pay rent under his charter, whether or not the ship is laid up after an accident, then neither the charterer nor the owner can sue the third party for the loss resulting from his negligence. The charterer cannot sue for the reasons just given, and the owner cannot sue because he suffers no loss.[12] But this result could be circumvented if charterparties were drafted so as to free the charterer from the obligation to pay rent while the ship is laid up after an accident at sea. The owner of the vessel could then sue the third party for all the loss caused by his negligence. So in the result this legal doctrine may be justified.

## Equitable obligations

There is one well-established area of the law in which equity can be prayed in aid to enable obligations to be enforced against third parties, even though those obligations appear to be of a contractual nature. Where information is given in confidence to one person, on the express or implied understanding that it is not to be divulged to anyone else, a third party who obtains the information with knowledge that it is confidential can be restrained by injunction from repeating it, or making use of it.[13]

---

[12] But the status of this rule does not seem as solid as it was once. See *Linden Garden Trust* v. *Lenesta Sludge Disposals* [1994] 1 AC 85, discussed *supra*, 362.

[13] The origin of this jurisdiction goes back to *Prince Albert* v. *Strange* (1849) 1 Mac & G 25. In modern times it has been applied in a wide variety of commercial and non-commercial situations. For some commercial cases (though not involving third parties) see *supra*, 104.

This principle is treated by lawyers as neither contractual, nor tortious, nor proprietary, but as arising from the equitable principles governing breach of confidence. This is, however, mere labelling. In fact the principles governing these cases are very close to contractual principles, because it is necessary to show that the information was given to someone who expressly or impliedly agreed to keep it confidential. This is not treated as contractual despite the element of agreement or promise involved, because there is no consideration as conventionally understood (though there is action in reliance—the very giving of the information) and also because the information is sometimes given in personal or matrimonial relations[14] which do not look contractual. None of this alters the substance of the matter, which is that agreements or promises not to divulge confidential information are enforced against third parties who receive the information with notice of its confidentiality.

---

[14] See e.g. *Argyll* v. *Argyll* [1967] Ch. 302; *Stephens* v. *Avery* [1988] 2 All ER 477.

# 21

# Termination and Rescission of Contracts

## I. UNILATERAL TERMINATION

GENERALLY speaking, of course, it is not open to one contracting party to terminate the contract unilaterally. Even breach of contract—as we shall see—must be accepted to terminate the contract. However, there are many contracts of a continuous nature in which the relationship is entered into without specifying any time limit, and yet which are clearly not intended to be permanent. In these contracts it is permissible for one party to give notice to the other of his intention to bring the relationship to an end. For instance, a contract of hire, a contract of agency, a contract of employment, a lease, or any other similarly continuous agreement, if entered into for an indefinite time, may be terminated by notice. The length of the notice, if not expressly agreed upon, will vary according to the circumstances of the case, but it must always be 'reasonable' and in certain contracts, like contracts of employment and leases, it has come to be more or less standardized by reference to the method of payment. So for instance at common law an employee paid by the week was normally entitled to at least a week's notice, and one paid by the month to a month's notice, but under modern legislation even an employee employed by the week will often be entitled to longer notice. It is not, of course, possible to determine agreements of this kind by unilateral notice where they are entered into for a fixed term, but if the relationship continues after the expiry of the term, it will usually be held to be 'at will', that is to say, terminable on notice by either party.

One apparent oddity of the law governing these continuous relationships is that it is only possible to give notice to terminate the relationship, and not to amend the terms. So, for instance a landlord at common law could not give notice of increase in rent; he had instead to give notice to quit and, at the same time, offer to enter into a new lease at a different rent, which the tenant might then accept or decline. But this came to seem very odd in modern times, so that in some cases statute now empowers a landlord to give notice of an increase in rent, though of course it remains open to the tenant to refuse to accept the change, provided he quits. In other contracts the common law rule continues. An employer cannot give notice to reduce an employee's wages (still less can he reduce them without notice); he must first give the requisite length of notice to the employee (which may involve him in paying redundancy money and other termination benefits) and then he may offer to re-employ him on different terms. Alternatively, the employer may seek the agreement of the employee to a reduction in pay, usually backed by warnings of what will otherwise ensue. If there is such an agreement, then that will be valid as a bilateral amendment to the contract, and there is no question of a unilateral variation. In other cases the difficulty may be got over if the original contract is made on the express terms that the rates of charge may be increased or reduced with (or without) notice.

The easy way in which continuous contracts can be terminated at common law reflects the classical tradition that contracts are a matter of assent, and when either party no longer wants to continue in a relationship with the other, he should be allowed ready escape. The period of notice is, in a sense, a short-term period in which the other party may then go into the market and obtain there some substitute. This means that although the parties to a contract of unspecified duration may reasonably expect it to continue for a long period into the future, neither party has a *right* to the protection of that expectation. His only right is to the period of notice, which gives him the chance to buy substitutes. In modern times, however, it has often been felt that this is unfair, and that long-continued and justified expectations are entitled to some legal protection. So, for instance, employees have been given many new statutory rights in recent decades, including especially a right to compensation for 'unfair dismissal' as well as to redundancy payments if their employment is terminated in many ordinary situations. Similarly, tenants have long enjoyed security of tenure under a variety of statutes. And this applies not only to the tenant of a dwelling-house, but also to agricultural tenants and even to the tenants of business premises, though the three legal regimes are very different from each other.

These statutory rights were created during the period when the principle of freedom of contract was at a low ebb, and it may be questioned by some whether they should be perpetuated in all circumstances. The need for them arises partly because the market in these matters is often very imperfect, so that it simply is not possible for one party to get what he needs elsewhere if his contract is terminated. In periods of high unemployment, an employee cannot always get another job when he is given notice, and in periods of great scarcity of rented accommodation, a tenant may not be able to find other premises if he is given notice to quit. On the other hand, the existence of these legally protected expectations is one of the very reasons the market works so badly. During the 1960s and 1970s the British labour market was almost frozen by the inability of employers to shed unnecessary employees—not indeed always or entirely because of legal protection, but partly or mainly because of trade union power; and the legal protection of tenants of houses (at absurdly low rents) is certainly one of the main reasons there is so little accommodation available for rent in Britain. So there has been some attempt to nibble away at the legal protection of these expectations by modern statutes—some reduction of the right to redundancy payments, and some possibility now of letting houses without the protection of the Rent Acts.

But some will think that, whatever the market situation may be, it is right that there should at least be protection against 'unfair dismissal'. At common law, if an employer gave the requisite notice, it did not matter what his reasons were for wanting to terminate the employment—whether he had good reasons, bad reasons or no reasons. This again followed the classical tradition—once the employer did not *want* to continue the employment, he was entitled to terminate it, whatever the reasons. But since 1971 an employee has been entitled to statutory compensation (from an industrial tribunal) for 'unfair dismissal', if he is dismissed for reasons which are unfair, *even if the requisite notice is given*. There is, however, no general requirement that a contracting party should act fairly (or even in good faith) in exercising his right to terminate a long-continued contract.

In most areas there has been no statutory protection of the interests of the parties in these contracts of unspecified duration, and occasionally, the results of an uncontrolled legal right of termination appear harsh.[1] In 'franchise contracts', for instance, where someone invests some capital in setting up a business in co-operation with a franchise company (such as a filling station, or a fast food outlet, or a hotel with a famous name), or where a commercial agent invests money and trouble in establishing a network of relationships on behalf of a commercial principal, the relationship is often terminable on notice (sometimes very short notice) and there is often no contractual restriction on the grounds on which notice to terminate can be given. This is another area in which the fundamental principle of freedom of contract appears sometimes to clash with simple justice. Although the economic arguments for freedom of contract may suggest that such contracts should be terminable for good commercial reasons, the law does not generally supervise the validity of the reasons at all, so termination for whim or caprice—the equivalent of the 'unfair dismissal'—here remains perfectly permissible in law.

Apart from these cases of continuous contracts, an express clause permitting one party to cancel the contract unilaterally, sometimes subject to various conditions, is not uncommon in practice. In particular, it will

[1] The EC Dir. on Unfair Contract Terms (dealt with *supra*, 312) includes in the list of suspect terms in the Annex a term enabling a seller or supplier to terminate a contract of indefinite duration without reasonable notice except where there are serious grounds; but because the Dir. only applies for the benefit of consumers not acting in the course of business, it is not likely to help in most of these cases.

often be found that wholly executory contracts are cancellable in this way, for in this case no loss (other than a 'loss' of expected profits) will be suffered by either party. In addition there are now cases where statute permits early cancellation of contracts, for instance, consumer-credit agreements obtained by 'door-to-door' salesmen. And even where the law provides no actual right of cancellation, it is still often the case that cancellation is permitted as a matter of practice and custom. For example, everyone knows that airlines will readily accept cancellations, provided, usually, that they are made in good time, although many reduced airline fares are now only available on the terms that bookings are firm and non-cancellable. In practice 'deposits' are often paid on the making of a contract, and (again, whatever the law may say[2]) it is commonly the case that the parties will rest content with a right to cancel subject to forfeiture of the deposit. But it cannot be assumed that because a deposit is forfeitable there may not be additional liability for damages if a party wrongfully cancels; people are sometimes surprised to discover that they have no right, for instance, to cancel reservations for holiday accommodation even on forfeiture of a deposit.

## 2. TERMINATION AND RESCISSION

Certain breaches of contractual duties (in the widest sense) give the innocent party[3] the right to bring the contract to an end, whether or not he has the further right to claim damages. Unfortunately, the terminology adopted by lawyers in this field has been neither uniform nor consistent, owing primarily to the historical difference between common law and equity, each originating in a different court. Thus, whereas common lawyers tend to talk of repudiating a contract, equity lawyers talk of rescinding or setting aside a contract. Further inconsistency arises from the special terminology used in relation to certain special contracts. For instance, in a contract of sale of goods, lawyers often talk of the buyer rejecting the goods rather than repudiating the contract, although this usually amounts to the same thing. Further confusion arises from the fact that lawyers use the word 'repudiation' indiscriminately to mean rightful and wrongful repudiation, and it may not always be clear which they mean.

Fortunately many of these problems have been cleared up by the decision of the House of Lords in *Johnson* v. *Agnew*.[4] A distinction was

---

[2] As to the legal position regarding forfeiture of deposits, see *post*, 438–9.
[3] But there is a strong rule of construction that a guilty party cannot rely on his own breach of contract to argue that the contract is terminated: *New Zealand Shipping Co* v. *Société des Atéliers et Chantiers de France* [1919] AC 1.    [4] [1980] AC 367.

here drawn between rescission of the contract *ab initio*, which prima facie has retrospective effect, and a mere subsequent termination of the contract. Where the whole contract is rescinded *ab initio* (for example, for pre-contractual misrepresentation), the principal function of the law is to restore the parties to the position they were in before the contract was made. Everything has to be undone, so far as practical, and no remedies for breach of the contract itself are available. So, for instance, a person who rescinds for misrepresentation cannot *also* claim damages for *breach of contract*. The two remedies would be inconsistent, because the innocent party would at one and the same time be asserting that the other party is guilty of failing to perform his contractual duties, while he would also be in process of removing those duties by rescinding the whole contract. The position is, however, complicated by the fact that damages may be recoverable for fraud or perhaps negligent misrepresentation, even where the contract is rescinded *ab initio*. This is because a claim for damages of this character is not based on the duties created by the contract: the innocent party is not demanding that the guilty party pay damages for failing to perform his promises, he is demanding that the guilty party pay damages for having misled him. It is not inconsistent at one and the same time to say: because of your misrepresentation, I want to rescind the contract *ab initio*, but you have also caused me loss by that misrepresentation and I claim damages for that.[5]

Where a contract is subsequently terminated for breach there is no *ab initio* rescission at all. The termination of the contract simply brings to an end any duty to perform obligations which have not yet been performed; and does not retrospectively eliminate the result of those breaches of contract which have already occurred. So in *Johnson* v. *Agnew* itself it was held that a buyer of land who acquiesces in the seller's failure to convey the land is not rescinding the whole contract *ab initio*, he is merely terminating the primary obligations (to pay and to convey) without in any way affecting his right to claim damages for breach of the contract.

We have classified the duties of the parties to a contract as those which arise under the contract, and those which arise independently of the contract. It must now be observed that, whereas a breach of one of the former duties only gives rise to a *right of termination*, and then only in certain circumstances, a breach of one of the latter nearly always gives rise to a *right to rescind*.

## Right to rescind

The latter cases may be disposed of first. There is, first, a general right to rescind for breach of any of the rules (mostly deriving originally from

---

[5] See e.g. *Archer* v. *Brown* [1984] 2 All ER 267.

equity) governing the way in which contracts are made. So pre-contractual fraud or misrepresentation, duress or undue influence, or other breach of a fiduciary obligation, prima facie confers an unqualified right of rescission. But in the case of misrepresentation, this is no longer always so today. Under the Misrepresentation Act 1967, a court may refuse to permit a contract to be rescinded for innocent misrepresentation (and may award damages in lieu) where it feels that rescission would be too drastic a remedy. But rescission remains the primary remedy for a breach of the duty of disclosure, where that exists, or an abuse of confidence by a person in a fiduciary position, or an exercise of duress or undue influence. The principles governing these duties have already been discussed, and it is only necessary to add three further comments here.

The first is that it is often unnecessary for the innocent party to do anything formal by way of rescinding the contract. In many circumstances, it is sufficient for him to defend an action for breach of contract by setting up the relevant facts as a defence. Merely pleading the facts as a defence is, in effect, treated as a way of rescinding the contract. Of course, where the facts are previously known it is unwise not to give notice of rescission, because the right may be lost or jeopardized by lapse of time, or by the possible intervention of third parties. And where the innocent party has transferred property to the other party under the contract, he may need the assistance of the court to get it back, but if the contract remains executory, he can sit tight, and await action by the other party.

The second comment which needs to be made is to draw attention to the importance of the distinction between executory and executed contracts in connection with claims for rescission. It is evident that rescission of an executed, or part executed, contract is often a *more* drastic remedy than merely awarding damages, while rescission of a wholly executory contract may well be a *less* drastic remedy. The point is that it is more trouble and may well cause more loss to attempt to unscramble the eggs once performance has begun. So one would expect the courts to be more willing to contemplate the remedy of recission *ab initio* where the contract remains wholly executory. Indeed, it was originally thought that rescission in equity was not available at all for innocent misrepresentation where the contract had been partly performed. This may well have been too rigid a rule and it was abrogated by the Misrepresentation Act 1967. So the courts now have power to order rescission even after a contract has been executed, but it seems very likely that in practice they will still tend to be more willing to grant the remedy where there has been no significant element of performance or reliance. Of course, this discussion only concerns innocent misrepresentation, as to which there is now the statutory discretion to award damages in lieu. In other cases, such as fraud or undue influence, the right to rescission *ab initio* remains unqualified, even where the contract has been executed, and even though in the result there may be serious difficulty in unscrambling the eggs.[6]

The third point to be made here is that (except in the case of misrepresentation which is now governed by a very complex regime of its own, and which is dealt with later[7]) rights of rescission are not usually accompanied by, or alternative to, claims for damages. Damages are (misrepresentation apart) only obtainable for a *breach of contract*, but the breach of a duty which arises independently of the contract is not treated by lawyers as a breach of contract. This can be a source of injustice, for example, where breach of a duty of disclosure leads to an insurance company's right to rescind or, in effect, to refuse to pay when an insured event occurs. Here the breach of duty may be relatively trivial, and justice could perhaps be better served if the court were able to award damages, or adjust the premium paid by the insured, while holding the insurer liable under the policy. But the court has no power to do this.[8]

### Right to terminate

A breach of a duty arising under the contract—that is *a breach of contract*—also gives rise to some difficulty. A breach of such a duty may take one of the following forms. It may consist simply in the non-performance of the whole contract. Alternatively, it may consist of a repudiation or refusal to perform. Again, it may take the form of defective performance. Finally, it may take the form of making a false statement of fact which is a term of the contract, that is (in the old terminology) a warranty or, more accurately, a promissory representation.

### (a) Non-Performance

The first case obviously causes no trouble in this context. Complete non-performance by one party naturally gives the other party the right to treat the contract as terminated. Indeed, it might be thought that the innocent party had no choice but to do so, without prejudice, of course, to any claim for damages he may have. However, the point is that the actual discharge of the contract cannot generally be effected by the unilateral action of the guilty party. If it should prove material, the dissolution will only date from the time when the innocent party has exercised his option to treat the contract as terminated.

---

[6] See *O'Sullivan* v. *Management Agency Ltd* [1985] QB 428, discussed further *post*, 411.
[7] See *post*, 441–3.
[8] See the comments of Lord Mustill in *Pan Atlantic Insurance Co Ltd* v. *Pine Top Insurance Co Ltd* [1994] 3 All ER 581 at 598.

## (b) Repudiation

The second case is almost identical to the first, and only requires a few words. Any intimation, whether by words or by conduct, that a party declines to continue with the contract is a repudiation if the result is likely to be to deprive the innocent party of substantially the whole benefit of the contract.[9] The principle itself is clear enough, although it is often difficult to apply in the circumstances of a particular case.

Indeed, there are a very large number of commercial cases which turn entirely on the application of this principle. What tends very often to happen in practice is that one party threatens to refuse to perform unless some condition is met, the other party declines to meet the condition, and the first then refuses to perform. Everything then hinges on whether the first party was entitled to demand that the condition should be met, and that often depends on careful examination of the terms of the contract, as well, perhaps, as on considerations of reasonableness.

In cases of this kind it is often immaterial that one or other party did not actually *intend* to sever the contractual relationship. If the threat is reasonably understood by the other party as a threat to deprive him of substantially the whole benefit of the contract, and it is an unjustified threat, then that will be sufficient to constitute a repudiation, and will justify the other party in throwing up the contract.

A repudiation by one party may occur before the time for performance has arrived. Such a repudiation is called an anticipatory breach, and it gives the innocent party the option of treating the contract as terminated at once and suing for damages immediately if he chooses or, alternatively, of waiting until the time of performance has arrived, and in the meantime calling on the other party to perform. However, if he waits, he keeps the contract alive for all purposes, and must himself remain ready to perform should he eventually be called upon to do so. So where charterers of a ship wrongfully repudiated by giving advance notice that they would not be ready to load when the ship arrived, and the owners refused to accept this repudiation, it was held that they had kept the contract alive, and therefore should still have brought the vessel into port to await loading.[10] This principle—that the innocent party must remain able and willing to perform if he keeps the contract alive—is, however, qualified by another principle, to the effect that, if the guilty party continues to make it quite clear that he will not perform, so that it would be a waste of time for the innocent party to make preparations for performance, then the latter can eventually abandon his attempts to perform.[11] This can either be seen as an ultimate

[9] *Federal Commerce & Navigation Ltd v. Molma Alpha Inc* [1979] AC 757.
[10] *Fercometal SARL v. Mediterranean Shipping Co SA* [1989] AC 788.
[11] *Ibid.*

acceptance by conduct of the repudiation, after its initial rejection, or as an act of induced reliance by the innocent party, which estops the guilty party from complaining about the former's inability to perform.

A further possible risk that the innocent party runs, should he choose to keep the contract alive between the date of an anticipatory repudiation and the date for performance, is that the contract may possibly become frustrated in the interim, in which case he will have lost his right to damages.

### (c) Defective performance

The third case of breach is that of defective performance, and this term is used in a wide sense to include all cases where there is a partial performance, or a complete performance which yet does not comply in all respects with the contract, such as belated performance. We have already discussed the distinction between conditions, warranties, and intermediate terms. As we have seen, breach of a condition always entitles the innocent party to terminate the contract, breach of a warranty never does so,[12] and breach of an intermediate term does so if the nature and consequences of the breach are sufficiently serious to justify this result. Where the breach justifies the innocent party in throwing up the whole contract, he has, once again, the choice between doing that or affirming the contract, while reserving any claim to damages. In some cases, too, he may be held to have waived the defective performance altogether, so as to deprive himself even of a right to damages.

### (d) Breach of a promissory representation

The fourth case is that of a misrepresentation of facts which is incorporated as a term in the contract, and thus becomes a promise. For instance, if a shipowner when chartering his ship states that it is at present in a certain port, this statement will normally constitute a condition of the contract, so if it is untrue, the other party can throw up the contract. It is also possible for a statement of fact to be incorporated into a contract as a warranty or (presumably) as an intermediate term. It was formerly arguable that a pre-contractual misrepresentation (which always gave rise to a right to rescind in equity) might lose this characteristic by being incorporated in the contract as a mere warranty. But since the Misrepresentation Act 1967 it is clear that the right to rescind is not lost in such circumstances.

---

[12] Insurance cases provide tiresome differences in terminology and possibly also of substantive law. In such cases it is well established that a 'warranty' is more like a condition, so that the insurer is not liable to pay claims which only arise from the insured's breach of warranty. Also, no specific repudiation is necessary: the insurer may simply refuse to pay a claim.

*Rescission, termination, and formation of contract*

Although the courts do not appear to have explicitly recognized it,[13] the principles governing rescission and termination for breach are closely parallel to the principles governing the formation of a contract, and therefore also to the principles governing the termination of a contract by agreement. In the first place, a person may be held to have repudiated a contract without intending to do so; it is not what a party intends that matters, but the reasonable interpretation that may be (and is) placed upon his words and behaviour by the other party. In the second place a breach or repudiation is treated very much like a contractual offer in that it has no legal effect until it is *accepted*. The other party is entitled either to accept or to affirm the contract, and thus in effect to reject the proposed termination. Thirdly, an acceptance may itself be express, or may be inferred from conduct. And fourthly, a party may be bound by an acceptance of a breach or repudiation either because he intended to accept it, or because he has led the other to believe that he intended to do so, and thereby induced him to act to his prejudice. This last possibility may be treated as an illustration of estoppel.

These principles appear to govern cases of rescission as well as many cases of breach and repudiation. As to rescission for misrepresentation, for instance, it was held in *Peyman* v. *Lanjani*[14] that the victim even of fraudulent misrepresentation must either rescind or affirm the contract (thus in effect rejecting the grounds for rescission). Although the court insisted that a person cannot be held to have intentionally affirmed the contract when he did not know of the fraud or of his right to rescind, they went on to hold that he may be held to have given the other party reason to think that he does intend to affirm, even where he does not know. This will not be binding on him unless and until it induces some act of reliance by the other party, whereas an express affirmation is binding forthwith.

That the same principles apply to cases of repudiation is confirmed by the decision of the House of Lords in *Fercometal SARL* v. *Mediterranean Shipping Co SA*.[15] Here it was again insisted that the innocent party must choose between keeping the contract alive for all purposes, or immediately terminating it, when there is a repudiation. If he keeps it alive he must remain ready and willing to perform himself, subject to the qualifications already discussed. So if he no longer is ready and willing to perform he may find that he is treated as being in breach himself.

These attempts to treat rescission and termination for breach as closely

---

[13] But for one dictum to this effect, see Winn LJ in *Denmark Productions Ltd* v. *Boscobel Productions Ltd* [1968] 3 All ER 513 at 527.    [14] [1985] Ch. 457.
[15] [1989] AC 788.

as possible to the principles governing the formation of contracts and termination by agreement possibly reflect the classical tradition. They seem prompted by a desire to see legal rights as deriving from the exercise of choices and intentional behaviour, rather than from conduct. They probably work well enough in most cases; but they do give rise to a number of difficulties. First, it must be appreciated that in this field—unlike the case of formation or termination of contract by express agreement—an 'acceptance' or a 'rejection' by inference from conduct is perhaps more often the rule than the exception. Thus it is often difficult to say whether a contract has been 'affirmed' so that the innocent party has lost his right to rescind or terminate.

Secondly, the rigid insistence that a contract can never be discharged by the unilateral breach of one party until it has been accepted by the other has caused a lot of trouble in employment contracts.[16] If an employee simply walks out after an argument and refuses to come to work again, few employers would see any necessity for giving notice to the employee that his breach has been 'accepted' and the contract terminated. Yet unless this is done there is a risk that the employment will be held not to have been terminated because the breach has not been accepted.

A third source of difficulty is that the innocent party is often placed in a dilemma, following a repudiation or breach, which does not always seem adequately allowed for by the courts. In a case like the *Fercometal* case, for instance, where the charterer wrongfully repudiates by saying that he cannot load the ship when loading is due, the innocent party is often placed in difficulties. On the one hand, he wants to claim damages for this breach, as he thinks it to be; but on the other hand, in the immediate hurly-burly of commercial activity it is not always clear what is a breach and what is a justified demand. So in such a case the shipowner may be desperately trying to do two things at once. He is trying to keep the contract alive, and so must be ready to perform if at the last minute the charterer says he will perform after all; and at the same time he is trying to ensure that, if the charterer fails to load, there may still be time to load the ship with another cargo. The innocent party can easily slip up in this situation, and may then be penalized either by reduced damages or even by being told that he cannot sue at all—as in the *Fercometal* case itself.

Some of these difficulties stem from the fact that English law makes no provision for a party to suspend performance when he has some reasonable ground for thinking that the other party may not himself perform. In the modern American law of contract this idea has been developed and there are some circumstances where it has clear utility; but in English law the

---

[16] See e.g. *Gunton* v. *London Borough of Richmond* [1980] 3 All ER 577. There have been many other cases centring round this difficulty.

innocent party must often take the risk of assuming that what has been done or said by the other party will ultimately be held to amount to a repudiation, and must then decide whether to accept this repudiation or try to salvage the contract.

In the above respects, the present rules may appear somewhat hard on the innocent party. But there is another respect—perhaps also a consequence of the close assimilation of these rules with those governing contract formation—in which the present law appears exceptionally favourable to the innocent party. The innocent party's right to terminate or rescind is very largely an absolute right, to be exercised at his complete free choice, just like the right to decide whether to enter into a contract in the first place. Certainly this is true of the common-law right to terminate, and although the right to rescind is an equitable remedy and is therefore in theory subject to the discretion of the court, it is in practice nearly always treated as just as absolute as the common-law right. This can have drastic consequences.

First, even if notice is required to terminate or rescind the contract, the innocent party does not have to give the guilty party an opportunity to rectify his breach or other wrong. Notice of instant termination or rescission is usually justified, although there are exceptions.[17] Secondly, it means that the innocent party is not bound to act reasonably, or even in good faith, except where statute provides otherwise, as with the remedy for unfair dismissal. If the guilty party is guilty of some trivial breach of contract (for instance, he performs a day or two late), the innocent party can terminate the contract even though the reason he wants to terminate has nothing whatever to do with the delay, as to which he may be quite indifferent. His real reason for doing so may be that the market has fallen and he wants to escape from a bad bargain. Similarly, if the guilty party has failed to disclose something which he should have disclosed, for instance, if an insured has failed to mention that his house has been burgled before, the insurer may repudiate liability, even though the claim is for fire damage and not for burglary at all.

There is another, closely associated, reason why these rules are exceptionally favourable to the innocent party. The rescission or termination of a contract will often cause loss to the guilty party which may be out of all proportion to the loss caused to the innocent party if he continues with the contract. Suppose, for instance, that goods are sold under a contract requiring them to be despatched from some distant overseas

---

[17] At common law (or in equity) notice to complete must be served where the complaint is of delay, giving the other party a reasonable time to complete if time is not of the essence, e.g. in many contracts for the sale of land: see e.g. *Graham* v. *Pitkin* [1992] 1 WLR 403. In other cases notice may be required by statute, e.g. under the Consumer Credit Act 1974.

country to an English buyer. If the goods fail in some trivial way to conform to the contract, or if they are despatched a day or two late, the buyer may suffer no, or very little, financial loss by accepting the goods. But if he exercises his right to reject them, the sellers may suffer huge financial loss. So far as they are concerned, the goods are in a distant land, earmarked for a particular buyer. If he does not take them the goods will remain perhaps in some port warehouse, subject to heavy charges; the sellers may have difficulty in finding agents to handle the goods; and they must then be resold perhaps in a falling market, with even more difficulty if the goods are unusual or were specially made to the buyer's order.[18] The law treats these factors as irrelevant: it does not attempt to balance the loss to the innocent party against the loss to the guilty party in determining whether there is a right to rescind or terminate.[19] This may well be unjust, and it may also be undesirable in the public interest. It is not desirable, economically speaking, for the law to sanction a result which causes a loss to one party greatly outweighing the gain to the other party, for this may lead to a net social loss.

But although the law ignores these factors, the parties themselves may choose not do so. Where the exercise of the right to rescind or terminate is likely to lead to a large difference between the gain to the innocent party and the loss to the guilty party, the parties may well attempt some renegotiation of their contract. The innocent party is, of course, in an immensely strong position to demand such renegotiation, such as a large discount off the price (if he is a buyer) or some other major concession if the contract is of a different character. There will often be difficulties in such renegotiation for a variety of reasons, but if they succeed they may have the welcome result of avoiding a social loss on the transaction. This may be desirable in itself, but it must lead to distributive consequences which are possibly also unacceptable. This is because the effect of such a renegotiation may be to give the innocent party compensation which is far higher than the damages which would be awarded if he sued for breach in

---

[18] See, for a good example, *Cehave NV* v. *Bremer Handelsgesellschaft (The Hansa Nord)* [1976] QB 44, where buyers (in Holland) rejected on trivial grounds goods imported by them, the goods were then stored by the port authorities and eventually resold by them by auction at a very low price, to defray port charges; the buyers actually bought the same goods at the auction and passed them on (without complaint) to their sub-buyers. Here justice was done (if at some perversion of legal principle) by holding that the buyers did not after all have any right of rejection.

[19] But in cases of misrepresentation, this is now subject to the Misrepresentation Act 1967 which gives the court power to award damages in lieu of rescinding a contract for innocent misrepresentation. This enables a court to balance the loss caused to the representee by continuing with the contract, and the loss which would be caused to the representor by rescinding the contract: *Sindall (William) plc* v. *Cambridgeshire CC* [1994] 3 All ER 932.

the ordinary way. Indeed, he is very likely to be able to make a significant profit from the defendant's breach of contract in this situation, something which is normally not permitted at all.

Although all this must be well known to practising lawyers and businessmen, it is almost never discussed in books on the law, or in legal cases raising these issues. But these extreme results may have been influential in persuading the courts to 'invent' the new category of intermediate term, where (as we saw earlier[20]) breach does not have these automatic and drastic consequences. Only where the nature and gravity of the consequences are serious enough to justify the result does breach of such an intermediate term give rise to a right to terminate. Hence in these cases the right to terminate is to some degree subject to judicial control; the court becomes judge of the gravity of the breach, and the matter is not left to the uncontrolled discretion of the innocent party.[21] But, of course, the earlier results remain wherever there is a breach of condition, or a right to rescind for some reason.

Although these earlier results appear to have been associated with classical contract law, and the invention of the 'intermediate' term may have been influenced by the general movement away from classical principles,[22] there does not appear to be any *necessary* connection between true freedom-of-contract principles and the idea that a right to rescind or terminate should be so absolute. In the absence of express stipulation in the contract, the consequences of a breach of contract (and *a fortiori* of a breach of a duty arising outside the contract) are for the law to specify. Even though the law is in theory based on what is presumed to be the intentions of reasonable contracting parties, it is far from clear that the present rules are justifiable. Do reasonable contracting parties want the right to behave in an unreasonable manner? Some might respond that what they want is rather the right to be the sole judge of what is reasonable, but this is an unacceptable claim—it violates the first principles of justice that a party should claim to be judge in his own cause. Nor does there appear to be any economic justification for permitting a right to rescind or to terminate to be used where it would inflict loss out of all proportion to the benefit to the innocent party. So any belief that the 'tough' rules of the classical law ought to be supported by those who adhere generally to freedom-of-contract principles appears to be an unfounded gut re-action.

---

[20] *Supra*, 176.

[21] Compare the HL decisions in *Reardon Smith Lines* v. *Hansen Tangen* [1976] 1 WLR 989 and *Bowes* v. *Shand* (1877) 2 App. Cas. 455.

[22] With *Bunge* v. *Tradax* [1981] 1 WLR 711 (*supra*, 174) perhaps indicating a reversion to classical principles?

## 3. THE EFFECTS OF TERMINATION

Where a contract is terminated without being rescinded *ab initio*, the normal consequences (unless the contract itself provides otherwise) are these. First, the guilty party is absolved from further performance of the primary duties under the contract, but these duties are replaced by the secondary obligation to pay damages. Secondly, the innocent party is also absolved from having to perform any duties not yet due under the contract, and is indeed freed from all further liability, subject to the question of obligations which had already accrued but not been performed. Thirdly, both parties may remain liable in respect of accrued obligations which should have been performed before the termination, but it remains obscure how far these obligations extend. Although it seems clear enough that the innocent party's previously accrued obligations remain binding on him even after the termination, it is uncertain how far the guilty party's accrued obligations remain binding and how far they are absorbed in the new secondary obligation to pay damages. This last point raises particularly acute difficulties in certain contracts of sale of goods, and especially in sales in which the price is payable by instalments. If the buyer is obliged to pay the price before the date for delivery and fails to do so, it is clear that he can be sued for damages for this failure. But is he still liable to pay the price? And if he has paid it, can he recover it?

In *Dies* v. *British & International Mining etc. Corp*[23] the buyers paid a large part of the price of goods in advance, and then defaulted in the payment of the balance, so the sellers refused to deliver the goods. The buyers admitted their liability for damages, but recovered their advance payment on the ground of total failure of consideration. In modern terms it would be said that the buyers' obligation to pay the whole price (including that part which had already been paid) was replaced by their liability to pay damages. But in *Hyundai Heavy Industries Co Ltd* v. *Papadopoulos*,[24] which was a shipbuilding case in which the price was payable by instalments as the work proceeded, the House of Lords held that the buyer could be sued for an instalment which fell due on 15 July, despite the fact that the seller exercised a contractual right of cancellation on 6 September. This seemed to follow from the newly established distinction between rescission *ab initio* and termination—the latter, not being retrospective, was thought to leave standing the accrued obligation to play the July instalment.

The distinction between these two cases was authoritatively explained by the Court of Appeal in *Rover International* v. *Cannon Film Sales*.[25] In this

---

[23] [1939] 1 KB 724.    [24] [1980] 1 WLR 1129.
[25] [1989] 1 WLR 912. It is doubtful if the earlier CA decision in *Damon Cia Naviera* v. *Hapag-lloyd* [1985] 1 WLR 435 (as to which see *post*, 439) can stand with this much better considered decision.

case the C company and the P company entered into a contract under which P was to distribute C's films in Italy. P was to pay in advance three instalments, the final one of $900,000 being due on 30 September 1986. P failed to pay this instalment and C treated this as a breach justifying immediate termination as it was expressly entitled to do under the contract. C thus became entitled to claim damages for its loss under the contract, but also sued for payment of the $900,000 in addition to the damages to which it was entitled. This further claim was rejected by the Court of Appeal which held that there was no consideration for this sum of $900,000, so that if it had been paid P could have recovered it (despite their later breach) on the ground of total failure of consideration. *A fortiori* the money ceased to be payable and could not be sued for once the contract was terminated. The *Hyundai* case was distinguished on the ground that in that case the contract was to *construct* and deliver the ship in question. In that case therefore the shipbuilders were providing consideration all along, as the construction of the ship proceeded. While the *Rover International* case is helpful in limiting the effect of the *Hyundai* decision, the latter is still liable to give rise to serious injustice in some situations, as for instance if the buyer in that case had been obliged to pay the whole price before the contract was repudiated.

As we have seen, in general, termination of the contract, unlike rescission *ab initio*, does not involve an undoing of what has already been performed under the contract. But there are some circumstances in which even termination does involve some attempt to undo an actual performance, and in these cases the distinction between termination and rescission is often obscured. The simplest example of this is the case of faulty or defective goods supplied under a contract of sale. If, as is likely to be the case, the fault or defect means that the seller is guilty of a breach of condition, then the buyer may terminate the contract, but in this event he must return the goods to the seller by rejecting them. He may then claim damages for breach of contract. It has never been suggested that because the seller's obligation to deliver the goods is due *before* the contract is terminated, therefore the buyer can terminate *and* keep the goods, while still suing for damages.

## 4. THE EFFECTS OF RESCISSION

The effects of rescission are, broadly speaking, the same whatever the ground on which it is sought, although there are certain differences in detail, and certain differences in the application of the same rules to different classes of cases. The first and most obvious result of rescinding a contract is that, so far as is possible, the position of the parties must be restored to what it was before the contract was made. Where it is completely impossible to do this, rescission may not be possible at all. For instance a buyer of goods who wishes to rescind the contract, whether on the ground of fraud or of innocent misrepresentation or of breach of any other duty arising independently of the contract, can only do so if he is ready and willing to restore the goods to the seller. If this is not possible, for example, because the buyer has already resold the goods to a third party, the contract cannot be rescinded. The buyer must then fall back on his remedy in damages, if any. More difficulty arises where rescission is only partially possible, as, for instance, where a person bought some mines from the defendant and wished to have the contract rescinded after the mines had been partially exploited. In such cases the principle to be applied is that there must be a substantial restoration of benefits received, but the application of the principle tends to vary according to the ground on which rescission is claimed. Where restoration proves impossible owing to the very breach of duty which is alleged to give rise to the right of rescission, as where a seller sells goods which belong to another, and are reclaimed by that other, there is no bar to a rescission of the contract so far as is possible.[26] So also, where there has been fraud, the court is much more willing to assist the innocent party than where there has merely been an innocent misrepresentation.

In the absence of fraud, rescission often requires a rough and ready adjustment of mutual benefits. For instance, in *O'Sullivan* v. *Management Agency Ltd*[27] a series of contracts between a young singer and his manager/agent for the exploitation of his songs were set aside after they had been fully performed, and the singer had achieved world-wide fame, even though restitution was not fully possible. In such a case, undoing the contracts is largely an accounting matter of paperwork. The manager/agent was ordered to return all payments received under the contracts, but was allowed to set off against this a reasonable allowance for his services. He was entitled to that because this, in turn, was a benefit rendered to the singer, and therefore some payment had to be made for it when the contracts were rescinded. In other words the contracts were substantially remade by the court, with the manager/agent's remuneration being drastically reduced.

A similar result was reached recently in *Cheese* v. *Thomas*[28] where a contract between a man and his great-nephew to a buy a house jointly, with each contributing substantially to the price, was set aside for undue influence. The house had lost approximately a third of its value but, because the nephew had been relatively innocent, the court ordered the loss to be divided between the parties in proportion to their original contributions.

[26] *Rowland* v. *Divall* [1923] 2 KB 500 (strictly, a case of termination, not rescission).
[27] *Supra*, n. 6.          [28] [1994] 1 All ER 35.

So stringent is the requirement that all benefits must be restored if a contract is to be rescinded, that it sometimes overrides even an express stipulation in the contract. If, for instance, the contract provides that on rescission the innocent party shall be entitled to keep any money received, this may amount to a forfeiture clause, which may be void.[29]

The obverse of the rule that benefits must be restored when a contract is rescinded is that an indemnity must be given in respect of all burdens that have been assumed under it. Generally speaking the right to such an indemnity is swallowed up in the much larger and more comprehensive right to damages which often accompanies a right of rescission. In many cases, however, there will be no right to damages when a contract is rescinded (for instance, for innocent misrepresentation). In these cases, therefore, the right to an indemnity may be important. This right is far less extensive than the right to damages, for it only covers burdens which were the necessary result of the actual contract itself, and not loss or damage which was the consequence of the facts misrepresented. For instance, where a person bought a poultry farm as a result of an innocent misrepresentation concerning the sanitation, and then claimed rescission of the contract, he was held entitled to an indemnity in respect of rates which he had paid, but not to damages in respect of loss of some of the poultry through disease.[30]

## 5. LIMITS ON THE RIGHTS OF TERMINATION AND RESCISSION

The rights to rescind or terminate a contract, whatever their source, are in all cases subject to certain restrictions. In the first place, as we have seen, if substantial restoration of benefits is not possible the plaintiff may no longer have the right to rescind at all. This limit on the right does not apply to all cases of termination because termination is not retrospective and, if there is a serious enough breach of contract, termination is a matter of right, however inconvenient and troublesome the subsequent adjustments have to be. But even the right to terminate may be lost in some cases, as we saw above, such as in contracts of sale of goods where, for example, it is not possible for the buyer to restore the goods. And as we shall see below, the right to terminate may also be lost in other ways which to some degree cater for the difficulties which can arise where the contract cannot easily be brought to an end in practice, such as by affirmation or waiver.

In the second place, the right to rescind or terminate a contract involves the exercise of a choice between affirming it and bringing it to an end. A person entitled to rescind or terminate a contract must make this choice,

---

[29] See *post*, 437, as to forfeiture clauses.
[30] *Whittington* v. *Seale-Hayne* (1900) 16 LTR 181.

and he cannot equivocate without danger of losing his right of rescission or termination. As we have noted, he has no right to suspend his own performance while he waits to see if the other party intends definitely to go ahead or not. So if he leads the other party to think that he prefers to carry on with the contract, subject to any claim for damages which he may have, he cannot afterwards turn round and insist on rescission or termination after all. What precisely amounts to an affirmation of the contract naturally depends on the type of contract in question, and the ground on which rescission or termination is sought. The general principles have tended to be worked out in detail in individual contracts, although there is still some residual problem arising from the fact that termination is a common law remedy, while rescission comes from equity. A simple modern example from the law of sale of goods (where the right to terminate is subject to express statutory rules corresponding to the common law doctrine of affirmation) is provided by *Bernstein* v. *Pamson Motors (Golders Green) Ltd*,[31] where the plaintiff bought a new car from the defendants for about £8,000, but within three weeks, and after only 140 miles had been done, the car broke down on a motorway and had to be towed away by emergency services. It was held that the buyer had lost his right to terminate (here, to reject the car) because he had had sufficient time to test the car for ordinary driving. Of course the plaintiff retained his right to damages.

As we have previously seen, it is now settled that a person cannot be held to have affirmed the contract or 'rejected' his right to terminate or rescind unless he was aware of the facts and of his rights, but even if he was not aware of them, he may lose the right to terminate or rescind by inducing the other party to act in reliance on the belief that he does not intend to terminate or rescind.[32] In some earlier cases in equity, other formulations are to be found, and there is much discussion of a principle of 'acquiescence' in some cases. There is also reliance on the concept of 'waiver' in many cases. But there is no reason to multiply doctrines and concepts unnecessarily, and it seems that today these cases of acquiescence and waiver may be explained as simple variants of the principle of affirmation.[33] Of course, in the case of waiver, it is necessary to distinguish between cases in which the right to rescind or terminate has been waived, and the possibility that the entire breach has been waived. The latter would deprive the innocent party even of the right to claim damages, and although such a waiver is perfectly possible, it is not lightly to be inferred.

There is some authority for suggesting that undue delay in exercising the

[31] [1987] 2 All ER 220.
[32] See the *Fercometal* case, *supra*, n. 10 and *Peyman* v. *Lanjani*, *supra*, n. 14.
[33] See e.g. Nourse LJ in *Goldsworthy* v. *Brickell* [1987] 1 All ER 853 at 873.

right to terminate or rescind may also deprive the innocent party of his right, though these cases may need re-examination today in the light of the modern authorities which distinguish so clearly between an intentional affirmation, and an affirmation which is binding by virtue of induced reliance or estoppel. Perhaps today it would be held that delay would only be treated as an affirmation of the contract if it could be brought within one or other of these two categories.[34] But it is possible that where the delay is inordinate—a matter of years rather than weeks or months—it might preclude rescission whether or not there was any intention to affirm, or any induced reliance.[35] This may seem hard where the innocent party acts with promptitude as soon as he discovers the facts, but there must be an end to transactions sometime, and the other party is entitled to assume that the innocent party is content with the contract if he does not act within a reasonable time after the contract was performed. But even if this is right, it is not apparently the law where fraud or some other deception is involved, such as an abuse of a fiduciary position.

The third general principle restricting the right to rescind is that a contract cannot generally be rescinded to the prejudice of innocent third parties. One kind of case where this produces important results is that of documents signed by a party who is deceived as to their contents by the fraud of another. Obviously the fraudulent party cannot sue on the documents; but if they are passed on to innocent third parties who act upon them then the deceived party will be liable unless he can rely on the plea of *non est factum*.[36] But the most common practical application of the principle is in the case of goods bought by fraud, and then resold to a bona fide purchaser for value without notice of the fraud. In such cases the third party gets a good title to the goods, and the innocent party to the original contract cannot divest the third party of his title by rescinding the contract. This rule only applies to cases where rescission is necessary, that is to say it has no application to contracts which are completely void. Where a contract of sale is totally void, whether because of mistake, or for any other reason, no rescission is necessary, no title passes, and the original owner can recover the goods even from an innocent third party. Nor does the rule apply to an assignment of rights, as opposed to a sale of goods, for, as we have seen, an assignment is subject to equities. Hence a contract can be rescinded to the prejudice of an innocent assignee.

---

[34] See also the cases on the possibility of inferring an abandonment of an arbitration from mere inactivity: *The Splendid Sun* [1981] 1 QB 694; *The Hannah Blumenthal* [1983] 1 AC 854; *The Leonidas D* [1985] 1 WLR 925; *Food Corp of India* v. *Antclizo Shipping Corp* [1988] 2 All ER 513.

[35] *Leaf* v. *International Galleries* [1950] 2 KB 86.

[36] *Saunders* v. *Anglia Building Society* [1971] AC 1004, *supra*, 184.

The above-mentioned principle is always stated as applicable to cases of rescission, and it is perhaps not wholly clear if it also applies to all cases of termination. In practice an innocent third party will usually have rights which prevent termination as much as rescission, certainly in cases of sale of goods, where the buyer may wish to reject the goods. For instance, if he has pledged the goods or documents of title to them, he will be unable to reject them so as to deprive the pledgee of his rights. Of course if the buyer has resold the goods the question will hardly arise, because there can be no reason why he should then want to reject them, at any rate, unless and until the resale is also rescinded and the goods are restored to him.

# 22

# Remedies for Breach of Contract

## I. THE PURPOSE OF CONTRACTUAL REMEDIES

CONTRACT law provides a battery of remedies as sanctions against those who breach their contracts. In one sense these remedies are remarkable examples of the willingness of the state to lend its assistance to the enforcement of private arrangements, and therefore a demonstration of the importance in our society of private arrangements for social and economic purposes. When a contracting party goes to law, and obtains a judgment against his defaulting partner, he obtains the right to the support of all the forces of the state to enforce that judgment. In the last resort bailiffs, sheriff's officers, the police, and even the armed forces can be called in to enforce that contract—and all this at the behest of a private citizen who has no official standing in the state. But in another sense the legal remedies available for breach of contract are very mild. It is (in general) no crime to break a contract. It is a crime to cheat or defraud someone, but it is not a crime simply to fail to pay a debt. It is not even a crime to refuse to pay a debt when the debtor is perfectly capable of paying it. So a breach of contract is not normally something of which state officials will take cognizance before the plaintiff obtains a judgment of a court and seeks their assistance in enforcing his judgment.

Moreover, even when the plaintiff comes to the court for assistance in enforcing his contract, it often seems that the court is not disposed to take a very serious view of breaches of contract. First (as we shall see), it rarely orders the contract to be performed—it is not generally the function of the court to compel the performance of a contract. The courts do have power to make a decree of specific performance (or to grant some other form of what is called specific relief) to compel the performance of a contract but this is rarely exercised except in certain limited classes of cases. Nor does contract law sanction the award of punitive damages, such as are occasionally awarded in tort, by way of punishment, to express the community's sense of outrage at the injuries inflicted on the plaintiff, or at the way he has been treated—as, for instance, where he has been assaulted by police officers. Indeed, even the award of damages for non-pecuniary loss, an everyday affair in tort law, is severely restricted in contract cases. The chief legal remedies for breach of contractual duties are rescission or termination of the contract, and an action for damages for the financial loss occasioned by the breach. But many breaches of contract cause no financial loss, and then only nominal damages can be recovered; and when that is the case it is debateable to what extent the contract was 'really' binding on the defendant.

Secondly, it is not even clear that a breach of contract is an *unlawful* act. The famous American jurist and judge, Oliver Wendell Holmes, used to argue that a contracting party was only bound *either* to perform his contract, *or* to pay for the loss caused thereby. Hence if he chose to pay for the loss, he did no wrong; he merely chose one of the two ways of performing his obligation. This is a point of view which might commend itself to an economist or a businessman even today. A businessman usually makes contracts in order to make a profit, and if the other party tenders him the profit, he is unlikely to complain that the contract has not been performed. So also, an economist might say that every contract has a monetary value, that every contracting party enters into a contract because he thinks that the performance of the other party is worth more to him than the cost of his own performance. Hence each contracting party expects to gain the difference in the value of the two performances—since the values are partly subjective, it is of course possible (and usual) for both parties to expect to make a surplus. So a contracting party who is paid damages or compensation representing this difference between the value (to him) of the two performances receives all that he expected to gain, and all that he is entitled to. Once this is done, no further sanctions are needed.

But this is not a view which has much support among English jurists and judges. They tend to insist that a contract does create a legal obligation to perform, so that a breach is an unlawful act, even though that unlawful act may not be visited with severe, or sometimes any, sanctions, if the defendant promptly pays up. And it is true that there are a number of specific legal rules which do appear to suggest that a party has a genuine obligation to perform his contract and that in some circumstances a breach of contract will be treated as something unlawful—for instance, the availability (albeit in only a few cases) of specific relief and the tort of interference with contractual rights do presuppose that a contracting party has a legal right to the performance of the contract, and his co-contractor a legal duty to perform it. But we have repeatedly stressed throughout this book that the law tends to distinguish in practice, and sometimes also in formal legal rules, between wholly executory contracts and partly performed contracts. Where the latter are concerned, the similarities between contract and tort (or equity, or restitution) are great, and in many such cases it would be hard to deny that breach of contract is indeed regarded as wrongful by the law, and requires serious and adequate sanctioning. On the other hand, as regards wholly executory contracts, there are many circumstances in which the legal sanction for non-performance are so weak that it cannot be said that Holmes's view has been totally rejected by the realities of English law, whatever the theory of the matter may be. Moreover, Holmes's views gain some support from the fact that the law does not in general distinguish between the contract-breaker who makes every good faith effort to perform his contract, and the contract-breaker who acts in cynical disregard of his contractual obligations, coolly calculating that it will be more profitable for him to breach than to perform. At this point it will suffice to give four examples, some of which will be discussed in more detail later.

First, in many executory contracts breach is not followed by any 'loss' as the law understands that term, and there is simply no legal remedy at all, other than a claim for purely nominal damages. A seller fails to deliver goods which are readily available in the market at the same price as the contract price. There is no effective legal sanction for this at all.

Secondly (and this is not just a matter of executory contracts), the sanctions imposed by the law for the non-payment of debts are very weak indeed. The creditor is entitled to sue for the debt and for any costs incurred, and he may sometimes obtain interest for the period during which the debt has been outstanding. But beyond this, the debtor will rarely be liable for any additional losses or inconvenience caused, nor is he liable to any sanctions, however unjustified or outrageous his behaviour may have been. An insurance company, for instance, which refuses to pay a manifestly due claim may cause great inconvenience and perhaps also financial loss to the insured, and their behaviour may be totally unacceptable in ordinary commercial and legal terms. Yet there is in English law no sanction for this, other than the payment of costs and interest.

A third situation illustrating the extreme weakness of contractual sanctions has recently come to light because the criminal law has been invoked to fill the gap left by contract law. A credit-card holder is often given a credit limit which he is contractually bound not to exceed, but if he does exceed it, no contractual penalty at all is incurred. The card holder has to pay the credit-card company, of course, but he would have to pay them that sum anyhow. So the imposition of the limit has no real penalty to it, so far as contract law is concerned. Perhaps for this reason, credit-card companies have invoked the criminal law by occasionally prosecuting for fraud those who exceed the agreed limits. Even this seemed a somewhat questionable proceeding, according to the Court of Appeal, which took the view that since the credit-card company would have to pay for the goods or services supplied in excess of the limit, no real fraud had been committed. But the House of Lords has taken a different view,[1] no doubt to the relief of the credit-card companies who would otherwise have been left without any sanction at all for breach of agreed limits.

---

[1] *R* v. *Charles* [1977] AC 179; *R* v. *Lambie* [1982] AC 449.

A fourth type of case which reveals the weakness of contractual sanctions is well illustrated by an American case from the last century. In *City of New Orleans* v. *Firemen's Charitable Association*[2] a contract was entered into between the plaintiff city authorities and the defendants for the supply of fire-fighting services. The defendants contracted to keep 124 men, a specified number of horses, and a quantity of hoses available for the fighting of fires. The plaintiff city claimed that the defendants had in fact maintained fewer men, horses, and equipment than the contract required, and thereby saved themselves some $38,000, but the plaintiffs did not allege, and presumably could not prove, that the defendants had failed to put out any fires as a result of this deficiency. It was held by the Louisiana court that the plaintiffs had no redress for this breach of contract because they had not proved any 'loss' resulting from it, a decision which is entirely in accordance with English law. The result certainly seems to indicate an extreme weakness in the sanctions sometimes available for breach of contract. We will return to this case later.

## 2. SELF-HELP

Before we turn to judicial remedies for breach of contract, it is advisable to examine the possibilities of redress for a plaintiff which do not involve going to court at all. Virtually everybody would prefer to obtain redress, if they could, without having to go to court. Courts are expensive, slow, and liable to make mistakes. Creditors, especially, are prone to think that courts are over-sympathetic to debtors, so they often seek some way of obtaining redress without having to sue for it, or, if they have to sue for it, of making the outcome of the proceedings as simple and inevitable as possible. For some centuries, indeed, a battle has raged between creditors (using this in a broad sense) who have sought to find some way of extra-judicial enforcement of their contracts, and debtors, who have tried to force creditors to go to court before they can exercise their remedies. It will be enough to give a few illustrations of this long history.

One of the most effective means of enforcing debts—though not other contractual obligations—was at one time imprisonment for debt. In its full glory, this system was self-help gone mad. The plaintiff only had to issue a writ claiming the debt (plus costs), and he could then proceed to arrest the debtor and incarcerate him in a debtor's jail. There the debtor remained as a prisoner of the creditor (not of the state) until he paid, or at least compounded with his creditor, or was released as an act of mercy by Parliament which every now and then emptied the debtors' jail of those who had been there over twelve months. But this form of imprisonment for

[2] (1819) 9 So. 486.

debt—before a judgment had even been given—was abolished in 1838. It remained possible to imprison a debtor long after that, but only after first suing and obtaining a judgment, so this had ceased to be a self-help remedy.

Another type of self-help remedy was (and still is, of course) to take some kind of security from the debtor. Originally, the creditor might demand a conveyance of some land, the debtor simply having the right to a re-conveyance if he paid off the debt when due. At first this was perhaps pure self-help. If the debtor failed to pay, the creditor simply retained the land by virtue of his conveyance. No legal or other action was needed. But then equity began to intervene, allowing debtors to pay off the debt after it was due, so the creditor never knew for sure whether his self-help remedy was secure. In order to prevent the debtor claiming to re-open the transaction beyond a certain point it became possible for the creditor to apply himself to a court of equity for a foreclosure decree, which would shut out the debtor if he still failed to pay after yet further opportunities. But this meant that the creditor was compelled to go to court to realize his security, one of the very things the security was designed to obviate. So the mortgage ceased to be a self-help remedy and foreclosure decrees became rather unpopular.

The next development was the mortgage which granted the creditor the power to sell the mortgaged property. From the creditor's point of view, this was far more satisfactory. Once the property was sold, the debtor could no longer demand further opportunities to pay off the debt and get his property back. Of course, the debtor had to be given the chance to contest a proposed sale, but this threw on to him the onus of taking proceedings. The creditor had no need to sue, and if the debtor failed to take proceedings, as most do, the remedy became a true self-help remedy once again. And so it remains today. Indeed, the mortgage of today often involves a two-stage self-help procedure. It is today very common for a debtor simply to deposit (say with a bank) documents, like title deeds or land- or share-certificates, as security for a loan. Rather than consisting of a long and complex security document, the modern mortgage or charge often consists of a simple deposit of documents with a very short, signed contract. This contract gives the creditor an irrevocable authority to execute a full mortgage or charge, as agent for the debtor, to itself, as creditor. This, again, is done as a pure matter of self-help, and once executed, the full mortgage or charge can be enforced by the power of sale. (Building society mortgages are not like this, however: they do involve a full legal mortgage from the outset.)

All these are traditional devices to enable creditors to enforce debts by self-help means. But there are many other possibilities of using self-help, some of which can be used for enforcing claims to damages, as well as claims to debts. Many of these are extremely simple, such as requiring advance payment; or, conversely, insisting that full payment will not be made until the other party has completely performed, or even (as is common with building and construction contracts) that a part of the contract price will be retained and only paid over several months after full performance is complete.

Other methods of self-help may involve some minimal degree of co-operation by third parties, but they can be designed so as to be almost entirely self-help remedies. For instance, it is now common in certain kinds of transactions to find that contracting parties are required to provide guarantors of unimpeachable integrity, such as leading banks or insurance companies. But what makes these remedies virtually a type of self-help remedy is that the guarantor is often required to agree to pay the claim (perhaps up to a specified maximum sum) on the mere demand of the creditor. So if the creditor claims that the other party is guilty of a breach of contract, he may simply write to the guarantor demanding payment and, with guarantors of this class, payment is assured. The guarantor will then claim an indemnity from the other contracting party, and that party may yet have a legal right to challenge the creditor's actions in claiming on the guarantee. But the onus of suing is on him and, in the meantime, the creditor has the money. To commercial people these are very important considerations indeed.

Many other kinds of self-help remedies exist, though they are not usually identified as such, or discussed together as involving similar principles. Rights of termination and of rescission, for instance, which were discussed in the last chapter, are self-help remedies. They do not require the assistance of the courts, although of course (like all self-help remedies) their use can be challenged in the courts by the other party. But this throws the onus of litigation on to that party, and the dislike of litigation is so great that the onus often means that there simply will be no action. At the least, shifting the onus can make a significant difference to the effectiveness of the remedy. So, for instance, some modern statutes (of a consumer protection kind) often do shift the onus, by requiring that a court order be obtained before certain remedies (otherwise self-help remedies) can be exercised. So, today, a landlord cannot lawfully throw a tenant out of a rented dwelling-house unless he first gets an eviction order from a court, no matter what the lease may say, and no matter how badly the tenant has behaved. So also, under the Consumer Credit Act a hire-purchase company cannot lawfully retake goods let under a hire-purchase contract after one third of the price has been paid, unless a court order is obtained. Today there is pressure to prevent electricity, gas, and water companies from cutting off supplies (again a form of self-help) without a court order, though at present no such order is required, and provided statutory procedures are observed, there is even a power of compulsory entry, by force if necessary, to effectuate this remedy.

All these restrictions on contractual self-help remedies raise similar issues to those which were discussed above,[3] in connection with the Unfair Contract Terms Act. Restricting the use of such remedies may eventually drive up the cost of the services for those who pay promptly. Court orders are costly and slow, and they often allow time to pay, during which further debts may be incurred, some of which may never be recovered at all. All these losses must, of course, ultimately be borne by the honest and regular payers of the services in question. Furthermore, if the use of self-help remedies is limited against debtors whose creditworthiness is low, the result may be that they are unable to obtain credit at all, or only on worse terms. If tenants cannot be evicted without court orders, landlords may take (have taken) to demanding deposits (or larger deposits) from tenants. In the case of gas and electricity supplies, the use of pre-paid slot meters is a far more effective way of ensuring payment by those with low creditworthiness than requiring court orders for disconnections. Thus statutory restrictions on self-help remedies like these need careful examination before they are introduced; it cannot always be assumed that they are in the real interest of those they appear designed to protect. On the other hand, as we have already seen, the law may at present go too far in making rescission and termination such uncontrolled remedies that reasonableness and good faith are irrelevant to their exercise.

Another kind of self-help remedy, which can be of great importance in certain situations, is the right of set-off. In the past, employers were often accused of abusing this right, by making unfair and unauthorized deductions from the pay of an employee (for instance, for alleged bad work, or for breakages or losses) and such deductions have been subject to legal control under the Truck Acts for many years. Recently, however, the Wages Act 1986 has liberalized the law a good deal, in the sense of modifying many of the former statutory controls, and leaving the matter largely (but not entirely) to the regulation of individual contracts of employment. One other interesting recent example of the use of the employer's right of set-off as a self-help remedy is provided by the case of local authorities who have deducted pay from teachers involved in 'industrial action'. Of course an employee who goes on strike gets no pay; but an employee who simply refuses to perform a certain part of his duties—a teacher who refuses to teach certain classes, for instance—poses practical problems for an employer. The amounts involved in each case are often small, and the number of cases may be very large, so legal action for breach of contract is hardly practicable. But it has recently been held that

---

[3] *Supra*, 308–312.

employers are entitled to deduct a proportionate part of the employee's pay as a set-off against such breaches of contract;[4] naturally, the employer will fix the way of calculating the proportion, leaving it to the employee to challenge him in the courts. So here the onus of litigation is left firmly on the employee.

Of course rights of set-off can exist the other way round—the debtor may be the person claiming a set-off and in that case a right of set-off may actually impede self-help by the creditor. A landlord, for instance, who wishes to exercise his self-help right to distrain on the tenant's goods (to seize them, that is, with a view to their ultimate sale) could be frustrated if the tenant was entitled to claim that the landlord was guilty (say) of breach of covenant to repair, and sought to set off that liability against his rent. But it has recently been held that the tenant is prima facie entitled to do this.[4a] In order to prevent this it is very common for certain types of contract (such as leases) to exclude rights of set-off, but very clear words are needed to achieve this result.[4b] It has also been held that a clause excluding all rights of set-off may fall foul of the Unfair Contract Terms Act, as being unreasonable and void.[5]

Another very common form of self-help remedy, which gives cause for concern in certain situations, is the forfeiture of advance payments or deposits. Some businesses (holiday companies, for instance) habitually demand 'deposits' or part payment in advance. If the company then claims a breach of contract by the other party, it may simply claim to 'forfeit' the deposit or advance payment. Here there is some measure of legal control, as we shall see later, in that some types of forfeiture are void, and advance payments (but not deposits) are recoverable. But in practice, because this is a self-help remedy, it is unlikely that many challenges will be made to forfeitures even when there is legal ground to do so.

There is a sort of half-way house kind of remedy in which legal action to enforce the contractual right may be needed, but the legal action is of a very simple type, in which procedures are streamlined, defences often shut out, and court orders easily obtained. Cheques and promissory notes and other bills of exchange, for instance, can be enforced by a very quick and simple procedure in the courts, which does not usually permit the defendant to raise any defence, except an allegation as to the very validity of the document in question. So a contracting party may demand bills of exchange or cheques in advance as a kind of half-way self-help remedy in some kinds of transactions. Even a buyer of goods who pays by cheque can be sued on the cheque in such a way that he cannot raise ordinary defences,

---

[4] See *Sim* v. *Rotherham Met. BC* [1987] Ch. 216; *Royle* v. *Trafford* [1984] IRLR 184.
[4a] *Eller* v. *Grovecrest Investments Ltd* [1994] 4 All ER 845.
[4b] *Connaught Restaurants Ltd* v. *Indoor Leisure Ltd* [1994] 4 All ER 834.
[5] *Stewart Gill Ltd* v. *Horatio Meyer & Co Ltd* [1992] 1 QB 600.

such as claiming that the goods were defective. He can still make such a claim; but not in the proceedings on the cheque. He must, in other words, pay first, and argue afterwards. This may seem odd, and it is perhaps unacceptable in consumer transactions; but it is more justifiable in commercial transactions because the whole point of demanding a cheque is to give the seller this degree of self-help entitlement.

Like the remedies of rescission and termination, all self-help remedies give rise to the possibility that they may be used where their use would cause more loss to the defendant than gain to the plaintiff. Indeed, they are often wanted for their deterrence value, precisely for this reason. A hire-purchase company which retakes a few pieces of cheap furniture or a battered television set, from the hirer is unlikely get much from reselling them, after payment of its costs. But the threatened loss to the hirer may be great enough to induce him to pay up. In such a case the remedy may not be unjustified (though it only remains self-help if one third of the price has not yet been paid, after which a court order is needed). But there may be other cases where, as with rescission and termination, the threat of using a self-help remedy may be made in order to extract compensation at a level higher than could be obtained in damages. This also may be thought to be a cause for some concern.

### 3. SPECIFIC PERFORMANCE AND INJUNCTION

As a general principle a person who complains of a breach of contract cannot compel the actual performance of the contract by the other party, but must rest content with compensation in terms of money. In certain circumstances, however, it has long been traditional to say that mere damages would be an inadequate remedy, and in these cases the court may grant a decree of specific performance or injunction, ordering the defendant to do, or abstain from doing, the very thing he agreed upon. The main sanction behind these decrees is the threat of imprisonment for contempt of court, but in certain cases it is now possible for the court to order the contract to be executed by its officials in the event of the defendant proving contumacious. This, of course, is only possible where the defendant's personal assistance is not required.

Broadly speaking a decree of specific performance is appropriate when the defendant has contracted to do something, while an injunction is appropriate when he has contracted to abstain from doing something, although it is also sometimes possible to obtain an injunction in such a form as virtually to compel the defendant to perform his contract—for instance, by drafting the injunction so as to forbid the defendant from using any property in a manner inconsistent with the contract. These decrees are discretionary in the sense that they cannot be claimed as of right (as damages can) and also in the sense that the court, in considering whether to grant them, can take into account questions of hardship and the like, which would provide no defence to an action for damages. On the other hand, as in the case of most judicial discretions, the broad principles on which the courts act are well settled, and there are cases where it is well known that specific performance will issue more or less as a matter of course, while there are other cases where it is perfectly well known that specific performance will never be granted.

For instance, specific performance is regularly granted, virtually as a matter of course, for the enforcement of contracts for the purchase and sale (or lease) of land and buildings. In such cases, discretion rarely comes into it, though one recent case shows that the old discretion to refuse specific performance in a case of great personal hardship still remains alive.[6]

The two main principles governing these remedies are, first, that they can only be granted when damages are inadequate and, secondly, that they will not be granted unless the court is in a position to see that they are executed. The first principle means that the court will never decree specific performance of an ordinary contract for the sale of goods which are readily obtainable elsewhere, and for which damages would, therefore, be perfectly adequate. So specific performance was refused even in the case of a contract for the purchase of a large machine, weighing over 220 tons, at a cost of some £270,000, and which could only be bought elsewhere with a nine to twelve months' delivery date.[7] But specific performance is granted more or less automatically of a contract for the purchase or sale of land (or a house), the theory being that no two pieces of land are quite the same, a not entirely convincing answer in modern times, especially where the plaintiff is the seller. Similarly, specific performance would be granted of a contract to sell a unique or very unusual chattel such, for instance, as a ship, which might not be easily obtainable elsewhere, though it would need to be shown that the ship had some special features rendering it uniquely suitable for the plaintiff's uses.

The second principle means that the courts will not normally decree specific performance of a contract whose performance would require constant supervision. Hence a contract of employment can never be specifically enforced, and a building contract only in very special circumstances. But although a decree of specific performance would be difficult to supervise, the same cannot be said of the negative injunction. Hence it is sometimes possible to prevent a person from breaking a

---

[6] *Patel* v. *Ali* [1984] 1 All ER 978.
[7] *Société des Industries Métallurgiques SA* v. *Bronx Engineering Co Ltd* [1975] 1 Lloyd's Rep. 465.

contract by injunction, where it would not be possible actually to compel the performance of the contract by specific performance.

This possibility has caused particular problems in employment contracts, where specific performance is never decreed, but where it is sometimes possible to obtain injunctions restraining the employee from working for one or more particular employers, so long as there is a distinct negative obligation not to take up such work.[8] The injunction, however, must never go so far as to impose on the defendant the choice of either working for the plaintiff or of starving, or even of remaining unemployed for any significant period of time.[9] And even where there is no risk of the employee starving (because, e.g., the employer is still paying his salary while he is on leave after notice to terminate) the courts are reluctant to grant an injunction unless there is good evidence that the employer will be significantly damaged or affected by what the employee wants to do.[10] Further, the courts are also unwilling to grant such injunctions where the relationship between the parties involves a high degree of mutual trust which has been destroyed, and where the injunction would almost certainly drive the employee to return to the employer. Indeed, a decree will not be granted if the practical result, looking at matters realistically, will be that the employee is virtually forced to return to work for the plaintiffs.[11]

Except in employment cases, there has in recent years been some slight tendency for the principles governing these equitable remedies to be relaxed. For instance, in *Beswick* v. *Beswick*[12] (as we saw earlier) the House of Lords permitted a promisee to obtain a decree of specific performance of a contractual obligation to pay an annuity, mainly because the doctrine of privity prevented the promisee (in her capacity as beneficiary) from enforcing the contract directly. This was something of an innovation, because hitherto the fact that damages are an adequate remedy has usually been regarded as a ground for *refusing* the equitable remedy, while it has not been previously decided that the mere fact that damages are an inadequate remedy is positively a ground for *granting* such a remedy.

Another interesting case is *Shell* v. *Lostock Garage*[13] where the Court of Appeal refused an injunction to restrain the defendant from buying petrol

---

[8] For one modern example see *Evening Standard Co* v. *Henderson* [1987] ICR 588.

[9] *Marsh* v. *National Autistic Society* [1993] ICR 453.

[10] *Provident Financial Group plc* v. *Hayward* [1993] 3 All ER 298. In this connection note the dictum of Dillon LJ at 304: 'It is very common for employers to have somewhat exaggerated views of what will or may affect their business'.

[11] *Warren* v. *Mendy* [1989] 1 WLR 853.     [12] [1968] AC 58.

[13] [1976] 1 WLR 1187.

from other suppliers in breach of its contract with Shell. The reason for the refusal was that Shell was supplying other rival petrol stations with petrol at such a low price that the defendant was unable to resell the petrol Shell sold him, because they were demanding a much higher price from him than from his local competitors. Although the Court of Appeal felt unable to imply a term in the contract to prevent Shell from behaving in this way, they nevertheless held that Shell's behaviour was so unreasonable that they would exercise their discretion to refuse an injunction. In theory Shell could still have obtained damages from the defendant, but in fact there was probably no loss at all, so effectively the Court denied a remedy for the breach of contract.

Other recent developments concerning equitable relief show an inclination to grant damages in lieu of specific relief for certain types of case (for example breach of a restrictive covenant) where in the past injunctions were granted more or less as a matter of course.[14]

It will be noticed that there is some inconsistency in the law's overall approach to contractual remedies. In the last chapter, and in the previous section, we saw that a party may be able to use self-help remedies like rescission and termination, even where their use would inflict loss out of all proportion to their value to the plaintiff. But this means that there is nothing corresponding to the adequacy principle governing decrees of specific relief—there is no general rule holding that rescission or termination cannot be invoked where damages would be adequate. Yet rescission and termination, like all self-help remedies, are tantamount to a form of specific relief. Indeed, they are even more potent than decrees of specific relief for, with these remedies, the plaintiff simply helps himself to what he claims to be entitled. But these remedies are available even where damages would provide a perfectly adequate remedy; the inconsistency in the law is compounded when it is recalled that rescission is an equitable remedy which could well have been made subject to the adequacy rule, in accord with general equitable principles. But this has never been done.

In modern times there has been a growing academic debate about the limited availability of decrees of specific relief. Some lawyers take the view—and it was a widely held view when the late proposed Contract Code was under discussion at the Law Commission—that specific performance ought to be the primary remedy of the law. A person ought, in principle, it was said, to be entitled to an order for the performance of his contract.

---

[14] *Wrotham Park Estate* v. *Parkside Homes* [1974] 1 WLR 798. This case was doubted in *Surrey CC* v. *Bredero Homes Ltd* [1993] 3 All ER 705 because of the way the judge assessed the damages. But if he had assessed the damages according to the *Bredero* decision, the damages would have been nil, in which case the judge might have felt it wrong to refuse an injunction. This seems to leave the judge in the dilemma of ordering houses to be torn down for breach of covenant or refusing all redress.

Even if this were the law, the experience of other countries suggests that it would not generally make a great deal of difference in practice to claims brought before the courts. This is because in most such cases, it is usually too late even to contemplate specific performance by the time the case is litigated, and the plaintiff has anyhow lost confidence in the defendant, and does not want him to perform further.

An opposite academic view is that the present rule is largely justified on economic efficiency grounds. According to 'the theory of efficient breach' it is desirable that a defendant should not be prevented by court decrees from breaking his contract where it is more efficient for him to do so than to perform. A defendant may be able to breach his contract with the plaintiff, and pay him adequate damages to compensate him, if he finds that he can use the resources he intended to use for this contract, with some third party prepared to pay more. Suppose S agrees to sell a machine to B1 for £100. B1 values the machine at £110, that is he expects to make £10 profit from it. Suppose then that B2 appears on the scene and thinks he can use the machine much more profitably than B1, so he offers S £150 for it. S can afford to sell the machine to B2, break his contract with B1, and pay B1 damages of £10. All three parties appear to be happy at this outcome. S gets more profit, B2 is happy, and even B1 gets the value of his contract, if not the performance of the contract. This is said to be an economically efficient result, because B2, being willing to pay more than B1, can be presumed to be able to use the machine more efficiently than B1. And because it is more efficient, it is presumptively in the public interest, as well as in the interests of the parties. On the other hand, if B1 were entitled to a decree of specific performance, then he would get the machine, and the more profitable use contemplated by B2 would never be achieved. So that would be an inefficient result.

Of course the law is not strictly concerned with economic efficiency arguments, but it is in general true that even the moral weight of a promise has little force in a case of this nature, where the defendant intends cynically to break his contract with the plaintiff because he can make more profit by doing so and paying damages than by performing it. So as a matter of law, the argument may be correct,[15] which is perhaps another illustration of the general weakness of contractual sanctions. However, the argument appears flawed as an argument about economic efficiency, at any rate, if pressed too far. In the example given above, if B1 gets the goods with the aid of specific performance, there is no obvious reason why he should not resell the machine to B2 and receive the extra profit for himself,

---

[15] But in fact the CA did grant an injunction to restrain a defendant doing this in one case (where, however, the property had passed to the buyer, and the seller no longer had any claim to the goods at all): *Redler Grain Silos Ltd* v. *BICC Ltd* [1982] 2 Lloyd's Rep. 435.

and no special reason to suppose that the cost of his doing so would outweigh the costs involved in S's selling the machine to B2. Still, in some broad sense, the argument may have some validity. The present law does mean that the mere fact that a person has a contract involving the use of certain resources does not discourage him from keeping an eye open for still more profitable uses of those resources.

There are also other circumstances in which the economic efficiency argument may be specially plausible. It occasionally happens that if the defendant actually carries out his contract there will be a net loss of value to the community, because the cost of performance will exceed the value of the performance when completed. In the Ocean Island case[16] the defendants were liable under some contracts which required them to restore the condition of the plaintiffs' land (on an island in the Indian Ocean) after it had been exploited for phosphates. In fact they left the land in a deplorable state, but it was proved that the cost of actual restoration would have been enormous—it would have involved shipping loads of soil from Australia—and would have far exceeded the value which the land would have after restoration. In these circumstances specific performance was ruled out as a matter of discretion; and this may seem a result dictated by efficiency considerations. But even here it is not certain that there would be anything inefficient about granting a decree of specific performance. Certainly it would be inefficient if the work were actually done in a case like this—society does not want to force somebody to use valuable resources in a wasteful manner—but it is not at all certain that granting the decree would actually lead to this result.

The reasons for this cast a whole flood of light on the nature of a decree of specific performance. The true nature of such a decree is not necessarily what it seems at face value. It looks like a simple order to carry out the contract; but it does not necessarily result in the contract being carried out, any more than an injunction is necessarily followed by observance. Decrees of specific relief give the plaintiff the right to place his own subjective value on the benefit he expected to derive from his contract, rather than accept the objective valuation involved when a judge assesses damages in accordance with the law. Once he has the decree, the plaintiff can, of course, 'sell' it, that is, he can renegotiate with the other party, but he now has a much more powerful bargaining position than if his only right was to claim damages. The position will be clearer if an example is given.

In the Ocean Island case, for instance, if the decree of specific performance had been granted, and if (to give some hypothetical figures) it had been estimated that the work would cost £10 million, while the land would have had an ultimate value of £2 million, it would clearly have been

---

[16] *Tito v. Waddell* [1977] Ch. 106.

worthwhile for both parties to renegotiate matters so as to save this possible waste of £8 million. Such a renegotiation would only require that the defendants offer the plaintiffs compensation of between £2 and £10 million, and a bargain could be struck which would be beneficial to both parties. So in the end the inefficient result—the actual carrying out of the work—would probably never occur. Of course, this is not certain. The parties might fail to reach agreement, because one or both might dig in their heels and try to strike too hard a bargain. But certainly a bargain seems highly probable in such a case; and if the court granted a decree expecting the parties then to negotiate over it, the court could always bang the parties' heads together later if it thought that they were being unreasonable about reaching agreement.

But although a decree of specific performance in such a case might then not lead to an inefficient result, it would certainly have major distributive implications—because it would amount to a decision that the plaintiff was entitled to share in the savings which would follow from the defendant's breach of the contract; and the plaintiff would then be able to get much larger damages from a renegotiation than he could obtain in an award from the court. It is not at all clear why the plaintiff should not have such a share, but we shall have to return to the point later when we consider the rules governing the award of damages in such a case.

For the moment, we return to decrees of specific relief, which we can now see afford some measure of protection for the plaintiff's subjective valuation of the benefits of his contract. Suppose the plaintiff contracted to buy a house for £100,000, and the seller failed to convey. If the market value of the house at the date when damages are assessed is (say) £105,000, then the plaintiff would recover £5,000 in damages. But the plaintiff may subjectively have valued the house at far above £100,000 or even £105,000. Precisely because a house is often unique, it is more likely that there will be wide variations in subjective valuations of its worth. Perhaps the plaintiff would have been prepared to pay £150,000 for it because of its unique ·features which attracted him. And even if he was not prepared to pay such a large sum (because he could not afford it) he may still feel that the house would be worth £150,000 to him, so that if he did obtain it, he would not willingly resell it for less than that sum. If so, damages assessed by the court would not adequately compensate him. If he obtains a decree of specific performance, however, he either gets the house itself, or he can negotiate a new deal with the seller, under which he is compensated to the full extent of his subjective losses.

In this respect, then, a decree of specific performance is like a property right. Just as the owner of property cannot (usually) be forced to sell it at some judge's valuation, but only at a price satisfactory to him, so also a decree of specific performance means that the plaintiff has a right which can only be taken from him if he is willing to sell at the price offered. A right to enforce a contract by an action for damages is different. Here the damages are assessed by the court in accordance with legal rules. The plaintiff's subjective valuation of what he had expected to receive under the contract is disregarded; he receives by way of damages the fair market value of his expectations (less the cost of his own performance), which may of course be very different from his subjective valuations. However, in the case of goods with a regular market price, it is unlikely that the subjective valuations of buyers and sellers will often be very different from those of the market. It is only likely that this will happen where the goods are unique or rare, so this may be a partial justification for the present rule.

### 4. THE ACTION FOR AN AGREED SUM

An action for an agreed sum (for instance a debt) is in many ways more like a claim for specific performance than an action for damages. It is an action to force the defendant to do precisely what he has contracted to do—that is, to pay over a specific sum of money. But such claims, though they do differ from claims for damages, have never been treated like claims to specific performance. They are available as of right, they are not subject to judicial discretion, and they are not, in general, subject to the restriction that they are only available if damages are an inadequate remedy. On the other hand, such claims also differ from claims for damages in a number of important respects which will be mentioned in this section. Apart from these substantive distinctions, the procedure for recovering an agreed sum is also simpler and, especially in uncontested cases, quicker than the ordinary action for damages. Where a defendant fails to appear in answer to a claim, for instance, judgment can immediately be given for the plaintiff if his claim is for an agreed sum; while if his claim is for damages, judgment can only be given for damages to be assessed, and even where the claim is uncontested, the plaintiff must produce some evidence to support his claim to the losses he seeks as damages.

The general principle is that in order to maintain an action for an agreed sum a contracting party must himself have performed his duties under the contract. Even if he has been prevented from doing so by the wrongful actions of the other party, he will not generally have an action for the entire sum of money agreed as the contract price. His remedy in these circumstances is an action for damages. 'You cannot claim remuneration under a contract if you have not earned it; if you are prevented from earning it, your only remedy is in damages'.[17] For instance, in a contract of sale of goods the seller cannot normally sue the buyer for the whole price if

---

[17] *Per* Lloyd J in *The Alaskan Trader* [1984] 1 All ER 129 at 134.

the latter refuses to take the goods, unless the ownership has already passed to him. If this has not yet happened the seller's proper remedy is an action for damages for non-acceptance.

However, there are some circumstances in which the innocent party can (it seems) go ahead and complete performance of his own duties under the contract despite the repudiation of the contract by the other party. If the innocent party does not require the co-operation of the other party to enable him to complete performance he can thus insist on performing and so become entitled to the agreed remuneration instead of merely to damages. This was decided by the House of Lords in the much-criticized decision of *White & Carter (Councils) Ltd* v. *McGregor*[18] in 1961. The chief reasons for the criticism are that it seems to encourage economic waste, because it enables the claimant for an agreed sum to evade the important principle—which we have yet to discuss—that a plaintiff must 'mitigate his damage', that is to say, must act reasonably so as to reduce his losses, and hence the damages. A reasonable plaintiff would presumably have realized that it would be a waste of money to go ahead and perform in this case, where the defendant had shown that he did not want the contract performed. But this principle was held inapplicable, on the ground that it only arises when the contract is terminated, while here it never was terminated—the plaintiff had refused to accept the defendant's breach. However, there were hints in this case that the result might be different where the innocent party had no 'legitimate interest' in performance of the contract. These hints were later acted upon in *The Alaskan Trader*,[19] where charterers in breach of contract refused to take a ship back after repairs, saying they had no further use for it. They would, of course, have been liable for damages, but the owners kept the vessel at anchor, fully crewed and ready to sail for the rest of the charter, and then claimed the entire rent due under the charter. It was held the owners had no legitimate interest in so behaving, and were limited to claiming damages. Clearly, this was a case of gross economic waste, and the court was right to penalize it.

In certain types of contract substantial performance will be sufficient to enable a party to maintain an action for the agreed remuneration, subject to any possible counterclaim for damages by the other party. In building and construction contracts, for instance, it would often be unreasonable to insist that nothing is payable until the work is absolutely and finally completed, because minor finishing off and rectification of defects are so common in such cases, and can easily be allowed for by a small deduction

---

[18] [1962] AC 413.

[19] *Supra*, n. 17; see also *Attica Sea Carriers Ltd* v. *Ferrostall Poseiden* [1976] 1 Lloyd's Rep. 250, where charterers had contracted to repair a ship before re-delivery, and it was found that the cost of repairs would be $2 m. while the value of the ship after repairs would only be $1 m.

(by way of damages) from the sum due. But part performance is not necessarily substantial performance. As a general rule part performance does not give rise to a right to part payment, at all events where the contract is entire and indivisible. For instance, if a builder contracts to build a house and leaves the work half-finished he is not (in the absence of express provision) entitled to any payment whatever for the work he has already done,[20] although in practice any substantial building contract will usually contain provisions for 'stage payments' as the work proceeds. Similarly, a builder may be unable to claim any payment at all if he contracts to install central heating in a house but makes such a bad job of it that the buyer has to pay several hundred pounds to have the work put right.[21] The justification for this rule (which permits one party to retain a benefit without having to pay for it, and which the Law Commission has accordingly proposed should be abrogated) seems to be penal or deterrent. This is contrary to the theory of contract law which is supposed to be purely compensatory, but there do seem to be cases where even contract law can legitimately find room for a small dose of deterrence, and this may well be one of them. However, it is true that the rule is apt to work hardship on occasion and it is now mitigated in two ways.

In the first place, part payment may be enforced if one party has received some benefit under the contract which he is not prepared to disgorge, although being in a position to do so. For instance, if a seller delivers part of a consignment of goods for which payment is to be made in one sum, but fails to deliver the rest, the buyer cannot keep what has been delivered and refuse to pay for it. He must choose between returning what has been delivered and claiming damages in respect of the whole contract, or keeping what has been delivered and paying for it, subject to his claim for damages in respect of the balance. This, however, can only be the case where the innocent party is in a position to return what has been given. It does not apply, therefore, where he cannot do so, as in the case of the builder who leaves a half-completed house on the other party's land or a defective central heating installation in the other's house. In this case the innocent party is perfectly free to have the work completed by someone else without incurring any liability to the original builder. In cases where this result seems intolerably harsh it may be possible to avoid it by implying a term requiring interim payments under the contract.[22]

In the second place, the general principle has been amended in respect of frustrated contracts. Where a contract is frustrated, the Law Reform

---

[20] *Sumpter* v. *Hedges* [1898] 1 QB 673.

[21] *Bolton* v. *Mahadeva* [1972] 1 WLR 1009 (the figure has been adjusted for inflation).

[22] As was done by the County Court judge in *Williams* v. *Roffey Bros* [1991] 1 QB 1, where this was not challenged on appeal. See *supra*, 133.

(Frustrated Contracts) Act 1943 enables the court, in its discretion, to order one party to pay for the value of any benefits he may have received before the frustrating event. Thus, to revert to the example of the uncompleted house, if the reason the work is not finished is a frustrating event, as opposed to a breach of contract by the builder, he may be able to recover a sum representing the value to the other party of the building as it stands. This, of course, may not be as much as the cost to the builder of what he has done. In *BP Exploration* v. *Hunt*[23] a very complex contract for the exploitation of an oil concession was entered into by the parties. The defendant received substantial benefits under the contract, while BP received very little in the early stages, the intention of the parties being that BP would be recompensed in the later stages when large-scale production was under way. But the concession was abrogated by the Libyan Government, thus frustrating the contract, and BP sought and obtained a large award from the defendant under the 1943 Act, for benefits conferred on him prior to the frustration of the contract. The judgment of Goff J in this case (which was affirmed on appeal) is the first major decision on the 1943 Act, and contains much learning on the nature of the rights created by the Act. In substance, the judge regarded the Act as creating a species of restitutionary right, governed by the usual principles of the law of restitution. We return below to some aspects of this branch of the law, and its impact on contractual cases.

The court is, however, powerless to assist a party who has spent money on the performance of the contract without actually benefiting the other party, unless (as we shall see shortly) something has been paid in advance. Thus if a person contracts to make machinery for another, and the contract is frustrated before any of it is delivered, no part of the agreed price can be recovered, notwithstanding that much money and work may have been laid out already on the machinery.

### Distinction between liquidated damages and penalties

It sometimes happens that the parties to a contract have themselves provided for what is to happen in the event of a breach by one or both of them. They may, for instance, expressly agree that if one of them breaks his contract he shall pay £100 damages to the other party. An agreement of this sort is in principle valid and unobjectionable, because there is no reason why the parties should not attempt to save legal costs by assessing, in advance, the compensation which will be payable in the event of breach, and the amount specified can then be sued for as an agreed sum. However, it is essential that the sum payable should really be intended as compensation, and not as a threat or penalty, held over the other party's

---

[23] [1979] I WLR 783, affirmed [1982] 2 WLR 253 and (on one point only) [1983] 2 AC 352.

head to compel performance. If the court thinks that the latter is the true position, the sum is a penalty, and is not recoverable. The innocent party is then left to his ordinary claim for damages to be assessed by the court in the usual way.

The distinction between a penalty and genuine liquidated damages, as they are called, is not always easy to apply, but the courts have made the task simpler by laying down certain guiding principles.[24] These principles must be applied by looking at the contract as a whole and construing the relevant clause as at the date of the contract, not as at the time of breach. First, then, if the sum payable is so large as to be far in excess of the probable damage on breach, it is almost certainly a penalty. Secondly, if the same sum is expressed to be payable on any one of a number of different breaches of varying importance, it is again probably a penalty, because it is extremely unlikely that the same damage would be caused by these varying breaches. Thirdly, where a sum is expressed to be payable on a certain date, and a further sum in the event of default being made, this latter sum is prima facie a penalty, because a very short delay in payment is unlikely to cause significant damage. Fourthly, the mere fact that the damages for a breach would be very difficult to assess does not mean that the agreed sum cannot be liquidated damages—on the contrary, this is precisely the situation in which the parties may reasonably wish to agree on the sum payable for breach. So, for instance, in contracts with public bodies (for the construction of roadworks or defence supplies or the like) where it would often be impossible to quantify the loss caused by delay or non-performance, liquidated damages clauses are almost universally used. Finally, the mere use of the words 'liquidated damages' is not decisive, for it is the task of the court and not of the parties to decide the true nature of the sum payable, and it would be easy to evade the principle if the parties only had to label the sum in the correct way in their contract.

The rule against penalties is an old equitable principle which was absorbed into the common law long before the classical period, and it survived that period although it manifestly involves a rare judicial power to override the express terms of a contract. But attitudes to the use of this power have fluctuated over the centuries and, as we have already noted, the 1980s saw a massive resurgence in belief in the principle of freedom of contract. Possibly because of this, an important decision of the House of Lords has recently limited the operation of the penalty rules. In *ECGD* v. *Universal Oil Products Co*[25] it was insisted that the penalty rule is only applicable to a sum of money payable on a breach of contract. It has no application to a contractual clause which provides for an agreed sum to be

[24] See in particular *Dunlop* v. *New Garage* [1915] AC 79.
[25] [1983] 1 WLR 399.

paid on any other contingency. In this case the plaintiffs only sought to recover their actual losses, so the actual claim was unobjectionable; but the defendants argued that, if the clauses in question were enforceable, there might be other circumstances in which sums vastly in excess of the plaintiffs' losses could be recovered. Further, although the event on which the agreed sums were payable here was not a breach of contract between the parties, it did involve a breach of contract with other parties, and the various contracts were all inter-related and inter-locking. All these arguments were rejected by the House of Lords in a decision which appears highly formalistic. Among other results, this means that a defendant may be better off if he breaches his contract, than if he does not. In the former event, but not in the latter, he may be able to invoke the penalty rules to save himself from severe consequences.

In many situations it no doubt makes perfectly good sense not to apply the penalty rules to sums which are not payable on breach, but on some other contingency. For example, the common practice by which credit-card companies charge interest on the whole balance if it is not paid off entirely each month could not sensibly be treated as penal. In a particular case it may be hard (if the debtor pays one day too late, for instance, or by mistake pays a few pence less than the due sum), but since the debtor's freedom from having to pay any interest at all is itself a substantial privilege it is in no way unreasonable to require the debtor to comply strictly with the terms on which the privilege is granted.

But in other cases it would be much more difficult to justify not applying the penalty rules to sums payable otherwise than on breach. It will be seen how easily the penalty rules can be evaded if the *ECGD* decision is followed through. For instance, a building contract might contain two clauses, (1) requiring the works to be completed by 1 January, and (2) providing for an agreed sum of £100 per day as compensation in the event of breach. That would clearly be subject to the penalty rules (though, of course, whether it actually would be a penalty would depend on the criteria listed above). But following the *ECGD* case the contract could be redrafted in a different form, combining the effect of the two clauses, but avoiding any suggestion that it would be a breach if the works were not completed by 1 January. So the contract could provide that the total price payable should be £X, but in the event of the works being completed after 1 January, the price would be reduced by £100 per day. According to the *ECGD* case, that would seem to evade the application of the penalty rules altogether. There is nothing fanciful about this example. In certain kinds of mortgages it has long been the practice to provide that the interest rate should be X per cent, but if the interest is paid punctually on the due date it should instead be X minus ½ per cent. This has long been upheld by courts of equity as not being penal.

Despite the *ECGD* case, the main body of the rules against penalties is well established, and still good law. But—perhaps also under the influence of the newly resurgent freedom-of-contract principles—recent years have seen a whole series of decisions which have nipped in the bud some less developed rules of a closely parallel character. These rules concern contractual forfeitures, that is to say, provisions which enable one party to retain property, or money, as a result of some breach by the other party, even though the result is out of all proportion to the loss sustained. Although these cases do not involve an action for an agreed sum, they are closely analogous to such cases, and it is convenient to deal with them here, in conjunction with the rule against penalties.

Historically, there was much support for a judicial power to override contractual forfeiture clauses, parallel to the power to deal with penalties. Penalties and forfeiture are, after all, very closely related. In essence they are often the same thing, the only difference between them being that the roles of the plaintiff and the defendant are reversed. In the case of penalties, one party is seeking to recover money from the other without having to prove the loss he has actually suffered; in the case of forfeiture, he already has the money or other property (in substance as security) and is seeking to keep it, while the other party is trying to recover it. The earliest example of these rules in fact concerned forfeiture, rather than penalty clauses. In mortgages, the property was usually declared to be forfeited if the debtor failed to repay the debt on the due date, even though the property might be worth much more than the debt itself, and the jurisdiction to relieve against these results is several centuries old. It was only later that this jurisdiction was actually extended to penalty clauses, originally in penal bonds, and later all forms of penalty clauses.

Even in relation to forfeiture (in the widest sense) there are some cases where the judicial power to grant relief is well established and, indeed, often now statutory. For instance, a landlord cannot forfeit a lease, whatever the lease may say, because of a breach of covenant by the tenant,[26] and there is even statutory jurisdiction to order repayment of the customary 10 per cent deposit paid on an exchange of contracts for the sale of land if the seller resells the land without loss, following breach by the buyer.[27] And more generally, it is accepted on all hands that a contract

---

[26] Law of Property Act 1925, s. 146. For a modern extension, see *Abbey National Building Society* v. *Maybeech Ltd* [1985] Ch. 190.

[27] *Universal Corp* v. *Five Ways Properties Ltd* [1979] 1 All ER 552. But in practice the customary 10% deposit is so well entrenched that it is hard to imagine a court holding that it is a penalty or ordering any of it to be refunded under the statutory jurisdiction. Contracts for the sale of land requiring forfeitable deposits of more than 10% must be justified by special circumstances, and normally such deposits will be reclaimable as a penalty subject to deduction for the seller's actual loss: *Workers Trust & Merchant Bank Ltd* v. *Dojap Investments Ltd* [1993] AC 573 (PC).

which provides for the forfeiture of possessory or proprietary rights may be challenged under the penalty rules. In Australia it has been held by the High Court that (even aside from the usual penalty rules) there is a wider equitable jurisdiction to relieve against forfeiture of property where the forfeiture would be unconscionable.[28]

But in recent years the House of Lords has several times refused to extend this jurisdiction to other cases, and insisted that contractual clauses must be strictly enforced. Thus a charterer of a ship (who does not usually have possessory or proprietary rights, but is a mere hirer in law) may find that the owner is entitled to withdraw the vessel under the charterparty if the rent is not promptly paid; and even though this may cause huge loss to the charterer, he has no claim to equitable relief outside the terms of the contract.[29] Some charterparties now contain an 'anti-technicality clause' to prevent this result where there is some 'technical' breach of contract, but not all do so. As with other examples of rescission or termination, these forfeiture clauses may enable a renegotiation of the contract under which the innocent party obtains compensation far in excess of the damages (if any) which could be recovered for the breach.

Similarly, the House of Lords has refused all relief to a contracting party whose failure to pay an instalment, under a settlement of a previous dispute, gave the other party the right to sever all ties immediately, and withdraw a licence to use a trade name which the guilty party had been exploiting.[30] Yet in a very similar case the Court of Appeal later found itself able to grant relief where a contract provided for forfeiture of a share in patent rights which were jointly owned by the parties, on non-payment of some relatively trivial sum by the guilty party.[31] Patent rights are a form of property, so a highly technical distinction now exists here between patent rights and mere licensing agreements which commercially are often almost indistinguishable from property rights.

So also the Court of Appeal has held that there is no jurisdiction to relieve against loss of a deposit payable under a contract, which is declared to be irrecoverable in the event of breach. So where a buyer contracted to buy a ship for $2.36 million, and to pay a deposit of 10 per cent of the price, and the contract expressly provided that if the buyer failed to complete the deposit would be irrecoverable, it was held that the deposit was forfeitable

---

[28] *Stern* v. *McArthur* (1988) 165 CLR 489.

[29] *The Laconia* [1977] AC 850; *Scandinavian Trading Tanker Co* v. *Flota Petrolera Ecuatoriana (The Scaptrade)* [1983] 2 AC 694. But the losses alleged in these cases were pure 'expectation' losses, and in one sense there was no 'forfeiture' at all here—they were simply cases of termination causing severe losses of expected profits. The result is more offensive where the losses are reliance or restitutionary losses which are truly being 'forfeited'.

[30] *Sport International Bussum* v. *Inter-Footwear* [1984] 1 WLR 776.

[31] *BICC* v. *Burndy* [1985] Ch. 232.

even though the seller had resold the ship at a small loss, much less than the amount of the deposit.[32] Indeed, in this case, because the buyer had not actually paid the deposit when he should have done, it was the seller who was plaintiff, suing for the recovery of the deposit, and yet this manifestly penal claim was upheld. This is an extreme case which appears inconsistent with other decisions and may well be wrong.[33]

A 'part-payment' is, however, generally recoverable, not because of the rule against forfeitures but because it is assumed that such a payment is not intended to be forfeited in the event of breach. The distinction depends on whether the payment was intended to be a security for the performance of the contract, in which case it is a 'deposit' and not recoverable, or merely an advance payment against the price, in which case it is recoverable if the contract does not go ahead. In practice a lot depends on the amount: small payments (such as 10 per cent of the price) are likely to be treated as deposits which may be forfeited, larger payments are more likely to be treated as part-payments.

As with other instances of judicial power to override the express terms of a contract, there has recently been much academic debate about the justifiability of the rule against penalties; and naturally, this debate has spilled over to raise questions about the recent trend to curtail the jurisdiction to grant relief in cases of forfeiture. These questions have already been discussed in Chapter 16, and here we need only repeat our conclusion which was that there really is nothing in the jurisdiction to strike down penalty and forfeiture clauses which is inconsistent with true freedom-of-contract principles. It is another of these mistaken 'gut reactions' to think that every case in which express contractual provisions are overridden by the law is a concession to sentiment.

## 5. THE ACTION FOR DAMAGES

The action for damages is the most general remedy recognized by the common law. Its primary purpose in the law of contract is to compensate the innocent party for the guilty party's breach of contract so far as money can do so. As we have seen, the law of contract does not (at least in theory) seek to punish; its purpose is compensation and compensation alone. Thus the exemplary damages which may sometimes be awarded in the law of tort as a sort of punishment are almost unknown in the law of contract. Only in the single case of breach of promise of marriage were such damages permissible, and this is the exception which proves the rule, for this action

[32] *Damon Cia Naviera* v. *Hapag-Lloyd* [1985] 1 All ER 475.
[33] It seems inconsistent both with the *Workers Trust* case, *supra*, n. 27 and also with *Rover International* v. *Cannon Film Sales (No. 3)* [1989] 1 WLR 912, *post*, n. 62, as to failure of consideration.

resembled an action in tort more than an action in contract. It has, in any case, now been abolished.

Furthermore, it is, in general, financial losses alone that the law of contract compensates with damages. Damages for physical injury (or damage to property) are recoverable in contract as in tort, and this includes also physical discomfort as, for example, where the owner of a house has to put up with having repairs done while he is in occupation, as a result of a breach of contract by a seller or builder. But beyond this, damages for pain and suffering or mental distress, are not generally recoverable for breach of contract,[34] though they are recoverable in those cases where tort and contract overlap, as with physical injury to an employee, and where no distinction is ever drawn between contract and tort. Damages for mental distress are also recoverable in contract in some rare cases where the whole point of the contract is to protect against mental distress (as where a plaintiff goes to a solicitor to get an order to prevent her husband molesting her[35]) or where the purpose of the contract is to provide especial pleasure such as a consumer contract with a holiday company. It has also become common for judges to award damages for 'inconvenience and vexation', which look very much like damages for mental distress in another guise, in some other consumer contracts, such as for the purchase of a defective car which breaks down on holiday,[36] or for the failure of a tradesman to make a proper job of some household repair. But it is now clear that such damages cannot be awarded in an ordinary commercial transaction, even where the plaintiff was in a sense just an ordinary consumer.[37]

We have already indicated at various stages in this book when the remedy of damages is available, and we need do no more now than collect these various cases together. In the first place, damages are the obvious remedy for a breach of contract, whether the breach takes the form of a breach of a promise to do something or a breach of a promissory representation that a certain state of affairs exists. Thus, broadly speaking, the action for damages lies for non-performance and for defective performance. On the other hand, damages cannot generally be recovered for breach of a duty arising independently of the contract—indeed the very term 'breach of contract' does not encompass these breaches of duty in ordinary legal parlance. The only remedy available here is rescission of the contract, although this may involve the recovery of any money which has

---

[34] *Addis* v. *Gramophone Co Ltd* [1909] AC 488; *Bliss* v. *SE Thames Health Authority* [1987] ICR 700; *Watts* v. *Morrow* [1991] 4 All ER 937.

[35] *Heywood* v. *Wellers* [1976] QB 446.

[36] *Jackson* v. *Chrysler Acceptances* [1978] RTR 474. There are scores of such cases (for relatively small sums) in the County Courts, which are noted in *Current Law* every year.

[37] *Hayes* v. *Dodd* [1990] 2 All ER 815; *Watts* v. *Morrow* [1991] 4 All ER 937; *Bliss* v. *SE Thames Health Authority* [1987] ICR 700.

been paid. So no damages can be recovered for duress,[38] undue influence, breach of a fiduciary duty, or breach of a duty of disclosure. The same used to be true also of non-fraudulent misrepresentation, but the law relating to damages for misrepresentation is now in a very complex state, and needs separate discussion.

### Damages for pre-contractual misrepresentation

Damages are always recoverable for fraudulent misrepresentation, and it is immaterial whether the statement was a term of the contract or not. Indeed, fraud is actionable even when divorced from contract, for it is itself a tort to cause damage as a result of wilful deceit. But at common law damages could never be recovered for innocent misrepresentation (unless the misrepresentation was incorporated into the contract as a promissory representation) and not until 1963 was such a remedy available for negligent misrepresentation. The refusal of any right to damages for non-fraudulent misrepresentation which was not incorporated in the contract was thought to be a source of injustice; and there have now been two important developments in this area. First, the decision of the House of Lords in *Hedley Byrne & Co Ltd* v. *Heller & Partners Ltd*[39] has established that there may now be liability for *negligent* misrepresentation in some cases. And secondly, the Misrepresentation Act 1967 gives a general right to damages to a contracting party who has been induced to enter into a contract through a misrepresentation made by the other party which he had no reasonable grounds for believing to be true. In effect, the Act permits damages to be obtained for negligent misrepresentation, just as if the misrepresentation were fraudulent; this has been held to mean that damages under section 2(1) are the same as damages for fraud.[40]

There is no doubt that the Act of 1967 has added greatly to the complexity of the law, which is now extraordinarily involved. And it may well be thought that the solution propounded by the Act is in any event not the best way of approaching the problem. Had the courts been willing to develop the law along more flexible lines, the Act could have been largely unnecessary. For where it is felt that the justice of the case requires that damages should be awarded for misrepresentation there seems no insuperable difficulty in treating that representation as 'incorporated' in the contract. It will be appreciated that the notion of 'incorporation in the contract' is itself a legal notion rather than a factual one. Unless a party has made it clear that he does not warrant the truth of a representation made

---

[38] But intimidation is a tort, and it is not clear what differences there are between the requirements of the tort, and the requirements of economic duress in a contractual context.
[39] [1964] AC 465.
[40] *Royscott Trust Ltd* v. *Rogerson* [1991] 3 All ER 294.

by him there is normally no problem in treating the misrepresentation as a term of the contract. And if he has made it clear that he does not take responsibility for the accuracy of the representation it may well seem unjust to hold him liable in damages even where he has been negligent. On the other hand, it is arguable that, even where a contracting party does not intend to guarantee the accuracy of what he says, the other party is at least entitled to assume that due care has been taken by the representor.

The 1967 Act also alters the law in another important respect. Whereas before 1967 a representee was always entitled to rescind a contract for misrepresentation, however innocent and however trivial, the court is now empowered to refuse to permit rescission and to award damages in lieu. If, for instance, a person buys a house on the strength of some relatively minor misrepresentation (e.g. as to the state of the drains) it would obviously be somewhat drastic to rescind the contract after the buyer had moved into the house. Most probably neither party would want this extreme result. Before 1967 the buyer would have had no remedy; now the court may order damages to be paid.

The Act has therefore cut across the traditional distinction between mere representations and contractual terms, though it has by no means abolished it. In particular, the *kind* of damages obtainable for pre-contractual misrepresentation (whether for fraud or under the *Hedley Byrne* case or under the Act) is different from the usual kind of damages obtainable for breach of contract. As we shall see shortly, the usual rule is that damages for breach of contract are designed to put the plaintiff in the position he would have been in had the contract been performed; but damages in tort (including damages for pre-contractual misrepresentation) are intended to put the plaintiff back in the position he would have been in if no tort had been committed.[41]

This does not necessarily mean that damages for lost profits (which are commonly awarded for breach of contract) can never be awarded for misrepresentation, but the basis of the calculation is different. Suppose, for instance, that A buys a business from B as a result of a fraudulent misrepresentation by B. If this is a breach of contract (that is, of a promissory representation) then A will be awarded damages to put him in the position he would have been in if the representation were true. So if A has made profits of £1,000 but would have made £10,000 if the representation were true then A would be entitled to damages of £9,000. But in an action for fraudulent misrepresentation A will be awarded damages to put him in the position he would have been in if the representation had not been made. This may be a difficult matter to assess because it may not be at all clear what in fact would have happened if the

---

[41] *East* v. *Maurer* [1991] 1 WLR 461.

representation had not been made. Perhaps A would not have bought that business but another. Then some assessment, however rough, must be made of the profits A might have been expected to earn in this other business.[42] Similar difficulties often occur in actions against professionals such as solicitors or surveyors where there has been misrepresentation, and it is necessary to distinguish between what would have happened if the contract had been performed (that is, if competent and careful advice had been given) and what would have happened if the misrepresentation had never been made.[43]

### Contributory negligence

Contributory negligence has never as such been treated as a defence to an action for breach of contract, as it used to be a defence to an action in tort. Similar results could sometimes be reached where the plaintiff was partly responsible for the damage by use of the mitigation principle (which we shall come to shortly) or occasionally by invoking causation and holding that the plaintiff was in fact the sole cause of his own loss. In claims based on misrepresentation, in particular, it was settled law that a defendant could not defend himself by arguing that the plaintiff should have discovered or realized that the representation was untrue.[44]

In modern times the question has been raised whether the Law Reform (Contributory Negligence) Act 1945 can be invoked to apportion the damages in a claim based on breach of contract where it is alleged that the damage which occurred was partly the fault of the plaintiff himself, and partly of the defendant's breach of contract. The present position appears to be that the Act can be invoked in cases where there is liability both in contract and in tort,[45] but not in cases where the liability exists solely as a matter of contract.[46] Nor can the Act be invoked in cases of fraud[47] but it may be available in some other cases of misrepresentation,[48] though the primary responsibility for a misrepresentation will always be on the representor. The Law Commission has proposed that the law should be amended so that apportionment of damages is always possible even in cases where the liability is solely contractual, at least where the liability is based on negligence.[49]

---

[42] *Ibid.*
[43] *Watts* v. *Morrow* [1991] 4 All ER 937.
[44] *Redgrave* v. *Hurd* (1881) 20 Ch. D 1.
[45] *Forsikringsaktieselskapet Vesta* v. *Butcher* [1988] 2 All ER 43; affirmed [1989] AC 852.
[46] *Bank of Nova Scotia* v. *Hellenic Mutual War Risks Association (Bermuda) Ltd* [1989] 3 All ER 628, reversed on different grounds [1992] 1 AC 233.
[47] *Alliance & Leicester Building Society* v. *Edgestop Ltd* [1994] 2 All ER 38.
[48] *Gran Gelato Ltd* v. *Richcliff (Group) Ltd* [1992] Ch. 560.
[49] Law Com. Report No. 219 (London, 1993).

## 6. EXPECTATION, RELIANCE, AND RESTITUTIONARY CLAIMS

### Expectation damages

The general principle of contract law is that the innocent party is entitled to damages for his 'loss', but losses are of various kinds. In particular, there is an important distinction between a loss of an expectation, and an actual loss which has resulted from action in reliance on the contract. Prima facie, the innocent party is entitled to full damages for his lost expectations, that is to say he is entitled to be placed by damages in the position in which he would have been if the contract had been fully performed. It must be said at once that this is a very extreme rule, which is exceptionally favourable to the plaintiff. For example, this rule enables a contractor to recover damages for his lost profit on a building contract if the other party repudiates the contract before the first party has lifted a finger to perform, or buy materials, or indeed act in any other way. Similarly, if a person contracts to buy a new car, and then changes his mind overnight and cancels the contract, the seller is in principle entitled to recover his anticipated profit on the transaction even though he has not, at the time of the cancellation, done anything whatever in pursuance of the contract. A person who books a table at a restaurant would in theory be liable to pay for the restaurant's loss of profit even though he cancels in sufficient time for them to be able to offer the table to other customers, so long only as the table in fact remains unoccupied because there are no other customers.[50] Damages of this kind are often called damages for lost expectations or 'expectation damages' or 'loss of bargain damages'.

It will be noticed that damages of this kind can be awarded even where there has been no action in reliance by the plaintiff, and no benefit received by the defendant; at this point it is relevant to recall the doctrine of consideration which in general requires some benefit or detrimental reliance to make a promise actionable. Yet in these circumstances, damages appear to be awardable even where there is neither benefit nor detrimental reliance. The plaintiff's bare expectations are protected. At one level this is explained by the fact that mutual executory promises (as we saw earlier) are treated as consideration for each other without inquiry into the question, how can such promises be beneficial or detrimental prior to any performance or reliance? But at another level, there is undoubtedly

---

[50] In 1987 newspaper reports appeared of a claim by a restaurant owner against some customers who had booked a table for a special New Year's dinner and then failed to show up, so the table remained empty. Such a claim is legally justified; but in strict legal theory the result would be the same even if the customers had cancelled in sufficient time, provided only that the owner was unable to get a replacement booking.

a problem about the recognition of damages for bare lost expectations. Liability of this nature, it will be seen, rests entirely on the promise or intent of the promisor: it does not rest on the fact that the plaintiff has relied on the defendant's promise or rendered some benefit to him, for in these actions on wholly executory contracts there is no benefit or detriment. It may seem at first sight that there is nothing peculiar about imposing liability on a contracting party just because he has made a promise or intended to assume the liability—after all it is, and remains, one of the fundamental objectives of contract law to give effect to mutual intentions, and so to protect expectations. But it is not always easy to justify awarding full expectation damages for breach of a wholly executory contract.

In the straightforward commercial contract where (say) a seller simply fails to deliver, the expectation damages rule may have some economic justification. In these cases the contract is in effect designed to shift the risk of changes in market prices after the making of the contract. And this shifting of risks may be assumed to be economically efficient in that risks are shifted in general to those who are best able to handle them. In such cases, commercial parties will normally be well aware of the nature of the risks, and also of the relevant rules of contract law. There is nothing especially esoteric about the expectation damages rule in ordinary commercial cases like these, and most businessmen are probably well aware at least that their expected profits are recoverable in law.

The expectation damages rule is also more defensible where the plaintiff has suffered substantial reliance losses. In complex contractual relationships, if the plaintiff has relied in various ways on a contract, and has in consequence suffered substantial loss from the defendant's breach, quite apart from any loss of expected profits, the expectation damages rule may make it much easier to compute the damages which should be awarded. In such a case it may even be suggested that the plaintiff recovers for his lost expectations in order the better to ensure that his reliance losses are fully compensated.

But it is not so easy to justify imposing liability for expectation damages in other sorts of cases. There are several reasons for this. First, except in straightforward commercial cases, a contracting party does not generally promise, or intend, to make himself answerable for the promisee's lost profits: what the promisor undertakes is to perform his side of a contract in return for the other side's performance. If he is in breach it is true that he cannot legitimately complain about being held answerable, but the consequences for which he is answerable are really determined by the law, and not by his intent or by his promise. A person contracts to buy a car: what he promises to do is to pay the price of the car, and he expects, of course, to receive the car in return. If he fails to take delivery then he may reasonably be held liable for losses suffered by the seller, but why should he pay for the seller's lost profits? He has made no promise to pay these profits. If he is made to compensate the seller for those lost profits it is because the law regards the potential profits as worthy of protection even before they have been earned, and not because the defendant promised to pay them. But this is, in effect, to treat the expected profits as earned before they have been actually earned.

In the second place, we must again stress a point repeatedly made during the course of this book—that contracting parties are very often liable for breach of contractual duties in which the element of assent is minimal—either because the terms of the contract have not been fully read or understood, or their significance grasped, or because the defendant is anyhow liable because he has induced reliance by the plaintiff in one way or another, rather than because of clear intentions.

One further example may here suffice to show how far the expectation damages rule goes in circumstances in which it may seem questionable. If a seller of goods is held liable for breach of an implied condition of fitness for purpose under the Sale of Goods Act (an everyday legal problem), he will prima facie be liable for damages to put the plaintiff in the position he would have been if the goods *had* been fit for their purpose. But it may happen that the only goods fit for this purpose would actually have cost far more than the goods sold.[51] So if the buyer is entitled to damages to put him in the position he would have been in if the implied condition had been performed he will, in the result, obtain the goods he wants at a fraction of their true price. If the seller really intended to assume this liability—if he had directed his mind to the possibility that the goods might be unfit, and had assured the buyer that they would be fit—it may be assumed that the contractual price would have reflected this risk, and included some sort of 'insurance premium' to cover it. So there would be nothing unfair about that. But in most such cases the seller does not direct his mind to the risk at all, the contract price probably does not reflect it, and the implied term is anyhow imposed under the Sale of Goods Act rather than arising from the intention of the parties. In such a case it seems very questionable whether the seller should be liable for the expectation damages of the buyer. The reason he is, nevertheless, likely to obtain such damages is that lawyers have persuaded themselves that contractual liability is always assent-based; yet, as this example shows, that is an elusive and treacherous idea which can easily be misapplied.

Still, it must be admitted that the expectation damages rule is widely applied (though not as widely as is usually thought—as we shall see) and

---

[51] See the Canadian case, *Sealand of the Pacific* v. *MacHaffie*, 51 DLR (3d) 702 (1974) on which this example is based.

widely supported. Until recently, there was one exceptional case where such damages were not obtainable under an ancient rule predating the emergence of the modern law of damages, namely the contract for the sale of land where the seller fails to convey because he is unable to do so for lack of a good title. Here, under the old rule in *Bain* v. *Fothergill*[52] (which actually goes back to 1776) the buyer could not get damages 'for the fancied goodness of his bargain' but could only obtain damages for his actual losses—legal expenses and similar costs. However, in modern times most lawyers regarded this rule as highly anomalous, and it was eventually abolished by the Law of Property (Miscellaneous Provisions) Act 1989.

It is worth adding that even an award of expectation damages does not necessarily protect the plaintiff's expectations fully. In *Moran* v. *University College, Salford*[53] the plaintiff was a student who had applied for a place at the defendant University College to study a particular course, and had been accepted as a result of a mistake. After the mistake was discovered the College refused to admit him, and he applied for a mandatory injunction to compel the defendants to accept him. In the Court of Appeal it was held that he might well have a right to damages (because the mistake would not necessarily have prevented a valid contract being shown) but it was inappropriate to award an injunction. There were other candidates for the course who had also been rejected by the defendants and who were better qualified than the plaintiff, and it would not be fair to them if the plaintiff were admitted. In a case like this even a generous award of damages would not really have protected the plaintiff's expectations, but it is also clear that there were good reasons for not protecting those expectations fully.

Another more common type of case where the expectation damages rule does not necessarily protect the plaintiff's expectations fully concerns damages for negligent advice, or for breach of contract for professional care. For example, in *Watts* v. *Morrow*[54] the plaintiffs bought a house for £177,500 on the strength of a surveyor's (negligent) report stating that the house was basically in good condition requiring only minor maintenance. In fact major repairs were required at a cost of £33,961. But it was also found that the house in its actual condition was worth £162,500, that is, only £15,000 less than the plaintiffs had paid for it. In an action against the surveyors it was held that the plaintiffs could only recover this sum of £15,000. The reason given for this is that a surveyor's duty in these cases is only to give reasonably careful and competent advice. He does not *warrant* the accuracy of his advice. If a seller sold a house in a case like this and *warranted* that the house was in sound condition the buyer would be

---

[52] (1874) LR 7 HL 158.     [53] *Independent*, 26 November 1993.
[54] [1991] 4 All ER 937.

entitled to damages to put him in the position he expected to be in if the contract were fully performed. But the surveyor's duty is more limited than this: the buyer who relies on his report is only entitled to be put in the position he would have been in if the advice had been carefully and competently given. In that case he would presumably not have bought the house at all, or would have paid £15,000 less for it. Whatever the reason, the upshot was that the plaintiffs' expectations (in the ordinary sense) were hardly fully protected. They presumably thought they were getting a house in basically sound condition for £177,500, but in fact they had to pay £162,500 (the price less the damages they received) plus £33,961 (for the repairs) to get what they expected to have under the contract. The facts of this case illustrate a very common problem in modern times, and the rule applied there has been followed in very many cases.

Similar results are found where a doctor is held liable for negligent treatment or misdiagnosis or the like. The plaintiff in such a case is not necessarily entitled to have his expectations fully protected but only to be put in the position he would have been in if the contract had been properly performed. A doctor who carelessly lets a patient think that a sterilization operation will be fool-proof does not *warrant* that it will be fool-proof. If the doctor had not been negligent the patient might not have had the operation, but if she would have gone ahead anyhow, then she has suffered no loss at all from the doctor's negligence. In no circumstances can she recover damages for the full cost of bearing and maintaining a child after the operation, which might be the true measure of protecting her full expectations.[55]

## Reliance damages

But if the case for awarding damages for lost profits or lost expectations is somewhat uneasy, the same is clearly not true of reliance damages or restitution 'damages'. Reliance damages are awarded for losses incurred by the plaintiff in reliance on the contract: these are 'real' losses in a much more tangible way than losses of expectations. The distinction is nicely illustrated by *McRae* v. *Commonwealth Disposals Commission*,[56] which has already been discussed in a different context. In this case, it will be recalled, the defendants sold a shipwrecked tanker which they advertised as lying on a certain reef in the Pacific, and the plaintiffs spent a substantial sum of money equipping a salvage expedition to go in search of the tanker. The shipwrecked tanker simply did not exist, and the plaintiffs were held entitled to damages. Here it was clear that the plaintiffs had incurred substantial expenses—real losses—in reliance on the contract, and the

---

[55] *Thake* v. *Maurice* [1986] QB 644.          [56] (1950) 84 CLR 377, *supra*, 221.

Australian High Court awarded these reliance damages to the plaintiffs. Their expectation losses were quite different. For their lost expectations consisted of the total expected value of the salvaged tanker *minus* the cost of the salvage expedition. However, it was impossible to quantify these losses because the venture was a sort of speculation and there was no basis for putting any sort of real figure on the expected value of the tanker. So in this case the court refused to award expectation damages. It seems clear that the claim for reliance damages in this sort of case has a much higher priority than the claim for expectation damages, and is more appropriate wherever the contract is of a speculative character.[57]

More generally, it seems that reliance damages are often recoverable as an alternative to expectation damages, if the plaintiff chooses to put his claim on that basis. But the plaintiff cannot claim on this basis where the defendant is able affirmatively to show that the plaintiff would have made a loss on his contract rather than a profit. In *C. & P. Haulage* v. *Middleton*[58] the plaintiff was granted a contractual licence to occupy the defendant's premises on a six-monthly basis. He spent money making the premises suitable for his work, even though the contract stipulated that fixtures were not to be removed. He was then ejected by the defendant ten weeks before the end of a six-month period, and claimed damages for breach of contract. It was held that he could not recover damages for his fixtures and wasted expenditure, because if the contract had been fully performed he would still have lost this money. A plaintiff, in other words, is not entitled to escape from a bad bargain by claiming reliance damages where the defendant is in breach. But if it is unclear whether the plaintiff's enterprise would have been profitable, he is entitled to claim reliance damages;[59] the onus is on the defendant to show plainly that the plaintiff's contract was a losing one.[60]

### Restitutionary claims

There is a third sort of claim which may be called a claim to restitution 'damages', though technically, in English law at least, claims of this kind are not generally regarded as claims for damages at all. A claim of this third kind arises from the possibility that the defendant has been benefited or enriched by a breach of the contract, and that he should therefore be made to pay the plaintiff for this benefit. There are two distinct ways in which the defendant may have been so enriched, however, and the law distinguishes sharply between them. First, the defendant may have been

---

[57] See also *Anglia TV* v. *Reed* [1972] 1 QB 60, where it was held that *pre-contractual expenditure* could be recovered in such an action, although such expenditure is not, of course, incurred in reliance on the contract.   [58] [1983] 3 All ER 94.

[59] *Anglia TV* v. *Reed, supra,* n. 57.

[60] *CCC Films* v. *Impact Quadrant Films* [1985] QB 316.

enriched by receiving or taking something from the plaintiff himself. And secondly, he may have been benefited by receiving or taking some benefit from a different source altogether.

The first type of case is very common, and is illustrated by the ordinary case of a plaintiff who has paid something under a contract where the defendant subsequently fails to perform at all. In this situation the plaintiff has long been recognized to have a right to recover his payment, not as damages for breach of contract, but in a quasi-contractual action or, as it would today be called, a restitutionary claim. From a very early date the common law recognized a quasi-contractual remedy for the recovery of money paid when the consideration for it totally failed. This action is not confined to cases of contract, although it finds its most frequent application in this field. It is, in many cases, an alternative remedy for a complete non-performance of a contract. Where money has been paid in advance by one party and the other party fails to perform, the innocent party may simply bring an action for general damages, which will include what he has paid, or he may be content with recovering what he has paid without making any further claim for damages. Thus if a buyer pays for goods which are not delivered he may sue for damages, or he may claim the return of his price on the ground of total failure of consideration.

In some cases the restitutionary remedy is available where no action can be brought for breach of contract, for the simple reason that there may in fact be no breach of contract, because there has been no contract or because there has been no breach or because there has been no loss. For example, an alleged contract may prove to be void owing to lack of a proper offer or acceptance, or a valid contract may fail to become operative owing to the failure of a condition precedent. In these cases there is a right of recovery of money as on a total failure of consideration, although there is no question of a breach of contract. Another illustration of this possibility is the case of the frustrated contract. If a person pays money under a contract which is subsequently frustrated before he has received any benefit from it, he cannot sue the other party for breach, because there is no breach, but he can recover what he has paid on the ground that there has been a total failure of consideration. For this reason it is frequently advantageous for a person who is content to recover his money to claim it on the ground of total failure of consideration rather than to sue for damages. If he takes the former course he establishes a good prima facie case simply by showing that he has received nothing for his money, whereas if he chooses the latter course he must actually prove that there has been a contract and a breach and some loss flowing from the breach.

The concept of total failure of consideration is a somewhat technical one. In particular there may be a total failure of consideration even though the defendant has actually done some work or expended some money in the performance of the contract, provided that what he has done has not enured to the benefit of the other party. For example, if a person orders machinery to be specially constructed for him, there will be a total failure of consideration if none of the machinery is delivered to him although work may have been commenced and money expended on it.[61] To establish a total failure of consideration it must basically be shown that the plaintiff has not received any part of the benefit bargained for—the fact that he may have fortuitously received some other benefit is irrelevant. So where payments are made under a contract which later turns out to have been void all along, the payments are prima facie recoverable for a total failure of consideration even though benefits may have been rendered to the payer under the putative contract.[62] Since the contract was legally void the plaintiff will not have received any part of what he bargained for. What he has received he did not bargain for—hence he in turn may have to repay or account for the value of any such benefits.[63]

On the other hand, if some benefit has been received under the contract, no matter how trifling, there is no total failure of consideration. In this case, just as there is generally no right to part payment for part performance, so also there is generally no right to part recovery for partial failure of consideration. Very often, this does not matter because the plaintiff will usually have an ordinary action for damages for breach, which will enable him to recover the value of the partial failure of consideration. But in some cases this will not be so. In *City of New Orleans* v. *Firemen's Charitable Association*,[64] which was mentioned earlier, the City was unable to recover damages from the defendants who had contracted to provide fire services, because they could prove no 'loss'; nor could they recover any part of the price they had paid, because there was no total failure of consideration. In this situation, the defendants' breach was entirely unsanctioned by the law, yet it was a serious, and presumably wilful, breach of contract, which may have exposed the City to considerable risk, even though the risk, by good fortune, did not materialize. The result seems unacceptable, and the law is seriously deficient in not affording some remedy in this situation.

---

[61] See *Fibrosa Spolka Akeyjna* v. *Fairbairn Lawson Combe Barbour Ltd* [1943] AC 32.
[62] *Rover International* v. *Cannon Film Sales (No. 3)* [1989] 1 WLR 912.
[63] *Ibid.*
[64] *Supra*, n. 2. But see now *Ferguson (D O) & Associates* v. *Sohl* (1994) 62 BLR 95 where the CA held that an overpayment under a building contract could be recovered even though there had been a substantial amount of work done because, as to the part of the work to which the overpayment related, there was a total failure of consideration. This is juggling with words to produce a total failure of consideration when there is manifestly only a partial failure of consideration and, if correct, will require the law on damages to be rewritten. Probably this decison only applies where it is possible to apportion the payments made so that an identifiable part of the sums paid can be regarded as paid without consideration.

Another problem arising from gains made by the defendant through his breach of contract concerns cases mostly of building or construction work, or contracts of a similar character. If a defendant contracts, say, to build a garden wall round the plaintiff's property at a cost of £1,000 (which is actually paid) and the defendant then breaches the contract, it may be found that the market value of the plaintiff's property is not reduced by £1,000, or anything like that sum—indeed, there could even be a net *increase* in the value of the property from the breach, as where the defendant contracts to paint the plaintiff's house to the plaintiff's own execrable taste. Obviously it would be outrageous and absurd to allow the defendant to retain the advance payment, and refuse to do the work at all, claiming that he had thereby saved the plaintiff some wasted expenditure. So in that case the money can be recovered as on a total failure of consideration, even though (in one sense) the result is to give the plaintiff more than his expectation rights, more than he would have had if the contract had been fully performed.

But suppose the defendant has partially done the work, or done it badly, the remedy as for a total failure of consideration is not then available, and the plaintiff must fall back on his claim for damages. Should the damages then be awarded on a 'diminution of value' basis, or on a 'cost' basis? If it is awarded on a diminution of value basis, the defendant may save himself a considerable sum (as in the *City of New Orleans* case) by breaching his contract, and this seems unacceptable. On the other hand, courts have been troubled about the thought of awarding damages on the 'cost' basis here for several reasons. First, because (as always) they are reluctant to award the plaintiff more damages than he has 'lost', more than his expectations, that is to say. And, secondly, because sometimes the cost is out of all proportion to the diminution in value, and it may seem inefficient to put pressure on the defendant to perform work which is of such little social benefit. Occasionally the courts have shown a greater willingness to award damages on a 'cost' basis if the plaintiff satisfies the court that he intends to have the work done after receiving the damages,[65] or even undertakes to do so, which takes care of the first of these problems, but hardly the second. But this seems an unsatisfactory result. The plaintiff's claim to damages should not depend on what he does with the money—he should not be able to increase the award by deciding how to spend it, nor should a converse decision reduce the defendant's liability.

Paradoxically, the law now provides some remedy to the plaintiff for

---

[65] See *Radford* v. *De Froberville* [1977] 1 WLR 1262. But the CA has now rejected this and insisted that the damages cannot be altered because of what the plaintiff does or does not intend to do with the money: *Ruxley Electronics and Construction Ltd* v. *Forsyth* [1994] 3 All ER 801.

partial failure of consideration in some cases where there has been no breach of contract at all. Where the contract is frustrated, the Act of 1943 enables the court to order part payment in the event of a partial failure of consideration. Thus if a house-holder pays a painter £500 to decorate his house, and the contract is frustrated after one room has been painted (e.g. by the destruction of the house by fire) a proportionate part of the £500 can be recovered. So if a contract like that in the *City of New Orleans* case was frustrated instead of being breached, it seems that the plaintiffs might be able to recover a proportionate part of the price they had paid.

However, the 1943 Act modifies the right to recover for total failure of consideration, as well as scaling down the newly provided right to recover for partial failure of consideration in one important respect. If the contract is not performed owing to frustration as distinct from breach, it seems particularly unfair to permit recovery of all the money paid on the ground of total failure of consideration if work has been done and money expended on the contract, even if the other party has had no benefit from the work and money. In this case, therefore, the Act of 1943 enables the court to permit some or all of the money to be set off against the cost of what has been done. To this extent, therefore, the right of recovery for total failure of consideration is impaired. And the same applies to the right to recover for partial failure of consideration.

The second type of restitutionary claim—where the defendant's enrichment has come from some other source—is much more restricted. Here we come up against a fundamental principle of the law, which some see as a further illustration of the relative weakness of contractual sanctions. If the defendant simply breaches his contract and proceeds to devote his time and resources elsewhere, any gains he makes from that other source are his, and the plaintiff has no claim to them.

Few would quarrel with this result where a contract of employment is breached, and the employee obtains another job, without giving notice. The employee may be liable to pay damages to the first employer for his breach, but the first employer has no restitutionary claim to the earnings of the employee, which he obtains from the second employer. Moreover, it seems that the law is the same even where the employee misuses confidential information which he has stolen or otherwise misappropriated on leaving his employment. The employer is plainly entitled to damages for any loss of business he can show was caused by the employee's breach of contract or breach of confidence, but he is not entitled to a restitutionary claim for profits made by the employee unless (as we shall see below) there has actually been a breach of a fiduciary duty.[66]

But it is not so clear that this result is acceptable in other cases. In *Surrey*

---

[66] *Universal Thermosensors Ltd* v. *Hibben* [1992] 1 WLR 840.

*CC* v. *Bredero Homes Ltd*[67] the defendants bought some land from the plaintiffs and entered into a covenant restricting the number of homes they could build on it. They breached this covenant and thereby made a handsome profit, but the plaintiffs suffered no pecuniary loss from the breach and it was held that they had no claim to any of the gains thereby made. If this is the law, it seems seriously deficient. Presumably the plaintiffs had some purpose in mind when they required the defendants to enter into the covenant in question. That purpose was defeated by the defendant's breach, and it is difficult to see why that should not be regarded as sufficient to justify an award of damages for loss. A contracting party is entitled to choose what price he wants for the property he sells, and if he chooses to take part of his price in the form of covenants like this, the law should recognize that they have value. This is particularly the case where public bodies (like the plaintiff County Council) are concerned because such bodies may well place a value, in the interests of the public at large, on environmental and other similar concerns where breach by the defendant does not cause monetary loss to the plaintiff. So an ordinary claim for damages seems entirely justifiable, but because of the difficulty in placing a monetary value on the loss, a restitutionary claim seems wholly appropriate as an alternative, and the law needs to develop along new lines to permit such a claim.

It is true that care needs to be taken if restitutionary claims are permitted more widely, in particular to ensure that inefficient uses of property and resources are not frozen by inappropriate contracts. We have previously encountered the suggestion that breaches of contract which are efficient ought to be permissible and even encouraged by the law. If a person discovers that he can devote his resources to a more profitable use after making a contract, he ought to be encouraged to do that, so long as he can pay off the first contracting party with ordinary expectation damages, and still make a profit. There are difficulties with this argument if pressed too far, but it is true that it might sometimes be felt oppressive if the mere making of a contract were so to bind a contracting party as to prevent all further initiative in the use of resources.

There are, anyhow, two exceptions to the present rule. In the first place, if the defendant has made a gain by breaching his contract, and the gain comes from the exploitation of the plaintiff's property, then a restitutionary claim will be available, even though there is no 'loss' and hence no claim to ordinary damages. If, in breach of contract, the chauffeur uses his employer's Rolls to take a party of friends for a day's outing, any payment he receives for this breach of contract will be recoverable by the

---

[67] *Supra*, n. 14. The earlier case of *Wrotham Park Estates* v. *Parkside Homes, supra*, n. 14, may no longer be good law.

employer.[68] Or again—though here the benefit comes from the plaintiff himself—A lets property to a tenant. The tenant remains in possession after the expiry of the lease. It is held that the landlord can recover rent (or damages as the equivalent) for this period even though there is no proof that the landlord has lost the opportunity to use or relet the premises.[69] This is regarded by English lawyers as a claim in tort for trespass, precisely because if the claim was made in contract there would appear to be no 'loss'. Yet surely the reality is that by recognizing and enforcing claims like this the courts are demonstrating that, even in contractual cases, damages ought (anyhow sometimes) to be awardable for benefits taken as well as for losses incurred.

The second exception concerns breaches of fiduciary duties. A contracting party who owes fiduciary obligations by reason of the nature of the contract or of the relationship between the parties, and who breaches these obligations, thereby obtaining gains from some outside source, will be liable to pay these gains over in a restitutionary claim. The agent who accepts a bribe from a third party, for instance, is liable to the employer in a restitutionary action even though no loss can be proved. Likewise, in a contract where the presumption of undue influence arises, any gains from outside parties are recoverable when the contract is set aside, even though there is no proof of any loss to the plaintiff.[70]

It is doubtful whether a breach of confidence could be sufficient for this purpose.[71] A person who wrongfully and in breach of contract or of confidence takes secret photographs of his clients and sells them for gain may well be outside this rule, and so may be free of any risk of a restitutionary claim for the gains he has thereby made. Similarly, it is unclear whether an employee or ex-employee who, in breach of contract and of a duty of confidence, publishes an account of some secret activities on which he was engaged, can be made to account to his employer for any profits he thereby makes. This question was not directly before the courts in the *Spycatcher* case[72] (in which the Crown attempted to prevent publication of the memoirs of a former security agent) but it was dealt with in the decision of the United States Supreme Court in *Snepp* v. *United States*.[73] The defendant here breached his duty as a former member of the CIA, by publishing a book based on his experiences, without clearance from the authorities. The United States Government did not claim that any

---

[68] The leading case is *Reading* v. *Attorney-General* [1951] AC 507, where a soldier used his uniform to assist in some illegal activities in Egypt.

[69] *Swordheath Properties Ltd* v. *Tabet* [1979] 1 WLR 285.

[70] *O'Sullivan* v. *Management Agency Ltd* [1985] QB 428.

[71] See *Universal Thermosensors Ltd* v. *Hibben, supra*, n. 66.

[72] See *Attorney General* v. *Guardian Newspapers* [1990] 1 AC 109.

[73] 444 US 507 (1980).

classified information had been divulged, but sued for the profits made by Snepp from his book. This claim was upheld by the majority of the court on the ground that the actual damage done by such breaches of contract was unquantifiable, and that a restitutionary remedy was preferable to the only real alternative, which was an award of exemplary damages. It seems that the case perhaps turned on the question whether the confidential information used by the defendant in his book was to be treated as though it was the 'property' of the United States Government, and only a minor extension of the existing law was required to support this result.

### The relationship between expectation, reliance and restitutionary claims

We have already noted a number of points at which these various possible claims intersect, and where it is accordingly necessary to decide which principle is paramount. As we have seen, the expectation damages rule is generally superior to the reliance damages rule in two senses. First, the general rule is that a plaintiff is able to claim expectation damages, and not merely reliance damages, and this is so even though the case is one in which the consideration for the promise sued upon is detrimental reliance, rather than an exchange of promises or benefits. So Mrs Carlill recovered the full £100 promised by the defendants, and not merely damages for the cost and inconvenience of using the smoke ball. Secondly, reliance damages cannot be claimed where, if the contract had been fully performed, the plaintiff would have made a loss. And the same is sometimes true of restitutionary claims, but it is not true where the defendant fails to perform at all.

But there is a broader sense in which the three kinds of claims probably have a different ranking from that which our treatment has so far accorded them. Indeed, there is surely one sense in which restitutionary claims have the highest priority, reliance claims the second, and expectation claims the lowest. This is simply because the restitutionary claim usually has the strongest appeal to our sense of justice, being closely linked to a proprietary claim, and involving (as it usually does) a loss to the plaintiff as well as a gain to the defendant. A plaintiff who pays money in advance, for instance, and who receives absolutely no return, whether because of breach or frustration, is generally felt to have a much stronger claim for the recovery of his money than a plaintiff who merely claims for expectation or reliance damages. And similarly, a claim to the return of money lent (though oddly it would not be regarded by lawyers as a restitutionary claim) is almost as indefeasible as a claim arising from rights of property— it could never, for instance, be defeated by a plea of frustration, and even where the contract is actually void, lawyers do their best to find ways of enabling the lender to recover his money if possible.

This priority is recognized by the law, in that restitutionary claims are sometimes allowed where no expectation or reliance damages are permitted—for instance where the agreement is void or illegal, or where the contract has been frustrated and there has therefore been no breach at all. Suppose A pays money to B in pursuance of a contract which turns out to be void, or perhaps is subsequently frustrated; clearly A cannot sue B for breach of contract. B's promise to perform his side of the bargain is vitiated by the mistake or the frustrating event, so A's lost expectations are losses which he must just put up with. But his claim to repayment of the money is evidently much stronger: for this money is a tangible loss to A and a tangible enrichment to B. So in this sort of case the money will often be recoverable, though English lawyers think of this as a restitutionary claim to recover money as on a total failure of consideration, and not a contractual claim to restitution damages. There is, however, no strong reason for refusing to call this a contractual action, any more than there is a reason for calling an action for damages restitutionary, merely because it sometimes embraces the return of money paid.

So also, in everyday life, contracts often fail for various reasons—strikes, bad weather, or other similar difficulties. In such cases there may well be no breach of contract (express or implied terms may excuse performance) but in practice it would be very rare for the recipient of an advance payment in such a case to refuse to refund the money. Here too, therefore, the restitutionary claim has a plainly higher priority than any claim for reliance or expectation losses.

There are also some circumstances in which damages for benefits or gains are recoverable where there is no reliance by the plaintiff. For instance, there are those cases, mentioned above, where the defendant has obtained money from some outside source, in breach of fiduciary obligations, and in which the money can be recovered by the plaintiff in a restitutionary action. So the fact that such a claim sometimes lies even in the absence of any expectation or reliance losses does seem to suggest that these claims have the highest priority in the law. Nor would this be surprising given that restitutionary claims are so closely associated with property rights. Property rights clearly have a higher priority in law than contractual rights. Property rights are normally based on possession, and they cannot be lost except by the consent of the owner. Contractual rights are usually concerned with the exchange of property rights, and often enforce some inchoate exchange, but essentially such rights are like an inchoate form of property, and therefore often, or even usually, less well protected.[74]

What then about the relationship between expectation damages and

---

[74] Of course *some* contractual rights do eventually become virtually the same as property rights—banknotes, for instance, were once contracts by banks to pay gold when called upon.

reliance damages? Now as we have already said, the general principle of English law is always said to be that damages are awardable for the plaintiff's lost expectations, and there is no doubt that, certainly in commercial cases, this principle is regularly applied and enforced. But at the same time it would be misleading to ignore the many circumstances in which this principle is not fully observed, and yet in which reliance (or restitution) claims may be permitted. Indeed, it may be suggested that, except in the straightforward, everyday, commercial contract, the expectation damages rule is frequently not followed at the present time. In this respect, the fortunes of the expectation damages rule (and the enforceability of wholly executory contracts) have been closely associated with the rise and decline of freedom-of-contract principles over the past two centuries.

The first and most important qualification to be made to the lost expectation principle is the rule that the plaintiff must 'mitigate his damage'. The plaintiff is required to take reasonable steps to protect his interests when the defendant breaks the contract, and he will only be entitled to damages for such losses of expectations as remain after he has taken these steps. To take a simple example, suppose a person is dismissed wrongfully from his employment where he has been earning £150 per week. His expectation *rights* are limited to the wages he would have earned while serving out the notice to which he was entitled; let us assume he was entitled to four weeks' notice, it would seem at first sight that he has lost the expectation of earning £600. But before the plaintiff can recover this (or indeed, any) sum as damages it must be clear that he has done his best to find alternative reasonable employment. If in fact the plaintiff has obtained a new job at the same (or a higher) wage, without any intervening time, then he will not have suffered any actual loss at all. If he is one week out of work while finding a new job, he has lost one week's wages and no more.

This principle is applied across the board to all contracts, and in practice makes a large dent in the theory that the plaintiff is entitled to damages representing his lost expectations.[75] A buyer fails to pay the price of goods not yet delivered: the seller has no right, in general, simply to sue for the price—he must first try to resell the goods and then sue for the deficiency, if any. A seller fails to deliver in breach of contract: the buyer must go into the market and look for alternatives. Only the remaining loss incurred after he has done this is recoverable as damages. A cargo fails to arrive in

---

[75] The mitigation principle is not confined to executory contracts but in practice it seems to be invoked more strictly against plaintiffs in such cases. Where the contract is part executed the courts appear less inclined to reduce the damages. See for one striking example *Hussey* v. *Eels* [1990] 2 QB 227.

time to be loaded on a ship in breach of contract: the shipowner cannot just sail away without examining the possibility of taking on an alternative cargo. And so on.

Now in all cases of this kind the extra expenses incurred by the innocent party in attempting to find alternatives are plainly recoverable as damages—these are actual expenses incurred as a result of the breach and are consequent on the plaintiff's reliance. So here one sees the reality of the law which is that reliance losses do seem to have a higher priority than expectation losses.

The mitigation principle is sometimes pushed so far that it seems almost to supersede the general principle altogether. In *Lazenby Garages Ltd* v. *Wright*[76] the defendant contracted to buy a second-hand car from the plaintiffs, who were car dealers, but then changed his mind and refused to take delivery. The dealers resold the car (without loss) and then sued the defendant for their lost profit on the sale. It was held that there was no loss of profit at all because the same car had been resold to another buyer without a lowering of the price. The plaintiffs argued that, if the defendant had taken this car, they would probably have sold a different car to the buyer who eventually bought it, so that they would thus have made two lots of profit. But the Court of Appeal rejected this argument, holding that a second-hand car was a unique chattel, from which only one lot of profit could be made. This is unconvincing, because very few second-hand cars are really unique in any relevant sense, and it is very likely true that the defendant's breach of contract did cost the plaintiffs a loss of profit. But it does not follow that the decision should have been otherwise. It is by no means obvious that the law ought not to limit the plaintiffs' rights in such cases to the actual costs (if any) incurred in making the second sale, in other words, to their reliance losses rather than their lost expectations.

An even more striking example of a breach of contract which left the plaintiffs remediless because of the mitigation rule is provided by *The Solholt*.[77] Here sellers had contracted to sell a ship to the defendants for $5 million, delivery not later than 31 August. In fact they were late in delivering the ship, and it was only offered to the defendants on 3 September. The buyers refused to accept it and, the market-price then having risen to $5.5 million, they claimed damages of half a million dollars. Prima facie this would seem to have been a simple case of lost expectation damages, but actually the buyers recovered nothing from an admitted breach. The reason for this was that the buyers made no attempt to mitigate their loss, after the refusal to accept delivery, which they could easily have done by renegotiating a new delivery date with the sellers. So it seems that a late delivery in breach of contract (unless the goods are

[76] [1976] 1 WLR 459.          [77] [1983] 1 Lloyd's Rep. 605.

urgently needed and must be replaced at once in the market) will often give no remedy to the buyer despite the fact that in theory he ought to obtain full damages for his lost expectation rights.

The general priority which claims for reliance damages seem to have over claims for lost expectations may also be illustrated by looking at claims which differ from ordinary commercial contracts, ordinarily made. Thus, claims against consumers, claims amongst members of a family, and so forth, are more likely to be dealt with by awards of reliance damages (or sometimes, restitutionary remedies) than by claims to the full amount of expectation losses. Indeed, in many of these cases the position in practice, and sometimes also in law, is that there is unlikely to be any recognition of a right at all unless there has been some element of performance or reliance. Wholly executory contracts in this sort of case are less likely to be found to exist in the first place, on the ground of a lack of intention to create legal relations, or uncertainty or other similar principles. Indeed, in such cases, wholly executory arrangements are very unlikely to be sued on at all. Even where contracts clearly exist, and may well be sued upon, the expectation damages rule is often severely restricted as in the case of liability for negligent advice or for breach of professional duties of care. We have already seen how in these cases the plaintiff's expectations are not really fully protected by the law.

This same general trend is also to be found in matrimonial contracts and agreements. First, there has been the abolition of actions for breach of promise—which were, in theory, designed for the protection of lost expectations. But, more realistically, there has been a massive movement in matrimonial causes away from the idea that expectations deriving from marriage are entitled to be fully protected. Few people any longer believe that a woman has the right to be maintained for life by her former husband at the standard of living she enjoyed when married to him. On divorce, it is now usually accepted that a woman has only the right to protection while she adjusts to her changed condition—which is in substance a protection of reliance rights, rather than expectation rights. Of course, expectations are not disregarded altogether. Where a marriage has been long-lasting, and expectations have crystallized into long-continued enjoyment, they tend to be stronger and more justified, and hence will probably receive greater protection on divorce. But bare expectations, derived simply and purely from the fact of marriage itself, are no longer regarded as entitled to such a high degree of protection. These changes in the protection accorded to expectations are reflected in the relevant legislation.[78]

Even in commercial contracts, it will be found that where something

---

[78] See the Matrimonial and Family Proceedings Act 1984, s. 3, replacing the old s. 25 of the Matrimonial Causes Act 1973.

unusual has happened—for instance, a serious case of mistake or frustration—there will usually be higher protection for reliance claims than for expectation claims. So, for instance, in the *McRae* case,[79] as we saw earlier, a claim for reliance damages was upheld in a mistake case, where the claim to expectation losses was denied. Although in practice this often seems to be what the courts actually do, it is not yet recognized that there is, in principle, often a *via media* between holding a contract to be void on one side, and holding it to be fully valid on the other. The *via media* is the road which enables the court to say, in effect: this is not a case where the contract is fully valid and where the parties' expectation rights deserve to be protected, but at the same time actual reliance deserves to be protected. What is surprising is that this is, in substance, precisely the result which is arrived at where tort law is invoked; but despite this fact, and despite the fact that contract and tort are growing closer together in so many areas, the application of pure contract doctrine still produces quite different results.

This divergence of approach between contract and tort is particularly striking in the case of misrepresentation where the two bodies of legal doctrine overlap so largely. In tort, there is no protection of bare expectations—even a fraudulent statement gives no right of action to someone who has not acted upon the statement, but who believes it to be true and thereby derives high expectations. Furthermore, even where the misrepresentation is acted upon, the representee can only claim for his reliance losses—his legal rights derive from the fact that he has been induced to act to his prejudice by the statement, and not from any expectations deriving from his belief in the truth of the statement. Now in contract law, many promises or agreements are actionable in substance because they are misleading, for precisely the same reasons as in tort cases. Wherever the promise or statement does not truly represent the intentional and informed assent of the promisor or representor—and this includes many cases of signed but unread contracts, of objective interpretation, of offers revoked too late, of agents who have acted beyond their actual authority, and of mistake and unanticipated consequences—he is held liable not because of his intentions, but because he has misled the innocent party. But in this situation, the result is sometimes quite different from what it is in tort law. The innocent party is entitled to have his expectations fully protected; the agreement is binding even if not yet acted upon, and damages for lost expectations and even, sometimes, specific performance, can be obtained.

A good example of this is the case of *Centrovincial Estates PLC* v. *Merchant Investors Assurance Co Ltd*[80] which has already been referred to

---

[79] (1950) 84 CLR 377, *supra*, 448.
[80] (1983) Com. LR 158, *supra*, 83. Compare *Moran* v. *University College, Salford, Independent* 26 November 1993.

in Chapter 3. Here the agent of landlords of a block of flats gave notice to the tenants of their proposed new rent under the rent review clause, and by mistake proposed a rent actually lower than the minimum rent already in the lease. The tenants immediately 'accepted' this offer, and the Court of Appeal held that they were entitled to do so (assuming they had no ground to suppose it was mistaken) even though the mistake was immediately disavowed, and the offer retracted before the tenants had acted to their prejudice in any way. Had the tenants sued for negligent misrepresentation they would not have had a leg to stand on, because their mere expectations would have been unprotected in tort. But because they were able to treat the representation as an 'offer' (though it was actually a peculiar sort of offer) they were able, by accepting it, to obtain protected expectations. The result seems absurd and unjustifiable on every count.

The difference between protecting expectations and protecting reliance in cases of misrepresentation is also relevant in certain restitutionary cases. In *Avon CC* v. *Howlett*[81] the defendant, an employee of the plaintiffs, was overpaid some sick benefit to which he was not entitled. He queried the amounts and was assured they were correct, so there clearly was a misrepresentation. He had also acted on the representation by spending part of the money (on unusual expenditure) so plainly his reliance was entitled to protection. But the question was whether he still had to repay the money which he had not spent. If the expectations raised by the misrepresentation had been protected, he could have kept it all, but if his reliance only was protected, he would have had to repay it. This question was not settled by the *Howlett* case which was inconclusive, and some technicalities of the doctrine of estoppel were thought to lead to the result that the defendant's expectations were protected; but this result again seems wrong and unjustified.[82]

There are also a variety of legal devices which need only brief mention here, which are invoked in various contexts to prevent the creation of liability on wholly executory contracts, and therefore liability for expectation damages. For example, there are contracts which cannot be enforced while still executory, unless they are in writing—such as contracts for the sale of an interest in land. Indeed, in these cases, the whole device of agreements 'subject to contract' (discussed at some length in Chapter 7) prevents agreements being treated as legally binding contracts until a very late stage in the proceedings—probably too late a stage. Then there is the

---

[81] [1983] 1 All ER 1073.

[82] See now the dicta of Lord Browne-Wilkinson in *Roebuck* v. *Mungovin* [1991] 4 All ER 568 at 575 suggesting that equitable (or promissory) estoppel could not be treated as protecting more than the plaintiff's reliance. See also the Australian High Court decision in *Commonwealth of Australia* v. *Verwayen* (1990) 170 CLR 394 where the majority held that estoppel only protects to the extent of reliance.

possibility of interpreting arrangements as unilateral transactions, and not bilateral contracts, so that they do not become binding until performed on one side or, at least, until performance has commenced. So, too, where continuing contracts are concerned, the implication of a right to terminate reduces the bindingness of the executory part of the contract, and in effect restricts the plaintiff to protection for the short time of the requisite period of notice—in effect protecting him for his reliance. And it is even possible to imply a condition precedent which prevents an agreement being treated as a binding executory contract in appropriate circumstances.[83] Then there are many modern statutes which confer 'cooling-off' rights on consumers, and entitle them to withdraw from contracts within a specified period (usually four days) if, on reflection, they choose to do so. These provisions usually apply only to agreements reached at the consumer's home (thus dealing with the over-pressing door-to-door salesman) or otherwise away from places of business.

Side by side with these developments, there has been another development in the law which actually leads to a greater degree of protection for certain classes of expectations—particularly, those deriving from the employment relationship, and those accruing to tenants. So we have seen how many modern statutes confer legal protection on these two classes for their expectations—for instance, in employment, by the law of unfair dismissal, and redundancy compensation and, with tenants, by granting security of tenure—but it is important to appreciate that these are not *contractual* expectations in the ordinary sense. Indeed, if they were, they would be protected by the ordinary law of contract, and would not require special statutory protection. But protecting these expectations, of course, is at the price of disappointing the expectations of the other party to the contract—when an employee is entitled to redundancy payments, his employer's contractual expectation of being able to dismiss his workforce with reasonable notice, but without compensation, is disappointed. What has happened in these cases, then, is that the law has protected expectations which do not derive from promises or contracts, but which are thought to be justified, *de facto* expectations, entitled to legal protection on non-contractual grounds. The protection of such expectations is, therefore, no argument for suggesting that contractual expectations should themselves always be fully protected.

One final question needs to be addressed here: is this trend towards less full protection for contractual expectations in conflict with the newly resurgent belief in freedom-of-contract principles? If so, this might suggest that the law is about to reverse direction here, once again. It is reasonably

---

[83] For a striking example see the Canadian case, *Custom Motors* v. *Dinwell* 6 DLR (3d) 342 (1975).

clear that the present trend is directly contrary to the trend which emerged during the classical period, when the protection of reliance (and of a right to recompense for benefits conferred) was gradually submerged beneath the rising tide of expectation-protection. So it might seem that the return to classical principles will lead, once again, to a greater degree of protection for contractual expectations, and less protection for reliance and benefit-based rights. Is this where the future will take us?

The answer to our question should really be implicit in what has already been said. In so far as the recent trend derives from some paternalistic element, some belief that parties who make agreements should not be irrevocably bound by the mere fact of the agreement, but should have time for reflection and withdrawal, then it seems clear that this trend is vulnerable to the renewed swing of the freedom-of-contract pendulum. So it seems probable that the present practice relating to 'subject to contract' agreements, for instance, will soon be revised so as to facilitate the making of binding executory contracts at an earlier stage than current practice permits; it seems possible that agreements interpreted in recent times as unilateral are more likely to be interpreted in future as bilateral, and hence binding at an earlier stage; it seems likely that continuing contracts will more often be interpreted as not terminable by notice; it is even possible, though perhaps less likely, that the move towards statutory 'cooling-off' rights for consumers in certain cases will peter out, and perhaps be reversed. Perhaps too, the belief in full expectation damages will once again revive, at the expense of the mitigation principle and other ways of cutting down such damages in practice.

On the other hand, in so far as the recent trends have begun to distinguish between genuinely promised results, intentional legal commitments, on the one side, and liability for misleading behaviour, for unintended consequences, for mistakes, for excesses of an agent's authority, and so on, on the other side, these trends do not appear to conflict in the least with the resurgence of freedom-of-contract principles. Quite the reverse, because in so far as these principles are associated with the goal of economic efficiency, they would seem to support this trend. Regrettably, as we have seen, the signs of this aspect of the recent trends are not encouraging.

## 7. CONSEQUENTIAL LOSSES AND REMOTENESS OF DAMAGE

In some cases another question has to be answered, and that is whether the defendant is liable for consequential losses, that is for additional damage caused as a result of the defendant's breach of contract. Such losses may, in one sense, be outside the scope of the anticipated contractual performance altogether, and may therefore lead to a liability in damages far exceeding the value of the contract. The simplest illustration of this possibility is the case of defective goods which cause physical injury or property damage to the purchaser. Damages in such cases may run into thousands of pounds although the inherent value of the goods may be trifling. This problem is known as 'remoteness of damage' because some kinds of damage are treated as too remote to be attributable to the breach of contract in question.

In the law of tort the subject of remoteness of damage has been bedevilled by theories of causation, but fortunately the law of contract has escaped these complications, although that does not mean that difficult questions do not still arise in this branch of the law. The principle to be applied in the law of contract is that the defendant is liable for all damage which he could reasonably have foreseen as a 'not unlikely' consequence of his breach of contract. This principle, usually known as the rule in *Hadley* v. *Baxendale*,[84] is frequently divided into two sub-rules. First, the defendant is liable for all damage occurring in the normal course of things as a result of the breach. This is just another way of saying that he is liable for reasonably foreseeable damage, for the normal is always reasonably foreseeable. The converse, however, is not true, because in particular circumstances a person may foresee the abnormal. This is accordingly the subject of the second rule in *Hadley* v. *Baxendale*, which states that a defendant is liable for damage occurring as a result of special or abnormal circumstances if, at the time of making the contract, he had sufficient notice of facts making the damage foreseeable.

The important case of *Victoria Laundries* v. *Newman Industries*[85] provides an excellent illustration of both branches of the rule in *Hadley* v. *Baxendale*. In this case the defendants had contracted to sell a large boiler to the plaintiff laundry company. The defendants were well aware of the fact that there was at the time an acute shortage of laundries, and that the plaintiffs were proposing to put the boiler into use at the earliest possible moment with a view to a rapid expansion of their business. When the defendants damaged the boiler in delivering it, with consequent delay in bringing it into use, it was therefore held that they were liable for the estimated loss of profits which the plaintiffs had incurred. On the other hand, the plaintiffs were not entitled to damages for the loss of certain highly lucrative dyeing contracts of which the defendants were ignorant.

The rule in *Hadley* v. *Baxendale* is not just an arbitrary, if convenient, formula. On the contrary, there is a strong rational basis for holding a defendant liable on the basis of the normal or foreseeable, and not the abnormal and unforeseeable. Indeed, the distinction between the normal and the abnormal, the foreseeable and the unforeseeable, is one which

[84] (1854) 9 Ex. 341.  [85] [1949] 2 KB 528.

runs right through the law of contract and, as we saw earlier, underlies the doctrine of frustration, as well as the principles of remoteness of damage. Generally speaking, it is the function of insurance contracts to take care of abnormal and unforeseeable risks, while it is the function of other contracts to take care of normal and foreseeable risks. To justify the principle as simply as possible, the price which the parties have agreed upon as representing the value of the goods or services being bought is calculated in the expectation of things turning out normally and not abnormally, or at all events in accordance with the foreseeable and not the unforeseeable. For instance, the cost of freight for the carriage of goods by sea is in the usual way calculated according to the actual cost (itself, of course, a difficult concept) plus a reasonable margin of profit. Certainly it is unlikely that any allowance would be made, for example, for the possibility that the cargo-owner might incur unforeseeable losses in the event of the cargo being delayed as a result of breach of contract.

But although there is therefore a sound rational basis for paying due regard to the foreseeable results of a breach of contract, it would be quite wrong to think that there are not other important factors to be taken into account such as (in particular) the nature of the contract. Some contracts, for instance, may be of a risk-allocation character, and the risks allocated may be of a general or even of an all-embracing kind. Then unforeseeable results must fall within the risks assumed. This is not a part of the law which can be satisfactorily solved by search for a single verbal formula, but unfortunately this is just what the House of Lords tried to do in the leading decision of *The Heron II*.[86] In this case damages were sought by a consignee of goods from a shipping company which was liable for late delivery. The question at issue was whether the shipping company was liable for losses resulting from a fall in the market price of the goods between the date when the ship should have arrived and the date when it did arrive. In this sort of case the conventional approach is not a great deal of help; such consequences may be more or less foreseeable, but it is hardly possible to pin down the requisite degree of foreseeability with mathematical precision. Yet this is just waht the House of Lords seems to have tried to do; the speeches in this case betray an excessive—indeed an almost obsessive—anxiety to find a single formula which expresses the degree of foreseeability necessary. Thus phrases such as 'in the contemplation of the parties', 'a real danger', 'a serious possibility', or 'not unlikely' are bandied about in the speeches in this case as though the whole law could be reduced to a single such formula. In the result the House of Lords seems to have settled on 'not unlikely' as expressing most accurately the necessary degree of foreseeability.

---

[86] [1969] 1 AC 350.

But with all respect to this august tribunal, it must be said that this is a very unsatisfactory case. Foreseeability is certainly important because (as we have said) prices are fixed on the basis of a foreseeable outcome; it would therefore generally be unjust to impose liability for unforeseeable consequences. But it does not follow that it is always just to impose liability for foreseeable consequences. Whether this is just may well depend to some degree on the nature of the contract and on whether the price of the goods or services in question is likely to be affected by the foreseeable consequences of breach. In a contract of sale of goods, for example, the price of the goods will normally reflect the scarcity value of those goods. In the *Victoria Laundry* case the sellers were selling a boiler for laundry use at a time when laundries were in great demand; plainly this fact would have affected the price at which the boiler was sold; and it was therefore reasonable to treat the seller as liable for lost profits arising from his delay in delivering the boiler. But in *The Heron II* the defendants were shipowners, and the service they were selling was that of carriage of goods. Now freight charges for the carriage of goods would not normally be affected by the value or scarcity of the goods being carried because these facts do not affect supply and demand of shipping space. Therefore a shipowner would not increase his freight charges to cover the additional risk of lost profits arising from fluctuations of market price in the goods which he carries. Nor does it seem desirable that he should be required to do so, because he does not have or profess the knowledge of relevant market conditions to enable him to gauge this additional risk accurately; nor would it be economically efficient for a shipowner to adjust his freight charges to the particular market conditions of the goods he carries. *The Heron II* is, it must be said, an illustration of serious deficiencies in the sophistication of common-law courts in dealing with what are at least partly economic issues.

Another case takes this principle to what are surely unacceptable extremes. In *H. Parsons (Livestock)* v. *Uttley, Ingham & Co Ltd*[87] the defendants supplied and installed a large hopper for holding animal foodstuffs for the plaintiff, a pig farmer. The defendants unfortunately left closed a ventilator at the top of the hopper (which could not be seen from the ground) with the result that some of the food became mouldy. The pigs became ill, and later a much more serious pig disease was triggered off by this first disease, and many of the pigs died. The farmer recovered substantial damages for all his lost and diseased pigs on the basis that these were foreseeable results. There does seem to be an air of unreality about the foreseeability test in cases of this nature. In one sense, everything that happens (except perhaps for voluntary human action) occurs according to

---

[87] [1978] QB 791.

the laws of the physical universe, and in so far as these are known (and for practical purposes, they are after all pretty well known today), virtually any result is foreseeable as possible from a base which supposes knowledge of the initial breach of contract. Thus, the only consequences that come to be regarded as unforeseeable are those where the train of events has been interrupted by conscious human interventions. This seems to go much too far. It would surely be more sensible in a case of this nature to ask whether losses from pig disease ought to be treated as part of the risks of farming, or of the manufacture and sale of animal food hoppers.

A more acceptable result was recently reached by the Court of Appeal,[88] where a holiday-maker told his travel agent that he needed insurance because he was subject to asthma. While he was on the holiday, some breaches of contract for which the defendants were responsible triggered off a bad attack of asthma, and the plaintiff claimed additional damages for this. But the court held that the mention of asthma to the agent was merely conversational, and not part of the booking arrangement (or, as we have suggested, it did not affect the price) so it did not bring into play the second rule in *Hadley* v. *Baxendale* and the defendants were not liable for it.

One powerful argument against these extensive liabilities for consequential losses is that insurance companies dislike them because of their open-endedness. It is difficult to buy unlimited insurance cover for liabilities of this nature because the insurer simply does not know what his maximum potential liability may be: in the old saying a kingdom was ultimately lost because of the absence of a horseshoe nail, and an insurer who insured the loss of the nail would be hard pressed to find sufficient premiums to pay out for a lost kingdom. Moreover, the cost of many small goods and minor services may become uneconomical if the supplier has to insure against potentially unlimited liabilities. One result of all this is that, in standard-form contracts containing exemption clauses, the one exemption which is almost invariably to be found is an exemption from liability for consequential loss or damage. And, as we have previously seen, it is very likely that these exemptions will in future be judged to be reasonable under the Unfair Contract Terms Act. But that naturally leads to the question, if they are reasonable when written into standard terms, why would they not be reasonable even if not actually written into the contract? Why, in other words, maintain these extensive liabilities for consequential loss, if the only result is going to be to force contracting parties to write them out of their contracts? Only those unfortunate enough to omit this precaution will then be hit with the ordinary legal liabilities.

---

[88] *Kemp* v. *Intasun Holidays* [1987] 2 FTLR 234.

*Consequential loss and the non-payment of money*

Where the defendant's breach of contract consists of a failure to pay some money when due, the law at present denies the plaintiff adequate and satisfactory remedies. In the first place, the plaintiff does not normally have a right to damages for consequential loss, following the non-payment of money. It may in some rare cases be possible to invoke the second rule in *Hadley* v. *Baxendale* where the defendant knew at the time of contracting that such a non-payment might lead to special losses, (for example, currency exchange losses[89]) but no damages are payable under the first rule in *Hadley* v. *Baxendale* for ordinary, foreseeable financial loss following non-payment of money.

Secondly, the plaintiff may sometimes be able to recover interest, in the discretion of the court, for the period between the time when proceedings are issued and the date of judgment, but the rules governing the right to interest are out of date, and often technical and arbitrary. An ordinary debtor can usually afford to pay his debts late, in the safe knowledge that no interest can be claimed against him, in the absence of specific contractual terms. The Law Commission published an excellent Report on Interest some years ago, in which carefully thought out and detailed proposals for reform were made. Regrettably, the Report has not been implemented for political reasons. The European Commission is now believed to be preparing a draft Directive which would entitle suppliers to claim interest on overdue invoices after a specified time.

[89] *Lips Maritime Corp* v. *President of India* [1988] AC 395.

# INDEX